W9-AAH-964

The
Gardener's Table

The
GARDENER'S

A Guide to

Natural Vegetable

Growing & Cooking

Richard Merrill and Joe Ortiz

TABLE

10 TEN SPEED PRESS
Berkeley/Toronto

© 2000 by Richard Merrill and Joe Ortiz

All rights reserved. No part of this book may be reproduced in any form, except brief excerpts for the purpose of review, without written permission of the publisher.

Ten Speed Press
P.O. Box 7123
Berkeley, CA 94707
www.tenspeed.com

Distributed in Australia by Simon & Schuster Australia; in Canada by Ten Speed Press Canada; in New Zealand by Southern Publishers Group; in South Africa by Real Books; in the United Kingdom and Europe by Airlift Books; and in Southeast Asia by Berkeley Books.

Text and cover design by Toni Tajima
Illustrations by Ann Miya, Santa Cruz, California

Library of Congress Cataloging-in-Publication Data on file with the publisher.

Thank you to *Food & Wine* magazine, Nancy Verde Barr, Flo Braker, Carlo Middione, and Sibella Kraus for permission to adapt several recipes for this book.

Some of the information in this book has previously appeared in *Organic Gardening Magazine*, *Kitchen Garden Magazine*, and the *Santa Cruz Sentinel*.

First printing, 2000
Printed in Canada

1 2 3 4 5 6 7 8 9 10 — 04 03 02 01 00

About the Nutritional Analysis in this Book

The nutritional information was calculated taking the following into account:

- Salt used to drain eggplant was not figured into the analysis because much of it is washed away before the eggplant is added to the dish.

- When a serving amount varies (serves 4 to 6, or a series of two interchangeable ingredients, like "chicken stock or vegetable stock"), the first one was used for the nutritional analysis.

- "Salt and pepper to taste" was not included in the analysis since the quantity is not determined.

- All "optional" ingredients (unless a specific amount is given) were not figured into the analysis.

- To significantly reduce sodium content in any recipe calling for chicken stock or vegetable stock, substitute low-sodium chicken broth for the stock.

This book is dedicated to children everywhere.
They are the seeds of the future. And to the child in all of
us, who is warmed by the life in the garden and the
love in the kitchen.

Contents

Acknowledgments

THIS BOOK WAS nearly ten years in the making, and we are greatly indebted to the many people who inspired and encouraged us to combine our fifty years of gardening and cooking experience in one book.

Mentors and editors: Martha Casselman, our dedicated literary agent, who always went beyond the call of duty; the memory of Alan Chadwick and Floyd Younger, who opened the garden gate for Rich; Drs. Monte Lloyd and Joe Connell, who taught Rich about the ecology dwelling in the garden; to Jay Leite, our accountant, friend, and confidant; and to all our friends at Ten Speed Press, especially editorial director Lorena Jones, publisher and vice president Kirsty Melville, editor Jason Rath, design director Nancy Austin, designer Toni Tajima, the late Celestial Arts publisher and vice president David Hinds, and owner Phil Wood.

Colleagues: Rosalind Creasy, friend and sharer of ideas and notes, and Shepherd Ogden, both of whose landmark books of the late 1980s started us all thinking about the forgotten link between growing and cooking; Louisa Beers, partner and general manager at Gayle's Bakery; Ann Miya, artist and friend, who rendered our concepts in this book; the horticulture faculty at Cabrillo College, especially Bonnie Faraola, Kathe Navarez, Chris Dye, Dave Seidman, John McKeon, John Foster, and Ernie Wasson; Robert Kourick, garden consultant and au-

thor; Jim Nelson of Camp Joy Farms; and Wendy Krupnick, formerly of Shepherd Seeds, for their knowledge of vegetables and for their help along the way; John Jeavons, for his inspirational work with intensive gardening techniques; Bill and Helga Olkowski, for their discussions about the garden's insect life; and our dear friend Renee Shepherd, for sharing seeds, recipes, gardening ideas, and many meals.

Experts: Bruce Butterfield of the National Gardening Association; amigo Bob Cantisano, Elaine Ingham, and Marc Buchanan for their advice about compost teas; Robert Engeland of Filaree Garlic Farms; Melanie Polk at the American Institute of Cancer Research; Joel Reiten, research manager of Territorial Seeds; Paul Relis and "Fitz" Fitzgerald of the California State Integrated Waste Management Board; Bob Scowcroft, executive director of the California Organic Research Foundation; Michael Sweeney, University of Santa Clara chemistry professor, for research information on the Maillard reaction; Lola Van Gilst and Leigh Ann Betters of the Produce Marketing Association.

Inspiring cooks: Nancy Verde Barr, for letting us adapt her eggplant recipe; Jesse Cool, for her creative vegetable concepts from Flea Street Cafe in Menlo Park; *Food & Wine* magazine for concept recipes; George Germon and Johanne Killeen, for earthy food in which everyday ingredients and inventive preparations take on special status; Molly Katzen, for blazing the way for vegetables as a part of life; Sibella Kraus, for her dedication to vegetables and permission to use several concept recipes; the *San Francisco Chronicle* for its excellent food articles and concept recipes; Deborah Madison for expanding many people's interest in cooking vegetables; Nancy McDermott, for her great books using Thai spices; Nancy Oakes and Bruce Aidells, for lavish home-cooked meals that prove that vegetables *aren't* always the only things in life; Mark Miller, for conjuring up the spicy flavors of the Southwest; Jacques Pépin, for showing us how to use less fat while retaining the integrity of the original recipe; Paul Shenkman and Kim Levin, from Pasta Moon in Half Moon Bay; Lindsey Shere, for her inspirations for fresh, seasonal fruits; Tony Tollner, restaurateur supreme from Carmel; Barbara Tropp, for giving us peasant Chinese cooking glorified and brought to a California-style interpretation; Viana LaPlace, for a moving book on vegetables; Carlo Middione, for savory vegetable inspirations and outstanding meals at Vivandi Ristorante; and Alice Waters, for championing fresh, seasonal vegetables.

Local chefs: Tom King, for recipes from Papa's Church and Paul Geise, for inspiring meals and ideas from Ristorante Avanti, both in Santa Cruz; Barbara Arroyo, head cook at Gayle's, who contributed many ideas and recipes; Rick Cunha, and the kitchen staff at Gayle's Rosticceria; and Flo Braker, for orig-inal concept recipes, especially the one for potato pancakes; Jack Chyle, Jim Denevan, Mimi Snowden, and Charlie Deal.

Recipe testers: Head recipe tester and confidante, Elfe Kuester, who not only tested our recipes many times, but contributed a few of her own. She also did the nutritional analysis and helped organize the other recipe testers, including Gretchen Collins, Matt Guerrieri, Sarah Jensen, Cyndi Freitas, Melinda Tao, Mimi French, and Pauline deVisser. Thank you all!

Family and friends: Our mutual friends and landscapers, Lisa McAndrews and Steve McGuirk, for their support and reassurance; Rich's lifelong friends Mimi and Alan Edgar, for their encouragement, love, and recipes; Bob and Jane Mangels, who can talk gardening while watching football; John Evarone, who provided Rich with a writer's paradise; Michael Lemos, the best home chef we've ever known, and the entire Harvest Club gang; Rich's children, Andre and Riana, and his grandchildren, Addison, Zoe, Adriane, Megan, Eric, and Cameron, for helping him discover the wonders of the garden anew with each generation; great pals and cooking inspirations Ginger Carlson, Christie Carlson, Charles Mostov, Jodi Alward, and Phil Basile; the gourmet group (Dunn, Bloom, Johnson, and Plager). *And finally,* those who deserve the most thanks—our wives, Yedida and Gayle, who are our chief editors, master muses, and best friends.

Foreword

by Rosalind Creasy

To be in a room with Rich Merrill and Joe Ortiz is always a memorable adventure. The energy level is palpable, the conversation arresting, and the food fantastic! And then there is all the fun—who else but this duo would glory over all the similarities between making soup stock and compost? Every few months my husband and I join Rich and Joe, their spouses, and seedswoman Renee Shepherd and friends in a gourmet garden gathering. Instead of a classic literary round-table we have a botanical and food free-for-all. The ideas fly around the room so forcefully I swear I've seen the centerpiece duck.

Given Rich and Joe's many talents I eagerly anticipated *The Gardener's Table*. After my first read-through I knew it would take an honored place among my most prized reference books. First, I heartily agree with the book's premise: that an environmentally friendly garden and delicious health-enriching foods are essential ingredients of "the good life." Further, like most of my favorite books, it is written from decades of direct experience and is packed with vital and eminently clear technical information, sidebars, diagrams, and easy-to-read tables. And as a cook I found this book a joy. It gives numerous solutions to the limitation of the kitchen garden, namely, its propensity to produce fabulous vegetables, but so often in odd-lots.

The scope of the book is significant. Rich, the passionate, hands-in-the-soil ecologist, deftly guides us through planning a habitat kitchen garden all the way to the harvest. Under Rich's direction our gardens take their place as wondrous pieces of a greater whole—the ecosystem. Instead of merely feeding your plants, you manage the soil for lasting fertility, and pests are controlled by creating garden microhabitats to attract beneficial insects and other friendly wildlife. Rich's lifelong interest in entomology gives the pest and disease section unique authority among garden books and promises to set a new benchmark in sustainable gardening.

Joe Ortiz appreciates fresh garden produce as few chefs do. Instead of pages of discrete recipes requiring exacting amounts, great care and passion are given to the strengths of garden cooking. He helps us create fabulous flavors by combining varying amounts of garden bounty. For example, while he includes wonderful individual recipes for salads and soups, he also shares basic flavor principles in his unique "recipe wheels" that explore a vast range of salad and soup combinations. Joe generously provides you with knock-your-socks-off party dishes, but his specialties and passion are day-to-day healthful foods with deep, intense flavors, many of which are inspired by Asian and Mediterranean cooking.

I certainly could have used this masterful book a decade ago. It would have short-circuited years of garden and kitchen trial-and-error. *The Gardener's Table* is sure to become a classic, a true marriage of the spade and the spoon.

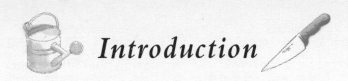

Introduction

THIS BOOK IS A collaboration of our two passions: gardening and cooking. It all started ten years ago in a lakeside cabin in California's Sierra Nevada. We had come to the lake for a week to relax and enjoy each other's company. The evening conversation began, as most good conversations do, over a delicious meal. We talked about the satisfaction we got from working in our kitchen gardens, the joys of sharing freshly cooked meals with friends and family, and the excitement of controlling, in some small way, the quality of the food we eat.

As we talked over the next few days, we realized that each of us had been influential in fostering new ways in which our community was thinking about food. Joe, through Gayle's Bakery and Rosticceria, had introduced people to the luscious foods of Europe and the Mediterranean and to new and savory ways of preparing them. Rich, as director of the horticulture department at nearby Cabrillo College, had worked for years with students and staff to change the basic design of the kitchen garden. Instead of perfect-looking rows of a few common vegetables and cottage flowers protected by chemicals, we sought more natural ways of growing all sorts of vegetables, hybrids and heirlooms, new and old, in a vegetable garden full of life and diverse plant habitats.

Back home, we often found ourselves sitting down over fresh bread from the bakery and slices of vegetables from the garden and talking about our experiences with cooking, baking, horticulture, and biology. We shared ideas as if they were appetizers or prized seeds. At some point, we realized that the languages of cooking and gardening were very similar and that they were not two separate crafts at all, but phases of the same nurturing process that links us to the garden and table.

In the years following that week in the mountain cabin, we've gardened, cooked, shared many memorable meals, and slowly transformed our experiences into the book you now hold. *The Gardener's Table* is for gardeners who love to cook and cooks who enjoy gardening.

The kitchen garden has been part of our culture since people first thrust a seed or tuber into the soil and tended the sprouts. In fact, the first farmers *were* kitchen gardeners, and from the beginning of our agricultural heritage, the home food garden has nurtured families, tribes, and civilizations.

In this century, the kitchen garden has gone through many phases. Most of these can be tied to our cycles of war, prosperity, and economic recessions. "Victory" and "recession" gardens have always been grown in times of hardship. What has been unique about the 1990s is that more people than ever are gardening even though it's a time of prosperity. Today, more than forty million of us tend food gardens.

Why are we gardening more now when we have less time and space to do so, and when it's easy to buy a wide variety of vegetables from the local market? There are probably several reasons, including our constant quest for Eden. Who doesn't go out to the garden just to get away from it all? We know that the garden is a place for quieting the mind and lifting the spirit, an oasis amidst the increasing hustle and bustle of modern life, where one is ensured the peace of mind that flows from a close connection with the life and times of nature.

There is also the thrill of growing and eating vegetables not available over the counter, from modern hybrids and ethnic edibles to the palette of rediscovered heirlooms. Varieties like 'Howling Mob' corn and 'Mortgage Lifter' tomato are earthly reminders of a heritage snatched from oblivion, of a time when people passed down seeds as family heirlooms out of necessity for next year's garden. By growing and saving these old-timers, we confirm their heritage and preserve the biodiversity they represent.

As we become more aware of the health benefits of growing and cooking fresh vegetables, we have begun to stay home more and rediscover the joys of sharing meals. Tasteless, processed foods are a thing of the past for many of us. Now we have fresh greens, vegetables, and herbs available from farmers' markets and natural food stores, plus garden-fresh cuisines served in restaurants all over the country. Exciting new types of vegetables and ways to prepare them are being discovered all the time. We've become aware of the nutritional value of fresh vegetables and their relation to our well-being. And when fresh vegetables are prepared just right, there is nothing quite like them. They become a renewed part of our diet.

Finally, for many of us, gardening is an opportunity to share in the stewardship of the environment. It's a central theme of this book—that is, that good gardening practices encourage biodiversity. By growing a wide variety of plants that are known to attract and sustain beneficial wildlife, we can have a strong effect on our garden pests and our local ecology. Annuals, perennials, herbs, and vegetables can lure predatory insects, spiders, insect-eating birds, and other local animals to help control garden pests. Our gardens become havens for the life all around us. Proper garden management also helps preserve and protect our precious resources of soil and water. Savvy gardeners now compost, not just to improve their soils, but also to ease the burden on landfills. They use natural pesticides and ecological techniques for their own health and the health of their neighborhoods.

Our title, *The Gardener's Table,* reflects the ways we have integrated gardening and cooking in our lives. This book is as much about the potting table as the dinner table and the similarity of activities performed at each. We believe that gardening, cooking, and eating connect long before they meet at the kitchen door. And if you're like us, the cycle starts all over again at the gardening cook's table because good food always sparks lively conversation and renews the passion for the gardening and cooking that fuel it.

Over one of our more memorable meals, the table topic turned to our prehistoric ancestors. We talked about how, as hunters and gatherers, they knew about every leaf, berry, nut, and tuber. They knew how to find them, pick them, and use them. Children were counseled about which plants to avoid and which to revere, and in this way plants became part of their lore and legend. For hundreds of thousands of years before we gew a thing, plant knowledge was at the core of human cultures. Plants gave people food, medicine, clothes, and shelter. It was a matter of life and death to respect them and know them. This once-urgent plant knowledge is lost in today's fast-paced supermarket world, but it lingers in our genes. Maybe this is why the search for our long-lost biological roots always seems to begin at the gardener's table.

1

Planning the Cook's Garden & Setting Up the Gardener's Kitchen

Designing a Kitchen Garden

Gardening is a process of discovery. Seeing an exciting new plant or someone's beautiful garden or going to a nursery can inspire us to go out and impulsively plop plants in the ground. A hit-and-miss approach to vegetable gardening is probably good enough for a few seasonal gardens and basic crops like summer corn and tomatoes. But if you want a steady supply of all kinds of vegetables in season, all seasons, if you want to grow a kitchen garden instead of just a few vegetables, you need a plan.

For one thing, vegetables are fast-growing, vulnerable, fussy plants that require constant pampering. No other kind of gardening requires as much attention to detail yet offers such health, bounty, and prompt rewards. With the time constraints of modern life, you especially need a garden plan to save time and make kitchen gardening not just more rewarding, but easier.

The first step in planning your kitchen garden is to ask some basic questions. How much time can you spend on gardening? How big do you want your garden, and where should it go? Do you want to plant in boxes, beds, rows, or containers, and how do you want to irrigate? Which vegetables do you want to grow, and how much of each should you plant? And what about the overall design? Are you interested in the beauty of an edible landscape or the convenience of a small vegetable patch you can tinker with on summer weekends? These are all *planning* questions.

No matter which kind of plan you adopt, expect it to change over time. Gardening is a process of discovery. Your design will be less than perfect at first. You'll plant some things too late and others too early, and you'll lose a few plants. Getting started is the hard part. As you continue to spend time in the garden and gradually refine things from year to year, you'll arrive at a scheme that is both efficient and satisfying.

UNDERSTANDING YOUR GARDEN ENVIRONMENT

A seasoned gardener moving to a new location faces the same challenges as someone gardening for the first time. They both have to learn about their regional and neighborhood environments: when it's going to rain, where the prevailing winds come from, and what the life cycles of local pests are. They have to learn where the shadows fall in their gardens and the dates of the first and last frosts. Most gardeners wind up becoming experts about their natural surroundings.

Local Weather

As the sun's energy enters our earth, it moves air and oceans to create weather. Winds whoosh from high pressure to low pressure, water evaporates and falls as rain, and temperatures go up and down. Patterns of weather are called climate, and climate affects everything in the kitchen garden: how fast seeds germinate, when particular insects emerge, and the date we choose to begin planting in

spring. Weather also accelerates many plant diseases, such as downy mildew and late blight. Gardeners know how important it is to understand their local weather patterns and they like to talk about the weather. That's why garden clubs, local nurseries, and fellow gardeners are often the best sources of information about the vagaries of your climate. With simple instruments, you can even begin forecasting your own weather.

DO-IT-YOURSELF WEATHER FORECASTING

A modest collection of weather gadgets takes the guesswork out of forecasting, and better prepares you for killer storms and wilting heat waves. You can spend anywhere from $150 to $5,000 outfitting a home weather observatory, but only a few simple devices are essential:

Barometers

A barometer is vital to even the most casual weather observer. The barometer measures changes in air pressure. Dropping air pressure usually indicates overcast or rainy weather, and rising air pressure means fair and sunny weather.

For most gardeners, a simple dial barometer is adequate. Try to find one calibrated in both inches and millibars (a unit of atmospheric pressure). The forecasting notes written on the faces of many home barometers—such as "stormy" and "fair"—are not very useful. The position of a needle on a barometer isn't as important as the direction it is moving, and this is what you need to focus on.

Because barometers measure air pressure, they are very sensitive to altitude. Follow your barometer's directions carefully and calibrate it accordingly. You can also calibrate it on a windless day to the same reading as announced by a nearby radio or television station.

Thermometers

Thermometers are handy for measuring the temperature of the air and the soil. There are plenty of inexpensive, easy-to-use ones available:

- **Maximum/minimum thermometers** are only slightly more expensive than common thermometers and much more useful. A "max-min" thermometer tells the present temperature as well as the lowest and highest temperatures over a period of time. This is useful because plants respond more to temperature extremes than to averages, so you need to know how hot and cold it gets over a period of time. For example, tomatoes rarely set fruit if the nighttime temperature stays below 50°. Max-min thermometers tell you when this begins to happen.

The most convenient max-min thermometer is the type with a U-shaped mercury tube (shown here), which measures minimum temperatures on the left and maximum temperatures on the right. As the mercury moves up and down each side, it pushes a piece of metal that remains in place to register the temperature. The thermometer is reset with a small magnet.

- **Air-temperature thermometers** should be mounted above the ground and out of direct sunlight preferably facing north. Some people simply attach them to the outside of the house, under an eave. Others make shaded, vented containers for them in the garden.

- **Soil thermometers** measure the changes in soil temperature that occur during the season (but at a slower rate than air temperatures change). Soil thermometers work like meat thermometers; they are simply stuck into the soil to the depth at which you want to measure the temperature. Seed germination and the presence of many soil diseases are governed by soil temperature.

Weather Vanes

A weather vane should be on your roof near your garden. Changes in wind speed and direction can give important clues to impending weather changes; that's why this device is called a weather vane and not a wind vane. Weather forecasting begins when you combine the information about wind direction and barometric pressure. If the air pressure is high and dropping *and* the wind is shifting from a familiar direction, you will know that you might be in for some bad weather.

FIG. 1-1:
Maximum-Minimum Thermometer

A Maximum-Minimum Thermometer with a current reading of 52° F and a previous minimum reading of 40° F.

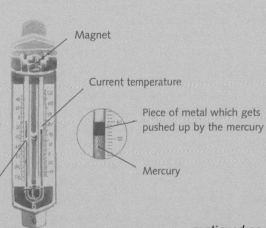

Magnet

Current temperature

Piece of metal which gets pushed up by the mercury

Mercury

Minimum temperature

continued on page 4

Rain Gauges

A rain gauge is useful because it tells you how much rainwater has fallen on your soil over a certain period of time. An inch of sudden rain can penetrate the topsoil, while two days of drizzle accumulates nothing. Most vegetables need approximately $1/2$ to 1 inch of water per week. Place your rain gauge in the garden and away from tall objects. To produce accurate readings, the gauge should be level and elevated off the ground.

Other Handy Forecasting Tools

There are many sources of information about your local weather patterns, like airports, boat harbors, and newspapers. Radio and television stations, some with around-the-clock regional forecasting reports, are great sources for short-term forecasts and measurements of high and low temperatures, rainfall, wind direction, humidity, and dew point.

Knowing your dew point is especially important because it tells you the temperature at which water starts to condense out of the air. If your dew point is above 32°, water will condense on your vegetables. If your dew point is below 32°, then the water *in* your plants will freeze first, killing the plants with the dreaded "black" frost. The worst condition for plants is not cold, but *dry* cold, and dew point is the best measure of this.

Your Plant Hardiness Zone

Hardiness zones tell which plants will grow where. If gardeners only grew native plants, plant hardiness would not be important. But gardeners want to cultivate nonnative vegetables, and they need to know what can grow where they live. The most commonly used reference is the USDA Hardiness Zone Map, which divides the United States into ten zones. Each zone corresponds to a range of average minimum winter temperatures, from Zone 1 (-50° to -40°F) to Zone 10 (+30° to +40°F). The map is available at most extension service offices, in libraries, and in many gardening books. The USDA scheme is useful in some ways, but very limited in others. For example, it puts the Olympic National Park in the same plant zone as parts of the Sonoran Desert.

At the other extreme, the American Horticulture Society (AHS) has developed a Plant Heat Zone Map based on the number of days per year above 86°F (30°C)—the temperature at which most plants experience damage to cellular protein. The AHS scheme recognizes twelve heat zones from cool summer areas with less than one day per year above 86°F (zone 1) to subtropical areas with more than 210 days per year above 86°F (zone 12).

The problem with both the cold and hot schemes is that extreme temperatures are only one of the many factors that determine how a plant grows. A more complete approach to plant climates has been devised by the editors of *Sunset* magazine, who organized the United States and southern Canada into forty-five climate zones based on temperature extremes *plus* rainfall, humidity, elevation, local topography, and nearness to bodies of water. The Sunset maps are described for the entire country in the *Sunset National Garden Book*, for the western United States in the *Sunset Western Garden Book,* and for the southern United States in *The Southern Living Garden Book* (see Bibliography, page 443).

Frost Dates and Growing Seasons

Most vegetables are sensitive to frosts. The number of days between the average last spring frost and the average first fall frost is the length of your growing season. Growing seasons can vary from 100 days in northern and mountain areas to 365 days in coastal southern California and southern Florida. Vegetable planting schedules often tell you to start seeds indoors six weeks before average last (spring) frost, or transplant twelve weeks before the average first (fall) frost. The key word here is "average." Since frost dates vary from year to year, you never know exactly when frost will hit. But if you know the *average* dates of the first and last frosts and keep your eye on the weather, you can at least beat the odds. For a list of vegetable planting schedules according to average frost dates, see pages 454–457.

Regional Microclimates

Microclimates are small climates within a larger climate. Available sunlight, slope of the land, bodies of water, and change in elevation create microclimates. If you live inland, on open, flat land away from mountains, chances are you have no obvious microclimates in your region. But if you live in a hilly or mountainous area, the valleys and ridges divide the landscape into warm and cool areas just a few miles apart. If you live by the sea or a large lake, high and low temperatures are tempered by the water. These moderate temperatures can extend the growing season of cool-weather vegetables, but shrink the season of warm-weather ones.

For example, in the area where we garden, the Monterey Bay of central California, a curving coastline, mountains, seasonal fog, and the Pacific Ocean all combine to produce a region of many microclimates. On the USDA map, the area includes two plant-climate zones. According to the *Sunset* scheme, the area includes four zones. The *Sunset* scheme is far more accurate than the USDA map, but if you talk to local gardeners and others who depend on the weather, it's clear the area has more like *eight* plant climates. In fact, your experienced gardening neighbor is probably the best microclimate expert.

Microclimates Around the Home

There are smaller, yet equally important microclimates around your home. Most mini-microclimates are caused by warm, reflecting objects or the movement of shadows around a house, which create hot and cold pockets on patios, decks, and throughout your yard. These patches of sunlight and shade not only shift during the day, but also over the seasons. In the winter the sun's path arcs in the southern sky near the horizon, reaching its lowest path on December 21 (winter solstice). As winter turns to summer, the sun creeps up the sky to the north in ever-larger arcs, until on June 21 (summer solstice) it reaches its highest point. (See the illustration of this on page 6.) Shadows of plants and structures shift accordingly. You should account for these changes when you choose where to place your kitchen garden. For example, as winter approaches, tall trees and fences begin casting shadows over previously sunny areas. In a yard with tall objects, there may be little space that gets enough hours of sunlight for vegetables to grow throughout the year. However, you don't have to plant all your vegetables in one spot. You can grow your tomatoes along the sunny border in the side yard and your greens in shadier places out back.

Around your house there are four basic microclimates: (1) a warm southern sun-facing side; (2) a cool northern shadow side; (3) a warm western side with afternoon sun; and (4) a temperate eastern side that may be warm or cool depending on how much sun it gets in the morning. Even these compass microclimates are very general because they change according to the seasonal movement of the sun in the sky—and because few houses are set on a straight north-south axis. For instance, the afternoon summer sun can actually reach the northern side of a house and sunburn summer greens planted in a pocket that was shady in the spring. On the other hand, the descending winter sun may cast shadows on your late-season vegetables

FIG. 1-2:
Seasonal Sun Path (Winter/Summer):
Changing shadows around
the home during the season

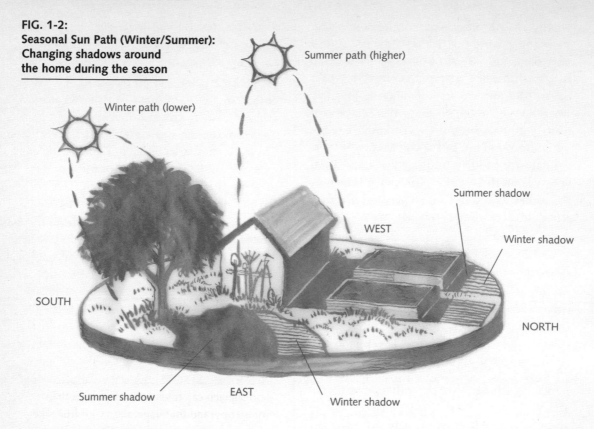

Summer path (higher)

Winter path (lower)

Summer shadow

Winter shadow

WEST

SOUTH

NORTH

Summer shadow

EAST

Winter shadow

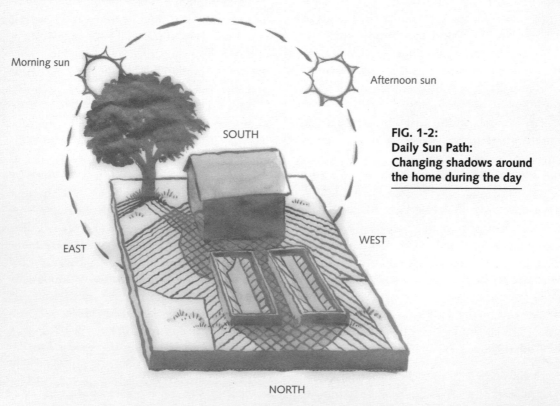

Morning sun

Afternoon sun

SOUTH

FIG. 1-2:
Daily Sun Path:
Changing shadows around
the home during the day

EAST

WEST

NORTH

and keep them from getting much-needed morning sun, which helps to protect against frost damage.

In some cases you don't have a choice where you put your garden. Your site may be limited to a balcony or small backyard. But if you do have enough space, start planning your garden by taking a stroll around your yard. The first thing you'll need to find is a sunny patch that gets at least 6 to 7 hours of sun per day during the time of year you want to grow vegetables. Sunlight is one thing even good gardeners can't grow! You can enrich soils and feed plants, but without enough light, vegetables will suffer. Fruiting types like tomatoes, squash, peppers, and beans will produce lush leaves, but little fruit.

If you look carefully, you'll notice that there are probably several different microclimates in your yard. It's well worth your while to discover where they are, because they'll let you grow things that the official zone map says you can't. A south-facing brick wall will absorb daytime heat and radiate it at night for tomatoes and eggplants. Shadows of hedgerows and other tall objects can overlap to create pockets of cool soil in the yard, perfect for summer greens. The mosaic of light and temperature around your home can make all sorts of planting opportunities. All you have to do is find them.

You can also help to create backyard microclimate in the following ways:

• Thin overgrown trees to allow more morning light to reach the planting area.

• Plant a windbreak, which can turn a cool, windy location into a warmer one.

• Paint fences and walls white to reflect extra light and heat.

There are a couple of ways to test for backyard microclimates. Try planting tender annuals like linaria or marigolds throughout your yard and watching them during the winter. Most plants may die, but the one surviving clump is probably rooted in a nice warm spot. Also, watch how frost melts on mornings after a freeze. Which parts of the yard warm up first?

When you do find a sunny patch, try to arrange your beds, boxes, or rows so that they run north and south rather than east and west. This way plants will receive a more even exposure to sunlight. In the winter, keep tall and trellised plants to the north end and leafy or root crops to the south. In the summer, place tall or trellised plants at the south end of the garden to shade areas for summer greens.

DEFINING SUN AND SHADE

Gardeners have coined a variety of terms to describe light in the garden. Although the terms are imprecise, they are useful. A general rule of thumb is that leafy crops like lettuce and spinach can tolerate shadier spots than root crops, and that vegetables with fruit, like tomatoes, peppers, and squash are sun lovers and need full sun.

Deep shade generally falls around tall objects, under eaves, or on the north side of buildings. The sun is blocked so that no direct light can fall on the plants; they only get indirect light. You may be able to grow hostas, mosses, baby tears, and ivy in deep shade, but not vegetables.

Partial shade means that an area gets full sun for part of the day and shade for part of the day. These conditions are typically found on the east and west sides of houses, trees, and tall barriers. The microclimate temperature depends on when the sunlight reaches the spot. On the east side of tall objects, sunlight hits in the morning when temperatures are low, making this a good spot for brassicas, alliums, most greens, and peas. The west side

continued on page 8

may be suitable for more heat-loving vegetables like tomatoes, beans, squash and peppers, depending on the available sunlight.

Dappled shade or filtered light happens when sunlight passes through porous materials like leaves, lattices, arbors, or shade cloth. The light in a dappled shade area is uniform but reduced—ideal for leafy greens, root crops, and other vegetables tolerant of lower light, like peas and leeks.

Full sun means at least 6 hours of direct sunlight per day. As noted before, most vegetables need full sun to grow well, though in summer, tall or trellised plants can extend the season by making partial or dappled shade for lettuce, carrots, greens, and the like (for more about this, see "Intercropping," page 32).

LIGHT NEEDS OF POPULAR VEGETABLES

Light Type	Vegetables
Partial or Dappled Shade (4 to 6 hours per day)	Beets, carrots, cauliflower, chard, chives, chicories, cucumber, lettuce, radicchio, arugula, onions, peas, spinach, and winter squash.
Full Sun (over 6 hours per day)	Beans, broccoli, cabbage, corn, eggplant, peppers, summer squash, and tomatoes.

Soil Drainage

The next thing to think about is your soil drainage. If you read the instructions on the back of vegetable seed packets, almost every one states "they need a rich, well-drained soil with uniform moisture." Some vegetables need less water than others, but none like soggy soils. Vegetables need both air and water around their roots. This means they need good soil drainage.

Wet or poorly drained soils are found in low spots in the backyard, on clay-filled dirt, under runoff from buildings, and around leaky irrigation systems. These areas retain water and keep the root zone wet.

There are three parts to understanding soil drainage. First, observe how your topsoil drains. Clay soils have a tendency to drain slowly; sandy soils drain rapidly. Regular additions of organic matter will eventually make both topsoils just right, so this is the easiest to fix.

Second, note that even with a sandy topsoil there may be underground layers of clay or rock, called "pans," that keep water from draining. A "claypan" is a layer of clay underneath the topsoil. If it's not too thick, a claypan can often be corrected by double-digging (see pages 65–66). If it's more than 1 or 2 feet thick, try growing a deep-rooted, green manure like clover or orchard grass (see page 127) to break things up. (It may take a few seasons to establish itself.) "Hardpans" are rocklike layers usually found in alkaline soils. For example, in the arid Southwest many areas have hardpans of chaliche, a cement-hard layer of limestone and clay that stops roots cold. Sometimes you can break up shallow hardpans with crow bars.

Third, if your soil is in a low-lying area, water will always find its way there. Under these conditions, either install buried drainage pipe to carry away excess water, garden in raised or boxed beds (see pages 10–12), or abandon the site.

There are several ways to assess your soil drainage:

- Dig around in your yard to see what the existing soil is like. What's growing there now? Lush growth or thick green grass probably indicates good soil drainage, but if there are only tough weeds or nothing much growing it's an indication of poor soil drainage and you'll have to take steps to improve it.

- Feel the topsoil to evaluate the texture, using the ball and ribbon method (see pages 54–55 for instructions). It's important to know whether you have a sandy or clay soil.

- Look for impervious layers beneath. Dig a 2- to 3-foot-deep hole (see pages 57–58) and look for layers of clay or sediment that might keep water from draining. This will let you know what your entire soil looks like, from top to bottom.

- Look at your weeds. Some weeds thrive in compacted or poorly drained soils (for more about this, see pages 59–60). A few isolated plants won't mean much, but if these weeds are the dominant ones growing, it may mean bad drainage.

- Fill a hole with water. A simple test will tell you if you have good drainage or not. Dig a hole about 1 foot deep and 6 inches across. Fill it with water and allow it to drain completely. As soon as it does, fill it again and see how long it takes to drain again. If it takes more than 8 hours, you may have to improve your drainage, grow in raised beds or boxes, or find another location.

Irrigation Water

Gardening books usually stress the importance of testing your soil, but it's surprising how many don't even talk about the quality of the water that comes out of your hose. Residential water is full of salts and other chemicals, and some of them not only harm plants, but build up in the soil and produce long-term problems. Most soil-testing laboratories can test your irrigation water. They'll let you know if you have too much chlorine, fluorine, salts, or sodium, or if your water pH is too acid or alkaline. If you have a standard water softener, your water may be high in sodium—an element harmful to plants. Unfortunately, there is very little you can do to improve the chemistry of your irrigation water. There are no cheap filters that can remove harmful chemicals in solution. However, you can reduce the effects of bad water on plants by improving your soil with aged organic matter (see page 104).

LAYING OUT YOUR KITCHEN GARDEN

The average person doesn't have the time to tend a large garden. Time, space, and convenience are now at the heart of any garden design, especially a kitchen garden, which requires so much care and attention. As we downsize our gardens and spend more of our time away from them, planting schemes have to conserve both time and space. Ask yourself: (1) how big do you want your garden? and (2) how do you want to arrange the plants?

The Size of Your Garden

When it comes to deciding on a size for your garden, think small. A common mistake that many beginning gardeners make is to start a garden that's too big and beyond their ability to manage it. A small, well-cared-for garden yields far more than a large, neglected one.

It's surprising how much you can grow in a small space. A well-tended plot of 10 square feet can produce most of the leaf and root crops for one person during a year. As you add larger vegetables, like tomatoes, corn, squash, and cole crops, more space is needed, but if you plan right you can come away with a big harvest on surprisingly little land. There are many fine gardening books that focus on small-space or container vegetable gardening (see the Bibliography, page 443).

The Shape of Your Garden

Kitchen gardens can take on any shape you wish, but some arrangements are more space-efficient than others. Arranging your vegetables is part esthetics and part practical management. There are three general approaches to setting out vegetables: in rows, in raised beds, and in framed beds.

Row method: The traditional way of growing vegetables in long straight rows with irrigation furrows between has only one advantage: it allows a gardener to weed with a machine by running a rototiller or tractor up and down the aisles. The row method is simply the design of large-scale farming being put to use in the garden. For most gardeners row planting wastes far too much space to be practical. A big country garden may have room for single narrow rows separated by wide paths. But in smaller spaces, wide, raised beds are far more efficient.

Raised beds: People have been growing vegetables in raised beds for centuries, from the kitchen plots of ancient China to the French market gardens of the nineteenth century. In this country, raised bed vegetable culture was popularized by central California gardeners in the early 1970s and dubbed the French intensive biodynamic method. Raised beds are typically 3 to 5 feet wide and as long as you want to make them. The paths between them are usually 1 to 3 feet wide. In this arrangement, vegetables are planted very closely in the beds and are tended from the paths between the beds.

There are several advantages to growing vegetables in raised beds:

1. **Saves space:** Since plants are grown close together and less space is devoted to paths, yields are 20 to 40 percent higher than for an equivalent area in single rows.

2. **Limits compaction:** Foot traffic is confined to the paths so that soil compaction is limited. You never have to walk on the beds, so the soil stays light and fluffy, allowing plant roots to grow better.

3. **Facilitates weeding:** The well-defined and narrow paths are easy to mulch, making weeding easier.

4. **Better soil:** The soil in the beds is above ground level, so it warms and drains quickly. This can often extend planting seasons and increase yields.

5. **More efficient cultivation:** You can concentrate soil-building efforts on the soil in the beds, rather than on the entire garden.

6. **Easier gardening:** The beds can be treated like individual plots, making fertilizer schedules and rotations easier.

Raised beds can be prepared with a rototiller or hand dug by the double-dig method. (For more about this, see pages 65–66, or refer to *How to Grow More Vegetables* by John Jeavons, for complete double-digging instructions.)

Framed beds: Framed beds are raised beds that are framed in wood, brick, hay bales or stone. They are basically large, bottomless, rectangular containers that let you pour good soil on top of the bed. They have all the advantages of raised beds and a few more:

1. **Lets you grow on poor soil.** Framed beds filled with your own topsoil blend are

FIG. 1-3: Raised beds

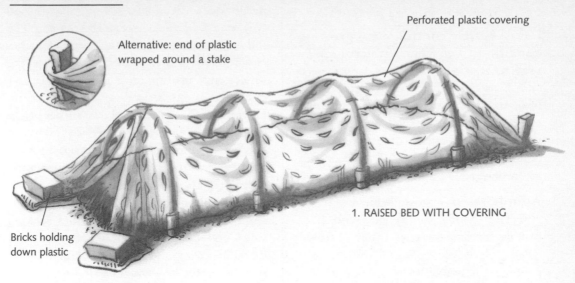

Alternative: end of plastic wrapped around a stake

Perforated plastic covering

Bricks holding down plastic

1. RAISED BED WITH COVERING

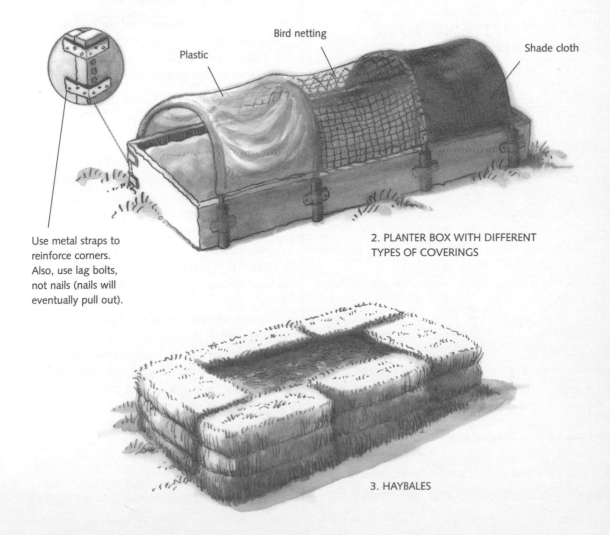

Plastic

Bird netting

Shade cloth

Use metal straps to reinforce corners. Also, use lag bolts, not nails (nails will eventually pull out).

2. PLANTER BOX WITH DIFFERENT TYPES OF COVERINGS

3. HAYBALES

often the only way to garden over heavy, poorly drained soils.

2. **Gives better control over growing conditions:** The framing material can be used to attach plastic sheets, row covers, and shade cloth for protecting crops from birds and deer and extending the growing season for both cool- and warm-weather vegetables. You can also use it to anchor netting underneath the bed to keep out soil rodents.

3. **Affords easier access:** Framed beds are especially handy for people who have trouble bending over, and they are used extensively in gardens that allow access to people with disabilities.

WATERING YOUR KITCHEN GARDEN

Most plants are about 90 percent water. Water carries nutrients throughout the plant and evaporates from leaf surfaces. This escaping water cools the plant and allows carbon dioxide to enter the leaves where photosynthesis takes place. Plants may often wilt in the heat of a hot mid-afternoon because they are giving off more water than they are absorbing. Under these conditions, the plants usually recover by late evening. But if plants wilt in the morning, the soil is probably too dry, and you should water as soon as you can.

For good growth, vegetables need about $1/2$ to 1 inch of water per week, or about 60 gallons per 100 square feet. One inch of rain will wet a sandy soil down about 12 inches, a loam soil about 8 inches, and a clay soil 4 to 6 inches. In areas where it rains throughout the year, a garden rain gauge is the easiest way to see if you are getting adequate water. If you have to supplement the rainfall in your area, be sure to follow these guidelines for using your water most efficiently.

Feel the soil. It's amazing how many people water their gardens on a regular schedule, without checking whether the soil really needs water. When in doubt, probe the soil with your fingers or dig a small hole in it. The soil may be dry on top, but damp a few inches down. In silt and clay soils, for example, the surface may dry up, crust over, and act as a mulch to keep the soil moist underneath. However, if the soil is dry 4 to 6 inches below the surface, it's time to water. Always ask yourself: "What's the moisture like at *root depth?*"

Apply water slowly, deeply, and uniformly. Plant growth, especially of vegetables, is interrupted if the soil is allowed to become very dry and then becomes soaking wet. Constant soil moisture is very important for rapid growth and best yields, especially for shallow-rooted vegetables like lettuces, brassicas, and alliums.

Apply water when the air is still. This way, water goes into the soil and is not carried away with the wind.

Water in the morning when the humidity is usually highest and the temperature is lowest. Watering in the middle of the day loses water to evaporation, and watering at day's end can encourage many foliage diseases.

Water fruiting vegetables just after blossoming. This is the most critical period.

Try to cultivate soil before you water. This way it can seep into the soil and not be blocked by any surface crusts.

Remember that the soil's organic matter is a water bank. Adding organic matter to your soil is a way to store and conserve water.

Avoid overhead watering. It's wasteful, can cause plant diseases, encourages weeds, and doesn't always place water where you want it—at the root zone. Irrigation water is usually full of salts, so overhead sprinkling is not the same as rain water, which is free of salts.

Ways to Water

There are several ways to water your vegetables. Some gardeners use bubblers on hoses to irrigate between rows of crops. Others simply sprinkle their plants with a hose or spray attachment. Flooding furrows between rows of plants wastes water and misses the main root zone. These methods are not the most efficient or desirable ways to water.

In many areas of the country where water is in short supply, or where summer rains are sparse, gardeners use a variety of drip irrigation methods for putting water right where they want it—at the base of the plant. Regardless of your climate, drip irrigation methods are the best way to conserve water and avoid plant diseases. Drip irrigation is more expensive than using hoses, but the savings in water and reduction of diseases more than makes up for it. Check with your local irrigation specialists or write one of the many garden suppliers listed on pages 451–452 for more information.

Six basic types of drip irrigation hardware, or systems, can be used in a kitchen garden: "spaghetti" tubing, porous hose, laser tubing, drip irrigation hose with punched-in emitters, in-line emitter tubing, and raised mini-sprinklers.

FIG. 1-4: Various types of "drip" and "localized" irrigation systems for raised-bed vegetable culture.

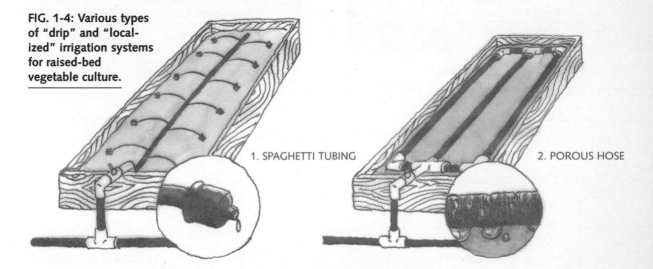

1. SPAGHETTI TUBING

2. POROUS HOSE

Spaghetti Tubing

Features

- Made with lots of pieced-together parts
- Uses emitters at the end of $1/4$-inch tubing
- Puts water right at the root zone

Disadvantages

- Tangles easily
- Difficult to weed and mulch around
- Easily sliced by garden tools
- Doesn't supply enough water for bigger plants
- Difficult to set up for annual plants

Porous Hose

Features

- Also called soaker hose
- Water oozes out of entire surface of hose
- Easy to install

Disadvantages

- Bulky and ugly
- Must be moved to weed
- Hard water seals pores with salts; needs regular flushing
- Flow rate varies from beginning to the end of the line
- Can only be used on level ground

Adapted from Kourik, R. *Drip Irrigation for Every Landscape and All Climates,* Metamorphic Press, Santa Rosa, California.

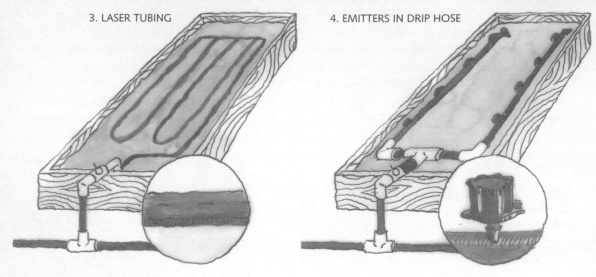

3. LASER TUBING   4. EMITTERS IN DRIP HOSE

FIG. 1-4, *(continued)*

Laser Tubing

Features

- Resembles spaghetti tubing
- Water comes out tiny holes every 6 to 12 inches along entire length
- Arrows printed on tubing for water-flow direction
- Easy to install
- Cheaper than porous hose

Disadvantages

- Clogs easily with algae, fine sediment, and salts
- Long lengths or steep hills cause large flow differences
- Tangles easily
- Difficult to weed around

Punched-In Emitters in Drip Hose

Features

- Emitters insert directly into 1/2-inch drip hose
- Emitters come in many sizes (1/2 to 1 gallon per hour)
- There are Pressure Compensating Emitters (PCEs), which keep flow consistent regardless of slope or hose length
- Simple to snake around vegetable beds
- Fittings don't leak
- Less likely to clog than porous or laser tubing

Disadvantages

- Costly, especially PCEs
- Stems of emitters grow brittle with age

5. IN-LINE EMITTER TUBING

6. MINI-SPRINKLER

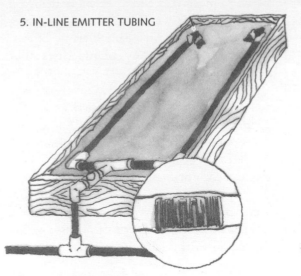
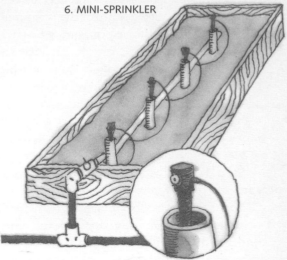

FIG. 1-4, *(continued)*

In-Line Emitter Tubing

Features

- $1/2$-inch tube with emitters preinstalled inside at regular intervals

- Emitters $1/2$ to 1 gallon per hour, at regular intervals of 12 to 36 inches

- Internal emitters are clog resistant

- Available both with noncompensating and pressure-compensating features

- Easy to install and snake around plantings

- Wet spots merge into continuous moist zone, thus moistening soil entire length of line and below surface

Disadvantages

- Needs extra planning for plants far apart

- Can't turn as small a radius as porous hose

- Not widely available

Raised/ Lowered Mini-Sprinklers

Features

- Punched-in, raised mini-sprinkler emitters that can also be lowered to soil surface

- Single line makes weeding easier

- In raised position ideal for sprouting seeds

- At lowered position can water larger, taller plants without wetting leaves

Disadvantages

- System is costly and installation is time consuming

- In raised position, wide water dispersion encourages unnecessary weeds

- Sprinkler emitters need regular attention with unfiltered, unchlorinated, or hard water

- Inconvenient to pull up, repair, and clean

CHOOSING WHAT AND HOW MUCH TO GROW

It may seem odd, but many gardeners choose vegetables and varieties that have captured their fancy for some reason, but when it's time to harvest they're really not so keen on eating what they've planted. To avoid this mistake, ask yourself which vegetables you actually eat. After you make your list of vegetables to grow, you need to figure out how much of each vegetable to plant. This is done in two steps:

Step 1: How many vegetables do you eat?

Try to estimate how much of each fresh vegetable you actually eat every year. (Processed vegetables like potato chips don't

count!) Do you eat one cabbage a month or two a year? All those carrots you munch on between meals may add up to more than you think. Start by writing down which fresh vegetables you eat on a daily basis.

Step 2: How many plants does that represent?

Once you figure out how much of each vegetable you eat, then translate that into the corresponding number of plants. This is easy for root crops like carrots and most leaf crops like lettuce, because one entire plant is a serving. But for potatoes and fruit-bearing crops, like squash and tomatoes that have many servings per plant, you need to convert pounds of fruit to number of plants. The information in the table below may help you

AVERAGE NUMBER OF VEGETABLES IN AMERICAN DIETS			
Vegetable	Average Annual per Capita Consumption (lbs) in Average Diet	Average Annual Plants in Average Diet	Average Annual Plants in "Natural Foods" Diet
Potatoes	49.2	10–15	15–20
Lettuce	24.9	30–40	50–60
Tomatoes	10.3	3–5	4–6
Onions	8.7	15–20	40–60
Cabbage	7.3	3–4	8–10
Carrots	6.1	25–30	90–120
Corn	5.7	3–4	10–15
Cucumber	3.8	1–2	5
Peppers	2.8	2–3	10–15
Broccoli	2.1	3–5	15–20
Beans	1.4	1–2	20–25
Garlic	0.8	4–8	10–20
Eggplant	0.5	1	1–3
Beets	n/a	n/a	30–40
Chard	n/a	n/a	3–5
Kale	n/a	n/a	10–15
Leeks	n/a	n/a	25–35
Spinach	n/a	n/a	15–20
Squash, summer	n/a	n/a	5-10

U.S. per capita consumption based on data from USDA Economic Research Service; USDA National Food Consumption Survey; *Produce Marketing Almanac*. "Natural foods" diet is based on the authors' survey of natural food stores and kitchen gardeners in Central California.

get started. The table includes the average number of plants eaten in a more health-conscious diet in which vegetables are a priority. Of course, a strict vegetarian diet would include even more vegetables, so plan accordingly.

GROWING VEGETABLE SEEDLINGS

Vegetables are easy plants to start, since over the ages, people have selected them to germinate and grow quickly. Most gardeners have experienced the frustration of losing their homegrown seedlings to overwatering, drying out, or pests. Like anything, young seedlings need regular care. Your local nursery has a selection of seedling vegetables, already to transplant. So why bother starting from scratch and growing your own seedlings? There are several good reasons!

1. **Homegrown seedlings make healthy plants.** Over the years, we have learned that the most efficient way to start vegetables is by planting healthy, homegrown seedlings. A few vegetables—like carrots, greens, and bunching onions—are, however, still easier to direct-sow.

2. **Homegrown seedlings give you more types of vegetables to choose from.** Local nurseries can't possibly carry the enormous variety of vegetables now available through mail-order seed companies (see pages 447–450), including vegetables of special flavor or pest resistance. Nor are they likely to carry those piquant nutritional greens, carrots with high beta-carotene, or ethnic or heirloom varieties. These vegetables you have to grow yourself. In fact, many people get hooked on growing their own seedlings because they want to experience a wider variety of vegetables.

3. **Homegrown seedlings extend the growing season and give you a bigger harvest.** When you plant out a seedling instead of a seed, you shorten the time the plant is in the ground. With fast-growing vegetables this can mean one or two extra crops per season.

4. **Homegrown seedlings conserve seeds and save money.** When you direct-sow in the garden, many seeds are wasted. Most seedlings are thinned or gobbled up by some hungry garden critter. This is why people are used to buying seed amounts suitable for broadcasting. But, when you grow your own seedlings, you can literally count the number of plants (seeds) you need, and buy accordingly, with very little waste (see page 18). As the cost of seeds continues to rise, counting seeds will amount to saving money.

5. **Homegrown seedlings make stronger, healthier plants.** Seedlings you grow yourself are generally healthier than store-bought and soil-germinated seedlings. If you do everything right and at the correct time, you'll have the healthiest seedlings money can buy and, best of all, you'll know exactly what went into growing them. Moreover, healthy seedlings grow into healthy plants. This more than makes up for the initial coddling they require.

6. **Homegrown seedlings avoid pests of emerging seedlings.** Newly sprouted seeds are susceptible to many diseases and pests. Fungus, snails, caterpillars, and birds all enjoy a good seedling meal. Large healthy seedlings that have been hardened-off are less likely to be attacked, or if they are nibbled on, they are more likely to survive.

7. **Homegrown seedlings protect your soil from diseases.** Some serious plant diseases can be introduced by store-bought seedlings. These include clubroot and yellows of brassicas, along with anthracnose, mosaic, and wilt.

QUICK-REFERENCE SEED FACTS

VEGETABLE	SEEDS PER OUNCE	GRAM	GERMINATION NOTES
Arugula[1]	15,000	550	Treat like lettuce.
Beans (snap)[1]	100–125	3–4	Treat roots with care. Direct-sow only after soil reaches 57°F.
Beets[1]	1,600	60	Soak seeds overnight. Direct-sow or transplant from peat pots carefully after spring frost. Germs cool or warm. Don't disturb roots.
Broccoli, cabbage, cauliflower, collards, kale[3]	9,000	300	Sprout seeds warm and grow-on cool (50°–60°F). Easy to transplant. Move quickly; don't let seedlings linger in pots.
Cabbage, Chinese[1]	10,000	360	Transplants poorly; for other see Broccoli.
Carrots[2]	25,000	820	Direct-sow on prepared seed bed. Keep seeds moist for 2 weeks.
Chard[1]	1,600	60	Handle seedlings carefully.
Chicory (endive)[2]	27,000	960	Treat like lettuce.
Chives[1]	25,000	900	Treat like onion; can also divide plants.
Chives, garlic[1]	6,700	240	Treat like onion; can also divide plants.
Corn, sweet[1]	120–180	4–6	Direct-sow, or sprout in peat pots for a few days. Transplants well if young.
Cucumbers[1]	1,100	40	Sprout in peat pots at 75°–85°F. Handle tranplants carefully.
Dandelion[1]	35,000	1250	Treat like hardy lettuce.
Eggplants[3]	6,500	230	In cool climates, prewarm soil with plastic mulch. Germinate at 80°F.
Leeks[1]	10,000	360	Transplants well. Keeps in pots for long periods.
Lettuce[1]	25,000	900	To sprout, needs light and 75°F. Grow-on cool (55°–65°F). For extended harvest, direct-sow some and transplant others for long harvest.
Mustard[1]	15,000	550	Direct-sow and thin quickly.
Onions (bulb and bunching)[1]	8,000	285	Direct-sow or transplant. Sprout at 70°F. Grow-on cool at 55°–65°F. Keep in pots for long periods.
Peas[1]	90–175	3–6	Direct-sow, but better tranplanted from peat pots.
Peppers	3,400–4,900	120–175	Transplants well. Presoaking seeds helps.
Pumpkins[1]	100–300	3–10	Direct-sow or transplant; sow in pots, and transplant quickly and carefully.
Spinach[1]	2,800	100	Direct-sow or transplant. Presoaking seeds helps.
Squash, summer[1]	80–190	3–7	Treat like pumpkins.
Squash, winter[1]	50–300	7–11	Treat like pumpkins.
Tomatoes[3]	8,000–14,000	285–520	Sprout at 75°. Grow-on at 65°F. with high light. Seedlings grow quickly. Transplants well; bury stems deeply.

1 = Can be directly sown or started indoors, 2 = Directly sown only, 3 = Start and plant out from individual containers

8. **Homegrown seedlings provide opportunity for recycling.** Gardeners who grow their own seedlings are always on the prowl for containers—large, flat, open ones for sowing their seeds and small, deeper, individual ones for growing the young sprouts. Many such containers are lying around the home, waiting to be recycled in the garden (see page 24).

9. **Homegrown seedlings provide special satisfaction and enjoyment.** You get to preserve the diversity of life, grow the variety that suits you, and reaffirm the future, all in one push of the seed.

What Is a Seed?

Seeds are alive. They are, in fact, living, breathing plant embryos. Within their hard shells they contain enough enzymes and food energy to carry them through germination and the first few days as an emerging seedling. The bigger the seed, the more the food. Seeds also have all the genetic information that will direct what they'll look like, which pests they'll resist, and how big they'll grow.

A seed is really a dormant plant, waiting for the right conditions to begin growing. This means anything that can break open the seed coat and let the plant embryo absorb water. As the seed swells, it bursts into germination. To break their seed coats, many perennial plants need all sorts of prodding, like fire, acid, light, dark, long periods of cold, scratching ("scarification"), or dark, cool, moist conditions ("stratification"). Fortunately, most vegetable seeds need only a warm, moist mix that is free of pests, to sprout up successfully. So, if you want to start your own vegetables, you'll need to locate a warm place with plenty of light, make suitable potting mixes, and find some containers.

A Warm, Well-Lighted Place

Onions, chives, and lettuce seeds germinate better if they have some light. All other vegetable seeds can germinate with or without light—they aren't particular. After seeds germinate, however, the sprouting plants do need light…right away. Young vegetables grow quickly, and if the emerging seedlings don't find light, they grow a pale, weak stem in search of it. Some seedlings can grow out of this early setback, but it's best to give them light from the moment you see the swollen seeds burst the top of the mix.

Try to locate a south-facing window with a porous curtain for bright, but indirect light. Remember, windows are vertical; they don't get as much sunlight as a greenhouse, sunroom, or outdoor cold frame with their sloping glass roofs.

If you don't have enough natural light to grow seedlings, try using artificial light. Fluorescent tubes are preferred over sunlamps or incandescent lights, both of which have poor colors and too much heat. As a general rule, vegetable seedlings need about 15 to 20 watts of light per square foot of growing area. A double row of fluorescent lighting tubes is usually enough for a row of flats about 16 inches wide. One tube should be a cool white tube with its bluish white light and the other a warm white tube with its tan or pinkish light. This gives plants a more complete light spectrum from violet to red. You can also use wide-spectrum light tubes specifically designed for growing plants indoors. Fluorescent tubes have a low light intensity, so hang the tubes about 4 inches above the plants. Be sure to keep raising the light as the plants grow, but always keep the lights closer than you think. Time your lights so that they don't shine more than 16 hours a day. Plants need to rest some in the dark in order to grow.

Since they need both light and heat, an ideal place for growing seedlings might be above a baseboard heater, or an air conditioner or refrigerator exhaust that is near a south-facing window with porous curtains, or in a well-lit bathroom or sun porch. But not everybody has these things. Since it's so important to keep within a range of temperatures to grow healthy seedlings, many gardeners buy commercial electric heating cables or waterproof rubber mats, connect these to a thermostat, and then locate the heat in the sunniest spot they can find. Resourceful gardeners might want to try water bed, yogurt, or hot pack heaters.

There are a few things about temperature worth mentioning:

• Some vegetables, like lettuce, cabbage, and turnips, will germinate just fine over a wide range of temperatures. Others, like tomatoes, celery, lima beans, and eggplant, are fussy and need more precise temperatures to sprout quickly. If you want most of your seeds to germinate as rapidly as possible, then you need to keep them at their optimum temperature (in their medium), which can range from 70° to 95°F. A constant temperature of 70° to 80°F is generally accepted as best for germinating most vegetable seeds. If you can't make the temperature optimum, at least make it constant.

FIG. 1-5:
Optimum mix temperatures for germinating vegetable seeds

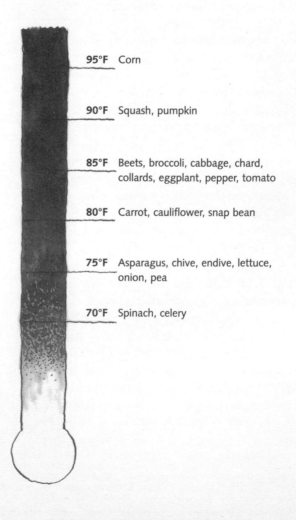

95°F   Corn

90°F   Squash, pumpkin

85°F   Beets, broccoli, cabbage, chard, collards, eggplant, pepper, tomato

80°F   Carrot, cauliflower, snap bean

75°F   Asparagus, chive, endive, lettuce, onion, pea

70°F   Spinach, celery

• The big difference between germinating seeds and growing seedlings (besides the medium) is the temperature. Seeds need constant warmth. But once they sprout, they not only need less heat, they also require a cool, dark period (i.e., night) to use the compounds made during the day's photosynthesis. Try to grow seedlings at 65° to 75°F during the day and about 5° to 15°F lower at night.

• As transplants approach the size for hardening-off, reduce all temperatures by another 5° to 10°. The process of growing vegetable seedlings is one of weaning the baby plant from a controlled, steady environment to the vagaries of the outdoors.

Potting Mix Ingredients

Potting mixes are blends of various ingredients for growing plants in containers. When you grow your own vegetable seedlings, you'll wind up using two different kinds of potting mixes. A nutrient-poor, somewhat sterile mix to germinate seeds (germ mix) and a richer mix with fertilizer to grow-on the seedlings (transplant mix). The major potting mix ingredients for holding water are peats, vermiculite, wood waste products, aged leaf molds, manures, and compost. And to promote good drainage, perlite and sand are commonly used.

Peat

Peat is a generic term for any plant material that partially decays underwater (for more about this, see page 105). Peats are known for holding lots of water and for being acidic and somewhat sterile. The properties of peat vary greatly, depending on the place where it is mined (principally Wisconsin, New Jersey, and Canada), the age of the peat, and the kind of plants in the bog. The most common type of peat used in nurseries comes from sphagnum moss. Research has shown that besides absorbing lots of water (up to its own weight), sphagnum peat moss (SPM) also has antibiotic properties that can reduce seedling "damp-off" diseases.

SPM has its problems, however. Once it gets dry, it is very difficult to get wet again, especially big chunks. This is why SPM should be sifted and mixed with other ingredients. SPM is becoming more expensive as prime deposits become depleted. It's getting harder to find the old, dark, and well-aged SPM that provides so many benefits to mixes.

For germination mixes it is best to sift peat moss through a $1/4$- to $1/16$-inch screen. Peat moss directly from the bag is typically too coarse for small seeds and tends to dry and crust.

Vermiculite

Vermiculite is a clay that is heated to about 2000°F. The heat vaporizes trapped water and literally pops the mineral layers apart, resulting in a light, fluffy, sterile product that retains lots of water. Being a clay, vermiculite also stores nutrients and provides a few of its own (notably magnesium). Small particles of sifted vermiculite are ideal for covering seeds.

Wood Waste Products

Wastes from the lumber industry are being used more and more as a substitute for peat moss in potting mixes. Most barks need to be sifted through $1/4$- to $1/2$-inch screens. Softwood barks (fir and pine) are preferred, but hardwood bark works just fine. Raw bark contains plant toxins that can harm young plants, so it should be aged or composted first (see page 132). Bark is preferred over sawdust because it decays quicker, contains antifungal properties, and doesn't have as much tannic acid. If you don't want to use peat moss, and you don't have access to aged fir bark, try making a soilless compost out of green wood chips or sawdust (see page 118) or both. After a few months, when the pile becomes dark and musty smelling, it can be sifted and used in both germination and transplant mixes.

Well-Aged Compost, Manure, and Leaf Mold

Some gardeners use leaf mold, very old steer manure, or compost in their mixes with great success, especially with brassicas and greens. Steer manure is preferred because it contains so much fiber. It should be dark and have an earthy and musty, rather than an ammonia, smell. The compost should have no soil in it...like the soil you find on the roots of weeds. For our mixes, we've used composted bark, green wood chips, and sawdust in place of peat moss.

There are a few precautions. The fresh leaves of some plants contain chemicals that inhibit seed germination (e.g., walnut, beech, and eucalyptus plus several Mediterranean-climate plants). As leaves decay, these chemicals are destroyed and rendered harmless in the mold, but beware of fresh leaves. Also, watch where you collect. In our area, rotting leaves of the California live oak, *Quercus agrifolia,* contain serious fungal diseases that can infect seeds and roots of other plants. If you collect leaf mold from the wild, be knowledgeable about local soil fungal diseases and which plants they attack. To be safe, limit your leaf mold to deciduous trees like sycamore, elm, maple, and birch.

Perlite

Perlite is a lava rock that has been expanded by heating, much like vermiculite. Each kernel of perlite contains a maze of sealed air spaces, which makes it 86 percent lighter than sand. Perlite retains a little water, but is used primarily to help mixes drain, to make them lighter, and to insulate them against temperature swings. After a year or so in containers, perlite compresses and loses its properties. This is not a problem with the fast-growing vegetables.

Sand

The word "sand" refers to bits of rock that range in size from $1/20$ mm to 2 mm ($1/16$ inch to $1/500$ inch, see page 53). Sand is used for drainage, and the ideal size is sand that is neither too large, which produces uneven drainage, or too small, which results in the sand floating to the surface of the mix. There are several kinds of sand.

- **Beach sand**: Most beach sand is actually quartz sand, which is what we think of when we hear the word "sand." *Beach sand should not be used in germination mixes.* It is usually too fine and may contain lots of salts.

- **Construction sand**: Although cheap and available, construction sand often has too many small and large particles. If you can sift out the extreme sizes, it's usable for germination mixes.

- **Crushed granite sand:** This comes from granite quarries and is sharp and angular, unlike beach and river sand, which is rolled over and over by water. It's this sharpness that makes it superior for drainage. Granite sand is not very uniform in size, so it may need sifting for potting mixes.

- **Plasterer's sand:** This sand is specially sifted to extract the large and small particles that hinder plastering work. It is excellent for drainage in all potting mixes.

Ingredients to Avoid in Mixes

Seedlings are especially susceptible to toxins, salts, and several diseases. For this reason, we limit the soil or fresh organic matter we add to our potting mixes. Soil has clay in it, which can get hard in just a few waterings, especially in small containers. Also, soil is not sterile, and it may contain seedling diseases. If you have a rich loam soil free of diseases, try the "with soil" transplant mix recipe suggested on the next page.

Recipes for Propagation Mixes

It seems that every gardener has a favorite formula for a potting mix to germinate seeds or grow seedlings. Regardless of the formula, an ideal mix should have the following properties:

• It should retain water.

• It should drain excess water and allow air to enter.

• It should be as lightweight as possible since containers often need to be moved around.

• It should be free of toxins, salts, and diseases.

• It should be free of large particles that impede germination or root growth.

A germ mix doesn't need nutrients. The seed has enough food stored for the first few days of seedling growth. Besides, for the short time they are in germination flats, you can easily feed the sprouted seeds with foliar fertilizers (see page 76). The role of the germ mix is to provide a clean, moist, and airy medium for the roots of sprouting seeds. The transplant mix, on the other hand, should have enough fertilizer to feed the baby plant. You can substitute sand for perlite, but the mix will be heavier and lose water faster. You can substitute old fir bark, compost, steer manure, or leaf mold for the peat moss, but be sure to sift it through a $1/4$-inch screen. Experiment by adding mixes of different ingredients to tall glass jars. Fill the jar with water and watch as the water percolates down through the mix. You'll soon learn to recognize the best mix with the ingredients you have.

Making Germination Mixes

We've tried many germination mixes over the years, and found this one the most reliable:

Germination Mix
    1 part vermiculite
    1 part perlite
    1 part sifted peat moss

With adequate warmth and light, virtually all vegetables germinate easily in this mix. Gather up your ingredients in the proper proportions *by volume* using bowls, buckets, or hands. Mix the dry ingredients together *thoroughly* until there are no clumps of any one material. (They don't call it a mix for nothing.) Set aside the amount you want to use immediately. The rest can be stored for several months if it's kept dry. Now dampen the portion you want. If you can, use warm water since it is more easily absorbed, especially by peat moss. Make the mix damp, but not soggy. Pick up a handful and squeeze hard. If water runs out, it's too wet. If not, you're ready to begin filling your germination containers.

Making Transplant Mixes

A transplant mix is different than a germination mix. Transplanted seedlings need something that drains better and provides more nourishment for the growing plants; a richer mix that is a little closer to soil. Some of our favorite transplant mix recipes are given below. A "part" can be any volume from a handful to a wheelbarrow full. Blend your dry ingredients thoroughly, using the same techniques described for the germination mix.

Standard Mix No. 1
    2 parts aged, sifted leaf mold, or soilless compost,
        or tree bark
    1 part sifted peat moss
    1 part perlite or sharp, medium-sized sand

Standard Mix No. 2
    4 parts aged, sifted compost
    2 parts sifted peat moss
    1 part perlite or sand
    1 part vermiculite

Mix No. 3 (Greens and Brassicas)
    1 part plasterer's sand
    1 part sifted leaf mold
    1 part aged, sifted, soilless compost or aged, sifted cow or stable manure

Soil-Based Mix (good for hardening off)
    1 part sharp, medium-sized sand
    2 parts aged, sifted compost
    1 part rich loam soil

Containers

When you finally get your seeds and mixes together, you're ready to start browsing for likely discards in which to grow your seedlings. It's nice to make use of the throw-aways that clutter up our households. For a germination flat, use a disposable aluminum pan, a recycled broiler pan, a dish pan, or a market pack (those small rectangular trays made of pressed fiber). Cottage cheese and milk cartons work well. Also, check with your local nursery. They often throw away carrying flats that are perfect for germinating seeds. Look for cut-off box tops ("beer flats") in liquor and grocery stores. Pie tins and egg cartons are too shallow and dry out quickly. If you want to use wood flats, they should be disinfected with a 10 percent chlorine solution every year. Over time, wood begins to decay and grow algae and plant diseases on its surface.

For growing-on seedlings, the container should be a couple of inches deeper than the germination flat. Plastic or paper milk cartons cut in half, with holes punched in the bottom, are as good as anything. They fit well under lights and make the best use of space. You can also use old clay pots, cracked kitchen bowls, yogurt and cottage cheese cartons, cinder blocks, old tires…the list goes on and on.

Some gardeners prefer to buy commercial container systems. There are several kinds.

Containers for Germination

- **Plug trays:** These are flats with several plant-holding cells molded into them. They can be plastic or foam. They are made so that you place a few seeds in each cell, and later thin the weak seedlings. The remaining young seedlings are easier to prick-out into transplant containers.

- **Drill flats:** These are flats with molded grooves about 1 to 2 inches deep running the length or width of the flat. In terms of conserving time, seeds, and space, these are probably the most efficient way to germinate seeds.

- **Germination flats:** These are regular flats molded out of plastic or wood fiber. Seeds are scattered on the surface or sown into dug-away drills.

- **Peat pots:** Large-seeded vegetables that transplant poorly (peas, beans, squashes) should be sown directly into peat pots (see below).

Containers for Growing Transplants

- **Plug trays:** See previous description.

- **Cell pack system:** Individual plant cells are variously arranged in small trays or packs, which themselves are placed in carrying flats.

- **Peat pots:** These are small containers made from pressed peat moss. The pots begin to decay in a few weeks if they are kept moist or in contact with the soil. This makes them especially useful for transplanting vegetables that don't like to have their roots disturbed like peas, beans, and squashes. Sow seeds of these vegetables into peat pots filled with transplant mix. Peat pots dry out very quickly unless they are grouped tightly together. So, bury the pots in a 2-inch layer of vermiculite, sand, or mix. Keep both the pots and medium moist until germination. In the short time it takes the seeds to sprout to a transplantable size, the pots will have just begun decaying as they are set into the ground. To ensure free root growth, tear off the bottom of the peat pot when you plant it.

Propagation Systems

Some gardeners prefer to invest in a commercial propagation system that includes any or all of the following parts: (1) premolded plastic containers that fit into a standard flat, (2) a

FIG. 1-6:
Different propagation systems
for growing vegetable seedlings

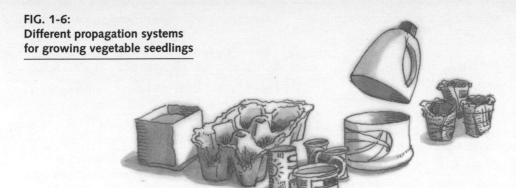

1. SIMPLE: RECYCLABLE GERMINATION FLATS AND CONTAINERS

2. INTERMEDIATE: COMMERCIAL FLATS AND CONTAINERS

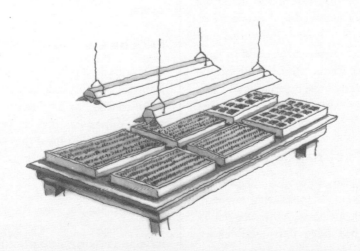

3. ADVANCED: COMMERCIAL PROPAGATION SYSTEMS

heating mat, (3) artificial lights, (4) and potting mixes and fertilizers. For a list of suppliers, see page 451–453.

Sowing and Caring for Seeds

You can either scatter the seeds over the entire surface, or you can sow in small rows or *drills.* Beginning propagators tend to sow too many seeds...it's human nature. It's also wasteful. Learn to estimate exactly how many plants you really want, and sow in drills whenever possible. You'll really save on seeds this way. Say you want ten broccoli plants. Most fresh vegetable seeds have a 70 to 95 percent germination rate. Older seeds or poorly stored ones may have lower rates. For this reason, sow 50 to 100 percent more seeds than the plants you want (i.e., fifteen to twenty seeds in this case). Some won't sprout, others will be spindly and a few will succumb to some disease or critter. If you've figured correctly, then you should end up with ten broccoli plants. By the way, twenty broccoli seeds weigh only about $1/400$ of an ounce.

Water your germination mix before you sow. Make sure it's damp, not soggy. Sow small dark seeds on a light material like sifted vermiculite or sand, and sow light-colored seeds on dark materials like moist peat moss. Large seeds are best planted in individual containers. Bury medium-sized seeds about three times the width of the seed and about $1/4$ to $1/2$ inch apart. Place the seeds individually, or tap them down the crease in the palm of your hand or the fold of a paper. Small seeds can be sown on the surface of the germ mix and watered into the mix very carefully with a fine mist nozzle.

Growing and Fertilizing Seedlings

The first leaf that comes out of the seed is the seed leaf or *cotyledon.* It looks different than the true leaves that follow. Most vegetables are *dicotyledons* and have two seed leaves. Corn, onions, and chives are *monocotyledons*

and have only one seed leaf. The next leaves to appear after the cotyledon(s) are the true leaves.

When sprouts show their first true leaves, they should be thinned if they are crowded. This will improve circulation and water uptake, and reduce diseases. To avoid disturbing the remaining sprouts, use a small pair of scissors and cut weaker plants off at the base, leaving the roots in the medium. Thin until you have about 50 percent more plants than you'll eventually need. There's still a chance you'll lose some.

Usually, new seedlings are moved, or pricked out, to larger containers when they have one or two pairs of true leaves. If you keep seedlings in the germination flat past this stage, you'll have to fertilize them. Since the germ mix is somewhat sterile and the seedling roots are still small, the most efficient way to feed sprouts is with a foliar fertilizer. You can do this with a spray bottle and diluted solutions of soluble kelp, fish powder, compost teas, or synthetic chemical blends (for more about foliar feeding, see page 76).

Most vegetables benefit greatly if they are pricked out and grown to transplant size for a few more weeks before being set out into the garden. In a deeper, nutrient-rich medium, the seedlings can develop strong roots, sturdy stems, and healthy leaves to set them on their course.

Pricking Out Seedlings

Every gardener has his or her own way of knowing when to transplant a sprout from the germination flat to a larger container. Some people do it as soon as the first true leaves appear. Others wait until they see subtle signs of plant hunger or stress. In general, for the vegetables that transplant easily, you can prick out sprouts safely after the first true leaves have appeared. In the end, it's a combination of when you can get to it, how the baby plants look, and if you have a place to grow them on.

Preparing the Transplant Containers

Gather your transplant containers together. They can be almost anything from Dixie cups to milk cartons to shallow cartons to fancy plastic cell packs. If the container has too many holes, line it with a double layer of newspapers. If it has no holes, make some.

Fill the containers with your transplant mix. If the mix is dry, be sure it's moist before you plant the seedling. Try filling all containers with a dry mix and then sprinkling them thoroughly all at once. Let them drain in the shade for 15 minutes or so. Now you're ready to transplant.

Transplanting Techniques

Most gardening books recommend that you thoroughly water your sprouts before pricking them out to avoid transplant shock. And this is certainly true. But if you can work quickly in the shade and into a moist transplant mix, try pricking out the sprouts with your germination flat on the dry side. It makes it easier to disentangle the roots and shake off excessive mix.

If you want to prick out quickly and efficiently, you'll need a tool to help you pull out the delicate sprouts from the germination container and plant them in their new con-

FIG. 1-7: Methods of sowing seeds and pricking out vegetable seedlings

1. HAND OR "TAP" METHOD:
    Tap cupped hand with opposite hand; let seeds fall out along crease of cupped hand.

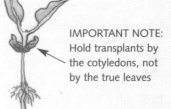

IMPORTANT NOTE: Hold transplants by the cotyledons, not by the true leaves

2. PAPER DRILL

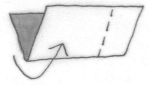

A. Fold paper in half lengthwise

B. Fold "tailpiece" to form a pocket for seeds

C. Tap end of paper drill to release seeds

3. PRICKING OUT

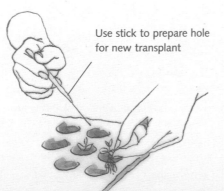

Use stick to prepare hole for new transplant

tainers. Gardeners have their own tried-and-true transplant tools, including pencils, popsicle sticks, screwdrivers, tongue depressors, butter knives, old plant tags, and many other things in that general shape. What you want is a tool that can help you gently lift the sprout from its tangle of roots in the germination flat, make a hole in the transplant container, and then help you backfill the soil around the roots of the new transplant.

Using your chosen tool, gently lift the sprouts from the germination flat. You may have to separate sections of mix and pull apart several sprouts. Don't pull up and down or straight apart. You'll tear the roots. Instead, take a section of several seedlings from a drill between both thumbs and forefingers. Now open your hands slowly like a book and the roots will gradually pull apart.

Move the sprouts quickly to the transplant containers. Even a few minutes of dry air will set them back, so you must *keep the roots moist at all times.* Make a hole in the mix of the transplant container. Holding the seedling by its seed leaf, set the seedling in the hole keeping the soil line where the stem and root meet, and backfill with mix. Don't push down, just gently tamp the container and water in the new seedling.

Growing and Fertilizing Transplant Seedlings

For best results, transplants need lots of light and a mix that stays moist. Try to keep the leaves damp with a spray bottle. At first, you may have to water and mist daily. The smaller the container and the warmer the mix, the more often you'll have to keep things watered.

Vegetable seedlings grow very quickly, and they aren't in their containers long enough to warrant amending the mix with lots of fertilizers, especially slow organic or time-release chemical fertilizers. You may get some results, but most of the nutrients will still be in the mix after the transplants are in the garden. To feed your transplants efficiently, drench or foliar feed with liquid organic fertilizers. Diluted fish emulsion (1 tablespoon to the gallon) is an excellent source of most nutrients, and so is kelp powder, fish powder, and manure teas. (For more about this, see page 72.)

Hardening-Off Seedlings

Before you move your seedlings outdoors, you should toughen them up by hardening them off. To make this transition as stress free as possible, you need to slowly get them used to where they are going. Hardening-off consists of two parts: getting the seedlings toughened up while they are still indoors, and carefully introducing them to the outdoors.

Preparing Seedlings for the Outdoors

To "harden-off" literally means to make the plant tougher. Vegetables don't have woody tissue, but they do have a tough tissue that protects them from weather and water loss. This hard tissue will start growing when the seedlings begin to experience modest stress from cold, light, or drought. If we give these things to the plant gradually and deliberately, then we are hardening-off the seedling.

A couple of weeks or so before you plan to transplant your seedlings outdoors, reduce water, fertilize less, and keep temperatures on the cool side. The plant can now slow its growth and put more energy into producing tough fibers for the outdoors.

Getting Seedlings Used to the Outdoors

Once the seedlings have endured a cool, dry week without fertilizer, they are ready to face outside conditions. This is the hard part because, to the eager gardener, the seedlings look ready. But they still need another week to get used to the full glare of the sun and the cold of the night. Begin with a few hours of sun exposure each day. Set them outside where they'll receive direct sun in the morning and bright indirect light in the afternoon. They will grow accustomed to the wind and cold that will hit them when they take up residence in the garden.

The Benefits of a Cold Frame

A cold frame is a shallow box set in the ground and covered with a sloping glass or plastic roof. When the roof is opened to varying degrees during the day, the cold frame becomes an ideal place to grow-on and harden-off vegetable seedlings. Most gardening books have descriptions of how to build cold frames. One good source is Poisson and Poisson's *Solar Gardening* (see the Bibliography, page 443).

Summary of Vegetable Seedling Production

- Always use clean containers. If necessary, soak them in a 10 percent bleach solution.

- Buy or make a sterile, soilless mix to germinate seeds. Moisten the growing medium before sowing.

- Sow seeds about $1/4$ to $1/2$ inch apart and at least that deep. Seeds sown too thickly will be difficult to pull apart as seedlings. The large seeds of squash, pumpkins, corn, peas, and beans are best sown in small individual containers where their roots remain undisturbed.

- Keep the medium evenly moist without over or underwatering. Never let the medium dry out. This may mean watering twice a day in hot, dry weather. Always water very gently, preferably with a mist sprayer.

- Vegetables germinate best with an even soil temperature between 70° and 80°F. Cooler and warmer temperatures will usually delay germination in all but a few vegetables. If

you have a heating mat, it will dry out your plants quickly; more heat means more water.

- After germination, thin crowded seedlings to 1 inch apart by clipping extra sprouts with scissors at soil level. Pulling them out can damage the roots of those remaing.

- After two to four true leaves appear, transplant corn, beans, peas, squash, and pumpkins to the garden. Other vegetables should be transplanted to a larger container for a few more weeks.

- Transplants should be fed with foliar fertilizers until they are ready for planting in the garden.

- One to two weeks before moving transplants to the garden, you need to harden them off. First, withhold water and fertilizer and cool the soil and air temperature down, then gradually begin moving the seedlings outdoors during the day.

Remember that you are taking a plant on a journey from an embryo to a young plant sturdy enough to make it on its own. The real trick is to keep the process going: prepare flats, sow seeds, germinate seeds, thin seedlings, prick out to larger containers, fertilize, harden-off, and transplant. Don't keep plants too long at any one stage. Some move through these stages at different paces, but each vegetable has a rhythm. For example, brassicas need to be pricked out, transplanted, and planted out on schedule. They can't dally in any one pot too long. Most greens are also that way. On the other hand, sprouted onions can stay in germination flats for weeks, especially if they are foliar fed. Growing vegetable seedlings is like having another garden. Each vegetable has its own needs.

SEASONAL PLANTING

It's one thing to figure out that you want to grow ten broccoli plants per year. It's quite another to plant them so they are ready when you want them. The problem is that some vegetables are in the ground a long time and others are in and out in a matter of weeks. You have to know the time period during which to plant. This time period varies from vegetable to vegetable and is related to their hardiness and how fast they grow.

Frost-Hardy to Tender

Vegetables come from all over the world, from the cool, foggy chalk soils of northern Europe (like cabbage) to the dry, winter-cold foothills of the Caspian Sea (such as garlic). Some grow best in the cool of spring, others need long, hot days to set fruit. Each vegetable has a favorite range of growing temperatures; that is, they have different types of "hardiness." The classification table below is a handy way to begin to figure out your own growing season for each vegetable.

When to Start Planting

Begin your seasonal planting schedule by grouping vegetables of similar hardiness and average time to maturity (see table below). This defines the time window for planting each vegetable, and gives you some idea of how long the vegetables will be in the ground. The table is meant to serve only as a general reference, because some vegetables are more flexible than others, and "early" and "late" varieties can stretch the season. This

---

DEGREE OF HARDINESS IN COOL-SEASON VEGETABLES
(Frost tolerant. Seeds germinate and roots absorb nutrients in cold soil. Most are shallow rooted.)

Hardy   (Endure normal frost. Safely planted 4 to 6 weeks before last spring frost. Can't tolerate hot, dry conditions.)

Asparagus	Collards	Kohlrabi	Parlsey
Broccoli	Dandelions	Leeks	Peas
Cabbages	Garlic	Mustard greens	Radishes
Chives	Kale	Onions	Turnips

Half Hardy   (Not injured by light frost. Sow or transplant 2 to 3 weeks before last spring frost.)

Beets	Celery	Chinese cabbage	Parsnips
Carrots	Chard	Lettuce	Potatoes
Cauliflower	Chicories		

DEGREE OF HARDINESS IN WARM-SEASON VEGETABLES
(Frost tender. Seeds germinate and roots absorb nutrients in warm soils. Most are deep rooted.)

Tender   (Injured by frost, but can withstand cool weather and soils.)

Beans, snap	Soybeans	Sweet corn	Tomatoes

Very Tender   (Injured by cool weather. Need warm soils to grow well.)

Cucumbers	Muskmelons	Pumpkins	Sweet potatoes
Eggplant	Peppers	Squash	Watermelons

explains the appearance of the same vegetable in more than one category. Estimate the date of the last spring frost and the first fall frost in your area. This information is available from national frost maps or your county extension service. Now refer to the Appendix for start-to-plant dates for various vegetables relative to the average dates of your first and last frosts. If you don't have any regional information on when to plant vegetables, this is a good place to start.

Plotting Your Planting Schedule

Begin by dividing your garden area into four areas, beds, or groups of beds, which we will call "plots." Each plot will eventually be planted in one of the four hardiness groups listed on page 30. For example, if you start your garden in late winter or early spring, pick your favorite vegetables from that seasonal group—say broccoli, cabbage, and chives—and plant in plot 1. Plant plots 2 through 4 in succession with appropriate vegetables as the season progresses. At year's end, after your fall planting, you will have expanded into your full garden size. Start small and grow with your garden.

In each plot, try to sow or plant out small amounts over a few weeks during the specific season. In the course of the first year, you will probably plant some vegetables too early or too late, but at least you'll get a handle on the time period for planting each vegetable. This

PLANTING BY SEASON AND HARDINESS
A seasonal planting plan for vegetables. Combines plant hardiness and time to maturity. A good place to start.

Planting Time	Short/Early Season (50 days)	Midseason (50–90 days)	Long/Late Season (> 90 days)
Late Winter to Early Spring (Plant as soon as ground can be worked in spring, 4 to 6 weeks before last frost.)	Arugula, Chinese broccoli, mizuna, scallions (sets), spinach, mustard greens	Broccoli, cabbage, chives, collards, dandelions, escarole, endive, kale, leeks (early), parsley, peas	Broccoli (late), brussels sprouts, cabbage (storage), leek, parsnips
Early to Midspring (Plant at average time of last frost.)	Beets, carrots (baby), bok choy, radishes	Beets, early potatoes, carrots, cauliflower, chard, Chinese cabbage, lettuce, radicchio, turnips	Onions (long day), celery
Midspring to Late Spring (Plant 2 weeks after the average last frost.)	Mustard greens, purslane	Beans, corn (early–midseason), early tomatoes	Late potatoes
Early Summer (Plant when weather and soil are warm.)	Mustard greens, purslane	Corn (main crop), cucumbers, eggplant, peppers, summer squash, winter squash (early)	Melons, onions (intermediate day), pumpkins, winter squash
Midsummer to Fall (second season where possible) (Plant from late June to early September, even later in mild climates.)	Arugula, beets, carrots, Chinese broccoli, cress, mizuna, bok choy, spinach, mustard greens	Beets, broccoli, cabbage, carrots, cauliflower, collards, kale, lettuce, spinach	Potatoes (winter), garlic

is the beginning of a continuous harvest, and a reliable planting schedule for where you live.

The fun begins as each plot is cleared for the next group of vegetables. For instance, plot 1, planted in late winter/early spring will be ready to plant again by early summer. At this point you have several choices: you could (1) plant more of what's in plots 2 through 4, (2) sow a cover crop, or (3) prepare plot 1 for late-summer crops.

The advantage of this method of seasonal planting is that it makes you start small and concentrate on a few crops, while it opens up opportunities to experiment and still plant your favorite vegetables. In time, as you refine your schedule, you'll settle into a routine and rhythm of seasonal planting of catch cropping, intercropping, and rotations.

Catch Cropping: Filling in the Gaps

Some vegetables grow faster than others so there are times of the year when gaps appear in the vegetable patch. These gaps can be used to grow—or "catch"—a crop of rapidly growing vegetables like Asian brassicas, beets, chicory, lettuce, mustards, spinach, and scallions.

Intercropping: Planting for Togetherness

If you want to make the most of your garden space, intercrop or plant two different vegetables in the same area. The trick is to grow vegetables that don't compete with each other. Common pairings combine tall plants and short plants, fast growers with slow starters. For example, if you grow carrots and radishes, the radishes will sprout much earlier, loosening the soil so the delicate carrot seedlings can sprout. If you grow leaf lettuce with head cabbage, the lettuce will be harvested by the time the cabbages are ready. Plant summer lettuce, spinach, or other greens with tomatoes, pole beans, cucumbers,

or corn. The shade of the tall warm-season vegetable helps keep the young greens cool.

ROTATIONS: YEAR-TO-YEAR PLANTING

Gardeners have long recognized the importance of rotating vegetables from year to year to maintain soil fertility and break cycles of pests and weeds. The notion of rotating crops conjures up images of something only big farms do, but it is one of the basic principles of sound kitchen gardening. Don't plant the same vegetables in the same place year after year.

It's important to remember that you're not only rotating vegetables, but also the way you fertilize, irrigate, and control pests. It's a seasonal dance in which plants *and* practices move from place to place and help create a new garden every year. Regardless of the size of your garden, it will benefit from the practice of rotation.

Principles of Rotating Vegetables

Figuring out rotations is one of the exciting challenges of kitchen gardening. Start by getting to know vegetables by their plant family (see page 34). Related plants usually have similar pests, needs, and tolerances, so they are typically rotated as a group. The next step is to learn how vegetables and vegetable families are rotated, based on the three aims of rotation: (1) to deter weeds, (2) to prevent a buildup of soil pests, and (3) to prevent a loss of soil nutrients.

Rotations for weed control

Rotations are especially valuable for breaking weed infestations. Say you have a serious thistle or quack grass problem. If you can follow an outbreak of these weeds with a wide-spaced vegetable like corn, tomatoes, broccoli, squash, or green beans, which create shade and can be weeded easily, or with leeks or potatoes, which need constant hilling-up, you can do a pretty good job of controlling weeds and preventing them from going to seed. These shade-producing, easy-to-weed vegetables are called "cleaner" crops.

Close-spaced vegetables like carrots, scallions, radishes, beets, and other root crops are more difficult to weed. They need a firm soil that is undisturbed during the season. They tend to leave the soil "dirty," or weedy, for the next crop. If you grow "cleaner" crops after these hard-to-weed crops, you can eliminate the buildup of weed seeds and a lot of garden work.

In some regions, there are seasonal factors to consider when planning the rotation to control weeds, since some weeds grow in winter and others in summer. Under these conditions, you want to break up winter and summer growing areas to avoid building up either winter or summer weed seeds (see Chapter 4 for more about this). For example, if part of your garden is especially rank with winter weeds, you can plant cover crops in winter and cleaner crops in summer to outperform these weeds. After a couple of seasons, you can plant the entire area with close-spaced root vegetables and have a clean plot.

Rotations for controlling soil diseases:

Some of the most serious plant diseases, like nematodes, wilts, and root rots, are found in the soil. Most soil diseases are specific to vegetables in the same botanic family, like members of the tomato, onion, and cabbage families. For example, a continuous planting of brassicas favors clubroot, while successive crops of tomatoes or potatoes in the same plot may cause a buildup of *Phytophthora* or other soil fungus diseases. Moving these plants around in the garden from season to season can interrupt disease cycles and thwart the buildup of soil microbes that plague these different vegetable families.

The same principle holds for insect pests and nematodes. Vegetable rotation makes it more difficult for emerging insects, like the Colorado potato beetle and cucumber beetles, to find their preferred food. Some pests build up so fast that dense planting can cause problems in one season.

Sometimes, a soil pest will prefer one vegetable over others in the same plant family, and this adds yet another layer of complexity to rotations. For example, potatoes are quite prone to late blight (*Phytophthora*), and commonly pass it on to peppers, eggplant, and especially tomatoes. Similarly, onions infect garlic and leek with nematodes. In these cases, the susceptible vegetable may have to be rotated away from its family members or grown in containers.

Although rotations can help control many pests, they don't always help. For instance, the fungus that causes *Verticillium* can attack several kinds of vegetables (including some weeds), and it can stay in the soil for a very long time. Some soil insect pests also may not respond to crop rotations, because they can move from crop to crop.

Rotations to prevent nutrient losses:

When we grow vegetables, we are actually growing a part of the plant that we intend to use, such as leaves stems, roots, or tubers. Each of these plant parts require different nutrients. Root vegetables, for example, need large amounts of potassium; fruiting vegetables need lots of phosphorous; and salad greens require high levels of nitrogen. This is why plants with the same edible part are often rotated together. Some vegetables, like corn and brassicas are "hungry" crops, as they need a lot of most nutrients, while legumes (peas and beans), actually add nitrogen to the soil. Most schemes for rotating vegetables are based on conserving soil nutrients. For information on nutrient demands of vegetables, see page 82.

VEGETABLES GROUPED BY PLANT FAMILY	
MONOCOTS (1-seed leaf)	**DICOTS (2-seed leaves)**
Asparagus Family (Asparagaceae) asparagus	**Cabbage Family (Brassicaceae)** arugula, bok choy, broccoli, cabbage, cauliflower, collards, kale, kohlrabi, mizuna, mustard, radish, roquette, turnip
Grass Family (Poaceae) corn	**Carrot Family (Apiaceae)** carrots, celery, parsley, parsnip
Onion Family (Alliaceae) garlic, onion, leek, shallot, chives	**Goosefoot or Spinach Family (Chenopodiaceae)** beets, chard, spinach
	Sunflower or Lettuce Family (Asteraceae) chickory, dandelion, endive, lettuce, artichoke
	Nightshade or Tomato Family (Solanaceae) eggplant, pepper, tomato, tomatillo
	Squash Family (Cucurbitaceae) cucumber, melons, pumpkin, squash
	Legume or Pea Family (Fabaceae) peas, snap beans, fava beans, lima beans

Putting It All Together

When we group vegtables by nutrient demands, they tend to fall into groups and plant families similar to those outlined for disease and weed prevention. This makes things easier when we try to put all this together in a general rotation scheme. Let's start with a simple four-year rotation plan, popularized by British gardening books. This scheme omits leafy greens, alliums, and warm-weather vegetables (to be added later), but it serves as a simple and practical introduction to the reasoning behind vegetable rotations.

Basic Four-Year Rotation

The first year, in plot 1 are potatoes, which are heavy feeders, do not like lime, and don't leave a legacy of weeds for the next crop. In plot 2 are brassicas, which are heavy feeders, simple to weed, require lime, and share similar soil diseases. In plot 3 are peas and beans, which need some lime, leave a clean soil, and supply it with extra nitrogen. In plot 4 are root crops, which are hungry for potassium, are awkward to weed, and need deep weed-

free soil. By moving the vegetables in the direction of the arrows each season, we achieve many of the benefits of rotation.

Let's examine the rotation closer. The potatoes follow into the brassica plot where they get the benefits of a clean, fertilizer-rich soil. The disadvantage here is that the potatoes dislike the lime applied to the brassicas, so it is important to prepare this plot with liberal amounts of organic matter. The brassicas, then follow the peas and beans where they get the benefits of the lime given to the legumes and the nitrogen the legumes leave behind. The peas and beans are then planted in the old root crop plot where they help clean up the weeds left behind. Finally the root crops follow into the potato plot where they profit from the clean field left by the cultivation of the potatoes.

Five-Year Rotation

Our next step is to include the vegetables that were left out of the 4-year rotation: leafy greens, alliums, and summer vegetables, and include a plot for cover crops. This will give

FIG. 1-8: Four- and five-year schemes for rotating vegetables in your garden

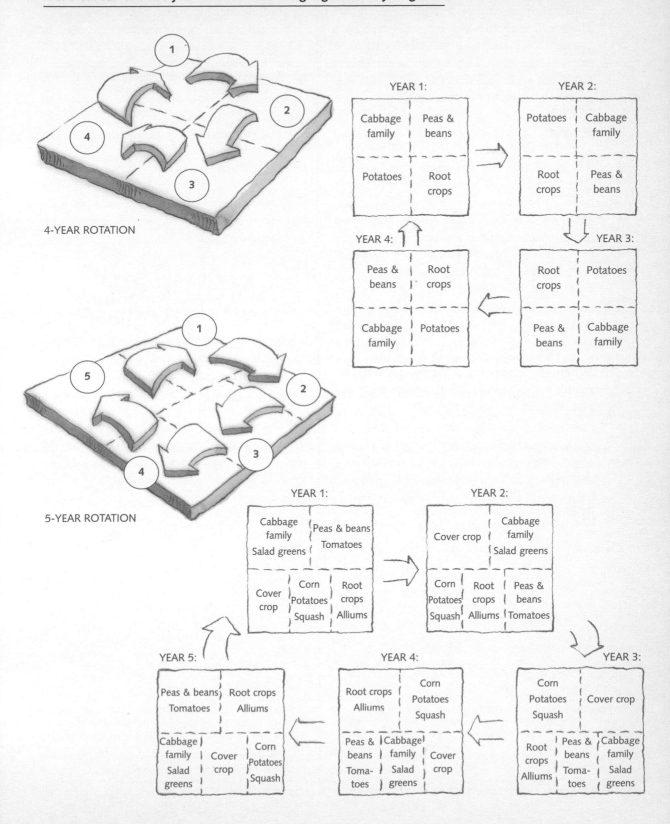

us a 5-year rotation. Let's see how they fit with the crops of our 4-year plan. The alliums grow well with the root crops because both groups are close-spaced vegetables that need careful cultivation. The alliums, however, require more nitrogen than the root vegetables, so they need to be fed differently.

Corn goes with potatoes, since they both need lots of nutrients and are cleaner crops. They are also easily cultivated and leave the soil in clean condition. Since they grow at different times of the year, there will always be room for catch crops in this combination. Also, it's best to keep potatoes away from other members of the tomato family because of common diseases like *Phytophthora*. Squashes also require large spacing, so we put them here, although we could just as easily combine the squashes with the peas and beans. Salad greens are grown with the brassicas, since both crops require lots of nitrogen and a well-cultivated topsoil. Salad greens are one of the best catch crops, so they can be grown almost anywhere. They grow quickly and can use the shade of other plants. Also, they don't tend to transfer diseases between themselves. Finally, tomatoes, peppers, and eggplant are placed with the peas and beans although, as already mentioned, the peas and beans could just as easily go with the squash family.

There is one other plot to make our rotation scheme complete and that is the use of cover crops and green manures described in Chapter 4. Cover crops add nutrients and organic matter to the soil and give it a rest between the heavy demands of vegetables.

With this general information, we can now place our vegetables in a rotational scheme that involves five rotational plots and nine vegetable groups.

Remember, this is just one way to do it. Consider your pests, what you're growing and the suggestions above to create your own year-to-year changes in the arrangements of your kitchen garden.

KICK BACK, RELAX, AND START PLANNING BEFORE PLANTING

One of the great joys of gardening is sitting alongside a winter fire with pencil and paper, poring over seed catalogs while drafting a spring garden plan and seasonal rotation scheme. Sometimes the plan doesn't make it off the paper, but when it does and it becomes a reality, it can change your lifestyle and provide you with the nutritious pleasure of fresh vegetables from season to season and year to year. The more you plan, the easier it is to grow a successful kitchen garden.

GROWING A NUTRITION GARDEN

It's hard to believe, but not long ago most doctors and health officials didn't acknowledge the relationship between diet and health. Now we know better. People whose diets are rich in vegetables, fruits, and whole grains have lower rates of cancer, heart disease, osteoporosis, hypertension, and other diseases. The latest estimates claim that fully one-third of all cancers are related to poor diet. It's now possible to say that we can influence our own well-being, simply by the choices we make about what and how we eat. And some of the most important foods we can eat for sound nutrition are fresh vegetables.

Scientists have found that there is more to foods than just vitamins and minerals. At least two other things are important:

Fiber: Fiber is the roughage of vegetables, which was once thought to be indigestible. We now know that roughage performs several beneficial tasks: (1) it satisfies appetite by giving people a feeling of fullness, which in turn can reduce the number of calories eaten; (2) it helps reduce cholesterol; (3) it helps regularity, which prevents various body chemicals from becoming carcinogenic; (4) it reduces constipation and hemorrhoids, and (5) it helps sweep away harmful bacteria from the intestine and colon.

Phytochemicals: Phytochemicals are natural chemical compounds found in all plants (*phyto* is Greek for "plant"). Some phytochemicals are such powerful disease preventers that drug companies are trying to synthesize and patent them. Phytochemicals are the ingredient in herbs that give them their healing and therapeutic power. Unfortunately, phytochemicals are rarely mentioned in common lists of nutritional value.

There are hundreds of beneficial phytochemicals. Some are essential to hormone regulation, others aid nerve impulses critical to mental and emotional well-being. Still other phytochemicals are able to prevent the spread of cancer cells. These include the flavonoids and lycopenes found in tomatoes and carrots; the allyl sulfides and allicins found in onion and garlic; the saponins found in peas and beans; and the isothiocyanate sulfur compounds of the brassicas. These recent discoveries aren't surprising, considering that most vegetables evolved from medicinal herbs.

One reason scientists are so excited about phytochemicals, especially a group called *antioxidants,* is their apparent ability to stop a cell from becoming carcinogenic. Oxygen, which we need to survive, can also damage the body when it forms "free radicals." These compounds damage cells and are believed to be involved in the causes of heart disease, cancer, tissue aging, and other ailments. Provitamin A (beta-carotene) is an antioxidant found in dark green and orange vegetables; vitamin C, vitamin E, and zinc, all of which have antioxidant functions, are found in most vegetables. Researchers are beginning to assign vegetables an "ORAC" value (Oxygen Radical Absorbance Capacity), which measures their ability to subdue free radicals. Vegetables with highest ORAC values include kale, spinach, broccoli florets, beets, and red bell peppers.

With all the interest in health these days, more and more gardeners consider their kitchen garden a source of sound nutrition and health. If you grow your own, you've got your own natural foods store in your backyard. Freshly picked vegetables can be much higher in nutrients than store-bought produce; once vegetables are harvested, their food value declines with time.

If you have limited space and time, the

continued on page 38

ideal vegetables are those that are easy to grow, produce quickly and abundantly, and are chock-full of nutrients. Unfortunately, it's hard to place an overall nutritional value on a vegetable, because so many things are important. Onions and garlic, for instance, are not terribly nutritious in terms of vitamins and minerals, but they contain important phytochemicals that may help prevent cancer and high blood pressure. Broccoli, which has long been known to be one of the most healthy vegetables, is praised even more today because it contains many cancer-fighting phytochemicals. Most of these facts are not yet on vegetable nutrient charts.

The table below lists those vegetables that are highest in common nutrients. Notice how certain vegetables keep popping up in each category. These are the foundation vegetables for a nutrition kitchen garden.

NUTRIENT VALUES AND YIELDS OF VEGETABLES

NUTRIENT	VEGETABLES WITH HIGHEST AMOUNT	NUTRIENT-RICH VEGETABLES WITH HIGH YIELDS
Vitamin A	Red and green chiles, dandelion greens, carrots, kale, cress, sweet potatoes, parsley	Carrots, kale, collards, sweet potatoes, spinach, mustard greens, dandelion greens
Vitamin C	Red and green chiles, beet greens, bell peppers, kale, parsley, collards	Kale, collards, chiles, turnip greens, spinach, mustard greens, cabbage
Vitamin B1	Green peas, pod peas, lima beans, garlic, turnip greens, dandelion greens	Peas, spinach, potatoes, corn, kale, collards, leaf lettuces
Vitamin B2	Turnip greens, cress, dandelion greens, parsley, kale, beet greens, mustard greens, red chiles	Spinach, corn, kale, leaf lettuce, turnip greens, mustard greens
Niacin	Green peas, red and green chiles, kale, Lima beans, parsley	Potatoes, kale, corn, turnip greens, collards, carrots, spinach
Calcium	Collards, kale, turnip greens, parsley, fennel, endive, spinach, Swiss chard	Kale, collards, leaf lettuce, spinach, mustard greens, turnip greens
Iron	Soybeans, lentils, lima beans, parsley, peas, beet greens, chard, spinach	Leaf lettuce, kale, collards, mustard greens, beets
Protein	Garlic, green limas, green peas, sweet white corn, kale, collards, broccoli, parsley, pod peas, spinach	Spinach, kale, legumes, collards, corn, potatoes
Fiber	Lamb's-quarter, chiles, green peas, lima beans, bell peppers, dandelion greens, garlic, broccoli, parsley, winter squash, kale, leeks	Carrots, onions, kale, collards, mustard greens, leeks, broccoli, parsley, bell peppers, green peas
Phytochemicals	Kale, beets, broccoli, and other brassicas, carrots, onions, garlic, peas, beans, tomatoes, peppers, orange squash	Carrots, cabbage, broccoli and other brassicas, onions, garlic, peas, and beans

Setting Up the Gardener's Kitchen

Before there was cuisine or kitchens, all you had to do was go into the surrounding landscape, pick something, and pop it into your mouth. In today's world, things are a bit more complicated, but even now we only need eight tools to cook vegetables: a chef's knife, a mortar and pestle, a pot with a lid, a vegetable steamer, a nonstick frying pan, and a cup and fork.

The chef's knife is used to chop, dice, mince, and julienne vegetables; the mortar and pestle are used to crush herbs, garlic, and seeds to use as flavorings; the pot with the tight-fitting lid and collapsible-basket vegetable steamer are used to cook vegetables without leaching out all the essential vitamins and minerals, vibrant colors, and toothsome textures; the nonstick skillet is used for sautéing vegetables and dry-roasting seeds; the cup and fork can be used to make dressings.

The following list includes these and several other kitchen tools that will make vegetable cooking easier and more fun.

BAKING DISHES AND PANS: Choose assorted sizes, in metal or ceramic, for roasting vegetables and baking gratins and pasta casseroles.

BAMBOO SKEWERS: Soak these before using for vegetable kebobs for grilling.

BAMBOO STEAMING BASKETS: Some stack so you can steam several different vegetables at once. Put vegetables in single layers for even cooking.

BLENDER: Use to purée soups and to emulsify salad dressings.

BOWLS: Assorted sizes are handy for making dressings, herbed salts, dry rubs, and marinades.

CANNING JAR: A small one with a tight-fitting lid can be used to mix dressings. Just add ingredients and shake. Leftover dressing can be stored right in the jar. To reuse, leave at room temperature for 10 to 15 minutes, shake well, pour over fresh greens.

CHEESECLOTH: Use to strain stocks.

CHEF'S KNIFE: Choose a 10-inch knife that weighs 7 to 8 ounces and is made of high-carbon steel. It's worth paying up to $60 for one, as it will last for twenty years.

COLANDER: Use to drain pasta, and to salt and drain zucchini and eggplant.

COLLAPSIBLE BASKET STEAMER: This simple device for steaming vegetables stores easily; make sure there's a metal stem in the middle with a wire ring for removing from pot.

COMPOST SCRAP PAIL: Aside from harvesting vegetables, this is the cook's primary connection to the garden, completing the cycle. (For storing kitchen scraps, see page 120.) We use a small plastic pail that goes right by the kitchen sink. It's easy to clean.

CONICAL STRAINER (CHINOISE): Use to strain stock.

CUP: An easy way to make a small amount of vinaigrette is with a fork and cup.

DUTCH OVEN: An enameled cast-iron pot, with tightly fitting lid; use for making stocks and for steaming vegetables. Buy several sizes.

FOOD MILL: This tool is hand-cranked, with an interior scraper over a perforated grater. Before the days of the food processor, this was the best way to purée rice or vegetables. A food mill is preferred over a food processor when you don't want the mixture to be overprocessed or inflated with air (e.g., mashed potatoes).

FOOD PROCESSOR: One of the great modern tools for chopping, mincing, puréeing. There are very small models. For small amounts of mincing, use a chef's knife.

FORK: Use (along with a cup) instead of a wire whisk and bowl for making vinaigrette.

GRATER, LARGE: Use to grate large amounts of cheese, beets, carrots, and fennel.

GRATER, SMALL: Use a handheld grater for small jobs like grating fresh ginger, cinnamon sticks, and citrus peel.

KNIFE SHARPENER: If you find whetstones hard to use, try a top-quality manual sharpener with two bevels. Running the knife across a butcher's steel after sharpening will true the edge.

MANDOLINE: A small adjustable slicer, suitable for making uniformly thin slices of vegetables.

MORTAR AND PESTLE: The best tool for grinding small amounts of flavoring paste, seeds, garlic, herbs, or spices when you don't want to get out the food processor.

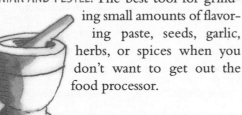

OMELET PAN: Any good-quality, 8-inch nonstick pan can be used for sautéing small amounts of food as well as for omelets.

PARING KNIFE: Use a 4-inch knife for small jobs, such as coring apples.

PEELER: A free-swivel type works great for most uses. A paring knife will do in a pinch.

PEPPER GRINDER: A small, cylindrical, hand-twisted grinder works well. Fresh ground pepper is far superior to preground.

RAMEKINS: Small individual ovenproof baking dishes.

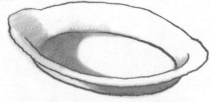

SALAD SPINNER: This is great for cleaning large amounts of lettuce, spinach, Swiss chard, and other greens. Or you can put washed greens in a towel and spin it around overhead (but do it outside!).

SALT DISH: Fill a small ramekin with kosher or sea salt; place near the stove to add pinches of salt to dishes in progress.

SIEVE: This is a small handheld wire strainer. Use one with fine mesh to strain small amounts of stock, mushroom juice, etc.

SKILLET, 12-INCH: A shallow, flat-bottomed pan used for frying and sautéeing. Choose a nonstick skillet.

SPICE GRINDER: An old manual or electric coffee grinder can be used for grinding seeds like coriander, cumin, and mustard and spices like cinnamon and cloves. Use only for spices (unless you like bizarre-tasting coffee!).

STOCKPOT: Use a 12-quart pot for simmering stocks and making stews.

TIMER: Eventually, you'll find that you like your vegetables and pasta cooked for an exact number of minutes.

TONGS: Long-handled metal tongs with long scalloped teeth are most versatile.

WIRE WHISK: A small 5-inch flexible whisk is excellent for making dressings. If you don't have one, a dinner fork will work just fine.

WOK: New nonstick woks with flat bottoms work well, not only for stir-frying vegetables but also for heating vegetables along with cooked pasta and a sauce.

WOK SKIMMER: Skimmers aid in stir-frying and in removing vegetables quickly from a pot or pan.

STOCKING THE PANTRY

The only ingredients you really need to cook vegetables are garlic, lemon, oil, vinegar, some herbs, salt, and pepper. Eventually, though, you'll get tired of all your vegetable dishes tasting pretty much the same. That's why it pays to have a well-stocked pantry. You'll need just a few shelves and a little room in the refrigerator to set it up. Start with the basics and add to them a few items at a time. Soon you'll have the ingredients to add great variety to your vegetable cooking.

When you're eating out and taste a new flavoring or combination, ask the waiter which seasonings were used. It's a good way to expand your repertoire and inspire experimentation. Try shopping at Asian, Latino, Thai, and Indian markets for a wealth of reasonably priced but uncommon flavorings.

Oils

CANOLA OIL: A good low-cholesterol oil to use for deep-frying or stir-frying. Better for you than most other oils.

EXTRA VIRGIN OLIVE OIL: Use this rich, dark green, fruity-flavored oil for seasoning, not for cooking; as a finish to many dishes; drizzled over salads; and in vinaigrette dressings. (All oils contain 126 calories and 14 grams of fat per tablespoon.)

PEANUT OIL: Use in Szechwan, Thai, and other Asian dishes. Can be used for high-temperature frying or stir-frying.

SAFFLOWER AND SUNFLOWER OILS: Mild in flavor and high in polyunsaturates, these oils can be mixed with stronger oils to flavor salads.

SESAME OIL: This oil comes in dark (Asian) and light varieties. Use Asian sesame oil as a flavoring in Chinese and Indian dishes.

VIRGIN AND LIGHT OLIVE OIL: This oil is lighter in flavor, higher in acidity than extra virgin, and better for cooking. Use to dress salads and for sautéing.

WALNUT AND HAZELNUT OILS: Nut oils can be used to dress salads; they complement sweet berry vinegars.

Vinegars

BALSAMIC VINEGAR: This is a sweet, aromatic, aged vinegar from Italy. Traditionally used with extra virgin olive oil for salads, it also can be used along with a squeeze of lemon juice to finish off sautéed vegetables.

CHAMPAGNE VINEGAR: This delicate, classy vinegar goes well with delicate lettuces and salads that contain fruit.

CIDER VINEGAR: This vinegar is too strong for most salads, but good for pickling.

MALT VINEGAR: This vinegar has a dark brown color, with a strong, sweet flavor. Good for hearty dressings and marinades.

RASPBERRY VINEGAR: Milder than red wine vinegar; excellent for salads that contain delicate greens or fruits.

RED WINE VINEGAR: A good basic strong-flavored vinegar for salads.

RICE WINE VINEGAR, PLAIN: This one is delicate, light, and sweet. Use in Asian-style dishes.

SHERRY VINEGAR: Use this good, rich-flavored wine vinegar in salads.

WHITE WINE VINEGAR: This vinegar is lighter in color and flavor than its red counterpart.

Dairy Products

ASIAGO CHEESE: This is a good, tangy substitute for Parmesan.

LOW-FAT MILK: This can be used to saturate white bread, which is then processed until smooth in a food processor and used, instead of heavy cream, to reduce the fat content in cream sauces.

LOW-FAT PLAIN YOGURT: This is an excellent substitute for mayonnaise. Mix with equal amounts of Dijon-style mustard and low-fat mayonnaise, plus a splash or two of both vinegar and olive oil and use as a low-fat dressing. Also, by itself, it can be drained overnight through cheesecloth to extract much of the liquid, then the remaining thick yogurt ("cheese") can be substituted for heavy cream.

PARMESAN CHEESE: Imported Parmigiano-Reggiano is the best and worth the extra expense.

PECORINO ROMANO CHEESE: This sharp grating cheese is often used as a substitute for Parmesan.

RICOTTA CHEESE: Low-fat varieties can be a savory substitute for cottage cheese.

Essential Fresh Produce

CHIVES: Use as a garnish for salads.

GARLIC: This is indispensable, in minced, chopped, or whole form. Roast or sauté in oil to make the flavor base for many dishes.

GINGER (FRESH): Ginger is great for stir-fry and Asian vegetable dishes; complements soy sauce and Asian sesame oil.

GREEN ONIONS: These are nice as a garnish for salads or potato dishes; great for adding flavor to soups.

LEMON JUICE AND PEEL: Use the juice and zest to add zing to marinades and dressings, pasta sauces, and sautéed vegetables.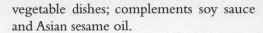

ONIONS: Sautéed in oil, these essential aromatic vegetables are used as a flavor base for many dishes, like stir-fries and pasta sauces.

SHALLOTS: Shallots are more subtle than onions, less harsh than garlic.

Pantry Essentials

Some of the following may need refrigeration after opening:

ANCHOVIES/ANCHOVY PASTE: Soak oil-packed anchovies in milk before using to draw out some of the salt. The paste can be used in tomato-based sauces or salad dressings.

BREAD CRUMBS (TOASTED): Making crumbs is a good way to recycle old bread. Crumbs are also a good substitute for Parmesan cheese in gratins as well as sprinkled over salads or sautéed vegetables.

CAPERS: Use these flavor enhancers for dressings, marinades, condiments, and pasta sauces.

DIJON-STYLE MUSTARD: This is an essential ingredient in many vinaigrettes.

DRIED HERBS: Keep a small number of jars of your favorites on hand as a backup for fresh herbs. Use one-third the amount as you would use of fresh. Replace once a year. Basil and rosemary should not be used dried, if you can help it.

KALAMATA OLIVES: Though high in fat, a flavor enhancer for salads or in marinades for chicken or fish.

KOSHER OR SEA SALT: This has better flavor than most table salts.

PEANUT BUTTER: A tablespoon goes a long way to flavor steamed broccoli stems or mixed sautéed vegetables. Use with peanut oil and a touch of soy sauce.

POWDERED VEGETABLE STOCK: This is available at natural foods stores. Add to water to make a quick stock.

ROASTED RED PEPPERS: Purchased in a jar or made at home (page 85), these are piquant condiments for salads and sandwiches and can be used to boost the flavor of a pasta sauce. Red pepper purée is useful condiment for sandwiches, or when thinned with stock and a touch of cream, as a spicy soup.

SOY SAUCE, LOW-SALT: This is just as good as the high-sodium variety. Adds a tang to sautéed vegetables, meat marinades.

SUNDRIED TOMATOES: Use this reliable flavor enhancer for salads and appetizers.

TAPENADE: A traditional olive paste that originated in Provence, tapenade usually contains black kalamata or salt-cured olives, anchovies, garlic, capers, olive oil, and herbs. It can be bought in small jars or made at home (see page 97). Use in salads, pasta sauces, and marinades.

VEGETABLE STOCK BASE: This is a paste of roasted organic vegetables from Germany (Instant Soup 'n' Stock); you can also make your own (page 87). Add to water to make a quick stock.

WORCESTERSHIRE: Add a splash to a Caesar salad dressing or a vegetable sauté.

Nuts and Seeds

High in fats, but if used sparingly as garnishes, they can add texture, flavor, and variety to many dishes.

MUSTARD, CORIANDER, AND CARAWAY SEEDS: Toast in a dry skillet to bring out the flavor. After toasting, grind to a powder to use in Asian or Middle Eastern dishes, or add whole as salad garnish.

PINE NUTS: Lightly toasted, these are great for adding to green or pasta salads. A primary ingredient in pesto.

PUMPKIN SEEDS: Toast and use as a garnish.

SESAME SEEDS, BLACK OR WHITE: Toast lightly and use as garnish for asparagus, broccoli, carrots, and other vegetables.

SUNFLOWER SEEDS: Use toasted or untoasted to add texture and flavor to vegetables, salads, and other dishes.

WALNUTS: Use toasted pieces as garnish for salads or gratins.

Fresh Herbs

BASIL: This is the essential ingredient in pesto sauce (page 87). Great as garnish for pasta and fresh tomato salads.

CILANTRO: Use this strong-flavored herb for Latino and Asian dishes. Use as a basil substitute in pesto.

EPAZOTE: This is a Mexican herb used to flavor beans and in tortilla soup (page 439).

FLAT-LEAF PARSLEY: Also called Italian parsley, this is better than regular, or curly, parsley, which doesn't chop well. Use for every type of dish from pasta to salads to gratins as a final garnish.

OREGANO: This herb is traditionally used in tomato sauces and on pasta and other Italian dishes. Different types (Mediterranean,

Greek, marjoram, etc.) display different sharpnesses of taste.

ROSEMARY: Use to flavor potatoes, lamb, pork roast, roast chicken.

TARRAGON: This is good in salad dressings and marinades for chicken.

THYME: This is good for topping pizza, in bouquets garnis, and in salad dressings and marinades (see pages 100–101).

Spices

BLACK PEPPERCORNS: Freshly ground pepper is far superior to the preground type in a jar.

CAYENNE PEPPER: Use in peach chutney, marinades for grilled vegetables, and vegetable chili.

CLOVES: Use just a pinch of ground cloves in tomato sauce, chutneys, and Asian dishes. It is one of the elemental spices in curry powder.

CORIANDER: This is also a curry powder component.

CUMIN: Use with corn, beans, and cilantro.

CRUSHED RED PEPPER FLAKES: Just a shake in a pasta sauce or vegetable sauté can lend a little heat.

CURRY POWDER: Use this variable mixture of cumin, turmeric, coriander, cloves, cardamom, fennel, ginger, fenugreek, and black pepper in salad dressings.

DRY MUSTARD: Use in Caesar salad dressing and in marinades for chicken or grilled vegetables.

NUTMEG (WHOLE): Use freshly grated on scalloped potatoes or to flavor any creamy sauce.

Thai and Other Asian Ingredients

CHILES, DRIED: These are found in cellophane packets in many supermarkets. Soften by toasting or soaking, or sauté in oil to flavor the oil.

CHILES, FRESH: Seed, mince, and use sparingly. Wash hands carefully after use.

COCONUT MILK: This is a milky white liquid used to flavor soups and sauces.

FISH SAUCE: Also called *nuoc mam,* this is a pungent sauce made from fermented anchovies. Use in marinades or tangy vegetable dressings.

GARAM MASALA: This is a hot aromatic mixture of roasted and ground cinnamon, cardamom, and cloves (can include other spices). Add to Indian dishes in the last minutes of cooking.

HOISIN SAUCE: This is a tangy-sweet sauce made with spices and ground soybeans. Use to accent marinades and stir-fries.

KAFFIR LIME LEAVES: Dried, these add lemon flavor to broths, curries, and cream sauces. Available in specialty foods shops.

RED CURRY PASTE: Made of red chile, onion, garlic, spices, and salt, this paste can be used to flavor pasta dishes, fried rice, and sautéed vegetables.

SAFFRON: This spice adds a bright yellow color and unique flavor to food. Comes in powder or threads; the threads tend to be fresher and more potent. Dissolve in liquid to release essence. Use in risotto and curry.

SOY MILK: This is a good substitute for regular milk if you like the flavor.

TAHINI: This is a sesame purée used to flavor Asian dishes.

TAMARIND PASTE: This is a dark brown, sour paste made from tamarind pods; dissolve and use in Asian dishes.

Pasta, Rice, and Legumes

ARBORIO: This medium-grain rice from Italy is used for risotto.

BEANS, DRIED: These include great Northern, white, pinto, kidney, cannellini. Use to add flavor, nourishment, and thickness to soups and pastas.

BULGUR: Whole wheat that has been cooked, dried, and cracked.

LENTILS: These are a good, quickly cooked bean substitute. For soups and lentil salads with vegetables.

PENNE: Use this tubular pasta for baked pasta dishes.

POLENTA: This coarsely ground yellow corn-meal is made as soft porridge or in firmer, cakelike form; goes well with chard, onions, and tomato sauce.

RICE: Besides using long-grain rice with vegetable stir-fries, or arborio rice in vegetable risottos, cooked rice can be used as a thickener for soups.

SOBA NOODLES: These Japanese noodles are made from buckwheat flour.

SPAGHETTI: This pasta is good to have on hand for quick pasta dishes, or to break into 2-inch pieces and add to soup.

WONTON NOODLES: Found in the Asian section of most supermarkets, these square, flat fresh noodles are ideal for homemade tortellini (pages 195–196).

BASIC VEGETABLE PREPARATION

Preparing vegetables can be therapeutic instead of a chore. Most people know how to chop, dice, and mince, but as Molly Katzen wrote in *The Moosewood Cookbook,* "The more shapes and sizes you can carve out of a vegetable, the more possibilities you will find for preparing it." And we would add, "for tasting it." More important, size and shape can also determine the quantity and quality of the nutrients a vegetable will retain during cooking. Finally, the right method of preparation, combined with the proper cooking method, can help provide optimum nutrition.

Here are a few ways to prepare vegetables, some hints for salad preparation, some ideas on preparing vegetables to retain nutrition, and notes on stir-frying.

Techniques

CHOPPING: Rest the knife against your knuckles and slide the vegetable out. This is safe and can be done almost without thinking once you learn how.

JULIENNE: To cut into thin (1/8-inch) strips or matchsticks. Use for stir-fries, crudités (raw carrots, bell peppers, zucchini, and the like). Cut the vegetables into 2-inch lengths with a thin knife or mandoline, then julienne into 1/8-inch pieces.

JULIENNING ONIONS:

First, peel, then cut down, top to bottom, into thin wedges. Separate pieces.

USING A MANDOLINE: A mandoline is an efficient tool for cutting thin, even slices. Wear an oven mitt on the hand holding the vegetable to safeguard against injury.

CHINESE-CUT CARROTS: Peel the carrot, then place on a counter. Cut diagonally, then rotate the carrot one-quarter turn and make another diagonal cut. Continue until done. The thick part of the carrot may be cut in half first to ensure that the pieces are relatively equal in size for even cooking.

PARING BROCCOLI STEMS: First cut into 1 1/2-inch lengths, then pare with a swivel vegetable peeler into oval nuggets.

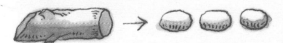

CUTTING POTATOES TO BE SCALLOPED: Peel the potatoes first, then slice into 1/8-inch-thick discs on a mandoline.

DICING: Cut vegetables (potatoes, zucchini, carrots, etc.) into 1/2-inch slices; cut lengthwise into 1/2-inch strips. Dice into 1/2-inch cubes.

DICING ONIONS: Cut off the stem and pointed bottom of the onion, then peel. Cut in half, then lay each half cut-side down on the chopping block, and cut 1/4-inch-wide strips into the onion to within 1/4 inch of bottom. Make another few rows of 1/4-inch-wide cuts at 90° angles to the first cuts. Roll onion over onto a cut-off-stem side and dice.

COINS: Cut carrots or broccoli stems in ovals or rounds 1/4 to 1/8 inch thick.

MINCING GARLIC: Break off the cloves and run them under water—this helps the peel come off and eliminates the garlic's sticky film. Flatten with the side of a chef's knife and peel. Cut into small strips one way, then the other. Mince by rocking the chef's knife back and forth over the garlic, then use the side of the knife blade to mash them, extracting the oil. Mince once more. Or use a garlic press.

PREPARING BEETS: For steaming, boiling, or roasting whole, leave stem and root end intact and skin on. To slice cooked or raw beets, first peel, then cut into 1/8-inch slices. To julienne, cut the slices lengthwise into 1/8-inch sticks, or dice into 1/4-inch cubes. Grate raw beets after peeling.

PREPARING BROCCOLI AND CAULIFLOWER: Run under cold water to wash. Break off florets and trim only the toughest bottom stems. Remove any unwanted stem leaves.

PREPARING CELERY: Wash and trim tops and bottoms slightly. For salads, cut into $1/2$-inch half-moon slices. For celery sticks, cut celery lengthwise into $1/2$-inch wide strips, then cut long strips into 3-inch lengths.

PREPARING WINTER SQUASH: For roasting, leave skin on, cut in half, and remove seeds and stringy pulp. For sautéing or steaming, cut in large chunks and peel off skin.

REMOVING LEAF STALKS FROM GREENS (SWISS CHARD, SPINACH, SORREL, RED CHARD, KALE): Either rip the stalk out with a sharp tearing motion, or lay the leaf down, folded over at the stem, and cut the stem out in a V shape with a knife.

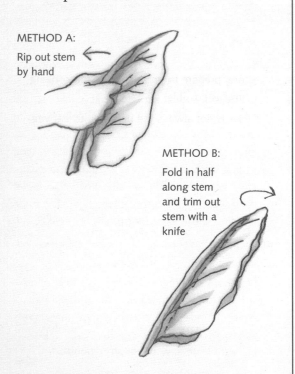

METHOD A:

Rip out stem by hand

METHOD B:

Fold in half along stem and trim out stem with a knife

SHREDDING GREENS (MUSTARD, SWISS CHARD, SPINACH, SORREL): This is also known as chiffonade. Wash and stem the leaves, then take three or four equal-sized leaves and stack them together evenly. Starting from one of the smaller ends, roll them up tightly into a small cigar shape. Then, starting at one edge of the "cigar," slice the entire roll into $1/16$-inch-thick slivers. Unravel the slivered rolls before cooking.

Roll up several leaves.   Slice into $1/16$-inch thick slivers.

SEEDING AND DERIBBING BELL PEPPERS: Cut in half. Remove the core, seeds, and ribs with a knife or your fingers. Lay each half cut-side down on the cutting board and julienne or chop.

SALAD PREPARATION NOTES

If you can develop the habit of washing, drying, and crisping salad greens right after you have picked them, you'll always have fresh clean leaves for salad. It's just as easy to clean three heads at once as it is to clean enough for one meal, and you'll probably use the same amount of water. When harvesting six or more heads at one time, leave at least three intact in a plastic bag in the salad bin of the refrigerator; this will keep the inner leaves fresh for several days.

Follow these tips for crisp, well-cleaned salad greens:

- Plunge freshly harvested lettuce heads into an outside sink or tub of water to remove most of the dirt that clings to the leaves.

- Remove any bruised, old, withered, and yellowed leaves. Cut out any large stems. Tear out the core and separate the leaves.

- For tight heads, like iceberg, endive, and cabbage, core the heads, then run cold water into the cut and over leaves. Invert to drain.

- Fill a sink or large bowl with cold water. Add the leaves and swirl them around. (Some cooks suggest adding about 1 teaspoon of vinegar to a sinkfull of water to help float away soil.) Soak for 5 to 20 minutes, then remove and set aside to drain.

- Water on lettuce repels the coating action of dressing and dilutes the dressing, so remove most of the moisture from leaves before serving (either by spinning in a salad spinner or drying with paper towels).

- Individual leaves may also be dried with paper towels or non-terrycloth dish towel.

- To crisp, wrap greens in a towel, roll tightly and chill in the refrigerator for at least 30 minutes. (Some cooks advise placing the towel-wrapped lettuce in a plastic bag.)

- If you put dried lettuce in plastic to store for several days, include a piece of paper towel to soak up excess moisture.

- If you will be using the lettuce in salads, go ahead and tear the leaves into bite-sized pieces no more than 1 hour before serving.

- If you are going to chop or shred the leaves, do so just before serving.

COOKING FOR NUTRITION

Once vegetables are harvested, their nutritional value is determined by the way they are handled before storage, length of storage, preparation for cooking, and cooking method. Here are a few facts to keep in mind:

- The nutrients in vegetables steadily decrease over time once they are picked.

- Cutting vegetables and storing them in the refrigerator reduces their nutrients. Therefore, prepare them as close to the cooking time as possible.

- Raw is not always the best way to eat vegetables; steaming broccoli and carrots, for example, makes the vitamin A in them more accessible to the body.

- Most vegetables retain more nutrients when cooked whole and unpeeled.

- Steaming and microwaving are preferred to boiling, baking, and roasting.

- Pressure cooking helps preserve nutrients.

- As long as vegetables are not burned or overcooked in the process, grilling is an acceptable method.

- Spinach is most nutritious when raw. Cauliflower and green beans are equally nutritious raw or steamed.

- Steaming is best for asparagus, peas, carrots, and broccoli.

- Stir-frying is acceptable for most vegetables as long as it is done at high heat and very quickly; extended cooking over high heat will destroy nutrients.

STIR-FRYING HINTS

Briefly stir-frying in a wok with hot oil is an efficient, timesaving, tasty way to prepare vegetables.

- Vegetable nutrients are best retained if the vegetables are not exposed too long to high heat.

- Cut vegetables into small pieces (this helps them cook quickly), and into similar shapes and sizes with the proviso that some denser vegetables (such as cauliflower and carrots) should be slightly smaller.

- Heat the wok before adding the oil, especially when cooking small amounts of vegetables. Heat oil until hot but not smoking before adding the vegetables.

- Always stir-fry vegetables over high heat.

- Cook only a few handfuls (8 or 9 ounces) of vegetables at a time to keep them crisp and colorful.

- Before removing vegetables, drip some water along the edge of the wok; this will enhance their color.

- Some recipes call for steaming vegetables for a few seconds first, so they will be al dente after minimal stir-frying. Steam each kind of vegetable separately, cooking denser vegetables a few seconds longer.

- Add fragrant ingredients like ginger, garlic, or crushed red pepper flakes after the vegetables have been cooking a few seconds. Push slightly cooked vegetables along the sides of the wok, add the fragrant ingredients, and then quickly toss everything together in the center of the wok, being careful not to burn the herbs (which will impart a bitterness to the stir-fry).

- Do not overcook. It's better to have vegetables that are slightly crunchy rather than mushy. Adjust cooking times according to your experience and preferences.

- Slightly toasted nuts (such as cashews or pecans) or seeds (like sesame seeds) can be added at the last moment or sprinkled over the vegetables just before they are served.

- Serve the vegetables immediately after removing them from the wok.

- Since stir-frying is a quick process, prepare all ingredients and sauces (including a mixture of 2 teaspoons cornstarch and water) in advance. Before adding the cornstarch mixture, stir it once quickly and remove the wok from the heat. Once the mixture has been added, the wok can be returned to the heat and the sauce will thicken without lumps. To give the sauce an appetizing shine, sprinkle a few drops of sesame seed oil into the wok after the cornstarch mixture has thickened.

- Add ingredients such as oyster sauce, tamarind paste, bean sauce, hoisin sauce, soy sauce, or other sauces separately or in combination after the vegetables are cooked. At the end of cooking, add a tablespoon of the cornstarch and water mixture to thicken the sauce and glaze the vegetables.

2

Understanding Soils and Fertilizers & Making Flavorings from the Garden

Introduction to Soils and Fertilizers

Good rich soil is the foundation of any garden; it is cherished by gardeners everywhere. Soil is a dynamic ecosystem containing rock particles, tiny wildlife, air, and water. It is a living medium of decay and renewal and a vital source of both plant and human health. Like any wildlife community, soil needs nurturing to stay healthy and productive.

For kitchen gardeners, good soil management is especially important because good food starts in good soil. Vegetables are hungry, fast-growing plants that don't grow well in poor soils. They need a constant supply of nutrients to thrive. They need rich soil!

The first step in good soil care is to figure out how much time and work your soil needs to make it productive. If you live on a deep loam with plants flourishing everywhere, consider yourself lucky. There's not a whole lot you have to do to make your soil grow a bounty of vegetables. However, most of us have soil that rates somewhere between okay and lousy—too much sand, too much clay, poor drainage, on a slope, or infested with

invasive weeds. Fortunately, almost every plot of ground can be pampered and transformed into productive soil. It may require some effort over a few years, but it can be done.

GETTING TO KNOW YOUR SOIL

Have you ever wondered where your garden soil came from, or how it got to be soil? The answer involves getting to know your soil and its important properties, such as texture, structure, profile, recent history, and chemistry. To really get to know your soil, you'll have to feel it, smell it, dig holes in it, ask your neighbors about it, identify its weeds, and maybe send it to a lab for analysis.

Feeling Soil Texture

"Texture" refers to the sizes of the rock particles in the soil. People are usually surprised to learn that soil comes from weathered rock. In fact, at one time there was no soil on earth, just rocks. But the forces of weather are relentless. Given enough time, the processes of freezing and thawing, heating and cooling, wind and rain crumble all rocks into soil.

The tiny rock particles that make up soil are classified according to their size. The largest are "sand" and range in size from 2 mm to $1/20$ mm ($1/16$ inch to $1/500$ inch). Smaller yet are silt particles, and the smallest are clay particles, about the size of a bacterium. The ratio of sand, silt, and clay particles is called the soil "texture," and it describes the way soil feels.

A soil that has approximately equal amounts of sand, silt, and clay is called "loam." It's the ideal texture to have because it combines the best qualities of sand and clay.

Telling Texture by Touch

To determine whether your soil texture is sandy, silt, clay, or loam, take a handful of soil and remove all pebbles, plant remains, insects, and anything bigger than the point of a ballpoint pen. Break apart all soft clods and remove all hard ones. If you can find a screen or sifter with mesh about twice the size of window screen (about 2 millimeters), sift your sample to remove any unwanted particles and help break apart soft clods.. Examine the soil sample when it's dry.

continued on page 54

TEXTURE AND PROPERTIES OF SAND, CLAY, AND LOAM						
TEXTURE	FEEL	WATER RETENTION	DRAINS WATER	HOLDS NUTRIENTS	WARMS IN SPRING	TILLAGE
Clay	Smooth, greasy, or sticky	Yes, but some hold too tightly for plants to use	Slowly; can form impervious layers	Yes	Very slowly	Difficult when wet, moist, or dry
Sand	Gritty, rough, scratchy	Poor, since particles and pore spaces are large	Yes, but often makes plants wilt rapidly	No	Rapidly	Easy when wet, moist, or dry
Loam	Neither gritty nor smooth predominates	Yes, with most water available to plants	Yes, at a rate plants like	Yes	In between	Easy when moist

FIG. 2-1: Rocks to Clay

All rocks eventually crumble into dust (clay) by the processes of weather and soil life

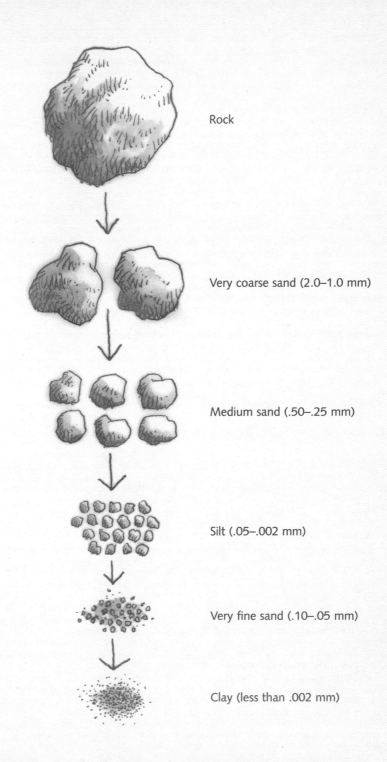

Rock

Very coarse sand (2.0–1.0 mm)

Medium sand (.50–.25 mm)

Silt (.05–.002 mm)

Very fine sand (.10–.05 mm)

Clay (less than .002 mm)

Sandy soil feels gritty, seldom forms clods, and makes a grinding sound when rubbed between fingers; very fine sand can be distinguished from silt in this manner. Dry silt feels smooth, like talcum powder, and the clods easily break into a soft dust that holds the impression of a fingerprint. Dry clay forms hard clods that are difficult to break.

Now wet the soil sample gradually, a couple of drops at a time, until it is moist but not soggy. Feel it, then try to roll it into a pencil shape. Sand is gritty and falls apart when you try to roll it. Wet clay feels sticky, even greasy. It rolls easily into a pencil-sized wire several inches long and becomes moldable. If you want a more accurate way to determine soil texture, see below and page 56.

Soils with different textures also have different properties. Sandy or "light" soils, have large pore spaces that make them well aerated. They also drain and dry out quickly and cool early in the fall. Fertilizers wash away easily and have to be replaced often. However, sandy soils also warm up early in spring and are easy to dig and till.

In clay soils, the clay particles are stacked on top of one another like tiny poker chips. There is so little space between the particles that they drain poorly. If you overwater clay soils, they become soggy, or "heavy," drowning plant roots and becoming difficult to work. Because they stay wet, clay soils warm slowly in spring, but stay warmer later in the fall. They also hold water and nutrients better than sandy soils.

The ideal soil texture is loam, which consists of sand, silt, and clay in similar amounts. When sand, silt, and clay are thus mixed, their drawbacks cancel out one another while their benefits remain.

It's very difficult to change soil texture. It would mean adding pure sand, silt, or clay to your soil. These would have to be spread in just the right proportions and mixed with painstaking thoroughness. Besides, the added particles wouldn't be covered with biological gums and resins, which give soil its structure. To improve your soil, you'll find it easier and more beneficial to improve the soil structure with organic matter.

The Ball-and-Ribbon Method for Determining Soil Texture

1. Scoop up a handful-sized sample of your topsoil. Clean and sift the sample as described (see the previous page) so that only sand, silt, and clay remain. The sifting will break apart all tiny clods, which can interfere with feeling the texture.

2. Take about a tablespoonful of your dry, sifted soil and moisten it gradually with an eye dropper. Knead the soil vigorously until all dry lumps are moist. If you use too much water, simply add more soil. The soil should be uniformly moist, not soggy.

3. Squeeze the sample in your fist and then open your hand. If the moist sample crumbles, you have a "sandy" soil texture. If it stays in a ball, you can proceed to estimate its texture by squeezing the sample upward into a ribbon. If it doesn't form a ribbon, then its soil texture would be classified as "loamy sand." If it does form a ribbon, then follow the procedures outlined on page 55. Practice making ribbons for a while. Try to make the longest ribbon possible, but allow it to break off naturally. Make at least six ribbons and take the average length. Then follow the procedures outlined.

FIG. 2-2: Determining soil texture (by the "feel" method)

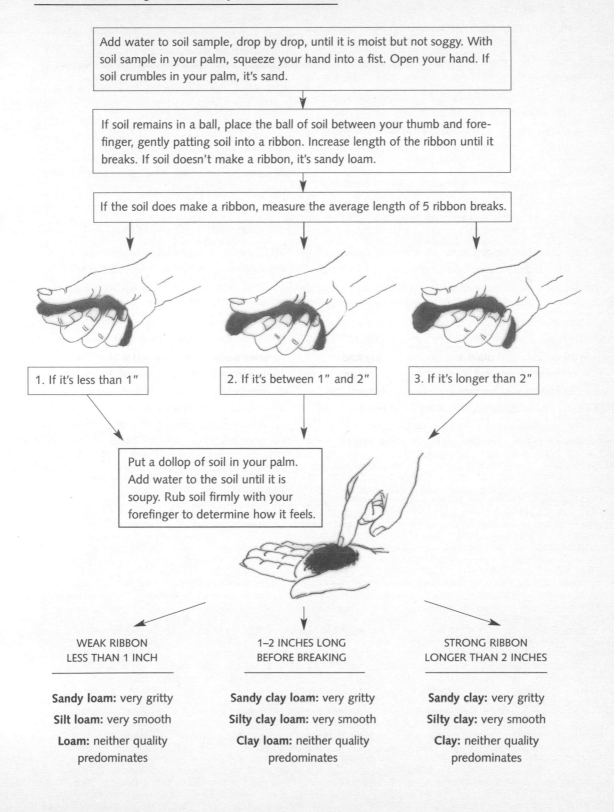

Add water to soil sample, drop by drop, until it is moist but not soggy. With soil sample in your palm, squeeze your hand into a fist. Open your hand. If soil crumbles in your palm, it's sand.

If soil remains in a ball, place the ball of soil between your thumb and forefinger, gently patting soil into a ribbon. Increase length of the ribbon until it breaks. If soil doesn't make a ribbon, it's sandy loam.

If the soil does make a ribbon, measure the average length of 5 ribbon breaks.

1. If it's less than 1″

2. If it's between 1″ and 2″

3. If it's longer than 2″

Put a dollop of soil in your palm. Add water to the soil until it is soupy. Rub soil firmly with your forefinger to determine how it feels.

WEAK RIBBON LESS THAN 1 INCH	1–2 INCHES LONG BEFORE BREAKING	STRONG RIBBON LONGER THAN 2 INCHES
Sandy loam: very gritty	**Sandy clay loam:** very gritty	**Sandy clay:** very gritty
Silt loam: very smooth	**Silty clay loam:** very smooth	**Silty clay:** very smooth
Loam: neither quality predominates	**Clay loam:** neither quality predominates	**Clay:** neither quality predominates

Soil Structure

Soil structure is formed when soil particles (sand, silt, clay) aggregate together into clods. If the soil doesn't have structure, it will just erode. Clay soil without structure forms a crusty surface, and pure sandy soil is like a sandbox. Soil structure is a by-product of organic decay. When soil microbes eat organic matter, they produce waste products that bind sand, silt, and clay particles together into clods, giving soil its structure.

Structure describes both the size and shape of the clods. They can be small or big, blocky or flat. The dirt clod you threw as a kid was probably a "medium-sized, blocky structure." An ideal soil structure is pea-sized or crumbly clods on the surface and larger, blocky clods in the subsoil. This combination of structures allows the soil to drain well and slows erosion. If you add organic matter to your soil on a regular basis, it will improve your soil structure. You can do this with mulch, compost, or green manures (see Chapter 3).

One of the reasons people dig the soil before planting is to break up the large clods that keep air and water from entering it. This is why gardeners like to brag about soil with a "crumbly" or "grainy" structure. Tiny clods not only let water percolate through the topsoil, they also hold water because of the organic matter binding the particles together.

Soil structure can be ruined if the soil is dug when it's too wet. Turning over soggy soils usually creates large clods, and if the soil is clay, the clods harden in the sun. On bare soil, hard rain can break apart the crumb structure and create an impermeable crust. Mulch helps to protect the soil surface from crusting by keeping the rain from beating apart small surface clods.

Reading Your Soil Profile

When most of us talk about soil, we're referring to the part we walk on, the topsoil. But you can't learn everything about your soil by standing on the surface, because there are layers upon layers below the topsoil that can hinder plant growth. Floods and winds deposit different soils, century after century, to make a "profile" of subsoils and former topsoils. As soils settle into layers, rain percolates down, carrying clay and dissolved minerals. Sometimes the clay accumulates in "pans," or impervious layers, that slow drainage and root growth.

THE PENCIL-WIRE METHOD FOR DETERMINING CLAY CONTENT

If you have a clay soil, the amount of clay can be estimated by the integrity of a moist sample rolled out into a pencil-shaped wire a couple of inches long. Place your soil wire on a flat surface and gently lift it up from the center with your thumb and forefinger.

IDENTIFYING CLAY PERCENTAGE BY PENCIL-WIRE PERFORMANCE

Pencil Wire	Clay %
Wire forms, but cannot be picked up	7–12
Wire forms and can be picked up, then breaks	12–18
Wire forms and can be picked up, but breaks when shaken	18–26
Wire forms, then bends and cracks, but doesn't break	26–35
Wire forms and can be picked up and bends, but doesn't crack	35–45
Wire forms and can be picked up, but doesn't bend	45+

If you have the time and energy to dig a profile, you can learn a lot about your soil. Along the side of the profile hole, you'll see a stack of two to four layers of different colored soils. The uppermost layer is the topsoil, or the "A" layer. It's where most of the biological activity takes place and nutrients are exchanged. Topsoils range in color from light tan to almost black; the darker the color, the higher the amount of organic matter. Most topsoils are just a few inches thick. If you have more than this, consider yourself fortunate. Below the topsoil is the light-colored subsoil, or "B" layer, which contains very little organic matter. It starts as soon as the darker color of the topsoil ends. Generally, subsoils will be either mostly clay washed from above or sand. Feel the texture of the subsoil. Does it feel gritty, like sand, or sticky, like clay? If the subsoil is mostly clay, it could be slowing drainage. Look for plant roots. Do they penetrate the subsoil? If so, that's a good sign. Look at the natural cracks along the face of the hole in the area of the subsoil. They will make shapes like blocks, columns, or plates. This is the structure of the soil. Clods shaped like blocks or columns drain water, while those shaped like plates slow drainage.

The minerals give subsoils their colors. Any red, orange, or yellow matter is iron. The specific color is a clue to how much air is in the subsoil. Red signifies iron oxide (the same as rust) and suggests that there is plenty of air; orange means a little less air; and yellow means that air is having a difficult time getting into the subsoil. If you see all colors, this means a variable or seasonal water table. White colors usually indicate calcium deposited from above.

If you dig past the subsoil, you may hit a compacted layer known as the "C" layer. The C layer is usually the remnant of an old topsoil that got buried, so there can be several C layers. If you have a soil thermometer, take the temperature about 36 inches down, usually in the area of the C layers. At this soil depth, the soil temperature stays about the same day and night, season to season. In fact, it reflects the average air temperature of your area.

When a building is constructed, sometimes the topsoil is carted away. After the building is finished, the plants around the building must grow in the subsoil that's left behind. If you've had trouble getting plants to grow around your place, you may be trying to grow them in the subsoil. Subsoils are typically low in nutrients, so plants will stay small and immature.

HOW TO DIG YOUR SOIL PROFILE

1. Choose a small plot in your garden. Mark out a 3-foot square with the edge of a shovel. If you can, try to orient one of the sides of the square to the south. This will give you light to see the face of the profile better. Begin digging the soil out of the square. If the soil is dry and hard, dig out as much as you can and set a slow-drizzle hose in the hole. Soak the area thoroughly until it is saturated (this may take several hours). Saturated soils glisten on the surface from the water at the top. Let the soil drain naturally until all the free water drains away. This can take a day or two on sandy soils or several days on clay ones. The soil should now be soft and easy to dig.

2. Dig out the top 4 to 5 inches of topsoil from the marked-off square and place it in a pile. Now, start digging a 1-foot-wide trench along the north side of the square, and start another pile. As you dig straight down the

continued on page 58

FIG. 2-3: Digging a soil profile and reading the layers of your soil

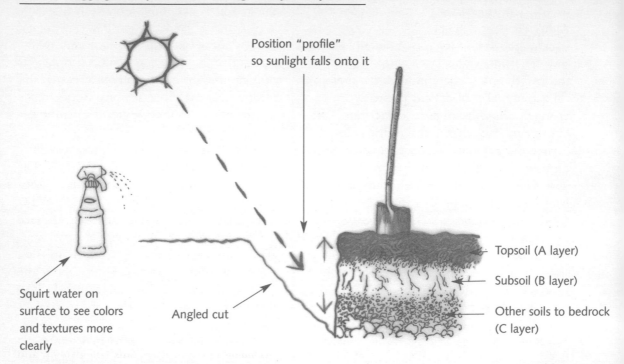

Position "profile" so sunlight falls onto it

Squirt water on surface to see colors and textures more clearly

Angled cut

Topsoil (A layer)

Subsoil (B layer)

Other soils to bedrock (C layer)

north side of the square, slowly widen the trench by digging at a 45-degree angle from the top of one side of the trench to the bottom of the other. When you're done, the sheer face of the soil profile will be facing the light of the sun, and your hole will be shaped like a bent V.

3. Look at your south-facing profile sometime around noon, when the sun is highest in the southern sky. To highlight colors, spray the side with a fine mist.

4. Be sure to fill the hole after you've poked and prodded the profile enough. Save the topsoil layer until last.

Using Local Soil Maps

Most soils in the United States have been "mapped" by the Department of Agriculture's Soil Conservation Service, which has identified the soils of every state and located them on county soil maps. The surveys de-scribe the profile of each soil type and tell something about the climate of the area. Here is a typical description of an area where we live: "Watsonville loam out of the Tierra-Watsonville complex, with a dark grayish brown, slightly acidic loam topsoil about 8 inches thick. The soil is deep, but drains poorly. The average annual rainfall is 28 inches and the mean annual temperature is 58 degrees, with a frost-free season of 245–275 days." This kind of general information is available free of charge to everyone.

County soil maps also describe the limitations of soils for uses like farming (and gardening), drainage for septic leach fields (and gardens), pond construction, wildlife habitat potential, and climate. They provide a broad, general look at the environment of your garden, as well as the potential of your soil.

You should be able to find a county soil map at a local library or at your U.S.D.A. Agricultural Extension Service headquarters. One handy feature is that they give the soil a capability class rating, which is an estimate of the time and energy necessary to make a soil productive. Ratings range from No. 1 (soils requiring very little energy to grow things) to No. 10 (soils on steep slopes with little prospect of supporting a garden).

Soil maps are made by people who take profile cores of typical soils. Maps are very general because only a few sites are sampled relative to the size of the county. For example, the soil map may say that you have Soil 348, but there's a fair chance you may be in one of the surrounding soils, so read about all of the soils in your immediate area. Maps also miss many of the subtle differences in soils created by the topography of ridges and valleys. These shortcomings aside, county soil survey maps are still a valuable source of free regional information.

Recent History of Your Soil

The soil in your garden has a recent history of either care or neglect, and it often helps to know about it. Some of the ways soil is commonly abused include:

- Overfertilizing or overmanuring it so that the soil is toxic with salts

- Overusing herbicides

- Poisoning it with motor oil by working on cars over it

- Filling in an old pond with bad fill dirt

- Dumping wood and barbecue ashes in the same spot for years

- Discarding toxic household cleaning products

- Digging used kitty litter into the soil, thinking it is good manure.

If you have places that don't grow plants, it may be caused by some of these, or other abuses. Have your soil tested, or talk to neighbors and previous occupants to see if they can help you with the recent history of your soil.

Reading Your Weeds

Many gardeners claim they can tell a lot about their soil by looking at the weeds growing in it. Weed scientists agree that many weeds can be reliable clues to soil conditions. However, just a few plants of any one weed are not enough; the weed needs to dominate the area. Also, perennial weeds, which regrow each year, are better indicators than annual weeds. Some weeds indicate more than one soil condition. For instance, dandelion (*Taraxacum officinale*), dock (*Rumex* spp.), and plantain (*Plantago* spp.) are good indicators of heavy clay, poorly drained, acidic soils.

The most obvious indicators are weeds found in wet, marshy soils caused by low spots or poor drainage. These include nutsedge (*Cyperus*), willow (*Salix*), purple loosestrife (*Lythrum salicaria*), marsh marigold (*Caltha palustris*), rushes (*Juncus*), bee balm (*Monarda didyma*), horsetails (*Equisetum*), and several species of boneset (*Eupatorium*). Also look for tiny mosses on the soil surface. If their greenish tinge persists into summer, this is another clue you have poorly drained soil.

Where burdock *(Arctium minus)*, pigweed *(Amaranthus* spp.*)*, lamb's-quarter *(Chenopodium album)*, chickweed *(Cerastium* spp.*)*, and purslane *(Portulaca oleracea)* grow very lush, the soil has good organic content and is well drained and fertile. It's interesting that many of these weeds are edible.

If a soil is low in humus or fertility, it's likely to be dominated by milfoil yarrow *(Achillea millefolium)*, fennel *(Foeniculum)*, sorrel *(Rumex)*, thistle *(Cirsium)*, black medic *(Medicago lupulina)*, crabgrass *(Digitaria)*, or chamomile *(Matricaria)*.

On heavily compacted soils, you're likely to find stands of thistle *(Cirsium)*, goose-grass *(Eleusine indica)*, knotweed *(Polygonum aviculare)*, annual bluegrass *(Poa annua)*, and white clover *(Trifolium repens)*.

If your soil drainage is good, some weeds may indicate whether your soil is acid or alkaline. Acid-loving weeds include red sorrel

(Rumex acetosella), plantains *(Plantago* spp.*)*, knapweeds *(Centaurea)*, and oxeye daisy *(Chrysanthemum leucanthemum)*. Weeds that suggest an alkaline soil include shepherd's purse *(Capsella bursa-pastoris)*, field pennycress *(Thlaspi arvense)*, chicory *(Cichorium intybus)*, and mugwort *(Artemesia vulgaris)*.

IS SOIL TESTING WORTH IT?

It's generally a good idea to test your soil every few years to see if it has enough plant nutrients and to determine properties like organic matter, pH, and salinity, all of which affect the availability of plant nutrients. You might be starting a garden on ground that has been in weeds for years. Such "native," or "fallow," soils are usually low in nutrients. Maybe your soil was abused by previous occupants or maybe it was overfertilized by well-meaning gardeners. A soil test will often help you sort out the recent past of your soil and give you recommendations for fertilizing.

There are many do-it-yourself soil-testing kits on the market. If you have a soil test kit with fresh ingredients, if you can keep your hands and all your tools clean during the chemical tests, and if you're happy with results measuring low, medium, and high, then test away. In the long run, however, local soil-testing labs have much better equipment, are far more accurate, and are more familiar with the mosaic of local soils. Their fertilizer recommendations are based on experience, not just numbers. Your local soil labs see the results of hundreds of tests of similar soils in your region and use this frame of reference to interpret their analysis and to recommend what and how much fertilizer you need.

A complete soil test measures macronutrients, micronutrients, pH, and salinity. To make it worth the money, your soil sample has to represent all the soil you want to use, not just the one spot you took it from.

How to Collect a Sample

Since a soil sample is only a fraction of all of the soil in your garden, you need to make sure that it represents your entire garden. If you take just one sample, then the results will reflect just the spot from which it came. Instead, you need to take several "subsamples" of topsoil from your garden, mix these together, and from this mixture draw the soil sample that is tested. Now your sample represents the soil of your garden.

Wait until the soil is moist, like a damp sponge, neither soggy nor dry. You can create this condition with proper watering (see page 57) or by waiting a few days after a heavy rain. To take subsamples, you'll need a clean bucket and trowel, a small plastic bag for each sample, and a tape measure. You'll need at least 10 subsamples, so take them from every row, bed, or box, or every other row, bed, or box. If your garden is large, divide it into a regular grid of 10 to 12 points.

At each spot, brush aside all surface debris, mulch, or sod. These exaggerate the nitrogen and organic matter results. Now dig your trowel 6 inches into the soil, at a 45-degree angle. This is your subsample. Don't touch the soil with your hands, and keep it away from all galvanized metal or brass, as these could contaminate your sample and throw off the results. Thoroughly mix all the subsamples in a clean plastic bucket with a clean implement. Remove about 1 cup of the mixed dirt and place it in a plastic bag. Keep the soil sample cool and out of the sun, and get it to a local soil tester as soon as possible.

SOIL pH

In the soil, plant nutrients cling to particles of clay and humus, where they are stored and picked up by plant roots. Each nutrient attaches with a different strength. Hydrogen clings more strongly than any other nutrient because it is small and abundant, so the amount of hydrogen in the soil controls the availability of all other nutrients. If the soil is too acidic, this means that the clay and humus particles are covered with hydrogen, leaving no room for other nutrients. If the soil is too alkaline, then calcium, magnesium, potassium, and sodium control the soil chemistry. Only when there is just the right amount of hydrogen will all nutrients be available to plants.

Hydrogen is measured by what the chemists call pH. The pH scale extends from 1 (very acidic) to 14 (very alkaline), with 7 being neutral. Most garden soils are in the range from 5 to 8, while most vegetables grow best in a range of 6.0 to 7.5, with 6.5 being ideal. Good soils are slightly acidic because the respiration of soil life produces slightly acid conditions. Thus, it's not surprising that humus has a pH of about 6.5.

Soil pH is determined by a region's climate, the local vegetation, and the minerals that make up the soil. Acid soils occur under most trees, especially pine or oak, because of their decaying litter. Sandy soils are usually acid because they drain away all the nutrients, leaving no competition for the hydrogen. In areas with heavy rainfall, soils will be on the acid side, regardless of their texture, for the same reason. Repeated use of most chemical fertilizers, especially sulfur and ammonia, can also make a soil acidic.

Calcium, magnesium, potassium, and sodium all make a soil more alkaline. This is why you find alkaline soils in arid areas where these nutrients evaporate at the surface, or on ground that has gotten too much calcium (limestone), wood ashes (potassium), or sodium/potassium fertilizers. Soil may also be alkaline if it is formed from bedrock with these elements in it, or is located near building foundations where water washes lime from mortar and cement.

If your soil is too acid, raise the pH by adding limestone, dolomite, or crushed oyster shells, all sources of calcium. Avoid quicklime and slaked or hydrated lime, which can burn plants and injure soil life. Wood ashes should be used sparingly since they're fast acting and can overload your soil with potassium. If you have a fireplace or wood stove, avoid burning brightly colored magazines and briquettes, and don't dump wood ash in the same place year after year. If your soil is too alkaline, lower the pH by adding sulfur. Some gardeners use vinegar on their alkaline soils at a rate of 1 pint of white distilled vinegar per 2 gallons of water.

The amount of sulfur or calcium you need to adjust your soil pH depends on your soil texture. Clay soils have more surface area than sandy ones and therefore need more fertilizer to achieve the same change in pH.

POUND OF SOIL SULFUR PER 100 SQUARE FEET NEEDED TO MAKE ALKALINE SOILS MORE ACIDIC

Change in pH Desired	Sandy	Loamy	Clay
8.5–6.5	1½	2	3
8.0–6.5	1¼	1½	2
7.5–6.5	1	1	1½
7.0–6.5	½	¾	1

continued on page 62

POUNDS OF LIMESTONE PER 100 SQUARE FEET NEEDED TO MAKE ACID SOILS MORE ALKALINE			
Change in pH Desired	Sandy	Loamy	Clay
4.5–6.5	12	20	27$\frac{1}{2}$
5.0–6.5	10	16	23
5.5–6.5	8	13	18
6.0–6.5	3	8	11$\frac{1}{2}$

THE LIVING SOIL

We know more about the soil on the moon than on the earth. Why? Because the earth's soil is alive, and this complicates everything.

During earth's early history, as rocky landscapes crumbled into soil, many creatures found that the new rubble was a haven of small air spaces that insulated them from the weather and hazards above. As each new wave of creatures evolved on land, some species hastened to the refuge of the soil and began their own evolution. Tiny bacteria thrived in the water film around clay and humus particles. Green algae swarmed in soil water. Fungi, with their threadlike strands, spread and ramified through the soil, holding it together. In time, worms, mites, miniature scorpions, insects, and rodents all carved out their niches and helped make the rubble come alive. This life turned the particles of rock into soil.

Every time you take a step in your garden, you walk on a web of life unlike any other. In 200 square feet of garden soil, more than 20 billion bacteria, 250 million fungi, 200 million protozoa (single-celled creatures), 3 million nematodes, 5,000 mites, and 2,000 earthworms can live. If you weighed all this life, it could weigh over 35 pounds and nearly 70 percent of that would be microbes.

Soil is literally a microbial culture not unlike those used to make cheese, wines, and bread. The cheese maker, vintner, and baker use certain fungi or bacteria to transform raw organic material into foods we enjoy. Likewise, soil bacteria and fungi transform soil's organic residues into humus.

As organic material decays, it releases plant nutrients. When microbes feed on organic matter, they add acids to the soil. These acids quicken the pace of decay, which means more nutrients. The acids also help to disintegrate sand and silt particles, and this also releases nutrients. In the end, rocks become clay and life becomes humus. This is the legacy of the living soil.

Each microbe has its own specific role in the soil. Some bacteria photosynthesize like plants, and others take nitrogen from the air and convert it to a form plants can use. These nitrogen "fixers" live freely in the soil and also on the roots of peas, beans, and related plants. Other bacteria take sulfur from rocks and make it into a usable form. Some fungi, called mycorrhiza, attach to plant roots in a mutually beneficial arrangement. They extend the roots of the plant and fend off diseases, while the plant makes food for the fungus. Some fungi eat wood, others eat nematodes, and some eat insects. There are very few things fungi can't eat.

Supported by this microbial foundation, several kinds of soil animals range through the

continued on page 64

FIG. 2-4:
Life in the Soil Profile

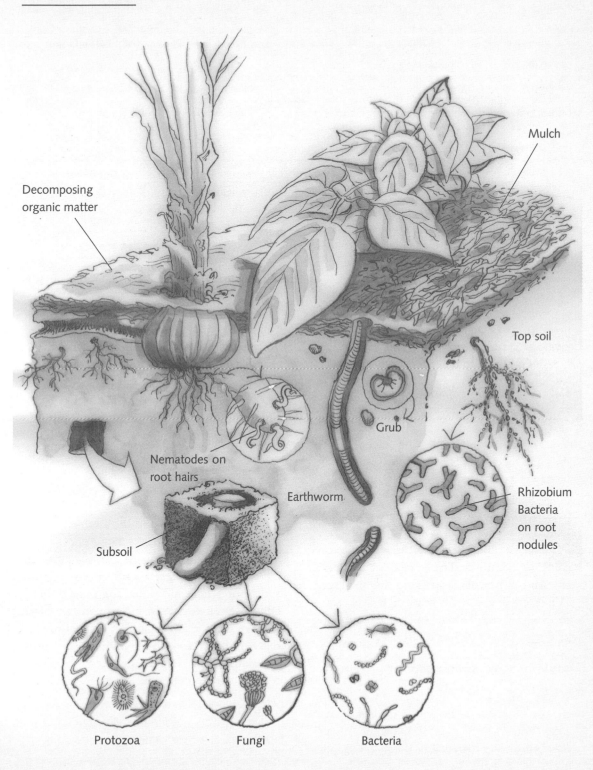

Mulch

Decomposing
organic matter

Top soil

Grub

Nematodes on
root hairs

Earthworm

Rhizobium
Bacteria
on root
nodules

Subsoil

Protozoa

Fungi

Bacteria

soil eating dead things or each other. Earthworms, millipedes, sowbugs, mites, and tiny wingless insects called springtails crawl and push their way through the microspaces of the soil looking for organic residues to eat. The residues are further attacked by microbes living in the intestines of these creatures. As soil animals defecate, their wastes become energy for a soil food chain: Earthworm castings are eaten by sowbugs, their wastes are eaten by soil mites, and their wastes are eaten by soil fungi. The final result is humus—manure from the soil's life.

Keeping things in check among all this living activity are a variety of soil predators like ground beetles and their larvae, subterranean crickets, tiny soil scorpions, predatory mites, and centipedes. They are the most visible indicators of a healthy soil. Soils with many species of predatory mites, for example, usually indicate a soil rich in other life. If you want to see a sample of soil critters, look in an old, moist compost pile or under thick leaf litter.

As gardeners, we are constantly reminded that a bountiful, sustainable garden depends on a healthy soil, which, in turn, depends on a rich population of soil life and a good supply of humus. In Chapter 3, we discuss several ways that you can get humus into your soil by recycling organic wastes around the home. In the meantime, remember that soil care is like any other form of wildlife management. If you nurture its home, the wildlife will take care of itself. Or to quote one gardener's saying, "Feed the soil and it will feed the plant," we would only add, "and you also."

PREPARING YOUR SOIL

Breaking ground is the symbolic beginning of a new garden or a new season. A loose topsoil means that seeds and seedlings will have an easy time establishing roots. We also dig and till to break open deeper layers of the soil. This helps air and water penetrate where they can feed plant roots and nourish soil life.

There are several ways to get soil ready for planting. Most of them involve digging. Other methods break up soil without digging. Gardeners don't agree on which method is best, but all techniques of preparing soils have one thing in common: They are done to aerate the soil without destroying its structure. Whether you do this with a shovel, a rototiller, by mulching, or by encouraging earthworms is a matter of choice.

Making Your Soil at Field Capacity

If your soil is hard and dry, start by sprinkling the area for several hours, or until it is saturated. You'll know it's saturated when the surface glistens. This means that all the pore spaces are filled with water. Now let the soil drain, two to four days for sandy soils and three to six days for clay soils. Wait about the same length of time after a heavy rainfall.

The soil is at the right point on the scale between wet and dry when a shovel goes in easily but the soil does not stick to it, or when you can pick up a handful of moist soil and squeeze it without water coming out. When the soil feels crumbly and moist, it's at *field capacity* and it's ready to work.

One of the easiest and most effective ways to get soil ready for spring digging is to apply a thick mulch in the fall. As it rots on the surface over the winter, the mulch protects the soil from winds and pounding rains while it attracts earthworms. In spring you can either remove the remaining mulch for compost or dig it into the soil. You'll find the soil much easier to work than unmulched soil. Some tried-and-true methods:

• Place layers of newspaper and cardboard on the soil and hold them down with thick hay or a light sprinkling of soil or sand.

• Cut your green manure (see page 130) at soil level in fall and let it lie on the ground over winter.

• Strew 2- to 4-inch-thick sections of alfalfa hay bales on the soil surface. If your area is windy, cover the mulch with a tied-down tarp that has a few holes in it.

Try to add compost and organic amendments while you are tilling the soil. When you dig up the earth and break up clods, air rushes into the soil. An aerated soil is one that decays organic residues quickly and recycles nutrients efficiently.

Digging Methods

No matter how you dig your soil, it's always best to do it when the soil is at field capacity. Dry soils are hard to dig into and will blow away with the wind, while wet soils throw up large clods and wreck the soil structure. Moist soils are perfect because you can slice into them a shovel's depth and break up clods easily.

Hand Digging

If you have a nice loam soil, or are starting a garden for the first time, hand digging to the depth of a shovel or fork may be enough. To loosen up soil by hand, you'll need a straight-edge shovel and a digging fork.

Begin by removing all rocks, rubble, weeds, and sod. Mark your garden off in strips a few shovels wide. Make your soil at field capacity (see the previous page). Then, simply turn over clumps of topsoil with your shovel and break up the large clods with a flat-tined digging fork. In a crumbly state, the soil can be moved and shaped with a flat-edged shovel and bow rake.

You can add compost or other organic amendments any time during hand digging. Spread it on the top before you start, or work it in as you dig.

Double-Digging and Raised Beds

Double-digging is a time-honored way of loosening soil deeply while incorporating organic matter and fertilizers. There are many ways to double-dig, but the steps are basically the same: (1) remove soil to the depth of a shovel; (2) use a digging fork to loosen the soil at the bottom of the dug-out trench; and (3) replace the topsoil, breaking up the large clods as you go. The main purpose of double-digging is to aerate the topsoil and subsoil while improving soil structure. It's also an excellent way to add fertilizers and organic amendments. When you are done double-digging a vegetable bed, you will have moved the topsoil about 3 feet forward and aerated the subsoil (see page 66). Double-digging is not for everyone or even every soil. It's a labor-intensive activity that shouldn't be done by people with a history of back problems. Also, deep sandy soil doesn't seem to benefit enough from double-digging to warrant all the work. However, shallow clay or silt soils are greatly improved by the technique.

DOUBLE-DIGGING DIRECTIONS

The following technique has worked well for us. First, mark off the width and length of your bed (we use string or limestone). The width can vary from 3 to 5 feet. If the soil is dry, give it a deep watering and let it drain for a few days, or until the top 12 inches are moist, not soggy (see "Field Capacity," page 64). Next, spread three or four wheelbarrows of compost or aged manure over each 100 square feet of your bed. Now you're ready to double-dig.

At one end of the bed, dig a trench to the depth of a spade 2 to 3 feet long down the bed. Take the soil from this trench and place it near the other end of the bed. Next, take a digging fork and thoroughly loosen the exposed subsoil in the bottom of the trench. This is the

continued on page 66

"double-dig" (a true double-dig removes soil to a depth of two spades, which is useful for perennials but unnecessary for most vegetables). At this point, some people add compost and soil amendments to the bottom of the trench; this helps improve the structure of the subsoil. Now score the edges of the bed with a shovel another 2 to 3 feet down the bed to mark off the second trench. Working across the bed, take your shovel and begin slicing off 2- to 4-inch pieces of topsoil down one shovel length. Throw the slices of soil straight in front of you to the opposite side of the first trench. Topsoil from the second trench will now begin to fill up the first trench. Break up all large clods with your digging fork as you dig.

Eventually, the first trench will be filled leaving a new trench in back of it. Loosen up the subsoil of the second trench with your digging fork, mark the edges for the third trench, and repeat the process. When you get to the other end of the bed, there should be an empty trench from your last dig. Fill this with the soil you moved from first trench. You'll notice that the soil in the bed is now slightly higher than it was when you started. This is because you've added a substantial amount of air to the soil, which is the basis of the "raised" bed.

Now you can shape and form the bed. When you are done, you will have moved the entire top 12 inches or so of the bed forward a few feet, broken up the subsoil, added organic matter, fluffed up the soil with air, and raised the soil level a few inches. In short, you will have created an ideal environment for vegetables to grow.

FIG. 2-5:
Preparing your soil
by double-digging

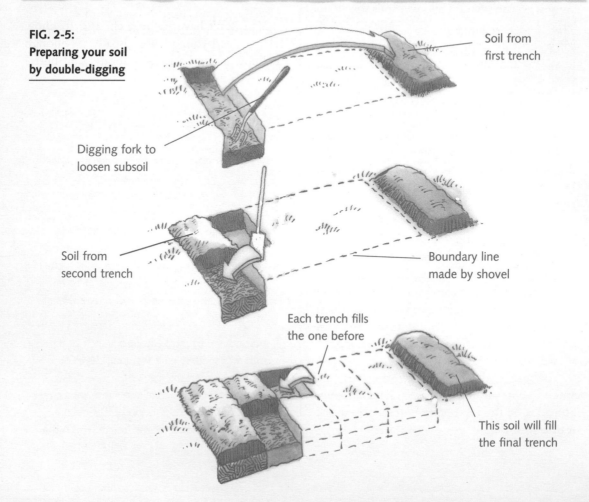

Digging fork to loosen subsoil

Soil from first trench

Soil from second trench

Boundary line made by shovel

Each trench fills the one before

This soil will fill the final trench

Rototilling

Some gardeners swear by rototillers, others swear at them. In our experience, one or two able people can hand dig a small garden (less than 2,500 square feet) without too much trouble. If the garden is in year-round production, hand digging is even easier because you only have to work small areas at a time. But if you're physically limited or have a large garden, a rototiller can be a very handy tool. They're especially useful for breaking up heavy, compacted soils and for incorporating green manures, compost, and fertilizers into the soil.

There is a negative side to rototillers. Some gardeners believe they pulverize the soil and actually harm its structure. They destroy earthworm passages, and as the tines rotate through heavy soil, they can create an impervious pan layer at tine depth. You also have to be mindful of all weeds that propagate by runners, like Bermuda grass and bindweed. A rototiller can cut these weeds into pieces that send out new plants everywhere. Rototillers are expensive to buy and rent, and like any good power tool, they need constant upkeep and attention. Also they are not used easily in contained beds. This is not a big problem, however, because other types of powered hand tillers are available for just that purpose; consult your local garden-supply shop for guidance.

No-Dig Methods

Some gardeners believe that the soil should not be dug up at all. They point to the model in nature of a thick leaf mulch protecting the soil and encouraging earthworms to aerate the soil.

In the "no-dig" method, a thick layer of mulch is applied to the soil year-round. The soil is not dug or turned in any way. The mulch keeps the soil moist and attracts earthworms to the surface. The earthworms aerate the soil with their vertical tunnels and create a crumb surface structure with their manure (castings). Vegetables are transplanted directly into the perennial mulch, which is pushed aside for direct sowings and fertilizing. As mulch is piled on each year, older mulch at the soil surface decays and, with the help of earthworms, is buried into the fabric of the soil. (See chapter 3 for more on mulches.)

FERTILIZING AND AMENDING YOUR SOIL

For many centuries, people knew that animal manures, blood, ashes, and other materials made plants grow lush and healthy. Anyone could see that plants flourished around animal droppings and carcasses, or in the wake of forest and grass fires. What they didn't know was that these apparent elixirs were simply concentrated sources of plant nutrients, or fertilizers.

You don't have to be a chemist to know how to feed your plants. Usually, it's enough to know a few basic facts about plant nutrients and fertilizers. What the kitchen gardener wants to know is

1. Which nutrients do my plants need?

2. Which fertilizer(s) do I use?

3. How much do I put on?

4. When and how do I put them on?

Plant Nutrients

Like us, plants need a balanced diet to stay healthy. In fact, both plants and people need about the same elements, just in different proportions. Of the more than 100 known chemical elements, only a dozen or so are considered essential, because without any one of them, plant growth is inhibited. It's convenient to place the major nutrients into five functional groups.

PRIMARY PLANT NUTRIENTS

NUTRIENT	FUNCTIONS	DEFICIENCY SYMPTOMS	NATURAL SOURCES
Nitrogen (N)	Makes plants green and leaves crisp. Aids growth of leaf and stem. Stimulates rapid, early growth.	Leaves pale green to yellow, especially lower ones. Stunted growth.	Organic matter, rain water, and nitrogen from air.
Phosphorous (P)	Crucial for root growth, seed formation, storing biological energy, and making cell membranes.	Leaves reddish purple, especially on underside. Small seed and fruit. Thin stems. Stunted growth.	Organic matter and rock phosphate minerals.
Potassium (K)	Helps disease resistance; production of strong stalks and roots; production of starches and oils.	Leaf edges scorched and curled. Stems weak. Stunted growth. Poor resistance to diseases.	Rock minerals of feldspar, mica, granite, and some clays. Organic ash.

SECONDARY PLANT NUTRIENTS

NUTRIENT	FUNCTIONS	DEFICIENCY SYMPTONS	NATURAL SOURCES
Calcium (Ca)	Builds cell walls. Part of many enzymes. Essential for N uptake and protein synthesis.	Weak stems with slow growth. New leaves curled with yellow spots and wavy margins. Roots stunted. Blossom end rot in tomatoes.	Rock minerals of dolomite, calcite, apatite, and some fieldspars.
Magnesium (Mg)	Essential part of chlorophyll. Aids seed germination and formation of fats and sugars.	Yellow mottling on older leaves with green veins and brown margins and tips.	Rock minerals of dolomite, serpentine, mica, and hornblend.
Sulfur (S)	Part of proteins and some vitamins. Essential for N-fixing in legumes. Flavors alliums and brassicas.	Resembles nitrogen deficiency. Older leaves yellow. Stems slender and hard.	Organic matter. Atmospheric sulfur fixed by microbes.

TRACE OR MICRONUTRIENTS

NUTRIENT	FUNCTIONS	DEFICIENCY SYMPTOMS	NATURAL SOURCES
Iron (Fe)	A nutrient for many enzymes. Hemoglobin in legumes. Chlorophyll synthesis.	Leaves are pale, spotted or yellow, especially new ones.	Organic matter and rock minerals.
Zinc (Zn)	Formation of growth hormones. Protein synthesis. Seed production. Metabolic enzymes	Leaves long and narrow, with yellow and dead spots, especially in late summer. In beans: seed leaves develop reddish spots. In corn: leaves develop wide stripes at bases.	Organic matter and rock minerals.
Copper (Cu)	Catalyst for enzyme and chlorophyll production and plant metabolism.	Slow growth, faded color, flabby leaves. In onions: outer skin is thin and pale. In tomatoes: leaves are curled and blue-green.	Organic matter and rock minerals.
Manganese (Mn)	Synthesis of chlorophyll and several vitamins. Carbohydrate and nitrogen metabolism. Helps vegetables keep better.	Slow growth, mottled yellowing of leaves. In onions and corn: leaves develop narrow yellow stripes. In spinach: leaves develop pale tips.	Organic matter and rock minerals.
Boron (B)	Protein synthesis. Starch and sugar transport. Root development. Fruit and seed formation. Water uptake.	Growing tips die back. Heart rot (hollow stems) and brown corky spots in root crops and brassicas.	Organic matter and rock minerals.
Molybdenum (Mo)	Crucial for bacteria that fix nitrogen in legumes.	Pale, distorted, narrow leaves with dry, rolled margins and yellow between veins.	Organic matter and rock minerals.

Nutrients from Air and Water

We work to make our soils breathe because air is an important fertilizer. It provides hydrogen (H) and carbon dioxide (CO_2), the source of all carbon (C) for making "organic" compounds plus oxygen (O) for the respiration of soil life. Legumes like peas and beans can also convert nitrogen (N) from the air into compounds plants can use through the action of bacteria living on their roots.

Primary Macronutrients

Macronutrients are the nutrients needed by plants in large amounts. Primary macronutrients include nitrogen (N), phosphorous (P), and potassium (K). The three numbers on a fertilizer package, called the "fertilizer grade," are the percentages of the primary macronutrients in the fertilizer. For example, a fertilizer grade of 5–10–15 contains 5 percent nitrogen, 10 percent phosphorous, and 15 percent potassium. Some gardeners refer to the fertilizer grade as the "N–P–K ratio."

Secondary Macronutrients

These include calcium (Ca), magnesium (Mg), and sulfur (S). Secondary macronutrients are important not only because they're plant foods, but also because they have a profound effect on soil pH. In fact, we use calcium and magnesium to make our soils more alkaline and sulfur to make them more acidic (see pages 61-62).

Primary Micronutrients

Micronutrients (or "trace elements") are needed in small amounts. They are a building block of vitamins, enzymes, and hormones, so they keep plants healthy, vigorous, and growing smoothly. Primary micronutrients include iron (Fe), manganese (Mn), copper (Cu), and zinc (Zn). Plants require more of these than other micronutrients, and they are easily applied.

Secondary Micronutrients

These include boron (B) and molybdenum (Mo). Only the smallest amounts of these nutrients are needed by plants. The most reliable source of secondary micronutrients is organic matter.

A micronutrient deficiency in plants is usually a sign that your soil is out of balance—that is, it's too acidic, too alkaline, too cold, or poorly drained. The problem can often be corrected by changing the pH and building the soil with humus rather than adding more micronutrients. Toxic amounts of micronutrients are often the result of adding animal manures from livestock that have them in their feed.

Micronutrients are common in organic fertilizers. If you need to provide a plant with a micronutrient quickly while you go about the longer term solution of changing your soil pH, you can use fish emulsion, liquid seaweed, or chelated fertilizers. Chelates (from the Latin for "claw") are organic chemicals added to nutrients to keep them available to plants, even when soil conditions are unfavorable. Look for "chelated micronutrients" in fertilizers at your nursery. The most common chelated nutrients are the primary micronutrients iron, zinc, copper, and manganese. They can be applied as a soil drench or sprayed on the foliage (see page 76).

Fertilizers and Soil Amendments

The words "fertilizer" and "soil amendment" are often used interchangeably, but there is a difference. A fertilizer provides nutrients to plants, whereas a soil amendment, like compost or aged manure, improves the soil's structure, enhances its microbial activity and stores water and nutrients (see chapter 3) for a productive *and* sustainable kitchen garden.

In nature, plants get their nutrients from many sources. Decaying organic matter, eroding rocks, air, and soil microbes all interact to provide most of the nutrients, while a tiny bit

FERTILIZERS AT A GLANCE

ORGANIC	PROS	CONS	FORMULATION	EXAMPLES
Plant and animal meals	Rapidly available fertilizers, some with micronutrients.	Availability depends on warm soils and a good population of soil microbes.	Dry, granular form.	Bone, cottonseed, blood, and soy meals.
Marine products	Best sources of micronutrients, plus plant enzymes and hormones. Some are water soluble for foliar feeding.	Costly (most kelp fertilizers come from Norway). Need sprayer for liquid forms.	Granular powder or liquid form used as foliar or drench.	Kelp powder, kelp meal, fish powder, fish meal, fish emulsion.
Animal manures	Cheap and available. Aged sources good for mulch.	Bulky. Fresh sources can have salts and toxic amounts of micronutrients.	Dry or fresh.	Chicken, horse, and cow manure.
Compost	Superior amendment for improving the structure, chemistry, and life of the soil.	Variable, depending on ingredients and age. Can spread disease when fresh.	Dry or fresh bulk.	Homemade from organic wastes. Also commercial brands.
Organic teas	When properly made, can directly provide nutrients, enzymes, and beneficial microorganisms.	Requires special apparatus to make and sprayers to apply. Highly variable.	Liquid form used as foliar or drench.	Made by soaking manures or compost in aerated water.
ROCK MINERALS				
	Good complement to organic fertilizers and composts. Good for long-term soil fertilizing.	Slowly available. Some, like greensand, are overrated and not useful in gardens of temporary use. Also less effective in poor alkaline soils.	Sand or powder form.	Granite dust, potassium sulfate, limestone, gypsum, rock phosphate, and colloidal phosphate.
CHEMICALS				
Soluble single nutrient	Concentrated sources of single nutrients; for specific deficiencies; for foliar feeding and chemical fertilizer blends.	Highly soluble. Easier to damage plants by over-application. May cause groundwater and pest problems.	Dry, granular form.	Ammonium sulfate (21–0–0), urea (46–0–0), ammonium nitrate (24–0–0), and muriate of potash (0–0–60).
Soluble complete nutrient	All nutrients available quickly. Used for hydroponics and container gardening or where frequent watering leaches nutrients.	Commonly misused. Strong dose can "burn" leaves. All problems of chemical fertilizers.	Dry, granular, and liquid concentrate forms.	RapidGro, Miracid, Miracle-Gro, and mixes of single nutrient fertilizers.
Partially soluble complete nutrient	For general garden use. Many formulations for specific groups of vegetables. Available over a longer period of time.	Cost per pound of nutrient is high. All problems of chemical fertilizers.	Dry, granular, and liquid forms, all slow release. Also pellets.	Vegetable food (5–1–10) and general-purpose plant food (8–8–8).
Slow release	Labor saving. Gradual feeding. Single nutrient or complete.	Expensive. Unpredictable—nutrient release depends on temperature and water. All problems of chemical fertilizers.	Pellet form. Chemical fertilizers encapsulated with coating so nutrients are released slowly.	Osmocote and Nutricoat (14–14–14) in 6-, 12-, and 18-month release formulations.

comes from rainwater. When we garden, we upset this natural balance and cycle of fertility. We grow hungry, fast-growing plants and take away the harvest; the soil is not recharged with plant food, so we have to add fertilizers and soil amendments.

FERTILIZERS BY NUMBER

Commercial fertilizers are labeled with the percentages of the three major nutrients they contain, always in the same order: nitrogen (N), phosphorous (P), and potassium (K). These are the three numbers you can see on the outside of a fertilizer bag. A 5–10–15 fertilizer contains 5 percent nitrogen, 10 percent phosphorous, and 15 percent potassium. These three numbers are called the fertilizer "grade," or the "N-P-K" ratio. A "complete" fertilizer contains all three major nutrients.

If you read the fertilizer label carefully, you'll often notice reference to other nutrients. Some fertilizers contain calcium, magnesium, or sulfur, while a few provide micronutrients.

Synthetic (chemical) Fertilizers

Synthetic fertilizers are plant nutrients manufactured from various acids, minerals, and ammonia, depending on which nutrients are needed. They include fertilizers like superphosphate, ammonium nitrate, and potassium nitrate. The first chemical fertilizer was manufactured in England around 1846, and was made from sulfuric acid and rock phosphate—today's superphosphate.

Chemical fertilizers are widely available, easily stored, convenient, and come in many grades. You can apply them in liquid, pellet, powder, or granular formulations. Most synthetic fertilizers dissolve in water and are rapidly available to plants. Some granular types are covered with resins or chalk. This allows them to slowly release nutrients over a period of several months. You can spray liquid forms on leaves as a foliar feed for an even speedier response (see page 76). Bagged chemical "vegetable food" is usually several chemical fertilizers mixed together to make a complete fertilizer (with nitrogen, phosphorous, and potassium).

Chemical fertilizers, however, have their downside. They tend to leach away readily to contaminate ground water, while they make the soil salty and alter its pH. They also make it easier for sucking insects like aphids, bugs, and mites to feed by increasing the fluid pressure of the plant sap. Chemical fertilizers, especially those with nitrogen, require a great deal of fossil fuel energy—a limited resource—to manufacture. It's not surprising that more and more gardeners are turning to natural organic and rock mineral fertilizers to provide plants with the nutrients they need.

Organic Fertilizers

Organic fertilizers are materials derived from once-living organisms. Their fertilizer grade depends on which part of the plant or animal the materials come from and how they are processed (see page 72).

Organic fertilizers, especially high-grade ones like liquids, emulsions, and "meals," don't provide organic matter for the soil. They're mostly made up of nutrient-rich soft cells and not the carbon-rich dead cells of twigs, sawdust, and other hard brown plant tissues, which are the foundation of humus. It's important to keep in mind this distinction

FERTILIZERS BY TYPES AND GRADES (%)

FERTILIZER	N (Ca)	P (Mg)	K (S)	TRACE	COMMENTS
ORGANIC					
Plant Meals					
Alfalfa meal	3	1	2	+	Good substitute for cottonseed meal. Natural plant growth stimulant triacontatol.
Apple pomace	2	1	1		Locally available.
Castor bean meal	5	2	1	+	Locally available.
Cocoa hulls	3	1	3	+	Locally available. May contain methyl bromide. Great mulch.
Cottonseed meal	7	2	2		Best complete plant fertilizer. May contain pesticides. Organic cottonseed meal is becoming available. Look for new organic meals.
Soybean meal	6	2	1	+	Good substitute for cottonseed meal.
Wood Ashes	0 (30)	0–1 (2)	4–10		Use wood and newspaper ashes only. Can make soil alkaline. Use only 2–4 lbs. per 100 square feet each year.
Animal Meals					
Blood meal	12	1	1		Fast source of nitrogen. May attract animals. Aids in decay of compost and high-carbon mulches.
Bone meal, steamed	1 (24)	15			Expensive; use for special things. Faster source of calcium and phosphorus than colloidal phosphate.
Feather meal	12				Lasts about 6 months. Great alternative to blood meal. Best as preplant.
Hoof and horn	10	2			Expensive, but rapidly available.
Oyster shell, ground	(38)				Organic liming agent: 96% CaCo₃.
Manures, Dry					
Horse	3	1	2	+	Look for stable manure with bedding.
Cow, dairy	2	1	2	+	Often sold packaged. Inexpensive. Watch for salts.
Chicken	4–6	2	2	+	Often sold packaged. Inexpensive.
Marine Products					
Fish emulsion	4–6	1–2	1–2	+	For drench or foliar application. Used in transplanting and for nitrogen, phosphorous, and micronutrients. Experiment with dilutions.
Fish meal	8–12	4–6	2–4	++	Locally available; great in fertilizer blends.
Fish powder	11	1	1	++	Soluble for foliar application. See kelp powder.
Kelp meal	1		3–4	+++	Great source of micronutrients and enzymes.
Kelp powder	1 (1)		2–3 (1)	+++	Great for foliar application. Lots of trace elements and growth hormones. Blend with fish emulsion or powder.
Compost	1.5	1	1	+	Commercial products of manure and yard waste are becoming more and more available. Highly variable. Easily home made.
ROCK MINERAL					
Chilean or sodium nitrate	15				Contains sodium; avoid using on clay soils. Only mineral source of nitrogen.
Dolomite	(25)	(12)			Liming agent with magnesium. Avoid using on soils with adequate magnesium.
Granite meal			2		Slowly available source of potassium. Two tons per acre; 20 pounds per 100 square feet.
Greensand		1.5	7	++	Mined seabed glauconite. Very slow, steady release of potassium.
Gypsum	(22)		(16)		For calcium or sulfur without changing pH. Sulfur will tie up excess magnesium. Helps to loosen up clay soils.
Phosphate, colloidal or "soft"	(21)	(20)			More available than rock phosphate on nonacid soils and no fluorine.
Phosphate, rock	(33)	(30)			Poorly available source of phosphorous, especially in acid or alkaline soils. May contain fluorine.
Potassium sulfate, sulfate of potash			50 (18)		Mined version of chemical fertilizer. Great source of natural potassium.
Sul po mag		(10)	22 (20)		Sulfate of potassium magnesia. Great if you need these three nutrients.
CHEMICAL					
Ammonium nitrate	32				Doesn't affect soil pH.
Ammonium sulfate	20		(23)		Strong acidifier.
Calcium nitrate	15/(19)	(2)			Tends to make soils alkaline; rapid source of calcium.
Potassium nitrate	13		44		Little effect on soil pH.
Superphosphate	(20)	20	(12)		Rapidly available potassium, calcium, and sulfur.

between organic soil amendments, which improve the life and structure of the soil, and organic fertilizers, which give nutrients to plants. They are not the same thing.

Commercial organic fertilizers are becoming more and more available, both in garden and mail-order stores. They're usually made of things that are recycled in the livestock and food industries, like composted or dried manures, animal meals (blood, bone, feather), plant meals (kelp, cotton, peanut), recycled leather or animal wastes (fish and fowl). Commercial blended fertilizers have a more reliable fertilizer grade than organic blends you make yourself (see pages 79–80), but they cost more. For convenience, we can separate organic fertilizers into four categories: Plant and animal meals, marine products, animal manures and composts.

- **Plant and Animal Meals:** These fine-textured meals are usually the waste products of food, feed, and livestock processing. They are relatively high in nutrients and low in organic matter. They act much like chemical fertilizers, except that they contain other nutrients in addition to nitrogen, phosphorous, and potassium. Bone meal is a great but pricey source of calcium and phosphorous. Blood meal is the richest source of organic nitrogen which makes it a valuable "starter" for compost piles (see page 112). Cottonseed, alfalfa, and soy meals are the major complete organic plant fertilizers.

- **Marine Products:** Fish and kelp ("seaweed"), both marine products, are fair sources of macronutrients but rich sources of micronutrients, plant enzymes, and hormones—more than any other natural fertilizer. Their value goes far beyond the traditional fertilizer grade.

Fish meal is a long-lasting source of most macro- and micronutrients.

Fish emulsion is a by-product of the fish meal industry. After the solids (which become fish meal) and the oils (used as oil stock) are removed, the remaining waste water is evaporated, leaving behind a thick, viscous product. Fish emulsion is generally graded about 5–2–2. If it's labeled much higher, it probably contains chemical fertilizers to give it a boost. Fish emulsion is easily mixed in buckets and tossed on the soil as a drench. If you dilute it enough, you can use it as a foliar spray, although pure fish emulsions may clog some sprayers.

Hydrolyzed fish powder is a specially treated fish product that is soluble in water and suitable for foliar feeding. Fish powder is about one-fifth the price of kelp powder. It lacks the growth hormones of kelp, but it is considerably higher in nutrients. This is why fish and kelp powder are such a useful combination in foliar feeding.

"Liquid Fish" is produced from fish by-products using a low-acid, low-heat process that ensures the natural organic compounds are left intact while eliminating harmful bacterial growth. It is an all-purpose water-soluble fertilizer with a low oil content that reduces odor and leaf staining.

Kelp is any one of several species of brown algae that grows in the cooler oceans around the world. Kelp fertilizers are a veritable treasure chest of micronutrients, plant-growth stimulants, vitamins, and chelating agents (see page 69), all of which greatly influence the health and vigor of plants. Vegetables are especially helped by kelp fertilizers. They keep these fussy plants growing quickly, while they reduce the effects of cold, heat, pests, and diseases. Kelp fertilizers can be costly, but they go a long way. Think of them as concentrated sources of things plants need that are *not* on the N–P–K label.

Kelp comes in three formulations: a dry meal, a fine soluble powder, or a liquid extract. The powder and extract can be used in foliar fertilizers. It's applied directly to the soil, and is one of the few organic fertilizers that can improve soil structure. It contains alginic acid, which binds soil particles together into granules and crumbs.

Kelp powder is made by drying and grinding seaweed to a fine powder that dissolves in water. It takes 200 pounds of kelp to make one pound of powder, so it needs to be diluted (use about $^1/_4$ teaspoon per gallon.) Kelp powder is useful as a root soak or foliar fertilizer. It provides some nitrogen and potassium, but its real claim to fame is as a source of micronutrients *plus* the chelating agents to make them more available. Used full strength, kelp powder can burn or mark leaves, so test on a few plants and dilute if necessary. It is often combined with organic teas and fish powder for a complete foliar fertilizer.

Concentrated liquid kelp is made in two ways. The Norwegian kelp is simply boiled down into a concentrate, whereas the Pacific brown kelp is digested with special enzymes to produce a concentrate of highest quality.

• **Animal Manures:** People have used animal manures as fertilizers since they began tending plants. The nutrient content of manure depends on the type of animal, its age, its diet, and how the manure was collected and stored. Fresh manures can be very salty or contain toxic levels of micronutrients, depending on what the livestock eats.

Bird manures have the highest amount of nitrogen and other nutrients, but very little carbon; they'll give you plant food but not organic matter. Horse, rabbit, and sheep manures have less nutrients, but more organic matter. Finally, the manure of goats, llamas, and cows, which are ruminants (they digest their food in several stomachs) have the least nutrients but the most organic matter (see page 72). In the long run, a mix of manures, such as chicken, horse, and cow, would be a better fertilizer than any of the manures by themselves.

If you use animal manures, let them age a few weeks to a few months before applying them. In a fresh state, they can burn plants. Also, some manures contain weed seeds and salts, which can also be neutralized some by aging the manure a bit. The best time to apply manures is the fall so that winter rains can leach the salts.

• **Compost:** Compost (see pages 107–124) doesn't have many plant nutrients, but it does provide quality organic matter. In this sense, compost is probably more of a soil amendment than a fertilizer; that is, it helps to build the life and structure of the soil more than to feed the plants directly. It's best to use your own compost, but commercial types are becoming more and more available. These include compost from recycled yard wastes, animal manures, and food processing wastes. In some areas, there is also compost from fruit pressings ("pomace"), like grapes and apples, plus spent compost from mushroom farms. In a fresh state, mushroom compost contains too many salts, so it should sit for a season before being added to the soil as an amendment.

The quality of compost is highly variable and depends on how it was composted, the materials used, and its age. If you buy commercial compost for your garden, be sure you look at it carefully and smell it first. If it is dark and crumbly with the musty odor of soil, then it is probably useful. However, in our experience, many commercial composts are hastily decayed and still smell like the products they were made from. This can mean that they still contain salts, tannic acids, and other toxins that need to be stabilized or eliminated by letting it decay longer.

The nutrients in manure are more available than in compost. However, compost has certain advantages over manure. Compost nitrogen is in a more stable form, so it won't easily evaporate or leach away. Compost also has more humus and beneficial microbes and fewer pathogens or weed seeds. The best plan is to add both aged manure and compost to your soil to gain the advantages of both.

- **Organic Teas:** (see pages 78–79)

Rock Mineral Fertilizers

Some rock formations are particularly rich in plant nutrients. These are mined and sold as rock fertilizers. Limestone and dolomite are examples. So is gypsum (calcium sulfate), a particularly useful fertilizer because it adds calcium or sulfur to the soil without affecting the pH. Gypsum also helps break up clay soils.

Rock phosphate is touted as a good source of natural phosphorous, and if allowed to mellow in good, neutral soil for a few years, it probably is. But in poor acid or alkaline soils, rock phosphate does not release phosphorous very well. A better choice is colloidal or "soft" phosphate. The particles are much smaller and available faster over a wider pH range than rock phosphate.

Granite dust from rock quarries has been used as a reliable and long-term source of potassium for centuries. The "dust" is actually clay and the potassium is available rather quickly.

Potassium sulfate is a mined rock fertilizer, but it is also manufactured as a synthetic fertilizer. It is readily available and has a neutral pH effect on soil. Potassium sulfate has one of the highest fertilizer grades of any "natural" fertilizer. Like blood meal and bone meal, it's great for fertilizer mixes because you don't need much of it. Even in the mined form, potassium sulfate should be treated like a chemical fertilizer.

Some rock mineral fertilizers are highly overrated. For example, the marine sediment called greensand is an iron-potassium silicate (glauconite) supposedly rich in trace minerals and potassium. But repeated tests have shown that the particles only release their nutrients over several years. Greensand is definitely for a well-grounded gardener.

Because rocks contain so many useful plant nutrients, it's not surprising that some people advocate grinding up plain old rocks to fertilize their soils. The first to recommend that gardeners "remineralize" their soils was Julius Hensel in his 1893 book, *Bread from Stones*. Hensel suggested the use of granite dust plus rock powders from glaciers and stream beds.

Rock mineral fertilizers seem to be more effective if they are added to the soil with organic matter. The organic matter acts like a glue and allows the rock minerals to mix in with the soil better. Organic matter also produces acids that speed up the release of nutrients from the minerals. This is why rock mineral fertilizers are so good in the compost. They don't add many nutrients to the pile, but each rock particle gets surrounded by organic compounds; this makes the mineral nutrients more available when you add the compost to your garden soil.

Natural Versus Synthetic Fertilizers

Organic and rock mineral fertilizers are often referred to as "natural" fertilizers, because they are not synthetic; instead, they're derived from the raw, natural products common in soil: crushed rocks and organic residues.

Whether you use chemical or natural fertilizers, it's important to be aware of the trade-offs. For example, the solubility that makes chemical fertilizers useful means that they can be easily misused and contaminate the soil or groundwater. Most chemical fertilizers acidify the soil, and their nutrients are too concentrated for soil life to use efficiently. Some, like superphosphate, calcium sulfate, and potassium sulfate, may be useful to jump-start problem soils. But in the long run, natural fertilizers provide a more balanced array of plant nutrients that don't leach away quickly. In a few seasons of diligent use, they'll be feeding your soil and your plants just fine, and you won't have to fertilize the soil every year.

METHODS OF APPLYING FERTILIZERS

The techniques and timing of fertilizer application have a language all their own. Here are the terms you'll need to know:

• **Broadcasting** involves spreading granular or powdered fertilizers evenly over the soil prior to setting seeds or seedlings. This method is convenient, but it wastes fertilizers, especially phosphorous and micronutrients, which are not that mobile in the soil. It also encourages weeds to grow between plants.

• **Drenching** involves pouring or spraying liquid fertilizers in a manner similar to broadcasting. It's a popular way to spread liquid chemical and fish emulsion plant foods, but results in the same inefficient dispersal as broadcasting.

• **Banding** is applying narrow bands of fertilizer where the seeds or plants are to be placed, or around plants in rows or beds. Banding conserves fertilizer by putting the food where it is needed. It's important to band fertilizers of nutrients that are immobile in the soil, like phosphorous, ammonia, and micronutrients.

• **Foliar feeding** involves fertilizing plants by spraying water-soluble fertilizers (organic or chemical) onto the leaf surface. This is rapidly becoming one of the most popular and convenient ways to fertilize plants. Chemical fertilizers are quite soluble and amenable to foliar spray, but more and more gardeners are turning to a new generation of organic fertilizers specially formulated or finely ground for easy application. These include compost teas (see page 78–79), fermented crop food wastes, plus kelp and fish powders. They provide a balanced diet of micronutrients along with vital plant hormones and enzymes.

The secret of the success of foliar fertilizers is how they enter the plant. Most plants can absorb nutrients through tiny holes, or pores, in their leaves, called stomata, as well as through their roots. Plants absorb foliar-fed nutrients twenty times faster than soil-applied nutrients, so foliar fertilizers are especially useful when the soil is cold, infertile, has a poor pH, or when the plant is under stress from drought or pest damage. Foliar fertilizers can also be timed to encourage the plant's growth at critical points like seedling, leaf growth, or flower, fruit, and seed formation. Foliar fertilizers are convenient and have many uses, but before you use them, consider some of the following handy hints:

1. Foliar fertilizers can be applied with most sprayers, but the finer the mist, the better the application. Inexpensive sprayers often produce droplets instead of a fine mist, wasting fertilizer and resulting in inadequate coverage.

2. Foliar feeding should not be done in the wind or in the heat of the day. The best times to spray are in the early morning and in the early evening when leaf pores are wide open.

3. Typical application rates for an average kitchen garden of 400 square feet could range between 1 pint and 1 quart, depending on the quality of your sprayer. Many higher quality mist sprayers could reduce this to one-quarter of the amount.

4. If you have hard or salty water, you'll need to clean your sprayer regularly to rid it of salt buildup. Use baking soda or a suitable cleaning agent. Hard water also makes water bead up and not spread out evenly and efficiently over surfaces. You'll need to add a surfactant or spreader, a chemical that keeps water from beading up. A good nat-ural surfactant is yucca extract, which is now available under various trade names (see Appendices, pages 451–453).

5. Some nutrients are picked up and moved through the plant better than others. Nitrogen, phosphorous, potassium, copper, magnesium, and zinc are easily absorbed by stomata, whereas calcium, magnesium, iron, boron, and molybdenum are not. If soil fertility is low, foliar fertilizers can have mixed results.

• **Fertigation** is the application of soluble fertilizer through irrigation lines (hose or drip).

Timing Applications

Preplant fertilizers are applied before seeding or transplanting, and are usually done during soil preparation. Preplants are commonly applied as a broadcast, band, or drench.

Starter or **"pop-up" fertilizer** is added with or near the seed for immediate use by the young seedling. Since small seeds have little food, starter fertilizers are sometimes used with small-seeded vegetables like carrots, celery, chicory, lettuce, and parsley. Starter fertil-izers are not usually needed for vegetables, however, because vegetables grow so quickly.

Split application is the process of adding fertilizer in two or more portions at different times during the season.

Top or **side-dressing** is the method of adding fertilizer while the crop is growing. The fertilizer can be dug in, banded, or added as a liquid. Simply scatter fertilizer on both sides of the row 6 to 8 inches from the plants. Rake it into the soil and water thoroughly.

BREWING COMPOST AND MANURE TEAS

For centuries, gardeners have mixed manures and composts in water, and used the rich brew as a liquid fertilizer. We now know that the water not only dissolves important nutrients, but under certain conditions, it also extracts vital enzymes and beneficial microbes, which gives a real boost to the plant's immune system. The effect of organic teas depends on the quality of the water used, the age and make-up of the organic material added, and the way it is brewed. Organic teas are best used with other organic liquid fertilizers like kelp or fish powder. You can apply teas as a drench, a side-dressing, or a foliar spray. Today, gardeners can use this old-fashioned fertilizer in new and exciting ways.

continued on page 78

Making Organic Teas

Soak-in-Water Method: The easiest way to make an organic tea is to toss some chopped-up plants (alfalfa and various weeds are popular) and animal manure or compost into a bucket of water and let it soak for a few days, which is about how long it takes for most of the soluble nutrients to leach out into the water. Try to use filtered spring or rain water, which will produce a richer tea. Add about 2 cups of organic matter to each gallon of water. You can also mix 1 tablespoon of molasses per 5 gallons of water to enrich the tea's microbial activity. Don't let the tea brew longer than a few days or it will begin to sour and smell. When it's done, scoop or drain out the liquid and pour it around your plants as a side-dressing. If you want to spray it on, you may have to strain it through gauze or screen. Follow standard practices for foliar spraying (see page 76.)

Soak-in-Bag Method: Most gardeners prefer to put their manures or composts in a porous bag made of muslin, burlap, or panty hose. The "tea bag" is hung in a container of water for 1 to 2 days. This produces a much cleaner tea than the soak-in-water method. Use 1 to 2 cups of material per gallon of water.

The trouble with these methods is that when you put organic substances into water, and let them soak for more than a few days, the air-loving (aerobic) microbes in the material pull all the oxygen out of the water. This turns over the production of the tea to air-avoiding (anaerobic) microbes, which produce an inferior tea. That is why we call these methods anaerobic. There is usually enough oxygen in clean water to prevent anaerobic teas from being produced for at least 24 to 48 hours. But after that, the quality of the tea begins to deteriorate. Anaerobic teas attract flies and have a foul odor—signs that the tea is too old or hasn't received enough air.

Aerobic Tea Method: The more air you put into your tea while it's brewing the better. This keeps it from going anaerobic, and allows time for enzymes, humic acids, and beneficial microbes to be extracted. Frequent stirring or bobbing of the tea bag helps incorporate air, but you can also use an aquarium air bubbler.

FIG. 2-7: Compost tea makers

1. ANAEROBIC:

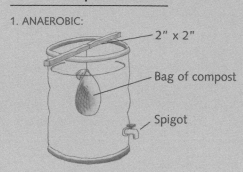

2" x 2"

Bag of compost

Spigot

2. AEROBIC:

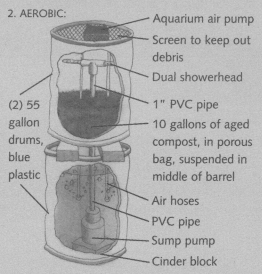

Aquarium air pump

Screen to keep out debris

Dual showerhead

(2) 55 gallon drums, blue plastic

1" PVC pipe

10 gallons of aged compost, in porous bag, suspended in middle of barrel

Air hoses

PVC pipe

Sump pump

Cinder block

You can make high-quality aerobic teas by placing your compost or manure in a fine wire or plastic mesh bag, and suspending it about 1 foot above the water container. Spray water over the tea bag using shower heads or better, porous pipe. Turn the water on and off several times a day or put it on a timer. Brew for up to a week or so. Adventurous tea makers can use a sump pump and container drums to continuously recirculate water over the bags.

Ingredients for Organic Teas

Like any tea, it's what's in the bag that counts. There are many types of organic teas, depending on the type of manure or compost used to brew it.

Manure Teas: Teas made from animal manures are richer in nutrients than compost teas because manures are fresher, nutrient-rich, and decay faster. They're a good source of nitrogen, phosphorous, potassium, and trace elements. Only a few manures, like horse, cow, and goat manures, are really suitable. Horse manure yields more nutrients; cow manures give more humic acids. Avoid the manure of chickens, turkeys, cats, dogs, and pigs. They can harbor pathogens and are difficult to work with.

Compost Teas: Teas made from fresh compost contain fewer nutrients than manures, but they do provide humic acids, which help plants to resist some diseases. Aerobic teas made from aged or suppressive composts (see page 123) contain more beneficial microbes, especially if they are allowed to brew for several days. Aged compost teas should be sprayed on leaves where the beneficial microbes can colonize leaf surfaces and help protect the plant against some leaf- and soil-borne diseases. In a real sense, aged compost teas are a concentrated inoculum of beneficial microbes. There are many benefits to organic teas, depending on how you make them.

MAKING BLENDS OF NATURAL FERTILIZERS

Blended fertilizers are the most efficient way to feed vegetables. Not all vegetables have the same nutrient needs, and they usually grow more vigorously when fed a particular balance of nutrients. Blends of natural fertilizers are becoming more and more available on the market, but they often don't have the exact grade or ingredients you want.

It's easy to make your own blended fertilizer. First, gather up your favorite natural fertilizers. Say that's blood meal (nitrogen), bone meal (phosphorous), and wood ashes (potassium). Next, make a table of the fertilizer grades of these fertilizers.

If you round the numbers a bit, you'll notice that the ratio of N (12%) to P (15%) to K (6%) in this situation is about 2 to 2 to 1. So if you mix equal weights (not volumes!) of each fertilizer, 1 pound for example, you'll have 3 pounds of a blended fertilizer with N-P-K nutrients also in a ratio of 2 to 2 to 1 and a fertilizer grade of 4-5-2 (see table below for percent nutrients in fertilizers).

Fertilizer	%N	%P	%K
Blood meal	12%	0%	0%
Bone meal	0%	15%	0%
Wood ashes	0%	0%	6%
	$12 \div 3 = 4\%$	$15 \div 3 = 5\%$	$6 \div 3 = 2\%$

continued on page 80

We can also say that the fertilizer grade of any blended fertilizer is the average of the individual fertilizer grades by weight. As an example, suppose you wanted a blend with more potassium to balance out the nutrients in the example above. You could double the amount of wood ashes, so that you would now have 4 total pounds of blended fertilizer with a grade of 3-4-3. The nitrogen and phosphorous grades are lower because you diluted the blend with more wood ashes, and the potassium is higher for the same reason.

Amount	Fertilizer	%N	%P	%K
1 lb.	Blood meal	12%	0%	0%
1 lb.	Bone meal	0%	15%	0%
2 lbs.	Wood ashes	0%	0%	12%
		$12 \div 4 = 3\%$	$15 \div 4 = 3.9\%$	$12 \div 4 = 3\%$

You can use this procedure to concoct almost any blend from a variety of natural fertilizers and to produce fertilizer grades for specific vegetable needs. Just remember that the nutrients of many natural fertilizers can vary a great deal from batch to batch. In other words, the fertilizer grades of your homemade blends are only as reliable as the grades of the individual fertilizers.

SOME BALANCED BLENDS (N–P–K Fertilizer Grades)

Balanced Side-Dressing 3–4–3	Alliums 4–5–2	Root Crops 3–7–9	Lettuce and Greens 6–7–2
1: blood meal	3: soy meal	3: cottonseed meal	1: fish meal
1: bone meal	1: soft phosphate	2: soft phosphate	1: bone meal
2: wood ashes	1: kelp meal		1: cottonseed meal

Some natural fertilizers seem to complement each other when they are mixed. For example, 2 parts blood meal, 3 parts bone meal, and 1 part kelp meal makes an excellent all-purpose fertilizer. So does 1 part kelp meal, 2 parts alfalfa meal, 4 parts soy or cottonseed meal and 1 part colloidal phosphate. Other combinations include blood meal, colloidal phosphate, and potassium sulfate; rock fertilizers and compost (the compost helps to release nutrients from the ground rocks); blood meal and alfalfa meal (fast and slow sources of nitrogen); fish powder, kelp powder, and compost tea (a balanced liquid fertilizer); and compost tea and fish emulsion, to name a few. The tables above can help you assemble your own assortment of special fertilizers for the kitchen garden.

SOME CONCENTRATED BLENDS

High-Nitrogen Fertilizer 11–1–1	High-Phosphorous Fertilizer 3–11–1	High-Potassium Fertilizer 2–3–7	Trace Elements 4–1–2
3: blood meal	2: bone meal	3: blood meal	2: soy meal
1: cottonseed meal	1: fish meal	3: soft phosphate	1: kelp meal
		1: potassium sulfate	

How Many Nutrients Do Vegetables Need?

Each part of a plant is hungry for different nutrients. Root vegetables need lots of potassium, but not much nitrogen. Salad greens are just the opposite, while potatoes, corn, and brassicas need plenty of everything. On top of this, vegetables that are closely related, like the alliums, brassicas, and legumes, have their own special nutrient needs. To help you get started, see the Nutrient Needs of Selected Vegetables chart.

When to Fertilize Vegetables

If you ask a dozen gardeners when they fertilize their kitchen gardens, you'll probably get a dozen different answers, ranging from "Whenever it's convenient" to "Every few weeks, just like clockwork." Here are some guidelines:

• Feeding all vegetables alike will overfertilize some vegetables and starve others. Each group of vegetables requires different amounts of nutrients in different proportions.

• When using chemical or high-grade natural fertilizers, timing and placement are important. You don't want to waste those valuable nutrients. If you're using rock mineral fertilizers or aged manure, timing isn't as critical because they are slow-acting, long-term sources of plant food.

• If you use organic fertilizers, make a distinction between fertilizers with high nutrients but very little organic matter, like blood meal and fish emulsion, and those with lower nutrients but higher amounts of plant fiber, like alfalfa hay, food wastes, and compost. Not all organic fertilizers provide organic matter.

• Some gardeners fertilize in the fall with rock fertilizers and composts, then let them mellow in the soil over the winter so that they will release nutrients in the spring. More concentrated fertilizers are reserved for preplanting and side-dressing vegetables as they grow during the season.

• The advantage to natural fertilizers is that they release nutrients over an extended period. If you fertilize year after year with any kind of fertilizers, you could easily overload your soil with too many nutrients. It's a common problem for garden soils to be overfertilized. To avoid this, have your soil tested every few years to see if your pH is on track, and if any nutrients are out of balance (see page 60).

NUTRIENT NEEDS OF SELECTED VEGETABLES				
CROP	NITROGEN DEMANDS	PHOSPHORUS DEMANDS	POTASSIUM DEMANDS	OTHER CRITICAL NUTRIENTS/COMMENTS
Alliums	Moderate–High	Moderate	Low–Moderate	Sulfur and micros, especially copper. Needs water and good drainage.
Asparagus	High	High	High	Deep-rooted perennial. Enrich prepared soil. High macros, low micros.
Beans	Low	Moderate	Low–Moderate	Calcium and micros, especially molybdenum and manganese. Slightly alkaline soil.
Beets	Low	Low–Moderate	Moderate–High	Micros, especially boron. Avoid fresh manure.
Brassicas (cabbage family)	High	Moderate–High	Moderate–High	Calcium, sulfur, iron, and boron. Kale and collards tolerate more acid soils.
Carrots	Low	Low–Moderate	Moderate–High	Tolerates acid soils, but needs good drainage. Avoid excess nitrogen.
Corn	High	Moderate–High	High	Zinc and magnesium. Side-dress when plants are knee-high.
Cucumbers	Moderate–High	High	High	Magnesium. High humus, tolerates acid conditions, and needs water.
Eggplant	Moderate–High	Moderate–High	Moderate–High	Tolerates acid soils and grows poorly in cold, wet soils.
Lettuce, Chicory	High	Moderate–High	Moderate–High	Calcium, manganese, copper. Needs water and good drainage.
Peas	Low	Moderate	Low–Moderate	Calcium, molybdenum, sulfur, and zinc. Good drainage and tolerates more acid soils than beans.
Peppers	Moderate	Low–Moderate	Moderate–High	Tolerates acid soils and needs good drainage.
Potatoes	High	High	High	Manganese. Prefers acid, well-drained soils.
Spinach, Chard	High	Moderate–High	Moderate–High	Micros. Prefers alkaline, well-drained soils.
Squash	Low–Moderate	High	High	See Cucumber.
Tomato	Low	Moderate–High	Moderate–High	Avoid excess nitrogen and watch for calcium shortages (blossom-end rot).

Making Flavorings from the Garden

How do we make vegetables taste good? One way is to use fresh seasonal vegetables in order to enjoy their true flavor and texture. Another way is to use concentrated flavorings made from vegetables, legumes, herbs, and spices to enhance fresh vegetables.

Being from the West Coast, we get much of our gardening and cooking inspiration from California. This state has always been heavily influenced by Mediterranean cuisine and horticulture because of similarities in climate and vegetable availability. California cuisine took its first inspirations from France and Italy, where the people revere fresh, seasonal vegetables. France and Italy have both given us flavoring techniques and ingredients. From France we've learned to use tapenade, bouquets garnis, *pistou* (a garlic, basil, and tomato sauce used in soups and on pasta), and *mirepoix* (a mixture of minced carrot, celery, and onion used as a garnish or as a flavor enhancer for many dishes). French chefs have also taught us about making and using reduced stocks as flavorings and how to use just the right herb for just the right dish.

Italian cooks have taught us how to make and use flavorings in the form of rich tomato sauces and pastes, herb salts, fruity olive oils, and aromatic vinegars.

Today, California cooking is also influenced by the cuisines of the Pacific Rim, the Southwest, and Mexico. Fish sauce, curry, ginger, soy sauce, chiles, and tomatillos are only a few of the ingredients from these cultures that are now basics in California cuisine.

Creative cooks also use dressings, condiments, marinades, and stocks to flavor their vegetables. For example, tapenade can be used to flavor pasta and pepper purée to flavor soup.

Herb salts, roasted vegetables, caramelized onions, oven-dried onions, mushroom concentrate, and other flavorings can lift everyday cooking to another level, lending deep, intense flavors to any dish. These flavorings also help maintain the integrity of fresh ingredients, because only a small amount is needed to provide added flavor. They can be stored in the freezer, refrigerator, or pantry, ready to be used in any number of dishes with fresh vegetables. And since you've prepared the flavorings yourself, you know they're healthy.

FLAVORINGS

Gremolata

Gremolata is a crushed herb salt traditionally used as a condiment for osso buco (braised veal shanks). It can also be used to season vegetable dishes, especially when no extra salt is desired in the dish.

MAKES 1 CUP

- $1/4$ cup grated lemon zest
- 4 teaspoons minced garlic
- $3/4$ cup minced fresh flat-leaf parsley

Mix all the ingredients together and store indefinitely in a jar in the refrigerator. A teaspoon or two (or just a pinch) can be used to finish any vegetable sauté.

Arista Gremolata

This gremolata is traditionally used as a stuffing for pork roast (arista), but it can be used to flavor virtually any vegetable dish, particularly potatoes or Swiss chard.

MAKES $1/2$ CUP

- 8 to 10 large cloves garlic, minced
- 2 heaping teaspoons minced fresh rosemary
- $1^1/2$ tablespoons salt
- 1 tablespoon freshly ground black pepper

Combine all of the ingredients in a small bowl. Use a teaspoon or two to flavor cooked vegetable dishes in the last few minutes of cooking. Keeps for several months stored in a jar in the refrigerator.

Ginger's Gremolata

Our friend Ginger Carlson learned how to make this mixture in Italy. She uses it to season vegetables, roast pork, and roasted chicken.

MAKES $1^1/2$ CUPS

- 1 cup kosher salt
- 2 tablespoons chopped lemon zest
- $1/4$ cup chopped garlic
- 2 tablespoons freshly ground black pepper
- 2 tablespoons chopped fresh sage
- $1/4$ cup fresh rosemary leaves

Combine all of the ingredients in a food processor. Process for 10 to 15 seconds, or until the mixture is ground into a fine powder. Store in a jar at room temperature for several months.

Use in pasta sauces, on roasted tomatoes and vegetables, in soups and in salad dressings, and to flavor sautéed spinach or Swiss chard.

Anchovy-Herb Paste

Garum *was an ancient Roman mixture used to flavor many dishes. The original used concentrated fish juice. The following method is a little more appealing to modern tastes.*

MAKES ⅓ CUP

> 4 cups grape juice or dry white wine
> 2 tablespoons anchovy paste
> 1 teaspoon minced fresh oregano

Heat the juice or wine in a small, noncorrosive saucepan over medium-high heat until reduced to ¼ cup. Combine the reduced juice, anchovy paste, and oregano. Use to flavor sautéed vegetable dishes, soups, or vegetable pasta sauces. Store in a jar in the refrigerator for several weeks.

Baked Onion Flakes

MAKES 1 TO 1½ CUPS

Preheat the oven to 200°. Chop 4 bunches of small scallions into ¼-inch rounds, including half the green stalks. Place the onions on an ungreased baking sheet. Bake for 30 minutes, or until pale in color but softened. Let cool. Break up the rings by rubbing them vigorously between the palms of your hands. Drizzle them with a little olive oil and rub the onions again to coat them.

Return the tray to the oven and bake for 50 to 60 more minutes, or until just browned. Watch the onion flakes carefully and do not let them burn. Store in a jar in the pantry for several weeks. Use as a base for salad dressing, sprinkled on top of a dressed salad, mixed with butter as a spread for onion bread, or as a seasoning for soups.

Roasted Red Pepper Purée

MAKES 1 CUP

Place 3 red bell peppers over an open gas flame and turn them until evenly charred, or char the peppers under a broiler, turning frequently to almost completely burn the skin. Place the peppers in a closed paper or plastic bag to cool. Peel, seed, and dice. Sauté the diced peppers in a medium skillet with 1 tablespoon of olive oil, 2 teaspoons of chopped fresh garlic, 3 tablespoons of minced thyme. Season with salt to taste. Purée in a blender or food processor until smooth.

Store in a covered jar in the refrigerator for several weeks. Use as a marinade and sauce for grilled vegetables, as a topping for grilled chicken breasts, as a spicy spread for a vegetable sandwich, or thinned with chicken or vegetable broth for a spicy summer soup.

Bouquet Garni

Bouquet garni, a handful of herbs tied together with string, is added to the pot to flavor soups and stews. In Provence a sprig of rosemary is included. Whole cloves and peppercorns also may be added; if so, tie the bouquet garni in a square of cheesecloth.

MAKES 1 BUNCH

> 2 bay leaves
> 2 sprigs thyme
> 4 sprigs flat-leaf parsley
> 2 sprigs tarragon

Tie the herbs together with kitchen twine and use to flavor soups. Remove before serving.

Hachis

Hachis, which means "a mince" in French, is a mixture of minced herbs that are used as a flavoring for vegetables. The simplest is a mixture of minced garlic and parsley sprinkled over salads or sautéed vegetables.

Another simple hachis is made with 3 to 4 minced garlic cloves, 2 or 3 finely chopped celery leaves, and a splash of olive oil. Use as a garnish, along with grated cheese, for Tuscan bean soups.

Bean Purée

MAKES 2 TO 3 CUPS

Cannellini beans, large white beans with a deep, savory flavor, are the base for many rustic soups, especially in Tuscany and Umbria. Any light-colored bean—navy beans, Great Northerns, pink beans, pintos, or flageolets—can be substituted.

Soak 1 to 1½ cups beans overnight (or cook a little longer on the day of preparation). Drain the beans and put them in 6 cups of water for every cup of beans. Cook until tender, about 20 to 30 minutes if they were soaked overnight; 40 to 45 minutes if not soaked (up to 1 hour for cannellini or kidney beans). Let cool. Add salt and pepper to taste. Process the beans in a food processor using chicken broth, concentrated vegetable broth, or water if necessary to thin. When done, the beans should be the consistency of very heavy cream.

Store in small jars in the freezer. Use as a base for vegetable soups, with cooked vegetables, as a base for a fresh bean soup, as a spread on *crostini* (toasted baguette rounds), or as a topping for pizza with vegetables.

Pumpkin and Sesame Seed Bread Crumbs

Try different combinations of ingredients for this topping: Substitute pine nuts for pumpkin seeds, sunflower for sesame seeds.

MAKES 3 CUPS

> 3 cups fresh bread crumbs
> ¼ cup pumpkin seeds
> ¼ cup sesame seeds
> 3 to 4 tablespoons low-sodium soy sauce

Preheat the oven to 350°. Combine all the ingredients in a bowl. The dry ingredients should barely absorb the soy sauce and not be too wet. Spread the mixture on an ungreased baking sheet and toast in the oven for 10 to 15 minutes, or until just golden.

Store for up to 1 month in a covered container or for several months in a jar in the freezer. Use as a topping for salads or vegetable or pasta casseroles, before baking. Or add 1 cup per loaf to bread dough in the final stage of kneading. Before the loaf goes into the oven, brush with egg wash or water and sprinkle with more crumbs.

Caramelized Onions

This preparation can be used to flavor and darken soups, to top pizzas, to garnish hamburgers or tofu burgers, or as an appetizer to serve with French bread.

MAKES 2 CUPS

> ¼ cup light olive oil, vegetable oil, or peanut oil
> 2 yellow onions, sliced thinly
> 1 tablespoon balsamic vinegar (optional)
> Salt and freshly ground black pepper to taste

In a heavy, nonreactive skillet over medium-low heat, heat the oil and cook the onions for 25 to 30 minutes, stirring continuously, until golden brown.

Splash with the vinegar and cook for 2 to 3 more minutes. Add salt and pepper. Store in the refrigerator for up to 5 days.

Mirepoix

A mixture of minced aromatic vegetables is traditionally used in France to enhance the flavors of meats, fish, and roasts. Combine equal parts minced carrot, onion, and celery. Sauté in a little olive oil and simmer gently in a covered pan until tender.

Use for braised vegetables, to start a soup, to flavor lentils, or a hundred other applications.

Roasted Mushrooms

This is a versatile condiment that can be used to boost the flavor of many dishes.

MAKES ABOUT 3$^1/_2$ CUPS

  2 pounds mushrooms, sliced (about 12 cups)
  2 teaspoons minced fresh thyme
  3 tablespoons minced fresh flat-leaf parsley
  3 tablespoons minced garlic
  6 tablespoons minced yellow onion
  1 teaspoon salt
  1 teaspoon freshly ground black pepper
  6 tablespoons olive oil

Preheat the oven to 375°. Toss the mushrooms in a bowl with all the ingredients except the oil. Drizzle the oil on top and toss well. Roast on a baking sheet for 15 minutes, tossing once. Bake for an additional 10 minutes, or until very dark.

Store in a sealed container in the refrigerator for up to 1 week. Use for sandwiches, as a condiment for salads, to top pizzas, or puréed with cream or milk as a pasta sauce. Their deep flavor can be extracted by boiling the mushrooms in water in the same way a stock would be made (page 88).

Fern's Pesto

Use this pesto at room temperature over cooked pasta, as a dressing for fresh or grilled vegetables, or as a garnish for soup.

MAKES 2 CUPS

  1 large bunch fresh spinach, chopped
    (about 3 cups)
  2 bunches fresh basil, leaves only (about 4 cups)
  $^1/_4$ cup minced fresh flat-leaf parsley
  2 cloves garlic, minced
  $^1/_2$ cup pine nuts
  $^1/_2$ cup olive oil
  $^3/_4$ cup (6 ounces) grated Parmesan cheese
  $^1/_4$ teaspoon salt
  $^1/_4$ teaspoon freshly ground black pepper

Place the spinach, basil, parsley, garlic, and nuts in a blender or food processor and chop fine. With the machine running, drizzle in the olive oil. Stir in the Parmesan, salt, and pepper. Store in a jar in the refrigerator for several weeks (or in the freezer for 2 to 3 months).

Roasted Vegetable Stock Base

MAKES $^1/_2$ CUP

You can find organic stock pastes in the soup section of most natural food stores, but you can also make your own. This recipe is ideal for vegetables that are a little past their prime, though of course, fresh vegetables can also be used.

  1 carrot, peeled
  2 stalks celery
  1 onion
  2 zucchini
  2 teaspoons olive oil
  Salt and freshly ground black pepper to taste
  Vegetable stock or vinegar, for thinning

Preheat the oven to 300°. Cut off any discolored or wilted parts of the vegetables, then dice the vegetables and place them in a baking dish. Drizzle with the oil and sprinkle with salt and pepper. Toss well. Bake for 2½ to 3 hours, turning several times.

Remove and mince in a blender or food processor, thinning with a little stock or vinegar. Return to a smaller baking dish and roast for another 30 minutes to 1 hour, or until the mixture is dark. Add water or stock so the mixture does not dry out or burn.

Store in a small jar in the refrigerator for several weeks, or in the freezer for several months. Use in soups and sauces.

Harissa

This condiment from North Africa and the Middle East is used to flavor couscous and meats.

MAKES 1 CUP

> 2 small red peppers, chopped and seeded
>
> 3 tablespoons minced fresh mint leaves
>
> 1 teaspoon ground coriander
>
> ¼ teaspoon cayenne
>
> 1 teaspoon cumin
>
> ¼ teaspoon salt
>
> ⅔ cup olive oil

Put all the ingredients except the oil in a blender or food processor and purée into a paste. Use a little oil if necessary to bind the ingredients together. Put the paste in a bowl or jar and cover with the oil.

Store in the refrigerator for several weeks. Use a very small amount in soups, risotto, pasta, or vegetable dishes, or as a condiment for grilled chicken or ribs.

Fines Herbes

The classic French mixture of minced fresh herbs is parsley, chervil, tarragon, and either chives or thyme in equal parts. Alternatively, sprigs of these can be tied together and used as a bouquet garni. Use in soups, quiches, omelets, chicken and fish dishes, and vegetable sautés.

Stock Reductions

Not only are stocks used as a base for soups and sauces, but they can be flavorings, too. The stock section (pages 138–140) fully explains how to make stocks. At this point, we just want to remind you of the virtues of stocks as flavor enhancers. You can reduce any stock to concentrate its flavor. Simply bring the stock to a boil in a nonreactive stockpot or saucepan over high heat. Then reduce the heat and simmer the stock until it is reduced to ¼ to ⅓ of its original volume. Cool and store in a tightly sealed jar in the refrigerator for up to 1 week or in the freezer for several months.

Reduce a chicken or vegetable stock to flavor pasta sauce. Reduce a fish stock with white wine added to use as a base for an herb cream sauce to serve with grilled salmon.

Mushroom Concentrate

MAKES 2 CUPS

Soak 2 ounces (2 cups, lightly packed) dried mushrooms in hot water to cover for 10 to 15 minutes, several times. Each time, strain the juice through cheesecloth and reserve the juice until you have 4 to 6 cups. In a saucepan, cook the liquid over medium heat to reduce down to 2 cups.

Or boil 1 pound sliced fresh mushrooms in salted water to cover (about 6 cups) for 15 minutes. After the mushrooms have been removed, cook the water over medium heat until reduced to 2 cups. In either case, the mushrooms can be used in soup or in pasta sauce.

Store the concentrated stock in a jar in the refrigerator for about 1 week, or in the freezer for several months. Use as a stock for soup or as a flavoring for vegetable pasta sauces.

Roasted Plum Tomatoes

This is a good way to cook a large tomato crop. This preparation can be canned or used fresh wherever a tomato sauce is called for—in soups or for pasta.

MAKES 2 TO 4 CUPS

- 20 to 24 plum tomatoes
- 3 cloves garlic, minced
- 6 to 8 fresh basil leaves, chopped
- 1 or 2 sprigs fresh rosemary
- 2 to 3 tablespoons olive oil
- Salt and freshly ground black pepper to taste

Preheat the oven to 300°. Choose a baking dish large enough to hold the tomatoes tightly standing up in one layer. Cut $1/2$ inch off the tops of the tomatoes.

Place the tomatoes in a single layer in the baking dish, cut-side up. Scatter the garlic on top along with the basil and rosemary. Lightly coat with the olive oil, then sprinkle with the salt and pepper.

Bake for $2^{1}/_{2}$ to 3 hours, or until dark and very soft.

Cool and store in an airtight container in the refrigerator for up to 1 week.

DRESSINGS

Dressings can be used to coat lettuce, to dress steamed vegetables, or as light, piquant pasta sauces. For salads, use heavier dressings—like honey mustard and green goddess—on heavier, more rugged greens, like romaine, endive, or chopped cabbage. Use vinaigrettes on delicate greens, like mizuna, baby greens, and dandelion greens.

Most dressings will keep for several weeks in the refrigerator, but they taste much better when made just before using. These recipes can easily be doubled or tripled. To use leftover dressing after it has been stored in the refrigerator for up to several weeks, remove the jar from the refrigerator and leave it at room temperature for 10 to 15 minutes. Then shake with the lid on just before using.

All dressings are a mixture of fat and acid, usually oil and vinegar or citrus juice in a ratio of 3 to 1. Salt and pepper are often added along with garlic and herbs. Some basic vinaigrettes might have a touch of prepared mustard or a squeeze of lemon juice along with the vinegar. Too much vinegar and dressing will be bitter, too little and it will be cloyingly oily. Make adjustments according to your own taste and experience. We think of dressings in three categories:

Vinaigrettes

These dressings are made in a bowl by whisking together all ingredients except the oil, then pouring oil in while whisking until the mixture emulsifies. Examples include Basic Vinaigrette (page 90) and Orange-Raspberry Vinaigrette (page 93).

Creamy Emulsified Dressings

These dressings are emulsified by beating vinaigrettelike mixtures into egg yolks, mayonnaise, or other fresh dairy products like yogurt and sour cream. The beating helps keep mixtures with natural emulsifiers creamy or thick. Examples include creamy Italian, Russian, and buttermilk dressings.

Purées

These dressings are made by puréeing vegetables and herbs in a processor or blender. Examples include Tomato-Basil vinaigrette (page 93) and pesto.

Basic Vinaigrette

*Use this recipe as a basis for your choice of varia-
tions, adding herbs and other ingredients as you
like or use as is.*

MAKES ¹/₂ CUP

1 clove garlic, minced
¹/₂ teaspoon kosher salt
¹/₂ teaspoon pepper
1 tablespoon freshly squeezed lemon juice
2 tablespoons red wine vinegar
¹/₃ to ¹/₂ cup olive oil

Crush the garlic and salt in a mortar with a
pestle or with a fork in a small bowl. Add the
pepper, lemon juice, and vinegar. Whisk in
the oil.

Lemon-Mustard Vinaigrette

This is a "light" recipe, as it uses less oil.

MAKES ¹/₃ CUP

1 teaspoon Dijon-style mustard
1 tablespoon balsamic vinegar
1 teaspoon red wine vinegar
Juice of ¹/₂ lemon
2 tablespoons olive oil
Salt and freshly ground black pepper to taste

In a small bowl, combine the mustard, vinegars, and lemon juice. Whisk in the oil. Add
salt and pepper to taste.

Refer to the Vinaigrette Wheel between
pages 308 and 309 to see how any of the
vinaigrettes on this page can be adapted in order to dress a variety of vegetables and other
dishes—from beets to potatoes, tortellini to
Napa cabbage.

Gayle's Dijon Vinaigrette

MAKES 1 CUP

1¹/₂ teaspoons Dijon-style mustard
1 tablespoon whole-grain mustard
6 tablespoons (3 ounces) red wine vinegar
1¹/₂ teaspoons sugar
³/₄ teaspoon salt
³/₄ teaspoon freshly ground black pepper
¹/₂ cup corn oil
¹/₄ cup olive oil

Mix all the ingredients except the oils in a
blender or food processor. Drizzle in oils
while the machine is running to emulsify.

Simple Vinaigrette

MAKES 3²/₃ CUPS

1¹/₂ cups red wine vinegar
2¹/₄ cups olive oil
2 teaspoons salt
1 teaspoon pepper

Place all the ingredients in a medium bowl
and whisk together.

Lemon-Mustard-Garlic Vinaigrette

MAKES ²/₃ CUP

1 garlic clove
¹/₂ teaspoon kosher salt
1 tablespoon freshly squeezed lemon juice
1 tablespoon balsamic vinegar
1 tablespoon Dijon-style mustard
¹/₂ cup olive oil

In a small bowl, mash the garlic together with
the salt. Add the lemon juice, vinegar, and
mustard and mix well. Gradually whisk in the
oil.

FIG. 2-8: The Mesclun Wheel

Mesclun (French for "mix") is a mix of greens that range from sweet to tart. Generally, the more tart the green, the more nutritious it is (in terms of vitamins, minerals, fiber, and phytochemicals). Thus, greens can be mixed for nutrition as well as flavor.

After greens (connected by the line) have been washed and dried, combine them in a bowl and toss with the suggested accompaniments (in bold face). Add the dressing (below the line) and toss once more. Sprinkle with the suggested garnish (in italics) and serve immediately. You can also make up your own combinations.

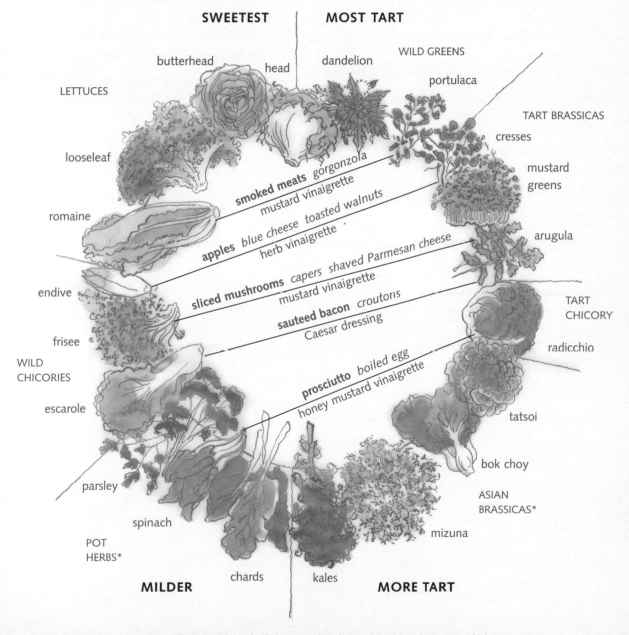

SWEETEST   MOST TART

WILD GREENS

butterhead   head   dandelion

portulaca

LETTUCES

TART BRASSICAS

cresses

looseleaf

mustard greens

smoked meats *gorgonzola*
mustard vinaigrette

romaine

apples blue cheese *toasted walnuts*
herb vinaigrette

arugula

sliced mushrooms capers *shaved Parmesan cheese*
mustard vinaigrette

endive

TART CHICORY

sauteed bacon *croutons*
Caesar dressing

frisee

radicchio

WILD CHICORIES

prosciutto *boiled egg*
honey mustard vinaigrette

escarole

tatsoi

bok choy

parsley

ASIAN BRASSICAS*

spinach

mizuna

POT HERBS*

chards   kales

MILDER   MORE TART

*normally served cooked, but can be slivered and used raw in salads.

Curry-Mustard Vinaigrette

MAKES ABOUT 1¹/₂ CUPS

- **1 tablespoon minced garlic**
- **1 tablespoon grated, peeled fresh ginger**
- **1 tablespoon Dijon-style mustard**
- **2 tablespoons minced scallions**
- **1 teaspoon curry powder**
- **2 tablespoons freshly squeezed lemon juice**
- **2 tablespoons red wine vinegar**
- **³/₄ cup olive oil**
- **¹/₄ cup crumbled low-fat feta cheese**
- **¹/₂ teaspoon salt**
- **¹/₂ teaspoon freshly ground black pepper**

In a small bowl, combine all the ingredients except the oil, feta, salt, and pepper. Whisk briefly to combine. Gradually whisk in the oil. Add the feta, salt, and pepper.

Asian-Style Vinaigrette

This is a wonderful dressing for julienned raw carrots or Asian noodles with poached fresh vegetables.

MAKES ABOUT ³/₄ CUP

- **2 tablespoons Asian sesame oil**
- **¹/₄ cup low-sodium soy sauce**
- **1¹/₂ teaspoons sugar**
- **¹/₄ cup freshly squeezed lemon juice**
- **1 tablespoon dry mustard**
- **1¹/₂ teaspoons minced garlic**
- **¹/₄ cup corn oil**

Combine all the ingredients except the oil in a blender. With the machine running, gradually add the oil.

Moroccan Vinaigrette

This is a good dressing for grated fresh carrots or beets, or tossed with steamed vegetables.

MAKES ABOUT ³/₄ CUP

- **1 tablespoon coriander seeds**
- **1 tablespoon cumin seeds**
- **¹/₄ cup freshly squeezed orange juice**
- **2 tablespoons grated orange zest**
- **¹/₂ teaspoon ground cayenne pepper**
- **¹/₂ cup light olive oil**
- **1 cup packed fresh mint leaves, minced**
- **Salt and freshly ground pepper to taste**

In a dry skillet over medium heat, toast the seeds until aromatic. In a medium bowl, combine the seeds, orange juice, zest, and cayenne. Gradually whisk in the oil. Add the mint, salt, and pepper.

Anchovy-Scallion Vinaigrette

Serve this on a Niçoise salad: steamed green beans, boiled potatoes, hard-boiled egg, tuna, and tomato wedges.

MAKES ABOUT ²/₃ CUP

- **1 recipe Basic Vinaigrette (page 90)**
- **3 anchovy fillets, chopped**
- **3 scallions, including the green tops, finely chopped**
- **4 sprigs flat-leaf parsley, minced**

Combine all the ingredients in a small bowl.

Orange-Raspberry Vinaigrette

Serve on a grilled-chicken salad with assorted greens, grilled vegetables, or thinly sliced red onions and slices of orange.

MAKES ABOUT 3/4 CUP

1 tablespoon minced shallot
2 tablespoons freshly squeezed orange juice
2 tablespoons grated orange zest
2 tablespoons raspberry vinegar
1/3 to 1/2 cup olive oil
1/4 teaspoon salt
1/4 teaspoon freshly ground black pepper

Put the shallot, orange juice, zest, and vinegar in a small bowl. Whisk in the oil. Add the salt and pepper and whisk once more.

Yogurt-Mustard Dressing

Use this in the place of regular mayonnaise.

MAKES ABOUT 1/3 CUP

2 tablespoons low-fat plain yogurt
1 tablespoon low-fat mayonnaise
1 tablespoon Dijon-style mustard
2 tablespoons white wine vinegar
1 to 2 tablespoons water
Salt and freshly ground black pepper to taste

In a small bowl, whisk together the yogurt, mayonnaise, mustard, and vinegar. Add water to the desired consistency. Add the salt and pepper. Keeps for a week in the refrigerator.

Shallot Vinaigrette

MAKES ABOUT 1 1/4 CUPS

1/3 cup thinly sliced shallots
4 teaspoons Dijon-style mustard
1/4 cup champagne vinegar
3/4 cup olive oil
1/4 teaspoon salt
1/4 teaspoon freshly ground black pepper

Whisk all the ingredients together or shake in a tightly closed jar.

Tomato-Basil Vinaigrette

This one goes well with crispy butter lettuce.

MAKES ABOUT 1 3/4 CUPS

1 tomato, peeled, seeded, and diced
1/2 cup packed fresh basil leaves
1 clove garlic
1 tablespoon grated Parmesan cheese
1/4 cup balsamic vinegar
1/2 cup olive oil

Combine all the ingredients in a blender or food processor and process until smooth, about 20 to 30 seconds.

Creamy Parsley Vinaigrette

Serve on salads or steamed vegetables.

MAKES 1 CUP

1/2 cup light oil
1/3 cup fresh parsley leaves, minced
2 scallions, minced
1/2 teaspoon salt
1/2 teaspoon pepper
2 tablespoons low-fat plain yogurt

Combine all the ingredients except the yogurt in a blender or food processor and mix well. With the machine running, slowly add the yogurt, blending thoroughly.

Mediterranean Vinaigrette

Use this dressing as a marinade for vegetables before grilling. Or use it to dress grilled, roasted, or fresh vegetables.

MAKES 4 CUPS

1 bunch mint, stemmed and minced
1¹/₂ cups extra virgin olive oil
1¹/₂ cups sunflower oil
1 cup white wine vinegar
2 tablespoons Dijon-style mustard
¹/₄ cup minced garlic
1 pinch crushed red pepper flakes
Salt and freshly ground black pepper to taste

Combine all the ingredients in a large bowl. Pour over sliced vegetables and marinate for at least 30 minutes. Drain the vegetables well before grilling to avoid flare-up of the fire. Brush the vegetables if necessary during grilling. Any remaining dressing can be used to dress the vegetables before serving.

Poppy Seed Vinaigrette

Use whenever a sweet-spicy dressing is called for.
MAKES 1¹/₂ CUPS

¹/₃ cup cider vinegar
1 cup corn oil
¹/₄ cup sugar
¹/₂ teaspoon salt
¹/₂ teaspoon dry mustard
2 teaspoons minced yellow onion
1 teaspoon poppy seeds

Put all the ingredients in a small bowl and whisk together.

Gayle's Green Goddess Dressing

MAKES ABOUT 2 CUPS

1 cup low-fat plain yogurt
¹/₂ cup low-fat sour cream
¹/₂ teaspoon minced garlic
2 anchovy fillets
¹/₄ cup minced green onions
¹/₄ cup minced fresh flat-leaf parsley
1 tablespoon freshly squeezed lemon juice
1 tablespoon tarragon or basil vinegar
¹/₄ teaspoon salt
2 grinds black pepper

Combine all the ingredients in a blender and blend well. Store for up to 1 week in a jar in the refrigerator.

Chinese Chicken Salad Dressing

MAKES 1¹/₂ CUPS

¹/₄ cup sugar
¹/₂ teaspoon salt
¹/₂ teaspoon dry mustard
2 tablespoons minced yellow onion
¹/₃ cup cider vinegar
1 cup corn oil
1 teaspoon poppy seeds

Whisk all the ingredients together in a large bowl.

CONDIMENTS

Condiments made from fruits, vegetables, or legumes are a good substitute for rich sauces; they add excitement to meals. Condiments can also be used to flavor vegetables. Try tossing a little tapenade (page 97) in a simple vegetable sauté, for example. Or you can use a condiment to create a dish. Red Pepper Purée (page 85) can be mixed with a little stock and low-fat yogurt to make a simple soup.

Some of the following condiments can be used as a topping for a salad, as a dip, as a marinade, as a garnish, or as a side dish for vegetables or an entire meal.

Roasted Eggplant Purée

Use as a topping for pizza or crostini.

MAKES 3 CUPS

- 2 eggplant
- 1¹/₂ tablespoons minced garlic
- Juice of 2 lemons
- 6 tablespoons minced fresh flat-leaf parsley
- 1 teaspoon salt
- 3 tablespoons olive oil
- 1 pound feta cheese
- 1 cup (8 ounces) kalamata olives, pitted and halved
- 8 ounces red onion, sliced (³/₄ cup)
- 2 bunches fresh oregano, chopped

Preheat the oven to 375°. Place the whole eggplant on a baking sheet and bake for 25 to 30 minutes, turning over during cooking, until the skin shrivels and the eggplant feel soft when squeezed. Let cool and peel.

Place the cooled eggplant in a blender or food processor. Add the garlic, lemon juice, parsley, and salt, and purée. With the machine running, drizzle in the olive oil. Store covered in the refrigerator for up to 5 days.

Divide the eggplant purée and spread on pizzas or crostini. Top with feta, olives, red onion, and oregano.

Roasted Pepper Sauce

Serve as a sandwich spread, a topping for grilled chicken, or a sauce for sautéed zucchini.

MAKES ABOUT 2 CUPS

- 5 red bell peppers
- 3 cloves garlic
- 2 tablespoons olive oil
- ¹/₂ teaspoon salt
- 1 teaspoon minced fresh marjoram, tarragon, or thyme
- ¹/₄ cup dry red wine

Cook the peppers directly over a gas flame until evenly charred. Alternatively, roast in a 350° oven 40 to 45 minutes or until skin is well browned. Place in a paper bag until cool. Peel, seed, and cut the peppers into strips.

In a large skillet over medium heat, cook the garlic in 1 tablespoon of the olive oil until golden. Add the peppers, salt, herbs, and wine. Cook for several minutes.

In a blender or food processor, purée into a smooth paste using the rest of the olive oil if needed. Taste and correct the seasoning. Store in a jar in the refrigerator for up to 10 days.

Spinach-Ricotta Spread

This is a good spread for all types of sandwiches, from vegetable to chicken.

MAKES 2 CUPS

2 bunches (1 pound) spinach, washed, stemmed, and chopped
¹/₂ teaspoon salt
1 tablespoon olive oil
3 cloves garlic, minced
1 tablespoon freshly squeezed lemon juice
¹/₂ cup low-fat ricotta cheese
1 pinch freshly ground black pepper

In a large skillet, cook the wet spinach over medium heat until wilted. Drain, cool, and squeeze dry. Add the salt and set aside.

In the same skillet, over medium heat, heat the oil and sauté the garlic until translucent. Add the spinach and sauté briefly. Add the lemon juice. Let cool. Add the ricotta and pepper and mix into a firm but spreadable paste. Store covered in the refrigerator for 3 to 4 days.

Onion Marmalade

Use to flavor roasted meats or as a garnish for a roasted-vegetable salad.

MAKES 1¹/₂ CUPS

2 tablespoons olive oil
6 red, yellow, or sweet (Maui, Vidalia, or Walla Walla) onions, thinly sliced
1 teaspoon salt
¹/₄ teaspoon freshly ground black pepper
2 tablespoons honey
1 tablespoon orange zest
2 tablespoons balsamic vinegar
1 teaspoon minced fresh thyme
1 teaspoon minced fresh sage

In a large skillet over high heat, heat the oil and sauté the onions for 8 to 10 minutes, stirring constantly. Add the salt, pepper, honey, and zest. Reduce heat to medium and cook for 5 minutes.

Add the vinegar and herbs. Reduce heat to low and simmer for 20 minutes, or until dark and thick. Store in a jar or covered bowl in the refrigerator for up to 1 week.

Pickled Onions

Use for sandwiches and salads, and as a topping for pizza.

MAKES 1 CUP

1 sprig thyme
1 sprig parsley
1 bay leaf
3 whole cloves
¹/₂ cup red wine vinegar
¹/₄ cup raspberry vinegar
¹/₄ cup sugar
¹/₂ cup water
1 pound onions (about 3), thinly sliced

Wrap the thyme, parsley, bay leaf, and cloves, in a square of cheesecloth and tie securely to seal as a boquet garni.

In a medium nonreactive saucepan, combine all the ingredients except the onions. Bring to a boil and set aside. Place the onion slices in a large, hot, sterilized canning jar.

While the vinegar mixture is still quite warm, remove the bouquet garni and pour the liquid over the onions in the jar. Let cool. Store in the refrigerator for up to 3 weeks.

Peach Chutney

Serve with grilled chicken breasts or as a topping for grilled pepper steak. Use also to accompany curries or sautéed vegetables, or on a grilled cheese sandwich along with caramelized onions.

MAKES 3 PINTS

- 2 pounds peaches
- 1 cup packed brown sugar
- 1 cup balsamic vinegar
- 2 teaspoons chile powder
- 1 teaspoon kosher salt
- 1 teaspoon coriander seed
- 1/2 cup golden raisins
- 2 tablespoons grated peeled fresh ginger
- 4 whole cloves

Drop the peaches one at a time into a large saucepan of boiling water, then quickly remove to a bowl of cold water. Peel, pit, and cut into 3/4-inch dice.

Put the brown sugar and vinegar in a medium saucepan and bring to a boil, stirring constantly. Add the peaches and all the remaining ingredients and stir to combine.

Reduce heat to low and simmer for 1 hour, or until thickened. Stir gently during cooking. Pour into 3 hot, sterilized pint jars and refrigerate for up to 4 weeks.

Tapenade

This Provençal olive paste can be bought in small jars, or you can make it at home. Use as a condiment for a plate of grilled vegetables, as a topping for grilled chicken, or to add zing to a vegetable pasta sauce.

MAKES 3 CUPS

- 4 cloves garlic, chopped
- 1 (2-ounce) can oil-packed anchovies, drained, washed, and patted dry
- 1/4 cup capers, drained
- 4 cups kalamata, niçoise, or salt-cured black olives, pitted
- 1 teaspoon chopped fresh tarragon
- 1 teaspoon chopped fresh thyme
- 2 tablespoons extra virgin olive oil

Combine all the ingredients except the oil in a blender and purée to a medium-fine paste. While the machine is running, gradually add the oil. Store in a jar in the refrigerator for several months.

Green Sauce

This is a piquant herb and vinegar sauce to accompany cold sliced roast meats, chicken, salmon, or cooked vegetables, or to use as a savory sandwich spread.

MAKES 1 CUP

2 slices white bread, crust removed
$^1/_4$ cup cider vinegar
$^1/_4$ cup olive oil
4 garlic cloves, minced
$^1/_2$ cup chopped fresh flat-leaf parsley
$^1/_2$ cup chopped fresh cilantro
4 green onions with tops, chopped
$^3/_4$ teaspoon kosher or sea salt
5 grinds black pepper

Soak the bread in the vinegar for 10 to 15 minutes.

In a blender, combine the bread and vinegar and all the remaining ingredients and purée until smooth. Add a little water if necessary for thinning.

Store in a jar in the refrigerator for several weeks.

Green Onion–Yogurt Dip and Sauce

Use as a dip for raw vegetables or chips.

MAKES 1$^1/_2$ CUPS

1 cup low-fat plain yogurt
$^1/_3$ cup thinly sliced green onions
2 tablespoons minced fresh cilantro
1 tablespoon fresh lime juice

Strain the yogurt overnight through a strainer lined with cheesecloth. Mix the yogurt with the remaining ingredients; taste and adjust the seasoning. Serve immediately.

Mustard-Dill Sauce

Use as a sauce for thinly sliced cucumbers.

MAKES $^1/_2$ CUP

$^1/_4$ cup Dijon-style mustard
1 teaspoon dry mustard
2 to 3 tablespoons sugar
2 tablespoons white wine vinegar
$^1/_3$ cup light vegetable oil
3 tablespoons minced fresh dill

In a small bowl, combine the mustards, sugar, and vinegar. Gradually whisk in the oil. Add the dill. Use immediately.

Muffuletta Spread

We use this at Gayle's for New Orleans–style muffuletta sandwiches. It can also be used in pasta salads.

MAKES 3 CUPS

1$^1/_2$ cups green olives, pitted
$^1/_2$ cup black olives, pitted
2 tablespoons capers
2 tablespoons minced cornichons
1$^1/_2$ teaspoons minced garlic
$^1/_4$ cup pimiento, chopped
5 peperoncini
$^1/_2$ cup diced carrots
$^1/_2$ cup diced celery
$^1/_4$ cup flat-leaf parsley leaves
1 tablespoon fresh chopped basil or 1 teaspoon dry
1 tablespoon fresh oregano or 1 teaspoon dry
6 tablespoons olive oil

In a food processor, process all ingredients except oil into a rough mince paste. Transfer to a bowl and stir in the oil.

Hummus

This is a great dip for vegetables or a spread for vegetable sandwiches.

MAKES 2¹/₂ CUPS

- 1 (15¹/₂-ounce) can garbanzo beans, rinsed and drained
- 2 tablespoons tahini
- 4 to 5 cloves garlic, minced
- ¹/₄ cup minced fresh flat-leaf parsley
- ¹/₂ teaspoon salt
- ¹/₄ cup freshly squeezed lemon juice
- ¹/₄ teaspoon ground cayenne pepper
- ¹/₄ teaspoon ground cumin
- 2 tablespoons minced scallions
- ¹/₄ cup olive oil

Combine all the ingredients except the oil in a blender or food processor and purée. With the machine running, drizzle in the oil. Store refrigerated in a tightly sealed plastic container for 1 week.

Salsa Fresca

This tomato salsa is a perfect low-fat condiment for corn chips, raw or grilled vegetables, or grilled fish.

MAKES 5¹/₂ CUPS

- 5 large tomatoes, finely diced
- 1 yellow onion, finely diced
- ¹/₂ red onion, finely diced
- 1 green bell pepper, seeded, deribbed, and finely diced
- 1 to 2 jalapeño chiles, seeded and minced
- 2 tablespoons fresh lemon juice
- ¹/₄ to ¹/₂ teaspoon salt
- ¹/₄ to ¹/₂ teaspoon freshly ground black pepper
- 2 to 3 cloves garlic, minced
- ¹/₂ cup minced cilantro leaves

Combine all the ingredients. Store refrigerated in a tightly sealed container for up to 5 days.

Herbed Croutons

Croutons are a good way to use up stale Italian or French bread. Serve warm or at room temperature on salads.

MAKES 4 CUPS

- 2 tablespoons extra virgin olive oil
- 1 tablespoon balsamic vinegar
- 2 tablespoons crushed garlic
- 2 tablespoons minced fresh herbs
- ¹/₄ cup water
- 1 teaspoon salt
- 4 cups bread torn into 1-inch pieces

Preheat the oven to 375°. In a large bowl, whisk together all the ingredients except the bread until well combined. Add the bread and toss with your hands until the bread is well coated with the liquid.

Place the croutons on a baking sheet and bake for 10 to 15 minutes, until they are golden brown and not too dry. Use these the same day you make them.

Mint Sauce

This is a sauce used in England as a dressing for Yorkshire pudding. It can also be served with roast lamb or grilled vegetables.

MAKES 1 CUP

- 1 cup malt vinegar
- 2 tablespoons sugar
- ¹/₄ cup minced fresh mint leaves

Combine all the ingredients in a small saucepan and cook over medium heat for 5 to 6 minutes. Use this sauce the same day you make it.

Garden Tomato Catsup

This is a spicy condiment to make when you have extra tomatoes from your harvest.

MAKES 3 CUPS

> **5 pounds tomatoes (12 large)**
> **1 yellow onion, chopped**
> **1¹/₂ tablespoons minced garlic**
> **1 cup red wine vinegar**
> **¹/₂ cup packed brown sugar**
> **2 teaspoons salt**

Blanch the tomatoes in boiling water for 1 to 2 minutes. Remove and set aside to cool. When cool enough to handle, peel the tomatoes and cut in half crosswise. Gently squeeze each half to remove the seeds. Purée in a food processor with the onion and garlic until smooth. In a small saucepan, mix the sugar and vinegar together, place over high heat, and bring to a boil. Reduce the heat and simmer 10 minutes, until reduced by half.

Meanwhile, place the tomato-onion mixture and the salt in a saucepan over medium-high heat and bring to a boil. Reduce the heat to medium-low and add the reduced vinegar to the tomatoes. Continue cooking for 30 to 40 minutes, stirring frequently, until the mixture is thickened to a catsup consistency.

Purée once more in a blender until very smooth.

Keeps for several weeks in a jar in the refrigerator.

MARINADES

Many marinades, condiments, and dressing are interchangeable, with some minor adjustments. Marinades, a mixture of oil and acid, add flavor; they also tenderize and lubricate foods.

While olive oil is the oil of choice for most marinades, you can also use safflower oil.

The acid for marinades can include red wine vinegar, balsamic vinegar, lemon juice, wine, yogurt, pineapple or apple juice, and soy sauce. Several different acids are often mixed in one marinade.

Aromatics and flavoring agents for marinades include garlic, ginger, shallots, onions, mustard, and herbs.

Use marinades the same day you make them.

Pineapple-Soy Marinade

This is great for grilled ahi tuna, swordfish, or halibut.

MAKES 3¹/₂ CUPS

> **2 garlic cloves, minced**
> **2 tablespoons minced peeled fresh ginger**
> **2 cups pineapple juice**
> **1 cup low-sodium soy sauce**
> **¹/₂ cup light olive oil or safflower oil**
> **1 teaspoon salt**
> **¹/₂ teaspoon freshly ground black pepper**

Mix all the ingredients together in a deep dish large enough to comfortably accommodate fish.

Marinate the fish 1 to 2 hours in the refrigerator, then grill over hot coals.

Yogurt-Mustard Marinade

This works well for chicken, but it also can be used for grilled vegetables.

MAKES 2¹/₂ CUPS

1 cup low-fat plain yogurt
¹/₂ cup Dijon-style mustard
¹/₂ cup red wine vinegar or cider vinegar
¹/₂ cup vegetable oil or light olive oil
1 teaspoon salt
¹/₂ teaspoon freshly ground black pepper

Mix all the ingredients together to a soupy consistency.

Marinate chicken or vegetables 1 to 2 hours. When grilling, make sure the chicken or vegetables are not too thickly coated with sauce, or it will drip onto coals creating unwanted flames.

Soy Marinade

Here's a recipe adapted from the Tassajara Zen Mountain Center, where they use it to marinate tofu before grilling. It can also be used for chicken, fish, or grilled vegetables.

MAKES 5 CUPS

1¹/₂ teaspoons ground cloves
1 tablespoon minced fresh oregano
1 onion, minced
1¹/₂ teaspoons minced garlic
1 teaspoon salt
¹/₂ teaspoon freshly ground black pepper
1 ounce dried mushrooms, rehydrated in 1 cup
    boiling water
1 cup low-sodium soy sauce
1 cup dry red wine
1 cup red wine vinegar
1 cup olive oil

Combine all the ingredients and whisk together until blended. Marinate tofu for 4 days before grilling. Marinate fish or chicken or vegetables for 2 to 3 hours or overnight in the refrigerator.

Moju

Use this as a basting mixture for chicken or as a sauce to pour over chicken or fish after it is grilled. For grilled giant prawns, replace the mint with flat-leaf parsley. Then, after grilling the prawns, place them on serving plates. Pour the mixture on top, then garnish with more fresh parsley.

MAKES 1¹/₃ CUPS

¹/₂ cup extra virgin olive oil
¹/₂ cup (1 stick) butter
4 to 6 cloves garlic, minced
1 cup minced fresh mint leaves
Juice of 2 lemons
1 teaspoon salt
¹/₂ teaspoon freshly ground black pepper

In a small nonreactive saucepan, melt the butter with the olive oil over low heat. Add the garlic and cook until translucent. Remove from heat and add the remaining ingredients.

Diavolo Marinade

Use this marinade for grilled chicken or vegetables.

MAKES 5¹/₂ CUPS

2 cups balsamic vinegar
2 cups olive oil
1 cup fresh lemon juice
¹/₄ cup minced garlic
2 tablespoons minced fresh rosemary leaves
1 tablespoon salt
1 tablespoon white pepper

Combine all the ingredients. For chicken, marinate no longer than 2 to 3 hours. (After 3 hours, the high-acid content of the marinade causes the meat to disintegrate.)

3

Nourishing Soil & Body

Making and Using Humus in the Garden

Long before people were growing plants, the soil was playing out its basic ecological role: decomposing organic matter into simple nutrients and recycling those nutrients back into plants. Every day, death and decay kept the nutrients cycling through endless generations. As plants evolved, they became bonded to the process of the soil's organic decay and to the conversion of microbes, plant bodies, and animal wastes into the dark, musty matter we call humus. Not only is humus at the heart of nature's way of renewal and life, it is also the basis of successful kitchen gardening.

The terms organic matter and humus are often used interchangeably, but they are not the same thing. Organic matter is the raw material you pile up in your compost bin or feed to earthworms. Humus is the dark, crumbly finished product. If you can identify the bits of organic debris in it, it's still organic matter. Humus is what organic material becomes when it is completely broken down. This distinction is important, so we need to take a closer look at the types of organic decay and the benefits of humus:

THE BENEFITS OF HUMUS

There are few panaceas in life, but humus is certainly one of them. It has the capacity to remedy virtually all of the undesirable traits of poor soils. Just as good soil is the heart of a healthy garden, humus is the soul of a productive soil.

Humus Builds Structure and Stores Water

Humus creates the porous, fluffy structure that's found in the topsoils of forests and prairies, and that all kitchen gardeners strive for. Most gardeners will tell you that after they dug in compost, their soil has a better structure, is easier to work, drains better, and doesn't need water as often. It is an example of nature's efficiency that humus improves both sandy and clay soils. Because humus is so fibrous, it breaks up dense clay, allowing air (an important fertilizer) to enter and water to drain. Since it is spongy and sticky with the by-products of decay, humus also helps bind sand particles while holding moisture that might otherwise seep away. No matter how bad your soil may be, humus can improve its structure and make it hold more water.

Humus Buffers the Soil Against Sudden Changes

One thing vegetables don't like is a soil that changes rapidly from hot to cold, wet to dry, or acid to alkaline. Like a sponge, humus soaks up water, which keeps the soil evenly moist and reduces sudden temperature swings. Humus also absorbs salts and other chemicals that might be brought in with irrigation water, manures, or fertilizers. In short, humus tempers, or "buffers," the soil environment and gives vegetables the stable root conditions they need to thrive.

Humus Nurtures Both Soil and Plants

Humus is a storehouse for plant food. It absorbs soluble nutrients that would otherwise leach away. Humus is also a matrix for beneficial soil life, and this leads to healthier plants. Tiny soil creatures, mostly bacteria and fungi, have a variety of ways to make a living that benefit plants. Many convert humus to available nutrients; others eat nematodes and disease fungi. Still others (mycorrhiza) grow on plant roots and help them take up nutrients and fend off disease microbes. Testimonials from gardeners about organic matter increasing plant vigor are likely due to these beneficial soil microbes, most of whom thrive in soils with lots of organic matter and humus.

THE MANY BENEFITS OF HUMUS

- Improves soil structure and makes soil easier to work.

- Opens up soil and improves drainage and aeration (important in clay soils).

- Increases soil's ability to store water (important in sandy soils).

- Increases the soil's ability to store heat (important in all soils, especially sandy ones).

- Serves as a reservoir for plant nutrients.

- Buffers the soil against sudden changes in water, temperature, and chemicals.

- Feeds and nurtures beneficial soil microbes and helps to suppress plant diseases.

- Helps neutralize the harmful effects of toxins and salts.

- Reduces erosion caused by wind and water.

THE FOUR PATHS TO ORGANIC DECAY

A good way to appreciate the ways that organic matter decays in nature is to imagine you're in a woodland area and you've come across a large pond. The plants at the edge of the pond are matted down into a wet, compacted mushy texture, much like a pile of kitchen garbage or fresh grass clippings. The carbon, nitrogen, and water are adequate for fast decay, but there is no oxygen. The result is a smelly incomplete decay, or *putrefaction*. Decay can take from months to years.

Looking out at the center of the pond, you notice tiny bubbles at the surface. This is methane gas produced by putrefaction of plants at the bottom of the pond. Because they are underwater, the putrefying sediments are called *peat*. Peats are very acidic and are not completely decayed. Look at peat of moss (peat moss) closely and you will see bits and pieces of the original moss plants. Peat moss is used to lighten and acidify soil mixes, but it is not humus. To see humus in nature, you have to look for places where there is plenty of air and only moderate water.

As you walk about the woods, you notice a fallen tree trunk rotting on the forest floor. It has taken decades to decay this far, and decades from now the once-proud trunk will disappear into the soil as crumbs of humus. This *dry decay* is very slow because the tree trunk is high in carbon and low in water and nitrogen, which have to be added by rainwater or animal droppings. Humus happens, but it takes generations.

Humus is made more quickly in places with a proper balance of carbon and nitrogen, lots of air, and moist (not wet) conditions. Nature shows us two examples. The first is leaf litter. If you scoop some up from the forest floor, you'll notice that at the surface you can see rotting leaves and twigs a few inches down. You'll see a dark, crumbly material with no recognizable bits in it. This is forest humus and the process that makes it is *humification*. The decay is complete and the smell is sweet and musty. Leaves are full of carbon, nitrogen, and water, and they fall to the ground so as to leave air spaces.

You can also find conditions for complete humus decay in the topsoils of grasslands. The fibrous, deep roots of grasses produce a rich, airy soil that allows dead plants to decay quickly in well-drained soil. This is why grasslands are so productive; their topsoils are high in humus. Leaf litter is nature's compost pile, and grasslands are nature's green manures.

TYPE OF DECAY	RATE OF DECAY	C/N	AIR/WATER	BY-PRODUCTS	EXAMPLES Natural	Residential
Humification	Weeks to months	Balanced	Normal/moist	• CO_2 • Humus	• Leaf litter • Grassland soil	• Compost piles • Worm cultures
Putrefaction	Months to years	High N	Low/high	• Methane • Sludges • CO_2	• Fresh manure • Compacted piles	• Wet garbage • Grass clipping • Septic systems
Peat decay	Years to decades	High C	Low/very high	• Methane • Sulfides • Peats	• Estuaries, bogs, lakes	• Bottom of garden ponds
Dry decay	Decades to generations	Very high C	Normal/dry	• CO_2 • Humus	• Fallen trees • Piles of branches	• Piles of twigs and branches

HOW ORGANIC MATTER DECAYS

All organic matter eventually decays. It may take a few months or several decades. How quickly and completely it breaks down depends on the interplay of four ingredients: carbon, nitrogen, air, and water. These elements have to be in just the right amounts for organic matter to decay quickly and completely into humus. This is the first principle of humus management. If one of these elements is absent or overabundant, decay to humus slows down or stops all together. It follows other pathways to decay.

WAYS TO MAKE HUMUS IN THE KITCHEN GARDEN

With all these benefits, it's not surprising that organic matter is at the heart of many gardening techniques and philosophies. Virtually every gardening book recommends its use. If we look closely at nature, we can see how organic matter is incorporated into the soil and note how gardeners have invented ways to mimic and accelerate these processes. For example, nature rarely keeps soil bare, but instead keeps it covered with a rich carpet of deep-rooted plants (green manures) or leaves and litter from the bodies of plants (mulch). As organic matter settles into the soil, earthworms digest it into tiny bits (vermicomposting) and microbes decay it into humus (composting). All of these methods of decay are available to the home gardener, and in this chapter we will describe them.

SOME TERMS DEFINED

Organic matter: The bodies and waste of once-living things. Kitchen scraps, grass clippings, weeds, leaves, sawdust, and animal manure are examples of organic matter.

Compost: Organic matter that has been decayed in constructed piles under ideal conditions of carbon, nitrogen, air, and water. Composting rids organic wastes of salts and toxins and pasteurizes many weeds and diseases. It creates a stabilized material that, when added to the soil, can decay rapidly into humus without upsetting the life and properties of the soil. Compost is not humus, but it is halfway there.

Humus: The end-product of organic decay, and the last stage in the decomposition of organic matter. In spite of decades of study, scientists are still not sure what humus is. It is probably a complex mixture of things that varies according to the type of organic matter that decayed and the organisms that made it. Whatever it is, all humus is brown or black, has a fine crumbly texture, and smells like fresh sweet earth. It is spongelike and holds many times its weight in water. It also attracts and stores many important plant nutrients.

Green manures: Plants that are grown in the garden and then dug in at season's end. The plant bodies provide fiber that breaks down in the soil to produce humus. Since most green manures have extensive or deep root systems, they represent one of the few ways that unavailable nutrients leached deep into the subsoil can be made available to plants. Some green manures also attract beneficial insects, which make them doubly valuable (see page 129).

Mulch: A protective layer of material that is spread on the surface of the soil. Mulch has many important advantages, like preventing water loss and holding in soil heat. It also cools the soil surface and attracts earthworms.

Vermicomposting: A method of making compost in worm cultures. This technique is especially appealing for people who live where bulky compost bins and unsightly heaps of organic wastes are not possible. The other advantage is that the manure from redworms, called "castings," is a bit closer to true humus than compost.

Compost tea: Made by soaking bags of compost in water to create a liquid rich in the nutrients and antibodies commonly found in compost. Compost teas are rapidly becoming an important and accepted method of using compost to not only fertilize plants, but to protect them from some diseases.

COMPOST AND COMPOSTING

The Bengalese call it "misrasher," the Arabs call it "samad a khdder," the Mandarin Chinese call it "gùn gē féi liào," and the Italians call it "concime." No matter how you pile it, compost is the foundation of a thriving kitchen garden. Compost can be defined as a pile of organic materials deliberately assembled for rapid decay. By piling up the heap carefully with an eye to proper moisture, mix of materials, and plenty of air, you can create the conditions that decomposing creatures love. They will rapidly render your pile of leftovers and yard wastes into rich, dark soil-building compost.

Compost, though, is much more than just rotted debris. The compost process prepares fresh organic wastes so that soil life can convert them efficiently into soil humus. Lots of organic wastes contain toxins, salts, pesticides, plus acid or alkaline materials, and other harmful chemicals that often go undetected. In a well-made compost pile, they are converted into harmless forms; that is, the or-ganic mass is "stabilized." When this stable compost is added to the soil, creatures there can begin to decay it into humus without being hindered by toxins. Thus, the organic materials are rotted twice: once in the compost pile to get it ready, and once in the soil to convert it into humus.

Composting used to be something only organic gardeners did; other gardeners sent their "wastes" to the dump, then spent money on chemicals to make their plants grow. For them, it was a matter of convenience.

Today, residential composting is becoming more and more popular, and the reason is simple: People know that if they really want to do something for the environment, they can begin in their own backyards by collecting their kitchen scraps and yard wastes and converting them into compost. Once you start looking around, you may be surprised at how much of what you throw away can be composted and turned into an elixir for your garden soil.

Basic Principles of Composting

Successful composters have an attitude: They know that composting is not a daunting task or something only alchemists can appreciate. It's easy, and it can be done in the smallest of spaces without odors or flies, and without complicated or expensive equipment.

Making compost means nurturing and watching over a living thing and is akin to making wine, cheese, or sourdough bread. Microbes do most of the work, but you have to feed and care for them regularly. People who compost also know that you don't always have time to do this. Once in a while a pile may get ignored, or scraps thrown away. In the end, composting is like any part of your lifestyle. If you learn the basics well, you will do it efficiently enough to fit it in; then it just becomes a habit.

There are as many ways to make compost as there are people who compost. Everyone has his or her own palette of special additives, combinations of ingredients, and personal touches. Maybe you've tried it and your compost remained a pile of smelly, cold wastes. You're not alone. There are many things to consider, like: How do I assemble the various wastes? How big does the pile have to be? Do I have to put it together all at once? Do I have to turn it? Many of these questions can be answered by simply understanding some basic principles. Then even a novice can coax a pile of garbage into compost.

Principle 1:

The compost pile is a living organism. Compost serves as home to hundreds of different organisms, including bacteria, fungi, earthworms, mites, sowbugs, and insects. Microbes eat the nutrients in the compost pile

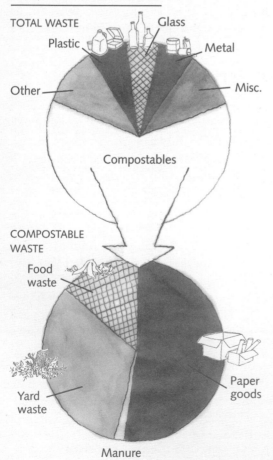

FIG. 3-1: **Waste of California**

TOTAL WASTE

Plastic

Glass

Metal

Other

Misc.

Compostables

COMPOSTABLE WASTE

Food waste

Yard waste

Paper goods

Manure

and store them in their bodies, where they are safe from rains and processes that wash nutrients away or release them into the atmosphere. In this way, compost microbes become like a slow-release fertilizer. When the compost is used on plants, nutrients are released when the microbes die and give up their stored foods.

As the compost microbes feed, they generate a lot of heat. Since organic matter is a good insulator, much of this heat is conserved in the pile. The temperature may reach 140°F, which attracts and nurtures a host of heat-loving bacteria and fungi that begin to break down hard-to-decay materials like twigs and sawdust. As decay continues, the temperature drops, and after a few weeks it returns to normal.

Heat is only generated when conditions are ideal. A casually thrown-together heap of weeds and such will decay slowly and generate little heat. The advantage of compost heat is that it greatly accelerates decay and can kill at least some weed seeds and diseases.

As the pile cools, soil animals will move in and help to break things down even further. Earthworms, mites, sowbugs, and other creatures eat organic matter, which is decayed by the bacteria in their guts. The waste they produce is eaten by other creatures. As the organic residues cascade down the food chain, all attached nutrients are consumed or used by plants and what remains is the stable, black, and spongy material we call humus.

Principle 2:

Compost life needs a balanced diet. Organisms in a compost heap are no different than us—they need a well-balanced diet to thrive. What they need is plenty of air, the right portions of carbon and nitrogen, and a moist (not wet) environment. If they get the right mix of these ingredients, they can decompose organic wastes quickly and completely.

Principle 3:

Compost life needs the proper mix of carbon and nitrogen. Every piece of organic material contains carbon and nitrogen in different ratios (abbreviated as C/N or C:N). Decay microbes prefer a diet with about thirty times more carbon than nitrogen (C:N=30). If there is too much carbon, decay will be very slow. If there is too much nitrogen, it will evaporate as ammonia gas, and decay will be incomplete. If there is just the right amount of both, then the nitrogen can provide the nutrients so that the carbon can become humus.

Nitrogen materials include blood meal, plant meals, animal manures, and young green plant wastes like grass clippings and leaves. Carbon materials are brown or dry and include straw, wood chips, sawdust, and dry leaves. For example, sawdust has about 500 times more carbon than nitrogen, or a C:N of 500 (high carbon), while blood meal has only about 4 times as much carbon, a C:N of 4 (high nitrogen). Virtually all organic materials fall within this range. A few materials have a balanced C:N (around 30) with a loose, moist texture, like broadleaf weeds, horse manure mixed with livestock bedding, and fresh deciduous leaves. These materials can be composted all by themselves with little fussing. Kitchen garbage has a balanced C:N, but it is too wet and mushy to allow air in. It needs to be mixed with a dry and fluffy bulking agent, like hay. Materials that are too wet, too dry,

and high in carbon or nitrogen, must be mixed together to achieve the proper balance of air, water, carbon, and nitrogen.

The carbon-nitrogen principle becomes obvious if you dig brown high-carbon stuff like straw or sawdust into your soil. Microbes will rob the soil of nitrogen to take advantage of the glut of carbon. This means less nitrogen for your plants. On the other hand, if you dig in high nitrogen sources like fresh chicken manure in the hopes of getting humus, you'll be disappointed. Most of the nitrogen will be taken up by plants or evaporated into the air. Without carbon, microbes don't have the material to make humus. Without nitrogen, they don't have the fuel. They need a balance of both.

Principle 4:

Compost life needs lots of air. The compost process requires plenty of air, since microbes of decay are "aerobic," that is, they need a free flow of oxygen like humans and other animals. Without adequate air, the compost is turned over to "anaerobic" microbes that thrive without oxygen. The result is a smelly mass of incomplete decay. There are three ways to get air into a compost pile: (1) Turn it frequently, (2) build it so that air can circulate naturally with perforated pipe or layers of twigs, and (3) force air through it with fans.

Principle 5:

Compost life needs plenty of water, but not too much. Water is vital to all life and especially to the decay microbes in compost piles. If the pile is too dry, decomposition slows way down. If the pile is soggy, it can't breathe; it will putrefy and attract flies. A compost pile should be like a wrung-out sponge: not too wet, not too dry. This is best achieved by gradually sprinkling the pile as you make it. But note that organic materials can absorb lots of water. What always surprises novice compost makers is how much water it takes to make a pile "like a wrung-out sponge." On the other hand, if you expect a downpour, cover your pile during the deluge and remove when the weather clears.

Principle 6:

Compost life works faster on smaller pieces of material. The smaller the pieces of organic material are, the faster they'll deay. Chopped, shredded, cut-up, or even bruised materials always decompose faster than whole pieces. This takes energy, whether it's yours or the gasoline of a chipper. Some gardeners prefer to simply pile up the whole pieces in careful layers, sift the compost when it's done, and let nature take its course.

Principle 7:

The more energy you put in, the faster the compost comes out. Composting can be fast and labor-intensive or slow and simple. The more energy you put into making the pile, the faster you'll get compost (see page 116). For example, if you simply toss your kitchen and yard wastes haphazardly into an open pile and let the rain add the water, then you'll get a cool pile with compost in a year or so. If you layer that same pile correctly, it will warm a bit and convert to compost in less than a year. "Carefully" means paying attention to the way you alternate layers of carbon or brown materials and nitrogen or green materials. It also means watering down dry layers as you go and inserting air pockets made of cross-layers of twigs and branches. These pockets take the place of turning by allowing carbon dioxide to escape up and out the heated pile and fresh air to move in. Turning a pile is optional if you put it together right and you're not in a hurry.

If you layer your wastes in contained bins and turn the rotting mass regularly, composting speeds up even more. When you turn a pile you do several things: (1) You purge excess moisture and let air into the breathing heap and, most important, you let carbon dioxide out; (2) you mix the ingredients; and (3) you move the outside material into the center of the pile. Turning a hefty compost pile is not for everyone. If they're made properly, compost piles do not have to be turned. They'll just take longer and decay won't be uniform throughout.

If you chop up or chip the materials into small pieces, the decay microbes can gain an even quicker foothold. Each increase in energy input makes the compost happen faster and more completely.

Principle 8:

Compost happens faster if you assemble the pile all at once. It's not always easy or convenient to have all your wastes at one time. Seasoned composters often stockpile or gather up their materials and build the pile all at once knowing that this will hasten decay. But as long as you pay attention to the mix of ingredients, you can construct compost piles in sequences of layers as wastes become available. Decay will just take longer.

Principle 9:

The size of the pile matters. Organic matter acts like insulation because of the air pockets it contains. If you want your pile to heat up, it needs to be at least 3 to 4 feet square to keep the heat and moisture in. A small pile may heat up a bit, but it won't sustain high temperatures long enough to do much good. A pile higher than 6 feet is difficult to turn and tends to compact too much at the base and go anaerobic.

FIG. 3-3:
C/N (Carbon/Nitrogen) ratios of compost ingredients

HARD BROWN

- Twigs & branches
- Small pieces of wood

SOFT BROWN

- Straw
- Paper
- Brown "wood chips"
- Pine needles
- Tree trimmings, chips
- Sawdust

HARD GREEN

- Evergreen trimmings
- Fresh corn stalks
- Mature weeds
- Green wood chips
- Dry hay

SOFT GREEN

- Grass clippings
- Fresh leaves
- Fresh young weeds
- Fresh legumes
- Spent crops

High C
High C/N
Humus

350 : 1

100 : 1

30 : 1

10 : 1

High N
Low C/N
Nutrients

RUMINANT HERBIVORES

Cows

Goats

(30–40 : 1)

NON-RUMINANT HERBIVORES

Horses

Rabbits

20–30 : 1

CARNIVORES

Dogs, cats

15–20 : 1

BIRDS

10–20 : 1

THE BENEFITS OF COMPOST

- Composting is a way to replenish the organic matter and nutrients that are removed when you harvest your plants.

- Composting is a way to recycle leaves, grass clippings, kitchen scraps, and other home wastes into a soil-building fertilizer.

- Composting is the best way to dispose of kitchen and garden wastes without using up our landfills.

- Compost saves money on fertilizers and soil amendments. As gardeners like to say: "Feed the soil, and it will feed your plants."

- Properly aged compost is only one step removed from humus. In time, it will give soil all the advantages of humus.

- There is growing evidence that well-aged compost can act to suppress certain soil diseases by feeding beneficial soil microbes. Fresh compost, just a few weeks or months old, is full of sugars that can encourage some diseases. But as compost ages, the sugars turn to starches, which seem to be preferred by disease-suppressing microbes.

Materials for Composting

If you have a garden, a yard, or a kitchen, you are already producing fodder for a compost pile. Yesterday's salad and vegetables, leaves from under your tree, twigs from those pruned roses, last Sunday's newspaper, lawn clippings—they can all be composted and returned to the soil instead of a landfill. The important thing is to use what you have available; special ingredients, like manure and commercial activators, are not necessary to make good compost. They just speed things up a bit.

To achieve the proper layering of the compost pile, it helps to categorize organic materials for simple reference. We have found it handy to separate wastes into six categories.

Activators

Activators like blood meal and plant meals are very high in nitrogen. They are best used to jump-start piles, especially when animal manures aren't available and there's lots of brown carbon materials in the pile. The term "activators" also refers to commercial products that claim to speed up and improve composting with special plant by-products or cultures of microbes. These may just be fine-tuners. We have found that the best activator for a compost pile is earthworm castings or compost from a previous pile.

Animal Manures

Animal manures should be evaluated from the viewpoint of three things: (1) the kind of animal it comes from, (2) its freshness, and (3) the amount of livestock bedding it contains. Birds like chickens, turkeys, and ducks deposit both urine and feces in solid droppings. For this reason, bird manure has the highest amount of nitrogen and the lowest carbon. It provides nutrients, but little material for making humus. At the other end of the manure spectrum are ruminants like goats and cows, which chew their food over and over and extract most of the nutrients in several stomachs. Their manure is high in carbon and low in nitrogen. Avoid cat manures. They can contain *Toxoplasma gondii,* a disease that sometimes can be transmitted to pregnant women and their fetuses. *Toxocara cati* is a roundworm, also common in cat feces, that causes similar problems in children. Keep the litter box away from children and out of the compost pile!

Manure that has been lying around for a while will lose much of its moisture and nitrogen. Fresh manure is moist and smells like ammonia. It will help heat up a pile. Aged manure won't bring much heat to a pile, but it's an excellent source of microorganisms and phosphorous.

Gardeners should avoid putting fresh manure on their soil. The best thing to do with fresh animal manure is to compost it. If you use manure in your compost, notice how much bedding material comes mixed with it. Stable-keepers often use wood chips, straw, or sawdust to help absorb urine and keep down odors. Urine-soaked bedding is a great source of nitrogen and carbon. Chicken manure often contains rice hulls or sawdust. Remember, bedding is a dry carbon source and can change the character of the manure. The carbon-to-nitrogen values of various (pure) manures are shown in the illustration on page 111.

Animal manures are not always available in many urban areas, and good compost can certainly be made without using them.

Soft Green Plant Materials

Soft green plant materials like grass clippings, alfalfa hay, young weeds and spent crops can be as high in nitrogen as some manures. They lack brown carbon material, but their freshness gives them plenty of water. Because they are so succulent, soft greens can often mat down and keep air from moving through the pile. They should be added in thin layers. To capture the most nitrogen for your compost pile, cover your scavenged soft green materi-

als with a tarp to retain their moisture and nitrogen until you are ready to add them to the compost. Kitchen scraps are best placed in this category.

Hard Green Plant Materials

Hard green plant materials include mature weeds, wood chips from treetops, leafy prunings, fresh cornstalks, and other plant wastes that contain both green and brown elements. Hard greens are important additions to the pile since they have a good carbon-to-nitrogen mix and their loose fibrous structure allows a free flow of air through the pile.

Soft Brown Plant Materials

Soft brown plant materials are in small, pliable pieces, like dry leaves, sawdust, bark, wood chips with little greenery, and straw. Most of these materials, especially straw and sawdust, can be soaked in a wheelbarrow, drained, and then added to the pile for best results. Soft browns can be stored easily for later use. For example, fallen dead leaves, sawdust, or wood chips stockpiled in autumn can be used for layering with soft green materials the following spring.

Hard Brown Plant Materials

Hard brown plant materials are very high in carbon because they are mostly pure wood. Twigs and branches don't break down very much during the lifetime of a single compost pile, but they are a very handy ingredient because they create pathways for free-flowing air. Plus, you can stockpile them quite easily.

Not all organic matter is suitable for composting. Around the home, unfit wastes will have to be separated out of your waste stream and treated otherwise (see the list of materials to avoid, page 115).

AVERAGE CARBON-TO-NITROGEN RATIOS OF VARIOUS COMPOST MATERIALS

TYPES OF WASTES	COMPOSTABLE MATERIALS	C:N RATIO
ACTIVATORS	**Animal wastes**	
High N	Urine	1:2
Low C	Blood meal	3–4:1
	Dry fish scraps	5:1
	Plant meals	
	Soybean meal	5:1
	Cottonseed meal	5:1
ANIMAL MANURES	**Manures**	
	Chicken manure	10–15:1
	Pig manure	15:1
	Horse manure, fresh	15:1
	Sheep, goat manure	20:1
	Horse manure with bedding	20–30:1
	Cow manure	25:1
GREEN PLANT MATERIAL	**Soft greens**	
	Alfalfa hay	15:1
	Grass clippings	15:1
	Seaweed	19:1
	Kitchen scraps	10–20:1
Balanced C:N	Green weeds	20:1
	Spent vegetables	20:1
	Fresh fall leaves	30–40:1
	Hard greens	
	Mature weeds (no seeds)	25:1
	Leafy prunings	35:1
	Leafy wood chips	40:1
	Dry hay or weeds	40:1
	Fresh stalks of corn, sunflowers, etc.	50:1
BROWN PLANT MATERIAL	**Soft Browns**	
	Dry leaves	60:1
	Old cornstalks	60:1
	Straw	70:1
	Newspaper	200:1
	Cardboard	250:1
	Brown wood chips	300:1
	Hard Browns	
Low N	Twigs and branches	400:1
High C	Sawdust	500:1

USE CAUTION IN THE COMPOST PILE

Do Not Use in the Pile

• Seed heads from invasive weeds (especially not in cool piles). You often read that the heat of compost will kill all weed seeds. This is true only if the heap reaches a very high temperature. In fact, most piles do not get hot enough to kill seeds; they merely remain dormant until the compost is spread. Pull weeds before they flower!

• Underground parts of invasive weeds, especially those with rhizomes (Bermuda grass) or deep sprouting roots (bindweed).

• Badly diseased plants. (Add only to the center of hot active piles.) Remember, some fungi that eat plants also thrive on organic matter. For this reason it's best not to add any diseased members of the tomato family, including potatoes and peppers, to the pile. Late blight is such a fungus.

• Cat, dog, pig, and human feces. (These can contain harmful pathogens. Don't put kitty litter in compost piles for the same reason.)

• Dairy products, greasy foods, and meat. (These decay slowly and attract scavengers and pests.)

• Coal and barbecue ashes contain sulfur oxides, which are bad for plants.

• Dishwater. Soaps contain grease, perfumes, and sodium.

• Magazines. Paper coatings and inks may be toxic.

Use Sparingly in the Pile

• Needles from pine trees (very slow to decay and often quite acidic).

• Fresh leaves from black walnut, red cedar, laurel, and eucalyptus trees (contain lots of tannins and other plant toxins).

• Fresh grass clippings. (Thick layers will mat down into a slimy mass.)

Making a Compost Pile

The challenge for a home composter is to learn how to achieve the proper proportion of carbon, nitrogen, air, and water without having to worry about the numbers. At first the categories of organic wastes come in handy. But with a little experience, and perhaps a few failed piles, you won't be conscious of measurements; a successful pile feels and smells just right.

There are no exact recipes for compost. Old-time composters like to talk of alternating "green" and "brown" materials in piles about 6 to 8 inches thick. Thin layers are important because it keeps complementary ingredients close together. You can use animal wastes like manures and blood meal to activate layers of carbon. The hard green layers usually take care of themselves. The real trick is in the proper layering and wetting of the pile as you make it.

Open, Unturned, Layered "Convection" Piles

Large, open compost piles have many advantages. They don't have to be turned, and they are ideal for recycling large amounts of yard and garden wastes. If you have lots to compost all at once, or if you have a big landscape, then an open, unturned pile might be best.

FIG. 3-4:
Energy & effort required to get fresh compost

ENERGY IN:

1. VERY LITTLE
Slowest method
(> 15 months)

- Haphazardly tossed
- Open piles
- Not turned
- No added nitrogen
- Rain watered only

2. LITTLE
Slow method
(12–15 months)

- Carefully layered
- Open piles
- Not turned
- No added nitrogen
- Watered while being made

3. MODEST
Average rate
(9–12 months)

- Carefully layered
- Open piles
- Not turned
- Nitrogen added
- Watered while being made

4. A LOT
Fast method
(6–9 months)

- Carefully layered
- In closed sided bins
- Turned periodically
- Nitrogen added
- Watered while being made

5. THE MOST
(< 6 months)

- Carefully layered
- Closed sided bins
- Turned periodically
- Nitrogen added
- Watered while being made
- Materials are chipped/chopped

An ideal location for such a pile is an inconspicuous, level area near the garden with ample available water. Try not to place your compost pile under trees, which can channel rainwater onto the pile and make it soggy.

- **Layer 1: The Foundation.** To lay the base, assemble available twigs, branches, stalks, and woody weeds. They should be from $1/4$ to $1/2$ inch thick and 1 to 3 feet long. Place these pieces crosswise in a layer about 1 to 2 feet thick. (Interestingly, this is the way ancient people made "bed springs" for their beds.) A base of intermingled coarse, woody materials serves as an airy organic scaffold for the pile above. As the pile ages, it settles, and so does a lot of water. The bottom of the pile needs to drain away water, let in air, and support a sinking pile. Without a porous and supportive base, material at the bottom of a pile can compact and putrefy. Don't water this layer. It'll get plenty of water from above.

- **Layer 2: Mature Weeds and Prunings.** This strengthens the foundation of the pile and begins the sequence of layers. Limit this layer to no more than 1 foot. Water lightly.

- **Layer 3: The Rest of the Pile.** Once the base is built, you can begin alternating layers of carbon- and nitrogen-rich materials. Make layers no thicker than 8 inches. Exact measurements aren't critical, but try to keep the brown and green layers equal and on top of one another. For instance, pile dry tall grasses on top of fresh weeds. Wet the brown grass layer until it's moist. As you stack your layers, interrupt the sequence now and then with a layer of twigs or stalks cross-layered like the base. These form air pockets and let air convect up through the porous twiggy base and through the pile. If you want a faster, hotter pile, simply add a handful or so of blood meal, ammonium fertilizer, or a few buckets of manure in and around each brown layer. Some commonly available compost materials are listed on page 118.

- **Watering the Pile.** Sprinkle the pile as you progress with your layering. Water less on the bottom than on the top, since gravity will pull water down through the pile. Be sure to water all of the dry brown layers thoroughly. They should have the feel of a wrung-out sponge, moist but not sodden. (Watch for water oozing out of the bottom of the pile). Beginning composters almost always put too little water on the brown layers and too much on the green.

After a few weeks, feel inside the pile for proper moisture. If you see lots of white fungal threads or ant colonies, this means that your pile is too dry. Remedy by adding some water (sprinkle the pile thoroughly).

The Compost Tractor: Moveable Compost Piles in the Garden

The open compost pile can also be used in a very efficient way within the garden. We have experimented with this method and found it to be a very convenient way to compost garden wastes while, at the same time, improving garden soil. The method is used in conjunction with raised beds.

Start by making a small open pile in much the same way we described for the open unturned pile. Construct the heap at the head of a raised bed that is at least 4 feet wide. Make the pile as wide as the bed, about 4 to 6 six feet long and at least 3 to 4 feet high. Use only landscape trimmings and spent crops, and try to avoid using activators and food wastes. This will discourage marauding animals from disturbing it. As you turn the pile, simply flip it so that it moves down the bed, and then start a new pile in its wake. Continue turning the pile down the bed until it is done. Then dig it in where it lies. There are several advantages to this method: (1) You don't have to haul your garden wastes very far; (2) your soil is directly nourished as the compost piles decay above it and "moves" down the raised bed; and (3) the older piles will serve as a habitat for many beneficial ground beetles and spiders (see page 171). We like to call this method the "compost tractor."

COMPOST MATERIALS

MATERIAL	COMMENT
Algae or seaweed	Fine micronutrient source. To remove salts, hose down or let rain fall on it before adding to pile.
Coffee grounds	Acidic source of nitrogen and phosphorous. Good earthworm food, since caffeine has been removed.
Corncobs	Use in twiggy, air-pocket layers.
Eggshells	Good source of calcium, but only if well crushed.
Fish scraps	Bury deeply in pile.
Grass clippings	Good source of nitrogen when fresh (green). Keep layers thin as they compact and stop air fllow. Don't use grass treated with herbicides.
Animal manures	See page 112–113.
Mushroom compost	Spent manure-straw from mushroom cultures. Contains salts and pesticide residue. Good soil builder when aged for several months.
Newspaper	Shred for compost, use shredded or fllat for mulch. Colored sheets okay.
Pinecones	Use in twiggy, air-pocket layer.
Pine needles	Acidic with tannic acids. Use sparingly.
Sawdust and wood shavings	High carbon; mix with nitrogen source. Avoid too much black walnut, red cedar, laurel, or eucalyptus trimmings.
Twigs and prunings	High carbon; slow to decay. Great for creating air pockets and pile foundations.
Wood ashes	Very alkaline; source of potassium. Use small amounts.
Vegetable leftovers	Good balance of carbon and nitrogen. Mix with alfalfa hay for perfect mix.

FIG. 3-5: Recipes for composting: **Two ways to use various organic materials for making compost. Each layer of material is described according to how much (+) or how little (–) carbon (C), nitrogen (N), air, or water it brings to the pile.**

KITCHEN SCRAPS WITH HAY

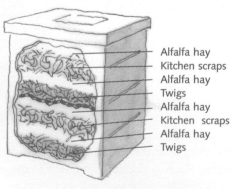

- Alfalfa hay
- Kitchen scraps
- Alfalfa hay
- Twigs
- Alfalfa hay
- Kitchen scraps
- Alfalfa hay
- Twigs

C	N	Air	Water	
++	+++	+	–	Alfalfa hay
+	+	– –	++	Kitchen scraps
++	+++	+	–	Alfalfa hay
+++	– –	++	– –	Twigs

PLANT WASTES WITH MANURE

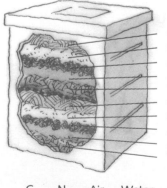

- Grass clippings, hay
- Sawdust, straw
- Manure
- Mature weeds, prunings
- Twigs
- Grass clippings, hay
- Sawdust, straw
- Manure
- Mature weeds, prunings
- Twigs

C	N	Air	Water	
–	++	–	+	Grass clippings, hay
++	–	+	–	Sawdust, straw
+	+++	–	–	Manure
+	+	++	++	Mature weeds, prunings
+++	– –	++	– –	Twigs

FIG. 3-6: Types of composters

OPEN

1. OPEN CAGE FOR LEAVES & LANDSCAPE TRIMMINGS

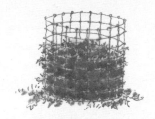

2. OPEN PILE AERATED WITH PERFORATED PVC PIPES

3. OPEN, UNTURNED PILE ("WINDROW")

Soil

Fresh weeds

Manure (or grass clippings)

Base of twigs laid in alternating directions

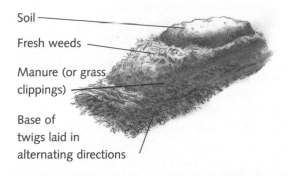

CLOSED BINS

1. HAYBALES

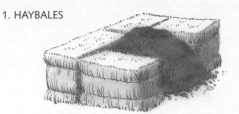

2. WOOD

3. BRICK

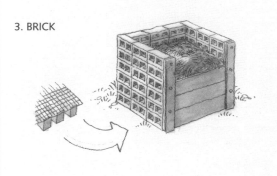

COMMERCIAL TYPES

The Compost Bin

If you like things a bit more tidy or want compost faster, then consider composting in containers. They have the added advantage of protecting the pile from marauding animals, while holding in heat and moisture better. The most popular containers are bins made of wood, cement blocks, or other suitable materials. You can also buy commercial compost bins (see pages 451–453). There are two types now available: stationary bins and tumblers. Many of these are reviewed and described in *The Urban/Suburban Composter* (see the Bibliography, page 443).

STORING KITCHEN SCRAPS FOR COMPOSTING

It's easy to accumulate and store your kitchen scraps if you do it properly. Simply take a 5-gallon bucket and place some sawdust on the bottom. Put your food wastes from day one on top of the sawdust and cover it completely with another layer of sawdust. Keep a tight-fitting lid on the bucket. By sandwiching your kitchen garbage between layers of sawdust you greatly slow down its decay and prevent its putrefaction and odors, which attract flies. Depending on the size of your family, you can store from one to several days' worth of food wastes this way. When the bucket is full, take it to your compost pile and add it as a layer between the layers of alfalfa hay or other bulky material. With all the sawdust, the contents of the garbage bucket are a little heavy on the carbon, so you might want to sprinkle some blood meal or fish emulsion on this layer.

Keep covered

Sawdust
Food scraps
Sawdust
Food scraps
Sawdust

Three-Bin System for Composting Kitchen Scraps

This is a method we have perfected over the years. It makes composting kitchen scraps easy and fool proof. Start with any closed container. It's important that the bin have a cover and solid sides to keep out animals looking for a meal. We prefer three bins side by side, since they make turning and storage so convenient. There's a nice three-bin design described in *The Rodale Book of Composting* (see the Bibliography, page 443), which can be built in one day for a modest price or with scrap lumber. You'll also need about two bales of alfalfa hay as an ingredient of the pile. This supplies nitrogen and carbon and acts as a bulking agent to keep the pile fluffy while it absorbs excess water from the kitchen garbage.

We have even built compost bins out of bales of straw stacked like bricks (hay decays too quickly). If you can find rice straw, the bales will last a year or so before decaying. Straw bale bins have two major advantages: (1) They are quick and cheap to build, and (2) they have tremendous insulation value and the bales themselves will generate heat as they decay. This makes them great for cold winter areas. On the other hand, piles in hay bales tend to dry out faster than those in wood bins.

Start your three-bin compost system in the following way: In the first (or left) bin, place twigs or other coarse materials on the bottom as described above. On top of this, place a 6- to 8-inch layer of alfalfa hay and water until moist. Then take your kitchen scraps and scatter them over the alfalfa layer. Cover the garbage completely with another layer of alfalfa hay and sprinkle it. This is your first series of layers; kitchen garbage sandwiched between two layers of alfalfa hay. You can add your kitchen scraps every day, or store them for up to a week in buckets layered with sawdust (see the sidebar below).

As you add your layers of alfalfa hay and garbage every few days, the pile will begin to settle almost as fast as you pile it up. It won't get hot at first and may even attract a few flies and ants. This is natural in the early stages. Flies and ants are attracted to the smell of exposed food wastes. Ants are a sign of a dry pile, so keep the pile moist and the garbage covered with the hay and this problem will be reduced as the pile gets taller. When the pile is about 2 to 3 feet high, it should start to heat up, to about 110° to 120°F, from the nitrogen in the alfalfa hay. If you add blood meal or other nitrogen activators to the hay layers, you'll get temperatures up to 140°F and a faster rate of decay.

When the first bin is nearly full, turn it into the middle bin and begin a second pile in the third (or far right) bin. When this second pile is ready to turn, move the partially rotted middle bin back to the first bin, and turn the second pile into the second (or mid-dle) bin. Start a third pile in the now-empty third (or far right) bin.

All three bins should now contain compost in varying states of decay. From this point, it's easy to cascade the aged pile in bin 1 to a holding area for further decay, then move the rotted pile in the middle bin to the first bin, and so on. Remember, as they decay, compost piles shrink considerably (by as much as 50 percent). Although you have less volume to turn, each shovelful gets heavier as the pile collapses and condenses.

There are any number of ways to move the piles around. The above method is only one example. With practice you'll settle into a routine that works for you. We have used this method of composting kitchen wastes for several years with great success. Once you do, however, you'll be amazed at how easy it is to generate compost year-round and not have to wait for seasonal supplies of landscape trimmings. The best part is that the food you decay becomes the food you eat.

FIG. 3-7: Compost turning sequence

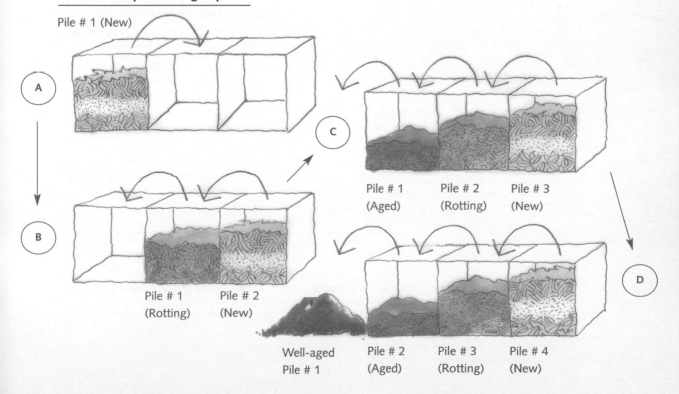

Pile # 1 (New)

A

B

C

D

Pile # 1 (Rotting) Pile # 2 (New)

Pile # 1 (Aged) Pile # 2 (Rotting) Pile # 3 (New)

Well-aged Pile # 1

Pile # 2 (Aged) Pile # 3 (Rotting) Pile # 4 (New)

Compost Pile Troubleshooting

A compost pile is really a small ecosystem, and when you fix one problem you often cause another one. For example, if your pile is not heating up, you may not have enough air. But that may be caused by too much water. Turning your pile will add air and help to dry out the composting mass, but you may also have to add a dry, absorbent bulking agent, like sawdust, peat moss, or straw, which is usually high in carbon. So you also have to add more nitrogen to readjust the C:N ratio. Alternatively, a cold pile may be caused by not enough nitrogen from green matter and/or manure, which is the same as too much carbon from brown matter. Here, all you have to do is to turn your pile while adding a strong nitrogen source like blood meal, fresh manure, or a chemical nitrogen fertilizer. With experience, it will be easy for you to tell exactly what is wrong with your pile if it doesn't decay properly. But remember, no matter what you do, your ultimate goal will always be to create ideal conditions for composting to take place; that is to balance the elements of carbon, nitrogen, air, and water. Don't allow too much or too little of any of these basic ingredients (see the table below for compost troubleshooting).

COMPOST TROUBLESHOOTING

PROBLEM	POSSIBLE CAUSE	SOLUTION
Pile not heating up	Not enough air.	Turn pile to aerate.
	Not enough moisture.	Turn pile, look for dry layers, and sprinkle.
	Too much moisture.	Turn pile, layering in dry bulking agent, or let it dry as you turn.
	Not enough nitrogen.	Add green matter, manure, blood meal, or other nitrogen sources.
	Pile too small (pile will not heat up if smaller than 3 feet square).	Gather more material and rebuild larger pile. Consider straw bale bins.
Pile smells putrid (like rotten eggs)	Lack of oxygen caused by too much water or compacted layers.	Turn pile, layering in dry bulking agent, or let it dry as you turn. Add twiggy layers within pile.
Pile smells like ammonia	Too much nitrogen and/or no gas-absorbing layer in pile, like soil or old compost.	Turn pile; add brown bulking agent and a little soil as layers.
Pile attracts flies	Exposed fresh kitchen scraps.	Keep meat, greasy foods, and dairy products out of the pile; bury other leftovers under soil and brown material as it is added to the pile.
	Too much nitrogen. Flies are attracted to ammonia, so see also "Pile Smells Like Ammonia."	Turn pile; add brown bulking agent and a little soil as layers.
Pile attracts ants	Exposed kitchen scraps, especially at edges of pile.	Keep meat, greasy foods, and dairy products out of the pile; bury other leftovers under soil and brown material as it is added to the pile.
	Pile is too dry. Ants are one of the best indicators of too little water.	Turn pile, look for dry layers, and sprinkle.

Using Compost

You've spent time and energy carefully nurturing the pile of yard and household wastes into sweet-smelling compost, and you want to be certain that it is used to best advantage. It needs to be parceled out carefully so that your soil and plants can gain from its many benefits. It's one thing to make compost, and quite another thing to know when and how to use it properly.

Unlike chemical fertilizers, compost does not produce instant results; its effects can't be seen in a single season. But if you apply compost season after season, both plants and soil will benefit in ways not possible with chemical fertilizers. Compost gives health, momentum, and sustainability to soil fertility.

When to Apply Compost

The best time to apply compost is when it's finished. But "finished" means different things to different gardeners. Compost is so valuable that we often push it into the soil before it has had a chance to completely decay and achieve its state of optimum use. Unfinished compost can retard the germination and growth of some plants, and in certain cases, can spread plant diseases. In our experience, there is no substitute for time. Some books describe making compost in as little as 14 days: Simply chop up your wastes, turn the pile like crazy, and presto: instant compost. Frankly, we find this idea rather silly. After years of making and using compost, we have found that, up to a point, the older the compost is, the better it is. By containing, activating, and grinding up your wastes, you can certainly speed things up. But what you speed up is not the production of humus, but the production of a stable material that can decay further into humus *in the soil;* this is a very important and often overlooked point. Once your compost loses the appearance of the materials that made it and begins to smell like soil, it enters a second phase of decay. Modern researchers call this phase the "suppressive" phase, because during this period compost decomposes further from a material high in sugars, favored by many disease microbes, to one high in starches, favored by the beneficial microbes that consume them. This is why we always recommend to people that when their compost first looks and smells finished, they should store it for a few more months before they use it. A cache of well-aged compost is a priceless resource for the kitchen gardener.

Mid-fall to early winter is perhaps the best time to add compost to your soil. By spring, it will have decayed enough in the soil to benefit early plantings of vegetables. You can also apply compost in late winter or early spring as you work the soil for the upcoming season. With soil temperatures below 50°F, soil compost decays very slowly, so time your additions accordingly.

During the growing season from spring to fall, compost can be added as a side-dressing for growing vegetables. It is especially valuable as a mulch or combined with phosphorous fertilizers because the compost renders phosphorous more available.

How Much Compost to Apply

Many gardening books tell you that you can't have too much organic matter in the soil. In our experience, this claim is quite misleading. Garden soils that are supercharged with organic matter can often tie up nutrients and lead to plant deficiencies. Speaking very generally, you want about 1 to 3 percent of organic matter (by weight) in sandy soils and 3 to 6 percent of organic matter in clay soils. Once you get to this level, then the regular addition of properly aged organic matter will keep you at this point. So, the answer to the question, "How much compost do I add to my garden?" depends on whether you are trying to increase organic matter or keep it at an optimum amount, and whether you have sandy or clay soils.

A useful but very general rule of thumb is

to apply the equivalent of 10 tons per acre per year of well-aged compost to clay soils and about 20 tons per year to sandy soils. This will keep you at an optimum amount of organic matter. If you are trying to increase your organic matter content, double these amounts. For convenience, you can think of each 10 tons per acre of aged compost as being equal to about one large wheelbarrowful (100 pounds) per 200 square feet, or one 5-gallon bucket per 20 square feet per year. In southern or warmer climates or areas of high rainfall, organic matter burns off more quickly, and you may have to double these amounts just to stay even. Remember, the addition of compost is a continuous process: The combination of hungry plants and regular irrigation greatly hastens the natural breakdown of humus. Most of the time you're adding compost just to keep your organic matter constant. Good health, ours or the soil's, requires constant tending.

VERMICOMPOSTING

Earthworms are amazing animals. They can consume their weight in soil and organic matter each day. During this prodigious eating, organic matter passes through their guts where it is ground up into tiny pieces, decayed further by microbes living there, inoculated with calcium, and passed out as manure. The manure, or "castings," of earthworms is the richest form of compost known. It contain five to ten times more available nitrogen, phosphorous, potassium and micronutrients than the soil the worms eat. It is much closer to humus than even aged compost.

Earthworms are found in almost every soil. You can often find them in compost piles burrowing and wiggling their way through the heap and liberating plant nutrients wherever they go. They usually enter from the soil beneath an open pile, but they can also enter a contained bin from soil attached to the roots of weeds. It is not surprising that people have devised a variety of ways to culture earthworms and in the process make a superior compost at an accelerated rate. Using earthworms to make compost is called vermicomposting.

Vermicomposting is a simple, efficient composting method that appeals to those who have limited space and still want to compost their food wastes. Getting started requires only a lidded container, the proper species of worm, some bedding for the worms to live in, and food scraps. Animal manures and supplemental foods like plant meals and grains can also be used.

The Right Worm

Red worms (or manure worms), not earthworms or "night crawlers," are the worms of choice for vermicomposting. The two best worms for composting are red worms (*Lumbricus terrestris*) and brandling worms (*Eisenia foetida*). Compost worms thrive in areas with high organic matter content, unlike the gray earthworms, which prefer to live in cool, undisturbed soil. Compost worms will naturally colonize a compost or manure pile as well as leaf litter under trees.

There are several ways to get a starter batch of red worms: You can dig them from a friend's colony; order them through the mail (see pages 451–453); or dig them from an old manure or compost pile. You can also attract native red worms by simply placing a bale of alfalfa hay on the ground for several weeks. Where the bottom of the bale rests on the top of the soil, you should find large numbers of red worms. One to two pounds of red worms (about 1,000 to 2,000 worms) are needed to start an average-sized home vermicompost colony. Red worms reproduce rapidly, and in a well-maintained system, they can live from one to five years.

The Container

Almost any wood or plastic container will hold red worms, but to work properly they need the following features:

- A tight-fitting lid and a bottom to protect the worms from weather and worm-eating animals like burrowing rodents. Drainage holes in the bottom keep the bedding material from getting soggy. This is important, since red worms can drown. The lid also protects worms from the light and the drying heat of the sun, and it keeps flies at bay.

- A depth of 12 to 18 inches. Red worms move to the surface at night to feed and go back down in the morning, sort of like ocean plankton. Anything deeper than 18 inches is unnecessary since this is the extent of their vertical movement.

- A general rule of thumb is to allow 1 square foot of surface area for each pound of food wastes added per week. For example, a 2 by 4-foot box (8 square feet) can accommodate 8 pounds of food wastes per week, the amount typically generated by 2 to 3 adults. A wooden box is preferable to plastic or metal because it absorbs and drains moisture better. But you can start your vermicompost operation in a plastic laundry tub, a tin bucket, a packing crate, and so on before you build something more permanent.

The Bedding

All sorts of bedding material can be used: leaves, peat moss, shredded newspaper—all provide worms with a damp, well-aerated place to live. The bedding material should be bulky and high in carbon, to provide a substance in which to bury your food wastes. Straw tends to mat down, so it should be mixed with other things. You can even tear cardboard into strips and use it. All dry bedding material should be soaked in water overnight before being added to the box. For example, we take bales of peat moss and soak them in 50-gallon drums before adding them as bedding to our 4 × 8-foot bins.

Together the bedding and the food scraps are a balanced medium of carbon and nitrogen, just like a regular compost pile. The air is added by the worms' activity. In a few months, the worms will eat their way through both materials and convert them into incredible compost.

Starting the Colony

Start by immersing the bedding material in water until it is thoroughly wet. Mix a small amount of soil into the moist bedding. Worms need grit from soil for their gizzards, the part of their intestinal tract that grinds up organic matter, like that of a chicken. Fill the container about half full with the bedding. Next, add your first supply of kitchen wastes, then add the worms, and top the bin off with a fresh layer of moist bedding. Put the lid on, place the container in a cool, accessible spot, and wait for the results.

Maintaining the Colony

As you add your kitchen waste, it's important to cover it with moist bedding material to prevent infestations of fruit flies. Seasoned vermicomposters keep a wet layer of newspaper on the top of the kitchen scraps. Since it's not always convenient to make bedding when you are adding the garbage, it helps to have some moist paper or pieces of burlap always ready in a storage container near the colony. For example, the next time you are ready to recycle your newspaper, tear it up, soak it in water, wring it out, and store it in a plastic trash bag placed next to the worm bin.

Red worms will eat most anything: fruit and vegetable scraps, grains, and breads. We've even had large colonies thrive on coffee grounds from a local coffeehouse. Some things, like onions and citrus peels, may have to undergo bacterial decay before they will

FIG. 3-8: Vermicompost

1. Push the worm compost to one side of the box.

2. Add fresh bedding to the empty half

3. Put kitchen scraps in fresh bedding only. Worms will move to the food side.

4. Remove the earthy compost & add fresh bedding to the cleared side.

be eaten, but they will be eaten. As with regular composting, though, stay away from meat, dairy products, and fatty foods. These break down slowly and attract unwanted wildlife.

Bury food scraps in holes dug into the bedding; don't spread it over the top. You want to keep the scraps covered with bedding at all times to avoid flies. Rotate food-burial sites evenly throughout the box. If you go away for a few days or even weeks, the worm colony will just slow down for a while.

If for some reason you are short on kitchen scraps, red worms will eat any nutrient-rich food like soy meal, cornmeal, animal manure, or chicken feed.

Other animals may set up house in the colony. Sow bugs also eat organic matter and contribute to the end result, so you can ignore them. Centipedes and black ground beetles eat red worms, however, so they should be removed.

Harvesting the Castings

After about 4 months, the castings should be ready to harvest. The easiest way to do this is to push all the material to one side of the box. Add fresh bedding to the remaining space and begin burying food only in this new material. Over the next month or so, the worms will migrate into the new material with the food. Now remove the old material and sift it through a $^1/_4$- or $^1/_2$-inch screen. Pull out any worms and large chunks of garbage, add fresh bedding to the empty side and begin adding food to it there.

Some vermicomposters simply dump the colony onto a flat surface in the sun, and mold it into a cone. As the sun heats the cone, worms migrate downward. After a few days, the top of the cone is harvested for its castings, and the rest of the cone, which is now full of red worms, is returned to the container to inoculate the next colony.

Using the Castings

The harvested castings will be dark and crumbly and should smell like good soil or aged compost. It is difficult to make enough earthworm castings to add to your garden soil. However, the castings make a mild, balanced fertilizer that is gentle enough to use in potting mixes, for seeds and transplants, and as a side-dressing for vegetables. It also makes an excellent compost tea. (See pages 77–79.)

GREEN MANURES

A green manure is any plant that is grown and then dug into the soil for its nutrients and organic matter. As early as 300 B.C., Greek naturalists wrote of "the ability of beans to reinvigorate the soil and manure the farm land," and noted that "beans and peas should be planted in light soil, not so much for their own value, but for the good that they do subsequent crops." The Greeks knew nothing of the bacteria growing on the roots of these legumes, which converted nitrogen from the air into a form that plants could use, but they saw the results.

Green manures are one of the most efficient ways to add organic matter to the soil. They are a fast and easy way to build up the soil, but they also have many other benefits, such as attracting beneficial insects (see page 171) and bringing up subsoil nutrients (see page 128). Although we tend to think of them as part of agriculture, it's entirely possible to use green manures in small garden plots, raised beds, and even containers. We encourage all gardeners to experiment with green manures and native grasses. Used properly, green manures are one of the most effective of all garden practices.

Green Manures for the Home Garden

For the home gardener, we can divide green manures into three groups: (1) cereals and grasses, (2) legumes, and (3) "other" crops.

- Cereals and grasses are valuable green manures because they grow rapidly and produce a lot of organic matter. Most grasses have extensive fibrous roots that pull a lot of nutrients from the soil and open it up to water and air. Sorghum or Sudangrass is a fabulous summer annual that grows quickly and produces lots of plant biomass. Common cereals like oats, wheat, and rye make great green manures, but the home gardener should also explore the potential of using grasses native to their area.

- Legumes are part of the Fabaceae family, which includes peas, beans, alfalfa, vetches, and clovers. The roots of legumes contain bacteria that convert nitrogen from the air to a form that plants can use. Some of the most popular legume green manures for home gardens are the vetches. They produce lots of organic matter, choke out weeds, and attract a variety of beneficial insects. Vetches need to be dug in before they go to seed, since they can become invasive weeds. They are usually planted with cereals, which support their upright viny growth. The sweet clover, *Melilotus alba* (white) and *M. officinalis* (yellow), have long taproots (like carrots) that open soils and "mine" the deeper soils for nutrients.

- Other plants: Almost any plant can be thought of as a green manure if it has lots of roots, grows quickly, and produces bulk. Sunflowers, mustard, kale, and *Phacelia* (bluebells) have all been used by farmers and gardeners. Our favorite "other" crop is the annual buckwheat *Fagopyrum*. It is a fast-growing, warm-weather annual that has the added advantage of attracting a variety of beneficial insects to its blossoms (see page 129).

Not all traditional green manures are suitable for the home garden. Many of the slow-growing clovers and perennials are difficult to fit into the rapid rotations and seasonal plantings typical of the kitchen garden. The green manures listed on page 129 are ones that we have grown and used over the years. Most of them are available in feed stores or from the suppliers listed on page 447–450.

BENEFITS OF GREEN MANURES

• Green manures are a very economical source of organic matter. Unlike animal manures, which are often hard to find or inconvenient to load up and bring to the garden, green manures make organic matter right in place. All you need is seed.

• When they are overwintered, green manures become a cover crop that protects the soil surface from erosion and harsh weather. Gardeners work hard to build up their soils, and green manures help to protect them.

• Green manures act as an insulating blanket and keep the soil warmer in winter, cooler in summer. This greatly encourages the activities of earthworms and other soil life.

• Many green manures have extensive root systems that reach deep into the subsoil, absorbing and bringing up valuable nutrients into their plant tissue. When the green manure is dug back into the soil or composted, these nutrients become available to shallow-rooted vegetables that would otherwise not be able to reach them.

• Certain green manures in the bean family (legumes) have the ability to capture nitrogen from the air and convert it into a form that other plants can use. Common green-manure legumes include peas, clovers, bell beans, vetches, and alfalfa.

• Digging in green manures can be timed to coincide with normal soil preparation activities in spring and fall.

• Green manures take up space and shade the soil. Many of them are good at suppressing or choking out weeds.

• Some green manures, notably vetches, clovers, bell beans, and buckwheat, attract a variety of beneficial insects to their flowers and stem nectaries (see page 171).

When Do You Dig in Green Manures?

This is not always an easy decision, since there are several considerations:

1. As plants grow, their carbon-to-nitrogen ratios change. Young plants are high in nitrogen and low in carbon. Mature plants in full bloom, however, are higher in carbon. When they are dug into the ground, they can provide the fiber for making humus, but they can also tie up nitrogen for a while. It is important that green manures not be allowed to become too mature and woody, since this can slow down decomposition considerably.

   The best time to dig in most green manures is just prior to the first flower bud ("pre-bloom"), when the carbon-to-nitrogen ratio is nearly balanced. Big, bulky plants, like bell beans and sorghum, should be dug in when they are knee- to waist-high.

2. Some green manures, like vetches and bell beans, can become very fibrous or viny and difficult to dig in as they get older. Vetches and grasses can also turn into invasive weeds, so it is important not to let them go to seed.

3. Annual buckwheat, bell beans, and some vetches all attract beneficial insects. They should be dug or tilled in gradually or in strips to give the insects time and opportunity to find other flower food.

SOME GREEN MANURES FOR THE KITCHEN GARDEN

CROP	SEED RATE (lbs per 1,000 sq ft)	WHEN TO SOW	HOW TO DIG-IN*	COMMENTS
GRASSES AND CEREALS				
Annual ryegrass (Secale)	4–8	Spring, fall (mild winters only)	1 or 2	Good winter cover in mild winter areas; not cold hardy. Good weed suppression. Likes lime.
Barley (Hordeum)	1–2	Spring, fall	1 or 2	Cold and drought hardy. Lots of fibrous roots.
Oats (Avena sativa)	2–3	Spring	2	Less cold hardy than ryegrass. More tolerant of wet soils than barley.
Ryegrass (Lolium multiflorum)	1–2	Spring, fall	1 or 2	Fast growing. Best mixed with annual legumes.
Sudan grass/sorghum (Sorghum bicolor)	1–2	Spring, summer	2	Vigorous summer green manure. Suppresses weeds. Needs warm, dry soils; dig in when waist-high.
Winter wheat (Triticum)	1	Fall	2	Best for cold-winter areas.
Zorro fescue (Festuca)	$1/2$–1	Spring, fall (mild winters only)	1 or 2	Fast, low-growing; drought and cold hardy. Great for dry, sandy soils.
LEGUMES				
Austrian peas (Lathyrus hirsutas)	2–5	Spring, fall (mild winters only)	3	Likes neutral pH. Stands heavy frosts. Grows well in mild winter areas. Dislikes heat and humidity. Smothers weeds.
Bell, horse, fava bean (Vicia faba)	2–5	Spring, fall (mild winters only)	3	Great for gardens. Tolerates acid soils. Makes large stalks, so dig in before it gets too large. Attracts beneficial insects.
Clover, crimson (Trifolium incarnatum)	$1/2$–1	Spring, fall (mild winters only)	2	Tolerates shade. Good for mild winter areas. Needs lime. Can be invasive.
Clover, sweet white (Melilotus alba)	$1/2$–1	Spring, fall	1	Annual with deep taproots good for breaking up heavy soils. Birds don't eat emerging seedlings.
Clover, rose (Trifolium hirtum)	$1/2$–1	Spring, fall (mild winters only)	1 or 2	Very drought tolerant. Tolerates poor soils but needs good drainage. Grows well with Zorro fescue.
Crotularia (Crotularia juncea)	1–2	Late spring, summer	2	Grows 5 inches in 70 days. Tolerates acid, poor soils. Prefers warmth, but grows in cool weather.
Vetch, common (Vicia sativa)	1–3	Spring, fall (mild winters only)	1 or 3	Common vetch has some cold tolerance; more than purple, but less than hairy.
Vetch, hairy (Vicia villosa)	1–3	Spring, fall (mild winters only)	1 or 3	Most winter-hardy vetch; best sown in fall with winter rye or wheat.
Vetch, purple (Vicia atropurpurea)	1–3	Spring, fall (mild winters only)	1 or 3	Least winter hardy, but most vigorous of the vetches.
OTHERS				
Buckwheat, annual (Fagopyrum esculentum)	1–2	Late spring, summer	1 or 2	Matures in 40 days. Crowds out weeds. Flowers attract beneficial insects. Fixes calcium.

*How to Dig In: 1 = spade or rototill; 2 = mow, then till; 3 = cut and compost tops, till in stubble.

How Do You Dig in Green Manures?

Rototillers are quite useful for digging in green manures, but not everyone has a rototiller, and in small gardens or framed beds rototilling is not always possible. If the green manure is young and small, you can usually dig it in with a shovel. You can also chop the tops with a power weeder, hoe, shovel, scythe, or machete, and then either dig them in, or gather them up for the compost bin. Remember that a large part of a plant's organic matter is in the roots, and these can be left to decay naturally in the soil, especially over winter.

As an example, this is how we dig in annual buckwheat. When first plants bloom, we dig 75 percent of the plants into the soil and leave 25 percent to attract beneficial insects. In the dug-in area, we sow another crop of buckwheat. As the remaining 25 percent of the crop goes to seed, we dig it in and replant with more buckwheat. In this way, organic matter is tilled in gradually, *and* there is always a source of flowers for beneficial insects. This process of replanting and tilling is repeated until 3 weeks before the first fall frost, at which time all of the buckwheat is dug in and the area planted in either winter vegetables or a winter green manure like bell beans, vetch, or winter wheat.

Another way to incorporate green manures is to cut the tops to the ground and leave them as a mulch on the soil surface for a few weeks or even over winter. This gives the plant tissues plenty of air and time to start decaying before you dig them in. It's also a handy way to deal with overmature green manures with tough stems.

When you dig or till green manures into the soil, it's important not to dig them in too deeply, especially in heavy soils. Organic matter needs plenty of air to decay properly, and when it's buried deeply in the soil, it decays very slowly.

Examples of Green Manure Plantings

In the home garden, green manures are useful in two ways. First, they are good to grow in those spots that you may not get to for a few years. They can improve the soil, reduce weeds, and generally get the area ready for those tasty vegetables to come. Second, green manures can be used as part of your seasonal rotation to clean and improve garden soils already in cultivation. Even in the smallest of gardens, green manures are a valuable addition to your landscape. Some of our favorite seasonal combinations for cool, temperate climates are described below.

In the Garden

- **Late spring/summer:** Start by planting successive crops of annual buckwheat every 30 to 40 days until a month before first frost. We let the buckwheat go completely to flower because the blossoms attract beneficial insects. Also, buckwheat stays fairly succulent, even as plants mature. We dig them in strips and plant anew in the dug-up earth. This encourages beneficial insects to hang around the area. If your buckwheat is in beds, just dig half the bed in at a time.

- **Fall:** In the fall we plant beds in combinations of vetch and winter wheat. The wheat grows very quickly and produces strong stems for the vetch to cling to. We plant a few beds just in bell beans. These beans attract beneficial insects, and the stalks of the mature plants make a great foundation for compost piles. The roots are dug in or left to decay over winter.

Other green manure combinations are red clover and ryegrass or vetch and ryegrass. The legume-grass combination is very efficient. The grasses mine the shallow soil with their extensive fibrous roots, and the legumes fix nitrogen and bring up nutrients from deep in the soil. White and yellow clovers are also valuable green manures for fall because, they grow quickly and their deep roots readily break up compacted, heavy soils.

Outside the Garden

• **Late spring/summer:** Our favorite summer green manures for marginal areas are crotularia and sudan grass. Crotularia, the most vigorous summer legume, will grow 5 to 6 feet within 2 months. It fixes lots of nitrogen and produces an abundance of organic matter. Sow crotularia in rows 2 feet apart since plants tend to smother one another with their extensive growth. Sudan grass or sorghum is the best summer green manure for producing organic matter and choking weeds. It also suppresses many soil nematodes. It goes to seed in 75 to 80 days, but we dig it in at about 50 days before it becomes mature with seeds and fibrous stems.

• **Fall:** White sweet clover is an excellent fall green manure for marginal areas because it has a deep taproot that can help break up compacted soils while adding nitrogen. Other annual clovers are also useful. Zorro fescue grass is a low-growing aggressive grass native to California. It has a massive fibrous root system that puts lots of organic matter into the soil very quickly.

MULCHES

It's not hard to imagine how someone discovered the wonders of mulch. Just go out into the woods and look at the ground. You'll see thin piles of organic materials everywhere: leaves, grasses, twigs, and branches. This is nature's way of enriching and protecting topsoil. The cloak of organic debris—or "mulch"—is part of a recycling process, a way station for nutrients on their path from living plants down through the life of the soil and back up through plants again.

You can see how mulch works by digging through layers of leaf litter, nature's finest mulch. As you poke down through the pile, the brown surface leaves soon become darker and broken up into tiny pieces that don't look like leaves at all. This is leaf mold. At the bottom, near the surface of the soil, the leaf mold has decayed and crumbled into dark, rich, fluffy material called "duff." As it decays further, duff settles into the soil where it is converted to humus by soil life. Humus gives nutrients to plants, and the cycle continues.

Benefits of Mulches

Mulch does more than just feed the soil. It also protects it from extremes of weather and losses from erosion. In the crisscrossing of their materials, organic mulches tend to form small air pockets. This makes them a natural insulator and explains why mulches keep the soil cool in summer and warm in winter. Mulches also absorb water. They can soak it up during wet weather and evaporate it away during drought, so that the soil stays evenly moist. Overall, mulch evens out weather extremes in the root zone, a condition all vegetables prefer.

The environment created by mulch also attract earthworms, which stay deep under bare soils to avoid the hot, dry conditions above. But under a mulched soil, they will come to the surface to enjoy the cool, moist carpet under the mulch as they feed on the duff and work it into the topsoil.

Some gardeners use mulch simply because it keeps the weeds down, especially annual weeds. Perennial weeds with deep roots or spreading stems are difficult to control with mulch, unless you really pile it on. As you weed an area, mulch over it. Soon, you will turn weeding into mulching.

For summer gardeners, mulch is a must. It keeps fruit off the ground and conserves soil water during the heat of the day. Mulch is great around tomatoes, pepper, squash, melons, bush beans and cucumbers. Resting on the mulch, fruit are less likely to rot. Also, constant soil moisture is essential for growing healthy, attractive tomatoes, peas, squash, and other fruited vegetables.

One final thought that often gets overlooked: Plants grown in mulch are not spattered by rain or hose water. This not only keeps plants clean, but it reduces some diseases that are transferred onto plants by splashing water.

BENEFITS OF MULCH

- Mulch conserves soil water. It acts as a barrier between the soil and the air. This reduces the evaporation of water from the soil.

- Mulch absorbs and stores water. It keeps roots moist during dry times and soaks up extra water during rainy times.

- Mulch tempers the soil environment. The air pockets in mulch insulate the soil against extremes of heat and cold so that the soil temperature is more constant than the air temperature.

- Mulch shades out weeds, which reduces garden work and water loss from the soil.

- Mulch helps reduce soil erosion. If the soil is covered, it's hard to wash away.

- Mulch keeps fruit off the ground. Fruit resting on mulch is less likely to get diseases.

- Mulch reduces splattering of disease spores and keeps soil off plants. Splattered soil is one way some diseases get onto plants.

Drawbacks of Mulch

Mulch can have its drawbacks. Sometimes you need to forgo it completely, use it with caution, or use it only during a specific time of the year.

- **Some mulches contain weed seeds.** Always treat your mulch as a source of weed seeds. Hay and spent weeds are primary culprits, but weed seeds are everywhere in mulch, so mulcher beware.

- **Mulch can keep the soil too cool or moist.** If your early spring is cold and wet, you may have to withhold mulch until the soil warms and dries a bit. Early spring mulches can often cause problems by slowing the natural warming of the soil.

- **Mulch can cause vegetables to rot.** Some vegetables are sensitive to winter moisture and may rot and die if water collects around their crowns (where stems and roots join). Keep mulches away from the base of plants whenever possible to avoid this problem.

- **Some mulches can rob the soil of nitrogen.** Some *fresh* woody mulches like sawdust and wood chips can use up the soil's nitrogen while they are decomposing. Eventually things will stabilize as the bottom mulch layers begin to decay at the soil surface, but in the beginning it could be a problem. If you see the yellowing of older leaves on plants growing in wood mulch, give them a dose of liquid nitrogen like fish emulsion, manure tea, or nitrate solution. This will also help the mulch break down faster.

- **Some mulches attract pests.** Mice and other rodents often burrow in deep, coarse mulches. Straw and hay can also become a refuge for snails and earwigs. Make it a habit to look through your mulch now and then and see what else grows there besides your plants.

TYPES OF MULCHES

Almost any material can be used as a mulch: large flat stones, cardboard, newspaper or even aluminum foil. But most practical gar-

den mulches are made of either plastics or organic materials. Each has its own advantages and disadvantages, so that they can often be used together in creative ways.

EFFECTS OF DIFFERENT MULCHES ON SOIL

MULCH	COMMENTS

FIG. 3-9: Mulches: The effects of three kinds of mulch on soil temperature & moisture.

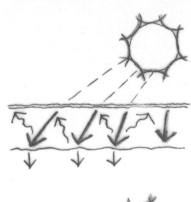

CLEAR PLASTIC MULCH

Sun shines through plastic, which traps heat, and warms the soil; plastic also traps evaporating water; warm, moist soil fosters early growth in cool seasons. Can encourage weeds. Dries quickly and protects fruit from rotting on the ground.

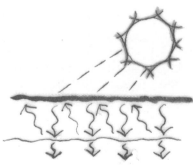

BLACK PLASTIC MULCH

Sun heats black plastic, which warms the soil, but not as much as clear plastic. Shades out weeds. Protects fruits from rotting on the ground. Breaks down faster than clear plastic.

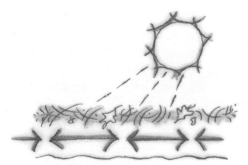

ORGANIC MULCH

Blocks sunlight from soil and keeps weeds down. Acts as an insulator when dry and as a water reservoir when wet. Protects soils against sudden temperature changes. Attracts earthworms and adds humus to the soil.

Plastics

Plastic mulches can't help enrich the soil, but they do have other uses. Clear plastic transmits sunlight to the soil, so it warms it considerably. This is why some gardeners use plastic mulches in the spring to speed up their early season vegetable seeds and then switch to organic mulches. Plastic mulch warms the soil early, and the organic mulch keeps it warm there the rest of the season.

Most clear plastic films will last for less than a year on top of the ground. Greenhouse films will last longer because they contain chemicals that prolong the plastic. Winds can flap plastic film to shreds overnight, so be sure your plastic mulch is secured at the edges with rocks, soil, or landscape staples.

Black plastic keeps light from reaching the soil, so it's good at keeping down weeds. It transfers less heat to the soil, and at a slower rate, than clear plastic. It also breaks down faster than the clear type.

All plastics conserve soil moisture, but they also keep outside water from getting in. You can perforate the plastic, and that of course allows weeds to grow through the openings. Some gardeners water by placing drip irrigation systems under the plastic mulch.

Organic Mulches

Organic mulches can be divided into three groups: tree products (bark, sawdust, and wood chips), plant materials, and aged compost. The value of tree products as a mulch depends on their size and how much nitrogen they contain. Small pieces with leaves or plant resins mixed in will break down quickly and make a great fine-textured mulch. One of the best is pulverized bark. It's not readily available in the fresh state, but you can buy it in bags at nurseries. It's best to age it a bit before applying it. The plant resins in the bark seem to provide enough nitrogen so that it decays fairly well all by itself.

Wood chips come in all sizes. Some are mostly brown and woody. Others have lots of leaves attached, and these are the ones to look for. More green means more nitrogen and faster, more even decay. Fresh sawdust should always be amended with nitrogen and aged before using. You can also mix the sawdust with coarsely sifted alfalfa hay to speed up the aging. This combination makes an excellent mulch. Sawdust from pines and other conifers decomposes slower than sawdust from hardwoods.

Among plant materials, one of the best mulches is alfalfa hay. It is widely available at reduced prices as "sour" hay, which has been rained on and is no longer suitable for livestock. A bale of alfalfa peels off conveniently from the ends into sections that can be laid directly on the ground. Try sifting alfalfa hay loosely through a $1/2$-inch screen. This is fine enough to spread amongst close-spaced plants while not giving snails and slugs the coarse, airy retreat they like. Sifted hay breaks down very quickly, and is a great way to add organic matter to your soil. As with all organic mulches, you need to watch out for weed seeds. You can use straw as a mulch, but it is a little different than hay. Straw is the stubble that remains after a grain has been top-cut, so it doesn't have as much nitrogen as hay, and takes longer to break down.

Leaves are an excellent mulch. Large flat leaves may mat down, whereas curly leaves make a more aerated mulch. Hulls from processed beans and grains are usually too light and fluffy. They just blow away. But they do work well if you mix them in with hay and other coarse materials. One convenient way to use plant materials for mulch is to simply cut your green manures or cover crops at an early stage and leave the felled plants on the ground (see page 130). The mulch can then be pulled aside so large seedlings can be planted directly through it.

Small twigs and branches from evergreen trees make an excellent winter mulch to protect and hold soil until spring. Your discarded Christmas tree can be cut up to make mulch for the rest of the winter.

SOME ORGANIC MULCHES

MATERIAL	ADVANTAGE(S)	DISADVANTAGE(S)	COMMENTS
Tree Products			
Bark, pulverized	Very attractive. Fine texture breaks down faster than bark chips.	Very acidic. Not widely available.	Apply 3 to 5 inches, may have enough resins to begin decay without added nitrogen
Chips from tree top-growth	Looks good. Contains nitrogen in leaves for rapid breakdown.	May contain black walnut or eucalyptus clippings.	Apply 4 to 5 inches, available from trimmers. Not all chips are alike.
Chips from bark	Looks good. Contains nitrogen in plant resins. Moderately quick to break down.	Expensive to buy. Fresh lots can have some plant toxins that inhibit growth for a while.	Apply 3 to 5 inches, available in landscape supply and lumberyards. Very popular mulch.
Chips from wood	Looks good. Permanent mulch for paths and walkways. Very slow to break down.	Contains little nitrogen. May rob soil of nitrogen at the start.	Apply 2 to 3 inches, available in landscape supply and lumberyards.
Sawdust	Easily available from lumberyards and cabinet shops.	Very high in carbon, so treat like wood chips. Can mat down when wet or blow away when dry.	Keep away from base of plants to lessen crown rot; get it aged or add extra N to hasten decay. Hardwood sawdust rots faster than pine or cedar.
Plant Materials			
Branches, evergreen	Widely available.	Some parts don't break down in a season.	Good as an overwintering mulch on next spring's plots.
Grass clippings	Widely available. Breaks down quickly.	Can mat down. Avoid grasses treated with herbicides.	Apply no more than 1 inch. Best mixed with other mulch materials as nitrogen source.
Hay, alfalfa	Not available everywhere. Contains nitrogen. Breaks down quickly.	Air pockets can house snails, slugs, earwigs. May contain weed seeds.	Apply 3 to 4 inches. Hay contains flower grains, unlike straw, so has better mix of carbon and nitrogen.
Hay, tall grass	Widely available. Contains less nitrogen. Moderately quick to break down.	Air pockets can house snails, slugs, earwigs. May contain weed seeds.	Apply 3 to 4 inches. Watch for weeds.
Hulls of buckwheat, cocoa, coffee beans, cotton, peanuts, etc.	Readily available in some areas.	Can mat down when wet, blow away when dry.	Best to mix with coarser mulches—improves their quality. Peanuts high in nitrogen very light so wind can scatter—keep moist.
Leaves, deciduous or "fall" trees	Nutrient-rich leaves feed earthworms, add organic matter quickly. One of the best mulches.	Flat leaves like maple may mat down if kept sodden. The leaves of some plants may have toxins that slow growth.	Apply 3 to 4 inches.
Leaves, pine needles	Light, usually free of weed seeds. Absorb little moisture. Don't pack down.	Slows down water penetration. Decay very slowly. Quite acidic.	Older needles less toxic to young plants. Watch acidity.
Paper (newsprint, cardboard, no color)	Readily available; can add trace minerals to soil.	Sheets may pack down and slowly decay. Wind can scatter. Slightly alkaline.	Use 5 or 6 pages or 4 to 6 inches of shredded (better) paper. Hold down with rocks.
Peat moss	Clean and free of weed seeds.	Expensive, acidic, very absorbent, and will not easily penetrate soil.	Good for improving clay or alkaline soils; not for general use.
Straw, grass	Easily available in some areas.	See "Hay, tall grass."	See "Hay, tall grass."
Straw, rice	Slow decay. Suitable for paths and walkways.	Not widely available. Very slow to decay due to silicon in tissue.	Best for permanent paths.
Compost			
Aged (more than 8 months)	Fastest way to get stabilized organic matter into the soil from a mulch.	Need to plan ahead to get aged compost, but it's well worth it.	Should have a sufficient heating period followed by at least 8 months of further decay.

Actually, there are mulch materials all around us. Each region of the country has its own locally available products. For example, you might have in your area apple and grape pomace, spent hops from microbreweries, wood chips and sawdust from lumber mills, rice hulls and commercial compost from chicken farms, or urban green wastes. Your quest for the perfect mulch begins at home.

Use fine-textured mulch around shallow-rooted vegetables, like onions and lettuce, where cultivation can harm roots. Examples include leaf mold; coarsely sifted alfalfa hay; bean and grain hulls; aged shredded bark, sawdust, or compost. These finer mulch materials are really useful among dense plantings.

Tips for Applying Mulches

You can use mulches in a variety of ways. Plastic mulches heat the soil early in the season and help you get that quick spring crop. Later in the season, after the soil has warmed up, remove the plastic and use organic mulches to retain the heat and keep the soil evenly moist the rest of the season.

The best time for applying organic mulches is in the late spring, after the soil has warmed. If you put them on too soon, they can keep cold soil from warming up. Place your mulch around the plant's drip zone. For most vegetables this is very near the stem. Try to keep mulch from touching the plant stem to avoid rots and diseases.

There is little point in mulching a dry soil, so water it thoroughly first. Think of your soil as a water reservoir with a top on it called mulch. In arid climates, mulching can be an important way to conserve water.

Mulch is more of a process than a finished product. It is continually decomposing at the soil interface, and it needs to be replenished. Make it one of your regular garden chores to stockpile mulch materials since mulch is probably the most beneficial way to add organic matter to your soil.

MANAGING YOUR GARDEN HUMUS

As we have seen, there are four major ways that kitchen gardeners can add organic matter to their soil: (1) compost, (2) vermicompost, (3) green manures, and (4) mulches. Those with yards and gardens can compost their home wastes in a variety of ways, grow green manures to dig into the soil, or pile on the mulch to protect and feed the topsoil. Even people living in apartments can make compost in earthworm cultures and use it to feed their container vegetables. All of these organic materials will become humus if converted properly. Compost and green manures can be added to the soil or used as a mulch, which will decay into humus, while the humus will retain nutrients and buffer the soil against extremes of weather and toxins. In the end, humus serves as a catalyst for the conversion of death into life.

The Basics of Ecological Cooking

Just as the life of the soil is based on ecological soil nourishment, vibrant kitchen garden cooking begins with the resourceful use of vegetables. In the gardener's kitchen, almost every part of a vegetable can be used in a variety of ways—whether as scraps to enrich the compost pile or the basic ingredients in stocks, which become the building blocks of nourishing, flavorful meals. A prime example of ecological cooking is the use of water, kitchen scraps, or fresh vegetables and the browning reaction to make stock.

MAKING STOCKS AND SOUPS

Water is just as important in cooking vegetables as it is in growing them. In 1746 M. Parmentier, a famous bread writer, called water "the principal food for all things living and the universal ingredient with capacity for giving life."

Water helps transform food during cooking. Not only does it change food from raw to cooked, thereby making it more pleasing to eat, more digestible, and (in many cases) releasing nutrients, it also helps us capture, preserve, and concentrate flavors and nu-trients. Five thousand years ago, when water was added to porridge, it enabled the grains to be transformed—first through sprouting, then through fermentation—into the first sourdough starter. Similarly, spirits such as whiskey are made through an interaction of water and grains. The method of whiskey production is a useful metaphor for understanding what creates flavor in soup.

The malting process for making whiskey starts when grain is soaked in water. The grain begins to sprout, and a process called auto-digestion takes place. The hydrated grain makes amino acids more accessible, which in turn, become the food on which the grain will feed itself as it grows. When dried in a kiln, sprouted grains (now containing readily accessible amino acids) become caramelized. This so-called "browning reaction" is what gives whiskey some of its deep color and flavor.

Raw vegetables contain water, and their nutritious elements—amino acids and starches—are readily accessible. When vegetables are roasted, sautéed, grilled—or cooked in a stockpot where the browning takes place at a slower rate—they caramelize in a similar fashion as do sprouted grains in the malting process. (The kilning process involves sugars reacting with amino acids.) This process creates a dark color (browning) and intense flavor. As we are told by aroma scientists, the flavors arising from the caramelization of amino acids and starches approach the taste of meat or chocolate, perhaps even those flavors we find in cabernet and zinfandel. Thus the same flavor-enhancing techniques used to bolster the taste, aroma, and color of whiskey is used in making stock.

So water is the agent or medium in numerous flavor transformations. First, of course, water is essential to growing the grains or vegetables. And water (either retained in raw vegetables or used to cook them) aids in caramelization by making active starches and amino acids readily accessible to a browning reaction when heat is added (by solubilizing them). Finally, water becomes the medium through which flavor and color are extracted when the vegetables are simmered for making stock.

Once the vegetables have released all their flavors, nutrients, and color into the water, they are removed so that the reduction of the stock can take place. The boiling down of the liquid concentrates the flavor and intensifies the broth, making it possible to use less volume to produce more flavor.

VEGETABLE STOCKS

If composting is the art of turning kitchen scraps into "black gold," then making stock is the art of turning vegetable trimmings into flavor. Stock is inexpensive and easy to make. Not only does it use scraps and leftovers, but it can help create deep, intense flavors.

Using vegetable scraps wisely is the experienced cook's sound practice of not allowing anything to go to waste. Mushroom stems, leftover leaves, withered onions and carrots, asparagus trimmings—almost any otherwise unusable vegetable part can be cooked in a large pot of water, extracting its deep flavors to make an earthy substitute for meat stocks. Vegetable stock can be used immediately or stored in the refrigerator or freezer. This flavorful liquid can be blended with fresh ingredients to elevate pan sauces, enhance braised vegetables, make quick soups, and enrich casseroles and risottos. Here are some tips for making vegetable stocks.

- Always wash vegetables before peeling. Use the peels, stem ends, and other trimmings for stock. You can use all fresh vegetables instead of scraps, or a combination. Always use a piece of celery and carrot to round out the flavor of leafy vegetables.

- Chop onion in large chunks or use onion skins. Onion gives an earthy, rich taste to vegetable stock and helps extend and broaden its flavor.

- Add one or two bay leaves to any vegetable stock. (Remember to remove them before the soup is served.)

- Use dried herbs at the beginning of cooking a stock or fresh herbs in the final stage. If you want an aromatic stock, use a mixture of thyme, oregano, and chervil. Avoid using too much rosemary, as it can add a strong medicinal flavor.

- Using lemon, apple, or pear peels can help mellow and round out flavors.

• Cook stock at a simmer. If the vegetables boil, they will begin to dissolve and create an undesirable sediment in soups.

• Freeze 2- to 4-cup portions in plastic containers, or strain cooled stock and pour into ice cube trays and freeze. Store in freezer bags to use with sautéed vegetables, pasta sauces, or risottos.

FISH AND CHICKEN STOCKS

Chicken and fish stocks often come in handy when preparing vegetable soups or vegetable pasta sauces. Here are some tips for stocks made with chicken and fish:

• For fish stock, use well-cleaned fish bones from mild white fish such as flounder or sole, not oily fish like salmon or mackerel, a touch of white vinegar, a few peppercorns, some dry white wine, and some chopped carrot, onion, and celery. Cook for 20 to 30 minutes, then strain. Cook again until reduced to the desired concentration.

• If you have shelled fresh prawns, don't discard the shells. Instead, cover them with twice the volume of water and cook for 30 to 40 minutes over medium heat. Discard the shells, then strain and reduce the stock to use in soups or pasta sauces.

• For chicken stock, always use the classic combination of carrot, celery, onion, and bay leaf. Try using chicken backs and thighs. They contain lots of flavor, are usually in abundance, and therefore much cheaper. Remember to skim off the film of impurities with a large spoon as it develops. Let the stock cool, then refrigerate overnight. Remove and discard the layer of congealed fat before use or further reduction.

Light Vegetable Stock

MAKES 6 CUPS

ESSENTIAL INGREDIENTS

2 garlic cloves

1 celery stalk, coarsely chopped

1 carrot, coarsely chopped

2 sprigs parsley

2 sprigs thyme

1 sprig marjoram

1 sprig savory

1 bay leaf

Salt and freshly ground pepper for taste

8 cups water

OPTIONAL INGREDIENTS

Leeks, with tops

Onion peels

Lemon rind

Well-scrubbed potato peels

Basil stems

Swiss chard scraps

Spinach scraps

Place all the essential and optional ingredients in a large stockpot. Bring to a boil, then reduce heat and simmer, partially covered, for 1 hour. Strain. Add the vegetables to your compost pile, or purée some for soup. Let the stock cool. Cover, and refrigerate for up to 1 week or freeze for up to 2 months.

VERDURA

By steaming vegetables instead of boiling them, you can retain more of their texture. Firm vegetables are commonly cooked this way in Italy, where the technique is known as *verdura*. Steam vegetables over boiling water in a covered container until crisp-tender. Sauté some minced garlic in olive oil until golden, then pour over the vegetables. Add some freshly squeezed lemon juice, perhaps a dash of balsamic or red wine vinegar, and toss and serve.

Roasted Vegetable Stock

MAKES 6 CUPS

ESSENTIAL INGREDIENTS

1 onion, coarsely chopped

1 carrot, peeled and cut into 1-inch lengths

1 stalk celery, coarsely chopped

4 unpeeled cloves garlic

2 to 3 tablespoons olive oil

Salt and freshly ground pepper to taste

8 cups water

$1/2$ cup dry white or red wine

OPTIONAL VEGETABLES

Parsnips, coarsely chopped

Turnips, coarsely chopped

Dried mushrooms, soaked in hot water, drained,
    and chopped

Fennel bulb, quartered

Fresh mushrooms, coarsely chopped

Apple, pear, and/or lemon peels

Preheat the oven to 300°. Place the onion, carrot, celery, and garlic and any optional ingredients in a baking dish large enough to accommodate them in one layer. Drizzle with the olive oil, then toss to coat. Add salt and pepper and toss once more.

Roast for 2 to $2^1/2$ hours, or until all of the vegetables are nicely brown.

Place the vegetables in a stockpot and add the water. Add the wine to the roasting pan and stir over medium heat to scrape up all the browned bits from the bottom of the pan. Add this liquid to the stockpot. Bring to a boil, then reduce the heat and simmer for 1 hour. Remove the vegetables with a slotted spoon and discard. Continue simmering the stock for 15 to 20 minutes. This stock is best when used immediately.

Roasted Mushroom Stock: Cover roasted mushrooms (page 87) with water in a saucepan. Bring to a boil, then reduce heat and simmer for 30 minutes. Remove the mushrooms and add to the compost pile, or purée and add to the soup. Cook the stock to reduce it. Use to flavor soups and pasta sauces.

CREATING YOUR OWN SOUP

To compose soup out of elements found on the following pages (or any number of other prepared elements you might have on hand), you'll need 2 to 4 cups of stock to use as a base. You can make a simple soup out of stock by itself or you can add a bit of cooked pasta or rice, garnished with chopped parsley. Or you can fortify a stock with puréed red pepper or puréed roasted carrots and a little cream.

For a well-rounded hearty soup, use at least 3 elements:

1. Stock

2. Thickener

3. Chopped freshly sautéed vegetables

You'll find that the potential combinations are almost infinite. See the Elements of Soup diagram between pages 308–309.

THE ELEMENTS OF SOUP

Soup can be made simply by following a recipe. Or soup can be made by combining a variety of already prepared ingredients or dishes, such as cooked vegetables, stock, thickeners and starches, flavorings, and fresh vegetables. By keeping these elements on hand, or making them as you need them, you can create your own inspired soups. Refer to the sidebar (opposite) and the Elements of Soup diagram between pages 308 and 309 to see how the following ingredients can be used for soup in a variety of combinations.

Cooked Vegetables

BEETS: Use roasted or boiled beets thinly sliced, diced, or julienned. Pair with cabbage, potato, or zucchini. Beets add flavor and rich red color to soups.

LEEKS: Leeks Vinaigrette (see page 422), simple steamed leeks, or leeks sautéed with a little olive oil make an aromatic base for soup. Combine with stock and boiled diced potatoes for a hearty meal.

ROASTED CARROTS: Add puréed or diced roasted carrots to any soup. For carrot soup, purée with stock, a little milk, cumin, mint, and sour cream or yogurt.

ROASTED VEGETABLES: Almost any vegetable can be roasted (see page 147). Purée roasted vegetables and add to any soup for flavor, color, and texture.

SAUTÉED CABBAGE: Cut cabbage into slivers. Combine with julienned onions and sauté briefly in olive oil, or steam and season with herbs and salt. Add to the soup in the final moments of cooking.

SAUTÉED GREENS: Use leftover or freshly cooked chard, spinach, bok choy—whatever is most abundant in your garden.

TOMATOES: Roasted, stewed, cooked into sauce, or freshly picked, peeled, seeded, and chopped. Add at the beginning or at the end of cooking.

Stocks

CHICKEN STOCK: An instant flavor enhancer, it has an unmistakable viscosity unachievable with vegetables.

FISH STOCK: This stock is made from fish bones and aromatic vegetables. Perfect for fish soups.

LIGHT VEGETABLE STOCK: This simple stock (see page 139) can be used for light soup.

MUSHROOM CONCENTRATE: Use to flavor most any soup or add sautéed fresh mushrooms as a base for a pasta sauce or mushroom soup (see page 88 for recipe).

ROASTED VEGETABLE STOCK: Deeply colored and richly flavored, this stock (see page 140) can be used for hearty soups and pasta sauces.

WATER: Use when liquid is needed and flavor is not. You can also use the water you've cooked potatoes or pasta in.

Thickeners and Starches for Soup

BEANS AND BEAN PURÉE: These classic additions provide flavor, substance, and protein.

BREAD, SOAKED IN MILK: This is a European technique used to thicken soup without using any heavy cream or a lot of butter. Cut off the crusts from 2 slices of French or white bread. Place the ramaining white crumbs in a small bowl and cover with 1 cup of milk. Soak for 10 to 15 minutes. Purée the milk and bread in a blender or food processor and add to soup.

PASTA: Add a handful of salad macaroni, pastina, or spaghetti broken into 2-inch pieces into soup before the final 30 minutes of the cooking process.

POLENTA: Use leftover polenta as a thickener.

If it is hard, rethin it with water and heat in a skillet over medium heat, or simply mash it with a fork.

POTATOES: Use leftover mashed, boiled, or fried potatoes or fresh ones. When puréed, they make a stellar thickener.

RICE: Purée leftover rice with chopped onion sautéed in a little olive oil. Add with stock to diced fresh carrots and/or zucchini. Rice can thicken most any soup.

Flavorings for Soup

(Most of these recipes can be found under "Flavorings from the Garden," on pages 83–101.)

BOUQUET GARNI: This is a simple but effective way to add the flavor of herbs to soup; tie herbs together and put them in the stockpot; discard before serving.

CARAMELIZED SHALLOTS, GARLIC, ONIONS: These add richness and substance to vegetable soups.

MIREPOIX: Minced aromatic vegetables (carrots, onions, celery, and garlic) sautéed in olive oil can start almost any dish, especially soup. Try minced celery tops and garlic sautéed in a little olive oil to top a bowl of soup just before serving.

PISTOU: This is a light, aromatic sauce used to garnish vegetable soup.

PESTO: Add this classic Italian mixture to soup at the table.

ROASTED MUSHROOMS: These provide an earthy flavor to any hearty soup, or they can be used to make stock.

ROASTED PEPPER PURÉE: Use to add flavor or as a garnish for soup. When thinned with stock and fortified with a little low-fat yogurt or a dollop of sour cream, it can be a soup by itself.

Fresh Vegetables

Add diced fresh vegetables toward the end of cooking a soup to provide flavor and crunch. Add fresh herbs in the last stages of cooking or as a garnish at the table.

QUICK SOUPS

Here are some fast combinations of various soup elements to make at the last minute. Or make up your own combinations.

QUICK BEET BORSCHT: Diced steamed or roasted beets, leftover mashed or scalloped potatoes, sautéed cabbage, light vegetable stock. Garnish with sour cream and chopped chives.

CREAM OF MUSHROOM: Puréed roasted mushrooms, bread soaked in milk, mushroom concentrate, sautéed fresh mushrooms.

PISTOU SOUP: Stewed tomatoes, steamed green beans and leeks, diced fresh vegetables, light vegetable stock. Garnish with additional pistou.

ROASTED VEGETABLE SOUP: Roasted vegetables (half puréed, half whole), roasted vegetable stock, steamed diced vegetables. Garnish with caramelized onions and minced scallions with tops.

TUSCAN MINESTRONE: Bean purée, whole cooked beans, sautéed spinach, stewed tomatoes, vegetable stock. Garnish with extra virgin olive oil and grated Parmesan.

Bean and Vegetable Soup (Minestre di Fagioli)

This is a good example of a recipe that is prepared all at once. But if you analyze it, you will see that it can easily be composed with the following ingredients: mire poix, bean purée, stock, roasted tomatoes, and cooked Swiss chard.

SERVES 6

6 tablespoons olive oil
1 large onion, finely chopped
1 carrot, finely chopped
2 stalks celery, finely chopped
4 cups cooked white beans
4 cups Roasted Plum Tomatoes (page 89) or fresh
   tomatoes, peeled, seeded, and diced
6 cups Light Vegetable Stock (page 139)
3 cloves garlic, minced
1 bunch Swiss chard, chopped

In a medium skillet over high heat, heat 4 tablespoons of the oil and sauté the onion, carrot, and celery for 4 to 5 minutes. Reduce heat to low and cook for 15 minutes.

Return heat to high and sauté the vegetables until brown. Let cool.

Place one-third of the beans, one-third of the tomatoes, the sautéed vegetables, and a little of the stock in a blender or food processor and purée. In a large skillet over medium heat, heat the remaining 2 tablespoons of olive oil and sauté the garlic and Swiss chard until wilted.

Place the remaining beans and tomatoes in a stockpot and add the purée and the remaining stock. Simmer over medium-low heat for several minutes. Ladle into soup bowls and top each with a little of the sautéed Swiss chard.

Per serving: 496 calories (158 from fat), 18.1g total fat, 2.9 g saturated fat, 2 mg cholesterol, 1690 mg sodium, 67.5 g carbohydrate, 11.1 g dietary fiber, 19.2 g protein

OTHER SOUPS IN THIS BOOK

Pasta and Lentils in Tomato Broth
(see Basic Pasta Sauces diagram between pages 308 and 309)

Roasted Broccoli Soup (page 399)

Cabbage and Potato Soup (page 403)

Soupe au Pistou (page 393)

Tuscan Minestrone (page 142)

Low Beet Borscht (page 395)

COMPOST OR SOUP?

Some scraps should go into the compost heap and some should be reserved for the soup kettle. As long as your garden clippings don't go into the landfill and your vegetable trimmings don't go down the garbage disposal, you are performing a recycling act that will enrich the soil in your garden or intensify the flavors in your cooking.

Even though we might create two seemingly dissimilar products—compost and soup—the processes are remarkably the same. The soup kettle and compost bin are two similar tools that help us convert organic matter into different forms. In the compost bin, biological heat helps create the dark, earthlike aroma and rich color of humus; in the soup kettle, the applied heat causes browning, which creates flavor.

The production of compost and soup are two similar processes: Both are linked by carbon and nitrogen. Since most of our foods and kitchen scraps contain both carbohydrates (sugars that contain carbon) and proteins (amino acids that contain nitrogen), most kitchen browning entails a reaction between sugars and amino acids.

Compost production, like soup making, takes place through the interaction of carbon, nitrogen, oxygen, and water, at temperatures between 80° and 150°F (whereas the cooking of the soup takes place between 210° and 212°F). An initial browning of some of the ingredients can give soup a rich color and flavor.

As any good cook will tell you, the basis for good soup is stock. And the basis for a good, rich stock is an extraction, usually done by simmering suitable vegetables or meats in water. It is good to know that an intense, dark, and flavorful stock—one that has the subtle flavorings of meat—can be created with vegetables alone (see Roasted Vegetable Stock, page 140).

Browning vegetables by roasting, grilling, or searing them in oil gives them a more intense taste and aroma. Once extracted into liquid, the same rich tastes and aromas will pervade the stock.

FIG. 3-10: Compost or soup?

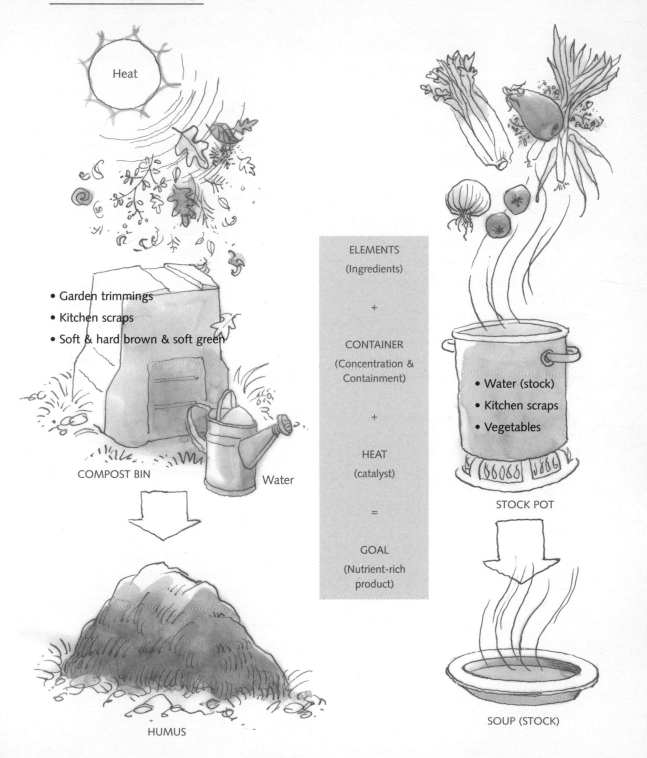

Heat

- Garden trimmings
- Kitchen scraps
- Soft & hard brown & soft green

COMPOST BIN

Water

ELEMENTS
(Ingredients)

+

CONTAINER
(Concentration &
Containment)

+

HEAT
(catalyst)

=

GOAL
(Nutrient-rich
product)

- Water (stock)
- Kitchen scraps
- Vegetables

STOCK POT

HUMUS

SOUP (STOCK)

Compost Soup

SERVES 6

This is not a soup made from compost, but a recipe for soup made the way compost is made: with heat and water. It yields a dark, earthy, intoxicating soup. The stock may be used in any dish that calls for a rich vegetable stock. Vegetable trimmings can be used in place of whole fresh vegetables.

STOCK

1 cup chopped fennel (optional)

2 cups chopped celery

2 cups chopped carrots

2 cups chopped onions

1 cup mushroom stems

4 cups assorted broken leaves and stems of
    spinach, chard, kale, or red chard

1 tablespoon Gremolata (page 84)*

1/4 cup olive oil

8 to 10 cups water

SAUTÉED VEGETABLES

1/4 cup olive oil

2 cups chopped onions

2 cups finely chopped carrots

2 cups sliced mushrooms

2 teaspoons Gremolata (page 84)*

1 cup finely chopped red cabbage

4 cups chopped Swiss chard, plus
    2 cups finely slivered for garnish

4 tomatoes, peeled and seeded

GARNISH

1 green onion

1 tablespoon olive oil

To roast the vegetables, preheat the oven to 450°. Place the vegetables in one layer on two baking sheets with the greens on one sheet and the rest of the vegetables on the other sheet. Combine the gremolata and olive oil and drizzle over the vegetables. Toss the vegetables to coat them with the oil mixture. Roast until dark brown but not burned (greens may take only 45 minutes, other vegetables may take as long as 1 1/4 hours). Toss the vegetables several times during cooking.

Place the roasted vegetables in a large pot with the water and simmer for at least 1 hour. Remove the vegetables and discard in your compost pail. Cook the stock over medium heat until reduced to about 6 cups.

To sauté the vegetables, place them in a small stockpot over medium heat, heat the oil and sauté the onions, carrots, and mushrooms until dark brown. Add the gremolata. Add the red cabbage and chard and cook for 5 minutes over low heat. Add the roasted vegetable stock to the skillet along with the tomatoes and chard.

To make the garnish, cut the green onion in half, then into 1/8-inch strips. Crumble the strips by rubbing a few at a time between your palms in a circular motion. Sauté these strips in the oil until just brown. Ladle the soup into bowls and garnish the soup with the finely slivered raw Swiss chard and the fried onion curls.

*NOTE: In place of the Gremolata, use a mixture of minced garlic, minced herbs, salt, and pepper.

Per serving: 138 calories (80 from fat), 9.4 g total fat, 1.3 g saturated fat, 0 mg cholesterol, 1162 mg sodium, 12.7 g carbohydrate, 3.9 g dietary fiber, 2.8 g protein

GRILLING AND ROASTING VEGETABLES

Ecological cooking means that when you have the oven on to roast a chicken or the barbecue going for a few salmon fillets, you make use of the heat to simultaneously roast or grill some vegetables.

With a minimum of preparation, you can roast vegetables slowly over spent coals or diminishing heat in the oven, or grill them quickly before the coals are ready for the main course. The heat from the coals seals in the juices and creates a smoky flavor in grilled vegetables, while roasting brings out vegetables' subtle flavors. In both processes, the caramelization that occurs adds flavor and rich, dark color.

GRILLING TIPS

• Some recipes recommend marinating vegetables 20 to 40 minutes before grilling. Others simply say to brush on a basting sauce while vegetables are on the grill. The advantage of marinating is that the vegetables are infused with more of the flavor of the marinade; the disadvantage is that the oil tends to make the fire flare up. We like to prepare vegetables right before grilling, lay them on the grill to sear them with the first flash of heat, then brush with marinade as they are turned.

• Use your favorite vinaigrette as a marinade, or simply use olive oil seasoned with herbs, garlic, salt, and pepper. If you don't want to marinate the vegetables, just brush them with a light coat of marinade or oil after they are cut. Good choices are Moju, Soy Marinade, and Yogurt–Mustard Marinade (page 101).

• Large vegetable pieces or whole vegetables tend to char on the outside and remain raw on the inside if not blanched or steamed first. Such vegetables you might want to blanch before grilling include leeks, asparagus, crookneck squash (halved lengthwise), large chunks or whole zucchini and carrots (not necessary for thin slices). Blanch or steam 3 to 5 minutes just before grilling.

• Don't just throw everything on a hot grill and pray that you have the time to turn it all; you'll get charred vegetables. Cook vegetables one variety at a time, starting with the biggest, thickest, and densest. Once cooked, they can be put on a serving platter or shifted over to the cool side of the grill while you cook the rest.

• Use bamboo skewers for certain vegetables (see below). Soak the skewers in water for 1 hour before using to keep them from burning. For easily turning chunks of vegetables, use two skewers instead of one. Thread different vegetables on separate skewers so they will cook more evenly, and to allow for different cooking times.

• Vegetables can be cooked over direct heat (with lots of turning) for a short amount of time or over indirect heat for a longer period of time.

To grill beets: Boil beets for 10 to 12 minutes, grill, turning often, until tender. Or quarter and thread onto skewers.

To grill bell peppers: Grill whole, turning often, or quarter and thread onto skewers.

To grill corn: Peel back husk, remove silk, and recover with the husk, tying with kitchen string to secure. Soak in water for 30 minutes. Grill in the husks for 10 to 15 minutes, turning often.

To grill eggplant: Slice at least 1/2 inch thick.

To grill fennel: Quarter the bulbs and thread onto skewers.

To grill garlic: Wrap the bulb in aluminum foil and grill over an indirect fire for 35 to 40 minutes. Or for the fast-roast method:

Wrap the bulb in foil and place on top of the lighted coals in a charcoal chimney for 15 to 20 minutes, or until tender.

To grill leeks: Grill small leeks whole. Large leeks, steam 10 minutes before grilling.

To grill onions: Quarter and thread onto skewers.

To grill potatoes: Cut into ½-inch-thick slices, or cut lengthwise into wedges, turning carefully so as not to break.

To grill zucchini: Cut lengthwise into ½-inch-thick slices.

To grill radicchio: Grill whole. Try stuffing them with cheese and/or wrapping them in a slice of bacon or pancetta. Serve with Anchovy-Scallion Vinaigrette (page 92).

To grill tomatoes: Grill large tomatoes whole; skewer cherry and plum tomatoes.

FIG. 3-11: Grilling wheel

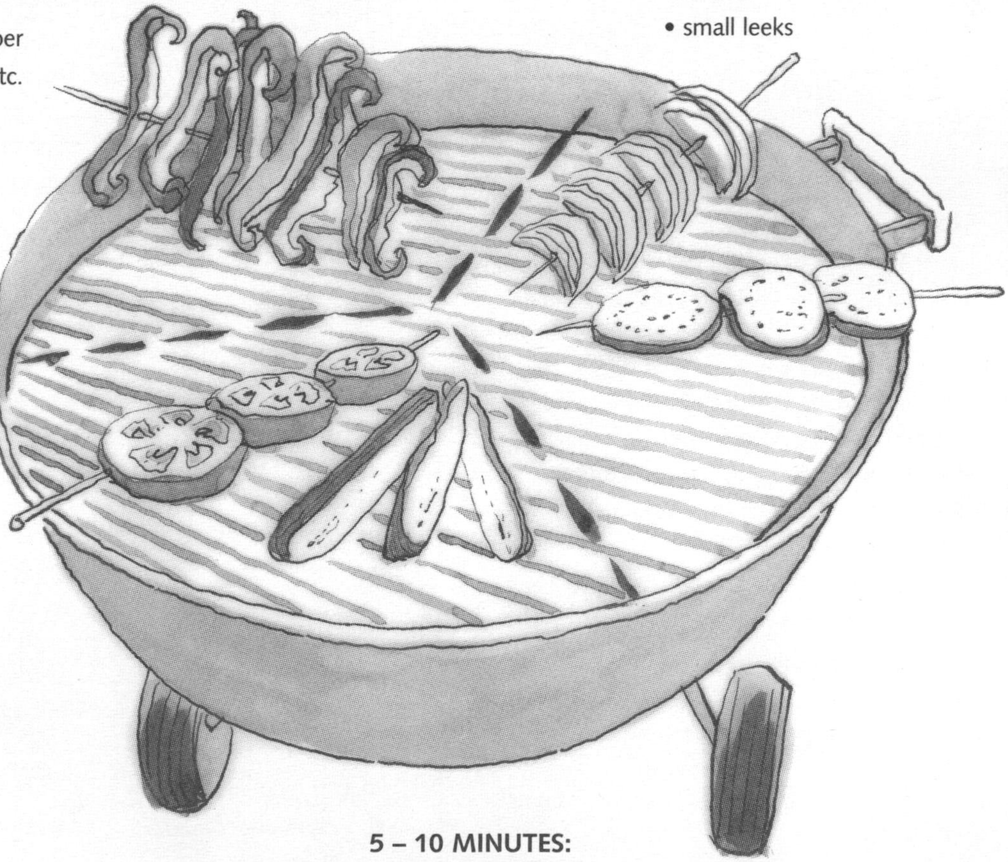

15 – 20 MINUTES:
PUT ON FIRST
• garlic
• bell pepper
• fennel, etc.

10 – 15 MINUTES:
PUT ON SECOND
• corn
• eggplant
• onions
• small leeks

5 – 10 MINUTES:
PUT ON AT END
• tomatoes
• zucchini

BATTLE OF THE BENEFICIALS

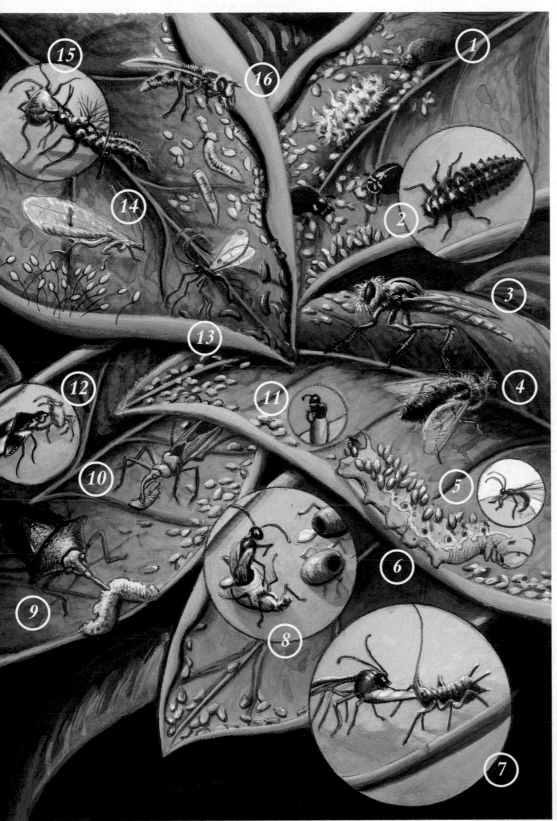

1. Mealybug destroyer (adult and larva)

2. Lady beetle eggs and larva

3. Robber fly

4. Parasitoid tachinid fly

5. Wasp laying eggs on caterpillar

6. Parasitoid wasp pupae on caterpillar

7. Adult wasp laying egg in aphid

8. Wasp emerging from aphid and aphid mummies from which wasps have emerged

9. Spiny soldier bug (eating caterpillar)

10. Assassin bug

11. Wasp hatching from parasitoid caterpillar

12. Pirate bug (eating aphid)

13. Adult aphid midge and eggs (orange)

14. Lacewing adult and eggs (on stalks)

15. Lacewing larva (eating aphid)

16. Syrphid fly and larva (eating aphid)

ELEMENTS OF THE NATURAL HABITAT KITCHEN GARDEN

1. Flowers that attract bees, butterflies, and beneficial insects:

   Euryops

   Hollyhocks (*Alcea rosea*)

   Sunflowers (*Helianthus*)

   Cosmos (*Cosmos bipinnatus*)

   Yarrows (*Achillea millefolium*)

   Sweet Alyssum (*Lobularia maritima*)

   Pincushions (*Scabiosa*)

   Mexican sunflowers (*Tithonia tagetifolia*)

   Spider flowers (*Cleome spinosa*)

   Buckwheat (*Eriogonum*)

   Goldenrods (*Solidago*)

   Chamomile (*Anthemis nobilis*)

2. Planter box with plastic covering (greenhouse effect)

3. Planter box (4' x 8', made up of 2 x 12s) with protective netting

4. Bunch grass (habitat for lady beetles)

5. Peas on trellis (grown on raised bed)

6. Birdhouses

7. Cover crop (vetch)

8. Uncultivated bed, with freshly dug-in cover crops

9. Tomato cages

10. Compost pile tractor

11. Newly tilled bed

12. Straw mulch

13. Pond (with shallow end for frogs and aquatic plants to shelter fish)

14. Undisturbed area (with weeds and upside-down flowerpots—habitat for spiders and ground beetles

15. Rotating crops (e.g., onions, cabbages)

16. Successive plantings of corn (also attracts beneficials)

PEST & DISEASE SYMPTOMS

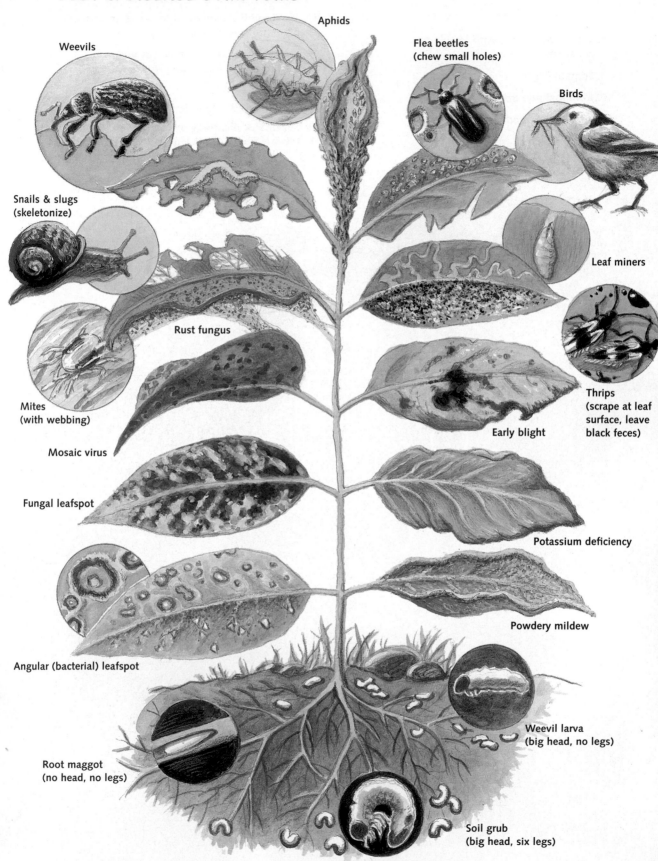

Weevils

Aphids

Flea beetles
(chew small holes)

Birds

Snails & slugs
(skeletonize)

Leaf miners

Rust fungus

Thrips
(scrape at leaf
surface, leave
black feces)

Mites
(with webbing)

Early blight

Mosaic virus

Fungal leafspot

Potassium deficiency

Angular (bacterial) leafspot

Powdery mildew

Root maggot
(no head, no legs)

Weevil larva
(big head, no legs)

Soil grub
(big head, six legs)

ROASTING TIPS

- Scrub vegetables well, using a bristle brush. No need to peel most vegetables.

- Cut vegetables into large, even chunks of about 1 to 2 inches. Or roast small vegetables whole.

- Adjust sizes according to how they might cook. For example, sweet potatoes, squash, and eggplants cook fast and can be in larger chunks.

- Before roasting, toss cut vegetables lightly with olive oil, then sprinkle with salt, pepper, and herbs.

- Toss the vegetables several times during roasting to avoid sticking and assure even browning.

- Test different vegetables with a fork, remove those that are done, and leave the rest in the oven. Most vegetables will take 30 to 40 minutes at 400°. Harder, denser vegetables like beets or turnips will take up to 1 hour in chunks or up to 2 hours if left whole.

- Some methods call for initial roasting at a high temperature (450°) for 10 minutes, then lowering the temperature to 350° for the remainder of the cooking. We suggest simply using whatever temperature you're using to cook your main dish. Or bake at 400° until cooked to desired doneness.

- If you do initial high-heat roasting, add flavoring ingredients that tend to burn, such as minced garlic and delicate herbs, toward the end.

- Don't dress the vegetables before roasting with mixtures that contain sherry vinegar, balsamic vinegar, or soy sauce, because they will burn in the pan.

- After removing the vegetables, add some dry white wine to the pan and stir over medium heat to scrape up all the browned bits from the bottom of the pan. Use as a sauce, add to soup, or use to dress roasted vegetables.

FIG. 3-12: When to Add Flavorings to Roasted Vegetables

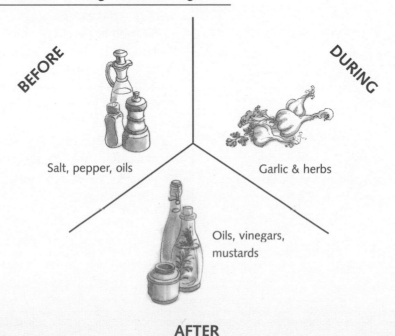

BEFORE

Salt, pepper, oils

DURING

Garlic & herbs

Oils, vinegars, mustards

AFTER

WAYS TO USE ROASTED VEGETABLES

- Right out of the oven: Place the roasted vegetables on a serving platter, sprinkle with a little raspberry or champagne vinegar or lemon juice. Add a few tablespoons of chopped flat-leaf parsley and serve.

- Warm or at room temperature: Arrange a serving platter in separate groupings of roasted vegetables, sliced tomatoes, assorted cheeses, and butter lettuce.

- For soup: Purée 1 cup of roasted vegetables, and coarsely chop 1 cup. Add both to your favorite soup stock and simmer over medium heat 10 minutes for the flavors to meld.

- See also Roasted Vegetable Stock (page 140) and Roasted Carrot Pasta Sauce (between pages 308 and 309).

Gayle's Roasted Vegetable Salad

Serve on a bed of mixed baby lettuce or butter lettuce.

SERVES 6

1 large yellow onion
2 large carrots (1 pound)
2 medium red potatoes (12 ounces)
1 medium summer squash (12 ounces)
2 medium zucchini (1 pound)
1 eggplant (8 ounces)
1 large red bell pepper, seeded and deribbed
1/4 cup extra virgin olive oil
Salt and freshly ground black pepper to taste
2 teaspoons minced garlic
2 teaspoons fresh lemon juice
2 teaspoons balsamic vinegar
1 tablespoon minced fresh oregano or basil

Preheat the oven to 375°.

Cut all the vegetables into 2-inch chunks. On one baking sheet, place the onion, carrot, and potatoes, drizzle with 2 tablespoons of the olive oil, and season with salt and pepper. Roast for 45 minutes.

On another baking sheet, place the squash, eggplant, and bell pepper. Sprinkle with the garlic, drizzle with the remaining 2 tablespoons of olive oil, and season with salt and pepper. Roast for 35 minutes.

Combine the vegetables on a serving platter and let cool slightly. Whisk together the lemon juice and balsamic vinegar. Drizzle the lemon juice and vinegar over the vegetables. Toss and garnish with the minced herbs.

Per serving: 188 calories (80 from fat); 9.5 g total fat; 1.3 g saturated; 0 mg cholesterol; 32 mg sodium; 24.7 g carbohydrate; 6.3 g dietary fiber; 3.9 g protein.

USING THE ENTIRE VEGETABLE

Not only is it ecologically sound to use the entire vegetable, it's also healthy and fun to find different ways to use things we'd normally throw away. Many people discard beet greens and broccoli stems, not realizing that they contain many nutrients that complement the other nutrients in the commonly consumed portion of the vegetables. In the end, we can always toss them into the compost pail, knowing that whatever we don't find a use for in the kitchen will eventually break down into humus for the garden.

Beet greens: Wash and remove the heavy stems. Cut the greens into fine shreds (page 48) and use to add color, flavor, texture, and nutrients to tuna salad or potato salad.

Boiled potato water: After you've boiled potatoes, don't discard the water. Use it (after it has cooled) to replace the water you use to make pizza dough.

Broccoli stems: Pare into nuggets, steam, and serve with soy sauce and ginger (page 398) or peanut sauce. Peel, cut into coins, and sauté with carrots. Julienne and use for vegetable pasta (page 152) or mixed-vegetable stir-fry.

Carrot trimmings: Some cooks say that carrot peelings make stock bitter; it's better to add them to the compost bucket and leave them out of the stock.

Celery tops: Chop and sauté along with minced garlic in olive oil for a few minutes. Use as a garnish for vegetable soup or minestrone. (Please note that some cooks advise against using celery tops for stocks as they tend to impart a bitter flavor. Toss them into the compost pail instead.)

Corn cobs: Reserve the cobs after slicing off the kernels and use them to make a corn-flavored broth (page 411).

Fig leaves: Use to wrap fish before grilling over charcoal. Tie with kitchen twine.

Onion skins: Wash onion well before peeling, then add the skins to the vegetables for making stock.

Rosemary stems: Throw on top of hot charcoal just before grilling vegetables.

Sorrel leaves: Use to wrap trout before grilling.

Swiss chard: Cut into fine shreds and add to tuna or potato salad. When making sautéed chard, coarsely chop the stems and sauté with onions for several minutes, then add the shredded leaves, which need less cooking.

COMBINING VEGETABLES FOR BETTER FLAVOR AND NUTRITION

Just as a gardener might combine vegetables in a bed for more efficient growing, a cook can combine them on the plate for better nutrition, flavor, color, and texture. Recent food research has revealed that plants contain beneficial chemicals called phytochemicals. They are not nutrients, like vitamins and minerals, yet they have been found to stimulate enzymes in the body that seem to bolster its ability to fight cancer and heart disease. Phytochemicals are being studied in foods long regarded as folk remedies, like garlic, soybeans, licorice root, broccoli, and flaxseed. Tomatoes, berries, and cucumbers are also being studied. Maximizing the power of phytochemicals is another incentive for not overcooking vegetables, because like some vitamins, the strength of many phytochemicals is diminished or lost through prolonged cooking.

Luise Light, executive director of the Institute for Science in Society, tells us that the "health benefits of eating plants can't be undertsood by measuring the amount of any one or one type of component. Food plants are complex and dynamic 'nutrition systems.' Plants contain 'mixtures' of compounds and the enzyme catalysts needed to make them bioactive." The key word here is "mixtures." That is, we may need to eat a variety of vegetables concurrently to maximize their healthful qualities.

Fortunately, vegetables can be easily combined to achieve a variety of flavors, colors, and textures. One of the joys of vegetable cooking is learning to combine several different (and differently prepared) vegetables in one meal. This appeals to our taste buds and basic need for a variety of tastes, and it can help us eat more vegetables at each meal. Combining for color also makes vegetables more esthetically pleasing and thus appetizing, and a variety of textures makes a meal more interesting.

FAVORITE VEGETABLE COMBINATIONS

VEGETABLE SPAGHETTI: Julienne carrots, red bell peppers, zucchini, broccoli stems, and onion. Steam first to soften, then stir-fry in light olive oil, adding soy sauce and minced ginger during the final minutes of cooking. Top with Turkey Bolognese (page 197).

ROASTED CORN AND RED BELL PEPPERS WITH WILTED GREENS: Roast several ears of corn over a charcoal grill, then slice the kernels off the cobs. Roast the bell peppers, place in bag to steam, then skin, seed, and cut into strips. Sauté julienned spinach, chard, or kale leaves (or use raw). Toss together in a bowl with a simple vinaigrette (page 90).

SWEET POTATO AND POTATOES: Sweet potatoes are rich in beta-carotene and can add phytochemicals to regular potato dishes. Sweet potatoes are also high in vitamin A, while potatoes are low. When making roasted, scalloped, or mashed potatoes, substitute sweet potatoes for half of the standard potatoes.

FENNEL COLESLAW: Make Christie's Coleslaw (page 157), but add 1/2 cup each shredded fennel, red cabbage, and carrots.

CARROTS, PEAS, AND TOMATOES WITH CHUNKY SAUCE: Peel several carrots and julienne into 2 by 3/4-inch pieces, then steam until tender. Steam fresh peas. Scald, peel, seed, and dice fresh tomatoes. Place a few cloves of garlic and 1 tablespoon of olive oil in a sauté pan over medium heat. Sauté just until translucent. Add carrots and peas, and mix several minutes over low heat. Add tomatoes to the pan. Season with salt, pepper, and your favorite herbs. Serve warm or at room temperature.

CARROT AND CABBAGE SALAD: Combine equal amounts of 2-inch-long carrot and cabbage shreds. Dress with Lemon-Mustard Vinaigrette (page 90), salt, and pepper.

JOE'S MIXED VEGETABLES: Combine equal amounts of diced zucchini, yellow squash, onion, and red bell pepper. Steam or stir-fry vegetables to desired doneness. Toss with diced grilled chicken or diced ham (optional). Splash with champagne vinegar and garnish with chopped parsley.

BEET AND CARROT SALAD: Grate or julienne raw beets and carrots, then leave raw or steam. Toss with a little vinaigrette. Place butter lettuce around the edges of individual salad plates and place the carrots and beets in the middle. Drizzle the lettuce with a little of the vinaigrette. Garnish with chopped chives.

THREE SISTERS WARM SALAD: Combine diced, sautéed squash, any type of cooked beans at room temperature, and lightly cooked corn kernels. Dress with your favorite vinaigrette.

TAPPING THE HEALTHFULNESS OF VEGETABLES

- Studies have shown that vitamin supplements don't always fight cancer as well as fresh fruits and vegetables.

- Steam or microwave vegetables to preserve phytochemicals, vitamins, and minerals. Some phytochemicals lose a little potency when cooked, others remain stable when heated, and still others, such as the *indoles* in broccoli, are freed when cooked.

- The jury is still out on whether raw or cooked food is better for us, although much research has shown that the beneficial enzymes of some vegetables are released when cooked.

- Until we know more, try to eat a variety of vegetables, cooked and raw vegetables, and all parts of most vegetables.

TIPS FOR COOKING VEGETABLES IN BULK QUANTITIES

Gardeners have a habit of overproducing certain vegetables. Why fight it? While you attempt to gradually diversify your planting and cooking patterns for the sake of your garden and your own health, why not experiment with ways to use all that zucchini or those bushels of onions? There are three main ways to use a big harvest:

1. Throw a party

2. Do some serious canning, preserving, and/or pickling

3. Make concentrated flavorings to enhance future meals (for instructions on making flavorings, see pages 83–101).

Large-scale cooking is not as difficult as you might think. There are a few secrets. First, test your recipes in small batches and then make adjustments until you achieve the right flavor balance. Then increase the basic recipe proportionally as is convenient. Begin by preparing all the ingredients, then cook them separately in manageable batches.

TIPS FOR PREPARING VEGETABLES IN BULK

- Use the following recipes for bulk preparation as your guidelines for cooking quantities of vegetables. Get familiar with at least a few of the recipes—then you'll be able to take any of the standard-proportion recipes in this book, or in any other book, and increase the batch size in accordance with the size of your harvest.

- When cooking in bulk, prepare everything before beginning to cook. Place all ingredients in separate bowls. Many very large recipes, such as Caponata Agro Dolce (page 156), can and should be made in one-third–sized batches. Since the key to this recipe is searing the ingredients over high heat, it would be impossible to do all at once. Transfer roughly one-third of the ingredients in each bowl into the pan and cook as indicated. Set the cooked portion aside and continue cooking the ingredients in batches. Mix the cooked vegetables, taste, and adjust for seasonings as necessary.

- When quadrupling (or increasing even more) a home recipe, it is not always necessary to increase the amount of flavoring ingredients like garlic, ginger, crushed red pepper flakes, cayenne, salt, and pepper in the same proportions as for the main ingredients. Always stand prepared to make adjustments.

- When dressing a salad or vegetable dish that has been tripled, use only part of the dressing at first. Then taste and add more dressing and seasonings as necessary.

- Most bulk recipes will last in the refrigerator for several days and can be frozen in airtight containers for several weeks. Dishes with cream sauces or soft cheeses don't freeze well.

There are many books on canning that describe the basic water bath method as well as more complicated techniques. We recommend you refer to *Stocking Up: The Third Edition of the Classic Preserving Guide,* for detailed instructions (see Bibliography page 444).

BULK RECIPES

Some of the following bulk recipes have been feeding a crowd at Gayle's Rosticceria for over twenty years. (We have intentionally omitted nutritional analysis for these recipes because of their specialized nature.)

Basic Vinaigrette

MAKES ABOUT 3¹/₂ GALLONS

9 cups olive oil
6 quarts plus 2 cups corn oil
6 quarts red wine vinegar
³/₄ cup salt
¹/₄ cup white pepper

Whisk ingredients together in a 5-gallon bucket.

Dijon Vinaigrette

MAKES ABOUT 2¹/₂ GALLONS

1 cup Dijon-style mustard
2 cups whole-grain mustard
3 quarts red wine vinegar
1 cup sugar
¹/₂ cup salt
¹/₂ cup pepper
1 gallon corn oil
2 quarts olive oil

Whisk together all ingredients except oils in very large mixing bowl or 5-gallon bucket. Drizzle in oil while whisking, and continue to whisk until dressing emulsifies. Store in the refrigerator for up to 1 week.

Gayle's BBQ Sauce

MAKES ABOUT 3¹/₂ GALLONS

Barbecue sauce isn't just for meat! Use this spicy sauce as a dressing for vegetables, too.

18 cups firmly packed brown sugar
2 gallons plus 10 cups red wine vinegar
36 cups catsup
³/₄ cup Tabasco sauce
9 cups Worcestershire sauce
2 ¹/₄ cups chopped garlic
3 pounds butter, browned

In large stockpot over medium-high heat, dissolve the brown sugar in the red wine vinegar. Bring to a boil and reduce by half, about 10 minutes.

In a large mixing bowl, combine the catsup, Tabasco, Worcestershire, and garlic. When the vinegar and sugar are reduced, add the catsup mixture and continue to boil over medium-high heat for 25 to 30 minutes, or until the barbecue sauce thickens enough to coat the back of a wooden spoon. Finish by whisking in the browned butter.

Roasted Plum Tomatoes

These tomatoes are one of the elements of soup and a good way to cook a large tomato crop. The preparation can be canned or used fresh wherever a tomato sauce is called for—in soups or for pasta.

MAKES ABOUT 8 CUPS

50 plum tomatoes
7 cloves garlic, minced
12 to 16 fresh basil leaves, chopped
2 to 4 sprigs fresh rosemary
6 tablespoons olive oil
Salt and pepper

Preheat the oven to 300°. Cut ¹/₂ inch off the tops of the tomatoes.

Place the tomatoes, cut-side up, in a baking dish large enough to accommodate them in one layer. Scatter the garlic on top along with the rosemary and basil. Lightly coat with the olive oil, then sprinkle on the salt and pepper.

Bake for 2¹/₂ to 3 hours, or until dark and very soft.

Caponata Agro Dolce

YIELDS 10 QUARTS

6 cups chopped yellow onion

12 cups diced eggplant

8 cups chopped zucchini

2 cups chopped roasted red peppers (page 85)

2 cups olive oil

1 cup chopped garlic

20 cups chopped tomatoes

1¹/₂ cups currants

5 tablespoons sugar

¹/₃ cup capers

5 tablespoons balsamic vinegar

Combine the onions, eggplant, and zucchini in a large mixing bowl. Heat one third of the olive oil in a large skillet over high heat. Add one-third of the one third of garlic and the mixed vegetables and sear. Transfer the garlic and vegetables to a large stockpot and repeat twice with each one-third portion.

Place the stockpot over medium heat and add the roasted bell peppers and tomatoes to the seared vegetables. Bring the ingredients to a rapid simmer, lower the heat, and add the currants, sugar, and capers. Simmer gently for 15 to 20 minutes. Stir in the balsamic vinegar, simmer for another 5 minutes, then serve.

French Onion Soup

SERVES 12 TO 14

This is a great way to feed a crowd and use up a lot of onions. The recipe can easily be cut in half or stored for several days in the refrigerator.

BOUQUET GARNI

1 bunch parsley

6 bay leaves

1 sprig thyme

1 clove garlic

¹/₂ cup butter

4 pounds white or yellow onions, thinly sliced

3 tablespoons sugar

2 cups dry white wine

1 quart beef stock

1 quart chicken stock or vegetable stock (page 139)

6 tablespoons black pepper

Salt

24 to 28 ¹/₂-inch-thick slices stale French bread

1 cup shredded Swiss cheese

1 cup shredded Monterey jack cheese

1 cup shredded Cheddar cheese

To make the bouquet garni, tie the herbs and garlic in a cheesecloth bag.

In a stockpot over medium-low heat, melt the butter and stir in the onions and sugar. Cook, uncovered, for 15 minutes stirring often. Add the wine and cook until reduced by half. Add the stocks, bouquet garni, and pepper. Simmer for 45 minutes. Season with salt. Remove the bouquet garni.

Divide the soup among 12 to 14 earthenware bowls. Top each with 2 slices of bread and the grated cheeses. Place under the broiler until brown on top. Serve immediately.

Christie's Coleslaw

SERVES ABOUT 60

DRESSING

7$\frac{1}{2}$ cups mayonnaise

8 ounces fresh ginger, peeled and finely chopped
(in food processor)

1$\frac{3}{4}$ cups sugar

1$\frac{3}{4}$ cups white wine vinegar

1 tablespoon salt

1$\frac{1}{2}$ teaspoons freshly ground pepper

SALAD

9 pounds cabbage, grated

4$\frac{1}{2}$ pounds carrots, peeled and grated

5 bunches cilantro, coarsely chopped

12 ounces scallions

1$\frac{1}{2}$ pounds roasted, unsalted peanuts,
coarsely chopped

$\frac{1}{2}$ pound candied ginger, finely chopped

Whisk together all the dressing ingredients in a 2-gallon container. Mix the salad with enough dressing (nearly all) to evenly coat the vegetables. Divide the coleslaw among four or five large platters. Sprinkle about 2 ounces of the candied ginger over each platter, and serve.

Fern's Pesto for a Crowd

MAKES ABOUT 24 CUPS

Gayle's mom made the best pesto, and we've been making it for Gayle's Rosticceria customers for some years now. Here's how to make it for your favorite crowd of basil lovers.

2 pounds 5 ounces spinach, washed and stemmed

3 pounds basil leaves

4 ounces flat-leaf parsley

1$\frac{1}{2}$ pounds pine nuts

8 cups olive oil

1 pound 12 ounces Parmesan cheese, grated

6 tablespoons chopped garlic

Salt

$\frac{1}{4}$ teaspoon powdered vitamin C (ascorbic acid powder)*

Chop the spinach, basil, and parsley in batches in a food processor, transferring the chopped greens and herbs to a very large mixing bowl. Place the pine nuts along with 2 cups of the chopped greens and herbs in the food processer and process until the pine nuts are finely chopped. Transfer the chopped pine nut mixture to the large bowl. Add the olive oil, Parmesan cheese, garlic, salt, and vitamin C. Mix by hand until evenly combined. Store in freezer bags or plastic containers in the refrigerator for up to 1 week, or in the freezer for up to 2 months.

*The vitamin C helps the pesto to maintain a bright green color.

4

Controlling Garden Pests & Feeding Kitchen Guests

Wildlife Management in the Garden Habitat

Sooner or later your garden will have pests, and you'll have to deal with them. The first step to safe and effective pest control is to learn about the natural history of your garden and the life forms that call it home. Many books are available that can help you identify major garden pests (see the Bibliography for specific titles). This chapter discusses pest managment in terms of up-to-date, safe, and effective methods that take the entire garden habitat into consideration.

In the last twenty years, we've learned that pest control is more about managing wildlife than killing it. The more you know about the habits and habitats of your garden pests and the natural history of your garden, the less you'll have to use pesticides.

For the home gardener, harsh pesticides are rarely needed. In fact, one of the joys of growing your own food is knowing that it isn't laced with dangerous chemicals. Much of the time gardeners use pesticides because they run out of patience or they aren't aware of all the options available. Some of these options are revived remedies from a time when there were only natural pesticides. Others are new and exciting, like beneficial insects, which are available through the mail, and "soft" pesticides made from special soaps, vegetable oils, and plant extracts. Sources for these and other natural pest controls are listed on pages 452–453.

WHAT IS A GARDEN PEST?

A "pest" is often described as a creature that damages garden plants. But "damage" means different things to different people. Some gardeners spray at the slightest sign of an eaten plant. Others are willing to tolerate more damage before they act. In the long run, a pest is more of a situation than a thing.

It helps to develop the attitude that pests are a challenge, not a problem. Try to see pest problems as part of your gardening education. Pests can be an indication of poor growing practices or a garden environment out of balance. This is why the first line of defense against any pest is to improve the way you select and care for your plants—that is, to consciously monitor your cultural practices. This applies to all four types of pests.

Weeds

Often described as plants out of place, weeds compete with vegetables for space, light, water, and nutrients. They also harbor other pests, especially if the weed is related to a vegetable. For example, cabbage aphids also thrive on wild mustard and radish. Some weeds are bad, but some are good: weeds can lure beneficial insects, concentrate subsoil nutrients, and cover bare soil. If you become familiar with the traits of your weeds, you can weed selectively so that they bring more benefit to your garden than harm. Of course, then they are no longer weeds!

Diseases

Plants, like people, get diseases. A disease is any condition that impairs normal function, thereby stressing a plant. Infectious diseases can be passed from one plant to another. Plant diseases are caused by viruses, bacteria, fungi, and other microbes. Some diseases are carried, or "vectored," by wind, water, certain insects, or nematodes; others lie dormant in the soil for years.

Plant Eaters

Also called herbivores, these are the animals that graze on roots, nibble on leaves, tunnel through stems, and bore into fruit. Small herbivores include insects, mites, snails, and slugs. In some areas, larger plant eaters, like deer, gophers, rabbits, and birds can also be a problem.

Environmental Stress

Plants become stressed by such things as extreme cold and heat, too much or too little nutrients, crowding, smog, salty soils, and low light. Plants need a favorable environment; if they don't get it, they become susceptible to disease and plant eaters.

WHY ARE "PESTS" PESTS?

Have you ever wondered why a certain insect or mite shows up in your garden one year, eating half of your crop, then disappears only to return a few years later? Or why your garden has a pest and your friend's garden doesn't? For safe and sensible pest control, you need to be able to answer a few questions. The answers begin with learning about four things that affect your garden and its wildlife.

Weather and Climate

All pests are strongly affected by the weather, some more than others—not just today's weather, but last season's as well. Cold winters kill off many pests, and warm winters encourage others to be a problem in the spring. Outbreaks of onion thrips and armyworms, for example, can be predicted from the previous winter's temperatures. If you pay attention to the patterns of your weather ("climate"), you'll soon learn how it affects the life cycles of the animals in your garden.

The Vegetables You Grow

Some vegetables are more susceptible to pests than others. Members of the cabbage family, like broccoli, cabbage, and cauliflower, are almost always attacked by aphids, loopers, root maggots, and caterpillars. Radicchio and garlic have few pests and usually require little care. Many vegetables have varieties that are resistant to pests and diseases, and these should be grown whenever possible (see pages 166–167).

Other Plants and the Design of Your Garden

If you grow only vegetables in your kitchen garden, chances are that you'll have lots of pests. But if you diversify your garden with certain flowers, herbs, cover crops, and even weeds, you'll have fewer pests from year to year. These "beneficial plants" provide sanctuary and food for beneficial animals like predatory insects, birds, and spiders.

The Health of Your Vegetables

Weak plants attract pests; healthy plants can better defend themselves when attacked. If the soil is poor or if plants are overwatered, underfed, or neglected, chances are you will have pests. *The primary way to deter garden pests is by keeping healthy plants in a thriving, diverse garden environment.*

INTEGRATED PEST MANAGEMENT FOR THE KITCHEN GARDEN

If you want to control pests without using pesticides, you need to consider the entire garden habitat. For example, the next time you go to pull up a weed, look again. It may be attracting some local insect predators searching for nectar or pollen to eat, or it may be bringing up valuable subsoil nutrients that can be composted and returned to the soil. It may have aphids, which can be an important food for beneficial insects. Do you kill all the aphids or keep a few around to feed the good insects? The answer depends on the situation.

Pest control with the entire garden habitat in mind is called integrated pest management (IPM). IPM is a way of looking at pest problems and finding the most effective ecological solution, one that will disrupt the life of the garden as little as possible. It is a different attitude altogether from trying to kill all pests, which we now know is neither possible or desirable. IPM seeks to manage pest numbers at a tolerable level. We don't see earwigs as a nuisance, spiders as scary, or aphids as the enemy. In IPM, all species are interconnected, and everything you do has an impact.

Elements of IPM in Kitchen Gardens

Grow healthy plants
Reducing pest problems starts with reducing stress on plants: giving them the best possible environment in which to grow. Begin with a healthy soil, grow the right varieties for your climate, rotate your vegetables to avoid soil pests, and keep plants evenly watered and properly fed. Healthy plants attract fewer pests.

TRICKS FOR OBSERVING TINY GARDEN WILDLIFE

Often we are so busy doing garden chores that we never take time to notice the tiny wildlife that is all around us. If you take a quick look around your garden, you'll see the obvious things like birds and butterflies. But the tiny creatures require a closer look.

Here are some ways to develop an "eye" and see the amazing world of insect wildlife in your garden. Start with insects, because they interact with everything and are large enough to see yet small enough to take you into another world. Once you learn how to see the insects, you'll notice other things you never realized were there. Here are a few tips for becoming a good observer:

FIG. 4-1:

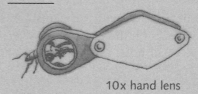

10x hand lens

1. Learn to look very carefully. Most insects are very tiny and cannot be seen easily with the naked eye. Some of the important parasitic wasps are the size of the period at the end of this sentence, and some insects are no bigger than this "a" during their early stages of life. You really have to look closely to see them. Use the right tools for observing like a magnifying glass, a zoom camera lens, or the best tool, a 10x hand lens. Be sure to hold the lens up close to your eye with the sun over your shoulder and your hand moving the lens back and forth to focus. It's tricky at first, but you'll soon get the hang of it. Start with an aphid-covered leaf. Under the hand lens, aphids look like a bunch of fat, green grazing cows with honey all over them. If you are fortunate you may see one giving live birth or being "milked" by an ant.

2. Look for insects both day and night. Different creatures are out at night. If you've never looked at your garden after sunset, you're in for an experience. Wrap the end of a flashlight with red cellophane to keep from disturbing the insects. You may even see the elusive critter that's been eating your lettuce.

3. Stare at flowers. Many flowers are very good at attracting insects. They provide refuge, nectar, pollen, and water for a host of different insects. Find a plant with clus-

Correct holding/viewing position

ters of small flowers, like yarrow, scabiosas, and wild carrots. Be still and just focus your attention on the flower for a while. Note the size, color, shape, and behavior of the creatures on the flower. Refer to books with good color photos (see pages 444–445 for recommended references). Don't just look at the insects but try to watch long and still enough to observe their behavior.

4. Start an "insectarium." Collect insects with nets or small jars. Place unknown specimens, eggs, and cocoons in a small glass jar or aquarium. Provide fresh vegetation and water, and wait to see what emerges. The next time you see the wormlike thing in the garden, you'll know what it's going to be-

come. Notice the eating patterns made by the insects. They eat in unique patterns of sucking or chewing, which will become signposts for future identification. Try putting an aphid-infested leaf in your insectarium for a few days. Aphids attract a host of beneficial insects that lay their eggs inside the aphids or near their colonies. In a few days you should see predatory maggot larvae of syrphid flies and aphid midges, alligator-shaped larvae of lacewings and lady beetles plus tiny parasitic wasps that have emerged from the aphid bodies.

Inspect your garden often

As plants grow, check for signs of damage on a regular basis. It's difficult to see pests during a casual garden stroll. Regard pest scouting as a specific garden chore, and set aside time to look for them. Observation is the key to the IPM method. Big things are obvious, but you have to look closely to see the little things; insects are tiny and they come in many forms. It takes a patient eye to see insects crawling and flittering about your garden.

You may not see a problem until it's obvious and hard to remedy. With practice you can enhance your powers of observation and, in the long run, your gardening skills. Once you learn the signs and symptoms of pests, you can identify your problem correctly and pick effective methods of control.

Look at the entire plant

Learn to separate symptoms into three categories: those from plant eaters, diseases, and cultural problems like water stress and low fertilizers. Notice differences in damage between old leaves and young leaves. Some diseases and nutrient deficiencies start on old leaves, some on new ones. Look at growing tips and undersides of leaves where many insects find food. Caterpillars often leave a greenish or brownish excrement that can be easier to see than the pest itself. Aphids and whiteflies excrete honeydew, which leaves a black "sooty" mold and a sticky film on leaves.

Sample efficiently

Unless you have a small garden, it's tough to look over each plant for pests. To save time, examine every third or fourth plant from top to bottom. In large plantings, check several plants on the outside and inside of the patch.

Identify your pests correctly and get to know their habits and enemies. You don't have to see the pest to know it's there. They can be recognized by the pattern of damage they leave behind. Weevils leave small scalloped chew marks on the edges of leaves, flea beetles leave small holes in the center. Snails make rasping marks with slimy trails leading up to the damage. Thrips make tiny scraping marks surrounded by dark drops of feces. (See "Pest and Disease Symptoms," between pages 148 and 149).

Place the blame correctly

Determine if the pest you see is actually doing the harm. For example, *isopods* (sowbugs and pill bugs) normally eat organic matter, but sometimes you can see them inside small holes of various fruit in the early morning. Chances are that the holes were made by slugs earlier in the evening and that the isopods simply moved in to gather moisture. Other times, if the fruit hasn't been harvested and is starting to rot on the ground, isopods can be the culprit. It all depends.

Disease symptoms are identified by color, shape, and size. Is the damage round, angular, or undefined? Does it look dry, powdery, or

FIG. 4-2: A guide to the many forms & shapes of insects

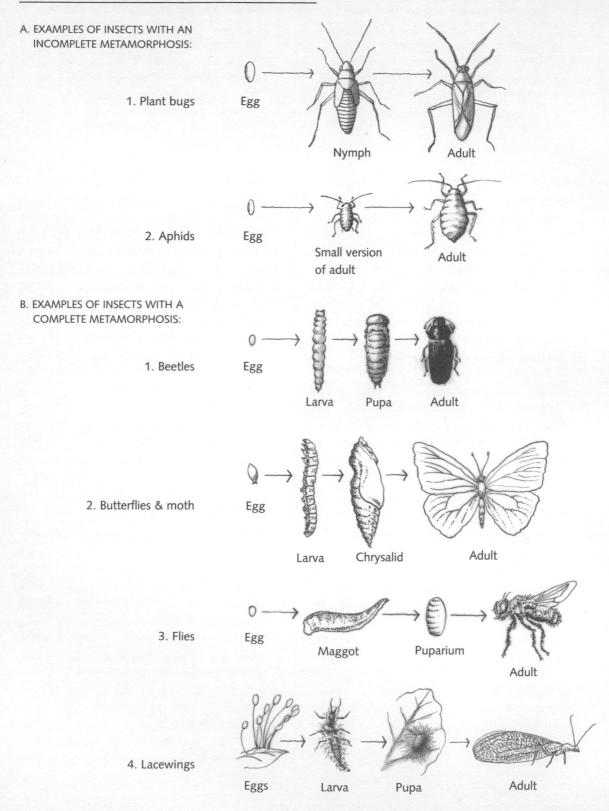

A. EXAMPLES OF INSECTS WITH AN
   INCOMPLETE METAMORPHOSIS:

1. Plant bugs   Egg   Nymph   Adult

2. Aphids   Egg   Small version   Adult
                           of adult

B. EXAMPLES OF INSECTS WITH A
   COMPLETE METAMORPHOSIS:

1. Beetles   Egg   Larva   Pupa   Adult

2. Butterflies & moth   Egg   Larva   Chrysalid   Adult

3. Flies   Egg   Maggot   Puparium   Adult

4. Lacewings   Eggs   Larva   Pupa   Adult

liquid? Does it occur on old leaves, new leaves, or the entire plant? Whether it's a rust, mildew, or blight, these are all important clues.

It's important to understand that a plant eater is only a *potential* pest. Tomato hornworms are huge caterpillars that look like they could eat an entire garden. In large numbers they can devour enough leaves to kill plants. In low numbers they can actually improve tomato yields by "pruning" plants. The hornworm is also a breeding host for parasitic wasps whose cocoons can be seen on the outside of the caterpillar's body. Sometimes the hornworm is a problem, sometimes it's a benefit. Observation and experience can tell the difference.

When you identify an insect pest, learn its habits and signs. Does it dwell on the soil surface, or does it hang out in the canopy of your plants? When did you first see it, and how long does it stay in your garden? These are the kinds of questions that can lead you down a path of gardening discovery.

Keep records

Pest activity varies with the weather and the season, but there is usually a pattern from one year to the next. If you note when you first see pests this year, next year's scouting will be much easier and more rewarding. We find it convenient to transfer our garden notes to a wall calendar, where we can see when activities begin to happen.

Establish your tolerance levels

How many lettuces can you stand to lose to gophers before you start trapping? How much of those eggplant or bok choy leaves can the flea beetles munch before the plants suffer? Balance the effects of pest damage against how much time and money you're willing to spend to fix it. Always consider the possibility that your pest is food for some predatory insect. It's a fine line between having enough pests to feed predatory insects and not so many that they injure your crops. If you're pa-

tient and trust the ecological integrity of your garden, it can often work wonders.

Treat safely and appropriately

In the IPM method, there are four types of control methods (discussed in further detail on pages 166–175).

1. Cultural controls: First and foremost, look at what you're growing, when you plant it, and how you care for it. This is often the cheapest and easiest way to control pests. The vast majority of pest problems are caused by putting the wrong plants in the wrong place at the wrong time, then not tending them properly.

2. Physical controls (traps and barriers): Traps are handy because they can also be used to monitor pests. Fences and row covers keep pests from getting to your plants.

3. Biological controls: These are predators and parasites that eat other animals. Some can be purchased through mail-order catalogs (see pages 452–453); others are part of your local landscape. They can be lured to your garden by making a home for them.

4. Chemical controls: Pesticides may have to be used if cultural, physical, and biological controls don't work. Begin with natural pesticides like soaps, oils, and botanicals. The very last option should be synthetic pesticides. IPM doesn't exclude the use of pesticides, but the goal is to solve the problem with the greatest safety and the fewest ecological side effects, a goal that makes pesticides a last resort.

Evaluate your treatment program

Continue to monitor your garden after you treat the problem. You may need to change your approach. Remember: Gardens do not have to be pest free, and some pests are necessary to feed beneficial insects. Strive for an ecological balance; IPM also stands for *intelligent* pest management.

The Four Types of IPM Controls

Sometimes it's difficult to know where to start if you have a pest problems and you want to control the safest way possible. It helps greatly if you consider the four types of control in the following priority:

Cultural Controls

Cultural controls are ways of taking care of your plants so they can resist pests and diseases, and of interfering with a pest's life cycle and behavior so they can't get to the plants.

• **Don't bring in problems.** Avoid infected seeds or sets. Use plant material that is certified disease free. Keep track of the seed companies you buy from, and note any bad germinations. Beware of compost materials, mulches, and cover crop seeds that may be contaminated with weed seeds.

• **Select your vegetable varieties carefully.** Choose insect- and disease-resistant strains whenever possible. Consult with neighbors, your county extension service, local garden clubs, and nurseries for regionally adapted varieties.

PEST-RESISTANT VEGETABLES

Primary Resistances (from breeding)

Many vegetable diseases can only be handled by planting resistant varieties that have been developed through careful breeding. Disease-resistant vegetables (with their seed catalog abbreviations) are listed below.

Vascular Wilts/Fungi

Fusarium verticillium, and other soil-borne fungi are some of the most difficult diseases to control. The fungi enter plants through the roots. Once the soil is infected, only resistant varieties can be grown with any success. The first symptom is rapid wilting on hot days as the small roots are destroyed. After that, the fungus moves up the plant and clogs veins in the lower leaves and stems, causing them to yellow, wilt, then turn brown and die. Cross-sections of infected stems reveal a ring of brown or reddish tissue. Fusarium wilts are more common in warmer climates (above 70°F). Verticillium is more common in cooler areas. Symptoms often start on one side of the plant.

🖉 Asparagus: Fusarium (F) 🖉 Cabbage: Fusarium yellows (F, FY) 🖉 Celery: Fusarium

(F) 🖉 Eggplant: Verticillium (V) 🖉 Pea: Fusarium (F) 🖉 Tomato: Fusarium, race 1 (F or F1), races 1 and 2 (FF or F2); Verticillium (V).

Leaf Spot Diseases/Fungi

Alternaria, alternaria stem canker, anthracnose, rust, angular leaf spot, northern corn leaf blight, and many others. Leaf spot diseases make it difficult for a plant to photosynthesize. All prefer situations of high humidity. Symptoms typically start at the base of the plant where air is damp most of the time. Alternaria leaf spot of potatoes and tomatoes is called "early blight." It starts as brown to black, round or angular spots, and is aggravated by high nighttime humidity and dew. Anthracnose is most serious in warm, damp climates. It leaves black sores on young stems at the soil line and on the leaves and fruit of cucumbers and beans.

🖉 Carrot: Alternaria (A) 🖉 Chinese Cabbage: Alternaria (A) 🖉 Corn: Northern Corn Leaf Blight (NCLB) 🖉 Cucumber: Anthracnose (ANTH); Angular Leaf Spot (ALS) 🖉 Tomato: Alternaria Stem Canker (A or AS)

Mildews/Fungi

Powdery mildew is actually a symptom produced by many different fungi. Usually, plants look dusted with a whitish powder on leaves and sometimes flowers. The disease slows photosynthesis and weakens the plant. Powdery mildew on tomatoes, eggplants, and peppers produces yellow patches on the upper surface of older leaves and not powdery growth. Unlike downy mildew, powdery mildew does not need moisture on the leaf surface and does well under dry conditions.

   Downy mildew produces yellow spots on the tops of leaves while the undersides are covered with a white, blue, or gray powder, especially after rain or heavy fog. DM destroys leaf tissue. It mutates rapidly, and resistant strains are hard to maintain.

   ◢ Bean: Powdery Mildew (PM) *◢* Cucumber: Powdery Mildew and Downy Mildew (PM and DM) *◢* Lettuce: Powdery Mildew (PM) *◢* Pea: Powdery Mildew and Downy Mildew (PM and DM) *◢* Spinach: Downy Mildew (DM)

Bacterial Diseases

Bacterial wilts of beans, corn, cucumber, and peppers clog up plant stems so that water and food can't reach the leaves. Besides a gradual wilting of the plant, infected stems will often "bleed" a sticky bacterial ooze after cutting. There are no resistant varieties for bacterial wilt of cucumbers. **Black rot** of cabbage and broccoli is identified by black leaf veins and yellowing of older leaves.

   ◢ Broccoli: Black Rot (BR) *◢* Cabbage: Black Rot (BR) *◢* Cauliflower: Black Rot (BR) *◢* Corn: Stewart's Wilt (SW)

Virus Diseases

Virus diseases are injected into plants by aphids, leafhoppers, thrips, and whiteflies. The viruses plug up the circulatory system of the plants. **Mosaic virus** produces yellow blotches on leaves that look puckered. Other viruses produce stunted plants with yellow and brown streaks on the leaves. There is no cure for viral diseases other than planting resistant varieties and establishing barriers for keeping insect vectors off the plants.

   ◢ Beans: Bean Mosaic Virus (BCMV) *◢* Corn: Maize Dwarf Mosaic Virus (MDMV) *◢* Cucumber: Cucumber Mosaic Virus (CMV) *◢* Lettuce: Lettuce Mosaic Virus (LMV) *◢* Pea: Pea Enation Virus (PEV) *◢* Pepper: Potato Virus Y (PVY); Tobacco Mosaic Virus (TMV) *◢* Potato: Potato Virus Y (PVY) *◢* Spinach: Cucumber Mosaic Virus (CMV) *◢* Tomato: Tobacco Mosaic Virus (TMV)

Secondary Resistances (from plant characteristics)

Have you ever noticed how certain varieties seem to escape insect attack better than others, when there's nothing in the seed catalog that says it should? You may have insect-resistant varieties growing in your garden and not know it. This is because plants use a variety of means including hairy leaves, chemical compounds, and thick fruit skins to protect themselves against pests. For example, if fruit worms or beet armyworms are a problem on your tomatoes, try thick-skinned types like 'Roma' or 'Red Cherry'. If aphids or leafhoppers are getting your snap beans, try varieties whose skin has tiny hairs like 'Provider' and 'Royal Burgundy'. Cabbage aphids prefer brassica varieties with curly leaves, so look for varieties with smooth leaves, like 'Red Russian' kale or many of the Asian vegetables. Red and purple varieties of many leafy vegetables seem to fend off a variety of insect pests. Some types of corn develop a resistance to the corn earworm by growing tight husks. Always grow several kinds of any one vegetable variety and you might find a gem.

- **Time your plantings to avoid pests.** Many times you can plant vegetables before their pests arrive for the season. Brassica seedlings planted early can usually escape damage from the cabbage root maggot, whereas seedlings set out later are often attacked. If you sow seeds of snap beans before the soil warms to about 58°F, they won't germinate and will probably rot or be eaten by the seed corn maggot. Sow later in warmer soils or use transplants.

- **Space plants carefully.** Dense plantings can create a weed-suppressing canopy, but they can also reduce air circulation and stimulate mildews and other diseases. Crowded plants are also weak and spindly and more prone to pest attack.

- **Take good care of your vegetables.** Plant them in a healthy, well-drained soil. Fertilizing and watering should be moderate and consistent to avoid sudden changes in growing conditions. Stressed plants attract pests. Keep the soil evenly moist, but never soggy. Give plants plenty of sun and always fertilize them carefully. Overfertilizing with nitrogen can cause soft, lush growth, which is very attractive to sucking pests like aphids. Just like people, plants can be harmed by too much food as well as too little.

- **Cull out stunted, diseased, and off-colored seedlings.** They will need more care in the long run. Bag diseased plants and discard them.

- **Trellis your climbing and vining vegetables.** Climbing vegetables include tomatoes, peas, beans, and cucumbers. Trellising not only saves space, but reduces disease problems because it keeps fruit off the ground and increases air circulation. Trim the foliage from the bases of trellised plants to allow air movement and to cut off corridors for crawling insects.

- **Keep down weeds that harbor pests.** Make a list of those diseases and insect pests that most seriously affect your plants. Find out if they overwinter on any of your local weeds, then be extra-vigilant about removing those weeds.

- **Practice good garden hygiene.** Keep garden tools clean to avoid spreading contaminated soil or diseases. Sterilize your equipment with 1 part household bleach diluted with 10 parts water. If you smoke, wash your hands before handling tomato family vegetables to prevent the spread of tobacco mosaic virus. Clean up wood piles, old pots, diseased plant remains, and other debris to eliminate pest breeding and hiding places.

- **Water carefully.** Avoid sprinkling your plants from overhead. Moist leaves encourage all sorts of plant diseases. A vegetable garden is a thirsty landscape. Vegetables are designed to take up and store water; that's what makes them crunchy and sweet. They prefer to grow in a soil that stays moist, not dry or soggy, so water deeply. Inspect regularly to see if the soil really needs water (see page 12). Compost and mulch can really help to stabilize the water in the soil so vegetables can grow quickly and without stress (for more about this, see Chapter 3).

- **Solarize your soil.** Weed seeds and several soil diseases can be destroyed or greatly reduced by covering moist soil with clear plastic during the hottest two to three months of the year. (for more about this, see page 186).

- **Rotate crops.** When the same type of vegetables are grown year after year in the same place, certain nutrients are exhausted and pests particular to those vegetables can increase to epidemic proportions. There are many schemes for rotating your vegetables in the garden, and some of these are discussed in Chapter 1.

- **Try to grow a diversity of vegetables.** Don't just grow several kinds of vegetables, but also an assortment of each type, like a few varieties of early cabbage or bush tomatoes. This will reduce pest damage to any one crop and give you more options for a healthy harvest.

- **Grow plants that attract and nurture beneficial insects.** Most gardens are teeming with native beneficial insects like lady beetles, syrphid flies, parasitic wasps, predatory bugs, and lacewing larvae. Many of these "good bugs" are attracted to certain types of plants and flowers (see page 189).

Physical Controls

Traps and barriers are fairly labor-intensive and require attention, but they work well in small gardens.

- **Handpick pests.** This is the most direct method of pest control and is especially useful for beetles, large caterpillars, and scale insects.

- **Wash off pests with a strong stream of water**. A handy method for aphids, scales, and other insects that feed in place.

- **Set up physical barriers to exclude hungry plant eaters.** Collars placed around seedlings discourage cutworms and root maggots. Fabric row covers, placed over crops, let light in but keep out weevils, flea beetles, and disease-carrying leafhoppers. Other useful barriers include fences to exclude deer; wood ashes and crushed eggshells, or other sharp or powdery material, to keep snails and slugs away.

- **Set traps.** Traps are an effective way to capture adult insects. They can also help you monitor how many pests you have and when they begin to appear in your garden, and therefore when you need to apply pesticides or release beneficial insects. For example, many gardeners use sticky traps or

light traps to tell them when thrips, aphids, or whiteflies may be a problem. Others use pheromone traps to detect when the adults of many garden pests are active. Pheromones are chemicals that animals use to communicate with one another. Copies of these chemicals are synthesized by laboratories and sold as lures.

Biological Controls

Animals that prey upon and eat garden pests are called "beneficials." These include insect predators and parasites, predatory mites, parasitic nematodes, insect-eating birds, toads, and several beneficial microbes (bacteria and fungi). There are several ways you can use and encourage beneficials in your garden.

- **Encourage beneficials by providing a diversity of plants and refuges in the garden.** You can make your garden a haven for native and released beneficials by taking simple steps to provide them with food, water, and shelter. The notion of designing your garden to attract insects may seem odd, but it really works. For more on this exciting approach to pest control, see page 187.

- **Encourage beneficials in the soil.** Certain types of compost can nurture beneficial soil microbes like predatory nematodes, predatory fungi, and disease-suppressing bacteria. Techniques for making "suppressive" compost are discussed in Chapter 3.

- **Buy and release beneficials.** Many beneficial insects, mites, nematodes, and microbes have been developed commercially and can be bought from mail-order catalogs. Should the home gardener buy beneficials for pest problems? It depends. First off, a beneficial insect is commercial because it can be collected or bred easily and shipped safely. Some of the best beneficials are the ones that can't be bought. They are insects that may be native in your garden, like syrphid flies, tachinid flies, ground beetles, several species of predatory bugs, and lady beetles. If your garden is a haven for native beneficials, you may not need to buy any at all.

If you do decide to buy beneficial insects, be aware that they are very active creatures, always on the prowl for food. If they don't find insects or flower nectar/pollen in your garden, they will fly to another area—your neighbor's garden, perhaps. The smaller your garden, the more likely this is to happen.

There are a few rules you should follow to make the beneficials you buy most effective. First, be sure you identify the pest carefully, because most beneficials attack only a particular type of pest. Find out as much as you can by talking to the supplier before you buy.

When the order comes, read the directions for handling and release. Every beneficial is unique and must be handled differently. Being shipped and confined in a package is very stressful for insects. Release them as soon as they arrive. If you can't do this, then keep them cool by storing them in the door shelf of your refrigerator. Release some directly on or near the infested plants; distribute the rest as evenly as possible throughout your garden. Once the insects are released, they will tend to seek out nectar and pollen rather than other insects, so be sure you have plenty of suitable flowers in your garden. In most cases, the insects you release won't do the bulk of pest control; with adequate flower food, they will mate successfully, and their youngsters will do most of the pest eating in the weeks to come. The thing to always keep in mind is that biological controls provide a long-term solution to pest problems, not a quick fix. You must be patient and willing to accept a tolerable level of pests.

Chemical Controls

Gardeners have been using pesticides for a long time to combat garden pests, from the garlic sprays our grandparents used to the synthetic pesticides of today. But the overuse of modern pesticides has caused health problems for people and the environment. Pesticides have their place, but only in a bigger management scheme where they are used strategically, not exclusively. Besides, for a variety of reasons, synthetic pesticides are becoming less and less effective.

- **Chemical pesticides cause resistance in pests.** Many pests, especially insects, mites, and weeds, have developed a resistance to the poisons that used to kill them. Gardeners and farmers have had to find new and stronger chemicals to combat them.

- **Chemical pesticides cause a resurgence in the pest problem.** Often, after using pesticides, pests return stronger than ever. This is called "resurgence." It is caused by the fact that pesticides tend to kill more beneficial insects than pests. At least two things can cause resurgence: (1) Beneficial insects are more active than plant-feeding insects, and in their wanderings they pick up more pesticide residue; and (2) being closer to the top of the food chain, beneficial insects concentrate pesticides in their bodies more than plant-eaters.

- **Chemical pesticides cause secondary pest outbreaks.** Sometimes after a pest is brought under control by lots of spraying, a new pest will appear that has not been a problem before. These "secondary" pests occur because the constant spraying has also killed their natural enemies and allowed them to grow to unusual numbers. It's hard to believe, but many of our most insidious pests (like mites) have been created by the misuse of pesticides.

MAIL-ORDER BENEFICIAL INSECTS FOR THE KITCHEN GARDEN

BENEFICIAL SPECIES	PESTS CONTROLLED	NOTES AND TIPS
Insect Predators		
Aphid midge (*Aphidoletes aphidimyza*)	Many species of aphids.	Release 3–5 pupae per plant; 2 releases give better results.
Convergent lady beetle (*Hippodamia convergens*)	Adults eat aphids, larvae feast on most soft-bodied insects.	May migrate from small gardens without plenty of insect food and plant nectar.
Lacewing (*Chrysoperla carnea, Chrysoperla rufilabrus*)	Adults and eggs of small soft-bodied insects like aphids, thrips, spider mites, and mealy bugs.	Shipped as eggs, larvae, or pupae. Distribute throughout garden. Often eaten by other beneficials. Good in small gardens with lots of flower nectar.
Mealybug destroyer (*Cryptolaemus montrouzieri*)	Mealybugs, aphids.	Will naturalize in warm winter areas, otherwise, release every year. Larvae look like mealybugs.
Minute pirate bug (*Orius*)	Small pests like thrips, mites, and insect eggs.	A few species of tiny bugs good for eating small things. Release 1–2 per plant. Attracted to pollen-rich flowers.
Six-Spotted Thrips (*Scolothrips sexmaculatus*)	Spider mites.	Package may include some spider mites.
Spined soldier bug (*Podisus maculiventris*)	Beetles, bugs, caterpillars.	Release 100 nymphs per 10 feet of garden row. Looks like a stinkbug with a spine on each side.
Wasp Parasitoids		
Braconid wasp (*Aphidius*)	Green peach and other aphids.	Several species lay eggs in aphids. Buy minimum order for garden. Adults attracted to plants in carrot family.
Chalcid wasps (*Aphelinus*)	Many aphids.	
Pediobius foveolatus	Mexican bean beetle.	Attacks larvae, so release must be timed to their presence.
Cotesia plutellae	Diamondback moth.	Several species attack the eggs of insects.
Dacnusa and *Diglyphus*	Leaf miners.	Several species.
Eretmocerus californicos	Outdoor whiteflies.	Attacks whitefly larvae.
Leptomastix spp.	Mealybugs.	Several species available.
Thripobiuis semiluteus	Thrips.	
Trichogramma pretosium	Many caterpillars	For general vegetables.
Trichogramma brassicae	Cabbage butterfly.	For brassicas.
Mite Predators		
Phytoseiulus spp.	Spider mites.	Can take weather extremes. Able to control pests in low pest numbers.
Metaseiulus longipes	Spider mites.	Tolerates weather extremes better than other mite predators. Able to control pests in low numbers.
Amblyseiulus spp.	Onion and flower thrips, plus other mites.	Consumes spider mites slower than *Phytoseiulus*, but is better when pests are low.
Nematode Predators		
Heterorhabditis and *Steinernema*	Soil insects: root weevils, crown borers, cutworms.	Need moist conditions and protection from sunlight; applied as a drench. Steinerema used for catepillars. Heterorhabditus used for beetles.
Bacteria		
Several types of *Bacillus thuriengiensis* (BT)	Caterpillars, fly larvae, leaf beetles, grubs.	Trade names: Thuricide, Dipel, MVP; in liquid or powder.

• **Chemical pesticide residue causes health problems to humans and the environment.** Several pesticides have been linked to a variety of human health problems including cancer. They can also damage the health of the environment by accumulating in food chains. If they get into the groundwater or are carried by air, they can do harm way beyond the borders of your garden.

Natural Pesticides

Natural pesticides are derived from plant, mineral, and animal products. Most of them are contact or stomach poisons. They are generally much safer than synthetic pesticides.

• **Sulfur.** Sulfur is probably the oldest natural pesticide in use today. The Greeks burned it to ward off insects. It remains popular because it's both effective and relatively safe. Sulfur is applied as a dust or wettable powder, and it's a good fungicide against powdery mildews, rusts, scab, and other plant diseases. It also works on some insects and mites.

Avoid breathing sulfur or getting it in your eyes. Always wear a dust mask and goggles when you mix or apply it. Overuse can make soil acidic. Avoid applying sulfur after an oil spray, since sulfur in oil will burn plant tissues. Use a plastic container; sulfur is corrosive to metals.

Copper is often added to sulfur, which makes it a more potent pesticide. Bluestone (copper sulfate) and bordeaux mix (bluestone with lime) are effective old-time fungicides.

• **Soap (Fatty Acids).** Soaps were probably discovered thousands of years ago when someone noticed that the animal grease and wood ashes in the old fire pit could be combined and used to rub away dirt. Even today, soaps are made by mixing the fatty acids from petroleum, animal fats, or plant oils with alkaline materials like wood ashes or lime. It's not surprising, then, that gardeners have been using soapy concoctions for centuries to ward off garden pests. As a pesticide, soap works by clogging the breathing pores of soft-bodied pests like aphids, caterpillars, thrips, mites, mealybugs, and whiteflies. They aren't as effective on beetles, scale, and insect eggs as oils. But if they are applied correctly, insecticidal soaps can help control the active stages of most soft-bodied insects.

There are three types of pesticidal soaps for different kinds of pests. **Insecticidal soap** is made from animal fats, which affects insects but not most plants. However, when using them around plants with dull or hairy leaves, keep in mind that normal concentrations of the soap may burn them.

Herbicidal soap is made from vegetable oils, like palm and coconut. Fats found in plants are good at killing plant cells, so apply your herbicidal soaps carefully around the plants you want to keep.

Fungicidal soap works by destroying the cell membranes of fungi. In the future, there will probably be a wider variety of fatty acids for more specific pests.

Soaps can't harm people, and they are completely biodegradable. Because they're a contact poison, they must be sprayed directly on the pest to work. So, if you apply soaps correctly, you are less likely to harm beneficial insects. Soaps don't corrode equipment.

You can make your own soapy pesticides from dishwashing liquids or Ivory soap (see page 174). Just remember that most cleaning soaps contain caustic chemicals, organic solvents, and degreasers, all of which have little effect on insects and may burn your plants. Commercial soaps are more pest-specific and less toxic to plants. Whenever you use soap sprays of any kind, it's best to test-spray a few leaves and note any damage.

- **Oils.** Mineral oils were used by the Romans to control various pests. Through the ages, people have used petroleum, kerosene, turpentine, and even whale oil to fight insect pests. Since 1940, refined petroleum oil has been used as a "dormant" spray on the wood of deciduous trees and shrubs. Dormant sprays, however, can burn leaves, so they have limited use. More refined petroleum oils, called "horticultural," "superior," or "summer" oils, can be sprayed on all kinds of plants year-round without burning leaves. Some "super-safe" summer oils are now made from plant oils like soybean, corn, and cottonseed instead of petroleum. You can also make your own vegetable-oil pesticide (see page 174).

Like soaps, oils kill pests by smothering, not poisioning. So a little dab won't work. You need to cover both sides of pest-infested leaves completely, especially when treating for aphids, mites, and whiteflies, which tend to dwell on the underside of leaves. Summer oil tends to kill the same kinds of insects that soap kills, but it does a better job on hard-to-get-to types like leaf miners, insect eggs, beetles, and scale. Summer oil doesn't burn plants as much as soap, although it can harm the green, waxy, leaves of plants like the brassicas or the hairy leaves of some squash.

Pesticidal oils are usually combined with water and a little soap to make them easier to spray. The mix should look like skim milk. To avoid burning plants, wait a few days between repeated sprayings and try to spray in the early morning or late afternoon, when temperatures are cool and dry. Avoid spraying when it's humid, cloudy, or overcast, and on plants that are under stress or in poor health. Be sure your spray container is well rinsed, especially if sulfur has been used in it recently; blends of sulfur and oil can burn plants severely. Although oils are chemically safe, they can cause eye and skin irritation, so always wear protective clothing and eyewear when using them.

You can make fungicides out of oils by adding common baking soda (see page 174). This concoction works against powdery mildews, early blight, and alternaria leaf blight.

The main advantage of soaps and oils is that pests are unlikely to develop resistance to them, because they kill insects by smothering them rather than by disrupting their biochemistry.

- **Botanicals.** Most plants contain natural chemicals that help them fend off pests. These chemicals can be processed and made into plant-derived pesticides, called "botanicals." Some botanicals, like sabadilla, have been used for centuries to control vegetable pests. Others, like neem, are new and exciting products. Always remember that botanicals are poisons; they are not selective about what they kill, including beneficials, and they should always be used with care. But they do have two important advantages. First, they break down rapidly into harmless by-products, unlike most synthetics. Second, because they are very complex chemicals, pests have a hard time developing resistances to them.

Botanicals are weak-acting pesticides and are often combined with synergistic chemicals to make them more effective. Some of these, like piperonyl butoxide (PBO), are quite toxic and not registered for use by many organic farming organizations.

RECIPES FOR HOMEMADE PESTICIDES

PESTICIDE	ACTIVE INGREDIENTS	TARGET PEST	PRECAUTIONS	FORMULATION/PREPARATION
Citrus oil	Linaloöl and d-limonene	Insecticide for leaf eaters like caterpillars, beetles, aphids, and mites.	Safe, but can irritate skin and affect cats.	Steep citrus peels in boiling water for 24 hours Strain, cool, and use.
Garlic	Allicin and sulfur	Insecticide for caterpillars, aphids, leafhoppers, whiteflies. Fungicide for brown rot, leaf spot, mildew, scab, and rust.	Keep away from eyes, wash hands.	Soak minced cloves in mineral or olive oil for 24 hours. Strain. Add 2 teaspoons of this oil to 1 quart water with a few drops of dish soap. Stir and strain again.
Hot pepper	Capsaicin	Ants, root maggots, soft-bodied insects.	Keep away from eyes, wash hands.	1 handful hot peppers blended in 1 quart water. Strain and spray.
Garlic and hot pepper	Allicin, sulfur, and capsaicin	See "Garlic" and "hot pepper." Combo is more effective on beetles than either by itself.	Keep away from eyes, wash hands.	2 cloves garlic plus ½ cup dried chiles in blender. Strain, add to 1 quart water, and spray.
Compost tea	Unknown	Early stages of leaf blight and powdery mildew.		Soak large cloth bag of aged compost in a bucket of water for a few days (see pages 77–79).
Oil fungicide	Oil and baking soda	Powdery mildew, alternaria, early blight.	May burn leaves of some plants.	4 tablespoons each of vegetable oil and baking soda, plus 8 tablespoons dish soap in 1 gallon water.
Oil insecticide	Oil	Mites, soft-bodied insects, beetles, scales.	May burn leaves of some plants.	1 cup vegetable oil and 1 tablespoon dish soap. Add 2 tablespoons of this to 1 cup water in spray bottle.
Soap	Salt of fatty acid	Mites and soft-bodied insects.	May burn leaves of some plants.	2–4 tablespoons liquid soap per gallon of water.

BOTANICAL PESTICIDES

NAME	SOURCE	TARGET PEST	COMMENTS
Citrus oils	Extracts from citrus peels	Aphids, beetles, caterpillars, spider mites, flies, fleas.	Not hazardous with normal use; dogs and cats should avoid.
Neem	Seed pod oil of South Asian neem tree	Aphids, mealybugs, caterpillars, beetles.	Stops feeding of many insects and halts growth of immature insects. Not toxic to birds or mammals, but may be toxic to fish.
Pyrethrin	Pyrethrum daisy flowers	Flying insects, thrips, leafhoppers.	Harmful to some beneficials. Acts fast and breaks down quickly.
Rotenone	Roots and stems of many tropical legumes	Many chewing pests like caterpillars and beetles.	Broad spectrum. Kills beneficials and very toxic to fish. Breaks down in a few days.
Ryania	Roots and stems of tropical South American shrub	Aphids, corn borers, leafhoppers, flea beetles, caterpillars.	Safe for beneficials. Slow acting. Most persistent of botanicals.
Sabadilla	Ground seeds of South American lily	Aphids, caterpillars, beetles, squash bugs, thrips, and grasshoppers.	Moderately toxic to people and pets; toxic to bees. Gets stronger with age.

USING PESTICIDES SAFELY

- When handling all pesticides, homemade or synthetic, respect them for what they are: poisons.

- Put all pesticides in one safe location where children, pets, and wildlife cannot reach them. Lock them up if necessary.

- Follow label directions carefully.

- Always leave chemicals in their bottles.

- Wear protective clothing and goggles whenever you spray.

- Use a good sprayer, one that has a pressure release button and is easy to carry. Never keep leftover pesticides in the sprayer. Wash it out immediately after each use.

- Spray on windless days and in the cool of the late evening to avoid drift on beneficial insects.

- Try to keep from spraying the heads of flowers. Many beneficial insects, including bees, are commonly found around flowers.

A Bevy of Beneficials

All plant pests have their own natural enemies that prey on them. For example, insects are attacked by bacteria, parasitic wasps, predatory insects and mites, plus reptiles and birds of all sorts. We call these creatures that help us control pests "beneficials." You can buy some from your local nursery or through the mail. But most garden beneficials are part of your local wildlife. They can be encouraged to enter your garden if you provide them with the right food and shelter. Whether you buy or lure beneficials, it helps to know a bit about their habits and haunts because they are the major players in the ecological balance of your garden.

Types of Beneficials

Beneficial insects eat the mites and insects that attack plants. They include everything from the popular ladybugs that eat aphids to the tiny *Trichogramma* wasps that parasitize insect eggs.

In the garden, beneficial insects generally roam within two kinds of environments. Some forage on the ground, like spiders, crickets, and ground beetles. Others look for prey in the foliage and canopy of garden plants, high above the ground. In this three-dimensional world, it requires lots of energy to maneuver through plants and forage for pests. As we shall see, canopy beneficials are best lured to the garden by the food of certain types of flowers, whereas ground beneficials are attracted to physical shelters ("microhabitats") near the ground (see pages 181–182).

Some beneficial insects are quite fussy about what they eat. They are specialists. Others feed on all sorts of pests. These generalists are important because they can survive when a food supply (pest) is low; there is always something else to eat. When pests flare up, the generalists are usually the first on the scene to help provide some control. Specialists, especially parasitoids, on the other hand, can react faster to rarer species or hidden pests. We need both the generalists and specialists to help us control garden pests.

Beneficial insects attack pests in two different ways: as predators or parasitoids. Predators either chew pests with their mandibles, or they stab them with tubelike mouth parts and suck them dry. Parasitoids lay their eggs in or on other insects. When the parasitoid eggs hatch, the larvae become predators and eat the insect from the inside out or outside in, depending on where the eggs are laid. A few flies and many species of tiny wasps are the major parasitoids.

Predators

An effective predator locates pests by hunting, ambushing, or trapping without spending too much energy. Some of the most efficient insect predators (syrphid flies, lacewings, and true bugs) lay their eggs near colonies of pests so that the hatching young don't have to go very far to find a meal.

- **Dragonflies (Odonata)** Called the "hawks of the insect world," dragonflies are fierce predators of many flying insects. Nymphs spend up to two years under water eating aquatic insects. If you have a pond with plants, it should attract dragonflies. They can range over half a mile from water.

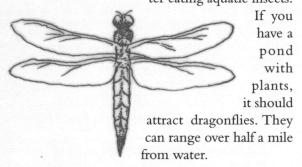

- **True Bugs (Hemiptera)** Most true bugs are plant feeders, but a few species use their prominent beaks to suck animal juices. Predatory bugs tend to be general feeders, but the smaller species have a limited diet due to their size.

The **minute pirate bug** *(Orius)* feeds on insect eggs, tiny insects, mites, and especially thrips. These tiny ¹/₁₆-inch predators are black and white as adults and an inconspicuous yellow as nymphs. They are one of the first beneficials to appear in spring. *Orius* eats pollen and nectar from goldenrod, daisies, yarrow, and corn. With a hand lens, you can often find the pirate bug at the ends of cornsilk looking for the eggs of the corn earworm. *Orius insidiosus* is commercially available.

The **big-eyed bug** *(Georcis),* is only a little larger (¹/₈ inch) and is an important predator of insect eggs (especially moths), mites, thrips, aphids, plant-eating bugs, leafhoppers, and other smaller pests. Their oversized eyes make them easy to identify, although you may need a hand lens.

Both adults and nymphs move rapidly and drop quickly from plants when disturbed. Big-eyed bugs eat plant nectar when pests are scarce. They like to lay eggs on goldenrod and pigweed.

Larger predatory bugs feed on small pests when they are young, but move to larger soft-bodied insects, especially caterpillars and beetle larvae, as they grow. Included here are:

1. The **assassin bug**, which, with its low profile, long legs, and pointed head, attacks almost any kind of insect, including other beneficials.

2. The **spiny stink bug** *(Podisus)*, which has recently been offered for sale as an insect predator. It is a large insect partial to caterpillars and beetles. There are many native species, and the value of store-bought releases is still unproven.

3. The **damsel bug** *(Nabis)*, which appears later in the year and hides in flowers to prey on aphids, leafhoppers, and caterpillars.

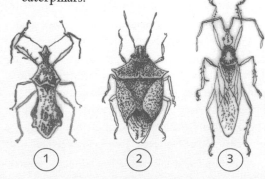

• **Beetles (Coleoptera)** With their bright colors, **lady beetles** are one of the most popular of all beneficials. They are found almost everywhere, and their presence is a sign of a healthy garden. The adults are specialists and eat mostly aphids, while the alligator-shaped gray and orange larvae eat insect eggs, beetle larvae, aphids, and other soft-bodied insects. There are several species of lady beetles, and each region of the country has its own native varieties. Along the West Coast, *Hippodamia convergens* migrates to foothill areas during the winter, where it hibernates in hoards and is easily collected and sold. However, releases of commercial *Hippodamia* are often unsuccessful. The hibernating beetles are full of stored body fat, and when they are released, they tend to be lethargic. Even when they are active, *Hippodamia* will fly away if there is not enough food in the area. There is also some concern about decimating natural populations of lady beetles. But with a good mix of suitable plants and flowers, you can encourage native or introduced lady beetles to stay in your garden, eat pests, reproduce and establish themselves.

Adult   Larvae

Perhaps the most underrated lady beetle is the **mealybug destroyer, *Cryptolaemus.*** It is commercially available for the control of mealybugs in greenhouses. In spite of its name, the mealybug destroyer is a generalist and an important predator of other soft-bodied insects, many of which are tended and protected by ants who milk them for honeydew. The ants attack insect predators that happen to prowl into the area, but not the larvae of *Cryptolaemus,* which look like mealybugs and in this guise can feed without being attacked by ants. You might say they are a wolf in sheep's clothing. Although commercial *Cryptolaemus* are expensive, they naturalize fairly easily in warmer climates, especially if there is a landscape with suitable plants and flowers.

 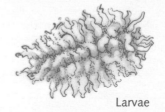

Adult   Larvae

Soldier beetles are common predators of aphids and other soft-bodied insects. These long, narrow beetles are often orange or red, with black or brown wing covers. They are especially fond of goldenrod and other plants in the daisy family (Asteraceae) plus milkweed and catnip. The larvae have a velvety surface and hunt like the adults.

Ground beetles (Carabids) are soil-dwelling beetles that are important predators of caterpillars, earwigs, snail eggs, and other ground-dwelling pests. Usually black and shiny, they have grooves on their wing covers and run quickly on long legs. You can encourage them in your garden by placing inverted flowerpots or other such containers in spots throughout your garden. Adults and larvae are most active at night and are commonly found in and around compost piles, coarse mulch, and leaf litter, looking for a meal.

Rove beetles are an underrated group of garden predators. They are small, slender, dark-colored beetles whose wings don't quite cover their abdomens, unlike most beetles. This allows them to be very active insects, running about with their abdomen raised. Rove beetles hunt at night. During the day you can find them around decaying material and under stones or other objects on the ground. Both adults and larvae are valuable ground predators of aphids, mites, slugs, snails, and fly eggs. A few species prey on cabbage root maggots.

- **Lacewings (Neuroptera)** There are many species of lacewings, but only a few, like the green lacewing *Chrysoperla carnea,* are commercially available. Fortunately, most gardens have many species of native lacewings in residence. The larvae are important general predators. When they are small, they eat insect eggs, mites, and thrips. As they grow, they attack larger soft-bodied pests like aphids, mealybugs, whiteflies, and small caterpillars. In an interesting twist, fresh releases of lacewing larvae can serve as food for other resident predators.

The larvae are difficult to see because they camouflage themselves with the cast-off skins of their victims. But if you look very closely around colonies of aphids you may see a small alligator-shaped larvae with a tapered hind end and a pair of icepick-like mandibles.

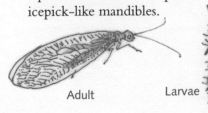

Adult   Larvae

Adult lacewings are delicate, slender, green to brown insects often found around lights at night. With their large transparent wings, it's easy to see where they got their name. The adults of most native species are predators. The commercial varieties eat nectar and pollen from flowers in the landscape, especially corn, sunflowers, grasses and legumes. Females lay eggs near patches of aphids. The larvae that hatch are strongly attracted to aphid smells and even eat nectar secreted by aphids.

- **Flies (Diptera)** The larvae of many flies are important garden predators. The best known and most popular are the **syrphid flies.** Syrphids are called "hover" or "flower" flies because the adults like to buzz around flowers in search of food. Most gardens have dozens of species of native syrphids about.

Adult syrphids are marked with stripes and splashes of yellow, white, and black. They have the appearance of a wasp or a bee, but a closer look soon reveals their short antennae, which are typical of flies. They come in all sizes and shapes, from stout and hairy to smooth and slender.

The adults feed on nectar and pollen from flowers, and if you look closely, you might even see them feeding from leaf surfaces where aphids have left a film of honeydew. Hovering and egg-laying require lots of energy, which is supplied by a steady diet of nectar wherever they can find it.

Not all syrphid flies have predatory larvae. Some species lay their eggs in damp places (including compost piles), where the larvae eat decaying material. The adults of these damp-area syrphids also frequent flowers. Syrphid flies are large, robust flies, beelike, with yellow and black markings. The predatory syrphids tend to be smaller, with flatter abdomens and light yellow, rather than dark yellow, markings.

Syrphid with
aquatic larvae

Syrphid with
aphid-eating larvae

The larvae are true maggots, only ⅛ to ¼ inch long with pointed, eyeless heads and legless bodies. They can be seen on aphid-covered leaves, swaying back and forth, hoping to bump into a meal. As the maggots get larger, they change color from white to tan to green to gray. You can't buy syrphid flies, but they are found everywhere. They are easily attracted to gardens by a variety of flowers, including many in the daisy family (Asteraceae), especially tansy, yarrow, and sunflower. They're also drawn to the carrot family (Apiaceae), the annual buckwheat *Fagopyrum,* the perennial buckwheat *Eriogonum,* and the ornamental ground cover alyssum (*Lobularia*).

The adults and larvae of several small, long-legged flies, called **midges,** are important predators but often go unnoticed. The adult looks like a small mosquito, dark on top and light underneath. Midges feed on mites and small insects. The larva is often mistaken for the syrphid fly larva. Some midges are commercially available. However, it is pinkish orange in color, and not gray or tan like the syrphid.

Parasitoids

Parasitoids lay their eggs in or on other insects. These eggs hatch into larvae, which eat the host. Two groups of insects have parasitoids: the flies (Diptera) and the wasps (Hymenoptera).

- **Fly Parasitoids (Diptera)** Fly parasitoids attack insects of all kinds, including termites, bees, ants, lady beetles, and scales. They also parasitize slugs, snails, crickets, and caterpillars. There are several families of fly parasitoids, but the most common are the **tachinids.**

You can't buy tachinids, but they are very common, and they can be seen in and around the garden. The adults resemble large, robust houseflies with a bristly abdomen. They eat nectar and pollen and they especially like the flowers of buckwheat, alyssum, corn plants, and various plants of the daisy family (Asteraceae). Tachinids lay eggs on caterpillars, Japanese beetles, crickets, and other insects. Each species tends to be a specialist. Don't kill a caterpillar with white eggs stuck to its back; they are probably tachinid eggs.

- **Wasp Parasitoids (Hymenoptera)** Most people are familiar with hornets, yellow jackets, and wasps because they can sting. The adult stinging wasps are predators of caterpillars and other insects, but they are not parasitoids. Wasp parasitoids include thousands of species of tiny nonstinging wasps that lay their eggs on or in other insects. When the eggs hatch, the wasp larvae become predators on their hosts. Some wasp parasitoids are generalists, but most are very particular about what they eat.

Many parasitoids are sold commercially. They attack beetles, leafhoppers, caterpillars, aphids, whiteflies, filth flies, and true bugs. In addition, most gardens have an arsenal of native parasitoids. Unfortunately, most of them are very difficult to see. You really need a hand lens to appreciate wasp parasitoids. Early in the morning you can see them waking up on the flowers of yarrow, Queen Anne's lace, and other flat flower heads. This is the time to get close to them, while they're too cold to move. The largest wasp parasitoids (Ichneumons) are the size of the smallest stinging wasp, $^1/_4$ to $^1/_2$ inch. They are common around fruit trees in spring.

The tiny *Trichogramma* **wasp** is the best known parasitoid. Smaller than a pinhead, "trichos" drill through other insect eggs, especially those of caterpillars, to lay their own eggs. These then hatch to eat the host's egg and emerge from it as adults. Trichos are shipped as pupae inside moth eggs glued to cards. Several species are available. Like many parasitoids, adult trichos feed on nectar from clusters of shallow flowers, including those in the carrot, scabiosa, and aster families. Releases of commercial *Trichogramma* will build up over time in gardens with beneficial plants and become established as native populations.

Other Beneficials

Although insects are the most common type of garden beneficial, they are by no means the only ones. Spiders, predatory mites, and certain microbes also have an important role to play in the control of your garden pests.

- **Spiders** Spiders are the most underrated and misunderstood of all beneficials. In spite of the fear surrounding spiders, they are some of the most important creatures you can have in your garden.

All spiders are predators. They hunt by trapping (webs), hunting (wolf spiders), and ambushing (crab spiders). They kill their prey with poisonous "fangs" called chelicera. Spiders should be left alone and never prodded, although very few spiders commonly found in the garden are dangerous. They feed on many kinds of garden pests during the day and night, and they flourish in a wide variety of garden habitats. Spiders fill many niches not filled by insect predators, and thus, round out the ecological balance of your garden.

Orb weavers spin the familiar flat spiraling sticky webs found on and between plants. They feast on leafhoppers, aphids, flies, and other small soft-bodied insects. Large species are commonly called "garden spiders."

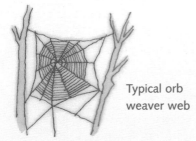

Typical orb weaver web

Combfooted spiders or **cobweb weavers** fling silk strands over their captives and build their irregular webs in fences, among rocks, and between low branches of shrubs. Their favorite foods are ants, beetles, and flies.

Funnel-web weavers hide at the narrow end of funnel webs amongst leaf litter, stones, low shrubs, and grassy areas. They are fond of moths, whiteflies, and grasshoppers.

Funnel web

Wolf spiders are ground hunters that don't weave webs. They prowl at night looking for aphids, beetle grubs, snail eggs, and fly larvae. When at rest, they stay under stones or dig burrows in uncultivated soil.

Jumping spiders and their close cousins the **Lynx spiders** are sun-loving, sharp-eyed hunters who rove around and pounce on their prey. Jumping spiders are typically brown, and you can often see them wandering around leaves, bark, or stones, bobbing their heads and trailing a silken thread behind them for security. Lynx spiders also hunt during the day, but they chase their prey over vegetation or lie in wait and jump out and attack. Both spiders feed on many pests that other spiders don't, like cucumber beetles, corn earworms, plant bugs, and weevils.

Crab spiders hold their legs outstretched and move about like a crab. They wait and ambush their prey on the ground or in flowers. Many crab spiders take on the colors of the flowers they inhabit. Because they hang out near flowers, crab spiders also eat beneficial insects, including bees.

There is another bonus that makes spiders superior predators; they are less likely to migrate from your garden when insects are scarce. Most spiders will simply slow down and wait for food to reappear.

To make spiders welcome in your garden, create a variety of microhabitats for the various kinds of spiders and avoid spraying pesticides. If you must spray, do so in the middle of the day when spiders are least active, and only spray severely infested plants. Don't blanket the whole garden. A good mix of tall and short garden plants, thick layers of mulch, in-garden compost piles, bundles of bamboo, and inverted flower pots are choice microhabitats for spiders.

- **Predatory Mites** Mites are a very large group of animals related to ticks and spiders. Most mites are quite small. Some eat organic matter, some eat plants, and some eat small insects and other mites. Predatory mites are an important part of the local wildlife, and they are in  every corner of your garden, from the topsoil to the compost pile to the canopy of your vegetable patch. Most predatory mites are large (for mites) and very fast moving. You can often see them amid colonies of spider mites.

Certain predatory mites (see page 171) are available from specialty suppliers (see pages 452–453). They are used mostly for controlling spider mites and thrips.

- **Beneficial Microbes** A garden teems with microbes: viruses, bacteria, fungi, and nematodes. They are in the soil, in compost piles, on leaves, around roots, in the morning dew. All groups of microbes have members that are good at eating other things. Some bacteria produce toxins that kill insects. A few soil fungi eat insects, nematodes, and mites, while certain soil nematodes eat soil-dwelling insects. This network of microscopic eaters and eaten is the foundation of the garden ecosystem.

A few beneficial microbes are available to the home gardener as "microbial pesticides" (see page 171). Although they can be effective if applied correctly, they are living things and lose their toxicity when they come into contact with ultraviolet light, plant oils, wind, rain, and other microbes. For this reason, they should always be considered only part of your garden's IPM program. They are especially valuable in the early stages of insect outbreaks and on small or immature insects.

Perhaps the most popular microbial is the bacteria *Bacillus thuringiensis* (BT), which produces toxins and helps control caterpillars, beetles, and fly larvae. BT is an effective, yet slow-acting stomach poison. Spray it on your plants where pests can eat it, and be patient. A growing number of BT varieties specially formulated for specific insects are now available.

- **Nematodes** are very small round worms found naturally in your soil. There are hundreds of species; some are beneficial and others are pests on roots of many plants. The predatory nematodes *Steinerema* and *Heterorhabditis* are sold commercially for the control of soil-insect larvae like grubs, cutworms, weevils, and maggots. They are shipped in a clay material that you mix with water and apply as a drench or spray on soil. Nematodes attack passing insects by wiggling inside of them through wounds or breathing pores. Once inside, the nematodes release their own unique bacteria, which kills the insect and turns it into a nematode nursery.

Beneficial viruses and insect-eating fungi are still in the developmental stages.

CONTROLLING WEEDS SAFELY

Ask most gardeners and they'll tell you that their worst pests are weeds. We have seen people give up on gardening because they didn't have the time or energy to keep weeds from enveloping their garden. Weed seeds are everywhere. They are mixed in the soil where they can lie in wait for years until you work them to the surface to germinate. They resprout from bits of roots, or they float in the air as wispy seeds. Birds drop them to the ground, animals carry them on their fur, and people bring them on their shoes and clothing. They are in your compost pile, in your mulch, and in that bag of cover crop seeds.

To make matters worse, gardens are an ideal habitat for weeds. The plants we call weeds ("plants out of place") are very good at invading patches of bare soil, then growing and flowering before other plants have a chance to root. They are very good at outcompeting other plants for water, food, and light. Many of them also harbor plant diseases and insect pests. It is for these reasons gardeners typically take a dim view of weeds. However, the same attitude that demands we eliminate all insects from our gardens requires that our gardens look like golf courses. This is neither possible nor in the best interest of your garden. What you need to do is separate the good weeds from the bad ones and give a priority to your weeding efforts (see page 184). The notions of "good" and "bad" can apply to the same plant in different situations. For example, plantain gives pollen to the predatory bug *Geocoris,* but in apple orchards this weed houses the apple aphid, a vector for apple scab disease. So before you go out and whack away every uninvited seedling, consider weeds in the same light as insect pests; keep some around for the sake of ecological balance.

Before agriculture, there was no such thing as a weed; there were simply invasive, fast-growing herbs that had a purpose in the grand scheme of things. Weeds are nature's way of preparing the soil for future plant communities. When weeds invade a bare disturbed area, they die, adding organic matter to the soil. As the soil improves, the way is paved for larger and deeper rooted perennials, shrubs, and finally, trees. Weeds are the first stage in the succession of bare land to a forest.

The same principle applies to your garden, only on a microscale. Essentially, your garden is a permanently disturbed area that serves as a haven for weeds. When you remove plant cover and cultivate, rototill, or trample the soil, you become a disturbing act of nature. You open the door for weeds to intrude and gain a foothold. To a weed, your garden is simply a highly disturbed plant community.

Benefits of Weeds

The presence of some weeds is not only inevitable, but actually desirable. Many weeds provide valuable services, and these should be considered before weeding with abandon.

Weeds Mine the Soil for Nutrients

Deep-rooted weeds penetrate the soil, and open up pathways for water to drain and roots to grow. The roots bring up nutrients that have percolated deep into the subsoil. These "mined" nutrients are stored in the weed's plant tissue for us to compost and put back into the soil. Since most deep-rooted weeds are quite invasive, they should be tolerated until they start to flower. After that, they become an official weed. So before they set seed, pull and compost them for the nutrients they contain.

Weeds Shelter Beneficial Insects

Many weeds provide a habitat for beneficial insects by offering food, drink, and refuge from bad weather and human activity. Wild carrots (*Daucus carota*) supply nectar and pollen for insect predators to eat, while wild mustards (*Brassica* spp.) are virtual storehouses for aphids that feed lacewings and other predatory insects. In California, various native bunching grasses (for example, *Koeleria*) serve as an overwintering home for migratory lady beetles.

Weeds Prevent Soil Erosion

All weeds eagerly cover bare ground and keep it from being blown or washed away. Some weeds, especially prostrate noninvasive ones like scarlet pimpernel (*Anagallis arvensis*) and Persian speedwell (*Veronica persica*), can keep patches of soil from eroding and drying out.

ASSESSING SOME COMMON GARDEN WEEDS

WEED NAME	PROBLEMS	BENEFITS	NOTES
Annuals			
Lamb's-quarter (*Chenopodium album*)	Harbors beet leaf miner.	Attracts beneficials. Deep roots. Edible.	Keep a few in flower, a few for young leaves, and weed the rest.
Purslane (*Portulaca oleracea*)	Invasive ground cover.	Edible and nutritious.	Harvest and compost, but keep from flowering. Edible ones need more water.
Sow thistle (*Sonchus asper*)	Invasive from seed. Large plant.	Aphid insectary plant.	Leave a few to grow but not flower; weed all the rest. Wind-borne seed.
Persian speedwell (*Veronica persica*)	Slightly invasive from runners.	Introduced as rock garden plant.	Keep well contained in a few spots for flower.
Winter Annuals			
Wild mustard (*Brassica* spp.)	Harbors cabbage aphids.	Aphid insectary plant. Edible.	Weed carefully and consistently with an eye out for aphids.
Groundsel (*Senecio vulgaris*)	Invasive from seed.	Easy to weed.	Low-priority weeding.
Chickweed (*Stellaria media*)	Seeds and creeping stems.	None apparent.	Weed constantly for compost.
Tansymustard (*Descurainia pinnata*)	Invasive from seed. Hosts diamondback moth of brassicas.	Aphid insectary plant.	Weed carefully and consistently. Look for aphids and beneficials.
Mallow (*Malva* spp.)	Invasive from seed.	Green manure prior to . seed formation.	Compost or dig in before flowering.
Oats (*Avena fatua*)	10-year seed dormancy. Hosts rust and aphids.	Aphid insectary plant and green manure.	Keep from going to seed. Mow at flower, for compost or mulch.
Biennials			
Poison hemlock (*Conium maculata*)	Poisonous. Invasive.	None apparent.	Top-priority weeding.
Queen Anne's lace (*Daucus carota*)	Slightly invasive. Harbors carrot rust fly.	Attracts beneficials. Nice cut flower.	Let several plants flower for beneficials unless rust fly appears.
Fennel (*Foeniculum vulgare*)	Difficult to weed out.	Attracts beneficials. Culinary herb.	Low-priority weeding.
Perennials			
Bermuda grass (*Cynodon dactylon*)	Highly invasive from rhizomes and seed.	Lawn grass. Rabbit food.	Top-priority weeding.
Bindweed (*Convolvulus arvensis*)	Highly invasive from deep rootstock.	None apparent.	Top-priority weeding. Likes disturbed soil.
Dandelion (*Taraxacum officinale*)	Invasive from seeds and deep rootstock.	Deep-rooted; young leaves are edible.	Top-priority weeding. Edible when grown, not collected.
Dock (*Rumex* spp.)	Invasive from rootstock.	Attracts beneficials. Young leaves edible.	Keep a few in flower, a few for young leaves, and weed the rest.
Mint (*Mentha* spp.)	Invasive from rhizomes.	Medicinal and flavoring herb.	Grow in containers under water faucets. Weed the rest.
Nutsedge (*Cyperus esculentis*)	Invasive. Prefers moist soils.	None apparent.	Top priority weeding.
Oxalis (*Oxalis* spp.)	Invasive. Seeds or tuberous roots.	Pretty flowers.	Easy to handpick, don't let go to seed.
Plantain (*Plantago lanceolata*)	Slightly invasive from seed.	Attracts small predatory bugs.	Let a few go to flower for beneficials; pick all the rest early.

Weeds are Barometers of Soil Conditions

Some weeds are particularly fond of certain soil conditions. In fact, the kinds of weeds growing in your garden can give you clues about your soil. For example, if red sorrel (*Rumex acetosella*) is common, your soil is probably acid and poorly drained. For more on how weeds can alert you to soil conditions, see pages 59–60.

IPM of Weeds

The principles of IPM described on pages 161–174 for plant-eaters can also be applied to weeds.

Take preventative measures

Start by making conditions inhospitable for weeds: (1) Keep bare soil planted with cover crops; and (2) for those weeds that thrive in alkaline, waterlogged, or compacted soils, correct these conditions. A rich, well-drained soil won't eliminate weeds, but it will discourage many invasive roadside types and give your vegetables a better chance at outgrowing the ones that do take hold.

Get to know your local weeds

During your regular scouting for pests, take notice of any new or strange seedlings that might appear. There are several good books that can help you identify common weeds from seedling to flower stage (see pages 444–445).

Learn the life cycles of your weeds and place them into five categories

1. Annuals (such as ryegrass and lamb's-quarter) are plants that live and die in a single season. If you whack off annual weeds at their base, they rarely resprout the same year. Annuals multiply by producing huge numbers of seeds that disperse easily and stay dormant for years. Weed these before they go to seed.

2. Winter annuals (such as mustard and sow thistle) germinate in the fall, grow in the winter, and set seed in the spring. They are among the first weeds to appear in the spring, so you can control them with a heavy fall mulch. In mild coastal areas, they may sprout whenever there's water.

3. Biennials (such as Queen Anne's lace and mullein) grow leaves the first year and shoot up the second year with a tall flower stalk. Treat biennials as perennials the first year and annuals the second.

4. Herbaceous perennials (such as dandelions and Bermuda grass) produce seeds, but they also shoot up from creeping underground stems (rhizomes) and deep taproots. Unless you remove the rhizomes and roots, perennials will probably resprout from hacked-off tops.

5. Woody perennials, such as blackberries, kudzu, and poison ivy, are some of the hardest weeds to eliminate; they should be weeded without hesitation.

Establish your tolerance levels

The key to safe weed care is knowing which weeds you can tolerate and which ones you can't. Consider the advantages and disadvantages of your local weeds. Some weeds are worth saving. Others have no place in the garden. Still others can go either way depending on the circumstances. The comments in the notes column in the chart "Assessing Your Garden Weeds," on page 184 gives examples of how one group of weeds might be assessed as part of a garden weed program.

Weed with Safe and Appropriate Methods

Weeding without using herbicides takes more time and energy, but creates a healthier garden. Following are some tried-and-true weeding methods.

- **Weed by hand hoe.** Fortunately, the common garden hoe is being replaced by more efficient weeders that are easier on the back. For annuals, use tools like the swan-neck and oscillating hoes that don't disturb the soil too much. You can also use razor-sharp shallow hoes as scraping tools. They are excellent for controlling annuals, which are killed when you cut their stems or crowns. Many perennials need to be dug up, roots and all, or else they will resprout from rootstock. Remember that it is much easier to remove weeds when they are young. Regular weeding is the easiest way to save time in the garden.

- **Always mulch.** Mulch smothers weeds and is one of the most effective tools for controlling weeds. Almost anything that stops light from getting to the soil will work, including plastic, newspapers, and boards. Geotextile weed mats, which are made from synthetic woven fabrics such as polypropylene, cover the soil but allow it to breathe. Organic mulches like rotted hay, lawn clippings, rice hulls, wood chips, or sifted compost have the advantage of adding organic matter to the soil. Be sure your organic mulch is free of weed seeds or you'll compound your problem.

- **Use living mulches.** Cover crops are often called "living mulches," because they can keep down weeds. Some gardeners "underseed" their vegetables with a cover crop. This is done by letting vegetables get established on weed-free ground, then broadcasting vetch or oats around the veggies. Look for living mulches that don't compete with your vegetables, but are tough enough to crowd out weeds. Try annual clovers and vetch around tomatoes and peppers. Oats and wheat are good at suppressing weeds among brassicas. If you sow them after the middle of summer, they'll die before they seed, giving you yet another layer of mulch. Grown this way, wheat and oats are good at keeping down winter annual weeds.

You can also use growing vegetables as a living mulch. In raised beds, place plants close together and arrange them to create a canopy that shades out weeds. This method works well if you water and weed your beds a couple of times prior to planting.

- **Practice solarization.** Solarization involves killing weed seeds by heating your soil to high temperatures for extended periods. Soil is usually heated by covering it with one or two layers of clear plastic film for 4 to 6 weeks *during the hottest part of the year.* For more penetrating heat, the soil should be watered thoroughly before covering. Solarization is less effective in cooler climates, where summers are below 80°F. It is good for vegetables that are especially difficult to weed, like garlic, onions, carrots, and salad greens; plant these into solarized soil during late summer and fall.

Solarization is quite effective with winter annual weeds, less so with summer annuals or perennials. Used in the heat of summer, solarization really gets to the seeds of winter annuals about to germinate in a few weeks. The seeds of summer annuals will die, but others will work to the surface by the time spring arrives. The roots and rhizomes of most perennial weeds aren't killed by solariziation.

- **Rotate crops.** Some vegetables are easier to weed than others. Tall ones like corn or trellised ones like peas and beans are easy. They also slow weeds by shading the ground. Plants that need hilling or digging, like leeks and potatoes, are easy to weed because you're always moving the soil around them. Wherever these vegetables grow you're likely to find fewer weeds than among lower growing, tightly packed vegetables like onion, garlic, carrots, and salad greens. If you rotate hard-to-weed vegetables with easy-to-weed ones, you'll save a lot of weeding time in the long run (see pages 32–36).

MANAGING PESTS WITH BACKYARD BIODIVERSITY

We know how important it is to protect and nurture biodiversity. Where better to start than in our own backyards? In nature, biologically diverse landscapes, with many species of plants and animals, have fewer pest outbreaks than landscapes with only a few species. Unfortunately, in our desire to keep tidy gardens we often destroy biodiversity. We eliminate plants and refuges that feed and shelter beneficials. The best way to shape the ecology of your kitchen garden is to provide what beneficial animals want most: food, water, and shelter. There are several ways to achieve this.

The Garden Plant Guild

The term *guild* comes from the crafts guilds organized during medieval times to protect workers from unfair competition. Botanists use the term "plant guild" to describe groups of plants that grow together in natural communities for mutual benefit. Plants in guilds depend on one another for shade, nutrients, and protection from pests; they complement each other's needs or make demands on resources at different times. These plants have evolved together because of mutually beneficial relationships.

We can imitate natural plant guilds in our gardens by planting tall or trellised plants to shade leaf crops in summer, by planting cover crops before planting heavy-feeding vegetables (see page 36), or by planting radishes among carrots to break open the soil. But the main elements in a garden plant guild are those plants that attract beneficial insects. Beneficials will always seek out a garden with the right lures: nectar, pollen, and juicy

insects. By using combinations of certain plants, you can provide these foods and create a biologically active garden environment. Think of three types of plants in a garden plant guild.

Pollen and Nectar Plants

Beneficial insects need lots of energy to find prey and lay eggs. They get this energy from the pests they eat. But when the pests are scarce, they fuel up on the male part of flowers, pollen (protein), and the female part of flowers, nectar (carbohydrates). Pollen is especially important for egg laying so that beneficials can quickly produce more generations of bug eaters. Nectar is in three places: (1) in floral nectaries inside the flower; (2) in extra-floral nectaries found outside the flower and on the margins and stems of leaves; and (3) in nectar-filled pests like aphids.

Insectary Plants

Some plants are just naturally pest-prone. In the plant guild they are called "insectary plants" because the gardener can use them as a source of insect food for beneficials, much like a commercial insectary.

Aphids are an easy food-pest to grow on insectary plants. They are found everywhere, they increase rapidly, and they have many natural enemies. In warm winter areas, broccoli, cabbage, nasturtiums, and tansy are attacked by aphids in late winter. These aphids are preyed upon by several beneficial insects. When spring arrives, the beneficials, having grown in numbers and fattened up on aphids during the lean winter, are better able to control spring pests. Golden yarrow (*Achillea filipendulina*), for example, attracts the lygus bug, which in turn lures many predatory bugs that eat it. Care must be taken in using insectary plants, because pests can get out of control, especially aphids.

Aromatic Plants

Plant-eating insects are very selective about what they eat, and they are strongly attracted to the smell of their favorite plants. Some smelly plants have aromatic compounds that actually repel plant eaters. Experiments have shown that odors given off by pungent plants can mask the attracting odor of vegetables, making it hard for the pest to find its favorite food. Common repellent plants include onions and tomatoes, many aromatic herbs and a few strong-smelling ornamental shrubs like *Tagetes lemonii* (Mexican marigold), *Aloysia triphylla* (lemon verbena), some of the ornamental sages, and *Artemesias*.

There is very little known about repellent plants, especially which plant combinations actually work or how much of each to grow. A lot of the companion-planting information of plants "liking" or "disliking" each other is probably based on mixing up the odor signals of vegetables and fragrant herbs to confuse pests—another reason to keep diversity in your garden.

Perennial Plant Refuges

During bad weather, perennial plants can be both food and protection for beneficial insects. Windbreaks, hedgerows, and flower borders give insects a place to spend the winter, a haven during lean times, and a retreat while you are cultivating, harvesting, or otherwise disturbing the garden. If your perennials include pollen and insectary plants, all the better. Even small patches of well-chosen weeds will feed the beneficial insects and wild bees that pollinate your garden plants.

Plant Families That Attract Beneficials

When beneficial insects are released or move into a garden, the first things they seek out are nectar and pollen from flowers. Most beneficial insects are very small and seem to prefer clusters of tiny shallow flowers growing horizontally like a miniature landing platform. Inflorescenses like this are typical of the daisy family (Asteraceae), the carrot family (Apiaceae), the teasel family (Dipsacaceae), the buckwheat family (Polygonaceae), and certain species of other families. Flathead inflorescences provide beneficials with a mini-meadow full of pollen and nectar.

Some plants also have stem and leaf nectaries outside of their flowers. These include corn, snap peas, peach trees, sunflowers, and *Vicia* (vetches and bell/fava beans). It's possible that these extra-floral nectaries lure beneficial insects that protect the plant. It's interesting that they also attract ants, which tend aphids for their honeydew. These aphids are eaten by many beneficial insects, and we might ask ourselves: Are aphids just insects acting like extra-floral nectaries? Some plant families, like carrots, have flowers with easy-to-access nectar. Other plants, like the tansy and chamomile tribes of the daisy family, have well-hidden nectar. So they only attract beneficials with special mouth parts, like syrphid flies and parasitoids. Likewise, not all species or varieties are equally effective at attracting beneficials. *Achillea millefolium* is preferred by syrphid flies more than other yarrows. Some varieties of *Ceanothus* sunflowers, cosmos, and goldenrods seem to attract insect predators better than other varieties. We are only beginning to understand these complex relationships between insects and plants. There are undoubtedly more beneficial plants out there, waiting to be discovered.

SOME COMMON GARDEN PLANTS THAT ATTRACT BENEFICIAL INSECTS

PLANT	COMMON NAME	TYPE OF PLANT
Apiaceae (carrot family)		
Ammi visagna	white lace flower	perennial, herbaceous
Anethum graveolens	dill	annual, herb
Angelica archangelica	angelica	biennial, herb
Apium graveolens	celery and celeriac	biennial, vegetable
Carum carvi	caraway	biennial, herb
Coriandrum sativum	coriander	annual, herb
Daucus carota	wild carrot, carrot	biennial cut flower, edible
Foeniculum vulgare	fennel	biennial, herb
Petroselinum crispum	parsley	perennial, herb
Asteraceae (daisy family)		
Achillea spp.	yarrow	perennial, cut flower
Anthemis tinctoria	anthemis, marguerite	perennial, border
Cosmos bipinnatus	cosmos	annual, cut flower
Helianthus annuus	sunflower*	annual, cut flower, edible
Heterotheca subaxillaris	camphorweed	annual/biennial weed
Layia platyglossa	tidytips	annual
Liatrus spicata	gayfeather	perennial cut flower
Rudbeckia hirta	black-eyed susan	perennial, herbaceous
Solidago spp.	goldenrod	perennial, herbaceous
Tanacetum spp.	tansy*	perennial, herb
Tithonia rotundifolia	Mexican sunflower	perennial grown as annual
Brassicaceae (cabbage family)		
Brassica niger	black mustard*	annual weed
Brassica oleracea italica	sprouting broccoli*	annual vegetable
Lobularia maritima	alyssum	perennial, ground cover
Raphanus sativus	radish and daikon*	annual vegetable, weed
Dipsacaceae (teasel family)		
Scabiosa spp.	scabiosa	annual, perennial cut flowers
Dipsacus spp.	teasel	perennial, herbaceous weed
Polygonaceae (buckwheat family)		
Fagopyrum esculentum	buckwheat, annual	annual summer cover crop
Eriogonum spp.	wild buckwheat	evergreen shrub
Polygonum aubertii	silver lace vine	perennial vine
Miscellaneous Plants		
Amaranthus spp.	pigweed	annual weed
Asclepias spp.	milkweed*	perennial
Chenopodium album	lamb's-quarter	annual weed, edible
Chenopodium ambrosioides	epazote/Mexican tea	annual culinary herb, weed
Euonymus japonica	evergreen euonymus	evergreen shrub
Rhamnus californica	California coffeeberry	evergreen shrub
Rumex acetosella	common sorrel	perennial weed
Salix spp.	willow*	deciduous large shrubs
Sambucus spp.	elderberry	evergreen shrubs
Spergula arvensis	corn spurry	annual weed
Taraxacum officinale	dandelion	perennial weed, edible
Tropaeolum majus	nasturtium*	perennial ground cover
Vicia spp.	vetches/bell/fava beans*	annual cover crop
Zea maize	188corn	annual vegetable

*Also serves as an insectary plant.

Resource Habitats

As we have seen, many plants provide water, food, and shelter for a variety of beneficial insects living in the plant canopy. Ground-dwelling beneficials, too, need permanent and reliable sources of food, water, and protection from the elements. Some ideas follow:

Water

All life needs water to survive, and active beneficial insects need more than their share. You can provide water by filling shallow birdbaths or large bowls with flat stones and water so that they can alight and drink without drowning. If you have the resources and space, ponds can provide a habitat for lots of beneficial wildlife like dragonflies, predatory flies, and toads. Insectivorous birds love to bathe and drink from garden ponds.

Mud is also important in your garden habitat. As water evaporates from soggy areas, it leaves behind salts that insects need to survive. Grow some watercress or mint in a shady area under a hose bib, or create a muddy shoal in your pond. You don't want too much mud, of course, but a little here and there is another way to nurture beneficials and wildlife in your garden.

Physical refuges

You can make artificial habitats for many beneficial insects that live on the ground. During the day, most ground predators like spiders, ground beetles, and rove beetles stay away from the hoe and tiller, by finding the permanent nooks and crannies of the garden. Things like path borders, year-round mulches, sod pathways, inverted flower pots, coffee cans, and statuary provide stable protected areas where beneficials can hide during disruptions like bad weather, cultivation, or spraying. These places can also become refuges for snails, slugs, and earwigs, so keep your microhabitats monitored. In time, they should attract more beneficials than pests.

Compost piles and mulch

Compost piles in late stages of decay serve as home to several beneficial insects like ground beetles, spiders, and predatory flies looking for things to eat. Try stacking a few small piles of aged compost in your garden as refuges for these important animals.

Designing a Kitchen Garden Plant Guild

Using the palette of known beneficial plants on page 189, design your plant guild around basic landscape elements. These might include:

- A flower border of alyssum, cosmos, goldenrod, scabiosa, tansy, yarrows, and white lace flower

- Successive sowings of herbs in the carrot family

- A patch of carefully chosen weeds

- Some vegetables gone to flower, especially broccoli, carrot, celeriac, lettuce, and corn

- Beds of cut flowers with lots of nectar and pollen

- Cover crops of annual buckwheat (*Fagopyrum*) in warm weather and vetch or horse beans (*Vicia*) in cool weather

- If space permits, a few shrubs, such as wild buckwheat, euonymus, and elderberry, to serve as a hedgerow shelter and food source.

Don't expect instant or even consistent results. Your plant guild is like a big bird feeder, only the birds are tiny insects. A plant may attract a beneficial in one area of the state but not in another. If you use beneficial plants instead of pesticides, you will probably have a few more pests, but they will rarely get out of control as they often do with pesticides.

Start by collecting information about the flowering period of beneficial plants in your area. Garden books tend to give only general information, which is not thorough enough to explain how and when local microclimates can cause plants to flower at odd times. You'll only know by planting and observing. Ideally, you want a constant display of beneficial flowers (nectar, pollen, and insectary) from early spring through the first chill of fall.

Get to know the beneficial insects in your area and notice which plants they prefer. Keep referring to the beneficial plants in the families mentioned on page 189. Also, watch native wildflowers, local weeds, and all plants with flat flower heads for visiting insects. If you see beneficials consistently around one variety of plant, chances are that you may have discovered something.

Reduce spraying. If you attract beneficials to your garden and then kill them with pesticides, you have accomplished nothing. All pesticides kill: This includes soaps, oils, botanicals, and synthetics. Use them very carefully in your garden. Always spot your spray where it is needed. An advantage to oils, soaps, and other contact pesticides is that they force you to do this. Never spray indiscriminately or around flower heads. Keep the beneficials alive.

Elements of the Habitat Kitchen Garden

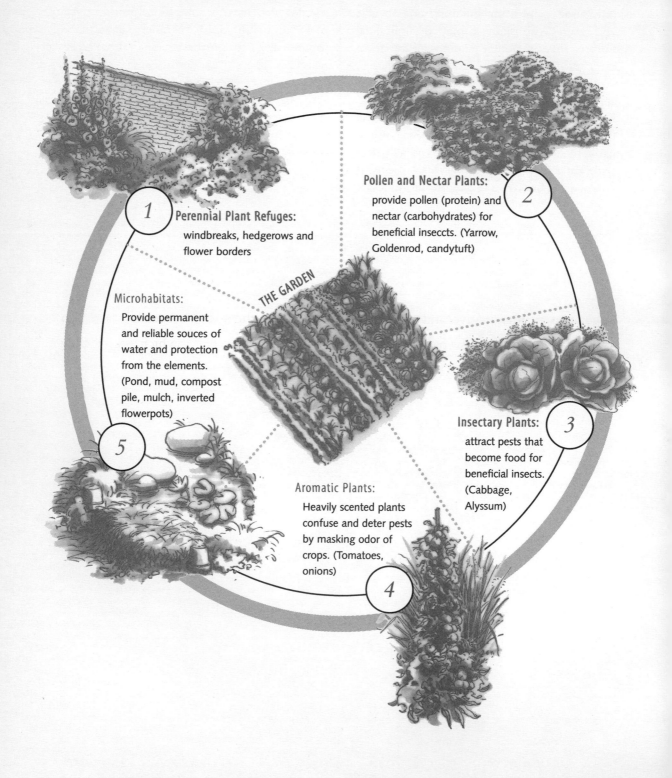

1 **Perennial Plant Refuges:** windbreaks, hedgerows and flower borders

2 **Pollen and Nectar Plants:** provide pollen (protein) and nectar (carbohydrates) for beneficial inseccts. (Yarrow, Goldenrod, candytuft)

3 **Insectary Plants:** attract pests that become food for beneficial insects. (Cabbage, Alyssum)

4 **Aromatic Plants:** Heavily scented plants confuse and deter pests by masking odor of crops. (Tomatoes, onions)

5 **Microhabitats:** Provide permanent and reliable souces of water and protection from the elements. (Pond, mud, compost pile, mulch, inverted flowerpots)

THE GARDEN

Feeding Kitchen Guests

As a cultural crossroads of diets, the Mediterranean shows us many ways to combine starches and vegetables. For centuries, various starches—from pasta to couscous, polenta to risotto—have been combined with a variety of fresh vegetables in imaginative and exuberant ways. By knowing a few basic Mediterranean-style recipes, which are easy to vary when you have a regular supply of freshly picked vegetables, your cooking is guaranteed to be flavorful, healthful, *and* visually exciting.

PASTA BASICS

There are three basic ways to prepare pasta: cooked and topped with sauce, baked with sauce, or cooked and then simmered in a skillet with the sauce until reduced (which we call the "infused" method for simplicity). Any pasta can be cooked until al dente, then topped with a cooked sauce. ("Al dente" is the term used to indicate the correct degree of cooking for pasta. When removed from the water and drained, pasta should not be mushy, but still firm to the bite or, literally, "to the tooth." Vegetables can also be prepared al dente, which means they retain their crunchiness when cooked.)

Baked pasta often consists of dried, shaped pasta—like ziti, penne, rigatoni, or farfalle—with lots of surface area so they hold the sauce well. In this method, the pasta is cooked until *very* al dente because it will be recooked in the oven. The al dente pasta is then tossed with sauce and possibly other ingredients. The entire mixture is either placed in a large baking dish or divided up among individual ovenproof ramekins (see page 41) and topped with a sprinkling of cheese or bread crumbs (or a combination) and fresh herbs. Then it is baked for 20 to 25 minutes in a 375° oven.

The pasta-infused-with-sauce method combines the pasta and sauce in a skillet for final reduction in order to create a more instensely flavored dish. For infused pasta, the sauce is made in the skillet, the very al dente cooked pasta is drained and placed in the skillet with the sauce, and a ladle of hot pasta water is added. The mixture is then cooked over medium-high heat to evaporate the liquid and bind the sauce to the pasta. The final cooking process also helps thicken the sauce.

In Italy, dried pasta is generally used to make infused pasta, because dried pasta is more durable and can withstand the extra cooking. Fresh pasta is usually served with cream sauces that are ladled on top of the pasta.

Most pasta sauces are based on either tomatoes, cream, or stock. Tomato sauces rarely use butter, while cream sauces usually do. Stocks can be used alone or with cream.

To make a healthy pasta sauce without cream, use olive oil and vegetable stock.

TIPS FOR INFUSING PASTA

First make a sauce in a skillet or saucepan. Then, in a separate saucepan, partially cook the pasta (2 to 3 ounces per person) and drain, reserving about 4 cups of the pasta water. Add the partially cooked pasta to the saucepan or skillet with the sauce and stir to coat it. Add a ladle or two of the pasta cooking water to the mixture. Over medium heat, stir the mixture as the liquid starts to bubble. The water, olive oil (used to make the initial vegetable sauce), and the starch from the pasta will begin to emulsify, creating a creamy sauce without butter. As most of the liquid evaporates, the flavors of the sauce intensify. For variations:

• Reserve some of the cooked vegetables used in the sauce before adding the pasta, then add to the pasta after it is infused, for crunch and texture.

• Bread crumbs can be used in place of, or in combination with, Parmesan cheese as a garnish.

• Minced fresh flat-leaf parsley, scallions, chives, or any assortment of herbs can be used as a garnish.

• Modify recipes by using more vegetables and less oil.

• Instead of pasta water, use chicken or vegetable stock as the final cooking liquid to infuse the sauce. See Basic Pasta Sauces illustration between pages 308 and 309.

Herb-Lemon Pasta

This recipe uses the basic technique of infusing pasta with flavor by cooking it briefly in the sauce (see page 194). This technique can be used to create endless variations of basic pasta dishes. See the Basic Pasta Sauces diagram between pages 308 and 309 for further suggestions.

SERVES 2

- $1/2$ cup packed arugula leaves
- $1/2$ cup packed fresh basil leaves
- $1/2$ cup fresh flat-leaf parsley leaves
- Juice and grated zest of 1 lemon
- $1/4$ cup extra virgin olive oil
- $1/2$ teaspoon salt
- 5 ounces dried spaghetti or penne pasta
- 1 cup low sodium chicken broth or vegetable stock (page 139)
- $1/2$ cup (2 ounces) grated Parmesan cheese
- Freshly ground pepper to taste

Combine the greens on a cutting board and chop them coarsely. Combine half of the greens in a blender with the lemon juice, 2 tablespoons of the olive oil, and the salt. Process into a purée.

Bring a large pot of salted water to boil, and add the pasta. Cook the pasta until it is very al dente, 6 to 8 minutes. Drain, reserving 1 cup of the pasta water.

Put the stock, the remaining 2 tablespoons olive oil, and the puréed greens mixture in a skillet over low heat. Add the drained pasta to the skillet and increase the heat to medium-high.

Add the reserved pasta water to the pan and cook the pasta, stirring, for 8 to 10 minutes, or until the liquid has almost evaporated. Taste as you go: the pasta is done when it's cooked to your liking. Add the remaining greens and stir until wilted. Turn off the heat and add half the grated cheese and the pepper, stirring a few times.

Transfer the pasta to bowls and garnish with the remaining cheese and the lemon zest. Serve immediately.

Per serving: 672 calories (325 from fat), 37.7 g total fat, 8.6 g saturated fat, 20 mg cholesterol, 2393 mg sodium, 62.6 g carbohydrate, 4.2 g dietary fiber, 28.1 g protein

Squash Tortellini

It's simple to make tortellini when you use premade, packaged wonton noodles, which are sold in most supermarkets. This recipe makes 40 to 50 tortellini, with some filling left over. Use any leftover squash and filling in soup.

SERVES 8 TO 10

FILLING
- 1 to 2 butternut or acorn squash
- 1 tablespoon olive oil
- Salt and freshly ground pepper to taste
- 1 cup grated Parmesan cheese
- $1/2$ cup toasted bread crumbs
- 2 tablespoons grated fresh ginger
- Half of 1 beaten egg

- $3^1/2$ to 4 dozen wonton noodles

SAUCE
- $1/2$ cup (1 stick) butter
- 6 to 8 fresh sage leaves
- 2 cups chicken stock (page 139)
- Grated Parmesan cheese, for garnish

To bake the squash, preheat the oven to 375°. Cut each squash in half and place the halves on a baking sheet, cut-side up. Drizzle with the olive oil and sprinkle with salt and pepper. Bake for 40 to 50 minutes or until very soft. Remove from oven and let cool. Scoop out squash from its skin and mash the flesh with a fork until smooth. Measure out 4 cups for this recipe.

Place the squash, cheese, bread crumbs, and ginger in a small bowl and mix until fully incorporated. The mixture should be a little dry and it should come together and hold its shape. Add part of the egg, just enough of it to make a thick paste that is soft but not runny.

To fill the tortellini, place 1 to 2 teaspoons (depending on the size of the noodles) of filling in the center of a wonton noodle. Fold the noodle into a triangle, with one edge slightly overlapping the other. Press the edges together to seal. Fold the corners at the ends of the longest side of the triangle up to meet and pinch together to seal. Allow tortellini to dry out slightly on a wire rack.

To make the sauce, melt the butter in a medium saucepan over medium heat. When the butter almost starts to bubble and smoke, remove it from the flame and add the sage leaves. Add the chicken stock and return the pan to the stove. Cook over medium heat just to heat through.

To cook the tortellini, set a large pot of salted water to boil. Add the tortellini, 8 to 10 at a time, and cook for 4 to 6 minutes or until they rise to the surface. Test tortellini by removing with a slotted spoon, draining, and tasting, making sure that the inner dough (where it has been folded over) is cooked. Drain finished tortellini before serving.

Place 4 to 6 cooked tortellini in a pasta bowl, and ladle 3 to 4 tablespoons of the sauce over the top. Serve with grated Parmesan cheese.

Per serving: 250 calories (157 from fat), 17.7 g total fat, 9.9 g saturated fat, 54 mg cholesterol, 953 mg sodium, 15.9 g carbohydrate, 1.8 g dietary fiber, 7.7 g protein

FIG. 4-3: Folding tortellini

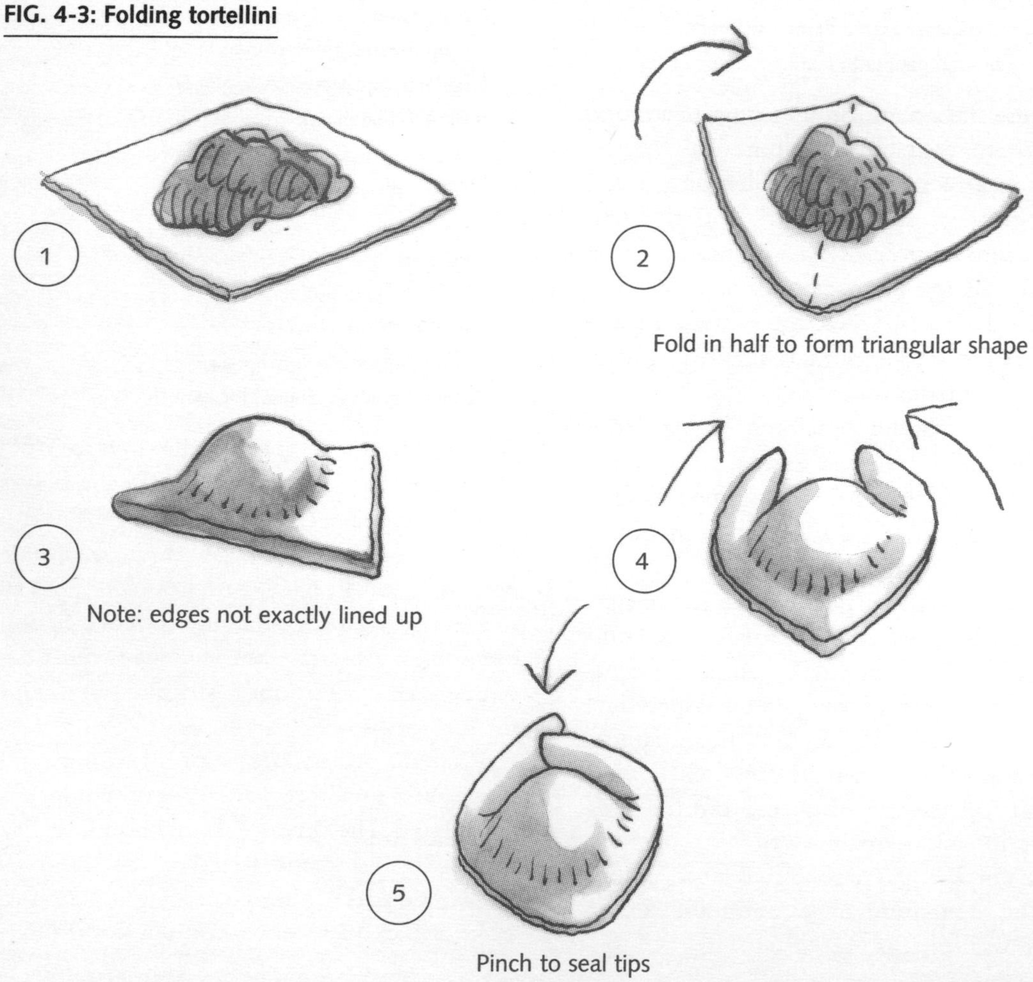

1

2

Fold in half to form triangular shape

3

Note: edges not exactly lined up

4

5

Pinch to seal tips

PASTA VARIATIONS

Roasted Vegetable Pasta Casserole:

Preheat the oven to 375°. Lightly coat 4 cups chopped vegetables—peeled carrots, potatoes, fennel, tomatoes, zucchini, eggplant—with olive oil. Then add whole and chopped garlic, thyme, oregano, parsley, salt, and pepper. Toss briefly. Bake for 30 to 40 minutes, or until golden brown, tossing occasionally.

Purée half of the mixture in a blender using a little vegetable stock or water to thin if necessary. Toss the remaining whole vegetables, the purée, and 12 ounces very al dente cooked farfalle or penne pasta together in a 9-by 12-inch casserole dish. Top with bread crumbs and grated Parmesan and bake for 35 to 40 minutes. Serves 2.

Turkey Bolognese Pasta:

Combine ¼ cup each finely chopped celery, carrot, fennel, and onion. Sauté in ¼ cup olive oil. Add 1 pound bulk turkey sausage, break up with a fork, and cook for 6 to 8 minutes, until it loses its pink color. Add 2 cups basic

Tomato Sauce (page 438) and cook over low heat for 10 to 15 minutes. Add salt and pepper to taste. Serve over 10 ounces cooked fresh fettuccine. Serves 2.

Farfalle al Forno:

Preheat the oven to 375°. Cut 1 cauliflower into florets and steam until tender. Cook 1 pound farfalle pasta until al dente, then drain. Set both aside.

Prepare a sauce by heating ¼ cup olive oil in a large skillet. Sauté 1 diced large onion until translucent. Add 6 chopped anchovy fillets, 4 cups basic Tomato Sauce (page 438), and ½ cup raisins.

In a large casserole, combine the cooked pasta, cauliflower, and sauce and toss well. Add salt and pepper to taste. Sprinkle with ½ cup pine nuts, ½ cup fresh bread crumbs, and ⅓ cup grated Parmesan.

Bake for 35 to 40 minutes, or until topping is crisp. Serves 4 to 6.

RISOTTO, POLENTA, PIZZA, COUSCOUS, AND PANINI

Risotto is an Italian dish made with arborio rice, a medium-grain Italian rice that forms its own creamy sauce as it slowly cooks. Almost any vegetable or combination of vegetables can be used in risotto. Usually the liquid used is either chicken stock or beef stock, but our method calls for low-sodium chicken broth or vegetable stock. To make risotto even more healthful, the basic version in this book uses less olive oil, butter, and Parmesan than most traditional recipes.

Polenta is a coarsely ground cornmeal that can be cooked to a porridgelike consistency, or molded, cooled, and sliced, then fried, baked, or grilled. Any version of polenta goes well with sautéed Swiss chard or spinach, tomato sauce, sausages, grilled chicken, or sauteed mixed vegetables.

Couscous is a traditional North African dish most often made with hard wheat semolina, but sometimes with barley or green wheat. It is a quick accompaniment to cooked vegetables.

Pizza can be topped with a multitude of vegetables and/or sauces, including caramelized onions and sautéed greens.

Panini are small Italian sandwiches made from a variety of bread rolls or small slices of bread. They make a particularly good snack when filled with roasted vegetables.

Risotto with Asparagus and Pine Nuts

This basic risotto can be cooked in about 40 minutes. The recipe can easily be doubled.

SERVES 4 TO 6

> 1/2 cup pine nuts
>
> 1 pound asparagus
>
> 4 cups low sodium chicken broth or vegetable stock (page 139)
>
> 1 white or yellow onion, chopped
>
> 2 tablespoons olive oil
>
> 1 1/2 cups arborio rice
>
> 1 cup dry white wine
>
> 2 tablespoons butter
>
> 1/2 cup (2 ounces) grated Parmesan cheese
>
> Salt and freshly ground pepper to taste

Preheat the oven to 350°. Place the pine nuts in a pie pan and toast until light brown, 8 to 10 minutes.

Snap off the large ends of the asparagus, peel the ends if they are thick and tough, and cut the asparagus into 3/4-inch pieces. Set the stalks and tips aside.

Heat the stock in a medium saucepan. In another medium saucepan, heat the olive oil over medium heat. Add the onion and sauté for 5 minutes, or until translucent. Add the rice and stir to coat. Continue cooking for 2 to 3 minutes, or until opaque.

Add the wine and cook, stirring, for several minutes, or until it is absorbed. Reduce the heat to low and add 1/2 cup of the stock. Stir until the stock is absorbed. Repeat this process until the rice is almost al dente, about 30 minutes. About 10 minutes before the rice is done, add the asparagus stalk pieces and cook and stir for 5 minutes. Then add the asparagus tips and cook and stir for 5 minutes, or until the rice is al dente.

Remove from heat and stir in the butter, toasted pine nuts, cheese, and salt and pepper. Serve immediately.

Per serving: 618 calories (252 from fat), 29.0 g total fat, 8.4 g saturated fat, 28 mg cholesterol, 351 mg sodium, 66.6 g carbohydrate, 2.6 g dietary fiber, 27.9 g protein

Baked Risotto

This dish can be made with any number of vegetables, including asparagus, peas, and artichokes. The addition of greens like Swiss chard or spinach makes the dish colorful and tasty.

SERVES 4

> 1 tablespoon olive oil
>
> 2 shallots, minced
>
> 1 cup arborio rice
>
> 2 cups low sodium chicken broth or vegetable stock (page 139)
>
> 1 cup fresh corn kernels (about 2 cobs)
>
> 12 to 15 string beans, cut on the diagonal into 1-inch pieces (about 1 cup)
>
> Salt and freshly ground pepper to taste
>
> 1/2 teaspoon freshly grated nutmeg
>
> Zest of 1 Meyer lemon
>
> 1/2 cup grated Parmesan cheese

Preheat the oven to 400°. Heat the olive oil in a large saucepan over medium-high heat, then add the shallots and sauté for 3 to 5 minutes, until translucent. Add the rice and stir until it is coated with oil. Add the stock, vegetables, salt, pepper, and nutmeg. Bring to a simmer.

Remove from the heat and add the lemon zest and 6 tablespoons of the Parmesan. Mix well.

Transfer to a 6- by 6- by 4-inch casserole dish or a 6-inch round by 3 1/2-inch high enameled dutch oven with tight fitting lit. Sprinkle the remaining 2 tablespoons Parmesan on top and bake, covered, for 35 to 40 minutes. Most of the liquid will be absorbed but the rice will still be moist. Serve immediately.

Per serving: 359 calories (75 from fat), 9.0 g total fat, 3.0 g saturated fat, 10 mg cholesterol, 274 mg sodium, 59.0 g carbohydrate, 3.7 g dietary fiber, 18.2 g protein

Zucchini-Mushroom Risotto

SERVES 4

- 3 tablespoons olive oil
- 3 cloves garlic, minced
- 2 zucchini or any summer squash, cut into coins
- 8 ounces mushrooms, sliced
- 2 teaspoons minced fresh thyme
- 4 cups low sodium chicken broth or vegetable stock (page 139)
- 1 yellow onion, chopped
- 1 1/2 cups arborio rice
- 1 cup dry white wine
- 2 tablespoons butter
- 1/2 cup grated Parmesan cheese
- Salt and pepper to taste

In a medium skillet over medium heat, heat 2 tablespoons of the oil, add the garlic, and sauté briefly. Add the zucchini, mushrooms, and thyme, and sauté until slightly brown, 5 to 8 minutes. Set aside.

Heat the stock in a medium saucepan. In another medium saucepan, heat the remaining tablespoon of olive oil over medium heat and sauté the onion for 5 minutes, or until translucent. Add the rice and stir, to coat. Continue cooking for 2 to 3 minutes or until the rice is opaque. Add the wine and cook, stirring, for several minutes, until the wine is absorbed.

Reduce the heat to low and add 1/2 cup of the stock. Stir until the stock is absorbed. Repeat the process until the rice is almost al dente, about 35 minutes.

Add the mushroom-zucchini mixture and cook 2 or 3 more minutes. Remove from the heat and stir in the butter and cheese. Season with salt and pepper to taste, and serve.

Per serving: 553 calories (200 from fat), 22.2 g total fat, 7.4 g saturated fat, 25 mg cholesterol, 353 mg sodium, 65.3 g carbohydrate, 1.9 g dietary fiber, 23.8 g protein

Saffron Risotto

This is a lighter version of risotto Milanese, which is usually made with beef broth, beef marrow, and a lot of butter.

SERVES 4

- 4 cups low sodium chicken broth or vegetable stock (page 139)
- 2 teaspoons saffron threads
- 2 tablespoons light olive oil
- 2 slices prosciutto, chopped
- 1 yellow or white onion, diced
- 1 cup arborio rice
- 1/2 cup dry white wine
- 2 tablespoons butter
- 1/4 cup grated Parmesan cheese
- Salt and freshly ground pepper to taste

Heat the stock in a medium saucepan. Dissolve the saffron in 1 cup of the hot stock and let soak for at least 15 minutes.

In a medium saucepan, heat the olive oil over medium heat. Add the prosciutto and onion and sauté for 5 minutes, or until the onion is translucent. Add the rice and stir to coat. Continue cooking for 2 to 3 minutes, until the rice is opaque. Add the wine and stir for several minutes until the wine is absorbed.

Reduce the heat to low and add 1/2 cup of the stock. Stir until the stock is absorbed. Repeat the process until the rice is almost al dente, about 35 to 40 minutes, using the 1 cup of saffron-infused stock last.

Remove from heat, stir in the butter, cheese, salt, and pepper, and serve.

Per serving: 373 calories (146 from fat), 17.2 g total fat, 5.8 g saturated fat, 23 mg cholesterol, 4895 mg sodium*, 41.4 g carbohydrate, 0.5 g dietary fiber, 18.4 g protein

*Sodium level of this dish can be greatly reduced by leaving out the prosciutto.

Mushroom Risotto

SERVES 4

  4 cups low sodium chicken broth or vegetable stock
     (page 139)
  3 tablespoons butter
  1 tablespoon olive oil
  4 scallions, chopped
  4 ounces shiitake mushrooms, stemmed and sliced,
     or 1 ounce dried mushrooms, rehydrated in hot
     water and drained
  1 cup arborio rice
  1/2 cup dry red wine
  1/2 cup (2 ounces) grated Parmesan cheese
  Salt and freshly ground black pepper to taste
  2 sprigs flat-leaf parsley, chopped

Heat the stock in a medium saucepan over medium heat. In a medium skillet over medium heat, melt 1 tablespoon of the butter with the olive oil and sauté the scallions until translucent. Add the mushrooms and sauté until brown, 5 to 8 minutes.

Add the rice and stir to coat. Continue cooking for 2 to 3 minutes, or until the rice is opaque. Add the wine and stir for several minutes, until it is absorbed.

Reduce the heat to low and add 1/2 cup of stock. Stir until the stock is absorbed. Repeat the process until the rice is almost al dente, about 35 to 40 minutes.

Remove from heat and stir in the remaining 2 tablespoons of the butter, the cheese, salt, and pepper. Garnish with parsley at the table.

Per serving: 476 calories (156 from fat), 18.6 g total fat, 8.3 g saturated fat, 33 mg cholesterol, 404 mg sodium, 63.3 g carbohydrate, 4.2 g dietary fiber, 23.3 g protein

Polenta

This recipe uses a mixture of polenta and fine cornmeal to achieve a creamy, porridgelike consistency.

SERVES 4

  6 cups water
  1 teaspoon salt
  1 cup polenta
  1 cup fine cornmeal
  1 1/2 cups (6 ounces) Asiago cheese, grated
  1/4 cup butter

In a medium saucepan, bring the water and salt to a boil. Gradually pour in the polenta and cornmeal, stirring continuously with a wire whisk. Decrease the heat to medium-low, continue to stir, and cook about 35 minutes, or until thickened but still smooth and creamy. During the last 5 minutes of cooking, stir in the cheese and butter.

Per serving: 525 calories (222 from fat), 24.5 g total fat, 14.8 g saturated fat, 69 mg cholesterol, 1180 mg sodium, 58.6 g carbohydrate, 7.2 g dietary fiber, 17.1 g protein

Polenta and Eggs

This is a wonderful and simple dish that makes use of leftover polenta. Serve it with sautéed mushrooms, spinach, or vegetables; or serve with sliced fresh tomatoes.

SERVES 2

  1 tablespoon butter
  2 cups leftover polenta, mashed
  2 eggs, lightly beaten (see note)
  Salt and freshly ground pepper to taste

In a medium skillet, melt the butter over medium-high heat. Add the polenta, stirring and breaking it up, until it is warm and soft like porridge. Pour the eggs into the pan of polenta and continue stirring over medium-high heat for 2 to 3 minutes, or until the eggs are incorporated but still creamy. Add salt and pepper, and serve.

NOTE: Those who are elderly, pregnant, or immunocompromised are generally advised to avoid eggs that are not fully cooked. Please keep this in mind when serving Polenta and Eggs.

Per serving: 475 calories (244 from fat), 27 g total fat, 15 g saturated fat, 277 mg cholesterol, 908 mg sodium, 39.7 g carbohydrate, 4.8 g dietary fiber, 17.7 g protein

Couscous

A very simple recipe for a North African dish that goes well with all sorts of vegetables.

SERVES 2

    1 tablespoon olive oil
    1 clove garlic, minced
    1 small onion, diced
    1 teaspoon ground cumin
    $^1/_4$ teaspoon ground turmeric
    $^1/_2$ teaspoon paprika
    1 pinch crushed red pepper flakes or cayenne pepper
    1 pinch ground cinnamon
    1 zucchini, cut into $^1/_2$-inch dice
    1 large tomato, diced
    $^1/_4$ cup currants
    1 cup low sodium chicken broth or vegetable stock
        (page 139)
    $^1/_4$ teaspoon salt
    $^1/_2$ cup couscous

In a medium skillet over medium–high heat, heat the oil and sauté the garlic and onion until translucent. Add the spices and sauté for a few more minutes while stirring.

Add the zucchini, tomato, currants, and $^1/_4$ cup of the stock. Simmer for 10 minutes, or until the zucchini is tender.

Meanwhile, bring the remaining $^3/_4$ cup stock to a boil along with the salt in a medium saucepan. Stir in the couscous, cover, remove from heat, and let stand for 5 minutes.

Fluff the couscous with a fork, then add the vegetable mixture and combine by mixing lightly. Serve immediately.

Per serving: 347 calories (75 from fat), 9.1 g total fat, 1.1 g saturated fat, 0 mg cholesterol, 304 mg sodium, 60.4 g carbohydrate, 6.3 g dietary fiber, 14.3 g protein

PANINI

Panini have become a popular snack in American restaurants and take-out shops. You can make panini with bread rolls purchased from your local baker or made at home.

Grilled vegetables are one of the main ingredients in panini of all sorts, whether or not they contain a slice or two of cooked ham, prosciutto, or cheese.

Here are a few ideas for panini fixings:

• Grilled eggplant and red peppers on grilled country bread, garnished with mixed baby greens and mayonnaise mixed with chopped capers

• Roasted mushrooms, watercress, and butter mixed with grated lemon zest on a flat Italian bread like *ciabatta*

• Sautéed spinach, sliced hard-cooked egg, mayonnaise, and tomato slices on a small egg bread roll

• Pickled onion, julienned red peppers, and thin slices of grilled chicken breast on thin slices of sourdough

• Smoked salmon, mayonnaise mixed with chopped capers, butter lettuce, and thinly sliced red onion on sliced challah with crust removed.

Little Pizzas

SERVES 6

DOUGH

1 tablespoon milk

1 tablespoon warm water

1 teaspoon sugar

1 package active dry yeast

3 cups all-purpose flour

1½ teaspoons salt

1 cup cold water

1 tablespoon olive oil

SUGGESTED TOPPINGS

Basic Tomato Sauce (page 438)

Roasted Mushrooms (page 87)

Grated pecorino Romano cheese

To make the dough, mix the milk, warm water, and sugar in a small bowl. Then sprinkle in the yeast. Stir and let stand for 5 minutes, or until creamy.

Put the flour in a large bowl along with the salt. Make a well in the center of the flour and add the yeast mixture and ½ cup of the cold water, whisking together wet and dry ingredients to prevent lumping. Incorporate the other ½ cup cold water and mix with a wooden spoon until you have a mass of shaggy dough.

On a floured work surface, knead the dough for 8 to 10 minutes, or until smooth and elastic. Add the olive oil by flattening the dough, pouring the oil on top, folding the dough several times, then kneading it a few minutes to incorporate the oil.

Cover the dough with a damp cloth or with plastic wrap and let rise for 1 hour, or until you can make an indentation in the dough with your finger and it fails to spring back.

Divide the dough into 6 equal pieces, round into tight balls, and place on a lightly oiled baking sheet. Cover with a damp cloth or plastic wrap and let rise for 1 to 1½ hours, or until doubled. (Or immediately after being formed into balls and covered, the sheet with the dough balls can be placed in the refrigerator for the final rising, for up to 3 or 4 hours.)

When ready, preheat the oven to 500° with a pizza stone inside if you have one. Flatten each piece of dough with your fingers and stretch over the knuckles of your hands to a 6- to 8-inch diameter. Place the dough on a baker's peel or a rimless baking sheet sprinkled with cornmeal (if you're using a pizza stone), or on a greased baking sheet. Spread the tomato sauce on the dough, then top with the mushrooms and cheese.

Slide the pizzas onto the stone or bake on the baking sheet for 5 to 6 minutes, or until crisp.

Per serving (with cheese and sauce): 482 calories (189 from fat), 21 g total fat, 10.8 g saturated fat, 51 mg cholestrol, 1266 mg sodium, 51.4 mg carbohydrate, 2.6 g dietary fiber, 21.7 g protein

ALTERNATE PIZZA TOPPINGS

- Beet greens, roasted diced beets, and chunks of feta cheese

- Sautéed spinach or Swiss chard, tomato sauce, and chunks of mozzarella

- Caramelized onions, pitted kalamata olives, and small chunks of Gorgonzola cheese

Vegetable Compendium

Vegetables in this compendium are grouped according to a combination of plant family and plant use. We find this a convenient way to describe vegetables, especially when speaking to both gardeners and cooks. Vegetables in the same plant family are likely to have common pests, suffer similar quirks, and need the same kind of attention. This takes a lot of the guesswork out of growing them. Where appropriate, we have discussed the common characteristics of the major plant families of vegetables.

Grouping vegetables by the part eaten is also handy. "You don't grow a vegetable, you grow part of a plant," goes the old saying. That part, whether root, leaf, or fruit, is what the cook uses in the kitchen. We start with underground vegetables, move up to the stems and leaves, and then to the fruit. Plant families are nestled in this scheme and the result, we hope, is a useful system for kitchen gardeners.

Table of Contents

WHY THESE VEGETABLES?

There are some vegetables—such as celery, turnips, radishes, and rutabagas—missing from this compendium. This isn't because we consider them unimportant. We simply chose vegetables that we grow in our gardens and use in our kitchens. We are especially excited about the growing popularity of Asian vegetables, exotic European greens, edible weeds, and heirloom varieties.

As we expand the vegetables in our kitchen gardens, we also expand the nutrients in our diet. Collards, cress, and bok choy may not be as popular to grow as tomatoes and corn, but they contain a wealth of nutrients: vitamins, minerals, fiber, and an array of disease-fighting antioxidants and phytochemicals. We owe it to ourselves to learn how to grow and cook all types of vegetables. Kitchen gardening is a never-ending experiment.

ORGANIZATION OF THE COMPENDIUM

The following sections explain what to look for in the compendium and how to use the information there. The vegetables are organized in three categories: "Underground Vegetables," "Leaves, Stems, and Stalks," and "Fruiting Vegetables." Each of these sections is further broken down into family or group names, and finally into individual vegetables.

THE NAMES OF THE PLANTS

Vegetables are listed by botanical name (genus, species, variety). We also list foreign-language equivalents of vegetables. The translations are formal rather than colloquial. We find these translations to be a handy reference as we read through the growing selections in seed catalogs and cookbooks.

INTRODUCTION

The introduction to each vegetable gives background information on the vegetable's history and uses. Knowing where vegetables come from and how they have been used in foods enriches our knowledge of this important group of garden plants. Some vegetables, like onions and garlic, have been in the human diet for thousands of years. Others, like snap peas and hybrid tomatoes, are recent additions to our cuisines. Whenever possible, we've included interesting historical tidbits about where a vegetable comes from and how it has been carried around the globe and used by people in the past. A vegetable's heritage can help explain a lot about how to grow and cook it.

CULTIVATION

Learning how to grow vegetables takes time. Vegetables are unlike any other garden plant: They grow quickly and demand lots of attention, almost like a pet. Everyone has his or her favorite vegetables and preferred ways of growing them. There is no single method in kitchen gardening, only a subtle blend of time, location, style, purpose, and cuisine.

One key to successful vegetable gardening is learning a bit about the natural history of each vegetable—in other words, how it grows. In this section we describe each vegetable's growth habits, plus its general temperature and soil preferences. We also make some general recommendations about the best time of year to plant each vegetable.

Since climate varies so much from place to place, the best reference point for knowing when to plant a vegetable is probably the average date of the first (fall) and last (spring) frost (see pages 455–457). Local microclimates and various garden structures can help you to extend your planting times, but average frost dates are a good place to start.

PLANTING

Here you will find instructions for direct-sowing or transplanting each vegetable. With few exceptions, the most efficient way to grow vegetables is to first grow them as seedlings in a protected place and then transplant them into the garden. This saves seeds and gives plants a head start against weeds and pests. Seedlings (started vegetable plants) are also easier to set out in whatever density or arrangement you want. Since seedlings mature faster than directly sown seeds, you end up being able to grow more crops in your garden each year. Every vegetable has a unique method for producing transplants, and these are described in this section.

SOILS AND FERTILIZERS

Here you will find a brief description of the type of soil each vegetable prefers, and recommendations for when and how to fertilize them. Remember, no matter its fertility, your soil can provide only so many nutrients. If you choose to grow your vegetables closely together for space-saving efficiency or convenience, your soil will have to provide more nutrients per unit of area than it would for more widely spaced plants. When determining how much fertilizer to use, consider not just your garden's total area, but also the number of plants per square foot.

NUTRIENT DEFICIENCIES

Vegetables require a steady supply of nutrients to grow at their best. When they don't get the food they need, they show typical signs of nutrient deficiencies. These signs vary from crop to crop. It's easy to confuse hunger signs with the symptoms of disease or environmental stress. For this reason we have included nutrient-deficiency charts for each type of vegetable to help you learn to "read" your plants correctly.

DISEASES AND PESTS

These sections include a brief description of the most common types of diseases and plant-eating pests. There are several excellent books that outline in detail the symptoms, biology, and control options for vegetable pests. (See the Bibliography, pages 445–446.)

RECOMMENDED VARIETIES

It's difficult to recommend vegetable varieties to gardeners because varieties tend to behave so differently from climate to climate; each region seems to have its own array of favorites. Also, vegetables come in all sorts of colors, shapes, and flavors, so the choice can be overwhelming. We have tried to include popular varieties from the major types of each vegetable as a starting point for gardeners. Other criteria include:

Open-Pollinated and Hybrid Varieties: Open-pollinated (OP) varieties are those that are naturally pollinated without interference from humans. OP varieties tend to be less vigorous than hybrids, and there is a great deal of variation in size and yield from plant to plant. However, since the seeds of OP varieties can usually be saved and sown the next season, vigorous varieties can eventually be selected. Since the plants have been pollinated naturally, their seeds also produce seedlings that look like their parents. In other words, they breed "true."

Hybrids, on the other hand, are the offspring of two parental lines that have been deliberately cross-pollinated by plant breeders. They may be uniform and possess special traits, but hybrids don't always produce viable seeds that can be saved for planting the next season. If the seeds are viable, plants tend not to share their parents desirable characteristics. That is, they don't breed true. In addition, hybrid seeds cost more because it takes skill and tedious handwork to produce them.

Hybrids are superior to OP varieties *for many vegetables in many cases for many purposes.*

For other vegetables or situations, OP varieties are as good as, or even better than, hybrids. Considerable effort is put into developing and promoting hybrids instead of OP varieties because it is more profitable for the seed companies to do so. This promotion has been quite successful, since most gardeners tend to believe that all hybrids are superior simply because they are hybrids. This may be true for most tomatoes and some broccoli, but it isn't true for all vegetables. We encourage kitchen gardeners to grow both OP and hybrid varieties whenever possible and judge for themselves. There are definite trade-offs.

To give kitchen gardeners a range of options, the table of recommended varieties for each vegetable lists both outstanding hybrid and OP types.

Heirloom Varieties: If you read an old seed catalog from the twenties or thirties, you'll notice that some of the varieties described, like Golden Bantam corn, Black Beauty eggplant, or Early Jersey Wakefield head cabbage arc still with us, but that most of the heirloom varieties have disappeared and been replaced by modern hybrids.

There is no precise definition of an heirloom. Some plant breeders consider heirlooms to be any open-pollinated vegetable that is over 75 years old. Others claim that true heirlooms are only those varieties that are exchanged between generations or lifelong friends. Nevertheless, most definitions skirt the fact that, like all plants, heirlooms change through the years and become genetically different from generation to generation. The Brandywine tomato that your grandparents grew is not the same variety available today. Heirlooms represent the past, but they are today's version of the past.

Whatever the definition, heirloom vegetables are more than just quaint anachronisms with nostalgic appeal. In recent years, a grassroots movement, led by home gardeners, a few seed companies, and forward-thinking horticulturists, has begun reintroducing old-fashioned varieties of vegetables. Today, heirlooms are found in more and more home gardens and seed catalogs. Many varieties have recently been reintroduced from seed stocks that have been preserved by immigrant families, tribes, and ethnic groups. These qualify as heirlooms because of their heritage, even though they may be new to the commercial trade. Still other heirlooms have been handed down as "land races," or varieties selected over generations and well adapted to particular microclimates and regions of the country. Most of these heirlooms you'll never see in any seed catalogs. The fun of growing heirlooms is uncovering their past and reaping their benefits. You're also preserving the heritage of a unique variety of food.

Days to Maturity: In seed catalogs you will often see a number in parentheses following the name of the variety. This number refers to the "days to maturity," which is typically measured from the time of seedling transplant (or direct-seeding) to the growth of the first edible portion of the vegetable (root, stem, tuber, leaf, or fruit). A variety may be classified as "early season" (short period of growth), "main crop or midseason," or "late season" (long period of growth). These categories are not precise to a definite number of days. The speed of plant growth depends on the time of year it's planted and the conditions of the soil, nutrients, weather, and so on. "Days to maturity" is most useful in establishing a staggered planting so that any one vegetable can be made available over a long period of time by planting, say, early, midseason, and late varieties, depending on where you live. For example, in foggy coastal climates or areas with a short growing season (high latitude or high altitude), warm-season vegetables such as corn, tomatoes, and melons are planted as early varieties, while cool-season vegetables are planted as early varieties for immediate use and late varieties for storage.

AAS winners. The AAS (All American Selection) award is given each year to outstanding varieties of garden plants, including vegetables. It is the Oscar of horticulture. The vegetable winners tend to be hybrids that are broadly adapted to many types of climates. Most of them perform very well under all sorts of conditions.

Our own tried-and-true favorites. Once you've grown a vegetable that performs for you year after year, you don't need a seed catalog description to convince you to grow it again. After years of kitchen gardening, we definitely have our own favorites, and these are included in our lists of recommended varieties.

Above all, experiment with new varieties and compare them to your current favorites. The best way to make a comparison is to grow a couple of varieties in the same part of the garden, at the same time of year, fertilizing and watering them equally so that their growing conditions are as much alike as possible. Seasons change from year to year—a hot summer now, a cool summer next year—and you may be surprised at which variety works.

ORDERING SEEDS FROM MAIL-ORDER CATALOGS

Every winter the arrival of seed catalogs lifts the spirit of gardeners everywhere with vivid descriptions of new varieties and old favorites. But before you rush out and buy more seeds than you'll need, consider the following pointers to make your mail-order shopping easier.

• **Choose from a variety of seed catalogs.** Today's kitchen gardener can choose from an unprecedented number of vegetable varieties. Besides the old standards our parents grew, we now have a wide assortment of recently discovered heirloom varieties, new and exciting Asian vegetables, and European greens. Add to this the growing number of regional varieties from seed-exchange programs and all the new hybrids being developed for disease resistance and nutrition, and you have quite a choice.

With so many options, you're not likely to find all your favorite vegetables in one place. Some large national companies have slick catalogs offering a blend of market and garden varieties. Others are more regional in scope and opt to carry varieties adapted to their area. Finally, more and more seed companies are offering heirloom varieties and coordinating national seed-exchange programs.

Note that the rising price of printing has forced many seed companies to charge for their catalogs; usually they're worth buying because they contain valuable cultural information. Think of them as inexpensive gardening books. Often the price is included in the first purchase. Major mail-order companies carrying vegetables for the home gardener are listed on pages 447–450.

• **Do your homework before ordering.** Check with fellow gardeners, regional references, your extension service, and local nurseries to see if the vegetables you want will grow in your soil and climate.

• **Read the catalog's ordering information.** Shipping times, seed substitutions, minimum orders, and return policies differ from company to company. Note if there are any speedy shipping options. They may cost a bit more, but in the spring, timing is everything.

• **Read plant descriptions with a grain of salt.** Seed companies are in the business of selling seeds, and sometimes their embellished descriptions border on sales hype.

• **A vegetable variety can carry two or more names.** Before there were seed companies, gardeners saved their own seeds from year to year. In time, new varieties emerged with features that were chosen by the particular seed saver. Over the years these home varieties, or "land races," were passed on to family, neighbors, and friends. As seeds circulated around, they were often named after their place of origin. When seed companies started to raise the seeds, they often retained these regional names. In other cases, they simply renamed the variety for marketing purposes. Bloomsdale Long Standing Spinach is also sold as Bloomsdale Long Standing Dark Green and American Bloomsdale Extra Long Standing. Among carrots, Scarlet Nantes, Nantes Coreless, Touchon, and Half-Long Coreless Nantes are all the same variety, while Rainbow Chard and Bright Lights are essentially the same multicolored chard. There are scores of such duplications in seed catalogs, so buyer beware.

- **Try to order what you need, not what you want.** With so many varieties to choose from, it's easy to go overboard and buy more seeds than you need. To avoid this, simply decide on how many plants you want of each vegetable, allow for loss, and buy just that amount of seed. For example, suppose you want to grow thirty plants of an early broccoli over the season. Double or triple this number to allow for losses in germination and transplant. That's sixty to ninety seeds. Broccoli has about 10,000 seeds per ounce, so you'll need about $100/10,000$, or about $1/100$ of an ounce. Seed companies sell seeds as fractions of an ounce, beginning with $1/2$, $1/4$, $1/8$, etc. The closest amount you can buy to what you need is $1/64$ of an ounce. Since not all seed companies will sell this amount of the variety you want, you may need to check through several catalogs. What you're trying to find is the seed company that sells your favorite vegetable variety in the right amount and at the best price. This usually means looking through several seed catalogs.

- **The early bird gets the worm.** Order your seeds and plant stock as early as possible. If there has been a bad seed crop, some varieties may run out soon, especially trendy hybrids and heirlooms. This is also true of potato sets, garlic bulbs, and other plant stocks that are available seasonally.

HARVEST AND STORAGE

The way a vegetable is grown, harvested, and cured determines how long you can store it. Proper storage, in turn, affects a vegetable's flavor and nutritional value. To get the most out of your kitchen garden, it's important to give as much attention to harvesting and storing your vegetables as you do to growing them. Although we make suggestions throughout the Compendium, there are some general rules to consider:

1. Preparation for storage begins in the garden. For example, you should stop fertilizing all long-storage vegetables (e.g. squash, onions, potatoes) after late summer; when these vegetables mature in high nitrogen soils, they tend to keep poorly. And don't water them for a week or so prior to harvesting. They keep better if their tissues aren't watery.

2. Harvest your vegetables at the proper stage of maturity. Recommendations are listed for each vegetable.

3. While harvesting vegetables with fruit, such as peas, beans, squash, peppers, and tomatoes, take special care not to damage or

bruise the fruit. A wounded vegetable is prone to rot and rapid decay in storage.

4. Some vegetables, such as onions garlic, squash, and potatoes, need to be cured before they are stored. Curing methods are listed for each vegetable where appropriate.

5. Harvested vegetables are not dead, but continue to grow in storage. Storing each vegetable under proper conditions of temperature and moisture will slow down this growth after picking and prolong the storage life of the vegetable.

6. Separate your storage environments into cool, moist areas, such as the refrigerator, and warm, dry areas such as the pantry.

STORAGE CHART

GROUP/VEGETABLE	STORAGE COMMENTS
COOL MOIST	
Leafy greens, such as lettuce, arugula, chard, spinach, cresses, endives.	Wash or soak briefly in light vinegar solution, drain or spin dry, place in a paper bag inside a plastic bag, and store in crisper.
Unhusked sweet corn, peas, brassicas, root crops.	Keep brassicas wrapped as they give odors to other produce. Root veggies may give flavors to leafy vegetables; store separately. Wrap root crops with tops in a damp towel and place in a plastic bag. Use corn and peas quickly since their sugars convert into starch.
Snap beans, cucumbers, summer squash, peppers.	Store unwashed in the warmest part of the refrigerator (in the door). Use immediately after removing from the refrigerator.
COOL DRY	
Ripe tomatoes, eggplant, winter squash, pumpkin, potatoes.	Store in cool place outside the refrigerator, such as pantry, garage, attic, closet, or basement. Cold temperature can cause injury.
WARM DRY	
Mature green or ripe onions.	Store in an open mesh container at room temperature. Keep away from direct sunlight.

Underground Vegetables

THE ALLIUMS (Onion Family)

Allium is the Latin word for garlic. Alliums include onions, garlic, shallots, chives, and leeks and the less familiar Egyptian, Welsh, and multiplier onions. There are over 450 species of the genus *Allium* including many varieties of ornamentals with colorful, round flower clusters.

Alliums have been cherished since antiquity because of their value to savory cooking and contributions to good health. Most vegetable alliums are native to central Asia, where nomads near the Caspian Sea grew garlic and onions over 8,000 years ago. Paintings show alliums being cultivated in Egypt as early as 4000 B.C., and there are historical references to garlic, onions, and leeks in the ancient cultures of Mesopotamia, India, and Greece.

The unmistakable odor of alliums is due to a sulfur compound called "allicin." Allicin is known to have antibiotic properties, making it a natural sulfa drug, able to combat infection. In addition, allicin helps break down fats in the blood and reduces the effects of high blood pressure and heart disease. Garlic also contains selenium, an important trace element that activates vitamin E and may prevent certain types of cancer. These and other alliums are being studied by the National Cancer Institute for their ability to stop carcinogens before they attack DNA.

Alliums are probably the most widely used vegetable for cooking in the world. They are a vital flavoring ingredient in Mediterranean, Asian, Southwestern, and many other cuisines.

Western cultures use alliums to spice up dishes, but rarely as a main dish. The average American eats less than 10 pounds of alliums per year. In Asia, alliums are eaten as vegetables in entrees. A typical person in China eats about a pound of onions and garlic per week.

CLASSIFICATION

Although botanically, alliums are distinct from one another, many common terms, such as *scallions, leeks, green onions, bunching onions,* and *multiplier onions,* are often used interchangeably, even in seed catalogs. "Scallions," for instance, can refer to onions that don't grow bulbs, or young shoots of bulb onions. The confusion comes from the fact that all alliums can form one or several bulbs, and that they all produce a similar odor. When ordering from catalogs, the best way to get the allium you want is to specify it by its botanical name (see page 212). The following two tables highlight two systems of allium classification. The first shows what is meant by the informal, common names in use, and the other lists the formal, botanical classifications.

ALLIUMS BY COMMON NAMES

NAME	DESCRIPTIONS FROM POPULAR USE
Bunching onions	Varieties of bulb onions that grow vigorous greens in bunches.
	Any of the multiplier onions that produce clusters of bulbs.
	The true perennial bunching, Welsh or Japanese onions that spread clumps of small-bulbed shoots very rapidly. It does not make large bulbs.
Chinese leeks	The garlic chive, *Allium tuberosum.*
Green onions	The greens of bulb onions; see also "bunching onions" and "scallions."
Multiplier onions	Often used as in bunching onions, but should refer to a cousin of the bulb onions, *Allium cepa aggregatum,* which grows many small edible bulbs and bunches of greens rapidly (potato onions); also used to describe shallots (*Allium cepa ascalonicum*).
Pearl onions	True pearl onions are cousins of the leek because they form just one storage leaf. Most "pearl" onions sold, however, are short-day bulb onions grown in the north where they form small bulb sets rapidly.
Scallions	The greens and bulbs of young bulb onions. See also "bunching onions."
Spring or salad onions	Scallions.
Welsh or Japanese bunching onions	Technically, the only true "bunching" onion, *Allium fistulosum,* a perennial. Can also refer to hybrid crosses of the seed onion, *A. cepa* with *A. fistulosum.*

ALLIUMS BY BOTANICAL NAMES

BOTANICAL NAME	COMMON NAME	OTHER NAMES
Allium ampeloprasum	LEEK GROUP	
var. *ampeloprasum*	Elephant garlic	Big-headed leek
var. *porrum*	Leek, true pearl onion	Leek, cocktail, pickling, or miniature onion
Allium cepa	BULB ONION GROUP	
var. *aggregatum*	Potato onion	Multiplier onion
var. *ascalonicum*	Shallot	Shallot
var. *cepa*	Bulb onion	Seed onion
var. *proliferum*	Egyptian onion	Multiplier, topset, walking, or winter onion
Allium sativum	GARLIC GROUP	
var. *sativum*	Softneck garlic	Braiding garlic
var. *ophioscorodon*	Hardneck garlic	Rocambole
Miscellaneous Groups		
Allium fistulosum	Welsh onion	Japanese or perennial bunching onion
Allium schoenoprasum	Chives	Chives
Allium tuberosum	Garlic chives	Chinese leek

CULTIVATION

Alliums are among the easiest of all vegetables to grow. These hardy biennials or perennials prefer cool weather. Since most of them store well, it's not difficult to maintain a year-round supply. Alliums like lots of sunshine and a soil rich in organic matter. The soil should be well drained and limed to give it a neutral pH. Alliums have shallow roots and narrow, skimpy leaves, so they don't compete well with weeds. Careless hoeing can damage the roots. For these reasons, alliums are a good crop to grow in raised beds, boxes, or containers, where weeds can be controlled more carefully. It's important to note that the edible portions of alliums (bulbs, cloves, or greens) are modified stems and leaves, not roots. Alliums need more nitrogen and less phosphorous or potassium than true roots like carrots.

Onion bulbs are the largest of the alliums. Garlic and shallots produce bulbs that split into equal parts, called "cloves." Multiplier onions grow clusters of small underground bulbs; a few also produce little aerial bulbs, or "bulbils," growing on flower stalks. Finally, most alliums at some time or another also grow tiny bulbs at the base of the mother bulb, called "bulblets."

Alliums are fun to grow because there are so many ways to propagate them. Onions, garlic, bunching onions, leeks, and some shallots can be grown from seed. The clumps of chives and Welsh onions can be divided. Garlic, elephant garlic, and shallots are started from their cloves, and bulb onions, potato onions, and leeks can be started from "sets." Sets are small dry bulbs grown the previous season by sowing seeds thickly and growing crowded bulbs quickly.

NUTRIENT DEFICIENCIES IN ALLIUMS

NUTRIENT DEFICIENCY	SYMPTOM
Nitrogen (N)	Growth stunted and pale; older leaves turn yellow and die back from tip.
Phosphorus (P)	Poor growth; leaves dull green; older ones die back from tip.
Potassium (K)	Older leaves die back from tip without first being yellow; plants look limp.
Calcium (Ca)	Young leaves die without yellowing; death of leaf tissue near stalk causes green ends to topple over.
Sulfur (S)	Leaves thick and deformed; new leaves yellow.
Magnesium (Mg)	Older leaves turn uniform yellow along entire length without dying.
Boron (Bo)	Look for regularly spaced faint yellow lines across leaves, which develop into cracks; young leaves mottled yellow.

DISEASES

Alliums are primarily affected by two types of diseases: leaf diseases and bulb rots. Leaf diseases include **purple blotch**, **botrytis**, and **downy mildew**. All three are caused by high humidity and water on the leaves, so avoid overhead watering and keep good circulation between plants with steady weeding and thinning. This will grow great alliums as much as anything else. Botrytis enters through plant wounds, so try not to injure your plants during cultivation. Purple blotch is carried on the seed, and resistant varieties are available. All leaf diseases should be controlled as soon as possible since the leaves are the future bulbs, cloves, and swollen stems of the mature plant. If leaf growth is inhibited, bulbs and the like will be small.

Two types of bulb rot affect onions and other bulbing alliums. **Pink root (Pyreno-chaeta)** infects roots, making them light pink to reddish. As the disease progresses, roots disintegrate and die. Pink root can live in the soil for long periods. It also occurs on plant debris, but not seeds. Alliums should not be planted for at least 5 years in soil where pink root has occurred. **White rot (Sclerotium)** causes yellowing of older leaves and a white mold on the bulb. Cool, poorly drained soils favor this disease. Destroy infected plants. Most root rots are discouraged by generous additions of aged compost, which stimulate beneficial soil organisms.

PESTS

Compared to other vegetables, alliums have relatively few pests. The most serious are onion thrips and onions maggots.

Onion thrips are tiny insects that also attack beans and cabbage. They transmit virus diseases and eat leaves. They can reduce yields significantly, but they rarely wipe out a crop if left alone. Thrips scrape the leaf surface with their unusual mouth parts and leave a silvery sheen in their wake. Also look for tiny black fecal spots. These very tiny insects are rapid breeders, so monitor with a hand lens early, since they can get out of control quickly. Use soap spray for small infestations and switch to botanicals when you can see damage with the naked eye from a few feet away.

The **onion maggot** is the larva of a small fly, which burrows into growing bulbs. Damage is worst in cool, wet weather. Onion maggots are preyed on by ground beetles. Row covers can keep adult flies off your plants. Red onions and Japanese bunching onions seem more resistant to the maggot than other alliums.

Garlic
ALLIACEAE (Onion Family)

Allium sativum sativum
(softneck garlic)
CHINESE: *da suan*
FRENCH: *ail*
GERMAN: *Knoblauch*
ITALIAN: *aglio*
JAPANESE: *ninniku*
SPANISH: *ajo*

Allium sativum ophioscorodon
(hardneck garlic)

When does a medicinal herb become a vegetable? When you eat a lot of it. Garlic, with its extraordinary value to our cuisines and health, surely should be a vegetable. Part of the appeal of garlic is the variety of its rich, resonant tastes. Minced garlic is hot and spicy, chopped or sautéed garlic is robust, boiled whole cloves have a mild taste, and grilled or roasted bulbs taste sweet and nutty. There is also a difference in taste between the varieties

and types of garlic ranging from staunch to sublime.

There's more to garlic than just flavor. For one thing, garlic is quite nutritious. Ounce for ounce, it has more protein and fiber than snap beans and more minerals than most greens. It's just hard to eat enough of it to count. One thing is for sure: garlic has proven medicinal value. Our ancestors had good sense when they regarded garlic as a charm against illness in their folk medicines. Like all alliums, garlic contains the smelly diallyl sulfides that act like a sulfa drug and give garlic its healthy traits. Research has shown that garlic can stop some microbial diseases like *Candida* yeast infections and ease other skin ailments better than some potent antibiotics. Garlic also contains allicin, which stimulates digestive enzymes, lowers blood pressure and cholesterol, breaks down lipids in the bloodstream, and may act like an antioxidant to build resistance against cancer. Each clove of garlic is a nugget of savory nutrition and lasting health.

Garlic is divided into two types: hardnecks and softnecks. Hardnecks get their name from a woody flower stalk that grows through the center of the bulb like the original wild form. The flower stalk doesn't actually bear a flower, but instead produces small aerial bulbs called bulbils. The hard stalk prevents the formation of small cloves in the middle of the bulb, so you get a few large cloves. The combination of large cloves, unique wild garlic

taste, and easily removed clove skins make hardneck garlic worth growing. Hardnecks are fussier about soils and climate than softnecks, preferring cooler temperatures, although a few varieties are suitable for milder, even coastal, climates. (See page 216.) Hardneck garlics are nicknamed "ophios," from their botanical name *ophioscorodon*.

Softneck garlics are the ones you usually see in the food store, large, plump, and full of cloves. Softnecks don't send up a flower stalk, which allows several small cloves to grow in the center of the bulb. Occasionally some of the Creole and Asian softnecks will bolt, but this is rare. Softnecks are best for braiding and storage. They are also less particular about soil and climate than the hardnecks. Most hardnecks are native to the garlic's homeland regions of central Asia and the old U.S.S.R., while softnecks are mostly cultivated varieties that typically hail from Europe and the United States.

Types of Garlic

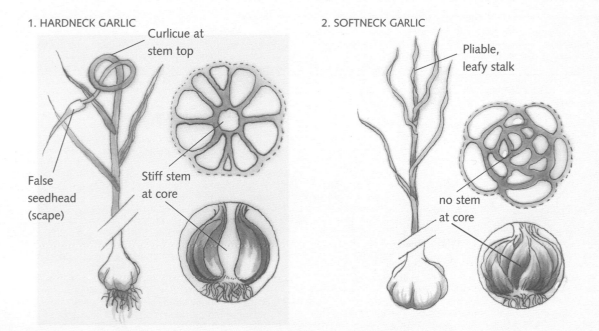

1. HARDNECK GARLIC

Curlicue at stem top

False seedhead (scape)

Stiff stem at core

2. SOFTNECK GARLIC

Pliable, leafy stalk

no stem at core

Adapted from Engeland, Ron. *Growing Great Garlic*. Okanogan, WA: Filaree Productions, 1991.

GARLIC TYPES	
TYPE	**DESCRIPTION**
HARDNECK ("Ophios")	
Allium sativum ophioscorodon Flower stalk hard	Types that retain characteristics of wild garlics from central Asia. Flower stalks harden through the bulb so that there are no small cloves in the center. Most varieties grow better in northern climates. Stores poorly.
Rocambole (Mediterranean)	Recognized by coiled garlic stalk; current gourmet garlic favorite: Superior taste in cold climates.
Continental (Central Asian)	From colder climates of interior Russia. Very spicy. Tall cloves and plants. Much like rocambole, but stores longer.
SOFTNECK	
Allium sativum sativum Flower stalk reduced or soft	Less sharp taste than hardnecks. Soft flower stalk doesn't penetrate bulb, allowing many small cloves in the center of bulb. Generally easier to grow, higher yields, more adaptable. Stores well, braids easily.
Artichoke (Italian Red)	Most widely adapted, largest bulb; vigorous. Judged best taste when eaten raw.
Silverskin	Smooth, tight skins for best storage. Widely grown in western U.S. Best for braiding. Good storage.

Adapted from Engeland, Ron. *Growing Great Garlic.* Okanogan, WA: Filaree Productions, 1991.

CULTIVATION

The first thing to understand about growing garlic is that it is a very adaptable plant. Soil and climate can change a variety's size and taste in just a few years of growing. This explains why the names of so many varieties are regional like California Early, Chinese Purple, Oregon Blue, Idaho Silver, and Leningrad.

Garlic is easy to grow. Bear in mind that it stays in the ground for 7 to 9 months, so you have to plan around it. Garlic likes uniform moisture and a well-drained soil rich in organic matter. It grows poorly in heavy soils with low fertility.

Garlic is typically planted in the fall and harvested in the early summer. In colder areas, it's planted in the early fall, when the soil is warm and roots can grow quickly. In warmer climates it can be planted until late November. The crucial element here is how soon winter cold sets in. In order to grow well, garlic needs to establish strong roots before the winter chill slows them down. In spring, garlic will continue to grow vigorously if it's fall roots are healthy and well established.

PLANTING

There are about 150 cloves to the pound, and 1 pound of cloves is enough to plant a 50-foot row. Larger cloves make larger bulbs. Smaller inner cloves are great for cooking but not planting. You can, however, sprout them for delicious winter garlic greens.

To plant garlic, just pull the large outer cloves from the bulb. Push them into the ground, blunt (root) end first, about 3 to 4

RECOMMENDED GARLIC VARIETIES

VARIETY	COMMENT
Hardneck	*Allium sativum ophioscorodon.* **Known as "ophio" garlic.**
Burgundy	Continental. Weak flower stalk. Grows in mild winter areas. Deep burgundy cloves.
Killarney Red	Large tasty cloves; grows in milder climates.
Red Rezan	Continental, from Moscow region. Dark purple; strong, lasting flavor.
Romanian Red	Continental, from Romania via British Columbia. Stores well; very pungent. Best in cold winters.
Russian Red	Russian heirloom rocambole. Great for storage; sharp taste; needs cold winters.
Spanish Roja	Spanish heirloom rocambole. Strong-tasting; grows in mild winter areas; easy to peel.
Softneck	*Allium sativum sativum*
California Early	Commercial California variety; large bulbs; stores well. Very adaptable; month earlier than late types; taste sharpens with storage.
California Late	Keeps well. Needs specific day lengths, so string out plantings. White skin with pink cloves; smaller, spicier, and 3 weeks later than Early.
Chet's Italian	Regional Washington state strain from Italian Purple. Stays mild tasting in mild winters; adaptable.
Creole Red	From California. Great mild, sweet taste; prefers mild winters and stores well; burgundy cloves.
Early Red Italian	Hot and spicy heirloom from Italy. Known as Early Red or Italian Purple; very productive.
Gilroy	Choice commercial strain from garlic center of America; easy to peel, adapted to mild winters.
Inchelium Red	From Washington state Indian reservation. Superior mild, sweet-tasting artichoke type; large bulbs; very popular.
Mild French	Deep purple color varies with climate. Best for hot, dry climates.
Nootka Rose	Adapted to Northwest. Productive and great for braiding.

inches beneath the surface. If you plant too deeply, sprouting will be delayed, too shallow, and the young stem will be weak. Plant cloves about 6 inches apart in rows 6 to 8 inches apart for easier weeding and care. For precise planting, it's better to push the cloves into the bottom of a 2-inch drill. This method makes it easier to count and to see where you've been. When all the cloves are planted, just cover the drill gently with your hands or the wrong end of a bow rake. After cloves are planted, give them one or two deep waterings, then keep the bed moist. You should see garlic sprouts in a week or two. Garlic loves a fine mulch of compost or aged manure. It keeps weeds down, retains soil moisture and serves as a refuge for predatory thrips that feed on onion thrips.

SOILS AND FERTILIZERS

Garlic cloves are actually swollen underground leaves. If early leaf growth is vigorous, the cloves will be big and healthy. To achieve this, side-dress garlic with fish emulsion, 10-5-5, or another nitrogen source every few weeks while it's growing leaves in the fall and early spring. Soybean meal is a natural, slow-release fertilizer that you can apply in the fall after cloves have sprouted. The meal will release most of its nitrogen in the warming soils of early spring to give your garlic a headstart. Stop all fertilizers after May.

For information on nutrient deficiencies in garlic, see "Alliums," page 213.

DISEASES AND PESTS

See "Alliums," pages 213–214.

VARIETIES

You can start garlic from store-bought bulbs; but only a few softneck types are available in food stores, and they're not certified free from disease. Most seed companies simply offer a generic "white" or "red" variety. If you want to experience the full gamut of garlic varieties, order from mail-order garlic suppliers (see pages 447–450), who now offer more than one hundred strains of both soft- and hard-neck types. These specialized nurseries have rediscovered almost-forgotten varieties and greatly expanded our choices.

HARVEST AND STORAGE

Garlic should be harvested when the cloves are tight in the bulb, or about 7 to 9 months from planting. To harvest garlic properly, it's important to understand that garlic leaves extend underground and wrap about the bulb during growth and storage. As garlic matures, its leaves begin to die from the ground up. The green leaves extend down to become solid bulb wrappers, whereas the brown leaves are wrappers that are dead below ground. So, it's best to harvest garlic, especially hardnecks, by counting the number of green leaves. If you wait until all the leaves are brown, the bulbs will be overmature, unprotected, and with the cloves wide open like flower petals. Start harvesting softnecks when there are 4 to 6 green leaves left and hardnecks when there are 6 to 8 green leaves left.

To check for maturity, pull a bulb out of the ground and take off the "wrappers" to see if the cloves are separate, fully formed but tightly packed together. If they are, then you're ready to harvest. Remember that the stalks of softneck garlic rarely get woody enough to pull the bulbs from the ground by hand; they should be dug up carefully in moist soil with a digging fork.

Once you've invested 7 to 9 months growing your garlic, you want to make sure it's cured properly for storage. If you harvested

Two ways to braid garlic:

1. BRAIDING THE STEMS

A. Start with three bulbs

B. Work in other heads of garlic, braiding like a hair braid

C. Braid to desired length, make a loop for hanging, secure with twine...

2. BRAIDING WITH STRING

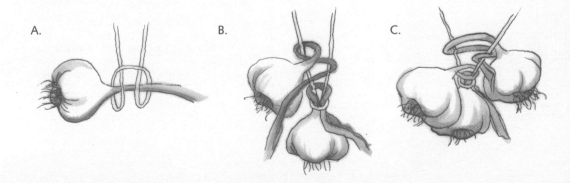

A.

B.

C.

correctly, with some green leaves, the bulbs will be too wet to store immediately. First, they need to be carefully dried.

Get the harvested garlic out of the sun as quickly as possible. Direct sun and heat shorten a garlic's shelf life. Move the bulbs, with stems attached, to a dark enclosure like a barn, garage, ventilated pantry, or toolshed. The area should have good air circulation and a near-constant temperature of 40° to 60°F. You can string a few bulbs together and hang them up, or place them on open screens above the ground. If you're in a hurry, lay plants in the field so that the bulbs are shielded by the leaves of the other plants in the row. But when the leaves decay and the bulbs are exposed to direct sun, bring them into a dark, cool place.

One of garlic's many advantages is that you can create regional strains simply by selecting tasty bulbs and storing them for next year's planting. Each garlic plant is a clone of its parent. However, garlic is a very adaptable plant, and it can vary if you change latitude, altitude, soil, climate, or growing methods from planting to planting. For example, you might find a purple-striped pungent bulb grown from a variety that is white and mild. When you save the purple-striped cloves and plant them next year, you have started the process of creating a new variety.

GARLIC GROWING TIPS

- Garlic is in the ground for 7 to 9 months. Plan accordingly.

- There are several varieties of both hard and softneck types. Experiment until you find the ones that grow best for you. In the kitchen, different varieties give a wide choice of garlicky flavors for your favorite recipes.

- Select large healthy cloves from bulbs that have been stored properly.

- Garlic needs well-drained soil, rich in organic matter.

- Plant cloves early enough in the fall to give roots a strong start in the warm soil before the winter cold sets in.

- Apply a fine mulch as soon as cloves sprout to discourage weeds, keep soil moist, and encourage predatory thrips.

- Stimulate and protect early leaf growth. The leaves are the future cloves. Fertilize with nitrogen early on.

- Examine regularly for onion thrips, snails, or other garden leaf-eaters.

- Weed often and carefully.

- Harvest when 40 percent of the leaves are dead.

- Harvest softnecks with a digging fork. Dry all garlic carefully out of the sun.

- Store bulbs in a cool, dark place.

Leeks
ALLIACEAE (Onion Family)

Allium ampeloprasum porrum
CHINESE: *jiu cong*
FRENCH: *poireau*
GERMAN: *Porree*
ITALIAN: *porro*
JAPANESE: *liiki*
SPANISH: *ajo porro*

Leeks are one of the most underrated of all vegetables. They are very cold-hardy and make an excellent substitute for onions during late fall and winter. In mild or coastal climates, leeks can be grown almost year-round. Whether they're braised, steamed, sautéed, or boiled, leeks have a unique creamy texture that will thicken soups and sauces with an unmistakable hint of onion. With their tall, thick stems and large, flat leaves in hues of green to blue, leeks give a special elegance to the edible landscape. Leeks are often considered "in the ground too long" and "fussy to grow" because they need to be blanched. But early varieties are now widely available and are not difficult to grow.

Leeks are much more popular in Europe and China than in America, although they are gaining popularity here. Like onions and garlic, leeks can be traced to the ancient cultures of the Near East.

CULTIVATION

Leeks are a winter-hardy biennial that require a longer, cooler growing season than onions. Most varieties will overwinter in the garden and grow to harvest size with warming spring temperatures. If they stay in the soil too long, they'll eventually grow seed and the stem will turn woody.

In colder climates, leeks should be planted in the early spring for harvest in late summer to fall. In warmer zones where frost is rare, leeks can also be planted in late summer to early fall and harvested all through the winter and into the following spring.

PLANTING

Leeks can be directly sown, but it isn't recommended. They germinate slowly and have a sluggish early growth, so the seedlings can easily be overwhelmed by weeds. If you must direct-seed, sow in early spring into a prepared seed bed, $^1/_2$ inch deep and $^1/_2$ inch apart in rows 12 inches apart, and press the soil firmly over the seed. Don't allow the seed bed to dry out before seeds sprout. Thin gradually to 2 inches apart.

Leeks grow best from well-rooted transplants, which are hard to find in most nurseries. To do it yourself, sow indoors February to March or 8 to 12 weeks before the last frost. Germinate at 70° to 80°F. To encourage roots, move to 3-inch-deep containers when seedlings are 3 to 4 inches tall. When seedlings are 8 to 12 inches tall, harden them off for a week. This hardening-off period is especially important for leeks. The warmth of indoors produces succulent seedlings that are susceptible to rot if they are transplanted immediately. After the seedlings have hardened-off, transplant outdoors 4 to 6 inches apart in rows 12 to 24 inches apart. To promote roots even further, place transplants into holes about 3 inches deep.

BLANCHING

In order to get the most out of leeks, the lower stem should be blanched. This keeps the stem white and tender instead of letting it grow green and tough. To do this, sow your seeds extra thickly. This makes the seedlings tall and lanky so there's a longer stem to blanch. There are three major ways to blanch leeks: dibbling, trenching, or hilling-up.

1. **Dibble method:** This works especially well with leggy seedlings. Simply transplant each into a deep dibble hole so that only an inch or so of leaves extends above the surface. This avoids the work of hilling-up.

2. **Trenching method:** Transplant seedlings into a small trench 6 inches deep and 6 inches wide, and fill it in as the plant grows.

3. **Hilling-up method:** Mound soil around the leafless part of the stem with each hoeing. Pull the soil or mulch up around the stem every few weeks to the point just before the leaves begin to fan out from the stalk. For late-winter varieties, continue hilling-up through winter. In dry summer areas, hill-up when the dry season begins.

SOILS AND FERTILIZERS

Leeks grow in many types of soils, but prefer a rich loam that is a little more alkaline than acid. They need plenty of nutrients and respond well to manure tea, fish emulsion, and other liquid organic fertilizers during the growing season.

For information on nutrient deficiencies in leeks, see the "Nutrient Deficiencies in Alliums" table on page 213.

DISEASES AND PESTS

See "Alliums," pages 213–214.

VARIETIES

There are about eighty varieties of leeks available. Most are open-pollinated, so you can save your own seed. In the past, most leeks were late overwintering varieties from colder climates, and were in the ground for nearly 9 months. The newer varieties are early and have a much shorter growing season. Two advantages to the new early varieties are that in colder climates they can be harvested before winter, and in warmer climates gardeners can sow late and harvest the next spring.

Whether you are endeared to the old standards like the giant Lyon Prizetaker or the succulent new early leeks like King Richard, you will be surprised at the variation in the shape, look, and taste of the different leeks now available (see page 223).

RECOMMENDED LEEK VARIETIES	
VARIETY/TYPE	**COMMENTS**
EARLY (summer, 65–90 days)	
King Richard	Since 1978. Upright, extra-long thin stems; not winter-hardy. Sow densely for mini-leeks.
Pancho	Heavy, thick stems resist bulbing. Disease-tolerant. Summer-fall harvest.
Titan	Very long and very early; a nice combination.
Varna	Fast growing. Slender and tall. Harvest anytime; not winter-hardy.
LATE (winter, more than 100 days)	
Broad London	Large-stemmed variety (1¹/₂″). Excellent puréed in soups.
Durabel	From Denmark. Slow growing, very winter-hardy, late bolting. Very mild, for winter salads.
Giant Musselburg*	Popular, broad-leafed, thick-stemmed type also called American Flag
Laura	Late-harvest leek, medium length and extra cold-hardy; harvest through winter.
Otina	Premium French leek. Very mild flavor.
Splendid	From Denmark. Rapid growing, medium height; overwinters in mild winter areas.

* Indicates heirloom variety

HARVEST AND STORAGE

Leeks are one of the most flexible vegetables to harvest. Depending on the variety, they can take anywhere from 50 to 140 days to mature after transplanting. You can harvest leeks anytime, although leeks really don't come into full flavor until after a hard frost. Cold weather seems to hasten the conversion of starch to sugar. When most vegetables are dead or dormant, the flavor of leeks is at its best.

Try pulling some early leeks when they are just pencil-sized as "baby" leeks, a tender delicacy. Otherwise, harvest mature leeks when they're 1 inch or more in diameter. Late varieties can be overwintered in just about any climate to provide eating through winter and early spring.

To store leeks, trim off the roots and all but about 3 inches of the greens. Wash carefully, air dry for a few days, and put them in the refrigerator crisper where they'll keep for up to 2 months.

LEEK GROWING TIPS

- Set out large, healthy transplant seedlings at least 8 to 12 weeks old with well-developed roots.

- Bury or hill-up the base of the stem as the leeks grow. This provides a longer and more tender edible stalk.

- Keep leeks weeded. They don't compete well with other plants.

- Leeks like constant moisture and fertilizer. To keep soil moist, add plenty of organic matter like well-rotted manure or compost.

- Better to harvest early than late. Young leeks are succulent and savory. Old leeks are tough and starchy.

Onions
ALLIACEAE (Onion Family)

Allium cepa var. cepa
CHINESE: *yang cong*
FRENCH: *oignon*
GERMAN: *Speisezwiebel*
ITALIAN: *cipolla*
JAPANESE: *tam an egi*
SPANISH: *cebolla*

Onions are one of the oldest and most popular vegetables. Praised by poets and cherished by cooks, onions have been used to flavor meals and cure ills for thousands of years. Their ability to outlast most other vegetables in storage has also added to their enduring popularity.

Onion comes from the Latin *unio,* meaning "one," since it is the only allium that produces just one large bulb. Unlike zucchini, you can never have enough onions, especially the storing types. Onions have few pests and are relatively care-free. Plants have small leaves and shallow roots, so they don't take up much room; grow them throughout your kitchen garden.

Onions can be enjoyed most of the year: scallions in spring salads, pearl onions in summer soups, sweet onions in midsummer sandwiches, and storage onions in the fall and throughout the winter. Whether they are sliced raw for salsas, caramelized for that "meaty" taste in soups, or marinated for grilling on the barbecue, onions can be enjoyed in a variety of ways. Ever notice that when a skillet of onions is sautéing, everyone around the place asks: "What smells so good?"

CULTIVATION

The bulb onion is a cool-season biennial, tolerant of frost. It grows best between 55° and 75°F. The "bulb" is actually layers of overlapping fleshy leaves at the base of the stem. Leaf growth in onions is important because the leaves later become the bulbs.

Onions are one of the few vegetables that are photoperiodic; that is, they only form bulbs when there are the right number of daylight hours, foggy or sunny (see page 226). Onions count the daylight hours. When the day length is just right, they stop making leaves and start making a bulb. If you plant too early, onions will go to seed instead of making bulbs. If you plant too late, you'll get lots of scallions and few bulbs. To further complicate matters, some varieties are more sensitive to day length than others. Good onion growing takes practice.

If you're just starting to grow onions in a new area, seek the advice of a local kitchen gardener and grow several onion varieties for comparison. More and more seed catalogs are offering onion varieties in terms of the day length and latitude at which they can be grown. After a few seasons of experimenting, you will discover the tastiest and most reliable onions for your area.

PLANTING

You can sow onions directly, transplant seedlings, or plant small starter bulbs, called "sets." Sets sprout quickly for fast scallions, and they produce bulbs about 3 weeks earlier than from seed. However, sets are notorious for bolting (flowering) before growing larger bulbs. For best results plant sets of average size ($^1/_2$ to $^3/_4$ inches). Small ones rot easily and grow slowly, and large ones almost always bolt. Plant sets as early as possible to give them plenty of time to bulb. You can find onion sets in nurseries starting in late winter.

If you sow directly, sow seeds $^1/_2$-inch apart and $^1/_2$-inch deep in drills. You can broadcast seeds for scallions, but bulb onions need even spacing to grow at their best. If you just want scallions, try broadcasting seeds and some sand from a canning jar with large holes in the top. It's very important to keep the seed bed moist. Sprinkle it with compost after sowing to hold in the moisture. When seedlings have sprouted four leaves, begin thinning, but not drastically at first. Thinning onions is a gradual process that can give you an extended supply of tiny to fat scallions. What's left in the ground will bulb up nicely. Ultimately, you want evenly spaced vigorous seedlings 3 to 6 inches apart, depending on the variety.

In the long run, transplants produce sturdier, more uniform plants than plants grown from seeds. To grow transplants, sow indoors 8 to 16 weeks before last frost for spring planting and in midsummer for fall planting. Germinate at 70° to 80°F. Give growing seedlings as much light as possible to avoid legginess. In 10 to 12 weeks they should be ready for transplanting. Harden-off for 3 to 5 days. Before planting, clip off the seedling tops to 6 inches to redirect the growth to the roots.

When you transplant, space onions carefully for best growth: 3 to 4 inches for most onions and 5 inches for the extra-large sweet and mild types. Since onions have shallow roots, be sure to bury them as deeply as possible, at least 3 to 4 inches.

SOILS AND FERTILIZERS

Onions grow in most garden soils, but they do best in well-drained, light loams rich in organic matter. Sandy soils usually can't hold enough water for onions to thrive. They prefer an even moisture at all times. Wet and dry conditions produce split and small bulbs.

Onions are heavy feeders and they grow best with constant food, especially a steady diet of nitrogen during early growth, plus some phosphorous and potassium prior to bulbing. Don't fertilize after the leaves begin to fade. This produces new leaf growth at harvest and more chance for rot in storage. Start mulching when the seedlings are about 4 to 6 inches. This helps buffer the moisture and temperature of the soil. About a month before harvest, remove the mulch.

For information on nutrient deficiencies in onions, see the "Nutrient Deficiencies in Alliums" table on page 213.

DISEASES AND PESTS

See "Alliums," pages 213–214.

VARIETIES

There are about 140 varieties of open-pollinated onions and just as many hybrid bulb onions. They come in sizes from tiny to titanic, shapes from round to oval to bottle-shaped, and in hues from white to tan to red. Traditionally, the colors of onions have signaled their use: red for sandwiches, salsas, and salads; white for boiling, creaming, and pickling; and yellow for most anything, but particularly for long-simmered sauces, stews, and soups. Although each color of onion offers different textures and tastes, the most important onion characteristics are pungency and response to day length.

RECOMMENDED ONION VARIETIES				
VARIETY/TYPE	GROWTH	FLESH/TASTE	STORAGE	COMMENTS
Intermediate Day	For areas 32–38°N latitude. Seeded or planted in fall for "early bulb" harvest in late spring through summer. Also planted in early spring for summer harvest.			
Australian Brown*	Early	Brown, strong	Long	Heirloom. Grows well in California. OP.
Buffalo	Early-mid	Mild	Medium	Earliest onion from seed. Plant late summer. Hy.
Fresno White	Mid-late	White, moderate	Short	Zesty, resistant to pink root. OP.
Italian Red Torpedo*	Mid-late	Red, mild	Short	Heirloom. Torpedo-shaped; good for sauces. OP.
Ringmaker	Early-mid	Yellow, mild	Med. to long	Best storing Spanish type. Large. Hy.
Spano	Late	Yellow, mild	Medium	Large bulb; good for different soils/day lengths. Hy.
Stockton Early Red	Early	Red, mild	Short	Common California variety. OP.
Walla Walla	Mid-late	Yellow, sweet	Poor	Gourmet heirloom onion from Pacific Northwest. OP.
Long Day	For areas north of 36°N latitude. Seed or plant in early spring for harvest in late summer to early fall.			
Ailsa Craig*	Mid-late	Yellow, med.	Med. to long	English heirloom favorite. Huge mild Spanish. OP.
Copra	Early	Yellow, mild	Long	Great early keeper. High sugar. Hy.
Early Yellow Globe	Early	Yellow, strong	Med. to long	One of the best early keepers. Widely grown. OP.
Kelsea White Giant	Late	White, sweet	Poor	Largest onion in world. Very mild. OP.
Mambo	Mid-late	Red, med.	Long	Best long-day red onion for storage. Hy.
Red Burger Master	Early	Red, sweet	Fair to med.	Large, great slicer for sandwiches. Hy.
Redman	Early	Red, med.	Med. to long	Earliest for 35°–55°N. Mellows in storage. OP.
Southport Red Globe*	Early-mid	Red, strong	Med. to long	Heirloom. Standard early red. OP.
Southport White Globe*	Mid-late	White, med.	Med. to long	Heirloom. One of the best for scallions and storage. OP.
Yellow Sweet Spanish	Mid-late	Yellow, mild.	Medium	High yields, good for bunching. Very large. OP.

Note: Hy = Hybrid and OP = open-pollinated.

* Indicates heirloom variety.

In terms of taste, there are two types of onions: the sweet, "eat 'em raw" kinds, and the pungent storage onions that make your eyes water. The strong flavor of storage onions is due to sulfur compounds, which act as natural preservatives against rot and decay. The sulfur compounds break down into *pyruvates,* which are used to measure the relative pungency of onions.

Sweet onions have few of these sulfur compounds. In fact, some of the most famous sweet onions in the world, like the Walla Walla (from eastern Washington), Vidalia (from Toombs County, Georgia), and Maui (from the slopes of Hawaii's Haleakala), are grown in and named after regions with low-sulfur soil. The Walla Walla is actually a French heirloom brought to Washington State by an early nineteenth-century emigrant from Corsica. Sweet varieties grow to be quite large with juicy, wide necks that invite disease. They should not be stored, but instead eaten quickly or preserved in relishes, salsas, and the like for later eating.

Onion varieties also vary in their response to day length (see sidebar, page 228). Some varieties are quite particular about the daylight hours they get before they "bulb up." Other varieties are less fussy and bulb up during a wide range of day lengths. These are the few "easy-to-grow" varieties sold in nurseries. If you want more choices, like the regional sweet, long-storing, big-bunching, or heirloom varieties, you'll need to order them from seed catalogs. The best way to find onions that thrive in your garden is to plant several varieties on the recommended planting dates. Use the general rules of thumb about day length and longitude in the table on page 226.

With onions, "days to maturity" doesn't mean much. Plants can be harvested at any stage, and the growing days vary greatly between fall- and spring-planted types. In spite of this, seed catalogs describe days to maturity from direct-seeding as early-storage onions (85–100 days), late-storage onions (100–115 days), sweet onions (110–125 days).

HARVEST AND STORAGE

As green leaves die back, nutrients move down into the bulb and promote flavor and dormancy for storage. Immature bulbs are good to eat, but they are not at the peak of flavor and storability. Mature bulbs are best harvested as the tops fall over and the bulbs pull easily from the ground. If the bulbs are hard to lift, this means the roots are still alive and giving nutrients to the bulb.

As soon as the onions are lifted, select strong, firm bulbs for curing. Place them on top of the soil for about a week. Move them to a dark, cool, well-ventilated spot for slow drying. Inspect regularly and remove any that have gone soft. When the onions are properly dried, they can be strung from a rope or woven together for more convenient storage.

ONIONS AND DAY LENGTH

Some plants are "photoperiodic." That is, they will only flower or bulb when the number of daylight hours is just right. If daylight hours are longer than a critical period then the plant is long day. If it's shorter than a critical period then the plant is short day. Poinsettias, for example, are short-day plants since they will only flower when they get *less* than about 9 hours of sunlight (around Christmas), and spinach is a long-day plant because it will only flower (bolt) when the day length is *more* than 11 hours. Onions are long-day plants, but they vary as to the hours of day length they need to bulb. Because day length changes with the latitude, it is convenient to divide onions into three ranges of latitudes.

Unfortunately, the terms used to describe these three types of long-day onions are *short, intermediate,* and *long,* adding confusion to the descriptions in seed catalogs. That is, you can buy an "intermediate-day" or "long-day" onion *variety* (see page 226), but they are both long-day *plants*. The intermediate-day variety needs more than 13 hours of daylight to bulb, while the long-day needs more than 14 1/2 hours.

ONION GROWING TIPS

- Plant the right variety for your latitude at the right time.

- Start with healthy, strong-rooted transplants.

- Space properly and set out transplants as early as possible, in weed-free, well-drained soil with organic matter.

- In mild winter areas, onions can be planted in the fall for winter and early spring harvests. In cold winter areas, plant in the spring.

- Keep onions well weeded. Their shallow roots do not tolerate weeds.

- Keep soil evenly moist. Water regularly and mulch.

- Encourage early leaf growth; the leaves will become the bulb. Side-dress with nitrogen as seedlings grow and be on the watch for early leaf damage by thrips, slugs, and other foliage-eaters. Remember, leaves become bulbs.

- Move storage varieties to a dark, cool, well-ventilated spot for slow drying. Remove any moldy bulbs.

ONION AND DAY LENGTH

TYPE	DAY LENGTH	LATITUDE
"Short" Long day	12–13 hours	24°–28° north latitude
"Intermediate" Long day	13–14 hours	32°–38° north latitude
"Long" Long day	14.5 hours or more	36° or more north latitude

Shallots
ALLIACEAE (Onion Family)

Allium cepa var. aggregatum
CHINESE: *fen nie yang cong*
FRENCH: *échalote*
GERMAN: *Eschlauch*
ITALIAN: *scalogno*
JAPANESE: *sharotto*
SPANISH: *chalote, escaluña*

MULTIPLIER ONIONS

Multiplier onions include shallots and potato onions, two varieties of *Allium cepa*, although some languages make no distinction between the two. Multiplier onions don't make flowers or seeds; they reproduce by making clusters of bulbs underground. Potato onions have round bulbs of different sizes, while true shallots have tapered cloves of equal size. Other differences are more subtle. The emerging leaves of the potato onion are bundled together in a sheath, while each leaf of a shallot has its own sheath.

Multipliers have been cultivated for over five thousand years and were brought to America by the first settlers. Around 1900, they gradually disappeared from seed catalogs and were replaced by bulb onions. Now they're making a comeback because people see that multipliers are hardier, more adaptable, more productive than bulb onions, and they have fewer pests (see pages 213–214). Multipliers can be left in the ground, but most gardeners lift the bulbs at harvest time, store some for eating, and replant the rest in fall or early spring.

Shallots were brought to Europe from western Asia by Crusaders, and quickly became part of European cuisine. They can be substituted for onions, and like all good flavor enhancers, shallots help lift many dishes from the commonplace to the extraordinary with a taste and aroma all their own. They multiply like crazy and are easy to grow. In effect, each clove grows a cluster (bulb) of new cloves. Once you start growing shallots, you'll find many ways to enjoy them and you won't need to buy them!

Shallots are a short-lived perennial. The bulb produces a cluster of six to twelve cloves, like garlic, but must be grown near the soil surface. The greens can be used like onion or garlic greens. The cloves have a unique zesty flavor that suggests a combination of all the alliums. They are a superb seasoning agent in sauces, soups, salads, and sautéed vegetables, and they cook down faster than onions or garlic.

CULTIVATION

The secrets of growing shallots are to choose large, healthy cloves, plant them as early as possible in the spring, and water and weed them. If a large clove is planted in rich soil, it will produce a strong cluster. If the clove is small or planted late or in poor soil, you will get a weak cluster.

As soon as possible in the later winter or early spring, poke cloves into a rich loam soil and space them about 6 to 8 inches apart. Keep the stem end of the clove even with the top of the soil. Deeper shallots form thick necks and don't keep well. Besides, as the clove cluster grows, it pushes itself to the surface anyway. Some people start their shallots early in boxes of sand, peat moss, and compost, and transplant them as soon as stems begin to sprout.

Shallots rot easily, so water them very carefully. Keep the soil moist, but never soggy. They need shallow cultivation and must be kept free from weeds. As the cloves multiply and grow, most of the plant will be above the ground. Do not cover the growing cluster with soil or mulch. This will make it rot!

VARIETIES

There are about fifteen varieties of shallots available in as many shapes, colors, and tastes. Some plants sold as shallots are actually crosses with bulb onions, so check the botanical name when buying. The true French, or Gray, shallot has a unique mild flavor preferred in French cuisine; it stores poorly. Dutch Yellow, with its onion flavor, is easy to store. Other good varieties are the Pear Shallots from Brittany, smaller round French Red shallots, Odetta's White, Jersey Shallot (the only one with seed), Atlantic (round, yellow, mild flavor), and Frog's Legs Gray.

HARVEST AND STORAGE

By the time the cluster of cloves matures, it should be clumped on top of the soil and opened up like flower petals. Shallots rot easily, and their growth habit keeps them high and dry. Help the process by drawing the soil away from the cluster as it grows. After the tops have died back, dig up the bulb clusters, keeping them intact. Clip the tops to within 1 inch of the bulb, and you are ready either to eat them or store them. To cure the bulbs, shake dirt from the roots and place them on a screen in a warm, dry, well-ventilated place for about 2 weeks. Then put the bulbs in paper bags and keep them in a cool, dry place (35° to 40°F) for winter. If you're saving shallot cloves to plant next year, set aside about one-sixth of your biggest, healthiest cloves and store carefully.

Potato Onions
ALLIACEAE (Onion Family)

Allium cepa **var. aggregatum**
CHINESE: *fen nie yang cong*
FRENCH: *oignon-patate*
GERMAN: *Eschlauch*
ITALIAN: *scalogno*
JAPANESE: *sharotto*
SPANISH: *chalote, escaluña*

Potato onions produce bulbs underground much like potatoes produce tubers. They are often described as the mildest, sweetest, most productive, and most disease-free of all the alliums.

We find it best to plant large bulbs in the fall around Thanksgiving and small ones in the late winter (warm areas) to early spring (cool areas).

CULTIVATION

Bulbs do not grow easily in heavy soils, so add plenty of organic matter, and raise beds to improve drainage if necessary. Large bulbs (2 to 3 inches) will produce a cluster of 8 to 10 smaller bulbs, while small bulbs (1 inch or smaller) will produce a few large bulbs. Plant a mix of bulb sizes 4 to 6 inches deep and you will have plenty of sets for replanting next season, plus a bounty of onions of varying size for eating during the year. Keep in mind that multipliers should grow near the surface. This produces larger bulbs with shorter necks that are less prone to diseases. They prefer cool weather. They should be ready for harvesting in July or August. The new bulbs develop just below the soil surface, and it is very easy to damage them, so weed by hand. Also, don't mulch during the growing season; it slows growth, and may cause rotting in wet years. Yields vary tremendously according to climate, soil, and culture. High soil sulfur will produce a more pungent taste.

VARIETIES

There are about a half dozen varieties available. They differ in color (yellow, white, and red), shape, and keeping quality.

HARVEST AND STORAGE

Potato onions should be dug as soon as the tops begin to die. The bulbs keep better if harvested while most of the top is still green. Potato onions don't keep well—especially large bulbs. Store smaller bulbs upside down in a cool, well-ventilated area.

Welsh, Japanese, or Bunching Onions
ALLIACEAE (Onion Family)

Allium fistulosum or **A. fistulosum x A. cepa** hybrids

CHINESE: *cong*
FRENCH: *ciboulette, ail-ciboule*
GERMAN: *Winterzwiebel*
ITALIAN: *cipoletta*
JAPANESE: *negi, nebuka*
SPANISH: *cebollete*

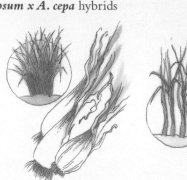

The "Welsh" onion is not from Wales; the name comes from the German word *welische,* meaning "foreign." This perennial or true multiplier onion is native to Asia and it has been the main garden onion of China and Japan since prehistoric times. Later, it migrated to Europe and became an important market onion.

Bunching onions have a unique mild flavor indispensable to Asian cooking. (Western cooking typically substitutes green onions.) The Chinese use the blanched bases of the stem. They are also a great substitute for chives, though a bit stronger in taste.

Welsh onions are very hardy and a handy source for winter onion greens. They have tall hollow leaves that grow in vertical masses nearly 3 feet tall with yellowish pom-pomlike flowers; they are splendid ornamentals in the edible landscape.

CULTIVATION

Bunching onions don't need quite as rich a soil as other alliums. They are propagated by seed or by dividing 2- to 3-year-old clumps. The seeds can be planted in the spring or fall. Germination is very erratic so sow seeds thickly. Cover with 1/2 inch of soil and thin to 2 inches apart. If you start with plants, 2 clumps of scallions will be big enough to divide within 2 years. If you start with a seed, a 1/4-ounce package will give you plenty of seedlings to supply green leaves the first year, and give you plants to divide the second year. For best results, grow in a well-drained, sunny spot, and give them some shade where summers are hot. They need little care beyond routine weeding and watering. In hot, dry climates the bunching onion will bolt to seed and go dormant. Spring rains soon bring it back.

VARIETIES

Seed Saver's Exchange lists thirty-six varieties of Japanese bunching onions, with a range of purposes such as multi-stemmed for leafy salad shoots (Asagi, Kyoto Market), single-stemmed for leafy scallions (Kuronobori), the Japanese nebuka types with their full leaf and white blanched stem (Tokyo Long White, Emerald Isle, Evergreen white bunching).

HARVEST AND STORAGE

Once established, the plant is perennial and produces a steady crop of scallion-type onions that can be harvested nearly year-round. The plant is very winter-hardy and widely adapted. In wet or mild climates, bunching onions grow slowly in the winter and may get a little strong to the taste. Store like onion greens (see page 210).

Chives, Garlic Chives
ALLIACEAE (Onion Family)

Allium schoenoprasum	**Allium tuberosum**
(common chive)	(garlic chive, Asian garlic)
CHINESE: *xi xiang cong*	CHINESE: *jiu cai*
FRENCH: *ciboulette*	FRENCH: *ail civette de Chine*
GERMAN: *Schnittlauch*	GERMAN: *Chinalauch*
ITALIAN: *cipollina*	ITALIAN: *cipollina chinese*
JAPANESE: *asatsuki*	JAPANESE: *nira*
SPANISH: *ceboletta, cebollino*	SPANISH: *cive chino*

Although they are both called chives and look similar, these two hardy perennials are different plants from different places. Garlic chive, *Allium tuberosum,* is from China where it has a long tradition of both culinary and medicinal use. In this country, garlic chives are best known as an ornamental herb. The common chive, *Allium schoenoprasum,* is native to North Africa and southwest Asia. It is the smallest and most subtle tasting of all the alliums. It has round hollow leaves, unlike the garlic chive, which has flat solid leaves. It sets seeds like crazy, so watch for unwanted clumps. Chives can be used raw in vegetable salads and egg dishes, sprinkled in soups, or added to cheese dishes and sauces.

CULTIVATION

Chives like a rich soil with plenty of water. They compete poorly with weeds. Remember, they're perennials, so prepare the soil well. To start chives, sow bunches of ten to twenty seeds in flats at 60° to 80°F indoors in early spring. When seedlings are a few inches high, lift them, trim roots to $^1/_2$ inch, and plant bunches 8 to 12 inches apart. Larger plants can be divided into smaller clumps of plants. Trim the root and most of the leaves. Replant the clumps about 8 inches apart.

HARVEST

Remove flower stems and flower heads as they appear, unless you want to save seeds. Flower production takes away from leaf growth. Cut the amount of chives you want with sharp scissors to about 1 inch above ground level, rather than cutting the tips of the entire clump. This will stimulate growth rather than disease.

TAPROOTS AND TUBERS

There are three kinds of underground vegetables: bulbs, tubers, and taproots. We've already described the bulbs of alliums as small underground stems surrounded by fleshy leaves. The layers of onions and the cloves of garlic are examples of these leaves. Tubers, such as potatoes and Jerusalem artichokes, are also underground stems, but they're not surrounded by fleshy leaves. The "eyes" you see on potatoes are buds or growth points, commonly found on all stems. When you cut a tuber into smaller pieces and plant them, new stems and tubers grow from the eyes. Because they're really stems, tubers can photosynthesize (turn green in sunlight). In potatoes, this green can be toxic, so tubers should be covered while they grow and always stored in the dark.

Taproots are the elongated primary root of a plant. Carrots, beets, and radishes are taproots. They don't have the eyes of tubers or the fleshy leaves of bulbs, although some taproots have a bit of stem tissue at the top. This explains the appearance of "green shoulder" on carrots (see page 240).

Underground vegetables have different fertilizer needs. Bulbs with their fleshy leaves, require more nitrogen than tubers and taproots, which require more phosphorous and potassium. It's good for gardeners to remember that not all underground vegetables are alike.

Beets or Beetroots
CHENOPODIACEAE (Goosefoot or Spinach Family)

Beta vulgaris var. *crassa*
CHINESE: *gen tian cai*
FRENCH: *betterave*
GERMAN: *Rote Rübe*
ITALIAN: *bietola da orta*
JAPANESE: *biito, kaensai*
SPANISH: *remolacha*

There doesn't seem to be anyone who feels neutral about beets. People either pine for their earthy, sweet taste or shudder at the thought. Nowadays, however, with new varieties that are earlier, sweeter, and more resitant than the old standbys, anyone can enjoy beets with homegrown freshness.

The beet, or beetroot, is closely related to Swiss chard and sugar beet and is a cousin of spinach and pigweed. It is really two vegetables in one: an earthy, sweet root and crispy, nutritious greens. The beet plant is native to the coasts of the Mediterranean Sea, where it has been used since prehistoric times. Early beets didn't look like the ones today. Back then they had small, bitter leaves that were cooked as a potherb and skimpy roots that were used as a medicine to reduce fevers and cure snakebites. The medicinal beetroot evolved into the vegetable beetroot as people began selecting for big and shallow-growing roots. By the time colonists brought beets to America, the roots were fat, carrot-shaped, and boldly colored, ranging in hue from purple to yellow, orange to white—much like the heirloom varieties that are popular today. The luscious round red beets we see these days are only about 200 years old.

Beets are popular in salads and soups. If you bake them, rather than steam or boil them, you contain their natural sweetness and lock in their nutrients. Bake beets whole; they lose some of their color and nutrients when they are cut and then baked. Try marinating these tasty roots or simply brushing them with oil before cooking. For added appeal, serve baked beets with candied ginger, nasturtium petals, shallots, mint, or dill. Mix grated raw golden beets in salads for an eye-catching, tasty treat. And don't forget the many ways to make both cold and hot borscht. Beets can be frozen, pickled, or canned. Store them like carrots (page 244).

Beetroots are high in fiber and contain modest amounts of calcium, iron, phosphorous, and potassium, plus vitamins A and C. The greens are among the most nutritious of vegetables, high in vitamins A and C plus calcium, iron, and potassium. Cook and prepare beet greens as you would spinach or chard.

CULTIVATION

Beets are a biennial taproot; like carrots, they thrive in a combination of warm days (60° to 70°F) and cool nights (50° to 60°F), and they can be fooled into bolting by cold spring weather. Beets go to seed if they are in temperatures of less than 50°F, or long, hot days above 75°F.

Many garden books recommend that you start sowing beets about 1 month before the last spring frost, but if the weather is cold and wet at that time, it's better to hold off until April. If beets are planted too early, they may chill and bolt to seed when the weather warms. You'll have the most luck if your seedlings get a lot of sun and the weather stays fairly mild. Beets take about 60 days to produce a crop.

Unlike carrots, beets can be easily transplanted. For an extra-early crop, start seedlings indoors March 1, or 5 to 6 weeks before the last frost. Grow indoors for 5 weeks and harden-off for 1 week before transplanting.

PLANTING

For a continuous supply of beet greens, baby beets, and mature roots, sow seeds at 2- to 3-week intervals until daytime temperatures creep above 70°F. Beets become tough and stringy if planted in the heat of summer (June to August). Otherwise they can be sown successively from late winter to late fall, depending on your location. The best time is when nights are cool and days are sunny and warm.

Beet seeds are notorious for "spotty" germination. This is because the seed is actually a dry fruit with two to six seeds inside and a dense corky coat on the outside. The seed coat contains a chemical that slows sprouting. Presoaking the seeds in water for a few hours before sowing will dissolve the chemical and soften the coat to improve germination. Sow seeds about 2 inches apart and $3/4$ inch deep into a damp seed bed. Seeds also must be in close contact with soil in order to germinate, so tamp down the seeds firmly after filling the drills.

To get good-quality roots, you need to thin seedlings diligently; first when they are 2 inches high and again when they are about 4 inches high. Most people don't thin their beets enough. Beets need at least 4 to 6 inches between seedlings to grow their best. The thinnings can be cooked, or if removed carefully, transplanted elsewhere in the garden. Beet seedlings are susceptible to seedling diseases like *Phythium*, so thin crowded seedlings and avoid soggy, cold soils.

Once your seedlings are established, it's important to supply adequate and constant moisture. Weed often and irrigate with drip or soaker hose, not with a sprinkler. Hoe the soil periodically to let water in, or mulch to hold moisture in. Rapidly growing beets are healthier, tastier, and less fibrous than those stressed by drought or extreme temperatures.

SOILS AND FERTILIZERS

Beets do well in most well-drained, moderately fertile garden soils with a pH near 7. They don't like cold, wet, acid soils, but they do tolerate quite a bit of salt in the soil. Fresh manure and high nitrogen will slow root growth and make them forked, misshapen, and "hairy." Like spinach, beets can accumulate excess nitrate in their leaves, so feed them carefully with organic nitrogen.

Beets do require lots of potassium, so dig in wood ashes, potassium sulfate, well-rotted manure, or another potassium fertilizer prior to sowing. Boron is important for root growth, and beets aren't very good at picking up boron from the soil. You can add a borax solution (see below) to help the problem. For the long haul, it's best to correct for a boron shortage by adding lots of aged organic matter to your soil, season after season. As boron is slowly released from the organic matter by soil microbes, the beets are able to get enough boron for healthy growth.

NUTRIENT DEFICIENCIES IN BEETS

NUTRIENT DEFICIENCY	DEFICIENCY SYMPTOM
Nitrogen (N)	Purpling or yellowing of older leaves, plus poor growth and small roots.
Phosphorous (P)	Smallest leaf veins purple on old leaf. New leaves completely purple.
Potassium (K)	Older leaves wilt and die back from tip.
Calcium (Ca)	Young leaves have purple-black hooked tips, which later die and develop rolled edges.
Sulfur (S)	Young leaves are narrow, stiff, erect, yellowish, and speckled with purple spots.
Magnesium (Mg)	Old leaves have yellowing and red spots between veins. Leaf surface bubbles up.
Iron (Fe)	Young leaves look bleached, old leaves have red tint.
Manganese (Mn)	Triangular leaves with leaf edges curled inward and with severe speckling between veins.
Boron (Bo)	Scattered black sores on the root. Young leaves reddish, with cat scratch–like streaks on stems.

DISEASES AND PESTS

Two diseases that threaten beets are black heart and curly top. For other diseases and pests that affect beets, see "Spinach," pages 306–307.

Black heart produces dark brown areas on the surface and inside of the root, posing a problem for beet growers. Sometimes it causes a hole in the middle of the root; it can also make the leaves develop brown edges.

Black heart is caused by a deficiency in boron, which is common in sandy, alkaline, or dry soils. If you have this problem, add as a preplant or side-dressing 1 teaspoon of household borax per gallon of water for each 30 feet of beets. If you amend your soil regularly with compost or rotted manure, you shouldn't have a problem with boron.

Curly top is a serious virus disease that attacks several plants, including beets and chard.

The disease stunts the leaves and roots. It also causes the leaves to roll upward and become brittle. On the underside of the leaves, it can cause small growths to develop. The disease is spread by the beet leafhopper, an insect that is a close cousin of the cicada and aphid. To keep leafhoppers off your plants, place fabric row covers over beets during the insect's months of greatest activity, around May through June (earlier along the coast).

VARIETIES

In 1888, Burpee Seeds listed twelve garden beet varieties. Today there are about one hundred varieties and some 85 percent are heirlooms. Hybrids are more expensive than OP varieties, but they offer better germination, faster spring growth, and disease resistance. Some hybrids are "monogerms," meaning that the seed ball contains only a single seed (Monopoly, MonoKing Explorer), which eases thinning and cultivation.

Not all beets are round and red; they come in several colors and shapes. The earliest beet roots were either pointed, like a top, or long like a carrot and in hues of yellow, orange, or white. Flat-topped beets, which were the first modern beets available, were popular for generations, but only a few are available now (such as Crosby's Egyptian). Today most varieties are round, with red, yellow, or white flesh. The whites are especially sweet because they were developed from sugar beets. Old-fashioned carrot-shaped beets have grown in popularity because they are tender and free of

RECOMMENDED BEET VARIETIES

VARIETY/TYPE	COLOR	COMMENTS
Albina Vereduna*	white	A pure white Dutch heirloom. Very tasty.
Chioggia*	red	Italian heirloom, dating back to 1880. Rosy pink skin and striped pink-white flesh. Flavorful leaves.
Crosby's Egyptian*	red	Early hybrid. Heirloom, dating back to 1880. Largest of early flat-top beets. Delicious and reliable.
Detroit Dark Red*	red	Heirloom, dating back to 1892. Old all-purpose variety for sweet roots and greens; fresh and canning.
Early Wonder Tall Top	red	Early. A favorite with eye-catching greens attached to small, flat-topped root.
Golden Beet*	golden orange	Old heirloom. Popular sweet, golden beet; doesn't bleed. Sow extra thickly.
Kestrel	red	Excellent baby beet with hybrid resistance.
Kleine Bol	red	Early hybrid. The "little ball" is an early, sweet, and tender baby beet.
Monopoly	red	Dutch breeding at its best. Monogerm (one seed per fruit) reduces thinning; tasty root and greens.
Pronto	red	Early hybrid. Great Dutch baby beet. Holds well in the field.
Red Ace	red	One of the best all-around beets; tasty greens and root. Stores well.
Spinel	red	Gourmet baby beet; very uniform.
Winterkeeper	red	Large roots for storing. Sow midsummer. Harvest late fall.
Carrot Shape		
Cylindra	red	Danish hybrid. Bright red for slicing and pickling. Stores well.
Formanova	red	Deep reddish purple, 7" long, tasty roots. Ideal for slicing, pickling, and preserving; smooth texture. Stores well.
Top Leaf		
Lutz Green Leaf*		Heirloom for fall harvest and winter storage. Grows large without losing taste. Great-tasting leaves. Roots store well.
MacGregor's Favorite*		Scottish heirloom with spear-shaped purple greens. Slow roots (90 days) are long and tapered like carrots.

* Indicates heirloom variety.

fiber. They are also easier to slice and prepare, which makes them great for canning. Other heirlooms include the sweet mild golden beet and the super-sweet Italian Chioggia, with its bright red exterior and rings of red and white on the interior. Whichever variety you choose, look for a smooth skin, a brightly colored interior, disease resistance, and mild, vigorous tops for eating.

HARVEST AND STORAGE

You can harvest beets anytime. When they're the size of a golf ball, you can pull them up and cook them, greens and all. With larger roots, you should probably cook the greens separately. Roots have the best flavor when they are about 3 to 4 inches in diameter. Early varieties, like Crosby's Egyptian, don't hold well in the ground and become rough and woody if not picked promptly. When you dig mature beets, remove leaves; otherwise they will take water from the root, making it shrivel. Be sure to leave 2 inches or so on the stem to avoid "bleeding." Beet greens can be wrapped in plastic and stored for several days in the refrigerator. For methods of storing beet roots, see Carrots, page 244.

BEET GROWING TIPS

- Grow beets in cool, moist weather and in well-drained neutral soils. For best flavor and texture, grow plants quickly.

- Be sure your soil has adequate potassium and boron, two nutrients beets really need. Use kelp, fish products, composted manures, wood ashes, potassium sulfate, or borax for lacking soils.

- To improve germination, soak seeds before sowing and tamp them well into the ground.

- Start sowing 2 weeks before last frost. Sow at 2- to 3-week intervals until summer's heat. Repeat in the fall.

- Thin gradually to at least 4 inches between seedlings. For greens only, leave seedlings 1/2 inch apart.

- Lapses in watering cause woody beets. Use fine mulch and anything else you can to encourage constant moisture.

- Weed early and then mulch; late cultivation can destroy shallow feeder roots.

- Harvest when beets are between the size of a golf ball and a tennis ball. Small baby beets are delicious, greens and all; remove greens from larger beets, but leave a little stem.

Carrots
APIACEAE (Parsley or Carrot Family)

Daucus carota ssp. _sativus_
CHINESE: *hu luo bo*
FRENCH: *carotte*
GERMAN: *Möhre*
ITALIAN: *carota*
JAPANESE: *ninjin*
SPANISH: *zanahoria*

The carrot is a swollen taproot native to Afghanistan (the white carrot is native to Europe). It probably evolved from a "weed" like Queen Anne's lace *(Daucus carota)*. During most of its early history, carrots were used as livestock feed and as a medicinal herb. The roots were prescribed for curing wounds, ulcers, stomach, kidney, and liver problems. People started eating carrots as a vegetable around A.D. 500.

Primitive carrots were yellow, orange, and red, or shades of purple and violet. These colors are still found in today's heirloom varieties. Orange carrots weren't developed until the 1600s by the Dutch. This came about because purple carrots gave soups and sauces an ugly color. With a steadfast pigment and much sweeter taste, the orange carrot quickly became a common food on the dinner tables of Europe. It was brought to the United States by early settlers, and today it is one of the most important root crops in the world.

In the garden, carrots are a versatile vegetable that make little demand on space. In a 16-square-foot space you can grow all the carrots you will need for a family of four in 1 year. Carrots grow in well-drained, average soils and they tolerate both cool and warm weather. In the kitchen, the carrots are versatile and quite nutritious. You can enjoy them freshly dug or from cold storage. They contain more sugar than most any other vegetable. You can snack on carrot sticks, sip carrot juice, or savor carrot cake. As an appetizer, main dish,

or dessert, carrots contribute health, color, and taste to any meal. They are also an important, aromatic foundation for stocks, stews, and soups. And like tomatoes, there is no substitute for just-picked carrots. When they are fresh, carrots, along with peas, are the closest thing to candy from the garden.

Carrots provide dietary fiber, minerals, thiamine, and riboflavin. Calcium pectinate, a type of soluble fiber in carrots, has been shown to lower cholesterol. Carrots are also one of the highest sources of beta-carotene, which the body breaks down into vitamin A. Beta-carotene lessens the tendency of malignant cancer cells to multiply. It is also a powerful antioxidant that prevents the formation of harmful free radicals.

CULTIVATION

Once past the seedling stage, carrots are easy to grow. If you don't harvest them all and let some flower the second year, the carrots' flat clusters of tiny flowers will lure many beneficial insects to your garden (see page 188).

Carrots can be sown from early spring through midsummer, but in cold spring soils, carrot germination can try your patience. Carrots sown in the late summer and early fall usually grow better, with fewer pests. Gardeners in very warm climates have to discontinue sowing in June or July, resuming in late summer for fall and winter harvests. If you sow your favorite varieties at regular intervals throughout the year, you'll soon discover the right time for sowing while assuring a steady supply of carrots.

Like beets, carrots grow healthier and tastier in regions where warm, sunny days are followed by cool nights. This type of weather allows carrots to photosynthesize like crazy during the day and put lots of sugar and starch into the root. During cool nights the carrot "rests" instead of burning up the sugar. The result is a sweeter, bigger carrot. These conditions usually come with spring weather, but they may occur during fall or even early summer, depending on where you live. Carrots are fussy about sudden weather swings. They will bolt with 6 to 8 weeks below 65°F or during long, hot days of summer.

PLANTING

The hardest part of growing carrots is getting them started. Carrots transplant very poorly (they become little corkscrews) so they should be sown directly into the soil. They are notoriously slow starters, and the seeds are very small. Try warming your soil by covering your moist carrot bed with plastic several days before sowing. This can speed up sprouting. We make drills with a bow-rake, sow seeds in the drills, and cover them with the other end of the rake. You can also make $1/4$-inch-deep holes or cross-hatches of holes in your damp bed. This will make sure that most of the seeds get buried.

If you don't mind thinning carrots, you can broadcast the seeds about $1/8$-inch apart on top of the bed and cover them with a thin dressing of soil or compost. You can try pelletized seeds or seed tapes, but they are expensive and come in only a few varieties. A lot of gardeners mix the seeds with an equal volume of coarse sand or fine vermiculite to spread the seeds out. Sow several times, 2 to 3 weeks apart. Each time, sow just enough seeds to keep you in carrots for a month or so, and you'll have carrots most of the year.

Carrot seeds take a week or two to sprout, so be patient. Since the seeds are so small, they need constant moisture with daily watering. Try covering your beds with burlap sacks or plastic to hold in the heat and moisture. Or sow a "breaker" crop of radishes with the carrots: The radishes germinate quickly, breaking the soil crust and making it easier for the carrots to sprout. Remember that thinning tends to disturb established seedlings, so water the remaining carrots after you thin.

When the carrots sprout, you'll probably also have a crop of baby weeds germinating with the carrots. Lose no time; get the weeds while they are small! Slow-sprouting carrots are one vegetable that can truly be overcome by weeds. As carrots grow, it is important to continue to keep the weeds down. When you weed, move soil or mulch over the top of any exposed root to avoid "greening" (green shoulders), which gives them a bitter taste.

SOIL AND FERTILIZERS

To grow into the delicate orange roots celebrated in seed catalogs and cookbooks, carrots need a well-drained, deep soil—the kind you can easily push a shovel into. If the growing root runs into a clod or stone, it will fork, so the ground needs to be free of obstacles to the depth of the carrots. In soggy soils carrots develop black spots near the top of the root that leave rotting cavities. To fluff up the soil, dig in plenty of aged compost or well-rotted manure a few weeks prior to seeding. Organic matter helps retain moisture, lightens the soil, and remedies any boron or manganese deficiencies. Avoid fresh manure; it gives carrots too much nitrogen, which can cause branching and hairy, fibrous roots. Keep soils slightly acid. Carrots respond poorly to foliar feeding, so keep soil charged with wood ashes, coffee grounds, bone meal, fish emulsion, and potassium sulfate to keep roots fed with plenty of phosphorous, potassium, and micronutrients. Potassium promotes healthy, sweet carrots. Fertilizing before planting is best, but you can side-dress with liquid fertilizer when the carrot tops are 6 inches tall. Carrots are hungry for the micronutrients boron and manganese. These are best provided by fish emulsion, kelp products, and compost.

CARROT NUTRIENT DEFICIENCY	
NUTRIENT DEFICIENCY	**SYMPTOM**
Nitrogen (N)	Fine pale foliage; small roots.
Phosphorous (P)	Purpling of older leaves in seedlings, beginning at margin. No yellowing.
Potassium (K)	Old leaves scorched at leaf margins; leaf stems look water soaked.
Calcium (Ca)	Rapid death of the leaf's growing point. Brown color to core of root.
Sulfur (S)	New leaves uniformly yellow and frail.
Magnesium (Mg)	Older leaves yellow with red tint at margin.
Boron (Bo)	Older leaves yellow and curled backwards. Roots may split to expose central core.

DISEASES

The major virus disease in carrots is **aster yellows.** Look for dwarfed, pale young leaves and a taproot covered with many hairlike roots, plus a bitter taste. The disease is spread by leafhoppers, so cover growing plants with row covers and destroy all infected plants. Resistant varieties include Chantenay and Scarlet Nantes.

The most serious disease of carrot roots is **black rot fungus (*Alternaria*),** which attacks the crown and is spread by water and seed. When infected roots are stored, they develop a white mold. Avoid overhead watering and destroy all infected plants.

Two fungi (*Cercospora* and *Septoria*) and a bacteria (*Xanthomonas*) cause **leaf spot** on carrots. The fungal spots are brown with a pale halo, and they can eventually cover the entire leaf. Bacterial spots are yellowish green and water-soaked. Protect carrots by removing all diseased leaves quickly and practicing 3- to 4-year rotations. Rain, wind, and dirty tools carry these diseases from plant to plant. Avoid working around carrots when the leaves are wet or wounding the plants in any way. Foliar sprays of compost tea or bordeaux mix used as a preventative fungicide prior to infection can reduce some fungi diseases, such as leaf spot, mildews, and rusts.

PESTS

Carrots are also vulnerable to a number of pests. **Root knot nematodes** are tiny wormlike animals that produce distorted roots with galls, forks, and tufts of side roots. Controls include rotating carrots with onions, radishes, and lettuce; soil sterilization; and digging in organic matter to stimulate soil fungi that feed on the nematodes.

Insects that eat roots are particular problems because as they feed, they make it easy for soil diseases to infect plants. There are three major insects that eat carrot roots:

1. The larvae of the **carrot rust fly (*Psila rosae)*** are pearly white maggots that tunnel in the lower part of the roots, leaving behind their rusty brown droppings. They feed on other members of the carrot family, including celery, parsley, and Queen Anne's lace. They are particular problems in the Northeast and on the West Coast.

2. The larva of the **carrot weevil (Listrono-tus oregonensis)** is a greenish white, legless insect with a dark brown head that feeds on crowns, lower stems, and the top part of the roots. Its tunnels are wider and higher on the root than those of the rust fly. Weevils also feed on other weeds and vegetables of the carrot family.

3. **Wireworms (Limonius)** are the slender, brown, leathery larvae of click beetles that can tunnel into and eat carrot roots. They feed near the soil surface during cool weather and burrow deeper in hot weather. For control, rotate carrots from season to season with green manures. Cover your plants with row covers to discourage the adult flies and beetles.

Also be sure to control carrot family weeds right away; sprays are not effective once the roots have been attacked. Drenching the soil with parasitic nematodes may give some control (see page 182).

VARIETIES

There are about 250 varieties of carrots available in the United States; most are open-pollinated. There are several hybrids, including new hybrid crosses between Nantes and Imperator carrots that are early, disease resistant, and high in vitamins. Carrot varieties are grouped according to shape and use. Some are long and skinny, some short and chubby, and some are almost as round as radishes. They come in all colors of the sunset, from pale creamy gold to deep red-orange.

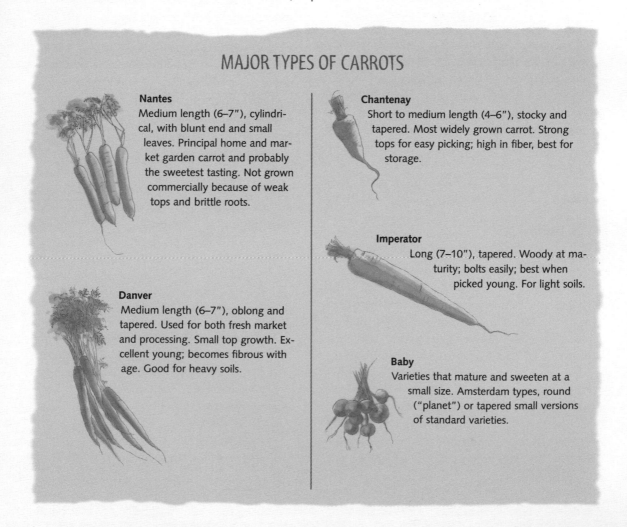

MAJOR TYPES OF CARROTS

Nantes
Medium length (6–7"), cylindrical, with blunt end and small leaves. Principal home and market garden carrot and probably the sweetest tasting. Not grown commercially because of weak tops and brittle roots.

Chantenay
Short to medium length (4–6"), stocky and tapered. Most widely grown carrot. Strong tops for easy picking; high in fiber, best for storage.

Imperator
Long (7–10"), tapered. Woody at maturity; bolts easily; best when picked young. For light soils.

Danver
Medium length (6–7"), oblong and tapered. Used for both fresh market and processing. Small top growth. Excellent young; becomes fibrous with age. Good for heavy soils.

Baby
Varieties that mature and sweeten at a small size. Amsterdam types, round ("planet") or tapered small versions of standard varieties.

RECOMMENDED CARROT VARIETIES

TYPE	VARIETY	COMMENTS
Nantes		cylindrical
Early, Hybrid	Napoli	One of earliest full-sized varieties. Strong tops. 7–9″
	Presto	Early French Touchon type. For bunching. 8″
	Nelson	Sweetest early Nantes for summer harvest. Strong tops for bunching.
Midseason, Hybrid	Ingot	The best for taste and nutrition. Extra-long Nantes; high in vitamin A.
	Bolero	Sweet, crunchy, and disease resistant. Taste improves with storage. Favorite in French kitchen gardens.
	Artist	Nantes x Imperator hybrid. Super sweet, stores well, resistant, and high in vitamin A. Good juicer.
Midseason, OP	Armstrong	Slim, orange, and sweet Dutch strain.
	Touchon	French heirloom. Very sweet. Grows poorly in cold soils.
	Scarlet Nantes	Old garden standard. Bright orange, good keeper; fresh, cooked, frozen. Dig, don't pull.
Late, Hybrid	Tomino	Uniform, high yield, very sweet and orange.
Danvers		long conical
Midseason, OP	Danvers 126	Since 1947, a popular high yielder. Suited to clay soils with its strong tops and roots. 7″. Thin early.
	Danvers Half Long	True-blue American heirloom, since 1871. Blunt end, nearly coreless. For clay soils.
Chantenay		short conical
Midseason, OP	Royal Chantenay	Good carrot for beginners. Good juicer and tolerates heavy soils.
	Red Cored Chantenay	Heirloom since 1929. One of the best-tasting carrots. Good for heavy soils. Gets sweeter in storage.
Late, OP Kuroda		Japanese. Very large (10″) and juicy. Slow to bolt in heat. Harvest in fall.
Imperator		long and tapered
Early, hybrid	King Midas	Earliest Imperator. Strong leaves; good for baby carrots.
	Imperial #15	Uniform short Imperator; resists bolting.
Midseason, OP	Imperial #58	Uniform short Imperator; resists bolting.
Late, OP	Gold Pak	Standard bunching Imperator for gardens.
Baby Carrots		
OP	Amsterdam Forcing	For forcing baby carrots. Matures well.
	Kinko 4″	Super early baby Chantenay. Harvest young.
	Minicor	Popular Dutch baby Nantes carrot, 3–6″. Great for canning.
	Thumbelina	AAS winner. Extra early, round gourmet carrot; best for heavy soils and containers.
	Rondo	French heirloom since 1850s. Round for heavy soils; very sweet.

Note: OP=open-pollinated

Choosing which variety of carrot to grow depends on what you want from your carrots and what kind of soil you have. It would be nice if you could plant just one variety and pull out a few early ones for baby carrots, the later ones for fresh eating and cooking, and some old big ones for keepers, but this isn't the case. If you want sweet baby carrots, you'll have to grow baby carrot varieties. The sweetness you taste in carrots is the root's food reserve. Immature carrots (as opposed to true baby carrots) are still growing and don't have the necessary sugars for great taste. Baby carrots ripen and sweeten quickly, but they don't stay sweet very long, so stagger your sowings every few weeks and harvest quickly. Storage carrots have been selected for their high fiber, low water, and long-lived sweetness. If you want to store carrots, grow storage varieties, especially the Chantenays. If you have a shallow or clay soil, you have a wide choice of short, round, and baby varieties to choose from. Chantenays are also good for heavy soils because they taper short, and their strong tops are less likely to break off when you pull them up. The Nantes are supposed to be the sweetest carrots for fresh eating, but most carrots can be grown sweet if you match the right variety to your local conditions and needs.

HARVEST AND STORAGE

Harvesting carrots is the fun part. They can be picked anytime, but mature carrots are usually ready in 2 to 3 months. A carrot's color is the best indicator of its ripeness. If it's pale orange, it won't be sweet enough. Carrots are sweetest at their mature size, and may only keep their flavor for a couple of weeks. Soak the carrot bed with water and let it drain for easy harvesting. Grab the green tops and gently tug with a twisting motion, loosing the soil first if necessary.

In mild winter areas, carrots can be stored in the ground and mulched over winter. You can also layer carrots in boxes of dry sand or double bag them. To do this, dig the carrots, air dry them for a week or so (do not wash), and remove all excess soil. If storage carrots have green tops, twist or cut off the leaves before storing. Otherwise, the greens will wilt and decay and draw moisture from the root. Place the carrots in a large paper bag punched with a few air holes and place the paper bag in a large plastic bag, also with air holes. Store the double bag in a root cellar or in the refrigerator crisper. Carrots will keep this way for 3 to 5 months.

Don't store carrots with apples, pears, or bananas that produce ethylene gases—this will hasten their ripening.

CARROT GROWING TIPS

- Select the correct variety of carrots for your soil and climate.

- Prepare the seed bed carefully. Remove all obstructions to root growth and load the soil with aged compost and wood ashes (potassium) for sweeter carrots.

- Stagger your sowing starting 3 to 4 weeks before the average last spring frost date for a sure and steady supply.

- Sow the seeds carefully and lightly mulch them to retain moisture and prevent soil crusting. Sprinkle daily and never let the seeds dry out. Germination may take 1 to 2 weeks, so be patient.

- Thin the seedlings early and diligently. Keep them well weeded. Avoid too much nitrogen and provide plenty of potassium and phosphorous.

- Side-dress with liquid fertilizer when the carrot tops are 6 inches tall.

- For a full, sweet taste, harvest carrots when they first achieve their full size. Carrot taste depends as much on timely harvesting as good culture. Drench the bed with water for easy harvest.

Potatoes
SOLANACEAE (Nightshade or Tomato Family)

Solanum tuberosum
CHINESE: *ma ling shu*
FRENCH: *pomme de terre*
GERMAN: *Kartoffel*
ITALIAN: *potata*
JAPANESE: *jagaimo*
SPANISH: *patata*

Potatoes are often neglected in the home garden because they're easy to buy and take up a lot of garden room. But potatoes are fun to grow, especially for kids. Slipping your hand under the loose soil and pulling up the first baby "new" potatoes of the season is like finding a buried treasure. Besides, there are only a few varieties in the store, such as russet baking, Kennebec all-purpose, or red boiling potatoes like Pontiac or La Soda. When you grow your own, you get to enjoy the hundreds of colorful and tasty varieties that are now available in nurseries and mail-order catalogs.

The so-called "Irish" potato actually comes from the high plateaus of Bolivia and Peru, where it has been cultivated for over 5,000 years. Potatoes were the staple of the Incas, who grew and ate hundreds of varieties; they even made a potato liqueur in some of the earliest known alcohol stills. Like its relatives, the tomato and pepper, the potato arrived in Europe with Spanish explorers. Within a few decades, it replaced the parsnip as the vegetable staple of Europe. The Irish were the first Europeans to grow the potato extensively, and to this day people still call it the "Irish" potato. Settlers brought the tasty tuber to North America, where it quickly became a mainstay of the New World diet. Today, of the eight major food crops on earth, seven are grains and the eighth is the potato.

In the kitchen, potatoes are very versatile. They can be fried, boiled, grilled, baked, or roasted. Potatoes are a basic ingredient in salads, casseroles, and chowders, and an excellent thickener for soups. The Irish have their stew, the French their gratins, the Italians their gnocchi, the Germans their potato pancakes, and the Americans their baked spuds.

Potatoes are very wholesome. They provide lots of complex carbohydrates, some protein, and good amounts of vitamin B-complex, phosphorous, and calcium. Most of the nutrients are near the skin, so don't peel if you don't have to. Remember, potatoes are low in calories if they aren't smothered in gravy, butter, or sour cream.

CULTIVATION

Potatoes are a cool-season perennial grown as an annual. They need full sun all day. If you grow potatoes in the shade, they become lanky and put their energy into leaves and not tubers.

In cold northern climates, plant potatoes from mid-April to mid-June or 6 to 8 weeks before the last expected frost. In warmer climates, potatoes can be planted anytime from February to mid-March for spring planting and again mid-July through early fall.

If you want potatoes all season, but you can only plant in springtime, try planting early midseason and late varieties one after the other. Plant early ones in late March, a week earlier in warm areas, and a couple of weeks later in the north. Harvest in June or July. Plant midseason types in early mid-April and dig in July or August. Plant a late variety in late April and harvest September through November.

One problem with planting late is that seed potatoes delivered then are still dormant and may fail to sprout. You can help the tubers break out of dormancy by keeping them in the refrigerator for 30 days before planting. Transfer them to a lighted place so they can sprout freely. Once sprouted, they can be planted.

PLANTING

Although potatoes grow underground, they aren't roots; they're actually the swollen end ("tuber") of skinny underground stems called rhizomes. They can sprout from growth points on their surface ("eyes"). Potatoes are grown by planting small whole potatoes ("seed potatoes") or pieces of whole potatoes known as "sets," each with one to three eyes. Once planted, the mother potato begins to sprout long, skinny stems underground (called rhizomes) and leafy stems above ground. As the days get shorter and cooler, the ends of the rhizomes swell up into tubers, which store food for the upcoming winter.

You can plant store-bought potatoes, although you risk disease. Just be sure they haven't been sprayed to prevent sprouting on the shelves. Most potato growers claim that whole seed potatoes grow more vigorously than sets. However, whole potatoes tend to grow lots of little potatoes from eyes grouped at the end of the tuber. Cutting seed potatoes into sets encourages all eyes to sprout normal-sized potatoes. If you decide to use sets, cut the potatoes widthwise into equal pieces with one to three eyes each. Smaller sets will give you fewer but larger potatoes. For best results, use medium sets about the size of a plum, and practice the cut-and-dry method. Let the sets cure in a warm place for a few days to callus and protect the cut ends once they are planted. To do this, expose them to light for 2 to 3 weeks. Sets treated by "chitting," as this technique is called, root quickly and mature earlier than those planted directly. Set seed potatoes about 12 inches apart in a 4- to 6- inch furrow. Plant them cut-side down, so the eyes are uppermost, and press them firmly into the soil.

You can buy certified seed potatoes at nurseries, through the mail, or you can make sets yourself.

As potatoes grow, new tubers form above the original seed potato. That's why gardeners have favorite methods for piling soil on top of the growing tubers. One standard method, called **hilling-up**, or hilling, is to dig a trench 6 to 8 inches deep, plant the sets about 12 inches apart in the bottom, then cover with 2 inches of good soil. As the plant grows, keep filling in the trench about every 2 weeks or so. When the trench is filled, keep mounding soil, compost, or mulch around the plant to form hills above the ground. It's okay to cover a few leaves. The hilling method not only makes room for more potatoes to grow on top of the original set, but also keeps light from reaching the tubers and turning them green. (This green tissue is mildly toxic and should be cut out before eating.) Hilling also protects the tubers from insects and airborne disease spores.

Some gardeners have shallow, rocky, or compact soil. For them potatoes can be grown by the **mulch method**. Place sets on the surface of the bed. Loosely shake a seed-free loose mulch like straw over the bed 6 to 12 inches deep. As the plants grow, continue to add more loose mulch, as if hilling.

You can also grow potatoes in containers. This is handy when your soil is infected with diseases like scab and late blight. Start by placing some clean soil into a large, deep container. Place the sets at the bottom of the container and gradually fill it is as though you were hilling-up.

Potatoes need about 1 inch of water per week. Too little water encourages scab, and too much water encourages foliar diseases. A thick layer of mulch helps keep moisture levels constant.

SOIL AND FERTILIZERS

Potatoes prefer deep, fertile soil with lots of organic matter. Never add lime. Make sure your soil phosphorous and potassium are adequate.

NUTRIENT DEFICIENCIES IN POTATOES	
NUTRIENT DEFICIENCY	**SYMPTOM**
Nitrogen (N)	Lower leaves pale yellow green.
Phosphorous (P)	Leaves curl with purplish color.
Potassium (K)	Leaves bluish; lower leaves turn brown at the edges; upper leaves curl.
Magnesium (Mg)	Lower leaves yellow with green veins; also curl up with brown spots.
Sulfur (S)	All leaves yellow.

DISEASES

Potatoes have more than their fair share of diseases. Blights, rots, and fungi attack the leaves and tubers of potatoes. Each region of the United States seems to have its own local potato problems, so we can only mention some of the major ones here. Your local nurseries, gardeners, growers, and extension service will all have good information for your area.

The best way to prevent the many diseases that affect potatoes is to keep the diseases out of your garden in the first place. Always use potato sets that are "certified" disease free.

Rotate potatoes throughout your garden, but keep them from following too closely behind tomatoes and peppers, which share many diseases.

Potatoes are susceptible to several **mosaic viruses.** Typical symptoms include a stunted plant with curled or puckered leaves that are mottled yellow. Mosaics are spread by aphids. Always destroy infected tissue. The virus can survive composting and stay viable for decades. The best approach is to vigilantly monitor and control sucking insects, use floating row covers to exclude them, keep plants growing vigorously, and grow resistant varieties.

A serious bacterial disease is **blackleg (*Erwinia*),** which causes yellowing of the lower leaves and upward curling of the top leaves. Soft black spots appear on the base of the stem near the soil line. Eventually plants wilt and die. Bacteria are spread on infected tubers and tools. Healthy plants can usually overcome infection. Avoid wet soils, overfertilizing, and bruised or uncertified sets. Also, sterilize your tools and grow resistant varieties.

Early blight (*Alternaria*) is a leaf-eating fungus, although the rough, sunken lesions it causes can also develop on tubers in storage. The first symptoms are dark leaf spots with a concentric "bull's-eye" pattern on older leaves. Spores overwinter in crop debris (including tomato-family weeds) and seeds, and they are mostly scattered by wind, but also by rain, tools, and flea beetles. Early blight spreads quickly, so it requires immediate attention. The fungus seems to affect weaker plants, so your best approach here is to culture your plants carefully. Keep rotating potatoes out of the same spot for 3 to 4 years, grow healthy plants of appropriate varieties, don't overhead water, and remove all infected plant parts.

Late blight (*Phytophthora infestans*) is the infamous fungus disease that caused the Irish potato famine last century. Late blight infects both leaves and tubers, and is a special problem when cool, moist nights are followed by warm, humid days. The leaves and stems develop water-soaked brown spots that quickly grow together. On the underside of leaves, the spots often grow a white mold. Tubers develop brown to purple sunken patches on the skin. Late blight only overwinters on living plant tissue, like tubers or plant debris, so always keep things tidy around potatoes, and compost diseased plants thoroughly. Late blight can come in on tomato or pepper seedlings, and be splashed from plant to plant with falling water, so don't water overhead. Choose resistant varieties and rotate for 3 to 4 years.

Vascular wilts are caused by two groups of fungi, *Verticillium* and *Fusarium*, which attack the roots and conductive tissues of plants. Early symptoms are yellowing of the leaves and curling or drooping of lower leaves; later the leaves die back from the margins. If you cut into the stem and look at a cross-section, it will be brown instead of a healthy green color. Tubers infected with *Fusarium* may show a slight pink color. Those infected with *Verticillium* will have dark streaking at the stem end. Both fungi are soil borne and persist for years, which makes them particularly hard to control. Although rotation may help, the disease cannot be eliminated completely from an infested garden. Try not to damage roots during weeding, and don't fertilize with too much nitrogen or fresh manure, which create favorable conditions for the wilts. Avoid bringing the disease into your garden on plants and soil, and look for resistant varieties. Unlike tomatoes, few varieties of potatoes are resistant to vascular wilts, especially *Fusarium*. For more on vascular wilts, see "Tomatoes," pages 355–356.

Scab (*Streptomyces scabies*) is a fungus that makes corky patches grow on tuber skins. The disease is not usually serious, but the lesions become points of entry for many other diseases, which will rot the tubers in storage. Scab spores overwinter on plant debris and in the soil for years. Choose resistant varieties and rotate for 3 to 4 years. The scab fungus avoids acidic soils, so don't lime or add fresh manure prior to planting.

Rhizoctonia (*Rhizoctonia solani*) is a fungus that attacks the seedlings, stems, and tubers of potatoes. It is part of the damping-off gang of several fungi that attacks and kills seedlings by girdling their stems. Tuber skins develop a dark spotting, which resembles dirt that won't wash off. Rhizoctonia is difficult to control, because, like scab, it can live for years in the soil, eating organic matter instead of plants. It likes high humidity, so keep plants generously spaced to ensure good air circulation. Avoid overhead watering. Rhizoctonia prefers dead organic materials and when soils are rich in organic matter, the disease may not infect living plants as much.

PESTS

Potatoes also have more than their fair share of pests. **Potato aphids** suck sap from leaves and make them curl downwards. You can see these tiny, pink and green, pear-shaped insects in clusters on the underside of the leaves. They attack related peppers and tomatoes as well as other vegetables and plants, especially roses and rose family members like *Potentilla* and apples. Potato aphids transmit virus diseases, so they should be discouraged even if they only do minimal damage. They like to feed on roses in spring and migrate to vegetables in the summer. For general aphid controls, see page 256.

Leafhoppers are cousins of aphids. If you watch patiently, you may see these small, wedge-shaped insects on the undersides of leaves. The insects suck sap and leave light green stipples at the leaf edges that soon brown, leaving what growers call "hopper-burn." Like aphids, hoppers transmit virus diseases, so they need to be controlled. Protect plants with row covers and spray early in the day with soap, oil, or botanicals, when hoppers are less active. Predatory bugs and lacewings (see pages 176–178) are especially fond of leafhopper eggs.

Colorado Potato Beetle *(Leptinotarsa decimlineata):* See "Tomatoes," page 356.

The **potato tuberworm** is found in areas of the South and in California. It prefers potatoes, but will attack most members of the tomato family. The tuberworm is a caterpillar that burrows through stems and nibbles at tubers. Adult moths overwinter on potatoes and in soil debris. In spring they lay eggs on potato leaves, or drop through soil cracks and lay eggs on the eyes of the tubers. Look for tunnels in the leaves and stems, and holes bored in the eyes of tubers. Destroy infected plants and tubers, and always check potatoes for larvae before storing. Add mulch and organic matter to keep soil from cracking, and always keep at least 2 inches of soil over growing tubers.

Wireworms are the larvae of click beetles. They are slender, smooth, tight-skinned, yellowish tan larvae that tunnel into tubers. Adults hang out and lay eggs in the soil. The larvae hatch and may live for 6 years before they pupate into adults. They can establish themselves in large numbers, especially in a spot previously planted in lawn or sod. If you're planting potatoes where grass used to be, till the area several times and plant sets in late rather than early spring. There are commercial predatory nematodes that will control wireworms (see page 182).

CULTURAL PROBLEMS

Green tubers occur when the potato's skin is exposed to light. Being a stem, the tuber can photosynthesize. (The green part contains toxic alkaloids that shouldn't be eaten.) To prevent this, be sure tubers are always covered with earth or mulch while they are growing.

Hollow heart refers to a tuber with brown, irregular cavities inside. The cavities develop when the plant grows too fast. This can happen if there is too much space between plants, if plants are overwatered or overfed, or if the mother sets are planted when they are too small.

Poor sprouting occurs when potato sets are kept too wet or planted in cold, wet soils. Under these conditions, soil microbes gobble up the potato sets before they can grow. To prevent this, pre-set your sprouts and wait until the soil warms to at least 45°F before planting out; water your sets carefully, and don't bury them too deeply.

VARIETIES

About 80 percent of the potatoes grown commercially are just a few varieties like Russet Burbank and Katahdin. However, hundred of exciting varieties are now available to the home gardener. Some are rediscovered heirlooms, others are brand-new hybrids, and a few are directly from South America. They come in unique shapes and colors, from purple, knobby "fingerlings" to round, red-skinned boilers to oval, brown-skinned bakers. You can grow potatoes you can't find in the grocery store, with flavors that store-bought spuds can't match.

From a cook's point of view, there are three kinds of potatoes:

1. Those with a thick skin and high starch content, like russets and some fingerlings. These are ideal for baking, mashing, and other dishes requiring potatoes that don't lose their shape when cooked.

2. Those with a medium starch content, such as the so-called "all-purpose" potatoes, which are used for baking, steaming, or grilling.

All-purpose

3. Those with a thin, waxy skin and low starch content, like the round red and white types, perfect for grilling, boiling, and roasting (that is, whenever a firm texture is important).

In recent years, as part of the growing popularity of specialty vegetables, new and hierloom varieties of potatoes have become more and more avail-

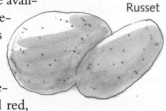

Russet

able. These specialty potatoes range in tastes and textures that go far beyond the usual red, white, and russets. In fact, specialty potatoes aren't new at all. They have been in regional cuisines throughout their homeland in South America for centuries. What's new is their mainstream popularity and availability in North American seed houses. There's the purple Peruvian with its oval shape, dark

Round Reds

blue skin, and deep purple, mealy flesh, which stores well. How about some of the sweet and nutty all-purpose potatoes, like Yukon Gold, Yellow Finn, or German Butterball, which usually win the taste tests. Or you might try the fingerling types like Russian Banana, Ozette, and Ruby Crescent. Fingerlings stay firm when cooked, making them great for potato salads and sautées.

Blue

Fingerlings are shaped like huge peanuts or knobs of ginger, and their skin varies from pinkish bronze to tan. They are heavenly when coated with olive oil and herbs and grilled or baked whole in aluminum foil.

Scores of other potato varieties, in addition to the ones we recommend, are now available from mail-order nurseries all over the country.

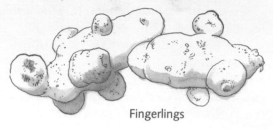

Fingerlings

HARVEST AND STORAGE

Many gardeners think that "new," or baby, potatoes gathered before the plant matures are the best potatoes. However, new potatoes store poorly because they have too much sugar. Storage potatoes should come from mature plants. Potatoes are mature when the tops die down. If the plants bolt, you can start harvesting about 2 weeks after the first flower opens. Be sure to dig the potatoes carefully, using a digging fork. Injured potatoes rot quickly. If you miss some potatoes in your harvest, they will be the next season's welcome volunteers.

Some potatoes store better than others. From the accompanying list, Norkotah, Goldrush, Butte, Katahdin, Caribe, and Red Norland are best for keeping. To store tubers, air-dry them for a few hours after digging and brush off all clinging soil. Then place them in a dark, dry, cool (60°F) place for 2 to 3 weeks. After this curing period, move them to a cooler (40°F) dark, humid spot with plenty of air circulation. Under ideal conditions, potatoes will keep for 4 to 6 months.

RECOMMENDED POTATO VARIETIES

VARIETY	SKIN	FLESH	SEASON	USE
High Starch (Mealy) for Baking				
Norkotah Russet	Brown	White	Early	Baking, frying, boiling, soups.
Goldrush	Brown	White	Mid	Baking, frying, soups, mashed.
Butte	Brown	White	Late	Baking, frying, soups, mashed.
Medium Starch (All-Purpose)				
Kennebec	White	White	Mid	Moist baker, good boiler.
Katahdin*	Tan	White	Mid	All-purpose boiling.
German Butterball	Tan	Yellow	Mid	Great baker. Best skin flavor.
Green Mountain*	Tan	White	Late	Moist baker, good boiler.
Yukon Gold	Yellow	Yellow	Early	Roasting, gratins, pancakes.
Caribe*	Violet	White	Early	Baking, mashed, steamed.
All Red	Red	Red	Mid	Boiling, salads.
Bintje	Yellow	Yellow	Late	Dry baking, frying, and roasting; gratins.
Yellow Finn	Tan	Yellow	Mid	Roasting, grilling, baking.
Low Starch (Waxy) for Boiling and Roasting				
Red Norland	Red	White	Early	Roasting, pan fried.
Red LaSoda	Red	White	Mid	Roasting, steaming, grilled.
Red Gold	Red	Yellow	Mid	Boiling, steaming.
Fingerlings				
Russian Banana	Yellow	Yellow	Mid	Roasting, sautéeing, and salads.
Ruby Crescent	Yellow	Pink	Mid	Roasting, sautéeing, and salads.
Peruvian Blue	Blue	Yellow	Mid	Roasting, sautéeing, and salads.
Caribe	Blue-purple	White	Early	Roasting, sautéeing, and salads.

*Indicates heirloom variety

Maturity dates are about 65 days for early, 80 days for midseason, and 90 days for late.

POTATO GROWING TIPS

- Buy certified seed potatoes every year to reduce chances of disease. Select the right variety for your needs and local conditions.

- If you cut sets from whole potatoes, put them in a warm place to callus over the cut ends and begin sprouting before planting out.

- Plant sets in an acidic lime-free soil. Bury them in a 6-inch trench. Fertilize with potassium and phosphorous, and hold back on nitrogen.

- Don't plant too early or spuds will rot in cold soil. Wait until the soil warms to 45°F.

- Hill-up around plant as tubers grow upwards to keep them from getting exposed to sunlight and pests.

- Side-dress when you hill-up the second time with fish emulsion or 1 pound of 5-10-10 per 30-foot row.

- Water well for 6 to 8 weeks after planting as tubers begin to form.

- Never plant potatoes in the same place for more than a year. Rotate throughout your garden.

- Avoid overhead watering, as this will stimulate many diseases.

- Harvest small ("new") potatoes 10 weeks after planting. Harvest storage potatoes after vines have died, when tubers will have tough outer skin. Dig them gently to avoid wounding the tubers. Eat damaged potatoes as soon as possible.

- To store, air-dry tubers, brush off clinging soil and cure for 3 weeks in a dark, dry, and cool spot. Store in a dark 40°F spot with good circulation.

Leaves, Stems, and Stalks

THE BRASSICAS (Cabbage Family)

According to Greek legend, Zeus was asked to resolve a difficult question. While he struggled to find the answer, he perspired the first colewort, the ancestor of all edible members of the cabbage family. The cabbage family (Brassicaceae) includes several of our most important vegetables, which we can divide into three groups:

1. The "European" brassicas, or "cole," crops, which include broccoli, brussels sprouts, cabbage, cauliflower, collards, kale, and kohlrabi. They all belong to the same species: *Brassica oleracea.* Many gardeners refer to them as *the* brassicas.

2. Asian brassicas: A host of vegetables that have been grown for centuries in China, Japan, and other parts of the Far East. Except for Chinese cabbage and mustard, Asian brassicas are relatively new to American kitchen gardens. They are very nutritious, and thrive in a wider range of climates than cole crops.

3. Miscellaneous "non-brassica" cabbage-family vegetables include arugula *(Eruca sativa),* radish *(Raphanus sativus),* upland cresses *(Barbarea verna),* garden cress *(Lepidium sativum),* and horseradish *(Armoraceia rusticana).*

European brassicas probably evolved from the wild sea kales still found along the Mediterranean coastline and the sand dunes of northern Europe. Each of today's modern cole crops is an exaggerated body part of the original ancestor: the loose leaves of collards and kale, the tight leaf head of cabbage, the flower buds of broccoli, the tufted stems of cauliflower, and the stem buds of brussels sprouts.

Most of the Asian brassicas originated from the turnip *Brassica rapa (campestris)* Some, like Chinese cabbage and bok choy, are favorites of the vegetable garden. Others are less familiar, but gaining in popularity, like tatsoi, choy sum, gai lan (Chinese broccoli), and komatsuna (mustard spinach).

The non-brassica cabbage vegetables are not discussed here, but arugula is included in the "Salad Greens" section of the Compendium.

The popularity of brassicas has a lot to do with their many health benefits. They're high in beta-carotene, vitamins B, C, and E, calcium, and dietary fiber. They're also rich in several phytochemicals that help the body fight cancer.

CULTIVATION

All brassicas grow best during cool weather in rich, limed soil. They are a little finicky when it comes to propagation. They like to germinate warm (75° to 85°F), but grow seedlings at cooler temperatures (55° to 65°F). In warm temperatures, seedlings will produce weak transplants, so it's important to remove brassicas from heat soon after they germinate.

SOIL AND FERTILIZERS

Brassicas are hard on the soil. They are heavy feeders, and they leave a wake of soil diseases. To keep brassicas producing year after year, it's important to rotate them in your garden. Never follow one brassica with another, and move them around from year to year so that they don't stay too long in any one spot (for more about rotating plants, see pages 32–36). Many rotation schemes call for planting green manures prior to planting brassicas. This helps provide extra nutrients and interrupts disease cycles.

It's important to grow brassicas in well-limed soils. They grow poorly and get diseased in acid soils. They are also heavy feeders and need a complete fertilizer (N, P, K), plus calcium, sulfur, and trace elements—especially boron and iron.

DISEASES

Cauliflower and **turnip mosaic (cabbage black ring spot)** are special problems on Asian brassicas. Infected plants have leaves that are mottled in a mosaic of light green or yellow with some black spots. The virus is spread by aphids, so floating row covers may help keep these vectors away. Avoid planting in old brassica beds and control cruciferous weeds, which act as reservoirs for the virus and aphids.

Black rot (*Xanthomonas campestris*) is a bacterial disease that favors warm, humid conditions. The disease is spread by splashing water from sprinklers or rainstorms. Bacteria infect the plant through pores or insect wounds at the leaf margins, and so the first symptoms appear as V-shaped, yellowish patches spreading inward on the leaves. Later, a unique network of black veins (the source of the disease's name) develops within the yellow areas. Black rot is carried on seeds and transplants, and it can overwinter on plant debris or cruciferous weeds. To control the disease, destroy infected plants, rotate brassicas at least every 3 years, control mustard and radish weeds, avoid overhead sprinklers, buy good seed, and select tolerant varieties.

Blackleg (*Phoma lingami*) is found east of the Rockies and along the West Coast. The fungus attacks all brassicas plus other cabbage family members like stock and sweet alyssum. It prefers cool, moist conditions. Symptoms appear as brown sores near the base of the plant, which soon grow to girdle the stem. Meanwhile, light brown spots appear on the leaf edges, while black dots (the fruiting bodies of the fungi) appear in the stem wound and leaf spots. As the fungus eats the water-conducting tissue, the plant wilts, topples, and dies. Spores are spread by wind, splashing water, infected seed, tools, and gardeners; they can live in plant debris for 3 years. There is no cure for blackleg, only cultural controls. Always buy reliable seeds, don't overhead water, avoid working among wet plants, destroy infected plants, and control cruciferous weeds.

Alternaria leaf spot (*Alternaria*) includes several kinds of fungus that infect the leaves of head cabbage, Chinese cabbage and, to a lesser extent, broccoli and cauliflower. They produce brown spots on leaves, stems, and seed pods. The leaf spots grow into large circles with a bull's-eye pattern of rings. A brown velvety mold grows on older spots. Spores spread rapidly in cool, rainy weather and are carried to adjacent gardens by air currents. The disease overwinters on seeds and plant debris, so all infected plants should be destroyed. Row covers may reduce incoming spores. We have had good luck with aged compost tea as a preventative organic fungicide for leaf spot (see pages 77–79).

Vascular wilts are fungi that destroy the water-conducting tissues of plants. They enter young roots and move up the water veins of the stems to the leaves. **Verticillium (*Verticillium dahliae*)** attacks all brassicas. Of the cole crops, broccoli seems to be most tolerant. Early symptoms are hard to see, but they start with irregular patches of yellow between the veins of lower leaves, often on just one side of the plant. If you cut off a stem cleanly, you'll see reddish streaks of the infected tissue in the cross-section, a sure sign of verticillium.

Fusarium *(Fusarium oxysporum),* or cabbage yellows, is another type of vascular wilt. It produces leaf and stem symptoms like verticillium, and it's hard to tell the two apart. However, fusarium favors temperatures between 75° and 85°F, and is a problem in the summer. Verticillium prefers temperatures between 60° and 65°F.

Wilts are spread by water, plus infected plants, soil, fresh compost, garden clothes, and tools, but not seeds. There are no real controls for vascular wilts except to grow healthy plants, and to avoid stressing them as they grow. Rotations aren't effective since wilts can live in the soil, munching on organic matter, for several years. Once a soil is infected, the only control is growing resistant varieties. Look for "yellow resistant" or the letters "F" and "V" in variety descriptions of seed catalogs (see pages 166–167).

Clubroot *(Plasmodiophora brassicae)* is a soil-borne fungus that attacks most members of the cabbage family. It makes plant roots grow large galls that are swollen at one end and tapered like a club at the other. Eventually, the roots rot. Above ground, the plant may wilt gradually and die. Controlling clubroot is difficult. There are many races, so "resistant" varieties respond differently in various regions. Also, the fungus is very persistent in the soil, especially warm, acid soils, so be sure to lime before planting, and keep brassica soils above a pH of 7.3; this usually prevents or controls the disease. Clubroot is transmitted by cruciferous weeds, infected soil, transplants, tools, or windblown dust, so keep things clean around the cabbage patch and remove all infected plants immediately. Rotations aren't effective because spores can survive in the soil for at least 7 years.

Sclerotinia *(Sclerotinia sclerotiorum),* or white mold, occurs on brassicas and other vegetables, especially lettuce (see page 283). During cool, wet, and overcast weather, the stalks, heads, and leaves of infected plants may be covered with a white, cottony fungal growth. The tissue beneath the growth turns soft and mushy. Hard, black resting spores are produced in or on the growth creating very unique symptoms. Sclerotinia survives in the soil for 3 to 4 years, so rotate accordingly. Keep the soil surface as dry as possible with a dust or organic mulch. Remove all infected plants, including the soil around the stem where spores may have fallen. Fungicides are effective in early stages.

Downy mildew *(Peronospora parasitica)* is a common brassica disease in coastal areas or in cool, wet weather. The fungus penetrates leaves producing a unique grayish white, powdery growth on the underside, plus irregular yellow spots on both leaf surfaces. These spots later turn purple. The infection can spread to stems and flowers, and show up as dark brown areas in the heads of cauliflower and broccoli. The wounds caused by the fungus are often invaded by other diseases. Spores are spread to other plants by wind, and the fungus can live in the soil for 2 to 3 years. Downy mildew must germinate in a thin film of water, so keep leaves dry and avoid sprinklers. Space your plants far enough apart to allow for good air circulation, practice a 3-year rotation, keep plants healthy to reduce infection, and in the fall, clean up and destroy all infected plants to remove overwintering spores.

Powdery mildew is a common fungus disease that affects many garden plants. Infected plants usually have a white powdery covering on the leaves that can be easily rubbed away, unlike downy mildew. Powdery mildew of brassicas *(Erysiphe cruciferarum)* is unsightly and may weaken the plant, but it rarely kills it. Spores overwinter on plant debris or other cabbage family plants. They are spread by the wind. Powdery mildew is one of the few fungus diseases that can thrive during hot weather. The fungus doesn't need wet leaves to germinate its spores, only the high humidity of muggy, foggy, or misty conditions. For control, keep good air circulation between plants and monitor them when humidity is high. Fungicides of all types are quite effective against early stages of powdery mildew.

PESTS

Brassicas are prone to many pests. Fortunately, most of them can be avoided by growing resistant varieties, setting out healthy transplants, rotating brassicas from season to season, avoiding overhead watering, and destroying infected plants. In our experience, no single brassica is most or least resistant to all the insect pests. The more primitive ones, like kale, mustard, and collards, usually have fewer pests, but not always. In some areas Asian brassicas can be hard hit by flea beetles and aphids. It's always good to grow several varieties of the same brassica. If you watch carefully, some varieties may stand out as being pest resistant and well adapted to your area.

Aphids attack cabbage and cause several types of damage. They suck plant sap, distort leaves, and make them curl. Some aphids (there are several types) also carry plant diseases. Colonies are often surrounded by sooty mold, a powdery black fungus that grows on their honeydew excrement, and slows photosynthesis. Sooty mold is a sign of aphids. The gray-green **cabbage aphid (Brevicoryne brassicae)** has a waxy covering that gives them a grayish white appearance. Aphids form dense colonies around the plant's newest growth and flowers. They rarely bother seedlings and seem to prefer larger plants. The **green peach aphid (Myzus persicae)** is also found on brassicas, although it is a more serious pest on lettuce and spinach. This aphid transmits several virus diseases of vegetables. It is pale green to yellow in color and it has no waxy covering like the cabbage aphid. It is usually found on the underside of older leaves, rather than on new growth, and it is common on seedlings.

Watch for aphids on transplants and remove or control cruciferous weeds like wild mustards and radish. Aphids have a special biology that enables them to reproduce rapidly, so be extra attentive. They have many natural enemies, such as lady beetles, syrphid fly larvae, and parasitic wasps; encourage these and other beneficials by growing plants that attract them (see pages 188–189) and by avoiding the pesticides that kill them. A strong spray of water can often wash away small colonies. If you use pesticides, use the contact types like insecticidal soaps or oils. This will force you to spray on the aphids and not the beneficials. Even then, always examine around aphid colonies for signs of beneficials before you spray (see page 187).

Caterpillars can do considerable damage, and it's important to begin controlling them when they are tiny larvae, not when you can see them from the next row over. Older caterpillars are quite resistant to most pesticides and tunnel into plants, making control difficult. It really helps to know a little about their ecology so you can begin to anticipate the problem.

The **cabbage looper (Trichoplusia ni)**, sometimes called the inchworm, is the larva of a night-flying moth. They are light green, with a white stripe down their side, and $1^1/2$ inch at full size. Their obvious looping motion while crawling helps to distinguish them from the cabbage worm. Loopers are serious pests since they eat more foliage than other caterpillars, and they can survive on other vegetables like lettuce, spinach, beets, peas, and tomatoes. Adults lay single, dome-shaped eggs on the underside of leaves. After hatching, the tiny ($1/16$") young larvae begin eating small holes out of leaf undersides. As the larvae grow, they move closer to the plant's center, gobbling up large ragged holes in the leaves. Leaf surfaces can be covered with green-brown excrement that is often mistaken for insect eggs. At this stage, they are hard to control.

The **imported cabbage worm *(Pieris rapae)*** is the larva of a white butterfly with one to four black spots on its wings that is often seen fluttering about the garden in midday trying to locate the mustard oil smells of brassica plants. Full-sized larvae are about 1 inch long and green with pale stripes on the back and sides. The caterpillars are sluggish, but voracious. They crawl normally and do not loop as they move. The pattern of eating and type of damage is similar to the cabbage looper.

Like aphids, caterpillars have many natural enemies, including virus diseases, spiders, predatory bugs, and parasitic wasps. Everything should be done to encourage these beneficials (see pages 187–188). Natural enemies are especially important in mild areas where pests can survive the winter. The commercial wasp *Trichogramma* (see page 180) is a useful egg parasite of many moths. When caterpillar larvae are small, you can spray them with the bacterial insecticide *Bacillus thuringiensis berliner-kurstake* (see page 182). Use row covers to keep moths and butterflies from laying eggs on plants. Most caterpillars are susceptible to botanicals like sabadilla, pyrethrum, and rotenone.

The brightly colored **harlequin bug *(Margantia histrionica)*** is a shield-shaped red-orange and black insect that is a major brassica pest in the southern half of the country. It also eats corn, eggplant, and potato. Both nymphs and adults suck the sap from various cabbage family plants, and they can often be seen eating together. Puncture wounds create a stippled pattern of yellow and green. Later, leaves become distorted, turn brown, and die. Adult harlequin bugs overwinter around old cabbage stalks and under debris. They emerge in midspring and first feed on wild mustards and radishes. After this first meal, they move into gardens in late spring and eat brassicas. Females lay eggs that look like rows of small, striped barrels. The simplest control is to remove bugs and their eggs by hand. There are resistant varieties of cabbages (Early Jersey Wakefield), cauliflowers (Early Snowball), kale (Vale), and collards (Vates). Harlequin bugs are difficult to control with pesticides. Fortunately, a number of insect predators like to feed on this showy pest of brassicas.

Several species of **flea beetles** attack brassicas. Most damage is done by the tiny hard adults. They feed on the underside of leaves, making many small round holes or pits. If you disturb them, they jump like fleas. The larvae are small, slender worms that feed on foliage, mine leaves, or eat roots, depending on the species. Flea beetles seem to prefer cabbage, Chinese cabbage, bok choy, and other Asian brassicas. For control guidelines, see "Eggplant," pages 365–366.

Leaf miners are very small, shiny black and yellow flies. Eggs are laid inside the leaf, through puncture wounds. These wounds also let in diseases. Upon hatching inside the leaf, the headless, legless maggot begins eating tunnels between the upper and lower leaf surfaces. The winding, whitish tunnels they make get wider as the maggot grows. Control is difficult once egg-laying has begun. Handpick and destroy mined leaves. Natural enemies, especially parasitic wasps are probably the most important control, so use your pesticides carefully and grow beneficial plants (see page 189).

Cabbage root maggot is a serious pest because once it gets to the roots, there's little you can do. They are particularly worrisome on transplants and young seedlings. The adult looks like a small housefly. Females are attracted to recently tilled soil and lay eggs at the base of brassica plants beginning in the spring. The small, white maggots hatch and crawl down to eat the roots. One defense is to keep the flies from getting to the plants. Place collars or tight mulches of tar paper, carpet, or cardboard around seedlings or cover your plants with row cover fabric. Leave seedlings covered for at least 6 to 8 weeks. Better yet, plant large, healthy seedlings as early in the season as possible, when root maggot flies aren't active. Most damage is done to small seedlings that are set out late in the season.

CULTURAL PROBLEMS

Tipburn can strike in hot, dry weather, affecting the new leaves of cabbages and collards. Like blossom-end rot in tomatoes, tipburn occurs when hot weather or acid soils make it difficult for the plant to take up calcium. Soils with lots of organic matter can also tie up calcium and make it temporarily unavailable. If you have tipburn, add a preplant fertilizer of bone meal, oyster shells, or other quick-acting liming agent. Use a foliar calcium or kelp fertilizer on growing plants until your soil comes around. On broccoli plants, tipburn is called "brown bud."

Hollow stem is a condition of cabbage, broccoli, and cauliflower. During rapid growth, the interior tissues of the stems collapse leaving hollow, light-colored cavities. The things that cause hollow stem are high temperatures and too much fertilizer, especially nitrogen. See also boron deficiency for more information.

Boron deficiency is an issue for plants in the cabbage family because they need more boron than most other vegetables. When they don't get it, their leaves get corky and their stems get hollow like hollow stem, only the cavities have a dark color. Prior to planting, add aged compost or manures, and foliar feed with liquid seaweed during early growth periods. Then, try applying a solution of 1 tablespoon household borax per gallon of water on 30 feet of plants.

BRASSICA CLASSIFICATION

BOTANICAL NAME	COMMON NAME	PARTS USED
Brassica oleracea	**European Brassicas**	
var. *acephala*	Kale, collards	Leaf
var. *alboglabra*	Chinese kale, Chinese broccoli	Flower shoot
var. *botrytis*	Cauliflower, heading broccoli	Flower stems
var. *capitata*	Head cabbage	Large stem tip
var. *gemmifera*	Brussels spouts	Axillary buds
var. *gongylodes*	Kohlrabi	Swollen base of stem
var. *italica*	Sprouting broccoli	Flower buds
Brassica napus		
var. *napobrassica*	Rutabaga	Root
var. *pabularia*	Siberian kale	Leaf
Brassica rapa (=campestris)	**Asian Brassicas**	
var. *chinensis*	Bok choy	Petiole, leaf
var. *japonica*	Mizuna	Leaf
var. *parachinensis*	Choy sum	Leaf, flower shoot
var. *pekinensis*	Chinese head cabbage	Large stem tip
var. *perviridis*	Komatsuna (spinach mustard)	Leaf, flower shoot
var. *rapifera*	Turnip	Root
var. *rosularis*	Tatsoi (rosette bok choy)	Leaf
var. *ruvo*	Broccoli rabe	Leaf, stalk, shoot
Brassica juncea	**Leaf Mustards**	**Leaf, stalk**

Edema happens when the roots take up water faster than the leaves can evaporate it, producing warty growths on the underside of the leaves. As the cells burst from too much water, the ruptured area becomes corky and brown. Look for edema when cool nights follow warm, humid days and the soil is wet. When this happens, reduce watering and keep air circulation high by weeding and thinning. Some varieties are more tolerant than others, so experiment with several types if your climate favors edema.

NUTRIENT DEFICIENCIES IN BRASSICAS	
NUTRIENT DEFICIENCY	**SYMPTOM**
Nitrogen (N)	Leaves pale green, becoming yellow, pink or purple. New leaves look gray, stiff, and waxy.
Phosphorous (P)	Muddy purple fllush on old leaves with no yellow; red curds in caulilower.
Potassium (K)	Margins of leaves are brown, curling upwards.
Calcium (Ca)	"Tipburn" on young leaves; older leaves are cupped and crinkled with tip burn.
Sulfur (S)	Young leaves are yellow with blue-green veins and cuplike growth.
Magnesium (Mg)	Older leaves are yellow with green veins. Purple blotches appear at leaf margin and between veins.
Boron (Bo)	Seedling leaves curl upward. Older leaves are yellow with green veins. Margins are purple and midveins are broad and swollen. Stems are cracked and corky on outside, with hollow dark lining inside.

Asian Brassicas
BRASSICACEAE (Cabbage Family)

The opening of China's borders in the 1970s was a cultural event in more ways than one. It also introduced American gardeners to the richness and versatility of Asian vegetables. Virtually every group of western vegetables—squashes, melons, beans, alliums, and brassicas—have counterparts in the gardens and cuisines of Asia.

Of all Asian vegetables, the brassicas are the most available and the easiest to grow. A surprisingly diverse group, they include the spicy fern leaves of mizuna, the succulent flowering shoots of Chinese broccoli, the crisp petioles of bok choy, the crunchy leaf heads of Chinese cabbage, and the loose, piquant leaves of many mustards.

Asian brassicas are ideal vegetables for the kitchen gardener. Most of them grow quickly and can tolerate cold weather, making them choices for fall and winter growing. They can be harvested at any stage of growth, from seedling to flower shoot, and they are extremely nutritious.

The ancestor of most Asian brassicas, the

wild turnip *Brassica rapa (campestris)* is originally from the Mediterranean, from which it spread both east and west. It still grows today in Europe as wild rape and in North America as field mustard. Original forms were probably used for oil seed, and the leafy types were selected later. Bok choy evolved in southern China around A.D. 500 and Chinese cabbages in northern China soon after. Some Asian brassicas, like komatsuna and mizuna, migrated to Japan very early. Chinese cabbage reached America in the late 1800s. Mustards evolved in the central Himalayas and from there spread to the rest of the world.

Asian brassicas can be eaten raw or cooked in countless ways. Whether they are boiled, sautéed, stir-fried, or fresh, they lend a sprightly, nutty, or sharp flavor and succulent texture to dishes. If you plan ahead, you'll always have some of these fast-growing vegetables. They are very high in fiber, calcium, and vitamins A and C. And when it comes to eating, the parts of Asian brassicas are interchangeable. You can grow them as a mature crop harvested at once, as a seedling for tasty baby vegetables, or as a "cut-and-come again" vegetable for the immature leaves and flower shoots. In addition, the flavor of Asian brassicas runs from mellow to mustardy. Chinese cabbages are the mildest, followed by mizuna, bok choy, tatsoi, choy sum, and mustards. With this versatility in taste and texture, it's no wonder that Asian brassicas are being used more and more in our diets.

CULTIVATION

Asian brassicas are a lot like cole crops: they prefer to grow in cool weather of 55° to 70°F. Both will bolt to flower if they get too warm or if they get too cold as seedlings. They both attract the same general pests and grow best in a rich, slightly alkaline soil with uniform moisture. What sets Asian brassicas apart is how fast they grow and the fact that you can usually eat the entire plant. They will usually flower faster than cole crops. Fortunately, the flower shoots are almost always edible, like a side shoot of broccoli.

Asian brassicas are more tolerant of the heat *and* cold than cole crops. You can plant earlier and later. In cold areas they are usually grown as a late-summer crop for fall or winter harvest. In milder places, most Asian brassicas can be grown as both a spring and fall crop.

You can really extend your season by covering Asian brassicas with row covers or plastic tunnels. Light frost won't harm them, but it will slow down growth. With protection, you can get several more weeks of vegetables.

PLANTING

See "Broccoli," page 265.

SOILS AND FERTILIZERS

See "Brassicas," pages 253–254. For information on nutrient deficiencies for Asian brassicas, see "Brassicas," page 259.

DISEASE AND PESTS

Speedy growing Asian greens are less troubled by insects than other brassicas, but they are vulnerable to the same pests. The most serious are slugs, aphids, caterpillars, flea beetles, and root maggots (see pages 257–258). Because of their ancestry, some of the Asian brassicas are prone to the turnip mosaic virus. For other pests, see "Brassicas," pages 256–258.

VARIETIES

More and more seed catalogs are offering Asian vegetables. Look for them under "Oriental Greens," "Specialty Greens," "Asian Vegetables," or just simply "Chinese Cabbage." There are also a few mail-order seed houses that specialize in Asian vegetables (see pages 447–450). As you look through the seed catalogs, you'll notice that their names may be given in Mandarin, Cantonese, Japanese, or English. Sometimes the Asian name will become a common English name like bok choy, komatsuna, mizuna, or tatsoi. These vegetables have aliases and alternative spellings. For example, pac choi, and pak choi are all different spellings for bok choy. Use the chart on page 262 to help you get oriented to the language of Asian brassicas.

The largest selection of Asian brassicas is among the Chinese cabbages. There are many varieties of tight-headed cabbages, including barrel-shaped types that are bolt resistant and good for early spring planting (Napa, Wong Bok), and tall cylinder types that are cold-hardy and best for late plantings (celery cabbage, tientsin, Michihli). Tight-headed varieties for many years were simply called Wong Bok or Michihli, hence the common names for these two types. But these have now been largely replaced by more temperature-tolerant, disease-resistant varieties. Currently, there are few loose-headed Chinese cabbages in catalogs, but more are available all the time.

Bok choy varieties include green-stem, white-stem, and soup-spoon types. Among the mustards, giant-leaf types give color and zest to salads. Look for more and more hybrids, especially Chinese cabbages, bok choy, and crosses between komatsuna and bok choy.

HARVEST

The best part about Asian brassicas is that you don't have to wait 2 months to start picking; you can harvest seedlings and outer leaves 20 to 30 days from planting. Cut early and often to keep them coming and let a few go to flower, which gives you a tart, broccoli-like vegetable.

A variety of Chinese Cabbage

Red round heart

Komatsu

Mizuna

ASIAN BRASSICA GROWING TIPS

- Plant Asian brassicas in warmer and colder seasons than cole crops. In time, you'll have your own favorites.

- Experiment with a wide variety of Asian brassicas, both in the garden and in your kitchen. You'll be richly rewarded.

- Planting, cultivation, and pests are much like cole crops.

RECOMMENDED ASIAN BRASSICAS

NAMES	VARIETIES	LATIN	CANTONESE	MANDARIN	JAPANESE	COMMENTS
Chinese cabbage, Pe Tsai	**Headed:** Napa, Spring Delight, wong bok, Michihli **Loose-headed:** Minato	*B. rapa pekinensis*	Bok choy, wong nga bok, Siew choy	Da bai cad, huang ya cai	Hakusai	Susceptible to soil diseases. Shallow-rooted, needs constant moisture and rich soil.
Bok choy (Chinese or celery mustard; loose-head or mustard cabbage)	**Green stem:** Shanghai, mei qing choy **White stem:** Bai cad, joi choi	*B. rapa chinensis*	Bok choy, pak choi, qing cai (green stem)	Bai cai (white stem)	Shakushina (white stem); chingensai (green stem)	Grows like Chinese cabbage but hardier; sharper taste. Harvest leaves and flower shoots.
Tatsoi tan tsai (Rosette bok choy; flat cabbage)	Tatsoi, vitamin green, tan tsai	*B. rapa rosularis* (= *narinosa*) (rosette)	Tai gu choi	Wu ta cad; tai gu cai	Tatsoi	Tolerates heat and cold; less likely to bolt and sharper taste than bok choy. Highly nutritious.
Choy sum (flowering white cabbage)	Tsai shim, hon sai tai	*B. rapa parachinensis*	Choy sum, pak tsoi sum tad	Cai xin, cai hon tsai tai (purple)	Saishin	Looks like flowering bok choy, grown for yellow flower shoots. In China, this is the most common vegetable. Sautée with garlic for best taste.
Komatsuna (Japanese mustard spinach)	Summer Sun	*B. rapa perviridis*			Komatsuna	Hardiest of the Asian brassicas; easy to grow and very productive.
Mizuna (Japanese mustard, kyona)	Tokyo Beau	*B. rapa japonica* (=*niposinica*)	Shui cai		Mizuna, kyona	Tolerates heat, cold, and variable soils. Plant most anytime. Most bolt resistant. Useful for intercropping.
Chinese broccoli (white flowering, Chinese kale)	Green Lance	*B. oleracea alboglabra*	Gai lohn tsoi, kailan	Gai fan, jie lan		Tolerates heat and cold; edible leaf, stem, white flower buds.
Gai Choy (Chinese mustard, mustard cabbage)	Green Wave, Osaka Purple, Red Giant, Green in Snow	*B. juncea*	Gai choy, kaai tsoi	Jie cad; gai cai	Karashina; takana	Robust plants grown for leaves and flower shoots. Very tangy. Grows best in warm, humid conditions.

Broccoli
BRASSICACEAE (Cabbage Family)

Brassica oleracea **var.** *italica*
CHINESE: *qing hua cai*
FRENCH: *chou brocoli*
GERMAN: *Brokkoli*
ITALIAN: *cavolo broccoli*
JAPANESE: *burotkorii*
SPANISH: *brocoli*

Brassica oleracea **var.** *botrytis*
Brassica rapa **var.** *ruvo*
Brassica oleracea **var.** *alboglabra*

It's hard to believe, but 75 years ago virtually no one in America outside the country's Italian community grew or ate broccoli. Then in 1923, an enterprising California farmer shipped crates of broccoli to Boston. It quickly caught on as an out-of-season fresh vegetable because it was easy to ship and freeze, and it slowly became a part of our diets. In the early '70s America's love for broccoli began to take off, and since then consumption has nearly doubled. Today it is touted as one of the most nutritiously important vegetables we can eat. If you can only grow a few vegetables in your garden, one of them should be broccoli. Broccoli translates from Italian as "little sprout," or "cabbage sprout," because it's known for its edible bouquets of flower buds or "florets." There are actually four vegetables called broccoli, and this leads to some confusion.

The annual **sprouting broccoli,** also called "Italian asparagus" *(Brassica oleracea* **var.** *italica),* forms a small, loose head on stalks that grow many side shoots. Most sprouting broccoli are planted in fall and overwintered for harvest the following late winter/early spring, hence their other name, "overwintering broccoli." A few varieties of sprouting broccoli, like Calabrese, Decicco, and Green Mountain have been selected for

their large heads and rapid growth, much like the regular heading broccoli.

The biennial (sometimes annual) **heading broccoli** *(Brassica oleracea* **var.** *botrytis)* forms a large, tight head on an edible stem with many or few side shoots, depending on the variety. This is the broccoli you normally buy in the store. Botanically speaking, heading broccoli is the same plant as cauliflower. What separates the two is that the broccoli head consists of flower buds, whereas the cauliflower head is made up of swollen flower stems with no flowers. Sprouting and heading broccoli are usually combined in seed catalogs under the same name. At other times, heading broccoli is included with cauliflower.

Broccoli rabe *(Brassica rapa* **var.** *ruvo)* looks like, and is, a sprouting turnip with many side shoots; there is no central head. Rabe is also called *cima di rapa* ("shoot of the turnip") or *rapini* ("little shoot"). It is native to Italy and has been popular there since Roman times. Some types are grown for their stalks (like an asparagus), others for their spicy leaves and tangy flower buds. All parts of the plants have the slight bitterness common to many European greens. The chopped leaves and small stems of rapini are commonly boiled in salt water to tame their taste and then added to soups.

Chinese broccoli (Brassica oleracea var. alboglabra), also known as Chinese kale, broccoletto, or gai lohn, is usually included under regular broccoli or Asian vegetables in seed catalogs (see page 262). All parts of this sharp-tasting, loose-growing broccoli are edible.

Broccoli is an important and versatile vegetable in the kitchen. The raw florets are delicious in salads or as crudités for hors d'oeuvre. The flower heads and stalks can be steamed, boiled, stir-fried, or sautéed. You can spice up cooked broccoli with grated cheese, nuts, lemon butter, or bread crumbs, or dapple it with a delicate hollandaise or tangy Asian sauce. You can also purée it for soups or soufflés and add it to omelets and quiches.

Broccoli rabe has several advantages over sprouting broccoli. For one thing it can be sown in fall and overwintered even in colder climates. Unlike fussier cole crops, it needs little fertilizer and it rarely attracts cabbage loopers and other pests. In the kitchen, the entire plant can be eaten: the flower buds and stalk, plus their young leaves make savory greens, a reward even sprouting broccoli can't offer.

CULTIVATION

Of all the cole crops, broccoli is generally regarded as being the easiest to grow and the most trouble free. Broccoli's requirements are similar to those of cauliflower, but it is not as fussy about weather, so it can be grown in more areas. Like all brassicas, broccoli needs uninterrupted growth and the cool, moist weather of spring and fall.

Broccoli needs diligent weeding; it doesn't like competition for nitrogen and nutrients. Weed carefully, since deep cultivation ruins feeder roots. Broccoli is a hungry plant that responds well to regular feeding as it grows. Keep broccoli rotated in your garden and out of areas where other brassicas have grown re-

cently. Diseases like black leg and clubroot can linger in the soil for years.

Broccoli matures quickly, so you can have a spring and a fall crop. Gardeners in the far north can nurse a broccoli crop through the summer. Along the coasts where long, warm autumns gradually turn to mild winters, gardeners prefer a fall crop. Soils are warm then, and pests are less severe than in spring. But for most gardeners, spring is the time to plant broccoli.

Spring crops should be started from transplants. Unlike cabbage, broccoli seedlings can be stunted by temperatures below 40°F. Start transplants indoors about 6 weeks before the last frost. In warm or coastal areas, this means starting in January and planting out in the middle of February (we use Valentine's Day as a reminder). In colder areas, start transplants in March and plant out from early April to early May. In areas with mild summers and cool, rainy winters (like the Pacific Northwest), broccoli can be directly seeded in April for summer harvest. Timing and weather are crucial to broccoli success, so make several plantings over extended periods to find the schedule that works for your area.

For fall broccoli, heat tolerance and timing are the keys. You can direct-sow or transplant at this time. The crop must be planted to grow during the heat of the summer and mature before the first killing frosts. Green Valiant and Eureka are especially good fall broccoli varieties. In the North and Midwest, plant around the summer solstice (June 21). For the Pacific Northwest, a mid-July planting will mature in October and November.

Broccoli rabe grows best and tastes best when raised and harvested in cool weather. Heat can make plants bolt, taste bitter, and grow smaller. Sow or transplant in early spring as for regular broccoli. If you live in an area where the ground doesn't freeze solid, you can also sow fall rabe about a month before the first fall frost for an early spring harvest.

PLANTING

Broccoli needs to head up in cool weather. In areas with early hot summers, plant in late summer, fall, or winter for winter or early spring harvest. Where summers are cool, you can transplant as late as mid-March for an early summer harvest, and again in late summer for a fall-winter harvest. In cold winter areas, set out seedlings about 2 weeks before the last frost.

Early broccoli should be started indoors in late winter to early spring. If you direct-seed them when gardens are warm, plants will make heads in the heat of summer and bolt to seed. Late varieties have a better chance from direct sowing during summer because they don't head up until the onset of autumn's cooler weather.

Broccoli grows best from transplants. Vigorous transplants survive the ravages of pests and weather better than newly sprouted seedlings. The most convenient way to start broccoli is in pots large enough to accommodate plants from sowing right through transplanting. Start by sowing several seeds in 3-inch containers with appropriate mix (see page 23). Seeds germinate best at 70° to 80°F, but as soon as they germinate, move them to a cooler location, 60° to 65°F. Warmer temperatures make the seedlings lush and soft, a condition that many pests enjoy. Give them bright light so they won't get leggy.

When seedlings are about 2 inches tall (after the second pair of leaves appear), thin out the weak ones, leaving two per pot to grow on for a week or two. To harden-off seedlings, hold back watering a bit and move the pots to a cold frame or other outdoor location for another week or two. After the third pair of leaves appears, fertilize every few days with a foliar feed of dilute liquid seaweed. When the seedlings are 4 to 6 inches tall (when the fourth pair of leaves begin to appear, or at 6 to 8 weeks old), you can transplant them to the garden.

Some gardeners prefer to transplant brassicas twice: first from a shallow germination flat into a deeper container, and then into the garden. This method is more time consuming, but it saves seeds and usually produces stronger plants. Whatever you do, the seedlings should not be kept too long in containers. If the seedlings start to get red tinges on the leaves, you are stressing the plants. The secret to growing healthy broccoli seedlings is to move them quickly through the stages from seed to seedling to hardened-off transplant to garden soil. Any hesitation will stress the plant.

There is one trick you might try to improve yields. At the four- to five-leaf stage, just before transplanting, pinch off the terminal buds of the seedlings. With some varieties, this could result in three or four medium-sized heads that have a greater combined yield than you'd get from one large head.

When you set out your transplants, keep in mind that the distance between plants determines the size of the heads. In our experience, a 24-inch spacing produces the largest heads and side shoots. However, if your garden is small, or you prefer smaller broccoli, set your plants closer.

SOIL AND FERTILIZERS

Broccoli has shallow, fibrous roots that need a rich organic soil from which they can easily absorb water and nutrients. Broccoli is susceptible to clubroot disease, which can be prevented by keeping the soil pH above 7.2. So prepare your broccoli bed with aged compost and some lime prior to planting. Broccoli is a heavy feeder, so pouring fertilizer on a small plant just before it heads up is a wasted effort. It needs plenty of nitrogen and trace elements throughout its growth. Water young plants deeply with dilute fish emulsion or manure tea about twice weekly for the first month after transplanting. This will supply the nitrogen and trace elements it needs. As flower stalks begin to form, side-dress with nitrogen fertilizer to get highest yields.

For information about nutrient deficiencies in broccoli, see "Brassicas," page 259.

DISEASES AND PESTS

See "Brassicas," pages 254–258.

VARIETIES

There are over eighty varieties of heading broccoli, and about two-thirds of those are hybrids. New hybrids of broccoli are being developed faster than for almost any other vegetable. You can now choose from a whole spectrum of colors, forms, and flavors beyond the green supermarket varieties.

Hybrids have larger, tighter heads and produce fewer side shoots than open-pollinated types. They are also more disease resistant, less fussy about the weather, and tend to mature at the same time. Open-pollinated types produce over longer periods and vary greatly from plant to plant. They are also less vigorous than hybrids, and only a few are reliable producers (see page 267).

The "ready-at-once" market hybrids are a good home garden choice if you're aiming to sell your broccoli, fill a freezer, or have a broccoli bash. If you want broccoli over a longer period, include some of the garden-variety hybrids and reliable open-pollinated strains listed on page 267. They give you an extended supply of broccoli heads followed by a delicious bonus of side shoots. If you favor side shoots, grow open-pollinated varieties like Decicco, Calabrese, or Purple Sprouting.

You can push your broccoli season even more by staggering your plantings and by growing several varieties with different maturity dates. In the early spring try a fast-growing variety like Packman, plus slightly later varieties like Green Valiant or Premium Crop. Always be on the lookout for early varieties that do well in your spring climate. Getting broccoli in early is often the only way to avoid pests like the cabbage maggot and harlequin bug. Early varieties should mature within 80 days to beat the summer heat, and they should be able to handle cold weather without buttoning (forming tiny, premature heads). If you grow fall broccoli and live in an area that gets late-summer rains, choose varieties that are not susceptible to downy mildew, like Shogun or Everest.

There are about ten varieties of broccoli rabe, all open-pollinated. The varieties are divided into two types best suited for specific seasons: rapine, or spring rabe, a quick-growing smaller type recommended for early spring sowing and summer harvest; and salade rappone, or fall rabe, which is sown in the fall for an overwintered spring harvest. Spring rabe will only overwinter in the mildest of climates.

HARVEST

To harvest broccoli at the peak of its flavor, cut the flower stalk when the flower buds are large and tight, and before any yellow flowers burst open. If the variety is one that produces side shoots, cut the central stem several inches below the head, using a sharp knife. The side shoots will produce smaller florets and greatly extend your season. If you cut some of the side stalks back to the main branch, the remaining ones will produce fewer but larger heads. And if you give the plant a light side-dressing right after harvesting the main head, your side shoots will produce longer.

RECOMMENDED BROCCOLI VARIETIES

VARIETY	TYPE	ATTRIBUTES AND COMMENTS
Broccoli rabe*	Open-pollinated	Italian heirloom grown for asparagus-like early spring shoots. Bolts easily.
Calabrese*	Open-pollinated	*The* Italian sprouting broccoli. Long growing with side shoots galore; good for freezing.
Decicco*	Open-pollinated	Italian home garden sprouting type, small central head, but lots of side shoots over long period; spring or fall.
Eureka	Hybrid	Improved variety for closer spacing. Good in raised beds for fall harvest. Downy mildew tolerant.
Everest	Hybrid	Downy mildew resistant. Small-headed for fall harvest.
Fall rabe*	Open-pollinated	Sow in cool fall for overwintering. Bolts easily in heat.
Goliath	Open-pollinated	Best tasting open-pollinated. Needs sandy soil and later sowings. Large side shoots.
Green Comet	Hybrid	AAS winner. For areas with temperature swings. Spring or fall; few side shoots. Cold and disease tolerant.
Green Valiant	Hybrid	Midseason type for summer planting. Frost tolerant and great taste. Huge heads and many side shoots.
Packman	Hybrid	Gardener's choice to start the season; very early. Sow later for larger heads; very uniform.
Premium Crop	Hybrid	Needs stable climate; freezes well; midseason type for spring or fall. Large heads. Disease and heat tolerant.
Purple Sprouting	Open-pollinated	Long growing, sprouting type. Very cold-hardy; must overwinter before heading in March/April.
Saga	Hybrid	Best variety for summer heat. Matures early.
Shogun	Hybird	Large head and side shoots; cold-hardy. Good fall type. Downy mildew resistance. Matures late.
Spring Rapini*	Open-pollinated	Italian heirloom. Most versatile rabe with tender flower shoots and mustardy leaves.
Umpqua	Open-pollinated	Best adapted open-pollinated type. Vigorous big head and many side shoots.
Violet Queen.	Hybrid	Early and easy-to-grow purple type. Often listed as cauliflower
Waltham 29	Open-pollinated	Compact open-pollinated variety, plenty of side shoots. Best variety for late summer or early fall harvest.

*Indicates heirloom variety.

BROCCOLI GROWING TIPS

• Vigorous and easy to grow, broccoli comes in many varieties, is delicious raw or cooked, and has extraordinarily high nutritional value. In warm areas, it is possible to grow two or three crops a year.

• For best results, grow seedlings by steadily moving them from germination tray to garden bed. Germinate in warm conditions and grow seedlings in cool conditions. Use foliar feed with kelp. Start spring transplants 5 to 7 weeks before the last spring frost, and fall crops 12 to 15 weeks before first fall frost.

• Prick out seedlings into cell packs after 3 weeks, and grow another 3 to 4 weeks. Harden-off for 1 week and plant out. Don't idle seedlings in containers for too long. Side-dress with nitrogen about a month after setting out transplants.

• Set transplants 6-24 inches apart, depending on the size of the head you want and the fertility of the soil.

• Always keep an eye open for pests and cultural problems. To avoid pests, plant strong seedlings into a rich, well-limed soil. Use row covers to keep out flying insects, and plant early to avoid root maggots. Don't overhead-water and keep plants well spaced. Like other brassicas, rotate broccoli throughout your garden to avoid disease buildups.

• Harvest for peak quality when the heads are tight and firm. It's okay if plants bolt because the yellow broccoli flowers are edible and can attract beneficial insects (see page 189).

Cabbage
BRASSICACEAE (Cabbage Family)

Brassica oleracea var. capitata
(common head cabbage)
CHINESE: *gan lan*
FRENCH: *chou cabus, c. blanc*
GERMAN: *Weisskohl, Weisskraut*
ITALIAN: *cavolo cappuccio*
JAPANESE: *kyabetsu*
SPANISH: *col repollo, repello*

Brassica oleracea var. sabauda
(savoy cabbage)
CHINESE: *zhou ye gan lan*
FRENCH: *chou de savoie*
GERMAN: *Wirsing, Welschahl*
ITALIAN: *cavolo verzotto*
JAPANESE: *saboi-kyabetsu*
SPANISH: *col de milan*

Head cabbage may not be as trendy as greens or heirlooms, but just try to imagine a kitchen garden without a cabbage patch. Long revered as king of the cole crops (or "Old King Cole"), cabbage is hardy and productive in the garden, versatile in the kitchen, and one of the few leafy vegetables that you can store. What's more, cabbage comes in colors of blue, green, and red and textures of smooth, waxy, and crinkled; it is an attractive addition to the edible landscape.

The word "cabbage" comes from the Old French word *cabache,* meaning "head." Wild cabbage, a winter annual native to the windy coastlines of Europe, is the likely ancestor of today's head cabbage. The Greeks, Romans, and Saxons all grew several types of open-headed cabbages and held them in highest esteem as a medicine for gout, headaches, and stomach problems. The tight-headed cabbage we grow today didn't appear until the twelfth century in Germany. Savoy cabbage, a separate variety, sprang out of Italian gardens and moved north into Europe around 1600. Cabbage was brought to North America by French explorers and early settlers, and Native Americans helped spread it across the continent.

Cooks value cabbage because it can be prepared in many different ways to produce a variety of flavors and textures. The zesty crunchiness of coleslaw, the mellow, soft-textured sweetness of cooked cabbage in soups and stews, the pungency of sauerkraut, and the spiciness of pickled red cabbage are only a few of the many ways you can enjoy cabbage.

Compared to broccoli or kale, cabbage is not particularly high in vitamins and minerals. But since we eat more of it, it can be a good source of vitamin C, beta-carotene, thiamine, iron, folic acid, and calcium. Savoy cabbage is a bit higher in nutrients. Cabbage has antibiotic and antiseptic properties. Research shows that cabbage boosts the immune system and contains chemicals that help fight ulcers. No wonder cabbage was known as the "doctor of the poor."

CULTIVATION

Cabbage is a hardy biennial and, true to its ancestry, prefers cool and/or coastal climates with a slightly alkaline soil. Cabbage tolerates freezing temperatures, but grows poorly in the heat. In order to head properly, cabbage needs cool weather in the range of 55° to 65°F.

Early to midseason varieties should be started 6 to 8 weeks before the last spring frost. In the north, these are summer and fall crops. In the middle latitudes, you can get a quick crop in spring, but the fall harvest will be better. In the south, early to midseason cabbages can be planted in late summer and again in mid to late winter. And in cool summer coastal locations, they can be grown most of the year. Late varieties are best for fall harvest. Plant them from early summer in the north to mid to late summer in warmer climates. Remember that cabbages are biennial. Don't set out transplants if you expect temperatures below 40°F, or they will bolt to seed.

An average head of cabbage goes a long way in the kitchen. Unless you need slaw for a block party, it's best to plant your cabbage by the time-release method (i.e., one or two plants every few weeks during the cool season). You can also plant early and midseason types at the same time to achieve a continuous harvest.

PLANTING

See also "Broccoli," page 265. Start seeds for early or midseason varieties in flats 6 to 8 weeks before the last spring frost. Transplant once into individual cells or pots after 2 weeks, and harden-off for 1 week after 5 weeks. Don't let the seedlings grow past their fifth true leaf or with a stem thicker than a pencil. Large seedlings tend to bolt.

Transplant seedlings 12 inches apart for early varieties, 18 inches for midseason types, and 24 inches for the huge, late storage varieties. Cabbages are sensitive to crowding. Some gardeners prefer to grow smaller heads for more practical use. To do this, plant at half the recommended spacing.

Bury transplants up to the first leaves, like tomatoes, to encourage more roots to grow. Cabbage likes a consistent supply of moisture, so mulch around each plant. Early varieties will split open if they grow under wet and then dry conditions. If root maggots are a problem, avoid mulch and place diatomaceous earth and wood ashes around the stem at planting time.

Although transplanting is the preferred method of growing cabbages, you can also direct-seed, especially fall crops. Sow thinly about three to four seeds per foot, $1/2$ inch deep. Thin to 12 to 24 inches apart in the row, as above.

SOIL AND FERTILIZERS

Slightly alkaline, sandy loams are best for cabbages, but they will grow in many types of soils. Like all brassicas, cabbages are hungry feeders with an extensive network of shallow roots. They prefer an evenly moist soil, not dry or soggy, with added compost or aged organic matter. This will speed up growth before the weather heats up, and fast growth is the key to getting good heads. Stay away from *fresh* manures. They encourage rapid growth and split heads.

Feed young seedlings with a bit of fish emulsion, compost tea, or kelp solution. What you feed them now will be stored in leaves and used to make heads later.

For information about nutrient deficiencies in cabbage, see "Brassicas," page 259.

DISEASES AND PESTS

See "Brassicas," pages 254–258.

VARIETIES

There are scores of cabbage varieties available in seed catalogs, and they are classified in many ways. Some gardeners arrange them according to head shape and texture: 1)round or "ballhead," 2)flat-headed, 3)cone-headed, and 4)savoyed (with thin, crinkly leaves). About 90 percent of today's varieties are ballheads. The only common cone-head cabbage is the heirloom Early Jersey Wakefield. Most flat-headed cabbages are the late storage types, which are rapidly disappearing from American gardens. In China, flatheads are the cabbage of choice; people there serve them cut in wedges the way we slice pie.

Cabbages can also be grouped according to maturity dates. Early, or "domestic," varieties like Stonehead have thin leaves and are small, fast growing, and very sweet—perfect for those who garden in raised beds with close spacing. All early varieties produce heads in the 3- to 5-pound range just 60 to 70 days after transplanting. Midseason vari-

eties have a sweet taste with thicker leaves, which makes them great for slaws. Most savoy cabbages are midseason types. If you have space for only one variety, choose a midseason cabbage. They will hold well in the garden, so you can harvest them over a long period. Some can even be stored for a short time.

Late, or "Danish," varieties are large, dense, and tightly wrapped. These are the long-storage cabbages best for winter keeping and making sauerkraut. Their flavor is improved by frost. Most flat-headed cabbages are late-season.

Savoy cabbages have thin, blue-green puckered leaves with a mild and unique taste. They store poorly, but are perfect for stuffing, cabbage rolls, and coleslaw. Late varieties have very tight, heavy heads, which are good for sauerkraut, slaw, and brief storage. They are not as hardy as regular cabbage, so look for recent cold-tolerant savoys like Wavoy.

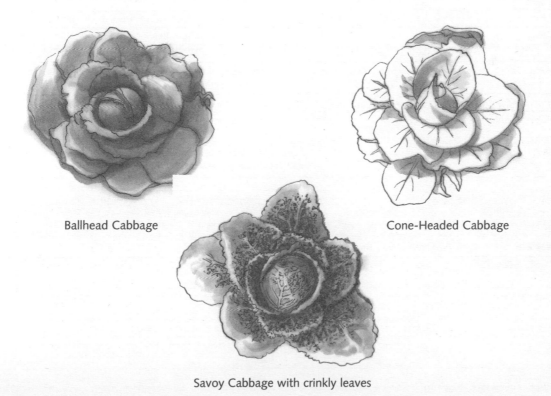

Ballhead Cabbage

Cone-Headed Cabbage

Savoy Cabbage with crinkly leaves

RECOMMENDED HEAD CABBAGE VARIETIES

Early Cabbage
Plant late winter to early spring for late spring, early summer harvest. Poor for storage; 60 to 70 days maturity.

VARIETY	TYPE	COMMENTS
Charmant	Green ball, hybrid	Suited to close spacing. Superior taste; eat fresh only.
Columbia	Blue-green ball, hybrid	Great-tasting summer cabbage. Good for coleslaw; yellows resistant.
Derby Day	Green ball, open-pollinated	Golden Acre type, very sweet, from England; uniform heads.
Early Jersey Wakefield*	Green conical; open-pollinated	Heirloom since early 1800s. 2-lb., cone-shaped, dark, waxy, and compact. Fall plant in mild areas.
Golden Acre	Green ball, open-pollinated	Small, 3-lb. gourmet cabbage; very sweet; pick early.
Jingan	Green ball, open-pollinated	Very early mild type from China; for extended harvest.
Lasso	Red ball, open-pollinated	Popular early red variety. 3-lb for salads, kraut, or cooking. Can be stored. Resists splitting.
Pacifica	Green, ball, hybrid	Superior taste, short core, holds well, multidisease tolerant.
Stonehead	Green, ball, hybrid	AAS winner. 3-lb. solid head. Dependable. Resists splitting.
Super Red	Red, hybrid	Highly rated early red. Round, medium size.

Midseason cabbage
Plant spring for late spring, early summer harvest, or plant midsummer for fall harvest. Short-term storage only; 75 to 90 days maturity.

VARIETY	TYPE	COMMENTS
Chieftain Savoy	Green, savoy, open-pollinated	Standard open-pollinated. Heat tolerant, resists splitting.
Gloria	Blue-green, hybrid	Medium size, great taste. Best for sauerkraut. Black rot resistant.
Julius	Savoy, hybrid	Finest early savoy. Holds well for extended harvest. Delicious.
Perfect Ball	Blue-green ball, hybrid	Large, vigorous, and tasty; for long summer-fall harvest; short-cored; yellows tolerant.
Ruby Ball	Red ball, hybrid	Superior early red with mild flavor. For extended harvest.
Ruby Perfection	Red ball, hybrid	Purple-red tight heads. Fall harvest for short storage. Resists splitting.
Multikeeper	Green ball, hybrid	Multidisease tolerant, short-term storage type; can also be cut fresh in late summer-fall.

Late Cabbage
Plant in summer for fall, winter harvest. Good for storage; 95 to 130 days.

VARIETY	TYPE	COMMENTS
Danish Bullhead*	Light green ball, open-pollinated	General purpose, especially good for sauerkraut, coleslaw, and cooking; holds into winter. Great for storage.
Late Flat Dutch*	Blue-green flat, open-pollinated	Heirloom since before 1840, still one of the best late fall and winter cabbages. 10-lb. flat heads.
Red Rodan	Red ball, open-pollinated	Vigorous, large-headed but tender.
Wavoy	Savoy, hybrid	Cold-hardy savoy for best winter salad. Dependable late winter harvest.

*Indicates heirloom variety.

HARVEST AND STORAGE

Cabbages should be harvested just before they reach full maturity. The head should be firm, but not at the solid bursting stage. This allows the cabbage to use stored nutrients during storage to keep growing.

Early and midseason varieties can be harvested by cutting the stems above the ground. The remaining stem will sprout a second crop of smaller heads in time for fall harvest.

For late or storage varieties, don't rush the harvest; your cabbages will taste better after a few frosts. If you don't have regular late frosts, then storage cabbages may have to be harvested before their time to avoid extensive pest damage.

If you do store cabbages, select only the ones with firm, dense heads. Trim off the stem and loose leaves. Cover with paper or plastic and place in a cool, humid, dark place with good air circulation.

CABBAGE GROWING TIPS

- Experience the diversity of cabbages by growing several varieties.

- Plan so that plants head up in cool weather (below 65°F). Start your transplants for early to midseason varieties 6 to 8 weeks before the last spring frost. Start late varieties in summer for fall harvest.

- To avoid pests, set out healthy 6- to 8-week-old seedlings in rich limed soil. Use row covers to keep out flying pests, and plant early to avoid root maggots.

- Rotate cabbages in your garden.

- Keep the soil around cabbages evenly moist and well weeded.

Cauliflower
BRASSICACEAE (Cabbage Family)

Brassica oleracea var. botrytis
CHINESE: *hua ye cai*
FRENCH: *chou fleur*
GERMAN: *Blumenkohl*
ITALIAN: *cavolfiore*
JAPANESE: *kalifurawaa*
SPANISH: *coliflor*

Think of cauliflower as a fussy, white broccoli without side shoots. Broccoli is made up of tightly bunched flower buds that will eventually form tiny yellow flowers, while cauliflower is made up of condensed flower stalks, called "curds," that will never flower. Once the central flower head is cut, cauliflower will not develop side shoots like broccoli. The taste is also different; the presence of chlorophyll gives broccoli a slight tang, while cauliflower tastes nutty-sweet.

Like other cole crops, cauliflower is native to Europe. Primitive cauliflower was first cultivated about 600 B.C. in the eastern Mediterranean. During the Middle Ages, varieties were developed that thrived in the cooler climates of Europe, resulting in the familiar white-headed types we know today.

The nutritional value of cauliflower is modest compared to that of broccoli. It does, however, have a unique combination of flavor and texture in cooked dishes, and can be used and prepared like broccoli.

CULTIVATION

Although hybrids show some heat and cold tolerance, cauliflower does best when daytime temperatures hover between 55° and 65°F. This is especially important when the curds are expanding. Try planting several varieties with different maturity dates to spread out the harvest and help you find those that are best adapted to your area. Then give this finicky vegetable what it wants, and it will give you beautiful, crunchy, sweet-tasting heads that you simply can't find in the market.

Short-season varieties of cauliflower (40 to 70 days) are usually seeded from January to April (6 to 8 weeks before the last frost) for harvest from April to July. Long-season types (70 to 120 days) can be sown anytime from June through August for harvest between fall and late winter. Fall crops avoid many of the serious cole crop pests like cabbage maggots and caterpillars. You need to be patient with winter cauliflower (180 to 260 days). They can take a long time to mature.

Regardless of when you plant your cauliflower, try sowing in successive plantings, a week apart, to prevent the chance of unfavorable weather conditions destroying your entire crop.

PLANTING

Grow transplants like broccoli (see page 265), only set out at the four-leaf stage. Cauliflower can't stand to be pot-bound, and if transplants become too large before planting, only small heads will develop. Space seedlings of most varieties 18 inches apart and the overwintering types 24 inches apart. Water young seedlings with dilute fish emulsion to get them off to a quick start.

SOIL AND FERTILIZERS

Like other cole crops, cauliflower has a weak root system, so it needs a rich soil high in organic matter for strong growth. Light, sandy soils can produce open curds; cauliflower prefers a heavy loam. Most cauliflower growers recommend composted manure as a source of nutrients. The soil should have a neutral or slightly alkaline pH, never acidic. A legume cover crop planted prior to the cauliflower crop is an excellent way to introduce or enhance the nitrogen and organic matter in the soil. Water with fish or seaweed emulsion during early growth to prevent nitrogen and micronutrient deficiencies. If you prefer dry mixes of fertilizers, try side-dressing with 6-6-6 natural mix (see pages 79–80) that contains chelated micronutrients. About one pound per 30 square feet should do it. Stop fertilizing a few weeks before the harvest.

For information on nutrient deficiencies in cauliflower, see "Brassicas," page 259.

DISEASES AND PESTS

See "Broccoli," pages 254–258.

CULTURAL PROBLEMS

Cauliflower is a challenging vegetable to grow. It demands more attention to soil preparation, planting dates, and care than most vegetables. It also reacts poorly to any kind of stress, be it heat, cold, drought, or lack of food. The heads of cauliflower stunt easily in cold weather or with low nitrogen, a condition known as "buttoning." "Ricing" occurs when curds loosen due to low temperatures or a late supply of nitrogen. The heads become discolored when they are exposed to sunlight due to poor leaf growth; acid soils will give the heads a brown or purple cast.

BLANCHING CAULIFLOWER

Direct sunlight discolors the cauliflower curd and can produce off-flavors. While curds are small, the inner leaves protect them from sunlight. But as the curds grow, they force the inner leaves apart. Some varieties, especially late ones, have very long, upright "wrapper" leaves that protect the curd until it is ready for harvest. These are the so-called "self-blanching" types. Earlier varieties must be blanched.

To blanch, gather the longest leaves together over the curd when it is about the size of a golf ball, and tie them with a soft twine, tape, or rubber bands. Since curds and plants grow at different rates, you will need to go through your garden every few days to retie each plant when the curd begins to show through the small central head.

VARIETIES

There are two basic kinds of cauliflower:

1. The early and midseason varieties, which produce white or purple curds, no side shoots, and don't require cold temperatures to form heads.

2. The overwintering varieties, which produce flowering heads (often purple) and side shoots and require winter cold to form heads.

Early cauliflower varieties (45 to 60 days) are best for spring growing and early summer harvest. They don't produce good wrapper leaves, and instead must be tied up for blanching. For a spring crop of cauliflower that matures before the heat of summer, plant early varieties like Snow Crown or Cashmere. The midseason varieties, or autumn cauliflowers, are usually sown in the late spring to summer and harvested in the fall. They are tolerant of cold temperatures and produce large wrapper leaves that self-blanch the head. Winter cauliflowers are grown a lot in Europe, and in mild winter areas, they're the easiest class of cauliflower to grow.

Romanesco is a *type* of green cauliflower with a unique pointy, spiraling head. It is often sold with broccoli in seed catalogs. It is not a specific variety, so expect a lot of variation if you order it. For a uniform Romanesco, try the dwarf variety Minaret.

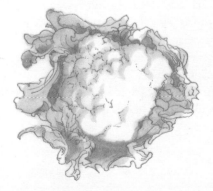

RECOMMENDED CAULIFLOWER VARIETIES		
VARIETY	**TYPE**	**ATTRIBUTES AND COMMENTS**
Andes	Open-pollinated	Midseason, self-wrapper type.
Armado Series	Open-pollinated	Several Dutch overwintering types bred to mature at specific spring dates; tolerate cold.
Burgundy Queen	Hybrid	Late, autumn type. Purple heads. Heat tolerant.
Cashmere	Hybrid	Early, very heat-tolerant spring type. Must be tied.
Dominant	Hybrid	Ideal fall type for arid areas.
Early Snowball*	Open-pollinated	Standard early cauliflower since 1888. Spring or fall in short-season areas.
Fremont	Hybrid	Midseason, autumn type. Very uniform under variable weather. Superior self-wrapper.
Minaret**	Open-pollinated	Smaller, more uniform Romanesco. Late spring for fall harvest. Cashewlike texture.
Purple Cape*	Open-pollinated	Sweet-tasting, purple, overwintering type. Ready in late February.
Ravella	Hybrid	Midseason, autumn type with large heads; tolerates frost. Can be sown in late spring.
Romanesco**	Open-pollinated	A type (not variety) of cauliflower with a beautiful large, pale green spiraling head.
Siria	Hybrid	Midseason. Heat tolerant. Vigorous self-wrapping type with large leaves.
Snow Peak	Open-pollinated	Extra-early and uniform spring type.
Snow Crown	Hybrid	Popular, extra-early spring type; uniform and tolerant of fickle weather. Very easy to grow.
White Bishop	Hybrid	Mid-early autumn type for summer planting. Heavy wrapper leaves for easy blanching.

*Indicates heirloom variety. **Often listed as a broccoli.

HARVEST

The most common harvesting mistake is leaving the heads on too long, which gardeners do in hopes the cauliflower will get as big as the ones sold in markets. It's difficult for home gardeners to give the fussy cauliflower the same rigorous care that growers do.

Cut cauliflower as soon as the head starts getting larger than a grapefruit. Focus on achieving the best taste, not the largest size.

CAULIFLOWER GROWING TIPS

• Grows like broccoli, but generally less tolerant of high and low temperatures.

• Two crops a year are possible in most areas. Start transplants 6 to 8 weeks before last frost in spring for summer harvest and again in mid to late summer for fall harvest.

• Early varieties must be tied up and blanched. Late varieties self-blanch with large wrapper leaves.

• For other hints, see "Broccoli," page 268.

Kale and Collards
BRASSICACEAE (Cabbage Family)

Brassica napus **var. *pabularia***	*Brassica oleraceae* **var. *acephala***
(Siberian or Russian kale)	(Scotch kale, collards, and borecole)
CHINESE: *xi bai li ya yu yi, gan lan*	CHINESE: *yu yi gan lan*
FRENCH: *chou à faucher*	FRENCH: *chou cavalier, c. fourrager*
GERMAN: *Schnittkohl*	GERMAN: *Grünkohl, Blätterkohl*
SPANISH: *col de la, Sibéria*	ITALIAN: *cavolo riccio, c. da foraggio*
	JAPANESE: *keelu, ryokuyô-kanran*
	SPANISH: *berza, col caballar*

Famed for cold-hardiness, kale (especially) and collards can be harvested even in the snow. Their taste is enhanced by winter chill. Collards are one of the few brassicas that also thrives in warm weather. Botanically speaking, the two plants are essentially the same and go by similar names in foreign languages. In northern Europe, the crinkled or curled nonheading types are known as Scotch kale or "borecole." Siberian kale is another species. It has purple stems and deep gray-green, frilly leaves; it is quite decorative in the garden. Unlike Scotch kale, the leaves of Siberian kale aren't curled and have a unique tender taste. Many people prefer their mild flavor to Scotch kales.

Kale and collards are cool-weather, nonheading cabbages that have been grown for at least 4,000 years. They are among the truly ancient vegetables and probably were the earliest cultivated forms of European wild cabbage. Types of kale and collards grow wild throughout Europe and Asia Minor. The Anglo-Saxons gave them the name cole worts or cole wyrts (cabbage plant), from which the name "collards" is derived. Collards were one of the first vegetables brought to America with the early settlers, and in the southern United States they have been a year-round staple vegetable for hundreds of years.

Kale and collards are among the most nutritious of all vegetables and the easiest of the brassicas to grow. The delicious greens are very high in vitamins A, C, and calcium. All kale and collards get tough sitting on supermarket shelves. But used the day of harvest, or after a few days of chilling in the refrigerator, they are one of the finest greens around. In the kitchen they can be eaten raw in mixed green salads or cooked as a potherb in a manner similar to spinach and chard.

Kale

CULTIVATION

Kale is a hardy biennial plant well adapted to growing in the fall. It will overwinter as far north as New England. Collards are a hardy, cool-season biennial that can withstand summer heat and short periods of cold as low as 10°F. Because they were adapted to both heat and cold, collards can be grown almost year round in areas with mild winters. In the north it is grown as a spring and fall crop, much like cabbage or broccoli. It can be planted in full sun to light shade.

In cooler areas, collards can be seeded 4 to 6 weeks before the last spring frost for summer harvest, in hot areas, plant midsummer for fall harvest, and in mild climates, plant in the fall for winter harvest. Kale can be scheduled similarly, but it is less adaptable to warm weather than collards. In cold climates, it is usually sown in early summer for fall and winter harvest. In hot climates, it should probably be limited to fall planting and early spring transplanting.

PLANTING

You can grow kale and collards from transplants or seeds sown in place. They are usually planted as a fall and winter crop. Direct-seed in the garden about 12 weeks before the first fall frost date, sowing seeds about 1 inch apart in rows spaced 24 to 30 inches apart. Thin kale to 12 to 15 inches apart in the row, and the larger collards to about 24 inches apart. You can also start them in flats and transplant seedlings to the garden (see "Broccoli," page 265). Siberian kale transplants poorly and is usually seeded directly.

SOIL AND FERTILIZERS

Like other cole crops, kale and collards do best in loamy soils with high organic matter and a good reserve of moisture. Acid soils limit production. Kale and collards are heavy feeders, needing substantial amounts of nitrogen. Little growth will occur during December and January, but in February, when plants pick up, side-dress with blood meal, fresh dry chicken manure, or other source of nitrogen. This will spur spring growth of tasty young greens. For information on nutrient deficiencies in kale and collards, see "Brassicas," page 259.

DISEASES AND PESTS

Collards and kale have very few pests compared to other cole crops. Aphids, flea beetles, and downy mildew can be occasional problems. The most serious pests are cabbage worms in summer. Also see "Brassicas," pages 254–258.

VARIETIES

There are about fifteen varieties of collards (three to six hybrids) and sixty or so varieties of kale (four hybrids). In general, the hybrids perform better under extreme conditions.

HARVEST AND STORAGE

Kale and collards should be harvested when plants are relatively young, or about 2 months after planting. You can harvest plants in two ways: (1) cut off the entire plant at ground level, or (2) periodically break off the outer leaves near the main stalk. Kale and collards produce leaves from the central bud. By harvesting the outer leaves throughout the season, successive plantings are not necessary for a continuous supply of delicious, nutritious greens. When you harvest the gradual way, be careful not to cut out the central terminal growth or leaf production will stop. Try the unopened flower buds of late spring kale from the previous fall planting. They taste like sweet broccoli.

Leaves should always be harvested before they become tough and stringy, and cooled rapidly after picking. To sweeten summer-harvested leaves, refrigerate for 3 to 4 days.

RECOMMENDED VARIETIES OF KALE AND COLLARDS

VARIETY	ATTRIBUTES AND COMMENTS
Scotch Kale	
Dwarf Blue Curled Scotch	Compact plants (12–15 inches) with blue-green, finely curled leaves. Extremely hardy and productive.
Green Curled Scotch	Heavily curled, yellowish green leaves.
Konserva	Popular Danish variety; broad, tall, dark green foliage, medium to well curled.
Lacinato*	Italian heirloom; "dinosaur" kale. 2-inch plants with dark blue-green straplike leaves. Very tolerant of both heat and cold. Very popular.
Winterbor	Tall (3 inches), well-curled blue-green leaves with extreme cold-hardiness. A favorite for tender winter greens. Hybrid.
Siberian Kale	
Red Russian	A tender, colorful specialty kale that many prefer over Scotch kale; leaves with purple, ragged edges and flat surface.
True Siberian	Largest roots of all kales; can be picked continuously throughout winter. Long, succulent stalks can be diced for salads.
Winter Red	Special strain of Red Russian; very disease-tolerant.
Collards	
Champion	Slow-bolting Vates type selected for compact growth under many conditions.
Georgia	The standard collard variety in the South; large, wavy blue-green leaves. Tolerates heat and poor soils.
Hicrop	Heavy-yielding hybrid with sweet flavor and slightly crinkled leaves.
Morris Heading	Wavy, green crinkled leaves, slow to bolt.
Vates	Fast-growing, large plant. Delicious and nutritious. Cold-hardy and disease-resistant.

*Indicates heirloom variety.

KALE AND COLLARD GROWING TIPS

- Kale and collards are cool-season vegetables, rich in nutrition. Collards are one of the few brassicas that you can also grow during hot weather. Both plants grow well in acid soils, unlike most other brassicas.

- Kale and collards are a bit easier to direct-sow than other brassicas. Otherwise grow transplants as in "Broccoli," page 265.

- For other cultivation, see "Cabbage," page 270.

SALAD GREENS

In the cold-winter areas of medieval Europe and western Asia, people would emerge from their starchy winter diet of grains, tubers, and roots craving a spring tonic of lively taste and vitality. They found it by tearing off the leaves and stalks of wild and cultivated vegetables and mixing them in a "salat" or salad. A typical salad might include wild lettuce and chicories, dandelion, cresses, purslane, arugula, sorrel, nasturtium and mustards. Each region developed its own unique combinations of greens depending on what was growing in the local gardens and landscapes. By mixing different plants, people could temper the bitter taste of highly nutritious greens like arugula, dandelion, and purslane with the milder flavors of lettuces and chicories. Salad greens also came in a variety of textures and a tapestry of red and green colors, which only enhanced their appeal.

Today, we see a renewed interest in all types of leafy vegetables. This is in sharp contrast to a generation ago when the basic salad consisted of tomatoes, celery, and cucumbers as a garnish to head lettuce. But now we know about the remarkable nutritional value and tantalizing tastes of salad greens. Chock-full of vitamins, minerals, and cancer-fighting chemicals, mixed greens are now in restaurants and food stores everywhere. In many seed catalogs, you can buy formulated mixes of greens called "mescluns" (meaning mix), which contain various combinations of European greens, Asian brassicas, cresses, lettuces, and a few wild plants. One company, for example, offers a mild Misticanza mesclun with four lettuces and five chicories; a tangy niçoise mesclun with endive, chicory, dandelion, cress, and arugula; and a Provençal mix with the blended tastes of chervil, arugula, lettuce, and endive.

Anyone can make a mesclun from the greens in their garden. Each mix of stems, leaves, and stalks will have its own unique textures, splashes of color, savory tastes, and combinations of nutrients. This is the alchemy of mixed greens.

As we learn more about the health potential of vegetable greens, and as more varieties become available, they'll continue to be growing favorites of cooks and gardeners. Salad greens give you a quick spring harvest, continuous high yields in small spaces, a cut-and-come-again crop, and a nutritious, low-calorie food that doesn't need cooking.

Lettuce
ASTERACEAE (Aster or Sunflower Family)

Lactuca sativa **var.** *capitata*	*Lactuca sativa* **var.** *longifolia*
(head and butterhead lettuce)	(romaine and leaf lettuce)
CHINESE: *wo ju*	CHINESE: *ye wo ju*
FRENCH: *laitue pommée*	FRENCH: *laitue romaine, chinchon*
GERMAN: *Buttersalat*	GERMAN: *Blattsalat*
ITALIAN: *lattuga a cappuccio*	ITALIAN: *lattuga romana, lattuga di taglio*
JAPANESE: *lotasu*	JAPANESE: *liifu letasu*
SPANISH: *lechuga acogollada*	SPANISH: *lechuga romana*

When we think of a tossed green salad, we think of lettuce. In spite of all the fancy new greens now available, lettuce remains the leafy soul of salads. We are all familiar with the crunchiness of crisphead, or iceberg lettuce, but there are others far better tasting and far more nutritious. They come in a variety of colors, textures, and flavors: red, bronze, lime green, dark green, buttery-smooth, crunchy, piquant, sweet.

Lettuce is a member of the aster family (Asteraceae), closely related to chicory, endive, sunflower, artichoke, and several troublesome weeds. In fact, if you go into your garden, you may see some weedy relatives of lettuce. The common or perennial sowthistle *(Sonchus)*, known as the "thistle without a painful prickle," is in the same "chicory" tribe as lettuce. The "wild" lettuce *(Lactuca serriola)* is a winter annual weed found in gardens throughout North America. It's native to the Mediterranean and Near East, and is the direct ancestor of today's lettuces.

Wild lettuce was drawn on Egyptian tombs around 4500 B.C., but it was probably used for seed oil and medicine, not food. The earliest mention of lettuce being grown to eat was around 500 B.C. The Romans enjoyed several kinds of lettuce, including one they found growing on the Greek island of Kos. It later became known as cos or romaine ("Roman") lettuce. Lettuce spread throughout Europe during the Dark Ages and was brought to North America by settlers.

Lettuce is not especially rich in vitamins and minerals, but it's a good source of roughage, which makes it important to our everyday nutrition. Leaf and romaine lettuces generally contain higher amounts of vitamins and minerals than head lettuces. Color, taste, and texture not only vary from variety to variety, but also from the outer leaf to the heart of each plant.

The great joy of lettuce is salads. The sweet flavor of young lettuce is especially good at mellowing out the zesty tastes of arugula, cresses, radicchio, and other piquant greens in salads or mesclun.

CULTIVATION

Lettuce is a cool-season annual and prefers cool temperature with daily highs in the range of 70° to 75°F and lows well above freezing, ideally around 50°F, with an overall daily average of 65°F. This range is typical for the central California coastal valleys, where the bulk of North American commercial lettuce is grown.

Lettuce is a fast-growing vegetable. You need to sow or transplant it every few weeks for a regular supply. Begin with early varieties, called "spring lettuces," that grow quickly in cool weather. Start plants 6 to 8 weeks before the last spring frost. These are followed in late spring by "summer lettuces," varieties that resist bolting in the heat of summer. Finally, cold-tolerant "winter lettuces" are set out in late summer and early fall for winter harvest in cold areas or for overwintering in warm ones. Winter lettuces are best protected from frost by covering them with floating row covers.

In some mild areas, lettuce can be grown almost year-round, but virtually all lettuces do best in cool weather. The heat of early summer can produce bitter leaves and trigger bolting in many varieties. In places with hot summer days and nights, lettuce growing is limited to spring and fall.

PLANTING

Lettuce can be directly seeded or transplanted. To seed directly, begin sowing in spring as soon as the soil can be worked. Sow seeds 1 inch apart in rows 12 to 18 inches apart. Cover seeds with only about 1/8-inch of soil, as they need light to germinate. Keep the seed bed evenly moist and shaded from direct sun. Thin young seedlings early, when they have two to three true leaves. Lettuce seed has an innate dormancy trigger that prevents sprouting when the soil temperature is above 80°F.

To transplant, start seedlings 4 to 6 weeks before planting-out time in early spring. Sow seeds on the surface of a flat and cover lightly with sifted peat moss or fine vermiculite. Keep the mix cool, below 75°F, until germination. Prick out 2- to 3-week-old seedlings to individual containers and continue to grow for 2 to 3 more weeks. Harden seedlings by reducing water and temperature for 2 to 4 days before planting-out. Transplant crisphead lettuce 12 inches apart and other lettuce 8 to 12 inches, depending on variety.

Sow or plant out every 3 weeks for a continual supply. While lettuce is first growing, it puts a lot of feeder roots into the topsoil. Weeding should be done carefully at this time. Later on, lettuce develops a rather deep taproot, and the plants can be weeded more vigorously. If you live near the coast or in a cool, moist area, don't mulch lettuce with a coarse material like straw. This will only encourage slugs and other leaf-eaters.

NUTRIENT DEFICIENCIES IN LETTUCES	
NUTRIENT DEFICIENCY	**DEFICIENCY SYMPTOM**
Nitrogen (N)	Foliage uniformly pale green. Oldest leaves are yellow, sometimes dying at tips. Reduced overall growth.
Phosphorous (P)	Reduced growth; plants fail to produce hearts. No obvious color changes.
Potassium (K)	Entire margins of older leaves die.
Calcium (Ca)	Puckering and death of margins of young leaves (tipburn).
Sulfur (S)	Young leaves are small, stiff, and pale with severe stunting.
Magnesium (Mg)	Older leaves with green veins, but yellow in between.
Boron (Bo)	Leaf tips die (tipburn) and pucker, much like calcium deficiency. But tissue death continues to the heart.

SOIL AND FERTILIZERS

Lettuces aren't terribly fussy about soil texture, but they do prefer a neutral soil. If your soil is alkaline, acidify it with organic matter or potassium sulfate. If it is acidic, add lime. Lettuce responds well to a preplant fertilizer. Work in a light dressing of steer manure or 3 pounds of 10-10-10 per 100 square feet prior to planting. Being a leaf crop, lettuce needs nitrogen while it is growing, so feed plants regularly with fish emulsion or another source of nitrogen.

DISEASES

Aster or **lettuce yellows** is a mycoplasma microbe spread by the six-spotted leafhopper. Symptoms are similar to mosaic virus, except the yellow leaves are twisted with a light brown gummy latex on the leaves. Leafhoppers pick up the disease from the surrounding Asteraceae weeds, so control these weeds and keep the hoppers off your lettuce.

Corky root is a recent disease caused by the bacteria *Corynebacterium*. Toxins of the bacteria stunt roots and reduce the growth of plants. The best controls are to increase the drainage and aeration of your soil.

Sclerotinia drop *(Sclerotinia sclerotionum)* is caused by a soil-borne fungus that is most active during cool, moist conditions, and in places where heavy rains occur during the growing season. It can become quite severe in beds repeatedly planted with lettuce. *Sclerotinia* only invades dead or dying tissue. Early symptoms include a white, cottony growth on lower leaves touching the soil. This distinguishes it from *Botrytis,* which forms a gray mold. *Sclerotinia* spreads to roots and up into the center of the head. Black fruiting spores develop on infected areas. *Sclerotinia* is hard to control because it lives in the soil, and it infects several other vegetables (such as tomatoes, squash, pepper, and celery). Spores are spread by tainted soil or they are shot into the air by fruiting bodies. Try to rotate lettuce every few years, look for tolerant varieties, destroy infected plants, and avoid close plantings in poorly drained soils. See also "Brassicas," page 255.

Botrytis gray mold *(Botrytis cinera)* is caused by a soil-borne fungus. Look for small, dark fruiting bodies ("gray" mold) and brown lesions near the soil line. Other symptoms and controls described for *Sclerotinia* (see above) apply to *Botrytis.*

Downy mildew *(Bremia lactucae)* makes pale or yellowish spots on upper surfaces of outer leaves and a white mold on the leaf underside. These spots become brown and make entry points for other diseases. The fungus overwinters on wild lettuce and plant debris. It thrives in the cool, damp weather of early spring and in close-spaced plantings. For control, see "Brassicas," page 255.

PESTS

One of the greatest threats to lettuce for home gardeners is from nibbling animals like rabbits, birds, and deer; erect fences, row covers, and other barriers to deal with these meddlers.

Aphids can form large colonies on lettuce and spread virus diseases; some species feed deep within the head, out of reach of predators or sprays. The **green peach aphid** *(Myzus persicae)* is the only transmitter of lettuce mosaic disease. It is hard to control because it attacks so many other vegetables besides lettuce. For control, see "Brassicas," page 256.

Several caterpillars feed on lettuce, including the **cabbage looper** (see page 256), **corn earworm** (see page 382), and the **beet army worm** *(Spodoptera).* The army worm is a robust brown caterpillar that feeds on many weeds and moves into gardens to eat lettuce. When it is young, it skeletonizes young leaves; as it grows, it moves on to the lettuce heart. These and other caterpillars can be controlled with handpicking, row covers, many natural enemies, and the microbial spray *Bacillus thuringiensis* var. *kurstaki* (BTK).

CULTURAL PROBLEMS

Tipburn is the rapid death of the margins of older leaves. It's due to fluctuating temperatures and soil moisture, which makes calcium unavailable to plants, especially head lettuce. Water your plants evenly and grow varieties resistant to tipburn (such as, Grand Rapids, Ithaca, Summer Bibb, and Canasta) or tolerant of warm weather.

VARIETIES

There are about 210 varieties of head lettuce (including Bibb), 95 varieties of leaf lettuce, and 70 varieties of romaine lettuce available. Some breeders place the total number of lettuce varieties at 800. All of them are standard open-pollinated types. The best homegrown lettuce patch contains many varieties.

Lettuces are divided into five major groups. **Head, Crisphead, or Iceberg:** Large, brittle, heavy leaves form a solid head tough enough to ship long distance. Lowest in food value. Takes a long time to mature and bolts easily in warm weather, so look for early resistant varieties. Homegrown icebergs taste much better than store-bought ones. Burpee introduced Iceberg in 1894, and it became so popular that its name came to stand for this type of lettuce.

Butterhead or Loosehead: The "gourmet" heading lettuce, characterized by loose, floppy heads of crumpled waxy leaves with a soft, buttery texture. As easy to grow as leaf lettuce, but less fussy than icebergs. There are two general kinds: (1) the Boston type, which has relatively large heads and light green leaves, and (2) the Bibb type, which has small heads with dark green leaves.

Romaine or Cos lettuce: Develops tall, loose heads of long straight leaves, with a heavy midrib. Outer leaves are coarse and dark green. Inner leaves are soft and blanched. Highest in nutrients and a favorite of salad aficionados.

Leaf Lettuce: Completely nonheading, the leaves are variable in shape and open outwards. The many varieties come in all sorts of textures, shapes, and colors. Most leaf lettuce withstand greater environmental variation than heading forms, and they mature faster than other lettuces.

French or Batavian Crisphead: Popular in European fresh markets, but not in the United States because they ship poorly. Combines crispness of romaines with the shape of butterheads. Better flavor and more heat tolerant than crisphead, but similar texture.

Read descriptions in seed catalogs for important characteristics like (1) resistance to tipburn and other diseases; (2) resistance to summer bolting; and (3) earliness.

HARVEST AND STORAGE

Lettuce can be harvested at any stage of growth. You can pick only the large outer leaves or slice the whole plant off about 1 inch above the soil line. This will prompt the plant to send out new growth. Mature heads of iceberg lettuce deteriorate quickly if the summer warms, while leaf lettuces stand well and can be harvested over a longer time. Clean harvested leaves in a weak vinegar-water solution, spin dry (wet leaves will rot easily), and store in paper bags inside plastic bags in the refrigerator. They will keep this way for 1 to 2 weeks.

RECOMMENDED LETTUCE VARIETIES

VARIETY	ATTRIBUTES AND COMMENTS
Butterhead	**50 to 60 days**
Brune d'hiver*	Cold-hardy French heirloom winter lettuce. Heading type intermediate between Bibb and romaine with red tinge. Fall, winter lettuce.
Buttercrunch	Continues Bibb line of summer butterheads. Dark green with compact heart. Crisp and sweet. Slow bolting. Spring or summer lettuce
Merveille des Quartre Saisons*	French heirloom Four Seasons that thrives year-round. Bright red with creamy heart. Outstanding.
Nancy	Big Boston for spring and fall. Firm green head, great taste. Resistant to mosaic virus.
Tom Thumb	Favorite baby type from English kitchen garden. Great for containers.
Winter Density	Unique large Bibb/romaine type—a tall buttercrunch. Very dark leaves. Grows year-round. Popular in Europe as Craquante d' Avignon. Fall, winter lettuce.
Looseleaf	**45 to 60 days**
Black-Seeded Simpson	Light green crinkly leaves. Longtime popular lettuce for spring and early summer; fast to grow and slow to bolt.
Deertongue*	American heirloom since 1740. Very tolerant of heat and cold.
Green Ice	Favorite for taste and heat-tolerance.
Lollo Rossa	Deeply curled, rose-colored leaves. Cut-and-come-again.
Oakleaf*	Heirloom since 1800. Attractive summer lettuce with deeply lobed leaves. Look for improved Royal Oakleaf.
Red Sails	AAS winner. Reliable red spring lettuce.
Salad Bowl	Deeply lobed, lime green leaves. Easy to grow. Heat tolerant.
Sangria	The fanciest red butterhead. Slow to tipburn and bolt. For spring and summer.
Crisphead	**40 to 60 days**
Ithaca	Very popular with good resistance to tipburn and bolting; early fast grower.
Salinas	Popular home garden type adapted to all weather conditions. Resists tipburn and bolting.
Summertime	Small, extra green, and heat-tolerant.
Romaine	**50 to 60 days**
Craquerelle du Midi	French summer cos. Also called Craquerela du midi, or "little cruncher of mid-France."
Little Gem	A 6-inch baby romaine. See Rosalito.
Parris Island Cos	The most popular standard cos lettuce. Slow-growing, tall, with creamy white heart.
Romance	Disease-resistant French cos. Smooth, tender leaves for special fresh use.
Romulus	Like Parris Island cos only lighter green and stands longer in the ground.
Rosalito	Compact, early red Romaine. Great for containers or for filling in garden space.
Rouge d'hiver*	Old French heirloom winter lettuce, red and hardy. Great for mesclun. Larger, slower to bolt, and redder than Rosalito.
Batavian	**50 to 60 days**
Centennial	Outstanding, with texture of iceberg and deeper flavor; harvestable any time.
Rouge Grenoblaise	Wine-red leaves. Plant in spring and harvest early as a leaf lettuce or let it head up.
Sierra	Summer lettuce. Fancy, bright green, dense Batavian with red tinge. Good for cut-and-come-again.

*Indicates heirloom variety.

LETTUCE GROWING TIPS

- Lettuce prefers cool weather and rich, well-drained soil.

- To experience the full range of color, taste, and texture available in lettuce, grow several varieties.

- Grow hardy fast-growing varieties in spring and heat-tolerant ones in shaded areas later to extend harvest into summer.

- Plant small amounts of lettuce every few weeks during the season to ensure a steady supply. Careful variety selection is important for growing lettuce over the entire season.

- To get the best germination from lettuce, keep soil temperatures below 80°F and give seeds some direct light.

- Harvest lettuce at any stage of growth by picking the outer leaves. Thick sowings can be grown as cut-and-come-again greens.

Chicories (Radicchio, Endive, and Others)
ASTERACEAE (Aster or Sunflower Family)

Cichorium intybus	*Cichorium endivia*
(radicchio)	(endive and escarole)
CHINESE: *ye ku gu*	CHINESE: *ku qu*
FRENCH: *chicorée sauvage a feuilles rouges*	FRENCH: *chicorée endive, c. frisée, scarole*
GERMAN: *Radicchio*	GERMAN: *Endivie, Endiviensalat*
ITALIAN: *radicchio*	ITALIAN: *endivia, scarola*
JAPANESE: *kiku-nigana*	JAPANESE: *endairu*
SPANISH: *achicoria de hoja roja*	SPANISH: *endivia, escarola*

The chicories are zesty-flavored relatives of lettuce. They have been more popular in Europe than America, but with a broadening American taste for choice salad greens, more and more people are growing and eating these nutritious vegetables.

The big surprise is how many different kinds of chicories there are, each with a different flavor, leaf shape, and color, from bright green to wine red. We can divide the group into its two species: perennial chicories (*Cichorium intybus*) and endives (*Cichorium endiva*), which are annuals. Broadleaf endives are known as escaroles; they look like a loose-head lettuce. Curly-leaf types are called endive or frisée and resemble leaf lettuce.

Perennial chicory, or succory as it once was called, is found throughout Europe in the wild state where it has been collected and used for thousands of years as a food and medicine. Cultivated types first appeared in sixteenth-century Germany and later in England and France.

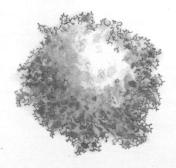

Most of the perennial chicories are grown as annuals. They have a wide variety of tastes, but always with a touch of bitterness that characterizes the group and gives a deliciously sharp bite to salads and mescluns. There are four major kinds. 1) The most popular is the heading type, or radicchio. Today this marbled burgundy and white salad green is rapidly finding its way into the precut salad business, kitchens, and restaurants. In Italian cuisines it is valued for use in antipastos, salads, pasta, and risotto. 2) The "cutting" chicories are leafy Italian heirlooms with a spicy taste. 3) The dandelion or asparagus chicory is grown for its succulent asparagus-like stems and dandelionlike leaves. Cutting and dandelion chicories are often called "spring" chicories because they can be overwintered and harvested in spring. Their ground-up roots have been used since ancient Egypt as a benefit for the liver and gall bladder. Today they are mostly used as a coffee substitute. 4) Witloof chicories are small, blanched tight-leaf heads that sprout from rootstock grown in darkness (see page 288).

Endive is native to Egypt or India. It was used by the Greeks and Romans and then migrated into northern Europe around the thirteenth century. It became a garden staple of England and France by the time of Columbus, and reached the United States in 1810. Endive is one of the traditional ingredients of mescluns, the popular salad mixes from Europe.

Chicories can be eaten raw or cooked. The endives have thicker, more resilient leaves than most lettuces, and they are useful as a leafy wrap for foods to be steamed. In fact, the tough outer leaves of escarole and endive can be cooked and used much like chard in soups, pastas, and casseroles. Raw chicories make a vivid seasonal salad using assorted leaves of green and red radicchios and the creamy pale hearts of endive. Dress with a vinaigrette of olive oil, mustard, garlic, and balsamic vinegar. Additions include toasted nuts, roasted red pepper, or goat cheese.

All chicories are very high in vitamin A and have good supplies of vitamin C and calcium. Escarole is higher in most nutrients than either radicchio or endive.

CULTIVATION

All chicories prefer a rather cool growing temperature of 55° to 75°F. The red radicchios are more fussy about temperature and are less adaptable. Rapid, continuous growth is essential for good yields and high quality.

The annual chicories (endive and escarole) can be planted in the cool weather of spring or fall with lettuces. Radicchio and other perennial chicories will bolt to flower as days get warmer and longer, so spring plantings are often disappointing. Sow seeds in midsummer for fall harvest, or early fall for overwintering.

Endives are grown just like lettuce, but are blanched when they begin to head up, in order to mellow the sharp flavor of the leaves. Transplant or thin seedlings to 12 inches and when the leaves touch, gather up the outer leaves and tie them together with string for a week or so. Or place a saucer over the center of the plant and leave covered for about 10 days.

PLANTING

Most chicories can be sown directly or transplanted like lettuce. Transplanting radicchio can be tricky and produce unstable plants. We've had the best luck transplanting smallish seedlings into moist soils on overcast days while disturbing the roots as little as possible.

SOIL AND FERTILIZERS

Endive and escarole prefer rich, slightly acid soils and respond well to side-dressings of nitrogen. See "Lettuce," page 283.

FORCING CHICORY

Witloof chicory has little nutrient value, but it is highly prized as a delicious and tender gourmet treat. Forcing chicory is exacting, but well worth the effort. There are two stages:

1. The preforcing stage: From late June to early July, seed is sown thickly in deep, fertile, light-textured soil. The object is to produce clean, well-shaped roots. Fertilizers should be low in nitrogen to avoid excessive leaf growth, but high in phosphorous and potassium to stimulate root growth. Seedlings are thinned to 6 inches and grown until late fall.

2. The forcing stage: Around Christmas, carefully dig up the plant, roots and all, and cut off the tops just above the crown. Plant the roots close together in a box of loamy soil with the crowns of the roots at soil level. Cover the box so the tight heads, or "chicons," can grow in total darkness to blanch, which prevents bitterness. Place the covered box in a place that stays above 50°F. Keep the soil moist. In 4 to 6 weeks, the chicons will be about 6 to 8 inches long and ready for harvesting. If you break off the chicons carefully instead of cutting them, a second crop will appear, smaller and looser but just as tasty.

DISEASES AND PESTS

Chicories are relatively pest-free, except for aphids and leaf-eaters like snails, slugs, and birds. Be careful with row covers, since high temperatures can make chicories rather bitter. See "Lettuce," page 283.

VARIETIES

Many of the most common radicchio varieties are named for towns in the Veneto region of northeast Italy—Verona, Castelfranco, Treviso, and Chiogga, among others—where radicchio is a vegetable staple. There are early, midseason, and large varieties, and breeders are constantly developing new hybrids. Radicchios range from difficult to easy to cultivate.

HARVEST

If chicories are picked quickly in the cool weather of spring or late fall, they are delicious. But if they stay in the ground too long or grow in warm weather, they become quite bitter.

Endive and escarole are annuals, so once you cut the plant for harvest, it won't resprout. Radicchio and the other perennial chicories will often resprout more leaves or heads if they are harvested carefully. When harvesting radicchios, remember that the prized edible heart forms just above the root and is exposed only after the outer leaves are stripped away. Cut radicchios near the ground to encourage more heads to grow.

If your perennial chicories bolt to seed in the heat, simply cut them back and the plants will make more growth once the weather cools.

RECOMMENDED CHICORY VARIETIES

PLANT	DESCRIPTION	PLANTING	VARIETIES
Annual Chicory			
Escarole	Broad, crumpled leaves. Deep hearted. Inner leaves well blanched.	Spring or fall. Avoid warm weather.	Cornet d' Anjou, Perfect
Endive, Frisée	Narrow, deeply curled leaves.	Spring or fall, avoid warm weather.	Galia, Fine Curled, President
Perennial Chicory			
Heading Chicory (Radicchio)	Least tolerant of temperature swings. Keep cool.	Plant midsummer to fall, some spring types.	Verona, Treviso, Guilio (spring), Chiogga, Marina, Inca, Bianca Milano (green)
Leaf or Cutting Chicory	Hardy and fast-growing; both rosette and upright varieties. Sharp, strong flavor.	Plant midsummer to fall, some spring types. Harvest young plants or snip leaves as they grow.	Grumelo, Spadona, Sugarloaf (Pan de Zucchero), Crystal Hat (spring).
Asparagus or Dandelion Chicory (Radichetta)	Edible leaves and flower shoots that resemble asparagus. Roots used as coffee substitute.	Plant midsummer for fall harvest, or early fall for spring harvest.	Dentarella, Putarella, Catalogna
Witloof Chicory	Forcing type for producing tight, blanched heads.	Sow June–July for root stock. Force roots winter-spring.	Witloof Zoom

Annual Chicory

Forced Chicory

Arugula
BRASSICACEAE (Mustard Family)

Eruca vesicaria* ssp. *sativa
CHINESE: *zhi ma cai*
FRENCH: *eruca, roquette*
GERMAN: *Garten-Senfrauke*
ITALIAN: *eruca, ruchette*
JAPANESE: *roketto salada*
SPANISH: *eruca, roqueta común*

Arugula, also known as salad rocket, roquette, or eruca (from Latin, "downy stemmed"), is a half-hardy annual, native to southern Europe. It is a wild weed in this area, and it has been harvested for thousands of years as a medicine, raw greens for salads, and a tangy ingredient in cooked dishes. Arugula has a stimulating effect on the circulation, appetite, and digestion. The leaves are rich in vitamins A and C and the minerals iron, potassium, and calcium. Arugula has a unique sharp, nutty taste that enlivens any dish. Its taste reminds you of its close cousin, mustard, only milder and more complex. Arugula has all the nutritional advantages of broccoli (see page 263), with an earthy, piquant taste. It is great as an ingredient in mescluns or in mixed green salads, stews, or soups. Stir-fried with garlic, olive oil, bok choy, and kale, arugula makes a complete and delicious antioxidant dish.

CULTIVATION

Arugula is in the cabbage family so it favors cool weather. In fact, it usually does best in partial shade. It's best to direct-seed arugula into a well-prepared seedbed in early spring or fall. In warm climates, you can probably get three crops a year: early fall, late winter, and spring. You can grow transplants like broccoli, but you need to harvest quickly, like bok choy. Harvest whole small plants or individual leaves of older plants. You can also cut off plants at ground level and they will usually resprout. Arugula also reseeds easily, making it a welcome addition to any kitchen garden: easy to grow, unique taste, and good for you.

NUTRIENT DEFICIENCIES

See "Brassicas," page 259.

DISEASES AND PESTS

See "Brassicas," pages 256–258.

WILD VEGETABLES

Many of the weeds growing in your garden are edible. In fact, there are over one hundred species of edible weeds in the United States. This shouldn't be surprising because most vegetables used to be weeds at one time. Some weeds have been bred to produce more edible varieties. These "wild vegetables" are among the most nutritious plants—rich in antioxidants, vitamins, minerals, fibers, and healthful fatty acids. It is amazing that such a nutritious group of easily grown plants should be the target of so many herbicides. Learn to include them in your kitchen garden and diet. Some are pleasantly bitter, some mustardy, some lemony, some tart and piquant, some strongly pungent. These vegetables add a delightful tang and nutritious component to many dishes.

Commonly available wild vegetables include dandelion, purslane, arugula, plantain, lamb's-quarter, miner's lettuce, curly dock, and "vegetable" amaranth. Most can be used as spicy, nutritious ingredients in salads, soups, and stews. Young plants can be boiled, sautéed, stir-fried, steamed, and eaten raw. They should all be harvested when they are young; the leaves quickly become bitter as they age.

Many of our wild vegetables have been improved with breeding to make them larger, more succulent, and more palatable. Seed catalogs are offering garden varieties of wild vegetables to complement their traditional vegetable selections. Some of the more common ones are described here.

Dandelion
ASTERACEAE (Aster or Sunflower Family)

Taraxacum officinale
CHINESE: *pu cong ying*
FRENCH: *pissenlit, dent de lion*
GERMAN: *Löwenzahn*
ITALIAN: *dente de leone, radichiello*
JAPANESE: *shokuyou-tanpopo*
SPANISH: *diente de léon, taraxacón*

Dandelion ("dente-de-leone," or "tooth of the lion," in reference to the leaf shape) is a perennial herb native to Asia, where people have been eating this "lawn pest" for over one thousand years. Dandelion has a long history as a cultivated culinary and medicinal herb (the species name means "remedy for disorders") with the ability to improve liver function, lower cholesterol and blood pressure, and stimulate urine production (hence its

French name, *pissenlit*). The edible flowers are one of the natural sources of lecithin, which prevents cirrhosis of the liver. Dandelions are the most common edible weed grown commercially in the United States. Several varieties are grown in gardens and blanched like endive (see page 288).

The traditional way to serve raw dandelion greens is in a salad with other spring greens, hard-boiled eggs, and herbs dressed with oil and vinegar. You can serve the greens in spring salad mixes or enjoy them simply sautéed with garlic and olive oil.

CULTIVATION

You can eat the young wild dandelion leaves growing in your garden, but many seed companies now offer several improved dandelion varieties that have thicker leaves, are slower to flower, and are less bitter than the wild plant.

To avoid bitterness, grow in slightly alkaline soils amended with aged compost. When the plants get large, simply cut the plant off at ground level and a whole new set of juicy young leaves will reappear. Since their roots can go down several feet, dandelions don't usually require fertilizing.

In colder climates, the perennial plants die back to the ground and reappear in early spring. French gardeners dig up some of the roots in fall, put a dozen or so in a window box, and eat the leaves all winter as they emerge. You can also blanch the leaves like Belgian endive by gathering up the outer leaves and tying them to cover the inner leaves.

HARVEST

Dandelion greens must be picked very young, before the plant has flower buds. Mature leaves are tough and bitter. Leaves from cultivated varieties are milder tasting and are often blanched to subdue the intense flavor.

Garden Sorrel
POLYGONACEAE *(Buckwheat Family)*

Rumex acetosa
CHINESE: *suan mo*
FRENCH: *grand oscille*
GERMAN: *Garten-Sauerampfer*
ITALIAN: *acetosa*
JAPANESE: *sorelu*
SPANISH: *acedera*

Garden sorrel is a robust perennial, native to Eurasia. Sourgrass, rumex, and dock are other names for sorrel, whose lemony flavor was used for centuries in European cuisine before citrus was introduced. In fact, the name sorrel derives from the old French word *surele,* meaning sour.

Sorrel is high in vitamin C and iron, and was once used as a cure for scurvy and anemia. Sorrel is also full of potassium, magnesium, antioxidants, and carotenoids. It has been used as a diuretic to eliminate toxins, and as a poultice to help heal skin problems. Sorrel is still a favorite in Europe, where it produces some of the earliest spring greens. It was introduced from Europe in the 1700s, and now grows wild throughout North America; it is also grown commercially. You may find sorrel growing wild in your garden as a "weed," but cultivated strains are bred for low oxalic acid content and less bitter taste.

Garden sorrel is a cousin of the French favorite bucklerleaf sorrel *(Rumex scutatus)* and the common garden weed, curly dock *(Rumex crispus)*. The tender fresh leaves are about 8 inches long and have an intense lemon flavor. Its pleasant tartness balances milder greens. Sorrel is used in soups, salads, purées, and sauces, and paired with fish, chicken, and eggs. Use sparingly in salads and generously in soups and sauces, especially with fish.

CULTIVATION

Start indoors or sow directly in mid-spring. Plant 8 inches apart in light shade. Regularly cutting the seed stalks increases yield, but good leaves will reappear in the fall even if plants bolt. Harvest side leaves until the plant becomes established; later it can be cut completely, right above the crown. Sorrel spreads easily, and established plants can be divided. The flowers attract beneficials, as do many members of this family. The deep taproots bring up nutrients from the soil.

Purslane
PORTULACACEAE (Purslane Family)

Portulaca oleracea sativa
CHINESE: *ma chi xian*
FRENCH: *pourpier potager*
GERMAN: *Portulak*
ITALIAN: *portulaca, porcellana*
JAPANESE: *tachi suberi hiyu*
SPANISH: *verdolaga*

Wild purslane is a prostrate succulent annual native to Europe, where it has been eaten for centuries as a treatment for arthritis and to promote general good health. Studies have shown that people who eat a diet rich in omega-3 fatty acids have lower cholesterol levels and fewer heart problems. These acids are found in seeds, wheat germ, and vegetable oils. Among vegetables, purslane has more omega-3 acids than any other vegetable, and six times the vitamin E content of spinach.

Purslane leaves have a mild nutty flavor and are a popular salad ingredient in Europe. They are eaten extensively in soups and salads throughout the Mediterranean. The Russians dry it or can it for the winter. In Mexico it is a favorite comfort food eaten in omelets, as a side dish, or in soups and stews.

CULTIVATION

Compared to the wild purslane, the cultivated variety is four times larger, much more succulent, and has a very upright growth habit. Sow seeds after danger of frost $1/2$ inch deep and thin to 4 to 6 inches apart. Purslane can also be transplanted. Pick as needed to within 2 inches of the base so that new leaves can grow. Purslane is sensitive to frost.

POTHERBS

What did people do before modern medicine? They practiced daily health care with local weeds and medicinal herbs. These were usually too bitter to eat raw, so they were slowly simmered in a "souper" or pot and called potherbs. A medieval souper of potherbs might have included borage, chives, fennel, marigold, cabbage, sorrel, dandelion, lovage, beet greens, and chard. Today we call it soup and make it an appetizer.

Because of their history, potherbs are usually thought of as vegetables that are cooked. This is not entirely true anymore, since most modern "potherbs," like the brassicas, spinach, chard, asparagus, and beet greens can also be eaten raw. What sets these vegetables apart for us is that they are usually better tasting when they are cooked. Our palates have evolved to avoid bitterness since it is often an indication of harmful alkaloids. Nevertheless, we have come to accept some bitterness in our food because it can be pleasant and also a sign of nutritional value. We do this by balancing bitter potherbs with other flavors. For example, collard, mustard, and beet greens are traditionally cooked with fruity olive oils and pungent alliums. We toss spinach with vivid vinaigrettes and cut the sharpness of chard with lemon juice, white wine, shallots, and chicken broth. A tasty potherb dish can always make a good meal better.

Asparagus
ASPARAGACEAE (Asparagus Family)

Asparagus officinalis
CHINESE: *lu sun*
FRENCH: *asperge*
GERMAN: *Spargel*
ITALIAN: *sparagio*
JAPANESE: *asuparagasu*
SPANISH: *espárrago*

Many gardeners will tell you that asparagus is the most delicious of all vegetables. It's also one of the easiest to grow if you have a sunny spot, well-drained soil, and some patience. "Asparagus" comes from the Persian and Greek words meaning "to sprout" or "burst forth," and the name sure fits. The early spring shoots ("spears") of asparagus have been considered a delicacy since ancient Greece. The Romans were the first to cultivate asparagus, but the Greeks and earlier people probably collected it from the wild.

Garden asparagus *(Asparagus officinalis)* is a hardy perennial that is native to the coastal areas around the Mediterranean Sea and Europe where it still grows wild in sand dunes, chalk cliffs, and dry meadows. There are over two hundred species of asparagus, and the fleshy young stems of many of them are edible. *Asparagus actifolius* is collected and eaten in Spain and Turkey.

Botanists used to place asparagus in the lily family (Liliaceae), but now it's in its own family, the Asparagaceae. Some familiar relatives of asparagus include several species of "asparagus ferns." Asparagus is also related to the common garden plants lilyturf *(Liriope),* Mondo grass *(Ophiopogon),* and Solomon's Seal *(Polygonatum).*

Asparagus requires an initial investment of time and soil preparation, but the dividends are worth it. New varieties and growing techniques make it more possible than ever to grow asparagus in the home garden. We now have high-yielding, disease-resistant varieties that can grow in heavy soils and warm winter areas, and that can be harvested early from shallow plantings. Beds have been known to produce for 15 years and more.

Asparagus has a combination of virtues. First, it's an epicurean delight with a truly heavenly taste and texture. Whether you steam, stir-fry, roast, or grill it, asparagus gives a regal touch to any meal. It's a good source of phosphorous, folic acid, and niacin and a modest source of fiber and vitamins A and C. It also contains rutin, a substance that strengthens capillary walls and reduces hemorrhaging. Asparagus is easy to grow if you take the time to prepare the soil and don't harvest the first year. The tall, feathery, graceful leaves and the female plants' red berries in late summer lend an ornamental look to any kitchen garden.

CULTIVATION

Asparagus is a "dioecious" plant; that is, plants are either male or female. You can recognize female plants in fall by their red berries. Female plants produce larger shoots ("spears"), but male plants produce more spears and live longer, because they don't use up energy making fruit.

Many gardening books will tell you that asparagus should be grown in areas where it freezes in winter, because its roots need a dormant period to keep producing. In our experience, cool winters that don't freeze simply shorten the life of an asparagus plant; they don't affect production much. Where winters are just plain warm, like the Gulf Coast states, asparagus growing is very limited, although even there new hybrid varieties, like the Jerseys, are being grown successfully.

With asparagus, you have to be very patient in the beginning. Your plants are going to be in the same space for many years, so the soil will need a special deep preparation. Also, you should wait to harvest for a year or two, so the plant can develop a strong root system. To do this, let the shoots form their green tops (ferns) the first year; these photosynthesize and feed the roots for next year's shoots. The second spring you can harvest for a month or so, but stop cutting when the shoots begin to get slender. This means the roots are running out of food and it's time to feed them by letting the shoots leaf out. After 3 years, the bed is usually ready for a full cutting. As plants grow larger over the years, you should be able to extend your harvest into early summer.

PLANTING

You can grow asparagus from seeds or "bare root" crowns. Crowns will usually produce spears about 1 year earlier than seed transplants. Regardless of what you plant, try to put your asparagus where it will get plenty of sunshine and not compete with tree roots. The soil should drain very well, since asparagus doesn't like to sit in soggy soils. If possible, dig lots of aged organic matter or compost into your asparagus patch before you plant crowns or transplants. This will help keep the soil loose over the years.

Planting crowns: Asparagus shoots grow from a group of buds at the top of a root mass, where the root meets the shoot, called a "crown." The crown is fed by several fleshy roots that ray out from the crown like the arms of an octopus. These crowns-with-roots are sold in nurseries as asparagus "bare-roots" or "rootstocks" anytime between January and March for spring planting. You can also get them from mail-order nurseries. Purchase only healthy 1-year-old crowns about the size of your hand. Older crowns are not better, just more expensive. If you have to delay planting, store them in moist sawdust or sand where they won't dry out. You'll need about 25 feet of asparagus (fifteen to twenty-five crowns) for an average family of three (one plant provides 1 to 2 pounds of spears). If you really like asparagus, double this planting.

Asparagus crowns are traditionally planted in deep trenches, and grown for 1 year before harvesting. But researchers and gardeners alike have shown that with some of the new hybrids, shallow planting and early harvest is just as productive, if not more so, than the old trench-and-wait method. Harvesting spears the first year may actually improve future yields by stimulating more buds to grow on the crown. There are more options now than ever for the asparagus gardener.

Some old gardening books tell you to plant asparagus crowns as deeply as 2 feet. Deeper crows produce thicker, fewer shoots. To grow the thinner, more tender shoots popular today, bury your crowns no deeper than 8 inches. Start by digging a trench 1 foot deep and 1 foot wide. Place 2 to 3 inches of well-rotted manure or compost in the trench (about 5 cubic feet per 25 feet of trench). Sprinkle 1 pound of bone meal or 2 pounds of colloidal phosphate for every 25 feet of row over the organic matter to help root growth. Churn up the soil, compost, and fertilizer with a cultivating fork or spade, then level it with a fork. Add 1 inch of clean, loose soil to keep young roots from touching the fertilizer. Mound the soil toward the center of the trench to about 8 inches below the surface so roots can spread downward. Now you're ready to plant the crowns.

If you have more than one trench, space them at least 3 feet apart. Asparagus roots grow deeply, but they also spread out in all directions and they don't like to compete with other roots.

Some gardeners like to soak the crowns in warm water for a few hours before planting. In the trenches, place plants 12 to 18 inches apart. Spread fleshy roots outward and downward over the ridge of soil in the trench. Cover crowns 2 inches deep with soil and water thoroughly. Keep a 3- to 4-inch trench above the plants. Don't expect shoots to appear for at least a month. For the first few weeks, most of the growth will occur in the roots. Fill in the trench gradually as shoots appear and grow into "ferns." Don't cover growing tips with soil. Let all the shoots grow into ferns the first year in order to build up

sturdy roots. Cut your first spears for the table the second spring.

Irrigate if winter and early spring are dry. Keep the bed well weeded. Feed and water regularly to build up sturdy leaves. Cut them in late fall when they turn yellow.

If your soil is shallow or heavy with clay, it might be easier to build 8- to 12-inch raised beds and place the crowns over a mound along the bottom of the bed (on top of the soil).

One advantage to the new strains of asparagus is that they're so productive you can plant crowns shallow and harvest spears the first year. This means less work and less waiting. Simply plant crowns 4 to 6 inches deep and only 12 inches apart. Harvest two thirds of your spears the following spring, but let the rest of the sprouts leaf out—some at the beginning, middle, and end of the growing period.

Some gardeners plant a dense, shallow bed of crowns next to their deep trenches. Small, tasty spears from the shallow bed are harvested and eaten the first year while the deeper crowns put on weight for future harvesting.

If your spears are getting too thin for your taste, but your roots are large and healthy, you may have to pile some more soil on top of the sprouts to fatten them up.

Growing transplants from seed: You can also grow asparagus from seeds. In some cases, you have no other choice because many new hybrids and older varieties are only available as seeds, not crowns. Seeds also cost less than crowns, and you're less likely to introduce diseases when using seeds. The dis-

advantages are that seeds can take several weeks to germinate in cold soils, plus you have to wait at least 1 additional year before you can harvest spears from transplants.

Eight to twelve weeks before the last spring frost, start seeds indoors in small containers like peat pots or cell packs. It helps to soak seeds for 2 days prior to sowing. Use sterile mix (peat moss, vermiculite, perlite) and bottom heat if possible since germination can take several weeks below 55°F, but only 7 to 10 days at 70°F. Plant only the strongest seedlings about 8 to 12 inches apart. Early in the following spring, crowns should be dug before the spears begin to poke through the soil. These 1-year-old crowns can then be transplanted to a permanent location and grown as previously explained. Keep nitrogen fertilizers low because they encourage shoot growth at the expense of root growth. Allow spear ferns to grow for 2 years before harvesting.

SOILS AND FERTILIZERS

Asparagus is not terribly fussy about soils as long as they are well drained. Plants can tolerate salty and alkaline soils better than most vegetables.

When preparing the soil for asparagus, you are building the foundation for years of production, so beds need thorough preparation prior to planting. In deep, sandy soils, this is a much easier task than in shallow, clay soils. Asparagus roots can grow several feet down, so if you don't have at least 2 feet of loose, workable soil, you might consider growing your asparagus in raised beds or boxes.

There are three steps in properly preparing soil for asparagus:

1. **Loosen the soil as much as possible and as deeply as possible.** Deep soil preparation is usually best done by hand since rototillers can't till deeply enough. The "double-dig" technique (see page 65–66) is the most efficient hand method

of loosening and amending subsoils. Some gardeners have been known to dig out entire beds of poor soil and fill them with better soil—just for the asparagus.

2. **Add large amounts of well-rotted compost or animal manure.** Nothing loosens up soil like aged organic matter. It's important to use well-rotted organic matter. Fresh stuff releases too much nitrogen and slows root growth. Try to get older organic materials deeper than a shovel's length. The well-aged stuff doesn't need as much oxygen since it's pretty well decayed. It can incorporate itself into the soil right away and begin loosening things up. Add fresher composts and manures to the topsoil. If you have a sandy soil, add about one wheelbarrow (four to five 1-gallon buckets) of aged organic amendments per 50 square feet—half in the subsoil, half in the topsoil. On clay soils, add about half a wheelbarrow per 50 square feet.

3. **Amend the soil with both quick- and slow-release, natural fertilizers, high in phosphorous and potassium and low in nitrogen to assure good root growth in the critical first few years.** You'll need to fertilize for the first year's growth and also supply some longer-acting nutrients for later growth. Just add them while you are digging and preparing the soil.

   One blend for the first year calls for 3 pounds cottonseed or soy meal (2 pounds fish meal), 2 pounds bone meal, 1 pound potassium sulfate, and $1/2$ pound kelp meal to make around 6 pounds of fertilizer for each 100 square feet of asparagus bed.

   For a slower release of nutrients during the next few seasons, also add 1 pound of colloidal phosphate and 3 pounds of granite dust for each 100 square feet of bed. The aged organic matter will supply the long-term nitrogen and trace nutrients while helping to release nutrients from the rock fertilizers.

The fertilizers you add during soil preparation will only last a few years. Beginning the second or third season, you need to side-dress the plants while they are growing. To encourage heavy top growth and thick spears, follow a twice-per-year fertilizer program. Make one application of 4-8-8 in the spring before shoots grow, and the second right after the last harvest is done.

Mulching is another important aspect of preparing the soil for asparagus cultivation. A common belief about growing asparagus is that it requires lots of water. However, gardeners in arid areas of the West, particularly where it doesn't rain in the summer, have found out that if you apply a heavy mulch over winter, it tends to hold the moisture from the winter and spring rains, making some of it available during the dry parts of the year.

Mulching also has the advantage of smothering weeds, which can be a big problem in the asparagus patch. The worst invaders are perennial weeds and asparagus seedlings from female plants. Mulching also helps to reduce cultivation, which can often damage roots.

DISEASES

Rust is a serious pest of asparagus, and resistance to this fungus disease is a top priority in the development of new varieties. Look for reddish brown streaks or spots on stems and leaves that turn black in fall. The best control is to plant resistant varieties.

Fusarium wilt appears as large lesions at or slightly below the soil line on spears. Fusarium fungi overwinter on crop debris and produce new spores when the weather warms. Rain, splashing water, and tools transmit the disease to new plants. Fusarium enters plants through wounds near or at the soil surface, so be careful while harvesting your asparagus. Since spores can stay viable for up to 10 years, the only satisfactory control is to plant resistant varieties like Martha Washington or the Jersey series.

PESTS

The most serious plant eater of asparagus is the **asparagus beetle** *Crioceris.* The **striped asparagus beetle,** *C. asparagi,* is reddish brown with black and cream-colored stripes on the wing cover. The **12-spotted asparagus beetle,** *C. duodecimpunctata,* is red-orange with twelve black spots on the wing covers.

Both adult and larvae chew holes in spears, causing brown blemishes. Later, they attack the stems and strip leaves from branches. Adults lay black, shiny eggs on the stems. The larvae hatch and feed on the spears for a few weeks. They are small, gray, and grublike. After feeding, they drop to the ground, pupate under the soil, and emerge as adults the following season.

The asparagus beetle is more of a problem in some areas than others. Start by covering your bed with floating row covers just before shoots break ground in the spring. Keep the covers on until after the harvest. Remove adults and larvae by hand, especially in early spring, to reduce the next year's population. In the fall, destroy all leaves, weeds, and mulch in the bed where adults overwinter. The tiny, naturally occurring parasitic wasp *Tetrastichus* feeds on eggs and larvae of the asparagus beetle. If infestations are particularly heavy, adults and larvae are easily killed with rotenone pesticide.

If you plant your asparagus bed in soil that hasn't been worked for several years, you may have trouble with **cutworms.** These voracious caterpillars chew holes in spears and can even topple them over. To clear the soil of cutworms before planting, scatter moist bran mixed with *Bacillus thuringiensis kurstaki* (BTK) a week before planting out, or drench soil with neem or a solution of parasitic nematodes (see page 182).

Onion thrips are minute insects that scrape away the stem and leaf surface and lap up the plant juices. They are difficult to see with the naked eye, but they leave a characteristic silvery, streaked appearance (see page 214). The only practical control is to spray with neem or pyrethrum, or hope they don't inflict serious damage.

VARIETIES

Some open-pollinated varieties, particularly heirlooms, aren't always available as crowns, and so must be grown from seed. In the early 1900s, two varieties of asparagus—the now famous Mary Washington and Martha Washington—were developed as strains resistant to rust disease, which was a serious threat to the varieties of the time. The home gardener was limited to these two varieties plus their improved strains for nearly three generations. In the 1950s, research at Rutgers and University of California yielded hybrids that were more productive, disease resistant, and grew better under specific regional conditions. The California types, like California 500 and UC 157 are especially adapted to the mild winters of the West Coast, the Jersey series is popular in the North and Southeast.

In 1984, the first generation of all male hybrids—Jersey Giant and Greenwich—were released. New varieties of asparagus are being developed all the time, so keep your eyes open for those adapted to your region of the country.

HARVEST AND STORAGE

Once your asparagus crowns have become established for a year, you can begin harvesting shoots the second spring. You can cut these for a month or so, but use common sense; every time you cut, you're taking strength from the roots below. After a month or so of harvesting, let the remaining spears develop into the attractive ferny stalks so they can soak up solar energy and replenish the crown for the next year's spears.

RECOMMENDED ASPARAGUS VARIETIES		
VARIETY	**RESISTANCE**	**COMMENTS**
Open-Pollinated		
Argenteuil*		French heirloom with thick, whitish stalks and purple tips. Great taste!
California 500	R	Adapted to Pacifiic Coast. Early Mary Washington with green tips.
Martha Washington*	R	Productive old timer with green tips.
Mary Washington*	R	Long-standing, standard commercial strain. Most widely available. Tips tinged purple.
UC 72	R, FW	Mary Washington type, well adapted to the West Coast and Southeast. Strong disease resistance.
Viking	R	Mary Washington type. Very stable open-pollinated variety. Hardier in cold climates than all-male hybrids. Good for freezing.
Hybrids		
Greenwich	R	First generation all-male hybrid for sandy soils.
Jersey Giant	R, FW, CR	First generation all-male hybrid with great flavor, yield, and resistance.
Jersey King	R, FW	Widely adapted, mostly male.
Jersey Knight	R, FW	Hybrid. Most disease resistant of the all-male hybrids.
Larac	R	A French hybrid that grows well in the Northwest. High yielding, so cut early, 3 years from seed.
UC 157	R	Commercial variety developed for mild winter areas. High yields in clusters.

R = rust; FW = Fusarium wilt; CR = crown rot
* Indicates heirloom variety.

In following years, you'll probably be able to stretch the harvest over 2 months or more before the roots weaken. If you want to extend your harvest for a few weeks, select two or three sturdy spears on each plant and let them grow their ferny leaves undisturbed while you continue to cut new spears. These "mother stalks" will help store energy for next year's shoots plus stimulate your plants to grow more spears during the current year. Always stop cutting when all the new spears are thinner than a pencil. This means the crown is played out for the season. Let all subsequent shoots go to leaf.

You can increase yields by using an old trick of the Amish farmers. They remove all the female plants—those producing red berries—leaving only the male plants to produce spears. Since male plants never go to seed, they put all their energy into growing fat, succulent shoots. Of course, you can achieve the same thing by growing all-male hybrids.

Early in the season, shoots may require cutting only every third day. But as the weather warms and plants grow faster, you may have to harvest every day, especially the new hybrids. Remember that when a spear is cut, it stimulates the crown to produce more buds, but cutting too many spears can rob the roots of nutrients. It's a balancing act that all asparagus gardeners soon learn.

The problem with a glut of asparagus is that it doesn't keep very well. You can freeze or can it, but asparagus wilts quickly when stored in the refrigerator. To avoid this, set stalks in a jar of water, like cut flowers, and cover them with a plastic bag. They'll stay crisp for 3 to 4 days this way.

ASPARAGUS GROWING TIPS

- Grow asparagus from seed or one-year-old crowns.

- Choose a permanent, sunny location, away from trees and in well-drained soil. Grow in raised beds if necessary.

- Before you plant, prepare the soil as deeply as possible. Amend with organic material.

- Coddle your plants the first year. Eliminate weeds and other problems that might slow growth.

- The first year, you want to grow only strong shoots with large leaves. This helps the crown store reserves of food so it can grow spears the next season.

- Start harvesting spears the second year from crowns, or the third year from transplants. Harvest only those spears thicker than a pencil. Cut spears at or just below soil line when they are 6 to 8 inches high.

- Thin out female plants to increase yields and reduce the need to weed out asparagus seedlings.

- Creeping perennial weeds have been the downfall of many an asparagus patch. Start early, and place a high priority on weeding the spears. Mulch deeply.

- New disease-resistant all-male varieties offer heavier yields with less care and a greater choice and opportunity for home gardeners.

Chard
CHENOPODIACEAE (Goosefoot or Spinach Family)

Beta vulgaris var. cicla
CHINESE: *tian cai*
FRENCH: *bette, bletta*
GERMAN: *Mangold*
ITALIAN: *bieta a foglia*
JAPANESE: *hudansöu*
SPANISH: *bleda, acelga*

Chard, also known as Swiss chard, sea kale beet, spinach beet, and leaf beet, is a rugged, deep-rooted, highly underrated vegetable. As some of its other common names indicate, chard is really a kind of beet that is cultivated for its large, hardy leaves. A very old vegetable, chard is native to the Mediterranean area, where it still grows wild on the Canary Islands. The Arabic name of the plant, *al-sila*, is derived from the Babylonian word *silq*, suggesting its ancient heritage. The Greeks wrote of garden chards in hues of red, light green, and dark green. The Romans were the first to cultivate it, and conquering barbarians scattered it throughout Europe.

Chard is a member of the goosefoot family (Chenopodiaceae), and next to beets, its closest relative is spinach. Chard is much less fussy about temperature, day length, and soils than spinach. You can grow it in partial shade and harvest it for a much longer time than either beets or spinach. Chard is a cut-and-come-again vegetable. Simply snap off the leaves and more will grow until winter. Chard is one of the easiest, most nutritious, and efficient vegetables you can grow.

Chard, spinach, and beet greens are similar in flavor, texture, and food value, and are often substituted for one another in cooking. Chard has a slightly earthier flavor, more body, and less water than spinach, so it doesn't shrink as much when cooked. Also, chard doesn't contain as much oxalic acid as spinach. This is important, because oxalic acid can take calcium away from the body—an undesirable feature, especially for pregnant or nursing women and elderly people, all of whom need to conserve their calcium (see "Spinach," page 304).

The young tender leaves of chard can be eaten raw, but older leaves need cooking. Most cooks separate the stalks from the leaves, since they have a different texture and cook more slowly. The stalks can be prepared by themselves like asparagus. The leaves can be steamed, stir-fried, braised, or baked. Use them in soups, pasta dishes, omelets, or as a spinach substitute in lasagna or spanakopita. Chard is delicious simply braised with olive oil and served as a side dish. The large, thick leaves of chard make excellent wrappers for fillings (cut out the thickest part of the stem first). Chard is a good source of vitamin A, calcium, iron, and fiber.

CULTIVATION

Chard is a biennial that flowers the second season after 6 to 12 weeks of temperatures below 50°F. It withstands both summer heat and light frosts once the plants are well established, but grows best in cool conditions.

Plant chard in the early spring, 3 to 4 weeks before the last spring frost, and at 10- to 20-day intervals after that. In mild coastal areas, chard can be planted most of the year.

Where summers are hot, you may have to take a summer recess and plant again 4 to 6 weeks before the first fall frost, from late summer in the North through midfall in the South.

PLANTING

Direct-seed chard or grow it from transplants. To sow directly, plant seeds $1/2$ inch deep and 1 inch apart; thin to 12 inches. Start transplants indoors 3 to 4 weeks before the last spring frost, and set out in rows 12 inches apart. Chard is a large plant and needs plenty of room to grow.

SOILS AND FERTILIZERS

Chard thrives in well-drained, rich, crumbly soil with a neutral pH. Before sowing seeds, mix about $1/2$ cup of 10-10-10 fertilizer for every 10 feet of planted row. If you use a preplant fertilizer, chard will rarely need side-dressing while growing.

For symptoms of nutrient deficiency in chard, see "Spinach," page 304.

DISEASES AND PESTS

See "Spinach" (page 304) and "Beets" (pages 236–237).

VARIETIES

If you've only eaten store-bought chard, you'll find that the difference between it and homegrown chard is striking. Commercial chard is rough and metallic tasting, while homegrown varieties are sweet and crunchy.

There are about forty varieties of chard currently available, and all are open-pollinated. Most of them have green leaves, although the stalks and veins range in

Red Stem Chard

color from shades of white to red. Other differences are the size of the plants and the shape and texture of the leaves, which range from large and flat to small and crinkly.

White Stem Chard

RECOMMENDED CHARD VARIETIES

VARIETY	COMMENTS
Argentata	Danish variety with narrow green leaves, and short, fat silvery white stalks.
Dorat	Danish variety with narrow green leaves and broad white stalks.
Fordhook Giant*	American heirloom from 1750, with large, crinkly leaves and long, narrow, snow-white stalks; cold-hardy.
French Swiss Chard	Tall plant with thick, white stalks and large, smooth leaves.
Lucullus*	Heirloom from 1914, with wide, thick, crinkled leaves and yellowish-white stalks.
Paros	French chard with large dark-green, crinkled leaves on thick white stalks; very resistant to summer bolting.
Ruby Red* (Rhubarb)	Heirloom from 1857; bright red stalk and leaf veins; for the edible landscape.
Silverado	Dwarfed, upright, slim white stalks with dark green, crinkled leaves; refined Lucullus type.
White King	A selection of Lucullus; large, thick stalks and dark green, very crinkled leaves; almost celerylike.

* Indicates heirloom variety.

HARVEST

Don't let chard grow too large or it will get tough and lose flavor. For the best quality, snap off individual outer leaves when plants are about 1 foot tall. Don't harvest leaves from the center of the plants, but allow them to develop. Chard is a cut-and-come-again green, because it will continue to replace harvested leaves despite heavy cutting. To harvest an entire plant, cut off all stalks 2 inches above the ground; a smaller second crop will follow. Few plants yield more food per area of garden with as little care as chard.

Under normal conditions, chard will bolt to flower the second season. If you remove the stalk before it has much chance to develop, your chard will probably give you another year of leaf growth. This doesn't always work, but it's worth a try.

CHARD GROWING TIPS

• Sow directly or set out seedlings, beginning in early spring and at 15-day intervals for 1 month. Plant again in late summer to mid-fall for a late-season harvest.

• Chard needs a regular supply of water to grow well. Mulch plants to conserve moisture, especially during dry spells. Water often.

• Harvest by snapping off the outer leaves of mature plant. Cut off entire plant 2 inches above the ground for a second growth.

Spinach
CHENOPODIACEAE (Goosefoot or Spinach Family)

Spinacia oleracea
CHINESE: *bo cai*
FRENCH: *épinard*
GERMAN: *Spinat*
ITALIAN: *spinacio*
JAPANESE: *hourensou*
SPANISH: *espinaca*

Spinach is an annual vegetable that grows best in cool weather. It is closely related to beets, chard, epazote, and quinoa, as well as the common garden weeds lamb's-quarter *(Chenopodium)* and Russian thistle *(Salsola)*. Spinach is native to Iran and was first cultivated by the Persians over 2,000 years ago. The Moors considered it a staple and took it to Spain in the eleventh century; from there it quickly spread to the rest of Europe. The colonists brought spinach to the New World, where it was listed in seed catalogs in 1806.

Spinach is used primarily as a cooked green (potherb) although it is also popular as a raw salad green. It contains a high level of vitamins and minerals, especially vitamins A and C, thiamine, iron, phosphorous, and potassium, and has a moderate level of protein. Although generally considered a very nutritious vegetable, spinach has one disadvantage. Look carefully at the leaves and you'll notice small white crystals embedded in the tissue. This is oxalic acid, which reacts with calcium to form calcium oxalate. Large amounts of this compound can interfere with calcium absorption, which is particularly serious for infants, nursing mothers, and the elderly. Spinach contains substantial amounts of oxalic acid, although savoy (crinkled) types are believed to have less than smooth-leaf types.

Most members of the goosefoot family, including spinach, are well adapted to salty soils and seaside habitats. They accumulate salts in their tissues, including nitrates from ammonium nitrate fertilizers. Nitrates convert to nitrites during digestion and result in the carcinogen nitrosamines. Because of this, it is important to use natural sources of nitrogen for spinach.

CULTIVATION

Spinach has a deep taproot with profuse side-branching. Although the taproots can grow several feet deep, most of the feeder roots are located in the top few inches of soil, so you need to cultivate with care. Since spinach doesn't compete well with weeds, it's important to mulch it whenever you can. Mulch also keeps the soil cool and moist—just what spinach likes.

Like the onion, spinach is photoperiodic, that is, it flowers in response to specific day lengths (see page 228). As day length approaches 15 hours, spinach plants will bolt to seed, especially if the temperature is above 70°F.

The key to successful spinach growing is cool temperatures and a day length of less than 14 hours. These conditions occur in spring and fall. In cool southern areas, where spring days are shorter, spinach can be planted up to early summer. Spinach can also be planted from September until the first frost for an early harvest the following spring.

In the spring, start planting about 4 to 6 weeks before the last spring frost, and keep planting successive crops for about a month. This will give you a continuous harvest throughout spring.

Fall plantings give a more sustained harvest than spring plantings. Sow seeds as soon as soil is cool enough in late summer, and continue sowing until the first frost. During summer in milder areas, sow spinach between rows of tall vegetables like beans, corn, and cucumbers to provide shade for the growing plants.

The sweetest tasting spinach comes from overwintered early spring plants. This is why some gardeners sow spinach while they are harvesting their fall crop. Most gardeners claim that fall-planted spinach is also easier to grow and more productive over a longer period than spring-planted spinach. Small seedlings will withstand frost better than larger ones. So try to sow about 3 weeks before the first fall frost. Keep these late seedlings on the dry side and don't fertilize with nitrogen, in order to harden them up for the winter cold.

PLANTING

Spinach may be direct-sown or grown from transplants. In either case, be sure to start with fresh seeds, as germination can decline by about 20 percent after the first year. Spinach seed is often treated with fungicides like captan or thiram, so if you want seeds free from these toxic chemicals, look for untreated seeds when you order.

Spinach seeds germinate best around 70°F, but will also sprout in cold soil better than most vegetables. Above 80°F, germination is poor and erratic. To direct-sow, place seeds 2 inches apart in drills (shallow furrows) 12 inches apart. Thin to 6 inches. If the soil is warm, pregerminate seeds on moist paper towels in the refrigerator for 2 days. This will break dormancy and encourage seeds to finish germinating even in warm soil.

Growing from transplants can help you gain a few weeks on the spinach season, as transplants will grow in hot soil while seeds languish. Start transplants in flats, cell packs, or peat pots. Grow inside in a cool location or outside in the shade. Harden-off transplants in the sun for a few days and plant out.

SOILS AND FERTILIZERS

Spinach can be grown in a wide variety of soils, as long as they are well drained. Sandy soils warm faster, so they will generally cause spinach to bolt earlier than clay soils. Spinach is very sensitive to acid conditions, so keep your soil pH above 6.0. If in doubt, add limestone prior to planting.

If your soil is nutrient poor, side-dress your seedlings when they are about one-third grown. Spinach needs lots of nitrogen and potassium. Use fish emulsion, wood ashes, or blood meal. If spinach doesn't get enough nitrogen early on, it will often go to seed.

NUTRIENT DEFICIENCIES IN SPINACH	
NUTRIENT	**SYMPTOMS**
Nitrogen (N)	Growth is stunted. Older leaves turn pale green and eventually drop off.
Phosphorus (P)	Stunted growth but no other symptoms.
Potassium (K)	Older leaves have brown patches all over and are droopy at the tips.
Calcium (Ca)	New leaves are very small, distorted, twisted, and pale green.
Sulfur (S)	Pale yellow-green in color, especially new leaves. Older leaves have brown tips.
Magnesium (Mg)	Older leaves have patches of light brown papery tissue that follow the small veins.
Boron (Bo)	Leaves are deformed, cupped upwards, and twisted. Leaf tips turn pale and brown, growing stem tips fail to develop.

DISEASES

Mosaic is a serious spinach disease caused by the cucumber mosaic virus, which is transmitted by the green peach aphid. Symptoms first appear on young leaves as a mottled puckering that soon moves to older leaves. The disease is more of a problem during long days and periods of high light intensity. The only long-term control is the use of resistant varieties like Winter Bloomsdale and Melody, plus careful aphid control. Use floating row covers to exclude these insects.

Curly top is a virus common in beets and spinach, especially in Western states. The first symptom appears when leaf veins on young plants turn milky white, followed by curling of the leaf margins. Young plants usually die, while older plants may survive but will be stunted. The disease is carried by the beet leafhopper, and no resistant varieties are yet available.

Downy mildew, or "blue mold," is caused by the fungus *Peronospora parasitica*. The disease first appears as yellowish patches on the upper side of leaves, which later turn black and die. The underside of the leaves may develop a bluish-gray mold. For controls see "Brassicas," page 255.

Fusarium wilt is caused by the fungus *Fusarium oxysporum*. The plant becomes pale green, and leaf margins roll inward as the plant withers and dies. The disease is both soil and seed borne, and it is common where soil temperatures are warm. The development of resistant varieties is still in the early stages.

White rust fungus (*Albugo occidentalis*) is an increasing problem in the Southeast and Midwest. Little white spots on the underside of leaves are the first sign of this disease. The fungus thrives in the 60° to 70°F range with high humidity. The leaves have to be wet for infection to occur, so water only in the morning so that leaves can dry out, or use drip irrigation. Don't plant spinach in the same place for more than 2 years in a row. Remove and destroy all infected leaves as soon as white spots appear. Control weeds, especially those in the spinach family, like lamb's-quarter, as they can harbor the fungus. Remove all plant debris from the garden in fall, since the fungus overwinters in garden refuse. Finally, try resistant varieties like Coho, Ozarka II, or Fall Green.

Rusts (*Puccinia* or *Uromyces*) are fungi that produce tiny orange raised spots or pustules on leaf undersides of spinach (rust rarely affects beets or chard). Spores are wind and rain borne, so there is little you can do to exclude it. The best remedy is good growing practices: avoid high nitrogen fertilizers and overhead watering, keep plants well spaced, and toss out infected leaves.

PESTS

The **green peach aphid (*Myzus persicae*)** is the most serious plant-eating spinach pest because it transmits several virus diseases. It attacks over two hundred species of plants, including potatoes, beans, beets, brassicas, cucurbits, eggplant, lettuce, and tomatoes. It can be distinguished from other aphids on spinach by its pale green to yellow color and three dark lengthwise lines on its back. For the general control of aphids, see "Brassicas," page 256.

The **spinach flea beetle (*Disonycha xanthomelas*)** feeds on the leaves of spinach, making small round holes. The damage is usually cosmetic, but smaller plants and seedlings can be destroyed. Use floating row covers to prevent adults from getting to leaves. Most larvae of flea beetles feed on roots, but larvae of *Disonycha* feed on leaves along with the adults. Little is known about the natural control of flea beetles, although native nematodes and parasitic wasps will attack the adults. If damage is extensive, use a pyrethrum spray.

Leaf miners are the larvae of certain flies that tunnel between the upper and lower surfaces of leaves. As they eat, they leave a whitish path through the green of the leaf. This path gets wider as the larvae grow. Leaf miners rarely cause significant damage, although they can make leaves unappealing. Pick and destroy damaged leaves to reduce the next generation of miners. Floating row covers can exclude the adult flies and prevent egg-laying. Leaf miners are less of a problem in fall and early spring.

The **beet armyworm,** the drab-colored caterpillar of a moth, eats large holes in the leaves of spinach, chard, and beets. Pick them off before they do much damage. Look for very small young caterpillars, $1/4$ to $1/2$ inch long. If they are a particular problem, spray with botanicals like neem or pyrethrin, or try the bacteria *Bacillus thuringiensis* (see page 182). The smaller you get them, the better. Large caterpillars (the ones you see when you look casually at your garden) are difficult to control with sprays of any kind.

VARIETIES

Cultivated spinach is normally dioecious, that is, there are both male and female plants. There are many gradations of "mostly male" or "mostly female" varieties, however, that are used to produce hybrids.

There are about fifty open-pollinated spinach varieties and slightly fewer hybrids, although hybrids account for over 85 percent of spinach seeds sold in the United States today. Until the 1950s, most spinach varieties came from Europe, even though they were low-yielding and susceptible to downy mildew. New modern hybrids have proven to be superior to such old standards as Bloomsdale Long Standing. They're more vigorous, uniform, and resistant to diseases and bolting, and most of them are well adapted to spring, fall, and overwintering.

Seed catalogs usually describe spinach varieties by leaf type. Savoy leaves are crinkled. They withstand cold better than smooth-leafed types. Savoy leaves can become encrusted with soil, however, making them a chore to clean.

If you want good fall spinach, it's better to select fast-growing varieties rather than bolt-resistant ("long-standing") ones, especially in cold-winter areas. The slow-growing bolt-resistant varieties might be stopped by winter freeze before they can mature, whereas fast-growing varieties won't bolt because they grow leaves when days are short and cool.

In many areas of the country, disease resistance is the most important criterion for spinach varieties. There are no varieties resistant to fusarium wilt, although several varieties seem to tolerate it (see page 308).

RECOMMENDED SPINACH VARIETIES

VARIETY	LEAF	RESISTANT	COMMENTS
Hybrid			
Avon	Semi-savoy, dark green	DM 1,2/MV	Very fast growing. Great taste. F,O, Sp
Hybrid #7	Semi-savoy	DM 1,2/MV	First hybrid with DM and MV resistance. F, O
Imperial Star	Smooth, thick, dark green	DM 1, 3	Best smooth-leaf type for year-round planting. F, W, ESp
Indian Summer	Semi-savoy	DM 1, 2 / MV	Very bolt resistant, erect habit. F, ESp, Su
Melody	Savoy, thick, dark green	DM; MV	Very popular Dutch type, AAS winner; overwinters well. F, O, Sp
Olympia	Smooth, deep green	DM 1, 2, 3	Spring and summer sowing, good DM resistance, very adaptable to year-round growing. Sp, ESu
Tyee	Semi-savoy	DM 1, 3	Bolt-resistant and great for fall and overwintering; high yields, bland flavor, spreading habit. F, O, Sp
Vienna	Heavily savoy, dark green	DM1, 2, 3/MV	Medium-large, erect plant for spring or fall planting, slow to bolt. F, O, Sp
Open-Pollinated			
Bloomsdale Long Standing*	Savoy, thick, dark green	MV	Heirloom since 1925, and the most popular nonhybrid spinach. F, O, Sp
Bloomsdale Savoy	Very savoy, thick, dark green		Heavy yields; great fresh or canned. F, O, Sp
Steadfast	Smooth, dark green		Bolt resistant, for late spring to early summer sowing; modest yield.
Viroflay*	Large, smooth, dark green		Heirloom since 1866. ESu

Disease resistance: DM = Downy mildew (races 1, 2, 3); MV = Mosaic virus

Grows best in: F = Fall; O = Overwinter (fall plant, spring harvest); ESp = Early spring; Sp = Spring; ESu = Early summer; Su = Summer

* Indicates heirloom variety.

VINAIGRETTE WHEEL

Take any basic vinaigrette (either Basic, Simple, Lemon-Mustard, or Gayle's Dijon Vinaigrette, page 90) and add the ingredients found in the diagram below to use as flavorful dressing for the vegetables found around the outer circumference of the wheel.

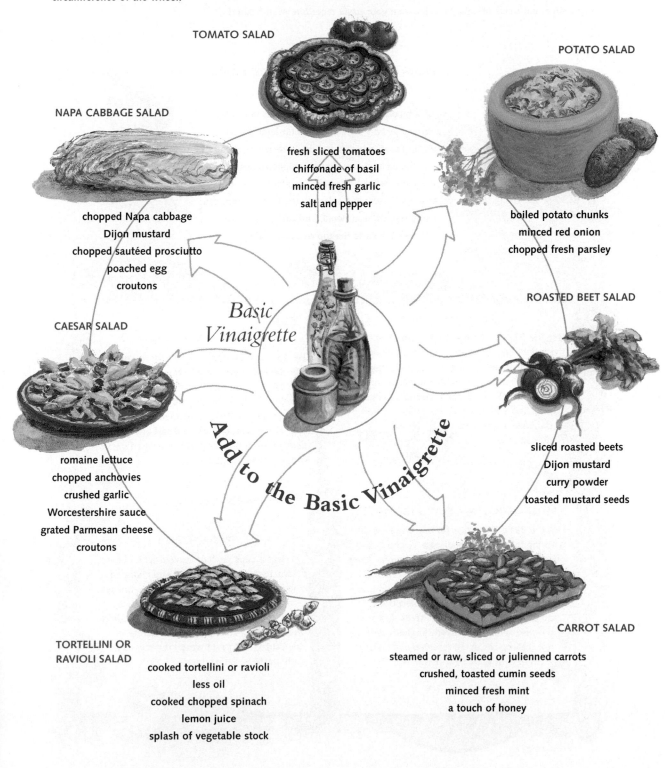

TOMATO SALAD

POTATO SALAD

NAPA CABBAGE SALAD

fresh sliced tomatoes
chiffonade of basil
minced fresh garlic
salt and pepper

boiled potato chunks
minced red onion
chopped fresh parsley

chopped Napa cabbage
Dijon mustard
chopped sautéed prosciutto
poached egg
croutons

Basic Vinaigrette

ROASTED BEET SALAD

CAESAR SALAD

Add to the Basic Vinaigrette

romaine lettuce
chopped anchovies
crushed garlic
Worcestershire sauce
grated Parmesan cheese
croutons

sliced roasted beets
Dijon mustard
curry powder
toasted mustard seeds

TORTELLINI OR
RAVIOLI SALAD

CARROT SALAD

cooked tortellini or ravioli
less oil
cooked chopped spinach
lemon juice
splash of vegetable stock

steamed or raw, sliced or julienned carrots
crushed, toasted cumin seeds
minced fresh mint
a touch of honey

BASIC PASTA SAUCES FROM YOUR GARDEN

A few basic techniques can be used to create countless variations of garden-fresh pasta sauces like the ones below. One of the most flavorful techniques is "infusing" pasta (see page 194). The basic technique is outlined here, along with several variations and recipes using other techniques. After you've perfected the recipes found here, use your imagination and sense of balance to broaden your pasta repertoire even further!

Basic Technique for Infusing Pasta
(see page 194)

Sauté a mixture of vegetables and herbs in olive oil, and reserve part of the mixture for later. Partially cook your favorite pasta, and drain, reserving a cup or so of the pasta water. Finish cooking the pasta in the skillet with the sautéed vegetables and the reserved pasta water. Cook until the liquid is reduced and the pasta is al dente, and add the reserved vegetables to the top of each serving.

GAYLES' PASTA ANNIE

Use the Basic Technique for Infusing Pasta with the following: Sliced mushrooms, chopped green onions, steamed asparagus tips, baby bok choy, tapenade (page 97), sundried tomatoes, chopped pitted kalamata olives, and 6 ounces penne pasta. Top with grated mozzarella, toasted pumpkin seeds, and lemon zest.

BROCCOLI GARLIC

Use the Basic Technique for Infusing Pasta with the following ingredients: 3 tablespoons olive oil, 4 minced garlic cloves, 1 cup steamed grated broccoli stems, 1/2 cup chopped fresh flat-leaf parsley, 4 cups steamed broccoli florets, 1/3 cup lemon juice, and salt and pepper to taste. Infuse 6 ounces partially cooked pasta using reserved pasta water.

SWISS CHARD, FAVA BEAN, AND ONION

Use the Basic Technique for Infusing Pasta with the following ingredients: 1/2 cup olive oil, 2 cups roughly chopped onions, 4 cups chopped Swiss chard, 4 cups shelled steamed fava beans, juice of half a lemon, a splash of balsamic vinegar, 2 tablespoons minced garlic, and chopped herbs. Infuse 5 ounces partially cooked spaghetti broken in 2-inch pieces using reserved pasta water. Serve with grated Parmesan.

PASTA FAGIOLI

Heat 2 cups each of cooked white beans; tomatoes, peeled, seeded, and chopped (page 438); sautéed Swiss chard or spinach; and vegetable stock in a medium saucepan. Infuse 10 ounces partially cooked spaghetti broken into 2-inch pieces, simmering in the sauce (and pasta water, if necessary) until pasta is done.

CABBAGE AND POTATO

Sauté 2 cups each julienne onions and thinly sliced cabbage in ¼ cup olive oil. Add 1 cup boiled sliced potatoes and cook until slightly crisp and warmed through. Add this mixture to the Herb-Lemon pasta recipe on page 195, when adding reserved greens.

PUTANESCA

Use the Basic Technique for Infusing Pasta with the following ingredients: 2 tablespoons olive oil; 6 cloves garlic, minced; 6 Roma tomatoes, scalded, skinned, seeded, and chopped; 18 kalamata olives, pitted and roughly chopped (page 438); 18 capers; and 6 anchovy filets. Infuse 5 ounces partially cooked pasta using a little reserved pasta water.

FRENCH PISTOU

Scald, peel, seed, and chop 6 to 8 plum tomatoes (see page 438). Combine in a small bowl with 2 tablespoons minced garlic, ½ cup chopped fresh basil, ⅓ cup olive oil, ½ teaspoon salt, and ¼ teaspoon pepper. Let sit for one hour so flavors can meld. Serve over 6 ounces hot, drained, cooked pasta. (See full Pistou recipe on page 393.)

PUTANESCA VERDE

Sauté 1 tablespoon olive oil, 1 tablespoon minced garlic, 2 cups slivered Swiss chard leaves, ¼ cup chopped fresh flat-leaf parsley, 2 tablespoons chopped capers, 12 small green olives, pitted and chopped, and the juice of 1 lemon for several minutes. Serve over 5 ounces cooked angel hair pasta and garnish with grated Parmesan.

PASTA AND LENTILS IN TOMATO BROTH

Use the Basic Technique for Infusing Pasta with: 1 tablespoon olive oil, 2 slices chopped prosciutto, and a mirepoix (page 87) made of 2 tablespoons each minced celery, onion, and carrot. Sauté briefly. Add 2 cloves garlic, minced, and ½ onion, julienne. Sauté 3 to 5 minutes. Add 4 medium tomatoes, scalded, skinned, seeded, and chopped (see page 438); ½ cup cooked lentils; and infuse 8 ounces partially cooked pasta using 2 cups pasta water.

ROASTED CARROT

In an oven at 425°, roast 4 cups carrots with a little garlic, thyme, mint, and olive oil until soft and brown. Mash half the carrots and add to a skillet with the rest of the carrots, a little stock, milk, and olive oil. Reduce slightly. Then infuse 5 ounces partially cooked rigatoni, using reserved pasta water if necessary.

ELEMENTS OF SOUP

Professional cooks often "compose" soups out of basic prepared ingredients they have on hand. You, too, can compose your own nutritious and tasty soups with any combination of the five basic elements: 1) stock, 2) cooked vegetables, 3) thickeners (or starches), 4) flavorings, and 5) fresh vegetables. You probably won't have all of these elements on hand at one time, but you might find many of them in your freezer, refrigerator, or pantry, having been canned from a previous season's harvest. By adding fresh diced or sliced vegetables from your garden, you can compose a soup in a matter of minutes.

When you look at your own soup recipes, analyze how the five elements are combined to make an aromatic, spontaneous meal. When you start to understand how soups are put together, you will be able to create your own recipes based on your own sense of balance, using the elements you've prepared from your own garden vegetables!

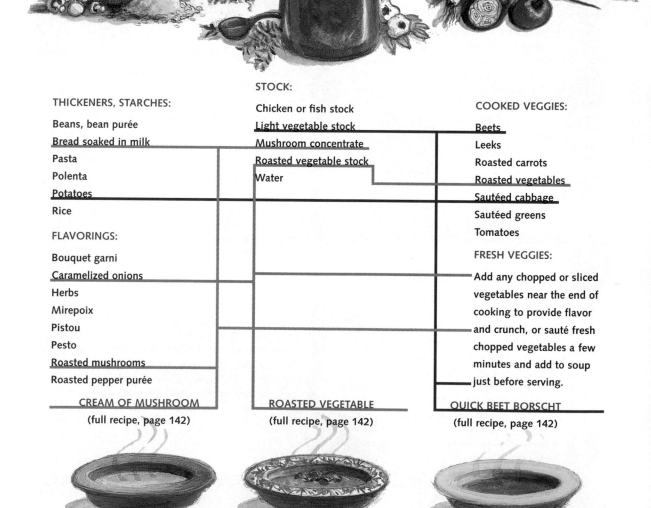

THICKENERS, STARCHES:

Beans, bean purée
Bread soaked in milk
Pasta
Polenta
Potatoes
Rice

FLAVORINGS:

Bouquet garni
Caramelized onions
Herbs
Mirepoix
Pistou
Pesto
Roasted mushrooms
Roasted pepper purée

CREAM OF MUSHROOM

(full recipe, page 142)

STOCK:

Chicken or fish stock
Light vegetable stock
Mushroom concentrate
Roasted vegetable stock
Water

ROASTED VEGETABLE

(full recipe, page 142)

COOKED VEGGIES:

Beets
Leeks
Roasted carrots
Roasted vegetables
Sautéed cabbage
Sautéed greens
Tomatoes

FRESH VEGGIES:

Add any chopped or sliced vegetables near the end of cooking to provide flavor and crunch, or sauté fresh chopped vegetables a few minutes and add to soup just before serving.

QUICK BEET BORSCHT

(full recipe, page 142)

You will find over 50 separate dishes that can be used to create soup in the sections on Stocks (pages 137-140), Flavorings from the Garden (pages 83-89), Condiments (pages 95-100), and the Elements of Soup (pages 141-143).

HARVEST

Like chard, spinach is a cut–and–come–again vegetable. Cut leaves from the outside of the plant and let the center leaves grow out to replace them. To harvest the entire plant, cut all the leaves to about 2 inches above the ground. This will encourage a new flush of growth.

SPINACH GROWING TIPS

- Spinach is sensitive to acid soils, so keep the pH at 6.5 to 7.5.

- Use disease-resistant varieties whenever possible as a first line of defense against diseases.

- Spinach bolts when days are around 14 hours long; warm weather will cause it to bolt faster.

- Spinach needs at least 6 weeks of cool weather from seed to harvest. Begin sowing in early spring. Sow again in August and September for the fall crop, and again from September until first frost for an early spring harvest.

- Take care cultivating spinach, as it has shallow feeder roots. Use mulch to smother weeds, conserve moisture, and keep the soil cool.

- Keep a watch out for aphids; they can transmit virus diseases. Use floating row covers to keep them off plants.

Fruiting Vegetables

LEGUMES

Beans and peas are members of the Fabaceae family, also known as legumes because of their podlike fruits. Legumes are unique vegetables because of their beneficial relationship with bacteria living on their roots. These bacteria convert nitrogen in the air to compounds that plants can use, which makes legumes far and away the best vegetable source of protein. Many legumes, like chickpeas (garbanzo beans), lentils, winged beans, cowpeas, and adzuki beans, are staple vegetables in other parts of the world. Legumes also include alfalfa, clover, and vetch cover crops; fenugreek, whose seeds are a key ingredient in curries; carob, whose seeds are made into a chocolate substitute; and several landscape plants such as acacia, mimosa, broom, sweet peas, and lupine.

The most common legumes in the kitchen gardens are peas, snap beans, soybeans, and fava beans. Peas and snap beans are especially popular. Fava beans were the only beans known to early Europeans, and their seeds date back to the Iron Age. Favas require mild coastal climates, so most of the United States is too hot or too cold for them. Soybeans require a hot, humid climate. Their fussy growth and low yield make them impractical for most small kitchen gardens.

KITCHEN GARDEN LEGUMES

BOTANIC NAME	COMMON NAME	PART EATEN
Pisum sativum	**Pea**	
ssp. *sativum*	Shell (English), snap	Pod, fresh seed
var. *macrocarpon*	Sugar, edible podded, snow, Chinese	Pod, young seed
Phaseolus	**New World Beans**	
Phaseolus coccineus	Scarlet runner	Fresh seed
Phaseolus limensis	Lima	Fresh seed
Phaseolus vulgaris	Snap, string, French; filet; flageolet; Kidney, black, navy, pinto, etc.	Fresh and dried pod Seed
Vigna/Cicer	**Old World Beans**	
Vigna spp.	Adzuki, mung, etc.	Dried seed
Cicer arietinum	Chickpea (garbanzo bean)	Dried seed
Vicia	**Vetch Beans**	
Vicia faba	Bell, horse, fava, broad, field	Young pod, fresh seed
Glycine max	**Soybean**	Fresh and dried seed

LEGUMES AND THEIR BACTERIA

Early Roman farmers knew that clover made the soil more fertile for crops that followed, although they didn't know why. The answer lies in the roots. Legumes are different from other plants because they have developed a mutually beneficial relationship with a group of bacteria called *Rhizobium*. These bacteria enter the roots of legumes, where they colonize and form pea-sized outgrowths called nodules. The bacteria harvest nitrogen from the air and convert (or "fix") it into a form plants can use. In return, *Rhizobium* receive carbohydrates from their host. Other plants also profit from legumes. As old nodules are sloughed off in the soil, nitrogen becomes available to nearby plants. If legumes are tilled back into the soil, succeeding crops benefit as well. In general, legumes that produce edible seeds, like beans, soybeans, chickpeas, and limas fix less nitrogen than those that are grown for their leaves, like alfalfa, clover, and vetch.

Inoculating Seeds with Bacteria

There are many species of *Rhizobium* bacteria and each one chooses a specific group of legumes with which to associate. *Rhizobium phaseolis* is the correct bacteria for beans, but peas require *Rhizobium leguminosarum*. Often these two bacteria are mixed to make an all-purpose pea and bean inoculant. Many older beans, like runner beans and heirloom varieties, are "promiscuous nodulators" and are able to use just about any strain of *Rhizobium* found in the soil. Newer varieties of peas and beans are more fussy about which *Rhizobium* they associate with, so they may respond better to inoculants.

Most soils have natural populations of *Rhizobium*. Some lack the bacteria, however, and you may have to inoculate your seeds by treating them with a dark powder containing the *Rhizobium* bacteria, available from mail-order seed companies and local nurseries (see pages 451–453). Simply place a tablespoon or so in a bag with moist seeds and shake them until they are well coated. When the coated seeds are buried, or when nodulated roots die, the soil will become infused with the *Rhizobium*. If you use *Rhizobium*, you should not use a high-nitrogen fertilizer, which inhibits their effectiveness.

Experts disagree as to whether inoculation is really necessary. Commercial pea and bean growers tend to fertilize with nitrogen and ignore inoculants. As a result, breeders look for peas and beans that are disease resistant, weather tolerant, and high yielding, but not necessarily good nodulators. Most heirlooms are better nodulators than recent types. If you're growing modern varieties in sandy, shallow, or poor soil or on a new garden site, you might try inoculating your seeds and looking for signs of successful nodulation.

There are a few important things to remember about legume inoculants:

- *Rhizobium* isn't very active in cool or acid soils.

- Peas require a different *Rhizobium* species than beans.

- *Rhizobium* can live in the soil for 3 to 5 years, so if you haven't grown any legumes in that time, it's better to inoculate.

- *Rhizobium* bacteria are living things. An inoculant may look like a powder, but it's alive. If you don't use it all immediately, be sure to refrigerate the rest. An inoculant that sits in the sun or on a nursery shelf for long periods is probably not viable. Always check your source.

continued on page 312

- If your soil has adequate *Rhizobium,* inoculating seeds will simply increase your yields a bit, like a fertilizer.

- High-nitrogen fertilizers tend to inhibit *Rhizobium* bacteria.

To see if your peas or beans have a good supply of bacteria on their roots, simply dig up (don't pull) a mature pea or bean plant as you harvest. You should see small whitish galls, or pealike growths, on the roots. These are the nitrogen-fixing nodules. Pinch some open. If they are white, then inoculation is poor. If they have a slight pink or reddish tinge, the bacteria are alive and well. The red color is caused by hemoglobin, which the bacteria produce to help harvest the air's nitrogen. Remember, the sign of good nodulation is the color, not the size.

SOILS AND FERTILIZERS

When you think about fertilizing peas, beans, and other legumes, consider the *Rhizobium* bacteria on their roots. Good supplies of phosphorous and potassium produce strong roots that can support large colonies of bacteria. The bacteria also need the trace elements iron and molybdenum to fix nitrogen, and a slightly alkaline soil to thrive. Trace elements are not available to plants in acid soil, so always correct acid conditions first.

DISEASES AND PESTS

Although peas and beans have some pests and diseases in common—like mildew, bean mosaic virus, and aphids—the differences are significant enough to warrant separate discussions under each vegetable.

NUTRIENT DEFICIENCIES IN PEAS AND BEANS

NUTRIENT	SYMPTOMS
Nitrogen (N)	Frail and light green plants; normally not a problem because peas get N from the air.
Phosphorus (P)	Slow growth, small leaves. Older leaves shrivel, beginning at edges, turn brown, and fall off.
Potassium (K)	Internodes of young leaves are very short. Older leaves have burned margins.
Calcium (Ca)	Young stems and leaf tissues wilt and collapse. Leaves yellow and margins have green veins. Pods and seeds are poorly developed. Older leaves turn brown and drop off.
Sulfur (S)	New leaves are very small. Plants are small and frail with vertical appearance because petioles slope at 45 degrees.
Magnesium (Mg)	Peas: Older leaves are yellow, with green veins and margins (unlike calcium deficiency). Beans: Upper surface of older leaves have rusty speckling (bronzing).
Iron (Fe)	New leaves curl downwards and are entirely yellow with irregular dead spots; older leaves are green.

Beans
FABACEAE (Legume or Pea Family)

Phaseolus vulgaris
  (French bean, string bean)
CHINESE: *cai dou*
FRENCH: *haricot vert, phaséole*
GERMAN: *Gartenbohne*
ITALIAN: *fagiolino*
JAPANESE: *ingen mame*
SPANISH: *judia común, faséolo*

If you haven't tasted fresh-picked home-grown snap beans, you're in for a surprise. Unlike fibrous commercial beans, which are bred for shipping, the beans you grow in your kitchen garden will be sweet, tender, and crunchy.

Beans are the most important source of vegetable protein, and one of the world's staple foods. Their pods and seeds are eaten throughout the world. The word *bean* actually applies to more than one group of plants. *Phaseolus* (snap, lima, pinto, navy, black, and runner beans) is the ancient bean of the New World, whereas *Vigna* (mung, adzuki, and garbanzo beans) is the ancient bean of the Old World.

Most beans require a long, warm growing season, but snap beans grow best in the short, warm seasons of otherwise cool climates. Snaps come in a bewildering array of heirloom and modern varieties that can be harvested from young pod to dry bean.

Snap beans are native to Central America. Fossil seeds dating to 5400 B.C. have been found in the Tehuaca'n Valley of Mexico. Native Americans grew snap beans among their corn, and New World explorers introduced them to Asia, Africa, and Europe. French Huguenot refugees first grew beans in Britain during the 1500s, hence the synonym "French" bean. They called the dried seeds *haricots* and the young pods *haricots verts*. Because they are very long and thin, and typically harvested when quite young, French snap bean varieties are also known as fillet ("small thread") beans. The pods and immature beans, eaten green before they dry, are called *flageolets* (which translates as "flutes"). The same bean was known in the United States as the green shell, snap, or string bean, not for its shape, but because of the fibrous strand that sealed each pod. Today most snap beans are stringless.

Snap beans are *Phaseolus* beans that are picked young, while the pods are still tender and edible. Most varieties can also be grown to maturity for their delicious and nutritious shell beans. These can be cooked fresh or dried and stored.

Green shell and dried beans are an excellent source of protein. In fact, a given weight of beans contain about 30 percent as much protein as steak, and none of the fat and cholesterol. Beans are high in lysine and thus complement corn and other grains, which are low in this essential amino acid. They are also a good source of vitamin B, calcium, and iron, and are second only to bran as a source of dietary fiber. The pods of snap beans have vitamins A and C, which the bean seeds lack.

Snap beans are best prepared simply. Steam them for a few minutes, then toss them with lemon, parsley, and garlic butter, and garnish with slivered almonds or crushed pecans. Or blanch them and serve with a vinaigrette.

Snap beans are also delicious in stews, soups, casseroles, and salads.

Dried beans are excellent cooked in soups and stews, or baked with honey or molasses and spices. To curb the flatulence that beans can cause, various cultures cook them with certain herbs (epazote in Mexico, winter savory in Germany).

CULTIVATION

The snap bean is a tender, warm-weather annual, which grows best in the warm seasons of otherwise cool climates. It prefers lots of sun and well-drained warm soil of 65° to 80°F. In cold soil, fungi, instead of *Rhizobium,* can colonize roots and plants will grow poorly.

Snap beans are an "in-between" vegetable. Adapted to the mild, constant temperatures of their native highlands of central Mexico and Guatemala, they don't like weather that is too hot or too cold. Air temperatures should not be less than 40°F at night or 60°F during the day. At the other end of the scale, the plants become stressed when days are warmer than 80°F. Temperature extremes will cause such problems as blossom drop, short and curled beans, poor yields, and deformed pods.

Always start your season with varieties advertised as "early." Try to plant dark-seeded types, like Royalty Purple, Provider, and Kentucky Wonder, as they're more cold-tolerant than the white-seeded types like Blue Lake. Also consider your soil texture: A sandy soil warms faster, so you can plant earlier than in a clayey soil.

Bush beans are an ideal vegetable for succession planting. Stagger your sowings every 2 or 3 weeks for a steady harvest during the season. Make the last sowing at least 3 months before the first winter frost for canning or freezing and for fall dishes. Summer heat in some areas will keep beans from bearing. Be patient. When temperatures moderate, your beans will flower and bear again.

PLANTING

Snap beans can be directly sown or transplanted. The key to rapid and successful germination is proper soil temperature. Germination in 60°F soil takes 2 weeks, and in 75°F soil it takes 8 days. If the soil temperature is less than 55°F, germination will not occur, and the seeds will rot or be eaten by seed maggots.

Use a soil thermometer and take the temperature a few inches underground about 1 week before the last spring frost. If it is less than 55°F, you can warm things up a bit with plastic film or a floating row cover secured over the soil surface. Also, try presprouting seeds in damp cloth (see "Peas," page 323). For better germination, plant bean seeds with the narrow side down. When seeds sprout, the embryonic root forces the seed up and out of the ground (unlike a pea seed, which stays in the ground), so this placement will aid germination.

Sow bush varieties 1 inch deep and 3 to 4 inches apart in rows 18 to 24 inches apart. When seedlings emerge, thin to 6 to 8 inches. Sow pole varieties 4 to 5 inches apart to grow up on poles or trellises. In high densities, bean plants will shade out weeds and conserve water. If densities are too high, however, air circulation will be poor and diseases will run amok. Proper spacing is an important part of growing snap beans.

For a faster and more reliable crop of snap beans, start plants from seedlings grown indoors (see "Peas," page 323).

Pole beans are one of the most space-efficient of vegetables. Every gardener has his or her own favorite way of trellising the wandering stems. See page 315 for more information on trellising.

BEANPOLES, TRELLISES, AND TEEPEES

Unlike peas, garden beans have few tendrils. They climb by wrapping their stems around long, thin objects, like beanpoles. The best time to set up poles and trellises for beans is right before you plant. Beans grow quickly and the young plants are brittle, so you don't want to work around them tying strings and pounding poles.

The bean teepees that are so often suggested in gardening books lend a quaint air to a garden, but they have some drawbacks. They don't use space very well, and the beans are often hard to see and harvest. Most of the space is at the bottom, where few beans grow. At the top, where most of the beans grow, the space gets very congested. Imagine pulling a teepee of poles apart and setting them in a row, and you'll see how much better trellises work than teepees.

There are several good methods. The most space-efficient system for harvesting and pest control is a row trellis made of wire or plastic mesh or poles tied to larger poles spaced about 6 feet apart. The mesh should be at least 6 inches square, or large enough to get a fistful of beans through. Alternatively, you can tie horizontal rows of string at the top and bottom of the poles, then zigzag more string up and down between them. Regardless of what your beans grow up, plan for a height of 6 to 7 feet for convenient harvest and pest control.

Examples of trellises

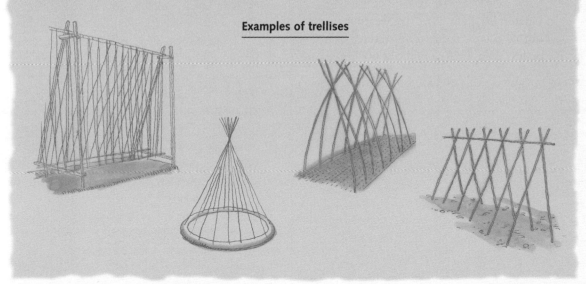

SOILS AND FERTILIZERS

Snap beans need a light but rich soil; cold, wet clay is deadly to them. Like most legumes, they need a neutral or slightly alkaline soil. Add only moderate amounts of fertilizer at planting time. Avoid high-nitrogen fertilizers, which discourage nodulation. Research has shown that regular foliar feeding with kelp extract during growth can increase yields by providing certain phytohormones.

Bush beans produce in a concentrated period of just 2 to 3 weeks. They appreciate side-dressings of 2-5-5 fertilizer at first flower bud. Pole beans produce over a longer time, so fertilize them more gradually.

For information on nutrient deficiencies in snap beans, see "Legumes," page 312.

DISEASES

Snap beans are subject to a number of diseases, but you can avoid most of them with good cultural practices. Don't grow beans in the same spot every year; rotate them throughout your garden. Leave open spaces between plants for good air circulation, and avoid cultivation when rain or dew is on the plants; this can spread diseases. Keep all bean plant residues out of the garden and in the compost bin. Avoid overhead watering, and always grow resistant varieties whenever possible. For added insurance, it's better to make several small plantings of many varieties at 2- to 3-week intervals. This way, if one planting is stalled by bad weather or pests, another will be coming along behind it to take its place. Finally, watch your seed sources. Many serious bean diseases are carried on the large seeds.

The **bean common mosaic virus (BCMV)** is such a serious disease that virtually all new varieties have been bred to be resistant to it. The disease is transmitted by aphids and carried on seeds and garden tools. Infected plants are stunted, with mottled yellow or green leaves that curl downwards. Many varieties will outgrow early problems if the plants are well watered and cared for. Most varieties are resistant to BCMV, but other viruses can be carried into the garden by aphids on surrounding weeds. The **bean yellow mosaic virus (BYMV)** causes bright yellow and green mottling on the leaves. It's transmitted by aphids, but is not carried on seeds. BYMV also attacks peas, sweet peas, and gladiolus, so avoid planting beans near these plants, and control for aphids. Always discard plants with an apparent viral disease. There is no cure for virus diseases other than using resistant varieties and eliminating the insects that carry them.

Bacterial blights overwinter on plant residue, so remove all spent bean plants from the garden. They're also carried on seeds; be careful if you save your own or swap seeds with others. Finally, avoid overhead watering and rotate beans through your garden.

Beans affected by **common blight bacteria (Xanthomonas)** have leaves and pods with spots that look water-soaked or greasy; brown sores also form on the stems and pods. BCM is especially severe in the hot, humid climate of the South.

Halo blight (Pseudomonas phaseolicola) is a bacteria carried on seeds. Affected plants wilt as the pods begin to develop. Pods, leaves, or stems will have greasy or watery spots surrounded by a pale green–yellow halo that fades into the green of the leaf. On pods, the halo is brown to red.

Anthracnose (Colletotrichum lindemuthianum) is a common fungal disease that develops quickly in cool, humid weather. Black, sunken areas with light centers show on pods, while the veins on undersides of leaves turn black. Anthracnose spores are carried on seeds and lurk in the garden on infected plant debris, so either dispose of it or compost it long and hard. Splashing water, tools, and gardeners can also help spread the disease from the debris. A few varieties of beans are resistant.

Root rot (Fusarium and other fungi) stunts plants or prevents the seeds from ever emerging. If your plant's roots are rotted or reddish in color, the cause is probably root rot, which is caused by soil-dwelling fungi. The best way to avoid it is to rotate beans every few years and sow seeds in a soil warm enough to facilitate quick sprouting.

Rust (Uromyces appendiculatus) can first be seen as reddish spots on the underside of leaves and on pods. Fungus rust spores can overwinter on plant residue and even beanpoles. If rust is a problem in your area, avoid high-nitrogen fertilizers, and space and water plants carefully. Don't water from overhead. Spray with sulfur or Bordeaux mix when spots first appear; this will kill new spores. Several resistant varieties of beans are available.

Powdery Mildew (Erysiphe polygoni) is

described in "Peas," page 325, and "Brassicas," pages 255–256.

PESTS

Beans, especially seedlings, are a favorite of slugs, snails, field mice, and birds. Cover young plants with bird netting or row cover, or handpick snails in the evening and early morning. Always protect your seedlings.

The **seedcorn maggot (*Hylemya cilicrura*)** is the larva of a fly and the cousin of the cabbage-root maggot. The seedcorn maggot eats organic matter, including seeds that are slow to germinate in cold soil. Grow beans from transplants or warm the soil with plastic, but avoid direct-sowing in cold soil, especially if it has lots of organic matter. If nothing comes up and you can't find the seed, the culprit is probably the seedcorn maggot.

Spider mites like hot, dry conditions, so they are usually found late in the season on downward-curled leaves with yellow stippling. Look *very* closely with a hand lens for signs of fine webbing on the underside of leaves around the veins; you'll see the spider mites and their eggs suspended in the webs.

A strong spray of water, weekly sprays of soap dilutions, or a spray of botanicals like neem and pyrethrin can control most mite problems, but you must be vigilant. When conditions are right, mites will breed faster than any insect. Early bean varieties usually escape attack because the weather is not yet warm enough. Mites favor plants coated with dusty soil, so keep a good mulch and the leaf dust down. Note that all recommended synthetic "miticides" also kill beneficial mites and insects.

Onion thrips are tiny pear-shaped insects that attack beans in the Western states. Affected plants will have leaves with retarded growth and white flecks. The symptoms resemble mite damage, and thrips are as tiny as mites. Thrips don't have any webbing, however, and they leave dark fecal pellets on the leaf surface. Also, thrips scrape and rasp the leaf surface away, whereas mites poke and puncture the tissue. Close inspection will reveal the difference.

Mexican bean beetles are voracious feeders in the eastern United States. Both the copper-colored adult and the spiny larvae devour leaves and young pods. Leaves look "skeletonized" and lacy, with just the veins remaining. Beetles overwinter in old bean plants, so a fall cleanup is very important. Row-covered plants and early-season varieties often escape damage. Commercially available wasps *(Pediobius)* that parasitize bean beetles are effective if used early (see page 171).

Leafhoppers and **aphids** are pests that feed by sucking plant sap, which stunts plants and causes curled and yellow leaves. Both insects also transfer virus diseases, so they are a double threat.

Adult leafhoppers are small wedge-shaped insects that jump around actively among the foliage when they are disturbed. You have to sit still for a few minutes to see them. Aphids are equally small pear-shaped insects that stay put in colonies. The bean aphid *(Aphis fabae)* is small and dark green. It also feeds on artichokes, asparagus, and members of the spinach family (chard, spinach, and beets). In diverse gardens, aphids and leafhoppers may be controlled by the presence of native beneficial insects and mites. You can also buy and introduce aphid midges, lady beetles, and lacewing larvae. Aphids and leafhoppers can be washed off with water and sprayed with insecticidal soaps or oils.

VARIETIES

Today there are over 600 varieties of beans available in the United States, including 227 shell beans (194 bush and 33 pole) and 374 varieties of snap beans (275 bush and 99 pole). All snap beans are open-pollinated, and many are important heirlooms. With so many types of beans to choose from, your preference will be based largely on flavor and regional considerations like climate and disease resistance.

Varieties are classified by growth habit (vine, bush), part eaten (young pod, full pod, green seed, or dried seed), pod color (green or yellow), and pod shape (flat, oval, or round).

Bush varieties produce clusters of flowers at the end of stems. These contain the plant's growth, make it look bushy, and force the plant to produce all of its pods early and over a short period. Bush varieties are the favorite of commercial growers, since they don't have to construct trellises, and harvesting can be done all at once.

Vine, or pole, beans grow their flowers on side branches. This allows the terminal stems to wind and weave. Pole beans produce later in the season than bush types, but they keep producing as long as the plant is growing. You don't have to bend over to harvest them, and many gardeners claim that pole beans taste better than bush types. The inconvenience of making a pole-bean trellis is offset by the superior flavor of the beans and the space-saving productivity of the plant. The high yield is due to the greater amount of leaf area exposed to the sun. A 10-foot row of pole beans growing up an 8-foot trellis has the same leaf area as 40 feet of bush beans. If you want to extend your bean harvest, mix the two when you plant. You'll get an early, concentrated harvest from bush varieties and a later, extended one from the vines.

Some varieties of snap beans can be eaten at each stage of development, from the immature pod to the dried seed. Other varieties have been bred to be eaten at one particular stage of growth. These varieties fall into four main groups:

1. Fillet beans, or *haricots verts*, as they are known in their native France, have very slender pods with slowly developing seeds. Fillet beans are true baby vegetables and are picked when they are no larger around than a pencil. They mature quickly and produce sugar at an early stage of growth. Most "baby vegetables" lack flavor, yet fillet beans pass the taste test with flying colors. On the other hand, they store and freeze poorly, and the window for harvesting is only a few days. For many gardeners, the fabulous taste of the fillet is worth it. For others, the fillet bean is too ephemeral, and the super-young pods of other varieties, which can also be eaten as mature pods, taste just as good. All fillet beans are bush types.

2. Snap or pod beans are picked when the pods are older but before the seeds develop. "Snap beans" are fresh, young pods that make a snapping sound when broken. The pods come in colors of green, purple, and yellow ("wax"), on bushes or vines.

3. Green shell, sometimes called "horticultural flageolet," beans can be eaten at any stage from fillet-sized pod to dried seed, but they are especially favored for their fresh seed. The beans are picked after the seeds are plump in the pod, but before they have dried. They are eaten and cooked just like lima and broad beans. Most flageolet beans are bush types, but a few are vines.

4. Dried beans are picked after the seeds are matured and dried in the pods. Many of our best-known dried beans, like kidney, navy, black, cranberry, and pinto, are simply snap beans that have been allowed to mature on the plant. Most of these can also be eaten as fresh seeds. Dried beans come in both bush and pole types.

In the future, look for bean varieties that are cold-tolerant and disease-resistant. Cold tolerance is difficult to breed into snap beans, but it is a highly desirable trait. Since beans are susceptible to many diseases, any degree of resistance or tolerance is also desirable. Future varieties will also fix more nitrogen.

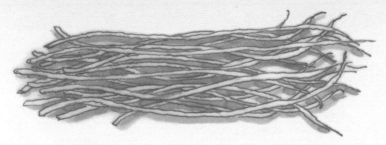

1. Fillet beans

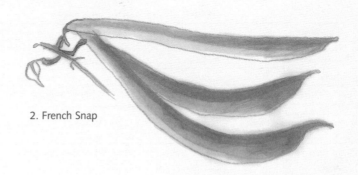

2. French Snap

3. Green shell bean

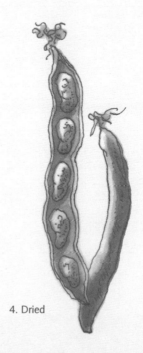

4. Dried

RECOMMENDED SNAP BEAN VARIETIES

TYPE/VARIETY	RESISTANCE	ATTRIBUTES AND COMMENTS
Fillet		
Tavera	A, BMV	Developed for French restaurant trade. Extra-short and slender. Small white seed.
Maxibel	A, BMV	Full-sized French fillet. Great taste. Keeps well.
Fin des Bagnols		Standard heirloom fillet bean from the 1800s.
Dorabel	BMV	French yellow (wax) fillet bean. Great taste.
Bush		
Black Valentine		Famous heirloom since 1850. Early snap, dried black bean for soups.
Bountiful		Heirloom since 1898. Flat pods. Tall bush. Early and productive.
Bush Blue Lake	BMV	Best tasting of this type. Standard for fresh, canning, or freezing. Slow to form seed.
Derby	BMV	1990 AAS winner. Vigorous bush with round, easy-to-harvest pods that set seed slowly. Great taste.
Narbonne	HB	Deep green. Slim, round pods. Very heavy yields. Eat fresh or freeze.
Provider	DM, PM, BMV	Round pods. Superior taste. Very early compact plant. Adapted to cool soils and diverse conditions.
Roma II	R, BMV	Bush Romano with flat meaty pods, green shell beans.
Tendercrop	BMV	Standard garden bush snap since 1958. Adapted to North, Midwest, and West. Holds well.
Tendergreen Improved		1933 AAS winner still delivers taste, disease resistance, heat tolerance, and early, heavy yields.
Topcrop	BMV	1950 AAS winner. Straight pods. Short harvest.
Wade	BMV, bean beetle	Straight, round pod. Great flavor, heavy yields.
Pole		
Blue Lake	BMV	Standard high-yielding pole bean. Round pods. Great climber to 7 feet.
Fortex		Early. Extra-long, round pods. Good eating, from fillet bean at 7 inches to fresh brown shell bean.
Hickman's		Heirloom. 12-foot vines ripen late. Fine for snaps and colorful dried seeds.
Kentucky Wonder Pole	R	Heirloom since 1850s. Popular pole bean. Strong, 5- to 7- foot plant. Good for snap, shell, and dried beans.
Cascade Giant		Improved from heirloom. Good for damp, cool soils. Pod mottled with purple.
Northeaster		Very early. Cold-tolerant. Flat pod. Rich flavor. Good for greenhouse culture.
Romano Pole	BMV	Classic Italian heirloom. Flat pods. Thick and meaty. Unique flavor. Snap or green shell beans.
Bush, Yellow (Wax)		
Brittle Wax		American garden heirloom since 1900. Long harvest. Good shell bean.
Dorabel	A, BMV, HB	Baby French wax with outstanding flavor.
Golden Wax	BMV	Superior bush wax. Early, suited to cold climates.
Goldkist	A, BMV, R	Long, slender gold-yellow pods. Superior taste. Harvest young.
Pencil Pod (Black) Wax	BMV, R	Highest quality. Heirloom since 1900. Best taste and texture. Very popular.
Roc d'Or	A, BMV	Long, straight, deep yellow pods. Germinates in cool soils. Pick early.
Pole, Yellow (Wax)		
Kentucky Wonder Wax		American heirloom since 1901. Everbearing. Good in cool climates.
Goldmarie		Golden Romano type. Use as snap or shell bean. Vigorous climber to 11 feet. Good in greenhouses.

A = Anthracnose; BMV = Bean mosaic virus; HB = Halo blight; R = Bean rust

RECOMMENDED SNAP BEAN VARIETIES, *continued*

TYPE/VARIETY	RESISTANCE	ATTRIBUTES AND COMMENTS
Purple Pod		
Trionfo		European heirloom with purple pods and leaves. One of the best. Turns green in cooking.
Royal Burgundy		Vigorous bush with dark purple pods that cook green. Great flavor. For cool soils.
Green Shell (Flageolet)		
Chevrier Vert		Classic French heirloom flageolet since 1880. Green shell or dried.
Vermont Cranberry Bush		Popular New England heirloom. Green shell or dried. Unique sweet taste. Hardy, easy to shell.
Lazy Wife		American heirloom since 1810 via Germany. First stringless snap bean. Late variety.
Horticultural King		Early. Known for large, early yields of delicious fresh seeds.
Tongue of Fire		Heirloom from Tierra del Fuego. Red-streaked pods good as snaps or dried green shell beans.

A = Anthracnose; BMV = Bean mosaic virus; HB = Halo blight; R = Bean rust

HARVEST

Whether you're growing fillet, snap, or shell beans, it's important to harvest at the right time. Remove all pods; this encourages the plants to produce more. Fillet beans must be picked every few days. For other snap beans, pick all pods before seeds begin to develop. If you miss a few, get ready for a different taste. Many bean aficionados like snaps with half-formed seeds inside, as they are rich and slightly starchy. Most snap beans will produce acceptable shell beans. If some seeds reach maturity, shell them and cook them with the pods or in stews and soups.

If you are growing a variety that produces both snap and dried beans; pick all the snap beans early in the season, then let the later ones mature at a slower pace. Snap beans have fragile stems. When you pull off the pods, use both hands, one to pick and the other to hold the vine steady. It doesn't take much effort to rip up entire sections of a bean plant in a haste to harvest its fruit.

SNAP BEAN GROWING TIPS

- Beans germinate poorly in cold soil. To plant early, set out transplants, or warm soil to 60°F with plastic mulch. Grow transplants in biodegradable containers like peat pots or bottomless paper cups to avoid disturbing the roots.

- Grow beans when day temperatures stay between 50° and 75°F. To help plants produce in hot weather, mulch the soil and keep it moist.

- Control watering when the plants are 1 to 2 weeks into flowering. Too much heat or water at this time can cause the pods to abort.

- Many bean diseases are transmitted on seeds. Get seeds from a reputable source, and be careful if you save or swap seeds.

- To avoid diseases, rotate crops, remove spent plants, avoid overhead watering, and grow resistant varieties.

- Harvest continually when beans are ready. Mature beans left on the plant will slow production. Cook them in stews and soups.

Peas
FABACEAE (Legume or Pea Family)

Pisum sativum sativum
(shell and snap pea)
CHINESE: *wan dou*
FRENCH: *pois potager, petit pois*
GERMAN: *Erbse*
ITALIAN: *pisello coltivato*
JAPANESE: *endou*
SPANISH: *giuisante*

Pisum sativum sativum var. macro carpon (Chinese or edible podded pea)
CHINESE: *tian cui wan dou*
FRENCH: *pois mange tout*
GERMAN: *Zuckererbse*
ITALIAN: *pisello mangiatutto*
JAPANESE: *kinusaya*
SPANISH: *guisante tirabeque*

One of the great joys of kitchen gardening is munching your way along a trellis of vine-ripened garden peas. Whether it's a shell pea (with edible seeds), snow pea (immature pea with edible pods), or snap pea (with edible seeds and pods), it's hard not to eat these delicious morsels before they get in the kitchen.

The garden pea has a long and noble history. Carbonized seeds discovered in Switzerland have been dated to 7000 B.C., making peas one of the few vegetables that can be traced back to the Stone Age. Native to an area stretching from northern India to Afghanistan, peas were cultivated by the Egyptians, Greeks, and Romans, though these were dried seeds that needed extended soaking before they could be eaten. It was not until the sixteenth century that tender varieties were bred to be eaten fresh. The snow pea was developed in Holland in the early 1600s. In 1787, the English began intercrossing varieties of peas, making them the first vegetable used to produce new varieties by controlled breeding. To this day, we call them "English" peas. In 1865, Gregor Mendel began his famous experiments with garden peas that were to lay the foundation of modern genetics. The snap pea was introduced to the gardening world in 1979. Peas have spanned the centuries, and they continue to be one of the most popular of vegetables.

Nutritionally, peas are important vegetables because of their high protein content. They are also a good source of phosphorous and vitamin B (thiamine, riboflavin, niacin, and pyridoxine), and a modest source of calcium and potassium. Wonderful eaten raw, quickly steamed, or stir-fried, peas add sweetness and texture to stews and soups, while pea sprouts give a unique texture and nutritious quality to salads.

CULTIVATION

The pea is a hardy cool-season annual that responds to both day length and temperature. Peas flower best during long days with cool temperatures. They grow best when the temperature is between 50° and 65°F; when the temperature exceeds 78°F, the plants suffer. Peas need as much cool weather as they can get in order to mature before sultry summer or frigid winter air makes them stop producing.

Peas are typically planted in the spring in most areas, and in the fall and early winter where there are few frosts. For a continuous harvest, sow several plantings of early varieties, like Knight and Sugar Bon, throughout the spring, along with one or two plantings of a later variety, like Alderman, Multistar, or Sugar Snap. Short, early types tend to ripen all at once, while tall varieties produce over a longer period. You can also make just one spring planting, with three or four varieties that mature at different times. This method is often preferred to succession planting in areas where warm late spring weather can cause second or third plantings to catch up with the first, resulting in a huge harvest of peas at one time.

It's important to trellis all varieties of peas, even the bush types. This allows you to grow more peas in less space, while guarding against rot and mildew by keeping the vines off the ground.

PLANTING

The trick to growing peas is twofold: germinate them successfully, then protect the young plants from munching animals, which crave the high protein and sweet taste of sprouting seedlings. Peas can be sown directly or grown from transplants. Direct-sowing, especially in the early spring, can be difficult, because pea seeds need a relatively warm soil to germinate (70° to 75°F), even though they grow best in cool weather (50° to 65°F). Consequently, many gardeners presprout pea seeds before they sow them, to get a jump on the season.

Many gardening books recommend soaking pea seeds in water for several hours to start them sprouting. But seeds can't absorb water this quickly; instead they may become waterlogged and suffer from "imbibition shock" by swelling too fast. In cold soil, they will then rot very quickly. A better method to "soak" seeds is to roll them in a damp cloth and place it in a warm, ventilated area. After a few days, the seeds will sprout, and can be directly sown

in the soil or in containers to grow transplant seedlings. Handle the sprouted seeds very carefully, though, because the embryonic roots and shoots are both brittle and irreplaceable.

To grow transplants, sow sprouted seeds in small containers. Peat pots are best, since peas do not like their roots disturbed, and peat pots can be set directly in the soil. Let the seedlings grow to at least 6 inches. Large transplants are less likely to get eaten, and they can be trained onto trellises much easier. Before planting, harden-off the seedlings for a few days in a cool space. If slugs, snails, or birds are a problem in your area, be sure to cover the seedlings with bird netting or a floating row cover to protect them from these marauders. Once seedlings are about 12 inches tall, they can usually outgrow most damage.

Peas do best when planted thickly. The optimum spacing is six to nine pea seeds or plants per foot of row, with rows 6 inches apart. Try not to thin peas, because this can damage the shallow roots.

It's important to rotate peas to different spots in your garden every season. Planting them in the same place year after year will inevitably cause disease problems, particularly root rot.

SOILS AND FERTILIZERS

Peas don't need much in the way of nitrogen because they make their own from bacteria living on their roots (see pages 311–312). They will, however, benefit from a boost of phosphorous and potassium, so add wood ashes and soft phosphate prior to planting, at a rate of 3 to 5 pounds per 100 square feet and then foliar feed with seaweed spray as the seedlings emerge. Peas need a good supply of trace elements to fix nitrogen, and fish emulsion or seaweed spray will provide them. Peas are sensitive to acid soils. If your soil pH is below 6.2, add limestone or dolomite (see pages 61–62). For information on nutrient deficiencies in peas, see "Legumes," page 312.

TRELLISING PEAS

Like their cousin, the snap bean, peas come in both bush and vine varieties (see page 327). Although seed catalogs describe the bush and short vine peas as not needing any trellis, most peas need some kind of support. Compact vines may do fine sprawling over each other at first, but wind and rain can entangle and mat them to the ground. They can also become top-heavy from the weight of ripening pods.

Peas climb by clinging with their tendrils. For bush and short vine varieties, simply stick firm, bare branches or brush cuttings into the ground, or tie a couple of horizontal strands of string between wooden stakes. For taller peas, use 6-foot fence posts and run three strands of plastic-coated wire between them. Starting 3 inches above the ground, zigzag strong string up and down between the wires so the tendrils can support the growing plants. You can also use plastic mesh or wire fencing between the stakes, but it is difficult to remove dead vines from these at season's end. Also, make sure you can get a fistful of peas through the mesh opening.

Examples of trellises for peas

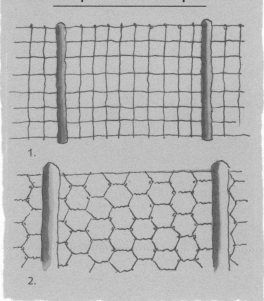

DISEASES

A number of virus diseases affect peas. They are all transmitted by aphids, including the pea, bean, and green peach aphids. **Pea enation virus (PEV)** is the most serious virus disease. The symptoms include yellowish spots on the top of the plant and clear spots on leaves that you can almost see through. Later on, the leaves are covered with bumpy, raised blisterlike wounds called "enations." The pods may become misshapen and split open. **Bean common mosaic virus (BCMV)** causes yellow mottling on leaves, which then become crinkled and stiff with curled edges. There are no controls for virus diseases except to grow resistant varieties and control for aphids (see "Brassicas," page 256, for more about this). Plant peas as early in the season as possible, before aphids are active.

Bacterial blight (*Pseudomonas pisi,*) is found everywhere except in arid Western regions. It damages the aboveground parts of the pea and produces large water-soaked spots on the pods, leaves, and stems. The spots turn brown and papery during dry weather. The bacteria is seedborne and survives in the soil and plant debris. It can also be spread by wind, water, insects, and gardeners tending plants, especially during cool, wet weather. To prevent infestation, buy your seeds from a reliable source, plant in well-drained soil, and after harvest, dig up and compost all pea plant debris. Clean all tools after using them around infected plants. There are no chemical controls or resistant varieties available.

Asochyta blight, or **pod spot,** is a seedborne fungus that affects peas in the central, southern, and northeastern states. Disease spores are also carried by wind and splashing water. Purplish to black irregular streaks appear on the pods and stems of affected plants. The controls are the same as for Bacterial blight.

Fusarium wilt is caused by the fungus *Fusarium oxysporum pisi*. It's quite widespread and causes stunting, yellowing, and a downward curling of the leaves. Another symptom is a reddish brown color on lower stems and upper roots. Transmitted by seeds, wind, or water, fusarium can remain in the soil for years, feeding on organic matter. It is more damaging in warm soils than cool ones. The controls are the same as for Bacterial blight.

Powdery mildew (*Erysiphe polygoni*) is common in warm, humid, or coastal climates. The fungus first appears on lower leaves as a white, powdery mold, usually on older plants late in the season. It is wind blown, but can also overwinter on plant debris and weeds. In later stages, the leaves develop yellow spots and drop off. Powdery mildew requires a thin film of water to spread, so it's a particular problem in foggy or humid areas of the South and along the East and West coasts. Powdery mildew spreads as the weather warms, so early planting helps to reduce the problem. Mildew is more serious where it's cool and shady and where plants are crowded, so plant in sunny areas of your garden and space plants for good circulation. Retard the spread of mildew by dusting with sulfur powder or spraying with compost tea, and repeat weekly as needed. Powdery mildew of peas can also attack and spread from snap beans, carrots, and brassicas.

PESTS

The **seed maggot** is the larva of a small fly (*Hylemya cilicrura*) that lays its eggs at the soil surface. The larvae bore into the seed before it germinates, especially in soils high in organic matter. Planting early or growing plants from seedlings is the best way to avoid this problem.

The **pea aphid (*Acyrthosiphon pisum*)** sucks plant sap and transmits the viruses that cause pea enation and bean mosaic. As aphids feed, leaves curl up, turn yellow, and wilt. The pea aphid is a relatively large, pale green aphid with black legs. The **bean aphid (*Aphis fabae*)** also attacks peas, but is darker and smaller and, unlike the pea aphid, feeds on plants other than legumes.

It's important to watch carefully for aphids and control them as soon as possible, as they increase very rapidly. Control them with soap, botanical sprays, or row covers, or by encouraging their many natural enemies, such as lady beetles, lacewing larvae, and parasitic wasps (see Chapter 4 for more about this).

The **pea weevil (*Bruchus pisorum*)** is a widespread problem. The small $1/4$-inch-long, dark brown adults feed on blossoms and lay orange to white eggs on the pods. The small, white grublike larvae bore into the pods and feed on the seeds. Adults overwinter in plant debris and are carried on seeds. Clean up all spent crops and cultivate the soil to eliminate overwintering adults. Buy seeds from reputable sources.

Other insects found on peas include **onion thrips** (page 214), **flea beetles** (pages 365–366), **cucumber beetles** (page 332), and **stinkbugs.** Exclude these pests with floating row covers.

VARIETIES

There are over 130 varieties of shell and snap peas, plus 60 varieties of snow peas on the market today. They are all open-pollinated. Technically, the shell pea is a different variety than the snow pea. The botanical difference between the two lies in the absence of a thin parchmentlike lining on the inside of the snow pea. In shell peas, this lining makes the pods unpalatable.

Shell pea varieties are classified by seed color, growth habit (bush or vine), and seed texture (smooth or wrinkled). Starchy peas have smooth seeds and are adapted to colder temperatures, while sugary peas have wrinkled seeds. A new type of shell pea produces large yields because its pods grow in pairs. Examples include Knight, Multistar, and Maestro. In 1986, another type of shell pea appeared in seed catalogs. Called the "afila," or semi-leafless, pea, this new type has several advantages over traditional varieties. Most of the small leaflets on the stem become tendrils, so that the plants entangle and form a self-supporting mass. This allows sunlight and air to circulate through the vines, helping to prevent diseases. Moreover, afila peas produce their pods at the top of the plant for easy harvesting, and they are resistant to powdery mildew. Novella II is one afila variety.

Shelling Peas

As soon as Sugar Snap hit the market in 1979, snap peas became standard fare in American kitchen gardens. In response to gardeners' demands, plant breeders have developed improved snap pea varieties with more

Snap Peas

disease resistance, larger pods, and shorter vines. Look for new semi-leafless varieties with increased pod size and disease resistance.

Snow peas are the original edible-pod pea, to be eaten while the pods are still flat. Breeders at Oregon State University have recently produced two impressive varieties: Oregon Giant and Oregon Sugar Pod II.

Snow Peas

Peas are self-fertilizing, and all varieties are open-pollinated. This means that it's easy to save seeds and begin developing your own local strains. Try to isolate your favorite varieties by at least 50 feet, or cage them to prevent the occasional visiting bee from mixing the varieties. Remember that many pea diseases are seed borne, so if you save your seeds, watch for signs of disease on plants you grow from your own seed.

HARVEST AND STORAGE

In order to reap the full flavor of peas, you must harvest them at the proper time. In fact, when you pick peas is often more important than the variety you plant. Peas are less flavorful before they mature, but they are also quick to convert their sugars to starch, leaving only a narrow time window for harvesting.

Harvest peas when they still have their bright green color; dull-colored pods with a waxy, opaque exterior ("netting") mean the flavor has already peaked. Peas can overripen in just a few days, so visit the pea patch regularly and when the peas are ready, harvest daily to encourage more production. Pick peas in the early morning, because the pods are crisper then and will keep longer. Put them in a paper bag and put that bag into a plastic bag. The paper bag absorbs excess moisture, while the plastic bag holds in enough moisture to keep the peas fresh.

PEA GROWING TIPS

- Purchase seeds from a reputable nursery, because many pea diseases are seed borne.

- Grow short varieties to save space and produce early harvests at one time. Grow tall varieties for larger, later harvests over a longer period of time. Always grow disease-resistant varieties when possible.

- Plant in well-drained, non-acid soil. Erect trellises for all varieties before planting.

- Sow as early in the season as possible and harvest before hot, early summer days. Where spring soil stays wet, grow peas in raised beds.

- Set seeds or seedlings in dense plantings no more than 2 inches apart. Protect seedlings with bird netting or floating row covers to discourage pests. Watch for and control aphids, which carry diseases.

- Avoid deep cultivation around plants, as the roots are shallow and tender.

- Harvest carefully when pods are well filled, but before they begin to harden or fade in color. Pick peas every day when they are ready.

RECOMMENDED PEA VARIETIES

VARIETY	TYPE	RESISTANCE	ATTRIBUTES AND COMMENTS
Shell Peas			
Alaska*	Vine, smooth seed		Heirloom since 1880. Named for a speedy steamship. One of the earliest of peas.
Alderman*	Tall vine, wrinkled seed		Heirloom since 1891. Standard for fresh, canning, or freezing.
American Wonder	Short bush		Extra-dwarf and early midseason pea. Drought tolerant.
Dwarf Telephone*	Bush	Fu	Heirloom since 1888. Late variety. Good yield.
Green Arrow	Short vine	Fu	Best taste. Low resistance. Long-bearing main crop. First double-podded pea.
Knight	Short vine	Fu, PE, PM	Popular, earliest large-podded pea. Great resistance.
Little Marvel*	Bush/short vine	Fu	Heirloom since 1900. Early, sweet, and tender. Heavy yields. Good freezer. Extended harvest.
Maestro	Short vine	Fu, PE, PM	One of the best all-around double-podded shell peas. Green Arrow type.
Multistar	Tall vine	Fu	One of the best late varieties. Double-podded.
Novella II	Short vine	PM	Outstanding afila pea.
Progress #9 Blue Bantam	Short vine, wrinkled seed	Fu	Vigorous, early large-podded pea. Standard early garden variety.
Thomas Laxton*	Tall vine	Fu	Heirloom since 1898. Good near coasts.
Top Pod	Short bush	Fu, PE, PM	Heat tolerant and disease resistant. Huge pods. Great pea.
Wando	Vine, wrinkled seed		Heat tolerant for late plantings. Great flavor.
Snow Peas			
Dwarf Gray Sugar*	Tall bush		Heirloom before 1773. Earliest and most dwarf of sugar peas.
Norli	Short vine		One of the best sugar peas for yield and taste.
Oregon Sugar Pod II	Bush	Fu, PE, PM	Multiple disease resistance. Best in its class. Good for freezing.
Oregon Giant	Short vine	Fu, PE, PM	First large-podded, sweet-tasting snow pea.
Snap Peas			
Cascadia	Short vine	PE, PM	Early, tasty, disease-resistant; second generation of snap peas.
Sugar Ann	Short vine		AAS winner. Best extra-early, short-vined snap.
Sugar Bon	Bush	PM	Earliest snap pea. Heat tolerant.
Sugar Daddy	Short vine	PM	First snap with stringless pods. Best snap for freezing.
Sugar Snap	Tall vine		Original snap pea. Good in heat and cold. Poor disease resistance.
Super Sugar Mel	Short vine	PM	Largest podded snap pea.
Super Sugar Snap	Vine	PM	Earlier and more resistant than Sugar Snap.

Disease resistance: Fu = Fusarium, PM = Powdery mildew, PE = Pea enation virus   * Indicates heirloom variety.

CUCURBITS (Squash Family)

Squash, melons, pumpkins, cucumbers, and gourds are members of the Cucurbitaceae family, also known as cucurbits. Plants in this family grow a gourdlike fruit, called a pepo, with a thick outer skin, large seeds, and a soft inner flesh.

Garden cucurbits come from all over the world. Cucumbers are native to India, muskmelons to Africa and India, loofah sponges to tropical Asia, watermelons to South Africa, and squashes to Central and South America. In spite of their varied origins, most cucurbits are warm-season tender annuals, thriving in hot, humid weather and disliking frost. This makes many of them suitable for greenhouse growing. Cucurbits tend to have a spreading growth habit and bear tendrils. Bushy and cold-tolerant varieties are becoming more available, so look for them.

This section covers summer squash, winter squash, pumpkins, and cucumbers. The first three are discussed under "Squash"; cucumbers are discussed separately.

KITCHEN GARDEN CUCURBITS	
BOTANICAL NAME	**COMMON NAME**
Cucurbita	**Squashes and Pumpkins**
pepo	Summer squash: zucchini, crookneck, scallop. Vegetable gourd. Field and pie pumpkins. Autumn squash: acorn, spaghetti, ornamental gourd.
maxima	Winter squash: buttercup, banana, turban, Hubbard, sweetmeat squash. Giant pumpkins.
moschata	Winter squash: butternut, melon squash. Cheese and Dickinson pumpkins. Golden cushaws.
Cucumis	**Melons and Cucumbers**
sativus	Cucumbers: slicing, pickling, yellow.
melo	Melons: Asian pickling, honeydew or casaba, muskmelon or netted melon. Armenian cucumber.
Others	
Citrullus vulgaris	Watermelons
Lagenaria siceraria	Bottle and dipper gourds.
Luffa cylindrica	Dishrag or loofah sponge.

CLASSIFYING AND CROSSING CUCURBITS

Cucurbits produce a bounty of large seeds, and gardeners are often tempted to save open-pollinated varieties for next year's squash patch. (Note: Don't save seeds from hybrids, as they will generally revert back to the inferior characteristics of the parents.) Cucurbit seeds are easy to swap, count, and trade, so they're a common barter item for seed savers. The problem is that most garden cucurbits are from a few closely related species that loosely interbreed with one another. If you save or exchange seeds, it's important to check out your source to make sure that interbreeding strains have been isolated from one another.

For example, if you grow zucchini and crookneck squash with a Jack-O-Lantern pumpkin and you plant the seed from their fruit the next year, there's no telling what you'll get. The problem is both these squashes are the same species *(pepo)*. A few plants may look like their parents, but most will be somewhere between a straight yellow "pumpkini" and a crooked green "zumpkin."

The potential for crossing can be summa-rized as follows: Any two or more varieties of the same species will cross with another (see page 328). For example, crookneck and scallop *pepo* squashes will cross, as will Hubbard and Buttercup *maxima* squashes. The major crossing that occurs *between* species is in the *Cucurbita*. Both *C. pepo* and *C. maxima* will cross with *C. moschata*, but *C. pepo* will not cross with *C. maxima;* that is, a pie pumpkin will not cross with a giant pumpkin. Melons and cucumbers *(Cucumis)* cross occasionally with one another but not with squashes.

The integrity of the seed you buy depends on how well the breeder isolated the desired variety from other cucurbits. If a strange squash creation grows from a seed gift or purchase, you'll know there was a cross somewhere.

Knowing the classification of cucurbits can help you in another way. In nurseries and seed catalogs, the common names "squash," "pumpkin," and "melon" are often used casually and interchangeably. The best way to get what you want is to specify a plant by its botanic name.

CULTIVATION

Except for some cucumbers, squash family plants are "monoecious;" that is, they have both male and female flowers on the same plant. Look carefully at your squash or melon plants in full bloom. You'll notice that some flowers have a swelling behind them and a short, thick center. These are the female flowers. The male flowers have no such swelling, but they do have a tall, thin center. If you want to hand-pollinate, cull flowers for better production, or harvest male squash blossoms without affecting the harvest, you'll need to know the difference.

Usually the first few flowers to appear on a cucurbit are male. Gardeners sometimes worry about this when they observe that no fruit is setting. In a short time, however, female flowers will appear.

Cucurbits are pollinated mainly by bees and beetles. Most of these pollinators are active in the early morning, so avoid watering your squash patch at this time. If you are in an area with few insects, you can be the pollinator. Simply cut away a new male flower in the morning and rub the pollen-laden stamen (the spur in the center of the flower) around the inside of a newly opened female flower.

PLANTING

Cucurbits can be sown directly or transplanted. If you sow directly, be sure the soil is warm. If the soil is cold, the seeds will rot. Warm the bed by covering it with clear plastic, or sow seeds in hills. If you save or trade seeds, dip them in a 10 percent chlorine solution before planting to prevent seed-borne diseases.

Cucurbits usually get off to a better start if they are grown from transplants. Start them indoors about the time of your last spring frost. Thinning disturbs the roots, so place one seed each in a peat pot filled with potting mix. Cucurbits need warm temperatures to sprout quickly. At 60°F, germination takes about 2 weeks, at 70°F it takes 1 week, and at 85° it takes 3 days, so keep seeds in a warm place with lots of indirect light.

Cucurbits have deep roots. Cucumbers, muskmelons, and summer squash, for example, can grow roots 3 to 4 feet deep; pumpkin, winter squash, and watermelon roots can grow even deeper. As soon as the seed germinates, the root starts growing faster than the shoot, and it quickly becomes crowded in small containers. Don't leave the seedlings of cucurbits in small containers for more than a couple of weeks. Be ready to set your seedlings 2 to 3 weeks after they sprout, or when the first pair of true leaves (the second pair of leaves) fully appear. Transplant 2 to 4 weeks after the last spring frost—earlier for sandy soils, later for clayey ones. Warm soils and warm nights are the keys to helping cucurbits off to a quick, healthy start.

NUTRIENT DEFICIENCIES IN CUCURBITS	
NUTRIENT DEFICIENCY	**SYMPTOM**
Nitrogen (N)	Uniform yellowing of older leaves.
Phosphorous (P)	Young leaves are dull emerald green.
Potassium (K)	All leaves light yellow, some with dead brown tissue on the margins.
Calcium (Ca)	Very young leaves have dead, brown tissue at their tips; patchy yellowing between the veins.
Sulfur (S)	Young leaves are a uniform pale yellowish green.
Magnesium (Mg)	Yellow and white marbled specks on older leaves, similar to mosaic disease, but also includes specks of dead tissue between veins.
Boron (B)	Cracks in young leaf stems. Cracks in fruit, especially cucumbers.

DISEASES

Cucurbits are pest-prone vegetables. As a group they tend to attract similar insects and diseases, though there are unique pest problems. Diseases include several viral mosaics, bacterial wilt, fruit rots, mildews, and leaf spots. Borers, squash bugs, and beetles are the major insect pests. Floating row covers help to keep out many insects; just remember to remove the cover at the first sight of female flowers so they can be pollinated. Otherwise you'll have to do it yourself.

Several virus diseases affect cucurbits. The most widespread is the **cucumber mosaic virus (CMV),** which is transmitted by aphids and both spotted and striped cucumber beetles. The virus also attacks many weeds, beans, peppers, spinach, and tomatoes, plus several flowers like aster, geranium, larkspur, marigold, and petunia. Infected seedlings turn yellow and die, while in older plants the virus causes stunting and a yellow-green mottling, distortion, and downward curling of the leaves. Also look for white blotches among raised, dark green blisters on diseased cucumbers. Infected summer squash is knobby and distorted. Control weeds in and around cucurbits. Watch for aphids (see "Brassicas," page 256), which carry CMV. Pull out and destroy all infected plants. Make sure your hands and any tools you have used around virus-diseased plants are cleaned before contacting other plants. Other virus diseases include **papaya ring spot virus** (formerly watermelon mosaic virus), which causes leaves to look like shoestrings, and **zucchini yellow mosaic virus.**

Bacterial wilt of cucurbits *(Erwinia tracheiphila)* causes wilting and death of the leaves and stems of most cucurbits, especially cucumbers and melons. The bacteria enter wounds caused by feeding insects and plant damage. Leaves wilt quickly, followed by a progressive death of the entire plant. Bacterial wilt is only found east of the Rockies. It can be distinguished from other wilts by the white substance that oozes out of leaves when they are cut open. The wilt bacteria overwinter only in the gut of the striped cucumber beetle. As beetles feed, the bacteria enter the wounds and infect the water-conducting tissue (xylem), which causes wilting. Remove all infected plants and protect young seedlings from beetles with floating row covers.

Angular leaf spot *(Pseudomonas syringae)* is a bacteria that attacks cucumbers, melons, and summer squash. Warm, moist weather and wet conditions in the morning favor the disease. The first things you see are sharply defined, irregularly shaped spots on the underside of the leaves. When leaves are wet, tearlike droplets may ooze from the wounds. Eventually the spots die out, leaving jagged holds. If the disease attacks the fruit, you will see distortion or rotting. The bacteria live on seeds and plant debris. Winds, splashing water, and working gardeners spread the disease from plant to plant. Buy reputable seeds, rotate cucurbits every 3 years, use resistant varieties, avoid overhead watering, and clean up all diseased crop residue.

Downy mildew *(Pseudoperonospora cubensis)* is a fungal disease of cucurbits, especially in the Gulf and Atlantic states. The first signs are angular yellow spots on the tops of older leaves, which turn brown on the underside. Sometimes a fine grayish mold also appears on the underside. Downy mildew is encouraged by rainy, humid weather with temperature in the 60s. Disease is borne on seeds and plant debris, so care must be taken not to spread it. Grow resistant varieties. For more, see "Brassicas," page 255.

If you overhead-water or live in areas with fog or high humidity, a single film of water can settle on leaves providing ideal conditions for **powdery mildew** *(Erysiphe cichoracearum)*. Leaves don't have to be wet for powdery mildew to take hold; even moist air provides a hospitable environment. In midsummer, look for circular white spots on the underside of older leaves. These spread quickly until a gray or white powder covers most of the plant. Growth soon slows and the plants may die. Disease spores are borne on the wind, in crop debris, and in weeds. The disease spreads rapidly when conditions are right. Grow resistant varieties and clean up crop residue. Encourage air circulation. A bordeaux fungicide is effective in stopping the spread of the disease early on. So is a mixture of water, oil, and sodium bicarbonate. Do not use sulfur on cucurbits; it will burn them.

PESTS

The **melon aphid** *(Aphis gossypii)* is found throughout the warmer regions of the United States. The pale yellow to black-colored insect colonizes the underside of leaves. The melon aphid prefers cucurbits, but it also feeds on other vegetables and weeds. As it sucks juices, the leaves become distorted and eventually die. Melon aphids are double trouble because they can also transmit cucumber mosaic and other virus diseases.

During most of the year, natural predators and parasites keep the melon aphid at bay. When a cool, wet spring is followed by a hot, dry summer, the numbers of melon aphids can explode. If so, spray with insecticidal soap or a citrus-based oil spray.

Squash bugs feed by sucking sap from leaves. A toxin that they carry makes the leaves turn black and die. These symptoms are called "anasa wilt" and resemble those of bacterial wilt. Adult squash bugs are about $3/4$ inch long, with a flat back and tan to dark brown mottling. The nymphs look like adults without the wings; small ones are green and red and larger ones are gray with dark legs. Look for reddish eggs on the underside of leaves beginning late spring.

Adults overwinter under plant debris, cold compost piles, rocks, boards, litter, and unfortunately, coarse mulch. The first step in controlling the squash bug is to keep the garden area as tidy as possible and to mulch carefully. Use a dense mulch like sawdust, grass clippings, or compost rather than straw or other coarse material that offers refuge for bugs. Protect young plants with floating row covers until they bloom. Several predatory insects eat squash bugs, so increase plant diversity and decrease spraying to encourage them. If you must spray, use insecticidal soap or rotenone on nymphs and sabadilla on adults.

Seedcorn maggots (Delia platura), or fly larvae, eat the large seeds of beans, corn, and squash when seeds are sown in cold soil. Large warm-weather seeds in cold soil are a banquet for creatures looking for decaying organic matter. To avoid the seed maggot, set out transplants or sow into warm soil.

If long, greenish yellow beetles with stripes or spots are munching on your cucurbit leaves, they are one of several species of **cucumber beetle (Diabrotica spp.)**. As a group, they often get confused with lady beetles. The adults eat pollen, flowers, and leaves, and also spread bacterial wilt disease. The larvae live in the soil and eat roots, so it's important to rotate cucurbits if you have this beetle.

East of the Rockies, the **southern corn rootworm (Diabrotica undecimpunctata)** is widespread except in the north, where it is limited due to the cold soil. Larvae attack the roots of squash, grasses (like corn), and beans. Adults eat the foliage of cucurbits, plus a broad range of other vegetables and garden plants.

The **western corn rootworm (Diabrotica virgifera)** eats squash blossoms as an adult, but the larvae feed only on corn roots. The adults have three black lines on their wing covers like the striped cucumber beetle, but with a difference. On the striped cucumber beetle the lines are straight, but stripes on the rootworm beetle are wavy. The **western spotted cucumber beetle** is a minor pest of squash along the Pacific Coast.

Striped cucumber beetles (Acalymma vittata) are a serious pest east of the Rockies, particularly in the Northeast. The $1/5$-inch-long yellowish green adult has a black head and three black stripes on its wing covers.

The beetle overwinters as an adult and begins feeding early in the spring on the leaves and flowers of several trees and shrubs. As squash plants emerge, the beetle moves to the seedlings. The larvae develop on and eat the roots of squash-family plants. The adults eat flowers and leaves; they also transmit both cucumber mosaic virus and bacterial wilt disease. Look for the adults at the base of plants or on the underside of leaves.

Cucumber beetles are difficult to control. The rich, moist soil that vegetables like is also favored by the beetle larvae. Start by protecting curcubit seedlings from flying adults with floating row covers. Keep them in place until plants bloom. Handpicking is difficult because the adults drop to the ground and hide. Natural enemies are usually not effective in controlling this beetle. Look for traps with the lure of the scent of squash (curcurbitacin) and mixed with insecticidal dusts. Botanical pesticides like neem will kill high numbers of adults.

The **squash vine borer (Melittia curcubitae)** is a pest found east of the Rockies, and it feeds only on cucurbits. The borer is a large dark-headed white caterpillar that bores into and eats stems and fruit; the stems wilt and die. You'll also notice piles of yellow-green material around holes in the stem. The adult is a large, beautiful black and orange moth with clear wings and long, narrow antennae. The adults lay eggs on the stems of cucurbits, preferring squash to pumpkin and pumpkin to cucumber. The caterpillars feed for a month or so, then enter the soil to overwinter.

To control the borer, till the soil deeply to kill all larvae. Many of the *moschata* cucurbits, like the butternut squash, are fairly resistant. Rotate cucurbits together well away from spots recently planted with cucurbits. Start plants early or late to avoid the borer's June/July activity period.

Other insect pests of cucurbits include **onion thrips** (see page 214), **pickleworms,** and **whiteflies.**

Squash
CUCURBITACEAE (Gourd or Squash Family)

Cucurbita pepo
    (summer squash)
CHINESE: *meiguo nan gua*
FRENCH: *courgette*
GERMAN: *Garten-Kürbis*
ITALIAN: *zucca, zucchini*
JAPANESE: *pepokabocha*
SPANISH: *calabacin, zapallito*

Cucurbita moschata
    (winter squash)
CHINESE: *zhong guo*
FRENCH: *courge muscarde*
GERMAN: *Moschuskürbis*
ITALIAN: *zucca moscada*
JAPANESE: *nihon kabocha*
SPANISH: *calabaza moscada*

Cucurbita maxima
    (winter squash)
CHINESE: *yin du nan gua*
FRENCH: *potiron, grosse courge*
GERMAN: *Riesen-Kürbis*
ITALIAN: *zucca gigante*
JAPANESE: *seiyou*
SPANISH: *calabaza grande*

Squash evolved in Central and South America over 8,000 years ago. Along with beans and corn, squash was a staple food of ancient America. This vegetable triumvirate, known as the "three sisters," nourished Native Americans for thousands of years and provided a food base for the Maya, Inca, and Aztec civilizations. European settlers quickly adopted squash into their diets, and it became a mainstay in pioneer and homestead gardens and storage cellars.

Current evidence suggests that ancient peoples first used wild gourds as rattles in ceremonies, then as containers for food and water. Later, squashes were probably grown for their protein-rich seeds long before their flesh was eaten. Today we tend to focus on the flesh and forget the seeds.

Squash comes in a wonderful diversity of sizes and shapes. From the ever-popular zucchini to the sunny crooknecks, pear-shaped butternuts, warty-skinned blue Hubbards, and disk-shaped, fluted scallops in white, green, and gold; there is a squash for everyone.

All garden squash and pumpkins are closely related and belong to one of three species, *Cucurbita pepo, C. maxima,* and *C. moschata* (see "The Three Species of Common Garden Squash," page 336). Each species has different growing, cooking, and storage qualities. You don't have to be a squash expert to tell the species apart. Simply look at the shape and texture of the stem (peduncle) where it attaches to the fruit. There are also differences in seeds and leaves. It's useful to know the species of squash if you are interested in saving seeds and avoiding unwanted cross-pollination (see "Cucurbits," page 329). Other than that, it's probably more important to know the vital statistics of each variety: appearance and taste; days to maturity; resistances; and growing conditions.

Many cooks have a limited repertoire of squash dishes. We all enjoy zucchini and baked winter squash and pumpkin pie during the holidays. But the truth is, squash is much more versatile than most people think. It usually takes only one helping of pumpkin bread, squash soup, or baby squash tempura to turn anyone into a squash lover.

Summer squash is usually cooked, but it can be eaten raw. In fact, the word squash comes from a Native American word meaning "something eaten raw." Sliced or grated, raw squash will pep up any green salad or cabbage slaw. Squash can be baked, grilled, boiled, sautéed, or stir-fried, and used in soups, salads, entrees, breads, or desserts. Only a few vegetables can claim such versatility.

Try cooking several varieties of summer squash—green, yellow, and white—together to make a colorful dish, then season it with herbs and spices. Summer squashes combine well with tomatoes, eggplant, bell peppers, onions, and pasta. Grill zucchini halves with a sprinkle of olive oil and garlic.

Some summer squashes are eaten when very small and their blossoms are still at-

Crookneck

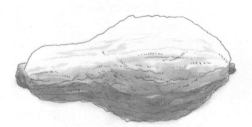

Butternuts

Hubbard

Yellow Scallop

tached. Squash blossoms give pizzazz to salads. They are also make great soup or can be stuffed with a favorite filling and sautéed or steamed.

Winter squash has a sweeter, firmer, drier flesh than summer squash. You can eat it plain or enhance its natural sweetness with cinnamon, honey, or pumpkin pie spice. Small squash that are halved and stuffed with seafood, vegetables, or grains make a savory one-dish meal. Add chunks of squash to stews and vegetable chowders. Winter squash is a perfect complement to the clean, sharp flavors of greens and brassicas.

Winter squash can also be mashed or puréed and topped with fruit, nuts, seeds, cheese, or bread crumbs. Almost any squash purée will substitute for pumpkin in cookies, cakes, puddings, and pies, and you can use it to thicken and flavor soups. One guaranteed winner is puréed squash thinned with broth and topped with yogurt and chopped parsley. Some gardeners prefer to store their winter squash as frozen purée. It lasts longer (up to a year), takes less space, and is always ready for quick use in baked goods and soups.

Squash provides a trio of cancer-fighting nutrients: fiber, vitamin C, and carotene (vitamin A). Winter squash is higher in fiber and carotene (which provides the orange color), summer squash in vitamin C. There's an added bonus. Pumpkin and other squash seeds contain a chemical (protease trypsin inhibitors) that may slow the growth of cancer, especially that of the prostate gland.

Curcurbita pepo

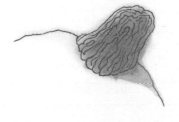

Curcurbita maxima

Curcurbita moschata

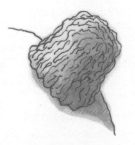

Curcurbita mixta

THE THREE SPECIES OF COMMON GARDEN SQUASH				
SPECIES OF CUCURBITA	**FRUIT STEM AND LEAF**	**SEED**	**PESTS**	**COMMENTS**
pepo				
summer squash, field and pie pumpkins, acorn and spaghetti squash	Fruit stem: hard with 5 sharp ridges that expand gradually to fruit. Leaf: triangular, saw-like edges; surface prickly, often irritating	Smooth, flat, and usually cream-colored with white margins	Susceptible to pests because of hollow, juicy stems.	Summer squashes don't keep well. Acorn types keep poorly and get stringy and less sweet with age.
maxima				
banana, Hubbard, buttercup, giant pumpkin	Fruit stem: round, smooth, with soft, corky texture; expands at the base. Leaf: hairy circular or kidney-shaped, ruffled edges.	Plump, smooth, and shiny white-brown, with . cream-colored margins	Susceptible to pests because of soft juicy stems. Borers, wilts, and rots enter stem wounds.	From South America. Tolerates cool weather best. Stores longer than *pepo*, shorter than *moschata*. Flesh is sweet, dry, and stringless.
moschata				
butternut, cushaws, cheese pumpkin	Fruit stem: hard and narrow with 5 ridges that expand at the base with knobs. Leaf: broad, heart-shaped, with five lobes; surface hairy but not prickly.	Small, beige, with grainy texture and brown scalloped margin.	Relatively resistant, especially to borers, due to hairy leaves and solid stems.	From tropical lowlands. Needs warm nights. Medium to large fruit, orange flesh. Best keepers. Taste sweetens with age. Green, tan, or mottled white rinds.

CULTIVATION

Squash are frost-tender, vigorous, annual vining plants with large leaves. They need warm weather; a sunny location; deep, rich soil; and plenty of air circulation. *Cucurbita moschata* (butternut squash) evolved in the tropical lowlands of Central America and grow best where nights are warm and days are humid. *Cucurbita maxima* (most winter squash) evolved in the foothills of Bolivia and Argentina. They can tolerate cooler and drier conditions. For the most part, all squash, including pumpkins, are grown in similar ways and suffer similar pests. The real differences among squash are the timing of the harvest and the way they are cooked.

In cold winter areas, squash are planted in the spring, 2 to 4 weeks after the last frost. In milder areas, summer squash can enjoy a second season in late summer and fall while the winter squash ripen.

PLANTING

Sow directly in the garden when all danger of frost is past. Place seeds about 1 inch deep in rows or hills 2 to 4 feet apart. Seeds germinate poorly in cool, wet soil (below 65°F).

To get a jump on the season, start your squash in individual pots 2 to 3 weeks before the last frost. Squash don't like to be transplanted and don't like their roots disturbed, so place just one seed in each container and use peat or paper pots, which can be set directly in the soil. Because squash have deep roots, they don't like to sit in containers long. When seedlings are at the three-leaf stage, soak the peat pots in water for a few hours, remove the bottoms, and plant out. If the weather is cool, harden-off seedlings (for detailed instructions, see Chapter 1, pages 28–29) before soaking the pots. Transplant carefully and avoid disturbing the roots.

Space bush types 18 to 24 inches apart.

ANOTHER WAY TO CLASSIFY SQUASH

Squash can also be classified as "summer," "autumn," and "winter" types. Winter squash are grown until they mature and are allowed to ripen on the vine. They are large plants with a sprawling, vining habit, and they may take up to 4 months to mature. The fruit has a hard rind and a dry, thick, mealy flesh. They will store for several months. Winter squash are found in all three species.

Autumn squashes include *pepo* species that are eaten after they mature but not stored for more than two months (acorn, spaghetti).

Summer squash are all *pepo* species and include zucchini, crooknecks, and scallop-type squashes. These should all be picked when the fruit are immature—the smaller the better. Because they are immature, summer squash plants are more bushy and contained than other squashes. The fruit has a thin, soft skin and loose, watery flesh. They grow quickly and store poorly.

Although you can eat an immature winter squash, it probably won't taste as good as a summer squash. Likewise, a summer squash you grow to maturity won't taste as good as a true winter squash.

Pumpkins are hard to classify since they occur in all three species: the *pepo* pie pumpkin, the *maxima* giant pumpkin, and the *moschata* cushaw pumpkin. The word pumpkin is derived from the Latin word *pepo,* referring to large melons. Squash were unknown in Europe until Columbus. Since pumpkins looked like melons, which had been in Europe for centuries, the name stuck. In the United States, "pumpkin" is used loosely to mean yellow, white, or orange-skinned round squashes grown for pies, carving, livestock feed, and contests. Like winter squash, pumpkins have a hard rind, but like summer squash, they store poorly.

Vining winter squashes need lots of room, and they are best planted in hills of three or four plants, spaced at least 4 to 6 feet apart.

The key step to growing squash is getting them off to a good early start. The challenge here is that the plants are very tender. You have a couple of options: Warm your soil with black plastic (clear plastic encourages weeds), or plant under floating row covers. The latter have the advantage of protecting plants from many early insect pests, like squash bugs and aphids.

As the squash grows, guide it by pinning down stems, buring them at regular intervals. Roots will form along the stem, which will help the plant absorb water and nutrients.

Almost everybody plants too much squash. One or two plants of any one variety at a time is plenty for a small family. The best ways to avoid the typical glut of summer squash are to stagger plantings at the beginning of the season and never grow more than a few plants at any one time. Temptation begins with large seed packets, so order small ones if possible.

SOILS AND FERTILIZERS

Squashes like a slightly acidic, rich, well-drained soil. The plants need plenty of moisture, especially after the first bloom, to keep the fruit coming. Squashes are also heavy feeders and prefer a slow, steady supply of nutrients. Provide both of these conditions with a good supply of compost or aged manure, and a preplant dressing of 5-3-4 natural fertilizer (5 pounds per 100 square feet) prior to planting.

For information on nutrient deficiencies in squash, see "Cucurbits," page 330.

DISEASES AND PESTS

See "Cucurbits," page 330–333.

VARIETIES

Gardeners who grow only a few varieties of zucchini, acorn, or butternut squash are missing most of the squash world. There are nearly three hundred varieties of open-pollinated squash now available (about half are pepo), plus a growing number of hybrids. Hybrids have two major advantages over open-pollinated types. They are reliably consistent, and they mature faster, meaning they can be grown where the season is shorter and the summers cooler.

Of all the vegetables, none can rival squashes for their dizzying diversity of shapes, colors, and textures. They grow as compact bushes or giant sprawling vines. They are egg-shaped, acorn-shaped, and bottle-shaped, small and smooth to huge and warty, and they come in every hue from red to green to orange to white. Some must be eaten within a few days, others keep for months. Growing several types of squash is one of the true joys of kitchen gardening.

Choosing which squash to grow depends on your tastes, your growing season, and the size of your garden. Although there are scores of varieties of summer squash, there is actually little difference in taste among most of them. Real taste differences, however, are found among winter squashes.

Winter squash seem to sprawl over everything in sight and take forever to grow. Besides, the size of the fruit can be intimidating. One trend in squash breeding has been to develop semivining or bush-type winter squash that produce smaller fruit in 70 to 90 days instead of 120 days. The problem is that most of them are more like a short vine than a bush.

They still sprawl, just not as far. And because they produce fewer leaves, they're not able to pump as much sugar and fiber into the fruit. The results are inferior taste and texture. Short-vined varieties also tend to set too much fruit at once, producing a glut.

Many experienced squash gardeners claim that it is a waste of time and space to grow the large Hubbard and banana squashes. They take up a lot of room, and their flavor is inferior to many other varieties. Acorns and buttercup varieties are preferred instead. For example, the new "sweet potato" acorn squashes like Delicata have a sweet flavor and dry flesh on smaller plants. And in terms of flavor and nutrition, buttercups may be the best winter squash you can grow. They don't keep as well as butternuts, nor are they as resistant to the squash borer, but their taste is without equal.

Sweet Dumpling

Buttercup

Banana

Acorn

GROWING GIANT PUMPKINS

Growing a really big pumpkin, say over 100 pounds, is not difficult, but it does require constant attention to detail. It's the kind of garden activity that families, neighbors, and friends can easily share, with a memorable reward at the end. To become an eye-popping behemoth, a pumpkin has to grow at a good, steady rate. Of the 120 to 130 days it takes to grow a giant pumpkin, the first 60 are the most important.

Step 1: Start with the right seed. You can grow normal pumpkins to a large size, but to grow giant pumpkins you need the right seed. Since 1979, the world's largest pumpkins (500 to 800 pounds) have come from the variety, Atlantic Giant. If you can settle for a more manageable bulk, say around 80 to 200 pounds, then try varieties like Big Max, Big Moon, and Mammoth Chile.

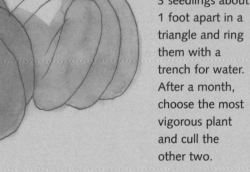

Step 2: Prepare soil the previous winter. Make sure you have a sunny spot large enough to leave at least 30 feet between plants; giant pumpkins need lots of elbow room. This may limit you to just one plant, but if you do it correctly, you won't need more.

Most giant pumpkin growers begin by dumping $\frac{1}{2}$ to 1 inch of well-aged manure and/or compost on the soil surface in early winter. This overwintering mulch protects the soil and brings earthworms to the surface. In spring, it is dug into the ground prior to planting (step 4).

Step 3: Start plants indoors. Giant pumpkins get off to a much better start if they are started indoors as seedlings and planted out at the three-leaf stage when the weather warms up.

Seeds of giant pumpkins are expensive, but you should start at least ten seeds for every plant you want to grow. The rule is to start lots of plants and keep only the fastest-growing ones, since rapid growth means bigger pumpkins. For more on growing cucurbit transplants, see "Planting," page 330.

Step 4: Dig in winter mulch and plant. In the spring, till or fork your winter mulch at least 6 inches deep. Place 3 seedlings about 1 foot apart in a triangle and ring them with a trench for water. After a month, choose the most vigorous plant and cull the other two.

Step 5: Keep on the lookout for borers, aphids, and beetles. Because they grow so rapidly, giant pumpkins are susceptible to pests. Borers are widespread; cucumber beetles and aphids transmit diseases.

Step 6: Give plants constant food and moisture. Another consequence of rapid growth is sensitivity to change. Giant pumpkins need constant moisture, a temperate soil, and a slow, uninterrupted flow of nutrients. A drip system underneath mulch keeps soil moisture and temperature even. Some growers even irrigate with warm water! Organic fertilizers

continued on page 340

provide a more moderate rate of nutrients than chemical fertilizers, which produce too much leaf growth and cause pumpkins to crack and split. Foliar feeding with fish emulsion or organic tea during early growth is recommended.

Step 7: Hand-pollinate. This is not necessary unless you live in an area with few insects. Simply use an artist's paintbrush to transfer the yellow, powderlike pollen of the male flowers to the top of the center of the female flower.

Step 8: Focus attention on one pumpkin per plant. When plants have three or four fruits, begin taking notice of their growth. Pull all flowers after the fourth fruit (don't cut the stems, as this invites pests). When the fruits are the size of a basketball, choose the largest from each plant and harvest the rest; this channels the plant's energy into one fruit.

As your pumpkin grows larger, check for signs of pests and cracks in the fruit. Cracks mean the fruit is growing too fast from too much water, so reduce your watering for a while. Be sure the fruit is resting on a thick, dry mulch, which will lessen the chances of it rotting. If all goes well, a time will come when you can no longer easily lift or roll the fruit, so plan accordingly. Have fun!

HARVEST AND STORAGE

Harvest summer squash when they are small; they'll taste better and you'll eat more of them. The skin of summer squash is thin and fragile, so try to avoid damaging it as you harvest. Place summer squash in plastic bags in the refrigerator crisper, where they will keep for up to 1 week.

In contrast, leave winter squash to mature on the vine. Harvest them when the rind is hard enough to resist denting with a thumbnail and the skin color is true. You can keep them on the vine as long as the leaves are healthy. But don't let them suffer a hard frost, as this will shorten their storage time.

Always harvest winter squash with a sharp knife and with as much of the stem attached as possible. This will lessen the chances of bacterial diseases entering the wound. Cure winter squash for a few days in a warm, sunny place to seal wounds and harden the skin, then store them in a dark, dry place at 50° to 60°F. Below 50°F winter squash tend to deteriorate.

Don't put winter squash on top of each other; allow air to circulate around each one. If care is taken not to bruise the skin, and all soil is carefully removed from the fruit, winter squash should store well for several months. Acorn squash will remain tasty until Thanksgiving, then go downhill after that. Buttercups are good through Christmas, while butternuts not only store well until the end of winter, but they also sweeten with age.

RECOMMENDED SQUASH VARIETIES

TYPE	COMMENTS
SUMMER	
Pattypan or Cymling	**Small, disk-shaped, and fluted (scalloped) squash.**
Peter Pan	Light green skin. Hybrid.
Scallopini	Vibrant, dark green skin. Hybrid.
Sunburst	AAS winner. Hybrid. Vivid golden yellow skin. Precocious yellow gene.
Yellowneck	**Pebbled skin and succulent yellow flesh.**
Seneca Prolific	Yellow straight neck.
Sundance	Full crookneck. Smooth skin. Hybrid.
Supersett	Fine-textured, nutty flavor. Semi-crookneck. Precocious yellow gene.
Zucchini	**Cucumber look-alike; classic summer squash.**
Arlesa	French courgette type. Easy harvest with few spines and open habit. Good for flowers.
Blackjack	Dark green hybrid. Long production. Open habit for easy harvest.
Butterblossom	Green zucchini; produces lots of male blossoms for eating.
Fiorentino	Italian variety with ridged fruits striped in greens.
Gold Rush	Golden hybrid zucchini. Sweet flavor. White flesh.
Roly Poly	Small, round zucchini popular in France as a *ronde courgette*.
Type 1406	Best taste. Sets seed without pollen, so keep row covers on past blossom stage.
WINTER	
Acorn	**Small, furrowed, acorn shaped. Pale orange flesh. Good for baking. Short storage. Good for cool weather.**
Bush Table Queen	Small fruit on semi-bush with 4-foot vines.
Delicata*	Heirloom *pepo* since 1894. 1- to 2-lb. oblong. Cream and green–striped with a sweet yellow flesh for baking.
Early Acorn	Large-fruited. Early hybrid. Semi-vining.
Golden Acorn	Orange rind. Moister, meatier flesh than other acorns.
Jersey Gold	Golden yellow hybrid. Eat as a summer or winter squash. Precocious yellow gene.
Spaghetti	Oval shape. 1 to 2 lb. fruit. Yellow rind. Stringy flesh cooks into spaghetti-like strands.
Sweet Dumpling	Small round *pepo*. Striped, cream-colored rind; very sweet flesh.
Table Ace	Best producer among small-fruited acorns.
Table Queen*	Original heirloom acorn since 1913. White rind. 1- to 2-lb. fruit. Best for baking.
Buttercup	**Midsized, decorative, squat shape. Green rind. Orange flesh is sweet and dry. Since the 1920s.**
Butterball Hybrid*	Late, semi-vining type. Highest yield. Best taste.
Emerald Bush*	Extra-early hybrid bush buttercup. Small fruit.
Semibush Buttercup*	Semi-vining. 4-lb. fruit.
Butternut	**Pear-shaped. 2 to 4 lb. tan rind and orange flesh with sweet, nutty flavor. Best for baking.**
Early Butternut	Extra-early, compact hybrid. Large 3-lb. fruit. More nutty flesh. Resistant to squash borer.
Ponca	Early, very tasty, small-fruited hybrid.
Puritan	An improved selection of the standard Waltham.
Hubbard	**Large, 10 to 15 lb. Sweet yellow flesh and blue-green bumpy rind.**
Gold Nugget*	Heirloom. Small 1-lb. fruit for 1 serving. Orange rind. Marginal taste.
Blue Ballet	Smaller, 4 to 6 lb., sweeter tasting Hubbard.

* Indicates heirloom variety.

continued on page 342

RECOMMENDED SQUASH VARIETIES, *continued from pg. 341*

TYPE	COMMENTS
WINTER	
Pumpkin	
Atlantic Giant	Grows to 400 lb. or more. Current world-record holder.
Autumn Gold	AAS winner. Hybrid. Precocious yellow gene. Semi-vining. 10 to 12 inches. Great for pies or carving.
Baby Bear	AAS winner. Semi-bush, 3 to 4 inches for pies or seed.
Baby Boo Mini	White rind. Early. Semi-bush. 3-inch fruit.
Big Max	Up to 100 lb.; good for pies.
Lumina	Glossy cream rind; plump, rounded shape. 12 inches. Good for pies.
New England Pie	The best for pies and canning. 6 to 8 inches.
Rouge Vif d'Étampes*	The Cinderella pumpkin. French heirloom since the early 1800s. Up to 15 lb. Vibrant deep orange. Low on taste.

* Indicates heirloom variety.

SQUASH GROWING TIPS

- During spring, prepare the soil by adding lots of aged manure or compost. A few weeks before planting, add a balanced pre-plant fertilizer. To warm soil for speedy early growth, cover soil with black plastic.

- Start squash by sowing directly into soil, or transplant into small mounds. Plant 2 to 3 seeds or transplants and thin to one. Allow 1 to 2 feet for summer squash and 2 to 3 feet for pumpkins and winter squash.

- Wait until all danger of frost has passed before direct-sowing or setting out plants. If you direct-sow, be sure the soil is at least 65°F and not soggy.

- One or two plants per person at a time is plenty. Avoid overplanting squash.

- Grow several varieties of squash for an assortment of colors and textures. Match the variety to the available space.

- Mulch to retain moisture and keep down weeds, but avoid coarse materials like straw and hay, as these act as refuges for some squash pests. Use sawdust, grass clippings, and similar materials.

- Keep moisture constant and provide a slow, steady supply of nutrients with side-dressings of organic fertilizer.

- You can store winter squash as a hard-shelled gourd or you can purée the cooked flesh and freeze it for future use in baked goods and soups. Before you store winter squash, cure it in a warm, well-ventilated spot for a week or two.

Cucumbers
CURCURBITACEAE (Gourd or Squash Family)

Cucumis sativus	
(if used as slicing cucumber)	(if used as pickling cucumber)
CHINESE: *hu gua*	CHINESE: *hu gua*
FRENCH: *concombre*	FRENCH: *cornichon*
GERMAN: *Salat-Gurke, Schlangengurke*	GERMAN: *Essiggurke*
ITALIAN: *cetriolo*	ITALIAN: *cetriolino sotto acete*
JAPANESE: *kyuuri*	JAPANESE: *kyuuri*
SPANISH: *pepino*	SPANISH: *pepinillo en vinagre*

"Cool as a cucumber" is an apt expression, as these close cousins of melons are mostly water and are often served cold. The cucumber is probably native to northwest India, where today it can be found in all sizes, shapes, colors, and textures. Although records of its use are sparse, the cucumber may be one of our oldest vegetables. It was reputedly grown in the fabulous hanging gardens of ancient Babylon, and by the beginning of Christianity's predominance it was already being grown in North Africa, Italy, Greece, Asia Minor, and Southwest Asia. The cucumber was so popular in ancient Rome that Emperor Tiberius developed the first greenhouses to ensure a constant supply. These were simply earthen pits, heated by composting manures and covered with sheets of talc or mica. The cucumber was brought to northern Europe in the 1300s, and Columbus planted seeds in Haiti. The first settlers in Massachusetts grew it in 1629.

Cucumber is probably best enjoyed raw in salads and sandwiches, or cut into sticks for dipping. And of course, gazpacho would not be the same without the cool, brisk texture of cucumbers.

Most regions of the world have their own version of cucumber salad. In India, cucumbers are combined with onions, tomatoes, cumin, cayenne, and lemon juice; in Japan julienned cucumbers are mixed with soy sauce, rice wine vinegar, and sesame seeds. Cucumber combines especially well with yogurt. Raita, the Indian condiment that accompanies hot curries, is a blend of yogurt, grated cucumbers, coriander, cumin, and pepper. Middle Eastern versions of this dish include raisins and walnuts.

Although less commonly cooked, cucumbers are quite delicious baked, boiled, braised in broth, sautéed, or steamed. Try hollowed-out peeled cucumber halves filled with your favorite meat, vegetable, or bread crumb mix, sprinkled with cheese, and baked until tender. Or cut cucumber into cubes or into balls with a melon baller, steam and serve with sour cream. The delicate flavor of cooked cucumber complements fish and poultry.

Cucumbers have little to offer nutritionally. Like melons, they are mostly water, with a moderate supply of vitamin C and iron. The vitamin A is concentrated in the rind, so the benefits of this nutrient are inconsequential if the rind is removed.

CULTIVATION

The cucumber is very frost-tender and likes warm weather. A creeping annual, it grows on sprawling, short to long vines with stiff hairs on the stems and leaves. Like other cucurbits, cucumbers are monoecious, with male and female flowers on the same plant. Since 1960, however, plant breeders have focused on developing "gynoecious" plants that produce mostly female flowers.

Don't start transplants earlier than 3 to 4 weeks before the last spring frost, or the plants will get too big and rangy and make transplanting difficult. Transplants are grown just like squash, and with the same considerations (see "Squash," pages 336–337).

In general, sow seeds or set out transplants in warm soil about 2 weeks after the average spring frost date. For a longer harvest, set out another crop 3 to 6 weeks later. Gardeners in coastal climates plant later in the spring or early summer to avoid powdery mildew. In areas with 5 or more warm months a year, a second crop can be planted after midsummer and picked before frost.

PLANTING

One of the most common mistakes gardeners make is planting cucumbers too close together. Most varieties need 12 to 18 inches between plants. Closer spacing encourages diseases and causes stress and poor fruit development.

Once the vines have grown to about 4 feet, you can control their growth and fruiting by pinching off the fuzzy tips of the vines. It's a good idea to keep plants and fruit off the ground by growing them in cages or up trellises. In fact, cucumbers are one of the few cucurbits that can easily be trellised, so it's good to take advantage of this. Trellising reduces diseases, conserves valuable garden space, and creates an early summer shadow for an underplanting of leafy greens.

SOILS AND FERTILIZERS

Cucumbers need the same kind of soils as other cucurbits: rich, well-drained, and slightly acidic loam. But there are other considerations. Cucumbers can develop a rather bitter taste, due to a compound called cucurbitacin.

Most of the bitterness is genetic, but excessive soil nitrogen can also make fruit acrid, so fertilize carefully. If your soil is poor, try side-dressing with a balanced fertilizer just before the vines begin to spread out and "run."

Water makes up 95 percent of a cucumber's weight, so plants need lots of water, especially when they are young and again after the first blossom. A sure sign of water stress is fruits that have become constricted or curved, as though cinched by a belt. Mulch only after the soil has warmed up, or else use clear plastic mulch.

For information on nutrient deficiencies in cucumbers, see "Cucurbits," page 330.

DISEASES AND PESTS

Like most cucurbits, cucumbers are subject to a host of diseases. Control these by growing resistant varieties, avoiding overhead irrigation, rotating crops, and swiftly removing all diseased vines from the garden. For specific controls, see "Cucurbits," pages 330–333.

VARIETIES

Until this century, cucumber varieties grew bent and twisted, with warty, thick skins, a slightly bitter taste, and a penchant for diseases. Modern breeding has given us the smooth-skinned, sweet-tasting, disease-tolerant varieties we enjoy today.

There are over 120 varieties of open-pollinated cucumbers, and about half as many hybrids. The seeds of some specially sexed hybrids are very expensive. For the money-wise gardener, the best bets are modern open-pollinated varieties with multiple-disease resistance, such as Poinsett 76 and Marketmore. Each region of the country seems to have its own favorite cucumber variety, so check with your local garden clubs and farm agents for advice.

Here are some terms that you need to know when choosing cucumber varieties:

- **Monoecious:** The ancient form of the cucumber. Most cucumbers are still monoecious; that is, separate male and female flowers are borne on the same plant. The female flowers produce the fruit, the male flowers provide the pollen, and insects do the pollinating. On monoecious plants, the male flowers are produced first.

- **Gynoecious:** From the Greek *gyne,* meaning "woman." Since 1960, plant breeders have been developing cucumbers that produce only female flowers, and therefore more fruit. Gynoecious hybrids must be planted with a few seeds of standard types to provide male flowers for pollination. For this reason, about 10 percent of the seeds in a packet of gynoecious hybrids will be monoecious.

The first blossoms of gynoecious hybrids are female (set fruit), unlike monoecious varieties, whose first blossoms are male flowers. Thus, gynoecious varieties mature earlier, yield higher, and have a much more concentrated crop than open-pollinated monoecious hybrids. Known as total hybrids, gynoecious varieties are also the most expensive.

- **Parthenocarpic:** This means that fruit can be produced without pollination. As a result, parthenocarpic varieties have no seeds, and they must be isolated from other cucumber types to avoid unwanted crosses. This type of cucumber is grown in greenhouses or under floating row covers, where natural pollinators are excluded.

- **Black- and White-Spined:** Many cucumbers grow small prickle-like "spines" from warts on their skins. The black-spined varieties are more primitive and turn yellow when they mature. The white-spined types are dark green when young and creamy green when mature. Both types of spines can be rubbed off easily.

- **Bush and Vine:** In 1977, Park Seed Company introduced the first bush cucumber, Bush Whopper. Today several varieties are available. Bush cukes may be full dwarfs, with a spread of 2 to 3 feet, or semi-dwarfs, with a spread of 4 to 6 feet. They have a shorter distance (called the "internode") between leaves on the vine. In this sense they are unlike bush varieties of tomatoes or beans, which are made compact by terminating their stem growth in fruits. Bush cukes produce earlier and have a more compact harvest than vine types, so many gardeners plant both types for an extended harvest. Some people claim bush varieties taste better.

There are five general types of cucumber varieties to choose from:

- **Slicing:** These cukes are about 6 to 9 inches long, with glossy, dark green, thick skin and tapered ends. Their thick skin protects them during shipping; slicing cukes should be peeled before eating. They are prolific and disease resistant, and they keep well.

- **Pickling:** These small white-spined cucumbers are used to make pickles. Small slicing cucumbers can also be pickled, but they are inferior to pickling cukes, which have a very thin skin and a flesh that absorbs brine more easily. Cornichons, the tiny, evenly shaped pickling cucumbers are picked when they are 1 to 2 inches long. Some gardeners grow pickling cucumbers to use as slicers. A pickler's flesh is smoother, more finely grained, and arguably more flavorful, and its thin skin doesn't have to be peeled.

- **Burpless and Nonbitter:** "Nonbitter" cucumbers lack the chemical cucurbitacin, which produces bitterness and gives some people a case of mild indigestion. The term "burpless" usually refers to thin-skinned, and therefore less bitter, Asian varieties. Not all burpless types are nonbitter; they just have lower amounts of the chemical. To make things more confusing, recent breeding has combined the attributes of Asian burpless types with traditional American slicers to create such varieties as Oriental Express.

The thin skin of nonbitter and burpless cukes means a short shelf life, so if you want to eat them, you'll probably have to grow them yourself. Since cucurbitacin also attracts cucumber beetles (and the diseases they carry), burpless varieties generally have little trouble with this pest. On the other hand, spider mites and small mammals seem to like the nonbitter taste.

- **Mideastern/Beit Alpha:** These are the finest-tasting slicing cucumbers. They have smooth, thin, nonbitter skins in hues of medium green. Their flesh is extra crisp and juicy, and they set seed very slowly. Unfortunately, they are not very productive or disease tolerant, and their seed is quite expensive.

- **Greenhouse Varieties:** Also known as English, European, or hothouse cucumbers, most greenhouse cucumbers are long parthenocarpic varieties from Europe with thin, tender skins. Since they don't need to be pollinated, these varieties can be grown in greenhouses and under cover and cloches, including row covers. Seeds are expensive, so the cash-conscious gardener should buy only greenhouse varieties if they are to be grown under cover.

HARVEST AND STORAGE

The secret to a good cucumber harvest is to pick continually, every day, if necessary. Pick slicers at 7 to 8 inches, picklers at 2 to 4 inches, Mideasterns at about 5 inches, and burpless cukes at 8 inches. Lemon cukes should be picked when they are light yellow. Once they are picked, dunk cucumbers in cold water for a few minutes to increase the quality and life of the fruit. Stored in a plastic bag in a refrigerator crisper, they should keep for about 2 weeks.

CUCUMBER GROWING TIPS

- Cucumbers come in several types of varieties. It's best to learn these before choosing what to grow. Always select disease-resistant varieties when possible.

- Cucumbers grow best with hot, humid days and warm nights. Plants are very sensitive to frost.

- Sow seeds outside only after danger of frost. The warmer the better.

- For earlier harvests, and to reduce pest damage, start seedlings indoors and plant transplants outdoors.

- Soils should be rich and well-drained.

- Keep soils evenly moist to prevent bitterness. Mulch 4 weeks after transplanting to conserve soil water.

- Side-dress with 5-10-10 just as vines begin to run.

- To hasten and improve production, harvest fruit as soon as they are ready.

RECOMMENDED CUCUMBER VARIETIES

VARIETY/ TYPE	HYBRID (H)/ OPEN-POLLINATED (OP)	RESISTANCE AND TOLERANCE	COMMENTS
SLICING			
Bush Crop	OP	A, ALS, D, M, P, S	Compact, dwarfy vines for containers and small spaces.
Dasher II	H	A, ALS, D, M, P, S	Top fresh market slicer in the U.S.; great for gardens. Small vines. Adaptable.
Fanfare	H	A, ALS, D, M, P, S	1994 AAS winner. Standard bush hybrid.
Lemon*	OP		Since 1894. Unique round, yellow type with burpless quality when small.
Long Green Improved*	OP		Since 1870. Good flavor for slicer. Warty but suitable for pickling.
Marketmore 76 or 86	OP	D, M, P, S	Improved OP types. Nonbitter flavor. Yields in hot weather. Main crop in North, fall crop in warmer areas. 86 bushier and earlier.
Poinsett 76	OP	D, P, A, ALS	Improved OP type with long, blocky fruit. M-susceptible. For Southeast and Atlantic Coast, but adaptable elsewhere.
Slice King	H	D, P	Gynoecious, compact dwarf plant.
Spacemaster 80	OP	M, S, P, D	Dwarf vines with no runners. Dark green, 6-inch fruit. For containers and small gardens.
Straight Eight*	OP	M	AAS winner, 1935. Standard smooth-skinned, black-spined variety. Vigorous.
Supersett	H	A, ALS, D, M, P, S	Gynoecious and monoecious mix for reliability and disease resistance.
Sweet Success	H		Parthenocarpic variety suitable for growing outdoors.
PICKLING			
Boston Pickling*	OP		Since 1880. Popular old reliable pickler. High yields if kept picked.
Bush Pickle	OP		Compact, dwarfy vines for containers and small spaces. Short production.
Conquest	H	A, ALS, D, M, P, S	Gynoecious. White spine. Superior modern pickling hybrid.
Cornichons	H	M, S, P	Traditional French hybrid; tiny pickler.
Little Leaf	H	A, ALS, D, M, P, S	Compact vigorous vine. Adaptable to many climates. Parthenocarpic. Resistant. Good pickler or slicer.
National Pickling	OP		Commercial type good for gardens. High yields.
Saladin	H	S, P, M, D	AAS winner. Curved and warty "pickle skin"; very productive.
BURPLESS			
Burpless	OP		Popular 8- to 10-inch fruit. Nonbitter skin.
Orient Express	H	A, ALS, D, M, P, S	Vigorous. Asian-American slicer hybrid. Can be pickled.
Suyo Long	OP		From China. Deeply ribbed, dark green skin; Asian type. 10 to 18 inches long. Seedless. Heat tolerant. Very popular.
Sweet Alphee	H		Tender, crisp, nonbitter. Best-tasting cuke. Monoecious; not for greenhouses.
Sweet Crunch	H		Superior gynoecious type. Vigorous plant with long picking period.
Sweet Slice	H	ALS, C, D, P, S	One of the best for home gardens.
Tyria	H		Dutch greenhouse (parthenocarpic) type. 1 ft. long; ribbed; dark green.

A = Anthracnose; ALS = Angular leaf spot; D = Downy mildew; M = Cucumber mosaic virus; P = Powdery mildew; S = Scab

* Indicates heirloom variety.

SOLANACEAE (Nightshade Family)

The Solanaceae, or nightshade family, includes three of the most popular vegetables in the world: the potato (page 245), the tomato, and the pepper (page 368). Other vegetables include the tomatillo (*Physalis*) and several species of the eggplant (*Solanum* spp.). Popular nightshade ornamentals include *Petunia, Datura* (trumpet vine), *Nicotiana* (flowering tobacco), *Physalis* (Chinese lantern), and *Cestrum*.

Many of the nightshade species contain chemical alkaloids, both medicinal and toxic. The family name, derived from the Latin *solamen,* meaning "quieting," refers to the narcotic effects of some of its plants, such as the roots of *Mandrabora* (mandrake), the sleeping potion of Juliet. There is also *Atropa belladonna* (deadly nightshade), which contains atrapine, a powerful muscle relaxant used in ancient operations. The green tissues of potatoes and tomatoes contain toxic alkaloids, and they should not be eaten. However, the fruits of tomato, pepper, and eggplant don't contain them. Potato tubers can become toxic if you expose them to enough sunlight to turn their skin green.

Nightshade vegetables tend to share the same kinds of pests: beetles, aphids, and caterpillars above ground and soil-dwelling diseases below ground, especially the fungi *Alternaria Phytophthora, Fusarium,* and *Verticillium.* These are hard diseases to control because the fungi can live in the soil for years eating organic matter, waiting to attack plants. This is why it's best to avoid growing a nightshade vegetable in the same place for more than one or two years. Rotate them throughout your garden from season to season (pages 32–36). Always look for varieties resistant to soil fungus diseases.

Tomato
SOLANACEAE (Nightshade or Tomato Family)

Lycopersicon lycopersicum (= esculentum)
CHINESE: *fan qie*
FRENCH: *tomate, pomme d'amour*
GERMAN: *Tomate*
ITALIAN: *pomodoro*
JAPANESE: *tomato*
SPANISH: *tomate*

The tomato is the most common vegetable in American kitchen gardens, and it's hard to imagine a vegetable patch without it. Tomatoes are easy to grow, versatile in the kitchen, and available in hundreds of varieties.

Native to Peru and Ecuador, the tomato

can still be found there in its lobed and marble-sized state. It was cultivated in Central and South America as early as the fifth century B.C. The Mayans called it *xtomatl*.

Spanish explorers brought the tomato to Europe in the 1500s and it was described by a botanist of the time as a yellow variety, hence the Italian name *pomodoro* (golden apple). Only the Italians showed any interest in this berry from South America. The rest of Europe considered the tomato a poisonous plant, probably because it was a cousin of the deadly nightshade weed. It was soon given the botanic name *lycopersicum,* which means "wolf peach." Ironically, it also acquired a reputation as an aphrodisiac and the names "love apple" and *pomme d'amour.*

The tomato arrived in the United States in 1710, more than 200 years after it had left its ancestral home. The wait seems to have been worth it since the tomato has deeply affected so many cuisines. Above all, it has found a second home in the Mediterranean region; here, garden-fresh tomatoes form a culinary union with garlic, basil, olive oil, and other herbs to make savory sauces and salads.

While the tomato has become more popular, today's supermarket varieties are pale and firm, and lack the vibrant color and luscious flavor of fresh-picked ripe fruit. Commercial growers choose varieties for yield and keeping quality, not always taste. The tomatoes are harvested when hard and green, so they can be packed without injury. The prematurely plucked fruit is then bathed in ethylene gas for several days to spur ripening, and stored in refrigerators, which robs it of any flavor. These kinds of store-bought tomatoes are tasteless and mealy and have fewer vitamins than the vine-ripened, juice-sweet types you can grow yourself.

The tomato is low in sodium, and a fair source of vitamins A and C, plus potassium and iron. The vitamin C is found mostly in the jellylike material around the seeds. Vitamin A content depends on the color; it's highest in orange varieties, followed by yellow, red, and then white.

The ancient fears about eating tomatoes were not completely ill-founded. Although the fruit is not toxic, the stems and leaves are. All the green parts of a tomato plant contain the toxin alkaloid tomatine, which seems to help the plant fend off some of its diseases. Tomatine is less potent than the alkaloids of the tomato relatives nightshade and belladonna, but it's best not to eat leaves or stems. Green fruit is all right.

For ease and convenience, few side dishes can beat a platter of sliced garden-ripe tomatoes topped with minced fresh parsley, tarragon, chives, or chervil; a dollop of mayonnaise seasoned with shallots, capers, or anchovies; or a simple vinaigrette. Serve cherry tomatoes as dippers on hors d'oeuvre trays, or grill them in kabobs.

Mature green tomatoes are easy to stew or bake. They can also be thickly sliced, lightly browned in vegetable oil, and sprinkled with orange juice, honey, or cinnamon. Try using mature green tomatoes in salsas or chiles, or as a substitute for tart apples in many recipes. Green tomatoes are excellent in guacamole, salsas, and uncooked relishes.

Ripe tomatoes can be stewed, baked, or boiled. They're especially good when served hot and covered with garlic and olive oil; grated Parmesan, Asiago, or Cheddar cheese; seasoned bread crumbs; or smoked salmon flakes in low-fat cream cheese. There are very few foods that aren't complemented by tomatoes.

CULTIVATION

The tomato is a tender perennial grown as an annual. If plants are kept warm during winter, they can sometimes produce for 2 or 3 years. Although varieties differ a bit, tomatoes generally set fruit in a very narrow temperature range. They need warm (not hot) days (70° to 80°F) and nighttime temperatures above 50°.

The nighttime temperature is crucial. If you start plants before the night temperature reaches 50°F, most varieties will just sit and sulk. Cool nights will also make blossoms drop off before they can produce fruit. You won't always get early tomatoes just because you plant early. Even early varieties need a minimum amount of warmth for growth, flowering, and pollen production. Cool, cloudy, or hot weather will slow down plant and pollen growth, delay fruit set, and cause some diseases.

Tomatoes are prone to several serious diseases that are rather difficult to control. Many of these are fungi that attack living plants, but that can also live for years in the soil, eating organic debris. There are only a few varieties resistant to these diseases, so you must both choose the right variety and watch your cultural practices very carefully.

Unless you plan on canning or drying tomatoes, try to resist the temptation to grow too many plants. While you should grow more than one variety for insurance, three or four plants at a time will give four to six people all the tomatoes they can eat.

PLANTING

Tomato seedlings are fairly easy to raise from seed. In warm climates, you can seed directly in the ground, but most people prefer starting seedlings indoors 5 to 7 weeks before the last spring frost. In our experience, transplanted seedlings seem to do better than directly seeded ones.

Sow seeds in a germination mix and prick out small seedlings to single containers. Tomatoes grow very quickly when they are young, and in low light they'll stretch and get lanky. Keep them in a heated, well-lit space for 3 weeks, and don't overwater them. Next, move them to a cooler location where the nights reach at least 60°F for another 3 to 4 weeks. When seedlings have four to eight leaves, they can be planted out. Plants that go to flower before being transplanted will suffer when finally set out. Smaller seedlings that have been hardened-off properly will usually catch up to and outproduce large heat-forced seedlings.

Unlike most vegetables, tomato plants can be set deeply in the soil, with the first leaves just above the soil line. Roots will form along the buried stem. When you place seedlings, be sure to leave plenty of room between the plants (2 to 3 feet for bush types and 3 to 4 feet for vine types). This allows for good circulation and reduces diseases. Some tomatoes will sprout suckers from their base. If they have a few roots, you can gently break them from the mother plant and transplant them to other spots in the garden. They may or may not take, but it's always worth a try to extend the tomato season.

SOILS AND FERTILIZERS

Tomatoes like a fertile, deep, well-drained soil that is slightly acidic but has plenty of phosphorous and calcium. Before planting, mix colloidal or super phosphate into the soil. This will take care of plants until the first fruits set. Feed once a month while the fruits are developing. Stop fertilizing when the fruits near mature size. Don't overfertilize with nitrogen, which will result in lots of leaves but very little fruit.

Every gardener seems to have a favorite method of watering tomatoes. Two rules are inflexible: (1) Don't overhead-water tomatoes. This encourages a variety of leaf and fruit diseases. (2) Tomatoes don't like soils that alternate between wet and dry. This leads to cracked skin, diseases, and misshapen fruit. Roots should be kept at an even moisture level by surface-watering mulched soil.

EXTENDING THE SEASON

One of the greatest challenges for kitchen gardeners is to harvest tomatoes as early and late in the season as possible. To extend the tomato season, grow both early and late varieties, and try one or more of a number of popular "season-extending" devices designed to help keep your tomato plants warm while the air around them is cool.

A. **Cloches:** (1) glass and (2) recycled kitchen containers

C. **Row tunnels**

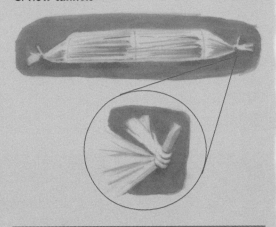

D. **Plastic and cloth coverings**

B. **Walls of water:** (1) Commercial and (2) homemade

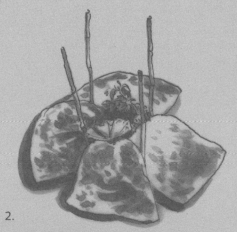

CONTROLLING TOMATO GROWTH

Tomatoes are rangy plants that will sprawl on the ground unless you give them support, especially vining varieties. It's important to keep tomato fruit off the ground so they won't be damaged by slugs, snails, cracking, diseases, and decay. In wet summer and fall areas, you can almost double your yield by keeping fruit high and dry. Unkept, spreading tomato plants are also a haven for various tomato diseases. If you do let tomatoes sprawl, be sure to keep the fruit from touching the bare soil by using a mulch.

Pinching out axillary growth.

Gardeners control tomato growth by pruning plants and/or containing them around stakes, up trellises, or within cages. Bush tomatoes are probably best caged and pruned to keep the plant's center open and freely circulating. Vine tomatoes can be pruned to focus growth into one or two stems and then trained up trellises or ground stakes. Trellises also conserve garden space and let the plant get the most amount of sunlight. In addition, the trellis makes it easier to spot plant-eating critters and diseases.

Pruning tomatoes for stakes and trellises produces an earlier although less productive crop than unpruned caged tomatoes of the same variety. In the end, it's all a trade-off between your time and an optimum yield. The bottom line: Keep the fruit off the ground.

Each gardener has his or her favorite way to get tomatoes off the ground. They range from the obvious to the inventive. We describe only a few here.

Pruning and Trellising

Some gardeners prune tomatoes, for several reasons: to increase air circulation and reduce diseases; to make harvesting easier; to divert more energy into fruiting; or simply to make room for more tomato plants. In general, bush varieties should not be pruned except to open up heavy growth in the center of the plant. This includes the short stocky types like Pixie, the loose bush types like Roma, and the semi-determinates (large bush types) like Celebrity. All vine tomatoes can be pruned to one or two leaders (main stems).

To prune a vine tomato, remove the axillary growth when it first appears (see illlustration). Axillary, or "sucker," growth comes from the axil between the side-branching (lateral) stem and the leaf. You can remove some or all of the suckers. If you remove all of them, you will have one strong vine that grows fruit on lateral branches. The vine is then tied to a trellis or stake for support. This "cordon" method will produce tomatoes earlier than a caged vine, so you should stagger your plantings. Some gardeners have found success by axillary pruning to two or three main stems for a bit more foliage that improves taste and reduces sunscalding of fruit.

In our experience, some vine varieties respond to pruning better than others, and an unpruned vine will bear fruit longer. Heavy pruning can cause fruit cracking and sunscalding; with fewer leaves for shade, there is more sunlight on the fruit and slower exchange of water. When there's a heavy rain or deep irrigation, the extra water then is taken up by the fruit, which swell and crack. Cracking is a serious problem in tomatoes, because the cracks are entry wounds for all sorts of pests and diseases.

Tomato Cages

As early as the nineteenth century, tomato cages were being constructed by driving three stakes in the ground around the plant and then circling the stakes with barrel hoops. Most commercial tomato cages today are too flimsy. Our favorite method of training tomatoes is to make a circular cage from a 6- to 8-foot length of 5- to 7-foot-high concrete reinforcing wire. The 6-inch mesh allows you to pick the tomatoes easily within the cage and to move stems around for training. To make the cylinder cage, bend the loose ends of wire from the first cuts into U-shaped hooks, wrap them over the other end of the mesh, and squeeze them together with pliers to form a tight clamp. Cut off the outside rung of wire from the end to make a row of wire "teeth" to stick into the soil, then anchor the cage into the ground by stepping on the bottom rung and forcing the protruding wires into the soil. It's important to keep the stems from growing out through the openings, so inspect your plants at least twice weekly and gently guide vigorous stems back into the cage. If the center of the plant gets too dense, prune some of the central branches to improve air circulation and make harvesting easier.

Tomato cage

Staking Tomatoes

Tomato stakes can be built easily from scrap and recycled materials. For strong bush (determinate) varieties, use a variation on staking called "string weaving." Drive sturdy 4-foot wood or metal stakes into the ground at the ends of each row and between every other plant. When the plants are about a foot tall, tie the end of a ball of sisal string to one stake about 10 inches above the ground on one of the end stakes. Weave it so that it crosses between plants—around the left side of one plant, then around the right of the next, and so on. Repeat with a second string 6 inches higher when plants are 1^1/$_2$ feet tall. If you go higher, don't weave; just string along the outside to contain the top stems.

String-weave trellis

Cordon trellis

NUTRIENT DEFICIENCIES IN TOMATOES	
NUTRIENT	SYMPTOMS
Nitrogen (N)	Tips of lower leaves are pale green, underside of leaves with purple ribs; with high deficiencies, leaves turn golden yellow and the stems become hard and bronzed
Phosphorus (P)	Reddish purple veins on the underside of lower leaves extending onto stems.
Potassium (K)	New leaflets of lower leaves are light yellow, some with dead brown spots and tissue on the margins; old leaves are ashen, grayish green. Fruit are greenish with large meaty centers.
Calcium (Ca)	Upper leaves are yellow while lower leaves remain green; terminal buds die and terminal stems get brown spots.
Sulfur (S)	Lower leaves become yellowish green; stems elongate.
Magnesium (Mg)	Pale-yellow areas between veins of leaves that turn into brown and black lesions.

DISEASES

Tomatoes are susceptible to many plant diseases. Several of these are either viruses or soil fungi, none of which can be controlled by pesticides. The only way to avoid them is by using resistant varieties. The disease resistances for tomatoes are noted by the letters V (verticillium wilt); F (fusarium wilt); N (nematodes, which are tiny wormlike root feeders that also carry diseases); and T, M, and TMV (tobacco mosaic virus). Resistances to other tomato diseases are more difficult to develop, but they are often present even though they are not listed. For example, Floramerica is said to possess a tolerance to more than fifteen diseases. Many varieties are resistant to fruit cracking, which is important in areas with rapid changes in temperature and soil moisture.

Tobacco mosaic virus (TMV) affects all nightshade vegetables. Unfortunately, the symptoms aren't very consistent. Look for light and darker green mottling on leaves; in cold weather, the leaves may grow very narrow, like a shoestring, and the fruit grow deformed with brown streaks inside. The virus can spread on seeds, but is most often caused by a smoker who touches a susceptible plant. To control, remove and destroy all infected plants at once. If you smoke tobacco, wash your hands or wear gloves before you enter the garden. Resistant varieties are available.

Look for the letters T, M, or TMV in descriptions. Keep plants growing quickly and vigorously.

Bacterial leaf spots: Two bacterial diseases attack tomatoes, beginning on the leaves and moving to stems and fruit. **Bacterial speck,** caused by *Pseudomonas syringae,* appears on leaves as dark brown to black spots surrounded by a yellow halo; stems show black sores. Fruit will have slightly raised black spots that look like fly specks. **Bacterial spot,** caused by *Xanthomonas campestris,* begins as dark, water-soaked circular spots on the leaves. Later, the spots turn angular and black, and eventually the tissue rots away. Fruit infection begins on green fruit as small black specks that enlarge to become scabby, craterlike sores. Leaf speck is favored by cool, rainy weather, whereas leaf spot occurs during warm temperatures. Both diseases are encouraged by overhead watering. Infection usually occurs through wounds caused by insects, wind, or cultivation. Control bad cases with bordeaux spray. Avoid overhead watering, dispose of all diseased plants quickly, and buy seeds from a reputable source.

Bacterial canker or blight *(Corynebacterium nichiganense)* is a widespread disease that attacks the circulation system of plants, so the first symptom is the wilting of lower leaves. The wilted leaves hang downwards, but their edges curl upwards. Often, only half of the leaf or plant will wilt. Light streaks may grow down the stem; these break open into cankers that bleed a yellow slimy ooze, a characteristic of many bacterial diseases. Bacterial blight is carried on seeds and can live in the soil for 3 years eating organic debris, so rotate your tomatoes regularly to avoid buildup. Otherwise, prevention is the only option since there are no known resistant varieties or chemical cures. Buy disease-free seed; control surrounding weeds in the nightshade family that can also carry it, like jimsonweed, horse nettle, nightshade, and nicotiana; sanitize tools with bleach; and remove and destroy infected plants quickly. The bacteria enters plants in water that seeps through wounds and leaf pores, so try not to work around plants when they are wet.

Alternaria, or **early blight** *(Alternaria solani)* is a widespread fungus that is less common in arid areas. Symptoms first appear on older leaves as irregular brown dead spots surrounded by yellow tissue. The spots have concentric rings like a dartboard. Spots on the fruit appear at the stem end as dark leathery sunken scabs. The fungus survives on seeds and decayed plant material in the soil. It grows quickly in warm, rainy, or humid weather and may require spraying with a fungicide. Buy disease-free seeds. No resistant varieties are available, although some varieties are more tolerant than others. Alternaria also affects peppers, potatoes, and eggplant. See also "Potatoes," page 247.

Anthracnose *(Colletotrichum phomoides)* is a fungus that attacks ripe fruit, leaving sunken circular spots that deepen, enlarge, and grow dark in the middle. Many minute dark specks are arranged in concentric rings within the spot. The fungus enters wounds on the fruit and survives on seeds and decayed plant material in the soil. Splashing rain or overhead watering carries the fungus from the soil to the fruit. Buy disease-free seeds. Practice crop rotation and avoid watering from above; there are no resistant varieties.

Fusarium wilt *(Fusarium oxysporum)* is a widespread, devastating disease of many plants in the nightshade family, including eggplant and pepper. There are at least three major strains. Symptoms begin with a yellowing of the older leaves or branches, producing a "yellow flag" appearance in the garden. Yellowing often occurs on just one side of a leaf or branch. The yellow leaves soon wilt and die, although they remain on the plant. To check for the disease, cut an infected stem in half lengthwise and look for a characteristic brick-red color running between the outside and the green center of the stem. The fungus is spread by seed, infected plant debris, tools, and irrigation water. It can live in the soil for 3 to 4 years eating organic debris, and it thrives best in warm, acid soils. Soil solarization (page 186) may suppress the disease, but the only reliable control is resistant varieties. Look for the letter "F" on variety descriptions or seed packets.

Phytophthora, or **late blight** *(Phytophthora infestans)* is the fungus that was the cause of the infamous potato famine of the nineteenth century. It attacks all nightshade vegetables, and it loves cool, wet weather. The first symptom is the bending down of leaf stems. Soon after, irregular dark green, water-soaked patches grow on the leaves. As the patches grow, they turn brown and paperlike. The fruit develops firm, large, irregular greenish-brown blotches with a greasy, rough texture. In warm areas, the fungus survives on weedy nightshade plants or potato and tomato volunteers. Infected potato tubers are a common means by which this disease invades gardens; spores are also carried long distances by storms. *Phytophthora* is very difficult to control. There are no resistant varieties, although some varieties seem more tolerant than others. See also "Potatoes," pages 247–248.

Septoria *(Septoria lycopersici)* is common in the eastern United States. It also attacks eggplants and potatoes. The first symptoms show up on the underside of leaves near the bottom of the plant: these are small, dark water-soaked areas that grow into circular spots with dark borders and a gray center peppered with tiny black specks. These specks distinguish septoria from early blight and bacterial spot. The leaves dry up and drop off the plant, which exposes fruit to the sun, causing sunscald. Septoria survives on plant debris or on wild tomato relatives like jimsonweed and nightshade, but it doesn't live in the soil. It thrives in warm, wet weather and can be splashed onto plants by rain or overhead watering. There are no resistant varieties. In extreme cases, bordeaux spray is effective if the disease is caught early enough.

Verticillium wilt *(Verticillium dahliae)* is a fungus that attacks over three hundred species of plants, including most members of the nightshade family, although it is rare on peppers. One obvious early sign is the wilting of older leaves. Later, large V-shaped yellow spots develop and the leaf dies, turns brown, and drops off. Eventually, the disease progresses up the plant. If you suspect verticillium, cut the base of a main stem. A speckled tan color, instead of a light green color, in the cross section indicates the presence of verticillium. It produces symptoms uniformly across the plant, whereas fusarium causes symptoms on one side of the leaf or on one branch. Verticillium thrives best in cool weather and enters the plant through the roots. It can live in the soil for several years. The only effective controls are resistant varieties and soil sterilization (solar or chemical). See also "Eggplant," page 365, and "Brassicas," pages 254–255.

PESTS

Many pests of tomatoes also attack other vegetables in the nightshade family, including peppers, eggplant, and potatoes. Refer to these vegetables for further information.

Spider mites are tiny creatures that attack during dry weather and feed on the underside of leaves, producing small white flecks. Spray daily with a high-pressure water spray. The **tomato russet mite** is even smaller than the spider mite. Common in the West, it seems to be spreading across the country. When russets feed, they start at the bottom of the plant and make leaves a dirty yellow-brown, almost greasy-looking. The dead leaves drop off, leaving the fruit exposed to sunscald. Russet mites usually kill the plant, so avoid growing tomato-family ornamentals, like *Datura*, *Petunia*, or *Salpiglossis*, on which they live. Predatory mites can keep up with russets in low numbers, but if they get out of control, use sulfur or a miticide.

Colorado potato beetle *(Leptinotarsa decemlineata)* is a yellow-orange beetle with tan stripes on its wing covers. It also chews holes in leaves. The brick red, hump-backed grubs can be controlled with neem spray or the bacteria *Bacillus thuringiensis* var. *San Diego.* Look for the insect's orange egg masses on the underside of leaves and crush them. Control the same as for flea beetles (see "Eggplant," pages 365–366).

Flea beetles *(Epitrix* **spp.)** feed on tomato foliage early in the season, often as soon as true leaves appear or when transplants have been set out. For other symptoms and controls, see "Eggplant" (pages 365–366).

When the corn earworm eats tomatoes, it is called the **tomato fruitworm** *(Heliothis zea).* It starts on leaves, but soon begins eating its way into fruit, usually at the stem end. It also eats broccoli, peppers, cabbage, and lettuce, and can do a lot of damage if left unchecked. Row covers can keep the moths from laying eggs, and *Bacillus thuringiensis*, if applied early, can kill most caterpillars that haven't burrowed into fruit.

Tomato pinworm *(Keiferia lycopersicella)* is another moth caterpillar that eats its way into the stem end of fruit. It is mostly a problem in the South and West. The pinworm is mottled and quite small ($1/8$ inch). It makes dark, narrow tunnels inside the fruit. Controls are similar to those of the fruitworm. In addition, there are also pheromone traps available for pinworms (see page 169).

Tomato hornworms *(Manduca* spp.) are voracious caterpillars that chew leaves and sometimes fruit. In large numbers they can defoliate plants. They are huge green caterpillars with diagonal stripes on their side and a long horn on the tail. Hornworms leave pellets of green excrement where they feed, and they are often found this way. The adults are large sphinx moths that are strong fliers and appear after dusk to feed on nectar. They are strongly attracted to light, and tomato plants around night lights are often heavily infested. Hornworm eggs and small larvae are eaten by many garden predators, such as spiders, predatory bugs, and lacewing larvae. But the most conspicuous natural enemy is a parasitic wasp that develops inside the caterpillars. When the wasp larvae eat their way out of the hornworm's body, they remain attached to their host and spin distinctive pale-colored cocoons. In this way, hornworms serve as a food source for a variety of beneficial insects. Hornworms are not usually a problem in spite of the amount of foliage they eat. In fact, they can often benefit the plant by pruning it. But they can get out of hand sometimes. Handpick hornworms in the early morning, or spray with *Bacillus thuringiensis,* to which they are very susceptible. Otherwise, control like other caterpillars.

CULTURAL PROBLEMS

Blossom-end rot starts as a dark, wet spot on the blossom end of the tomato (opposite the stem end). The blemish may stay dry or become wet and mushy as it grows over the fruit. This disease is a result of calcium deficiency and may be caused by stunted or damaged roots or a soil that is low in calcium or very acidic. The most likely cause is uneven soil moisture, which makes it hard for the plants to take up calcium, especially early varieties in wet soils that are hit by a dry spell. This is why mulches are so helpful when you grow tomatoes: They keep the soil evenly moist, and they smother weeds so there's less chance of root damage during cultivation.

In **catfacing,** the blossom end of the fruit is deformed by rough brown spots, swollen outgrowths, and a puckered surface. It's caused by cold days and nights when the flower buds are forming. It may mean that you started your garden a little too early, or that you need an earlier variety. The fruit is still edible.

Cracking refers to open wounds, either radial (from stem to blossom end) or concentric (around the fruit). Radial cracks are caused by high temperatures and bright light, while concentric ones tend to form when rain follows a dry spell. Other diseases can enter crack wounds, so grow crack-tolerant varieties, keep your soil evenly moist, and shade your plants in very hot weather.

Sunscald occurs when tomatoes get too much sunlight. Look for a blistered, shiny light area on the sun side of the fruit. Tomatoes typically get sunscalded when plants lose leaves through pruning or disease.

VARIETIES

There are literally thousands of tomato varieties. The gene bank in Gatersleben, Germany, maintains over twenty-five hundred varieties as a "heritage of mankind." Seed Savers Exchange lists over 640 open-pollinated varieties in this country alone. They range from ancient lobed heirlooms to modern smooth hybrids, from regional favorites to commercial standards, and from container-sized bushes to rangy vigorous vines. The fruit varies from grape-sized currants to melon-sized beefsteaks in red, pink, orange, yellow, green, black, and white. There is truly a tomato for every taste and every location.

Fully ripe tomatoes come in a variety of solid and striped colors: white, yellow, orange, pink, red, green, and black. The orange color, called beta-carotene (vitamin A), is the same pigment-vitamin found in carrots, squash, sweet potatoes, and other orange vegetables. Orange tomatoes tend to be higher in vitamin A than other colors. White tomatoes have a gene called Gh, for ghost, which breaks down chlorophyll but does not make carotene. Tomatoes of different colors also add greatly to the eye appeal of salads, sauces, and main dishes, so be sure to try varieties other than red tomatoes.

Successful tomato growing begins by choosing the right varieties for your locality. Each area of the country has its own favorite regionally adapted varieties, so begin by talking to neighbors, garden clubs, and county farm agents about which tomatoes grow best where you live. Whether you have warm or cool summers, and which diseases (fusarium or verticillium) are prevalent in your area are important factors. With tomatoes, it's always a good idea to experiment, so leave room in your garden for a diverse tomato patch in which you can test new varieties against old favorites. Since seasons change from year-to-year—a hot summer one year, a cool summer the next year—you may be surprised at what works.

Most gardeners will admit that although hybrid tomatoes are disease resistant and reliable, the open-pollinated types have the best flavor. Heirlooms such as Brandywine, Roma, Camp Joy Cherry, Marmande, Stupice, and Jubilee are renowned for their taste, and some of them should be included in every kitchen gardener's palette of tomato varieties.

The varieties you choose also depend on how you will use the tomatoes. Large, fleshy flattened types are best suited for ketchup and tomato paste. Large-lobed heirlooms with many cavities can be torn apart without a knife and popped into the mouth. Paste tomatoes are ideal for drying and making sauces, pastes, and purées. Some tomato varieties are piquant and meaty and ideal for sauces and salsas. Others are best used for canning or pickling. There are even large tomatoes that can be stuffed and baked like bell peppers.

If you have lots of space, plant a combination of early, midseason, and late varieties, both bush and vine, for a long, luscious supply from early summer through late fall. If you have limited space, try container varieties or certain viney types that, when staked and pruned properly, require less room (see pages 352–353).

Tomatoes are prone to a variety of serious diseases. Always look for resistant varieties, especially if your area is home to verticillium or fusarium wilts. In the long run, this is the only way to deal with these soil-borne plant diseases.

Early varieties should be planted if you live in short-season, cool-summer areas, or coastal regions where warm temperatures are delayed until fall. In places where long warm summers are common, late varieties grow well.

Bush varieties usually fruit earlier than vine tomatoes, but are productive for a shorter time (4 to 6 weeks as opposed to 8 to 12 weeks). They should be staggered throughout the season. They also need less support than vine varieties. If you plan to carry spring-planted tomatoes through until fall, consider a series of vine varieties with different maturity dates, like Early Girl (early), Better Boy (main crop), and Big Girl (late).

Plant breeders are always looking for improved tomato varieties, and the kitchen gardener should check seed catalogs for new introductions. Tomato breeding programs are working on (1) varieties resistant to more difficult diseases such as late blight *(Phytophthora),* bacterial diseases, and viruses other than TMV; (2) large-fruited, early-to-bear varieties; (3) early, disease-resistant plum types for fresh eating rather than processing; (4) extra-dwarf types; and (5) highly flavored, sugar-rich types. The future of tomato varieties is almost limitless.

BASIC TOMATO TYPES

Slicing tomatoes are big enough to slice and tasty enough to eat raw. They are great for salads and sandwiches, and for baking and stuffing. They come in all sizes, from 6 ounces to large beefsteaks weighing over 2 pounds. Small-fruit varieties are easier to grow, take up less room in the garden, and are more adaptable to temperatures than large slicers.

Paste tomatoes are rather dry and mealy, and contain fewer seeds and less juice than slicers. As a result, they are easier to dry and to cook into ketchup, sauces, pastes, and purées. Either bush or vine, they come in yellow and red and in two basic shapes: plum (also called Roma) and pear.

Cherry tomatoes are small and grow in large clusters. They can be bush or vine, and come in several colors. Cherry tomatoes don't suffer from blossom-end rot and are generally earlier and tastier than other tomatoes. Many cherry varieties, like Pixie and Small Fry, are exceptionally sweet when fully ripe, and are excellent for containers, small garden spaces, hanging baskets, and for overwintering in the home or a protected sunny space. While you can't slice cherries, they are great for salads, hors d'oeuvres, kabobs, and snacking.

Tomato Growth Habits

Indeterminate, or vine, tomatoes do not flower at the end of the main stems, but on lateral stems, while the main stems keep growing just like any other vine. Indeterminates produce higher yields over longer periods and may be from 5 to 9 feet long. They should be pruned, staked, or trellised to keep the fruit from touching the ground.

Determinate, or bush, tomatoes produce flowers at the ends of the main stems. This encourages lateral growth and a compact plant 2 to 4 feet tall. Determinate tomatoes set fruit early and all at once, and because of their bushy growth, they are better caged than staked or trellised. They also tend to stop producing at the onset of hot weather, so you should choose several determinate varieties with different maturity times.

Semi-determinate tomatoes are determinate plants that produce lateral flower buds before the stems end in a flower cluster. In other words, they are just big bushes.

Dwarf tomatoes can be either bush or vine, but the length of the stem between the laterals (the "internode") is quite short, making these varieties suitable for small spaces and containers. "Dwarf" refers to the size of the plant, not the fruit.

RECOMMENDED TOMATO VARIETIES

VARIETY/TYPE	HYBRID (H)/ OPEN POLLINATED (OP)	FRUIT	RESISTANCE	COMMENTS
Early Red Slicing (50–60 days)				
Bush				
Bush Beefsteak	OP	Medium		Early beefsteak type; compact plant and high yields. Popular in Northwest.
Earlirouge	OP	Medium-large	V	Sets fruit in heat or cold; tasty and peels easily for juices and soups.
Siletz	OP	Large beefsteak		Acid taste; yields in cool weather; great slicer.
Ultra Girl	H	Medium	V, F, N	Semi-bush; widely adapted; very popular.
Vine				
Burpeeana Early Pick	H	Medium-large beefsteak	V, F	Early hybrid; developed for Western growing.
Champion	H	Medium-large beefsteak	V, F, N, T	Popular sandwich tomato; larger than Early Girl and earlier than Better Boy.
Dona	H	Medium-oblate	V, F, N, T	French market–garden variety; sweet/acid flavor.
Early Cascade	H	Clusters of medium fruit	V, F, A	Vigorous vine; for slicing, canning, or sauces; favorite of many home gardeners.
Early Girl Improved	H	Small-medium globe	V, F, F	Most reliable type in a wide range of climates; standard of early slicing tomatoes.
First Lady	H	Small-medium globe	V, F, N, T	Has everything: earliness, disease and crack resistance, tasty fruit, lengthy yield.
Stupice*	OP	Small fruit		Best-tasting, most reliable early heirloom; high yields even in cool weather.
Main-Crop Red Slicing (70-80 Days)				
Bush				
Campbell 1327	OP	Medium-oblate	V, F	Popular for canning and crack resistance; very adaptable.
Cavalier	H	Medium	V, F, N, T, A	High yields of firm fruit on compact vines.
Celebrity	H	Medium	V, F, N, T	1984 AAS winner; great flavor; widely adaptable.
Floramerica	H	Large	V, F	1978 AAS winner; high yields; mild flavor; fresh, canning, or juicing; widely adapted.
Marmande*	OP	Medium ribbed globe	V, F	French garden heirloom; semi-bush; highest-quality flavor.
Olomovic	OP	Medium-ovate		Czech variety; sets well in cool summers.
Vine				
Better Boy	H	Large globe	V, F, N	Very tasty, meaty fruit; long yield; needs support, like Big Boy, but earlier.
Carmello	H	Medium globe	V, F, N, T	French garden variety; fragile fruit; great taste; crack-resistant.
Champion	H	Medium globe	V, F, N, T	Very popular for taste and disease-resistance; very adaptable.
Double Rich	OP	Large		Very high in vitamin C; very productive.
Late Red Slicing (>80 days)				
Bush				
Cal-Ace VG	OP	Large	V, F	Bred for the West, but grows everywhere.
Stakeless	OP	Medium-large	F	Vine grows without support; for small gardens.

RECOMMENDED TOMATO VARIETIES, *continued from page 360*

VARIETY/TYPE	HYBRID (H)/ OPEN-POLLINATED (OP)	FRUIT	RESISTANCE	COMMENTS
Late Red Slicing (>80 days), *continued*				
Vine				
Big Girl	H	Large globe	V, F	A Big Boy with resistance; mild flavor, vigorous grower; widely adapted.
Burback Red Slicing*	OP	Medium		Since 1915; developed by Luther Burbank; high in amino acids; stocky vine.
Lady Luck	H	Medium	V, F, N, T	Touted as "best late variety for local home gardens."
Super Beefsteak	OP	Extra large	V, F, N	Huge flavorful fruit; needs long warm season.
Colored Slicing Tomatoes				
Bush				
Caro Rich	OP	Orange; large		Very high vitamin A; late.
Vine				
Brandywine*	OP	Pink; large globe		Renowned for its taste of sweet and tart; may crack; large vine; main crop.
Evergreen	OP	Green		Only tomato that's green when ripe; mid-season.
Golden Boy	H	Yellow; large globe		Large vigorous plant, mild flavor, main crop.
Golden Mandarin Cross	H	Yellow; large		Best-tasting yellow tomato; dense foliage for safe fruiting; great garnish; main crop.
Jubilee*	OP	Gold-orange; medium-large		1943 AAS winner; remains most popular yellow slicer; mild flavor; main crop.
Lemon Boy	H	Bright yellow; medium	V, F, N	First true yellow tomato; mild flavor, crack resistant; long production; late.
Orange Queen	OP	Medium orange; oblate		Earliest orange slicing tomatoes.
Pink Girl	H	Pink; medium-large	V, F, T	Best pink hybrid; large fruit; mild flavor; crack-resistant; long harvest; late.
White Beauty	OP	White; medium-large		Great taste with high sugar and few seeds; low in vitamins A; enlivens salads; late.
Cherry Tomatoes				
Bush				
Basket King	H	Red; clusters of 2-inch fruit		Very early; for hanging baskets; cascading clusters of fruit.
Baxter's Bush Cherry*	OP	Red; clusters of 2-inch fruit		Earliest open-pollinated cherry tomato; needs no support; vigorous and productive; great taste.
Chello	H	Yellow; clusters of 1-inch fruit		High yields; viny bush; for salads and snacks; early.
Small Fry	H	Red; clusters of 1-inch fruit	V, F, N	AAS winner; high yields; compact vines; for containers and small gardens; early.
Sweet 100 Plus	H	Red; clusters of medium fruit		The standard of large-fruited cherry tomatoes rank growth needs support; high vitamin C; early.
Patio Prize	H	Red; clusters of 2-inch fruit	V, F, N	A better Patio, great for large containers; erratic, but taste is worth it; early.

continued on page 362

RECOMMENDED TOMATO VARIETIES, *continued from page 361*

VARIETY/TYPE	HYBRID (H)/ OPEN-POLLINATED (OP)	FRUIT	RESISTANCE	COMMENTS
Cherry Tomatoes, *continued*				
Vine				
Camp Joy Cherry	OP	Clusters of 1-inch fruit		From California biodynamic farm collective; superior taste, extended production; main crop.
Pink Cherry	OP	Pink-red; 1-inch fruit		Very productive; good for salads and pickling; main crop.
Red Cherry	OP	Red; 1-inch fruit		Vigorous vine; one of the best large-plant cherry tomatoes; main crop
Paste/Drying				
Bush				
Bell Star	OP	Red; plum		Large paste for canning or juice; for containers and cool climates; early.
La Roma	H	Red; oblong; small-medium	V, F	High-yielding, hybrid Roma; early.
Milano	H		V, F	Early Italian; great for drying, sauce, paste.
Napoli VF	H	Red; plum	V, F	Viny bush; like Roma VF but earlier, shorter yield, and smaller fruit; main crop.
Principe Borghese	OP	Red; plum		The sun-drying variety in Italy; meaty with little juice; main crop.
Roma VF	OP	Plum/pear; blocky	V, F	Viny bush; versatile, popular; for drying sauces, juicing, and canning; main crop.
Ropreco	OP	Red; plum		Earliest paste tomato; big yields; good taste; great for sauces.
Royal Chico VF	H	Bright red	V, F	Very compact with large fruit; outstanding for paste or canning; main crop.
Sprinter	H	Globular		High yields; great taste for paste; main crop.
Super Italian*	OP	Large fruit		Italian heirloom; large fruit makes sauce fast; ripens after picking; main crop.
Viva Italia	H	Red; pear	V, F, N	New hybrid paste; lots of sugar; sets in heat; fresh, canning, or freezing; late.
Vine				
Nova	H	Red; pear; oblong		Earlier than Roma; same taste; good for cool climates; main crop.
Red Pear	OP	Red; pear		See "Yellow Pear"
San Marzano	OP	Bright red; pear		For dry, warm climates; large vines; long yields; mild flavor and meaty texture; late.
Yellow Pear*	OP	Yellow; pear		Earliest yellow pear; fresh canning, and pickling; needs support; main crop.
Yellow Plum	OP	Yellow; plum		Mild flavor for salads, canning, and pickling; main crop.

Disease Resistance: V = Verticillium wilt; F = Fusarium wilt; N = Nematodes; T = Tobacco Mosaic Virus

Fruit Size: Cherry/pear/plum 1–2 inches; small 2–4 inches; medium 4–8 inches; large 8–16 inches; very large 1–2 pounds

* Indicates heirloom variety.

HARVEST AND STORAGE

Tomatoes continue to ripen after they're picked, but only if they are mature. After pollination, the flower's ovary swells rapidly into a hard, dark green fruit called an "immature green." As the tomato loses its chlorophyll (the source of greenness) and begins producing other pigments, it slowly lightens from deep green to lime green to almost yellow. This is the "mature green" stage. Further color changes produce streaks of pink at the blossom end of the fruit, which is now called a "breaker." Immature green tomatoes will not ripen off the vine under any circumstances, but mature greens and breakers will.

When the nighttime temperature is consistently below 50°F, vine-ripening time is over for tomatoes; you might as well harvest them all. Although immature greens cannot be ripened, they can be used to make relish. You can hasten the ripening of mature green or breaker tomatoes by putting them in a paper bag with an apple or a banana. This traps the fruit's natural ethylene gas and speeds up the ripening. Place the container in a cool (60° to 75°F), dark place. If you have both breakers and mature greens, put equal numbers of each in a container. The breakers will give off enough ethylene to ripen the mature greens.

Cold temperatures slow down ripening, so don't put unripe tomatoes in the fridge unless you want to keep them that way. Cold temperatures also destroy the chemicals that give mature tomatoes their essential flavors, so store them in a cool, but not cold, dark place until you need them.

Both slicing and paste tomatoes can be canned. Cherry tomatoes, being smaller, have a high ratio of seeds, juice, and skin to pulp, so they should be eaten fresh.

For a long time it was believed that non-red tomatoes were low in acidity. As such, they could be eaten by people with sensitive stomachs, but not used for canning because they didn't have enough acid to prevent food poisoning. According to studies by the USDA, however, there is probably as much variation in tomato acidity due to climate, soil, and culture as to color differences. On the average, red tomatoes are just as acidic as white, green, pink, or orange ones. It is far more important to pick tomatoes that are not overripe and to follow the recommendations for reliable canning methods.

TOMATO GROWING TIPS

- First and foremost, fit the proper variety to the local climate, prevailing diseases, and available space.

- Tomatoes need at least 6 hours of sun a day; they don't like shade at all.

- Grow tomatoes from transplants that have been well hardened-off.

- Don't try to rush the season; wait until nights get above 50°F to plant. Early varieties set fruit at lower night temperatures. Extend production by growing early, mid-season, and late varieties whenever possible.

- To conserve garden space and keep fruit off the ground, cage bush varieties and prune vine varieties so they can be tied to trellises or stakes.

- Don't feed the plants too much nitrogen. This makes leaves at the expense of fruit.

- Avoid overhead watering, which encourages several diseases.

- Tomatoes continue to ripen after they are picked, but only under certain conditions (see text).

Eggplant
SOLANACEAE (Nightshade or Tomato Family)

Solanum melongena
> (aubergine, melongene,
> brinjal, and Italian squash)

CHINESE: *qie zi*
FRENCH: *aubergine*
GERMAN: *Eierfrucht, Aubergine*
ITALIAN: *melanzana, petonciano*
JAPANESE: *nasu*
SPANISH: *berenjena*

Many gardeners would agree that, with its many shapes, colorful fruit, and vivid purple flowers, the eggplant is one of the most attractive vegetables in the edible landscape. In fact, until this century, American gardeners valued this ancient Asian vegetable more as an ornamental plant than as a versatile food.

The eggplant is probably native to the dry hillsides of eastern India, where it was first described in Vedic writings from the sixth century B.C. Related species of eggplant are popular in Southeast Asia. The eggplant was not known in Europe until Arab traders brought eggplants to Spain in the twelfth century A.D. By the eighteenth century, it was an established food in France and Italy, and in 1806 it was introduced to the United States as an ornamental curiosity. In Europe, large oval varieties were developed. In Asia, where food is sliced and stir-fried at high temperatures, long, narrow types are still preferred. Today, eggplant is grown in most warm regions of the world, and is widely used in Asian, Middle Eastern, and Mediterranean cuisines.

When it was first introduced in Europe, eggplant was called *mala insana* in Spain, *melazana* in Italy. Both names loosely translate to "mad apple," because people believed that eating eggplant would cause madness. After all, it was related to the tomato, which, at the time, was believed to be poisonous.

Eggplant is not particularly nutritious, but it is very filling and its firm, meaty texture makes it an excellent grilling and baking vegetable. Charred on the grill, eggplant takes on a unique smoky flavor. Eggplant can be served as a main dish, an appetizer, a side dish, or as an ingredient in meat or vegetable dishes.

Although the eggplant is not terribly popular in the United States, many other cultures seem to have their own favorite eggplant dish. The French cook it with summer vegetables to form the colorful Provençal stew ratatouille. In the Middle East, it is charred, mashed, and combined with sesame paste (tahini), olive oil, garlic, and lemon juice to make the zesty spread baba ghanouj. In Greece, it is part of the savory casserole dish moussaka. In India, mashed baked eggplant is mixed with yogurt and seasoned with cumin and coriander. And Italy, of course, has the famous eggplant parmigiana and caponata.

The spongelike flesh of eggplant soaks up stocks, cooking juices, and oil. In fact, eggplant has been described as a black hole into which infinite quantities of cooking oil can disappear, so care must be taken by those following a low-fat diet. Many recipes call for salting eggplant before cooking it, then rinsing it to wash off the salt. This draws out some of the moisture and produces a denser flesh, which absorbs less fat during cooking;

it also eliminates much of the vegetable's natural bitter taste and mellows its flavors a bit. If you're going to cook eggplant in oil or mash it up, you might want to try the salt method. Otherwise, we find it unnecessary. Our favorite way to prepare eggplant is to lightly brush thin slices with olive and mashed garlic, and then grill or stir fry them quickly.

CULTIVATION

Like the tomato, the eggplant is a tender perennial grown as an annual. A bushy, somewhat sprawling plant, its fruits can vary in shape from oval to oblong, in a wide variety of colors.

Eggplant requires lots of heat, and needs 3 to 4 months of warm weather to produce well. It thrives best at 78°F during the day and 68°F at night. It is especially sensitive to low temperatures, more so than either peppers or tomatoes. Large-fruited varieties need more heat than those with smaller fruits, so select the latter where summers are short.

PLANTING

For best germination, eggplant needs warm soils ranging from 75° to 80°F. For this reason, the seeds are usually started indoors 8 to 10 weeks prior to the estimated last spring frost date. The seeds take 10 to 14 days to germinate. Keep the soil moist but not soggy, because the seedlings are prone to damping off. The seedlings need to be exposed to strong natural or artificial light before being set out; a cold soil can shock them. When transplants have six true leaves, place them in full sun and slowly reduce watering to harden them off. Plant seedlings 2 to 3 feet apart and use floating row covers to retain heat and keep out various pests like flea beetles.

SOILS AND FERTILIZERS

Eggplant is a heavy feeder. Boost your soil with blood meal, bone meal, and kelp to supply the necessary nutrients. Some gardeners also feed plants with liquid fish emulsion every 2 weeks to ensure that they are well fed. The fruit can become bitter if the plants don't get enough water, so mulch, water often, and add organic soil amendments like aged manure and compost. For information on nutrient deficiencies in eggplants, see "Tomatoes," page 354.

DISEASES

Tobacco mosaic virus: See "Tomatoes," page 354.

Verticillium wilt *(Verticillium* spp.) is one of the most serious eggplant diseases. No eggplant is resistant to verticillium, but there are ways to increase yields by helping the plant to "outgrow" the disease. This means planting early varieties in warm soils and fertilizing regularly to spur rapid growth, before the disease can gain a foothold. Mulch with black plastic to keep the soil warm. Early low-yielding Italian types are more tolerant than the late varieties with white and lavender fruit. See "Tomatoes," page 356, for more information.

PESTS

Colorado potato beetle *(Leptinotarsa decimlineata)*: See "Tomatoes," page 356.

Several species of **flea beetles *(Epitrix* spp.)**, tiny black and brown jumping beetles, are generally regarded as the eggplant's worst insect pests. Badly infested plants have leaves that are honeycombed with tiny shot holes from the feeding insects. Flea beetles also attack many other vegetables, weeds, and ornamentals. To prevent damage, avoid stressing transplants by hardening them off and planting large sturdy seedlings in warm soils. Cultivate the soil in fall or early spring to disturb overwintering adults. Cover seedlings with floating row covers. If necessary, spray with rotenone or pyrethrum.

Spider mites: See "Tomatoes," page 356.

VARIETIES

Everyone is familiar with the dark purple pear-shaped eggplant, but the fruits may also be white, green, black, pink, red, orange, or variegated lavender and white. There are about sixty open-pollinated varieties of eggplant and several hybrids. The two basic types are the domestic, or Italian, eggplant, which is oval or round with a glossy black or white skin, and the Japanese, or Asian, eggplant, which is elongated and comes in many colors. A host of specialty varieties includes miniature plants in a range of shapes and colors, among them the lavender and white Italian Rosa Bianca. Smaller eggplants are generally sweeter and more tender than the larger varieties.

Eggplant has gained popularity in the United States, thanks to the introduction of early-maturing, disease-resistant hybrids that set fruit over a wider range of temperatures.

Japanese

Bianca Ovale

Florida High Bush

White Egg

Rosa Bianca

RECOMMENDED EGGPLANT VARIETIES		
VARIETY/TYPE	**HYBRID (H)/OPEN-POLLINATED (OP)**	**COMMENTS**
Oval, Bell-Shaped		
Black Beauty*	OP	Dark purple, standard late variety for areas with long summers. Offered since 1902.
Black Bell	H	Dark purple, best midseason Italian type. Small fruit.
Blacknite	H	Dark purple with early, large fruit. Best large oval variety. Resistant to the tobacco mosaic virus.
Italian Pink Bicolor	OP	Combines great colors and tastes.
Listada de Gandia*	OP	Bicolor lavender. Variable colors. Best in southern areas. Very tasty.
Osterei	H	White, small, oval fruit. Good for containers.
Rosa Bianca*	OP	Italian heirloom, light pink and white shades; mild flavor, no bitterness.
Turkish Orange*	OP	Turkish heirloom. Round, tomatolike fruit. Harvest when green. Susceptible to flea beetles.
Long, Cylindrical		
Agora	OP	Purple, bitter-free Italian type. Upright bush.
Casper	OP	White midseason variety.
Dusky	H	Purple-black, popular, pear-shaped, mid-early variety. Resistant to the tobacco mosaic virus.
Ichiban	H	Great purple, mid-early Asian variety.
Neon	H	Dark pink. Bitter free.
Orient Express	H	Purple-black, very early variety. Good in cool weather.
Thai Long Green*	OP	Light green, very hardy, and excellent for stir-frying.
Violetta de Firenze*	OP	Lavender and white bicolored Italian heirloom. Needs plenty of heat. Very tasty.

* Indicates heirloom variety.

HARVEST AND STORAGE

Harvest eggplant when the skin is still glossy. If the skin is dull and the seeds are large and dark, the flesh is overripe and will probably be bitter. The thin skin is easily injured, so take care when picking the fruit, and try to leave the green "calyx" cup attached to reduce injury. Use pruning shears to snip off the rough stems.

Eggplant doesn't store very well, but you can keep them for several days in a dark place.

EGGPLANT GROWING TIPS

- Start plants indoors 8 weeks before the last spring frost. Germinate at 75° to 85°F. Eggplant needs warm soils to grow, so transplants work best.

- Transplant seedlings into pots. Set out plants with at least six leaves and only when night temperatures are above 55°F.

- To avoid serious diseases, don't push your eggplants to grow during cold weather. Warm up the soil with black plastic, foliar feed biweekly, and grow during the warmest time of the year.

- Harvest when the fruits are small and glossy.

Peppers
SOLANACEAE (Nightshade or Tomato Family)

Capsicum annuum var. grossum
(bell, sweet, pimiento pepper)
CHINESE: *tian jiao*
FRENCH: *poivre d'Espagna, paprica*
GERMAN: *Gemüsa-Paprika,*
Spanischer Pfeffer
ITALIAN: *peperone*
JAPANESE: *piiman; shishi tôgarashi*
SPANISH: *pimiento, paprica*

Capsicum annuum var. longum
(cayenne, chile, or hot pepper)
CHINESE: *chang la jiao*
FRENCH: *poivre di Cayenne, piment d'oiseau*
GERMAN: *Cayenne, Vogel, Gewürzpaprika*
ITALIAN: *pepe di Cayenne, peperone rabbioso*
JAPANESE: *nagami-tougarashi*
SPANISH: *chile, pimiento picante*

Capsicum frutescens
(tabasco and habanero pepper)
CHINESE: *xiao mi jiao*
FRENCH: *piment, pilli*
GERMAN: *Tabasco Pfeffer*
ITALIAN: *tabasco, peperone ornamentale*
SPANISH: *tabasco; chile; guindilla*

If someone asked you which is the fastest growing vegetable in popularity, you might be hard pressed to guess peppers. Between 1976 and 1986, consumption of peppers in the United States more than doubled. And it's still going up in what can only be described as a growing affection between Americans and peppers. It's amazing how they've slipped into our diets. Peppers are in curry powder, chile powder, cayenne, pizza pepper, paprika, pimiento, pickles, stuffed olives, Tabasco sauce, dips, and a bewildering array of salsas. Raw, baked, fried, grilled, or stuffed, the native American pepper is now more than just an ethnic spice. It has moved into the mainstream of our diets. The '90s will go down as the decade in which salsa became more popular than ketchup.

Peppers are native to Latin America, where people have been growing them since at least 7000 B.C. By 5200 B.C. people were cultivating several species in neolithic gardens throughout Central and South America. When Columbus arrived in the West Indies, he found natives growing the plant, which they called *aji (ah-hee)*, or chile, the Aztec word for "red." They used the large pungent berry to spice up an otherwise bland and saltless diet. They also valued it as a medicine; peppers helped them digest their bulky foods and cool their bodies with sweat. To Columbus, the New World pepper had the sharp taste of the Old World black pepper, but with a broader range of flavor. Columbus called it "pepper," after the black pepper of India he had been seeking, to the confusion of generations to come.

From Spain, the pepper spread rapidly. Wherever it landed, it revolutionized the cuisine of the area, especially in Slavic countries, the Mediterranean, China, India, and Southeast Asia. Today, peppers continue to be used the world over as a medicine, condiment, spice, and vegetable. Ironically, the United

States may be one of the last countries to fully embrace this wonderful vegetable.

The name *Capsicum* comes from the Greek word *kapto,* meaning to bite. But giving popular names to peppers is not always straightforward. In Hungary the word "paprika" means pepper, and in this country it's a variety of sweet pepper popular in condiments. In the United States, the anglicized spelling "chili" and the Spanish "chile" are used, while chili also applies to various stews of meats, beans, spices, and peppers. In Mexico, they say "chile" to mean both hot and sweet types; it's also used descriptively, as in chile verde, or with its place of origin, as in poblano chile. To make it even more confusing, the same variety can have different names for young green, red, dry, and fresh forms. For example, poblano is the fresh green form of a long semihot pepper; when dried, it is called "ancho." Fresh green Anaheims are called "chiles verdes." Fresh red ones become "chiles colorados." If they are dried, roasted, and peeled, they are called "chiles pasados." The fresh pasilla pepper becomes a "cholaca" when it is dried. A smoked serrano chile is called "mora moritas," and a smoked jalapeño is called a "chipotle." In places where peppers are appreciated for their range of tastes and uses, the people are very careful about how they describe their pepper pods.

Peppers get their heat from a compound called capsaicin (cap-SAY-uh-sin). Most of this fiery stuff is found in tiny blisterlike sacs in the light-colored ribs on the inside of the fruit (the placenta). These sacs are easily broken if rubbed, and they can cause a burning sensation in your skin, mouth, or eyes. Always wear gloves when you prepare hot peppers, or wash your hands afterwards. Generally speaking, the hottest peppers are thin-skinned with many ribs. Contrary to public opinion, there is very little capsaicin in the seeds or skins.

Until 1980, the heat of peppers was measured by taste tests—useful but not very ob-jective. A better way of measuring pepper pungency is to analyze capsaicin levels in parts per million. The levels are expressed as Scoville units, the standard index (see below).

Peppers hit their peak heat just as they are turning from green to red (or another color), and the hottest peppers are usually at the bottom of the plant. The heat of a pepper is strongly affected by the age of the plant, as well as the soil and climate where it is grown. The real secret is hot nights that stress the plant and make it produce more capsaicin.

The flavor of peppers is contained mostly in the outer skin, not the inner wall. The skin is also a source of vitamins, especially vitamins A and C. For maximum nutrition, don't peel your peppers.

THE SCOVILLE SCALE

CHILE	RATING	SCOVILLE UNITS
Habanero, Bahamian	10	300,000–100,000
Chiltepin, Thai, santaka	9	100,000–50,000
Pequin, cayenne, tabasco	8	50,000–30,000
De arbol	7	30,000–15,000
Serrano, yellow wax	6	15,000–5,000
Jalapeño, mirasol	5	5,000–2,500
Sandia, cascabel, rocotillo	4	2,500–1,500
Ancho, pasilla	3	1,500–1,000
Anaheim, New Mexico chile	2	1,000–500
Pepperoncini, El Paso, cherry	1	500–100
Sweet (bell), pimiento, banana	0	100–0

In the kitchen, peppers are one of the most versatile and nutritious vegetables you can have. You can eat them raw, cooked, or pickled. Serve thick-walled sweet peppers raw in salads or as a garnish, or cook and stuff them with elegant stews or last night's leftovers. You can also sauté sweet peppers as a condiment for other dishes and as an ingredient in hundreds of ethnic recipes. Dried peppers like cholacas and anchos can be ground up and combined with other spices to make chile powder or puréed into a chocolate-like paste called "pisado chile." In Mexico, this paste is widely used as a flavoring in dishes. Fresh and cooked chiles can be puréed with tomatoes, tomatillos, onions, and herbs to make a bevy of salsas from mild to fiery hot.

Like celery and onion, pepper is a highly aromatic vegetable, which also boosts the tastes of other ingredients. When peppers are heated in vegetable oils, the capsaicin breaks down into vanillin, which is known to draw out flavors in foods. Peppers also slows the oxidation of cooking oils, so hot pepper oil doesn't go rancid as quickly as plain oil.

The pungent lure of the chile pepper also goes beyond the dinner plate; peppers have a variety of nonfood uses, appearing in muscle ointments, self-defense sprays, food coloring, petroleum jelly, throat gargles, cosmetics, and insecticides (see page 174 for more about the latter).

Peppers are one of the best natural sources of vitamins A and C. Vitamin A helps maintain normal vision. It is also an antioxidant that helps fight cancer and contributes to the health of bones and teeth. Vitamin C promotes growth and helps in tissue repair, especially in blood vessels. In general, both vitamins increase as peppers range from green to red fruit and from sweet to hot. Ounce for ounce, a hot red pepper has more vitamin A than carrots and more vitamin C than citrus fruit. The recommended daily allowance of vitamin A can be satisfied by eating about a tablespoon of fresh red chile sauce.

CULTIVATION

Peppers are tender perennials grown in temperate regions as annuals. They can be directly seeded or transplanted, depending on soil temperature and growing season. Generally speaking, peppers are started 8 to 12 weeks before the last spring frost, and hardened-off for 2 weeks prior to setting them out in the garden. Hot peppers often take longer to sprout and grow than sweet types, so plan accordingly. Pepper seeds also germinate very slowly in cool soils, so if you don't have warm soil in late spring, it's best to start seedlings indoors 6 to 8 weeks before transplanting them out into the garden. Peppers don't set fruit very well below 75° or above 85°F. Fruit set is also reduced by extremes in soil and weather conditions. Optimal temperature for seedling growth is quite high, 86°F.

Each species and variety of hot pepper has the potential to be hot, which is only realized with the correct combination of temperature, soil, and season. But one thing we have noticed over years of growing peppers: Once the fruit sets, the hotter the climate, the hotter the pepper.

Although peppers require warm weather to grow best, you can help things by making your soil warm with mulches (see page 133), growing the right varieties for your area, and starting with seedlings that are strong and well hardened-off. Once vigorous transplants start growing in a warm soil, peppers are fairly easy to grow.

PLANTING

To really enjoy the great diversity of pepper types, you'll want to grow your own transplants from seed. Peppers are a tricky vegetable to germinate, and the seedlings are rather weak plants. For really successful growing, you need to pay special attention to early growth. The seeds of peppers, especially the hot ones, go dormant if they are stored below 85°F. That is why most pepper seeds you buy seem to take so long to germinate. This dormancy is necessary for the plant's survival but it makes for a slow sprout. To get your seeds to germinate faster, you'll have to soften or nick the seed coats before they can begin absorbing water. To soften the seeds, scatter them on a wet towel or piece of paper, roll it up, and place it in a dark, warm spot for a couple of days (see page 376). You don't want to sprout the seeds, just soften their seed coats. To nick the seed coat, either cover the seeds with a towel and gently roll them with a rolling pin, or place the seeds in a tall jar lined with a roll of rough sandpaper, coarse side facing in, and shake the jar for a few minutes.

Sow seeds $1/4$ inch deep and 2 to 4 inches apart in a germination container. When seedlings are 2 inches tall and have their first true leaves, transplant them to individual cell packs or containers. From here, seedlings can take several weeks to reach transplant size. When they are about 5 to 6 inches tall, harden-off transplants by holding back on water (never let them wilt) and growing on in cooler location (70°F), being careful that night temperatures don't fall below 60°F.

Transplant to the garden in full sun when the soil is warm. As a general rule, it's time to set out peppers when the soil 4 inches below the surface is at least 65°F at 8 A.M. Below 55°F, roots will not develop. If the soil is still cool, plant out in raised beds, warm the soil with black plastic, and cover seedlings with a fabric row cover. Set plants 12 to 18 inches apart. Space as close as possible; research has shown that close spacing produces more and larger fruit. Don't mulch until the soil is thoroughly warm, and don't overfertilize with nitrogen at this point. It leads to lush growth and a poor fruit set. The key to successful early growth of peppers is a well hardened-off seedling with strong roots set into a warm soil.

SOILS AND FERTILIZERS

Peppers prefer a sandy loam or loam soil. They grow especially well in raised beds where the soil is warm and drains well. Peppers are fertilized much like tomatoes, except they don't need as much nutrients. Hold off on nitrogen until the plants are 2 months old. Then side-dress with a 5-10-10 fertilizer. As flower and fruit begin to develop, side-dress again. In light or low-nutrient soils, you can help growth by foliar feeding with calcium nitrate, liquid fish, or seaweed fertilizers. Magnesium is critical, so in magnesium-poor soils, when plants begin to blossom, dissolve a teaspoon of Epsom salts (magnesium sulfate) into a spray bottle and spritz the leaves. This helps to encourage an early and abundant fruit set. For information on nutrient deficiencies in peppers, see "Tomatoes," page 354.

DISEASES AND PESTS

Most cultural problems, diseases, and pests that affect tomatoes also attack peppers (see pages 354–357). Liquid rotenone and floating row covers will reduce most insect pests if used early in the season. Whenever possible, use disease-tolerant or resistant varieties, practice good sanitation, and don't plant peppers where other nightshade family vegetables, such as potatoes, tomatoes, or eggplants have grown within the last 2 years.

VARIETIES

There's a staggering range of pepper shapes, colors, sizes, and flavors available to today's home gardener. There are over five hundred open-pollinated varieties, and one hundred hybrid varieties. From small and round to large and blocky, white to purple, and sweet to sweltering, there's a pepper for every taste.

The many shapes of peppers have evolved from their cherrylike ancestor in four major ways:

1. An elongation into conical shapes that are short and narrow (serrano, jalapeño), medium (cayenne), and long (Anaheim, pasilla)

2. A gradual tapering into wide conical forms from small (habanero) to large (pimiento and poblano)

3. An overall enlargement from small round shapes (cherry, cascabel, rocotillo) to tomato shapes and the lobed, blocky shapes of the sweet bells

4. The long, full shapes of the large manzana and Italian peppers

Most peppers are green in the immature stage but turn red or brown as they mature on the plant. However, today's sweet peppers also come in a rainbow of colors including white, yellow, orange, brown, purple, and black, and are as attractive on the bush as they are in fresh salads and sauces.

Although peppers are versatile, some varieties have special uses. Thin-skinned ones like Paprika, are better for drying, frying, and cooking. Thicker-skinned, sweet, and succulent types like Sweet Banana, Sweet Italian, Bell Star, Cal Wonder, or the yellowish Aconcagua are best to eat fresh, sautéed, grilled, or roasted, and they're great for stuffing and for making relishes. Heart-shaped Pimiento is just right for canning and Sweet Cherry is perfect for pickling. For a rich red color and sweet taste in salads and omelets, try Pimiento (also found as a stuffing in olives). And if your summers are short, try the new generation of early bell peppers like Ace.

The famous Hatch peppers refer to the Anaheim varieties grown at various farms in Hatch, New Mexico, like Big Jim, New Mexico #9, and Sonora. These and other hybrids generally provide less blossom drop during cool nights, more disease resistance,

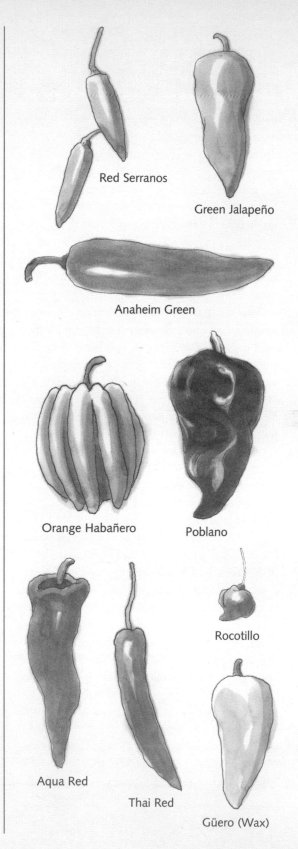

Red Serranos

Green Jalapeño

Anaheim Green

Orange Habañero

Poblano

Rocotillo

Aqua Red

Thai Red

Güero (Wax)

RECOMMENDED PEPPER VARIETIES

TYPE/VARIETY	HYBRID (H) OR OPEN-POLLINATED (OP)	HEAT	COMMENTS
BELL GROUP			Large, lobed, blocky fruit, like a bell.
Green to Red			
Ace	H	1	Extra early, even in cool climates; large yields; early red.
Belle Star		1	TMV resistant; early; thick-walled, large fruit.
Big Bertha	H	1	Popular, large, deep bell; main crop.
Bull Nose Hot		3	A hot, bell-shaped pepper.
Cal Wonder	OP	1	Popular in cooler regions of the west, but adaptable; thick walls for stuffing.
Northstar	H	1	Early to turn red in cool climates; TMV resistant.
Red Dawn	H	1	High yields; great taste; best early red.
World Beater*	OP	1	Tall plants; heavy crop; large fruit with thick flesh; main crop.
Other Colors			
Chocolate Beauty	H	1	Best-tasting brown bell; very high in vitamin C; main crop.
Golden Bell	H	1	Judged the sweetest and most vigorous golden bell.
Golden Summer	OP	1	Deep gold when ripe; TMV resistant.
Ivory	H	1	Turns ivory white at early harvest.
Lilac Belle	H	1	Matures from ivory to lavender to crimson; large fruit.
Orobelle	H	1	Yellow when ripe; strong plants.
Purple Beauty	OP	1	Best OP purple strain; small and prolific; thick flesh.
Yellow Belle	OP	1	Yellow variety of Cal Wonder.
OTHER SWEET PEPPERS			
Aconcagua*	H	1	Large, long, and contorted; tender and sweet for frying and grilling; green to red.
Corno di Torro*	H	1-2	Italian "bull horn" frying pepper; "Giallo" is yellow and "Rosson" is red.
Gypsy	H	1	Bred for flavor; medium, wedge-shaped, and thin walled; TMV resistant; yellow to red.
Italian Sweet	OP	1	One of the sweetest peppers; dwarf, upright plant.
ANCHO/POBLANO GROUP			Large, thin-walled, and heart- or wedge-shaped; essential to Mexican cuisine. (Green to Reddish Brown or Brown)
Ancho (many types)	OP	2	Lobed, heart-shaped, and wrinkled; sweet flesh, hot pith; the relleno pepper.
Mulatta Isleno	OP	2	Ripens brown; used in mole sauces; widely adapted in warmer climates.
Pasilla Bajio	OP	2	Long cylindrical fruit; great for drying; smoky flavor.

continued on page 374

RECOMMENDED PEPPER VARIETIES, continued from page 373

TYPE/VARIETY	HYBRID (H) or OPEN-POLLINATED (OP)	HEAT	COMMENTS
ANAHEIM/NEW MEXICO GROUP			**Long, thin, green tapered; essential to Southwest cuisine. (Green to Red)**
Anaheim TMR 23	OP	2	Productive California chile.
New Mexico #9	H	2-3	Moderate heat; dry powder a must for chile; Hatch variety.
Paprika Supreme	H	1	For drying and grinding into powder.
Sandia	H	3	All-purpose; Hatch variety.
CAYENNE GROUP			**Small, round to slightly flat fruit; dries poorly. (Green to Red)**
Long Red Cayenne*	H	4	Ancient pepper for drying and chile powder.
Ring of Fire	OP	4	Pencil-thin, earliest cayenne; great for dry powder.
CHERRY GROUP			**Large, blunt-end, irregular fruit; thin wall; very tasty. (Green to Red)**
Cuban	H	2	Smaller Cubanelle.
Cubanelle	OP	2	Long, green, sweet Italian for frying.
Pepperoncini	OP	1	Great for pickling and salads.
JALAPEÑO GROUP			**Rounded and conical with smooth skin and a thick wall; will not dry. (Green to Red)**
Early Jalapeño	OP	4	Earlier and smaller than Jalapeño.
Ole Jalapeño	OP	4	Large, early, and hot.
Tam Jalapeño	OP	2	A mild Jalapeño.
PIMIENTO GROUP			**Large and thick-walled with green conical shape. (Green to Red)**
Pimiento L	OP	1	TMV resistant, thick-walled pimiento.
Pimiento Red Heart	OP	1	Judged best-tasting sweet pepper.
WAX/BANANA GROUP			**Small to large, long, conical; shiny, waxy skin. (Yellow to Red)**
Hungarian Wax	OP	3	For canning, pickling, and fresh use; 6-inch tapered fruit.
Ivory Banana	H		Earliest yellow banana; high sugar.
Sweet Banana*	H	1	Since 1941; 7-inch pointed fruit; very popular; all-purpose.
SMALL HOT GROUP			**Small, pungent, thin-walled, tapered fruit.**
Chiltepin*	OP	4	Grows in Southwest; reseeds; great in containers.
Serrano	OP	4	Slim, dark green, and very hot; for salsas and picking.
FRUTESCENS **HOT GROUP**			**Small, very hot** *Capsicum frutescens.*
Habanero	OP	5	The hottest pepper; for sauces and oil extraction; green to orange or red.
Tabasco	OP	5	Several varieties of this classic super-hot pepper.
Arledge Hot*	OP	4	The "Louisiana hot" pepper.

Heat: 1 = sweet; 2 = mildly hot; 3 = hot; 4 = very hot; 5 = be careful **TMV** = Tobacco Mosaic Virus * Indicates heirloom variety.

and earlier and larger yields. However, open-pollinated varieties are often better tasting and more variable in shape and color, and you can save their seeds.

Besides the two popular species of peppers, *Capsicum annuum* (sweet and hot peppers) and *C. frutescens* (tabasco and habanero pepper), there are also other species of peppers worth growing if you can find the seed: *Capsicum chinense, C. baccatum* (the aji pepper), and *C. pubescens* are popular in South America, but only available from a few U.S. seed companies. The "flaming canary" chile, *C. pubescens,* is said to be the hottest pepper in North America.

Each region of the country seems to have its own favorite varieties of pepper, so check with neighbors, garden clubs, and your county Agricultural Extension Service. For hard-to-find varieties, look to specialty seed houses offering peppers (see pages 447–450).

HARVEST AND STORAGE

Peppers are fully ripe when they change from green to red (some types turn orange, yellow, or brown-purple). Once they change colors, sweet peppers become sweeter, hot peppers become hotter, and both types increase their vitamin A and C content. It's important to harvest your peppers regularly. This will keep plants producing. When you harvest peppers, be careful not to break the branches. Injured plants invite diseases. Use a sharp knife or scissors. Ripening will continue after harvest, so keep your picked peppers in a cool place, or they will overripen. For most peppers there is a simple rule: Harvest some to serve green, and let others mature to a shiny red. That way you mix flavor, heat, and nutrition. Hot peppers can be dried for a long-lasting supply. Pick them after they turn red or orange and dry them where it's warm and the air circulates well. You can thread peppers onto a string and hang them in the kitchen for an eye-catching store of your favorite

chile within arm's reach. A familiar sight in the Southwest are long *ristras* (Spanish for "string") of brilliant red chiles strung up and hung to dry after the fall harvest. If you want to make ristras, it's important that you choose the right pepper. A thick-walled variety like jalapeño or serrano will rot before it air-dries. Chiles destined for air drying must have a thin flesh. Strung on cotton string (small chiles) or twine (large chiles) and suspended in a well-ventilated indoor location, they will lose moisture over 1 to 2 months, darkening in color and deepening in flavor. It's also important to use chiles that are fresh from the vine, so that the stems are still fresh enough to be pierced with a needle. Some chile aficionados bind the stems with string, claiming that puncturing the stems hastens rot.

In cool or humid areas, drying peppers can be tricky. You might try the following technique when the sun is not so helpful. Quarter harvested red peppers lengthwise and remove all seeds. If necessary, freeze them until you have enough to dry. If you have sunny weather at harvest time, you can sun-dry peppers on a screened tray. Otherwise, dry them in a food dryer, or on a baking sheet in the oven at 175° maximum. Peppers contain a lot of water, and drying them at a high temperature can ruin their flavor. If you want to make and use powdered chile, the peppers should be cracking dry. However, if you leave them in the heat too long they will lose flavor.

If you want to make a chile powder or paprika, don't grind the dried peppers all at once. Finely crushed dried pepper deteriorates quickly. Instead, use a mortar and pestle and pulverize only as much as you need. A pinch of salt in the mortar makes it grind and pour easily. If you really treasure fresh chile powder, this is the way to get it.

You can also store chiles as a paste that can be used to enliven soups, stews, and sauces. Start by removing chile stems and seeds. Toast the chiles in a dry skillet over moderate heat until they puff up and soften; don't let them burn. Pour boiling water over the chiles and let them stand for 30 minutes or so. Purée the soaked chiles in a blender. The paste can be stored in the freezer or refrigerator until needed.

Some peppers, like the jalapeño, have flesh that's too thick to dry normally. These peppers are dried by a smoking process that was in practice when Cortés arrived. Smoked peppers, especially jalapeño, are called by their ancient Aztec name of "chipotle," and they lend a unique, smoky flavor to salsas and cooked dishes.

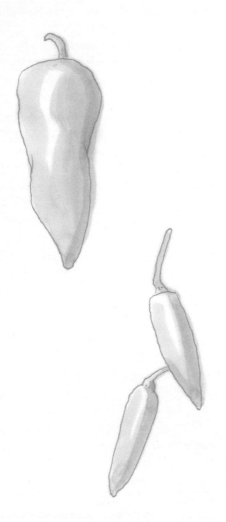

PEPPER GROWING TIPS

- Peppers are one of the few vegetables whose seed have to be coaxed out of dormancy. To soften the seed coat, place seeds in a wet towel for a few days before sowing.

- Peppers germinate very slowly in cool soils, so start them indoors about 6 to 8 weeks before the last spring frost. Optimum temperature for germination is 85°F, and even then sprouting may be variable. To keep seeds warm, hang a lightbulb over the flat, or use an electric heating coil under the flat.

- Give seedlings plenty of light, and don't let them stretch. Stocky strong transplants perform best and give the highest yields. Don't overwater seedlings as they are very susceptible to root rot.

- Transplant to the garden when the soil is warm. If the soil is still cool, plant out in raised beds and warm the soil with black plastic. The key to successful early growth of peppers is a well hardened-off seedling set into a warm soil.

- Side-dress with a 5-10-10 fertilizer about 2 months after planting out and again as plants begin to flower.

- Mulch plants once the soil has warmed up.

- Pest problems are similar to those of tomatoes.

- Harvest carefully since injured plants are more vulnerable to disease.

- Most peppers eventually turn red on the vine, producing a sweeter or hotter flavor with higher levels of vitamins A and C.

CORN (Grass Family)

What would summer be like without the sound of corn stalks rustling in the breeze or the incomparable taste of freshly picked corn plopped into a pot of boiling water? Easy to grow and easy to cook, this native New World grass has become a highlight of the home gardening season and a symbol of our kitchen garden heritage.

As a vegetable, corn is in a class by itself. It's the only vegetable that is also a cereal—that is, it belongs to the same plant family as wheat, rice, barley, and oats. And unlike other New World vegetables like peppers and tomatoes, corn wasn't widely accepted in the Old World, even though it had nourished North American Indians as well as the Incas, Mayas, and Aztecs for thousands of years. It wasn't easily suited to the kinds of grain dishes that Old World cultures were used to, like pasta, bread, and pilaf. However, when settlers began occupying North and South America, they found the natives growing corn from southern Canada to Brazil. Corn grew faster and required less space than either wheat or rye, and pioneers soon accepted it as a new staple in their diet. They learned from the Native Americans how to grow it, cook it, store it, and process it into flour and cereal. In the kitchen, the European ingredients of animal and dairy products were combined with corn to make many of the popular corn dishes we eat today. More than any other vegetable, corn is a testimony to the union of New and Old World cuisines.

Native Americans called corn *mahiz*, which means "our life"; the word is the source of corn's popular and botanic names.

The ancestry of corn is somewhat of a mystery. Wild maize has never been found, although a close relative, *teosinte (Zea mexicana),* grows wild in Central America where it was first cultivated approximately 7,000 years ago. Through thousands of years of selections and improvements, teosinte and primitive maizes were gradually transformed from loose-headed grassy forms into the modern large-eared varieties of field, dent, sweet, and popcorns.

Today we see corn in all sorts of processed foods such as microwave popcorn, tortilla chips, dry cereals, cornmeal, cornstarch, polenta, masa, margarine, and corn oil. In the kitchen we use corn to make breads, chowders, custards, fritters, and relishes, and as a welcome ingredient in stews, soups, salads, and succotash. An ear of sweet, crisp corn, freshly picked from the home garden and rushed to the kitchen, is still one of the traditional symbols of the American kitchen garden.

Sweet Corn
POACEAE (Grass Family)

Zea mays **ssp.** ***rugosa***
CHINESE: *yu mi*
FRENCH: *maïs sucré*
GERMAN: *Zuckermais*
ITALIAN: *mais zuccherino, m. dolce*
JAPANESE: *tomorokoshi*
SPANISH: *maíz dulce*

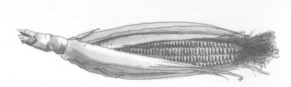

Sweet corn does not have the nutritional value of the mature field corns. Compared to other vegetables, it has modest amounts of vitamin A, thiamin, and riboflavin, but lots of protein, phosphorous, and carbohydrates.

There are two nutritional problems with corn. It's low in niacin and the amino acid tryptophan, which helps us utilize niacin. A shortage of niacin in the diet produces pellagra, a nutrient disorder that is found in poor areas of the world where corn is eaten as the only staple. Native Americans avoided this disease in a couple of ways. First, they soaked their corn in the wet ashes of various shrubs, trees, and seashells. This removed the outer hull, released extra niacin, and made the corn easy to cook. Today, hominy and masa are made much the same way, only with lime. This age-old tradition of preparing corn with alkaline solutions was a major step in making corn more nutritious.

Native Americans also combined corn with beans, a vegetable rich in both niacin and tryptophan. Combinations of legumes and grains for a complete protein are found throughout the world; there's rice and soybeans in China, wheat and pulses in India, succotash in America, and lentils and millet in Africa.

Whole dried corn can be ground into a meal and cooked in hot water to form a thick porridge. It is called "mush" in England, "polenta" in Italy, and "putu" in certain parts of Africa. Corn can also be processed into hominy and cooked like a grain. Hominy is used whole or cracked into grits and used as a cereal, side dish, or base for puddings, muffins, and breads.

CULTIVATION

Corn is a tender annual that can handle cool weather better than most warm weather vegetables. It is surprisingly easy to grow if you pay attention to a few important details like choosing the right variety, germinating seeds in warm soils, enhancing wind pollination, and controlling some particularly ornery pests.

Sow corn seeds when the soil has warmed to at least 60°F. This usually occurs a few weeks after the last spring frost. If you are impatient, try warming your soil with plastic mulch for a week or so during sunny weather. If you get an early warm spell, you can usually sow corn seeds 2 to 4 weeks earlier than usual. Plant successive crops every 2 weeks through midsummer, or until about 90 days before first frost. Choose an early variety for the last planting. If you want to plant a supersweet variety (sh2), remember they can cross-pollinate with normal and sugar-enhanced varieties (su and se), producing tough, starchy kernels for both types (see page 380). This is usually less of a problem in small garden plots than large fields, but to avoid cross-pollination possibilities, time your plantings to ensure that there are at least 2 weeks between the pollination periods. For example, you could plant a late supersweet

variety that matures in 85 days at the same time as an early normal type that matures in 70 days.

SKIMPY EARS AND GAP-TOOTHED COBS

Anyone who has ever grown corn has experienced the problem of more cob than kernel: stunted, misshapen ears with just a few plump kernels at the base of the cob. Usually this condition is due to incomplete pollination.

Corn is an unusual grain in that the plants bear the male organs (the tassels) and female organs (the cob or ear) in separate flowers on the same plant. This configuration is known as *monoecious,* from the Greek for "one house." Most grasses are "perfect flowered," bearing male and female organs within the same flower. This unusual trait of corn not only places it within its own botanical tribe, but means that it has its own peculiar way of pollination.

The ear is actually a compressed flower stalk, with female flowers (the kernels) arranged in pairs along it. The tassels at the top of the plant hold thousands of tiny male flowers, which shed clouds of pollen. Wind blows the pollen onto the sticky "silks" of the ear, down which the pollen travels to fertilize the kernels.

Each silk is connected to a pair of female flowers (future kernels) on the cob. If a flower is not fertilized, it leaves a gap on the cob. On the farm, where corn is planted in large fields,

there's so much pollen in the air that pollination is inevitable. In the home garden patch, lots of pollen is produced, but wind whisks it away, out of reach of the corn silks. In heavy rains or with overhead watering, pollen is hurled to the ground before it can attach to the silk.

If you plant corn in a long and narrow row, this also decreases pollination. If you plant in blocks instead of long rows, and face the shortest edge in the direction of prevailing winds, you increase the likelihood of complete pollination and a full ear of kernels. Any creature that eats corn silk, like earworms, corn aphids, earwigs, and grasshoppers, will also hamper pollination.

The home gardener can make sure that all silks get their fair share of pollen by hand-pollinating the ears. After the tassels have emerged and begun to spread open, they start to produce thousands of golden yellow pollen grains. When this happens, simply grab the tassel, bend it over and gently shake it over the silks of the emerging ears below. You can also break off tassels in the middle of your plot and shake them onto ears at the edge of your plot to ensure that every silk in your corn patch is pollinated.

PLANTING

Corn needs a warm soil to germinate (65° to 75°F). If you sow your seeds directly, wait until your soil warms to at least 60°. Set seeds

about 1 inch deep and 4 to 6 inches apart. Thin the strongest seedlings to 1 foot apart.

In short-season areas, or where soils stay cool into the summer, start corn seedlings inside in a warm location. When seedlings are about 4 inches high, plant them in moist soil about 1 foot apart. Plant the seedlings in blocks, rather than long rows, to enhance pollination (see sidebar), and isolate normal and sugar-enhanced varieties from supersweets and popcorns to prevent unwanted crosses and starchy-tasting corn.

Optimum growth for corn takes place from 75° to 85°F, but cool nights are important during harvest, slowing maturity and increasing sugar content. Roots are relatively shallow and sparse; they stay mostly at the top 18 to 24 inches of soil. To prevent damage, avoid deep hoeing.

Because corn is wind pollinated, many gardeners try to crowd their corn plants into tight spaces. But be careful. Corn needs room to grow and gather sunlight; it should be planted in rows 3 feet apart with seeds or seedlings about 1 foot apart in rows. Try to plant your corn in several small blocks close together, rather than one large block. This way you'll expose your corn plants to the maximum sunlight while you optimize for pollination. You'll need about 4 ounces of seed to plant four 25-foot rows, yielding about one hundred ears of corn, depending on the variety.

SOILS AND FERTILIZERS

Corn can be grown in almost any type of soil. Early types prefer fine sandy loams, and late varieties grow best in heavy loams.

Corn is also a heavy feeder. It needs nutrients, especially nitrogen, throughout its growth. Corn experts recommend a preplant fertilizer of fast-acting nitrogen like chicken manure, blood meal, fish emulsion, or cottonseed meal or the equivalent of about 1 to 2 pounds of 5-10-10 per 100 square feet. Sidedress when the seedlings are about 6 inches high and again when the plants just begin to form tassels. Sweet corn doesn't have a particularly high demand for trace elements, but it does need a great deal of water, about 1 inch per week. Don't water overhead as this will reduce pollination and increase diseases.

NUTRIENT	SYMPTOMS
Nitrogen (N)	Common in humid regions and in acid, sandy soils; plants are slender; leaves turn pale green to yellow in a "V" from the tip backwards with reddish veins; kernels poorly developed in rows.
Phosphorus (P)	Uniform deep purpling, especially of older leaves and leaf sheaths of young plants; kernels poorly developed and absent from tip of cob.
Potassium (K)	Death of the margin of older leaves from tip backwards; short stems and small ears with pointed tips.
Calcium (Ca)	New leaves are twisted and shriveled at tip and trapped inside blade of next oldest leaf, making it buckle; leaf margins puckered and wavy.
Sulfur (S)	New leaves a golden yellow, especially at the base; old leaf bases red.
Magnesium (Mg)	Parallel yellowish-white stripes between green veins (interveinal chlorosis) of older leaves, followed by reddish tints on edges and tips of these leaves.
Iron (Fe)	Interveinal chlorosis on new leaves; common in artificial media.
Zinc (Zn)	Broad bands of whitish tissue on the lower half of emerging leaves in the young plants, especially in cool, damp weather and alkaline soils; reduces pollen production and stem height.
Boron (Bo)	Reduced pollen production; sparse ears, especially at tip, which is pointed; short stems; irregular white spots on youngest leaves, which merge to make raised, waxy stripes.

NUTRIENT DEFICIENCIES IN CORN

Corn can serve an interesting function in the garden. The leaf-veins of corn are parallel, which makes nutrient-deficiency symptoms more obvious and easier to read, especially for nitrogen, phosphorous, potassium, or magnesium. If you don't grow corn to eat, you can grow it as an indicator of your soil's fertility— a sort of "canary crop." If you learn to recognize the signs of hunger in a corn plant, you'll begin to see them in your other vegetables.

DISEASES

For **bacterial or Stewart's wilt** *(Erwinia stewartii),* look for long, irregular brown streaks up to 1 inch wide on the leaves. Plants may be stunted and produce few ears, or wilt rapidly and die. Brown cavities occur inside the stalks near the soil line. This disease is common throughout middle America from the Rockies to the Atlantic seaboard. It is carried by cucumber and flea beetles (see pages 332 and 365–366), and bacterial wilt is most severe in places where these beetles survive mild winters. Early yellow varieties of corn are especially vulnerable. The only way to deal with this disease is to control the beetles, remove and destroy all infected plants, and grow resistant varieties like Miracle, Tuxedo, and Silver Queen.

Seed and seedling rot diseases are caused by several soil- and seed-borne fungi. They are favored by cold, wet conditions. Since most gardeners sow corn directly, most seeds come coated with a fungicide to protect them from these diseases. You can avoid seedling rot by using treated seeds or growing untreated seedlings indoors.

For **smut** *(Ustilago maydis),* look for black puffballs full of black powdery spores on cob tips, stalks, and tassels. They are spread from plant to plant by wind, water, and manure. Smut favors warm (80 to 90°F) weather. Commercial corn seeds are often treated with fungicides like thiram or captan that prevent this seed-borne disease from surviving. Smut is also spread by spores blown in from neighboring fields. Cut off smut balls before they break open; avoid manure if smut is a problem in your area; clean up all plant debris after harvest; and look for resistant varieties.

The reddish spots of **rust disease** are spread during wet, hot weather and becomes especially noticeable toward the end of summer when night temperatures drop and overnight dew helps spread the disease. The rust fungi are some of the most notorious diseases because they mutate rapidly and penetrate the leaf surfaces through natural openings. Rusts are susceptible to copper-based fungicides (for example, bordeaux). Grow resistant varieties; set out plants for good air circulation; water early in the day and avoid overhead watering.

PESTS

Raccoons and birds have an uncanny sense of when the corn is ready. Raccoons will pull back husks and devour kernels. Birds, especially house finches, blackbirds, starlings, and crows, can peck holes in husks and eat corn ears and tassels. To avoid their damage, wrap duct tape or packing tape around the ear about 1 inch above the stalk and another piece 1 inch below the tip of the ear. You can also tie paper bags over each ear a week before harvest, but after tassels begin to brown. Bird netting works for birds, but raccoons are clever creatures and you may have to tie the netting down a bit.

If you see ants crawling up your corn and the plants turn yellow and wilt during the midday, suspect the **corn leaf aphid** *(Rhopalosiphon maidis).* Look for small, bluish-green aphids feeding in the masses of leaves and the upper part of the stalks and tassels. Ants carry the aphids to corn and tend them for their honeydew. To control the aphids, you have to control the ants. Use boric acid baits, and destroy ant nests in the soil with deep cultivation before planting next year. Plant early and provide good growing conditions.

Earwigs (Forficula auricularia), the familiar ³/₄-inch-long, dark, elongated insects with pincers on their rear ends, are fond of climbing up tall plants like corn, where they chew and eat the silk and hamper pollination. They rarely eat the kernels. Earwigs have extremely wide food tastes. Besides plants they also eat insect eggs and small, soft-bodied insects like aphids, another pest of corn; controlling earwigs can sometimes be a tough call.

In coastal or cool humid areas, earwigs can be quite numerous. If they are literally dropping out of the husks and chewing the silks to a nubbin, place earwig traps among your plants, and shake them out into soapy water in the early morning. You can make traps out of rolled-up newspaper, wet towels in a shallow box, or short pieces of bamboo or old garden hose tied up together. One effective trap is a 1x1-inch wooden stake, about 8 inches tall, with wetted gauze wrapped around the top, and a paper cup placed over it. During the day, earwigs crawl up the stake to find refuge and moisture on the covered wet gauze, from which they can be removed the next day.

Corn earworm or tomato fruitworm (Heliothis zea) are striped yellow, brown, or green caterpillars and are the most serious pests of corn throughout North America. They also eat sunflowers, tomatoes, eggplant, and squash. On corn, caterpillars enter the ear at the silk end, so they are often seen around the tip of the ears when the husks are pulled back, or when just-picked corn is being husked. The adult is a night-flying, light gray moth that lays its eggs on corn silks and underneath leaves. The caterpillars feed on silks, causing poor pollination, and on the growing kernels. Undamaged portions of the ear are perfectly edible. This is why many gardeners tolerate the pest and cut away the damaged tip before cooking.

If you have an uncontrollable problem with the earworm, there are several things you can do. The first step is to prevent moths from laying eggs on the silk. Do this by dropping mineral oil on the tassels as soon as they appear or when you see the caterpillar's sticky frass on the silks. Also, don't leave night lights on near the corn patch. This will attract moths. Honeydew from corn aphids also attracts the moths, so it helps to control the aphids. Several small predatory insects like pirate and big-eyed bugs thrive on caterpillar eggs so encourage these beneficials by introducing them into the garden or planting flowers that attract them (see pages 188–189). A tachinid fly parasitizes the larvae. Other natural predators include lady beetles, Trichogramma wasps, and lacewing larvae.

Once caterpillars have infested the ears, but after the silks start to dry, treat the tips of each ear, inside the husks, with the microbial insecticide *Bacillus thuringiensis kurstaki* (BTK). You can also plant varieties that feature tight husks that cover the tip of the ear well. In warm areas, where earworms survive the winter, early and late plantings suffer the most damage. BTK is harmless to humans.

The **European cornborer (Ostrinia nubilalis)** is a pinkish caterpillar with a dark brown head and two rows of dark spots along the side. These spots distinguish it from the earworm, which has lateral stripes. It is a pest throughout North America, except in the far West and Florida. Small larvae eat shot holes in leaves and larger ones tunnel into stems and leave tassels broken and ear stalks bent. They also enjoy feeding on peppers, beans, and tomatoes. Early plantings of corn are most affected because larvae survive the winter in corn plants and debris. Young stages of the borer don't like extreme temperatures, and they drown during heavy rains. Thus, they are inhibited by dry summers, cold winters, and cool, rainy weather in the early summer.

Control the cornborer by destroying all corn plant debris at the end of the season. Treat ear shoots and centers of leaf whorls with rotenone or neem at the first sign of borers, or when 10 percent of the ears show silk. This is one of the most effective ways to control them. Following harvest, chop up and remove or compost all corn stalks.

Like the earworm (see page 382), eggs and young larvae of the cornborer are eaten by many small predatory and parasitic insects, and these should be encouraged. In areas where borers are a major problem, remove tassels from half of your plants before pollen is shed. This removes many larvae and leaves enough tassels for pollination.

Several species of the **spotted cucumber beetle,** or **corn rootworm** *(Diabrotica),* attack corn, including "Southern," "Northern," and "Western" varieties (see also "Cucurbits," page 332). The pale green or brownish adults eat leaves, leaving ragged holes in the center; they also eat tassels and silk, producing malformed ears and undeveloped kernels. In the West, they are less of a problem. Adults lay eggs in the soil at the base of the corn plants, and the white, brown-headed larvae feed on roots. Larvae don't have fat legs on the rear half of their body like caterpillars. Rootworms are most common where corn has been grown in the same place for several seasons. Late planted corn and corn under drought stress are the most susceptible.

To control rootworms, don't plant corn in the same place for more than 2 years. Rotations are very effective since eggs are laid around the base of the plant. Parasitic nematodes applied to moist soils have had mixed results. Since cornborer eggs are preyed upon by predatory soil mites, the addition of aged organic matter to soils, which increases the food of the mites, has shown some success.

If seeds do not germinate, even in warm soils, you may have wireworms (the larvae of a beetle) or the seedcorn maggot (the larvae of a fly) eating your seeds. **Seedcorn maggots** *(Hylemya platura)* are small (1/4 inch), white, legless cousins of the cabbage root maggot. They normally eat organic matter and will also eat large, slow-sprouting seeds before they can germinate. They can be a particular problem in cool soils with lots of organic matter.

Wireworms are long, shiny, and brownish, and they eat seeds early in the season. Infestations are highest in soils where lawn was previously grown or in soils high in organic matter. The best defenses against these subterranean marauders is to sow seeds in warm soil (above 65°F) or set out transplants. Avoid adding manure just before planting and apply parasitic nematodes to moist soils.

CULTURAL PROBLEMS

For information on poorly-filled ears, see page 379.

Lodging occurs when plants topple over in heavy wind and rain. Corn plants have shallow roots and lodging can be a common problem in regions with strong summer storms. To prevent lodging, go easy on mulching your plants until the end of the season, after the tassels show. You can also give the plants added support by either hilling them up or planting them in 4-inch trenches and filling in as the seedlings grow.

VARIETIES

Corn is classified into several distinct types based on use and the characteristics of the kernel. Many of these can be grown by the home gardener.

Popcorn (var. *everia)* ears are short, the flesh of the seed is hard, and its skin is thick. When kernels are heated, trapped steam makes them explode into puffy white flesh. Popcorn is one of the earliest cultivated types of corn.

With **flint, ornamental, and Indian corn (var.** *indurata),* the flesh of the seed is hard, and it is difficult to grind when it's dry—like flint. The kernel is smooth and the skin is thick. These are vibrant, colorful types of corn with ears of many shapes, and names like Strawberry, Wampum, Fiesta, and Seneca Indian. Many varieties can be ground for flour or cornmeal.

Dent or field corn (var. *indentata)* ears are large and the kernels, which have a soft, starchy center, shrink when they dry, developing a dent. Sweetest of the mature corns, dent grinds easily into cornmeal for baking and cereal.

Flour corn (var. *amalacea),* a favorite of the Seneca Indians, is a soft-flesh, thin-skinned corn that is easily ground into a fine flour.

Sweet corn (var. *rugosa)* is actually an immature field corn with a high sugar content. The seed flesh is clear, the kernel is wrinkled, and the seed skin is variable in thickness.

Sugary, sweet forms of corn occurred throughout history. Mayas valued them for making alcoholic drinks. However, sweet corn was routinely rejected as a staple, because it couldn't be stored for long. Not until settlers were introduced to sweet corn by Native Americans did it become popular.

Today's common sweet corn can be traced to a single Iroquois village in central New York. The first modern reference date for sweet corn is 1779 with the introduction of Susquehanna or Papoon. By 1900 there were sixty-three cultivars of sweet corn, including the still-favorite heirlooms Country Gentleman, Golden Bantam, and Stowell's Evergreen. The first hybrids sweet corn was introduced in 1924 by the Connecticut Agricultural Experiment Station.

Generally speaking, the later the variety, the bigger the ear and the taller the plant. Early varieties rarely get taller than 5 to 6 feet, while some late varieties can reach 8 feet or more. Yellow varieties keep longer than whites or bicolors.

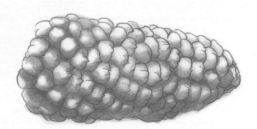

1. Example of nonhybrid (uneven row)

3. Bi-color

2. Strawberry corn

4. Yellow sweet (even row)

5. Silver Queen—white sweet (even row)

SWEET, SWEETER, AND SWEETEST

The sweetness of corn is determined by genes as much as by growing conditions. In recent years, plant breeders have introduced a number of new hybrid corn varieties with lots more sugar and the ability to stay sweet longer after harvest. These new cultivars are described by the symbol of their gene.

- "Normal sugary" (su): Normal hybrid sweet corn. Kernels contain moderate but varying amounts of sugar, depending on variety. Sugar converts to starch quickly after harvest, but the varieties are generally earlier and the seeds tend to germinate better in cold soils. "All Sweets" (su++) are unique high-sugar normal types that survive early summer heat better than the sugar-enhanced types (se).

- "Sugar-enhanced" (se): This gene modifies the normal sugary gene (su), by slowing the conversion of sugar to starch after harvest rather than increasing the sugar of the kernels. The (se) varieties are hybrids between (se) and (su) parents. The (se+) varieties are "fully sugar-enhanced" with even more tenderness and sweetness. The (se+) is a hybrid between two (se) parents. Neither (se) hybrids needs to be isolated from normal (su) hybrid sweet corn. For the home gardener seeking really sweet corn, the (se) varieties are probably the best bet since they are more cold-hardy and have a stronger corn taste and crisper texture than the true supersweets (sh2). Note that (se) hybrids are more sensitive to weather changes than (su) types, so you may end up making several successive sowings of both to assure a constant harvest.

- "Supersweets" (sh2): Also called "shrunken" because of the appearance of the kernel. This gene creates very sweet kernels that convert sugar to starch very slowly after harvest. These are the true "supersweets." The (sh2) hybrids must be isolated from all other types of corn, especially (su) and (se) hybrids, since cross-pollination will result in rough, starchy kernels. Also, the (sh2) varieties are less vigorous than other types. They need moist, warm soils to germinate and extra fertilizers to grow well.

- Within these three main categories, there are still other varieties, like the "Sweetie" supersweets that have both the (su) and (sh2) genes.

There are scores of varieties of sweet corn available, including heirlooms, modern open-pollinated types, and old favorite hybrids. Choices are more confusing now with the new generation of extra-sweet varieties. Although supersweets are unique and interesting, from a home gardener's perspective they seem a bit overrated. They were developed just 30 years ago to solve the problems of commercial shippers and processors. However, in terms of flavor right off the plant, they certainly haven't made old-fashioned varieties obsolete. If you have to buy your corn in stores, then look for supersweets. They retain their sugar much longer than normal corn varieties. Also, supersweets keep longer and let you stretch the season a bit, which makes them great for canning and freezing. But if you pick your own corn just before you cook it, normal sugar varieties are just as tasty and much less fussy to grow.

RECOMMENDED SWEET CORN VARIETIES

VARIETY	TYPE**	EAR	ATTRIBUTES AND COMMENTS
Early (60 to 70 days)			
Earlivee	su++	yellow	Standard early (su) with extra sugar. Needs lots of fertilizer.
Honey Cream	su	white	Super early with dwarf stalks. Great for small gardens.
Quickie	se	bicolor	Earliest bicolor. Short (5-foot) sturdy plant. Good in cool soils.
Seneca Dawn	se	bicolor	Best tasting early (se) bicolor. Good for short seasons.
Seneca Horizon	su	yellow	Largest ear of any early (su) type. Rust resistant.
Sugar Buns	se+	yellow	The sweetest, most tender early corn.
Midseason (70 to 80 days)			
Ambrosia	se	bicolor	Widely adaptable. Smut and rust tolerant. Tender and sweet.
Double Gem	se+	bicolor	Perfect for home and market garden.
Golden Bantam*	su	yellow	Since 1902. First popular yellow sweet corn.
Golden Jubilee	su	yellow	For cool coastal areas. Great flavor. Resists lodging. One of the all-time greats. Since 1950s.
Kandy Korn	su	yellow	Delicious 8-inch ears on 7-foot burgundy stalks.
Lancelot	se+	bicolor	Tolerant of rust and drought. Very sweet taste.
Platinum Lady	se	white	One of the best midseason (se) whites.
Silver King	se+	white	Disease-resistant (se) version of Silver Queen.
Tuxedo	se	yellow	Rust and smut resistant. Great flavor. Great for dry soils.
Zenith	sh2	yellow	Rust resistant. Supersweet flavor.
Late (more than 80 days)			
Black Aztec*	su	white	Legendary variety from before 1860. Eat sweet in early stages. Turns blue-black and suitable for cornmeal.
Country Gentleman*	su	white	Standard garden, open-pollinated, late white corn. Since 1891. Great taste. Good for canning and freezing.
Honey 'n' Pearl	sh2	bicolor	1988 AAS winner.
How Sweet It Is	sh2	white	1986 AAS winner. First popular (sh2). Long shelf life.
Howling Mob*	su	white	Since 1904. Similar to Silver Queen but more adaptable.
Merit	su	yellow	Good for drought gardens.
Miracle	se+	yellow	Improved Golden Jubilee. Very popular.
Silver Queen	su	white	The standard late white corn. Needs warm soils.
Stowell's Evergreen*	su	white	Since 1853. 1934 AAS winner. Huge ears and kernels.

* Indicates heirloom variety.

** See page 385

HARVEST

The days to maturity listed in seed catalogs are good approximations, but corn's actual growing season varies a great deal according to climate, maturing faster in warmer regions. A much better way to know when to harvest your corn is to watch it and feel it.

After the silks have dried and turned brown or black (18 to 24 days after they first appear), feel the tips of the ears to see if they are full. A rounded shape below the husk means the ear is ready. Pull back the top of the husks and press a thumbnail into a kernel. It should squirt a milky liquid. Corn that has stayed on the plant too long and is starchy can still be used to make chowders, fritters, and other cooked dishes.

With open-pollinated corn, each plant tends to ripen at different rates. Hybrid corn ripens much more uniformly. The best open-pollinated corn stays ripe for only 3 to 5 days and then goes starchy, but plants are ready at different times. The sugar-enhanced hybrids stay sweet on the plant for 4 to 6 days, and the supersweets stay sweet for a few days more. For each variety and type of corn, there is a surprisingly brief time window of maximum sweetness that is best learned with trial and error.

CORN GROWING TIPS

- Corn needs warm soil (at least 60°F) to germinate, especially late and supersweet varieties, so monitor soil temperatures carefully for rapid germination. In cold soils or early season, set out 10-day-old transplants.

- Plant your corn to avoid cross-pollination between incompatible types and to prevent tall, late varieties from shading crops that need light.

- For a continual supply of corn and the longest harvest possible, plan on at least three plantings. Sow first indoors, 2 weeks before the average last frost date; then do an outdoor sowing of several varieties maturing at least 1 week apart when soils have warmed to 60°F; and finally do an outdoor sowing of a favorite late variety.

- Plant corn in small blocks of at least five rows with 2 to 4 feet between rows and 1 foot between plants. This will optimize pollination and access to sunlight.

- Corn is a heavy feeder, so use preplant fertilizers and side-dress plants when the seedlings are about 6 inches high and again when the plants just begin to form tassels.

- Avoid damage to shallow roots; hoe once when plants emerge, and again when plants reach 1 foot tall. Hill up around each plant to prevent them from falling over.

- Monitor regularly for pests and nutrient deficiencies. Corn is a demanding crop, but gives you a great deal in exchange for special attention.

- Sweet corn has a time window of only a few days when it is at its sweetest. Harvest when ears are completely filled out and a punctured kernel shows a milky white liquid. Eat as soon as possible after picking. Use older, starchy ears in soups, stews, and chowders.

Recipes from a Green Kitchen

The following recipes are designed to utilize the fresh produce you grow in your garden. These recipes are low in cream, butter, and cheese to reduce fat and to let the flavors of the vegetables dominate. Feel free to add or substitute other vegetables you have on hand, depending on the bounty of your garden. The following recipes are organized alphabetically by the vegetable they highlight.

ARUGULA

To prepare: Wash and tear off large, withered leaves and trim stalks. Cut into chiffonade (see page 48 for directions) and sprinkle on salads. Chop raw and serve with chopped fresh tomatoes on pizza after it has come from the oven.

To cook: Sauté in a little garlic and olive oil.

Arugula and Mushroom Salad

SERVES 6

2 bunches arugula, trimmed and washed
1 head frisée lettuce, torn into bite-sized pieces
8 ounces cremini or white mushrooms, thinly sliced
1 cup walnut pieces, toasted
$^1/_3$ cup olive oil
$^1/_3$ cup walnut oil
$^1/_2$ teaspoon kosher salt
$^1/_4$ to $^1/_3$ cup raspberry vinegar
$^1/_2$ cup grated Parmesan cheese

In a large bowl, combine the greens, mushrooms, and walnuts and toss. Drizzle on the oils and toss again. Add the salt and vinegar and toss. Divide among 6 plates, garnish with the cheese, and serve.

Per serving: 392 calories (333 from fat), 38.7 g total fat, 5.1 g saturated fat, 7 mg cholesterol, 317 mg sodium, 5.7 g carbohydrate, 1.7 g dietary fiber, 9.6 g protein

ASIAN BRASSICAS

To prepare: Discard withered leaves and wash dirt from stems.

To cook: Chop larger leaves coarsely; leave small shoots whole. Steam, braise, or stir fry.

BASIC BRASSICA RECIPES

Napa Cabbage Salad

Take equal amounts shredded carrots and napa cabbage and dress with a mixture of white wine vinegar, sugar, minced garlic, and minced fresh gingerroot. Toss well. Season with salt and pepper to taste and refrigerate for up to 4 hours.

Braised Choy Sum with Mushrooms

Wash and dry choy sum shoots and tie into small bundles with kitchen twine. Place the bundles upright in a pan large enough to hold all of them and add 1 inch water. Add a little peanut oil, some sliced mushrooms, and finely sliced onion. Cover and simmer until the stems are tender, about 10 to 12 minutes.

Chinese Cabbage with Yogurt

Sauté some chopped onions in a little oil; add shredded cabbage, caraway seeds, salt, and a little water. Simmer until tender.

Prepare a dressing of low-fat plain yogurt, chopped fresh mint, and crushed garlic. Pour the mixture over the cabbage in the sauté pan and stir over low heat just long enough to heat through. Season with pepper and serve.

Stir-Fried Tatsoi

SERVES 4

- 1 whole tatsoi (about 1 pound)
- 2 tablespoons peanut oil or corn oil
- 2 tablespoons low-salt soy sauce
- $1/2$ teaspoon granulated sugar
- $1/2$ teaspoon cornstarch mixed with $1/2$ teaspoon water

Cut the tatsoi into quarters, wash, and drain. In a wok or skillet over high heat, heat the oil and stir-fry the tatsoi for 3 to 4 minutes. Add the soy sauce and sugar, then cover and simmer for 1 minute, or until soft.

Uncover and stir-fry for 2 to 3 minutes. Stir in the cornstarch mixture and stir-fry until tatsoi is translucent.

Per serving: 82 calories (59 from fat), 7 g total fat, 1.2 g saturated fat, 0 mg cholesterol, 374 mg sodium, 4.1 g carbohydrate, 1.2 g dietary fiber, 2.2 g protein

Chinese Cabbage and Cashews

SERVES 4

- 2 tablespoons peanut oil
- 1 pound Chinese cabbage, coarsely chopped
- Salt and freshly ground pepper to taste
- 2 garlic cloves, minced
- $1/4$ cup cashews
- 2 tablespoons dry white wine or water
- 1 teaspoon Asian sesame oil

In a wok or large skillet over high heat, heat the oil and stir-fry the cabbage for 2 to 3 minutes. Add the salt, pepper, and garlic, and stir-fry for another minute or two.

Add the nuts and white wine and stir-fry for 1 minute. Add the sesame oil and serve immediately.

Per serving: 137 calories (106 from fat), 12 g total fat, 2.1 g saturated fat, 0 mg cholesterol, 19 mg sodium, 5 g carbohydrate, 1.5 g dietary fiber, 2.9 g protein

ASPARAGUS

To prepare: With a sharp snapping motion, break off 1 inch of the lower end of each asparagus stalk. If stalks are thick and hard, peel each with a swivel peeler.

To steam: Steam over boiling water in a covered pot for 8 to 10 minutes until just crisp-tender.

To grill: Grill over medium coals, basting with olive oil and turning often so as not to burn.

To store: Store upright in a container of water in the refrigerator for several days.

Grilled Asparagus with Shallots and Parsley

SERVES 4

- 1 ¹/₂ to 2 pounds thin asparagus, trimmed
- 3 teaspoons peanut oil
- 2 shallots, minced
- 3 tablespoons minced fresh flat-leaf parsley
- Salt and freshly ground pepper to taste

Coat the asparagus with 1 teaspoon of the oil. Grill over a hot charcoal fire turning frequently, until crisp-tender, about 8 to 10 minutes. Do not burn.

Transfer to a bowl and dress with the remaining 2 teaspoons oil, the shallots, parsley, and salt and pepper. Toss briefly to coat. Transfer to a platter and serve.

Per serving: 61 calories (29 from fat), 3.6 g total fat, 0.6 g saturated fat, 0 mg cholesterol, 5 mg sodium, 6.4 g carbohydrate, 2 g dietary fiber, 2.5 g protein

BASIC ASPARAGUS RECIPES

Asparagus with Hoisin Sauce and Red Onion

Trim and steam asparagus until crisp-tender; set aside. In a skillet, prepare a sauce by first sautéing finely chopped red onion in a little olive oil. Add a tablespoon or so of hoisin sauce, a little lemon juice, and enough water to make a light sauce. Add the asparagus and sauté briefly just to coat. Serve as is or with a light sprinkle of toasted sesame seeds.

Asparagus with Tarragon Vinaigrette

Trim and steam 1 bunch of asparagus until crisp-tender. Place on a serving platter. Mix together 1 tablespoon white wine vinegar, 2 to 3 tablespoons olive oil, 1 tablespoon minced fresh tarragon, and salt to taste and pour over asparagus. Turn to coat evenly. Serve immediately, or refrigerate for several hours so that the flavors can meld. Serves 2.

Grilled Asparagus

Use 15 to 16 grilled asparagus (see recipe this page) and ¹/₂ roasted red pepper (page 85), peeled, seeded, sliced into thin strips. Sauté 1 cup sliced mushrooms in a little olive oil until just browned. Toss the asparagus, peppers, and mushrooms with 2 tablespoons champagne vinegar, 1 tablespoon olive oil, and salt and pepper to taste.

Asparagus with Anchovy Paste and Garlic

SERVES 2 TO 4

- 1 bunch asparagus (³/₄ pound), trimmed
- 1 tablespoon butter
- 2 tablespoons olive oil
- 3 cloves garlic, minced
- 2 tablespoons anchovy paste
- Juice and grated zest of 1 lemon
- ¹/₄ cup minced fresh flat-leaf parsley
- Pepper to taste
- ¹/₄ cup toasted bread crumbs

Steam the asparagus over boiling water in a covered pot for 8 to 10 minutes, or until just crisp-tender. Remove from the steamer.

In a large skillet, melt the butter with the oil over medium heat and sauté the garlic until translucent. Add the anchovy paste, lemon juice, zest, and parsley. Add the asparagus and cook for 2 to 3 minutes. Add pepper.

Place in a serving bowl and garnish with the bread crumbs.

Per serving: 295 calories (191 from fat), 22.8 g total fat, 5.6 g saturated fat, 15 mg cholesterol, 181 mg sodium, 20.2 g carbohydrate, 2.3 g dietary fiber, 7.8 g protein

GREEN BEANS

To prepare: Snap off the stem end with a sharp motion.

To steam: Steam over boiling water in a covered container for 8 to 10 minutes, or until just crisp-tender.

To boil: Plunge the beans into a large pot of salted boiling water and cook for 3 to 4 minutes, or until crisp-tender. Drain and run the beans immediately under cold running water. Drain again. The beans will be a beautiful dark green. Use as is in salads, or reheat in butter or olive oil with fresh herbs just before serving.

BASIC GREEN BEAN RECIPES

Green Beans with Ginger

Dress hot cooked green beans with plain rice wine vinegar (or red wine vinegar) plus a pinch of granulated sugar, soy sauce, and shredded fresh gingerroot. Add salt and pepper to taste.

Green Bean Salad

Toss hot cooked green beans with mushroom slices that have been sautéed in olive oil. Add a pinch of grated orange zest and garnish with orange zest curls.

Green Bean and Onion Sauté

Boil 8 ounces green beans until crisp-tender, then rinse in cold water. Sauté 1 diced yellow onion in 1 tablespoon of olive oil until golden brown. Add the beans and cook over medium heat until the beans are hot. Dress with a dash of lemon juice and balsamic vinegar and serve immediately.

Green Beans with Potatoes and Tomatoes

SERVES 6 TO 8

This is good as an entrée with some crusty bread and a green salad. Add ¹/₄ teaspoon New Mexico chile powder for some extra zip, if you like.

- 1 pound Romano beans or regular green beans
- 2 large potatoes, peeled
- 2 tablespoons olive oil
- 1 onion, chopped
- 2 cloves garlic, minced
- 4 tomatoes, peeled, seeded, and chopped
- 1 to 2 tablespoons minced fresh basil
- 1 teaspoon minced fresh mint
- 2 tablespoons minced fresh flat-leaf parsley
- 2 teaspoons honey
- ¹/₂ teaspoon salt
- Freshly ground pepper to taste

Break the beans in half. Cut the potatoes into 1-inch cubes and soak in cold water for 15 minutes.

In a large pot or skillet over medium heat, heat the olive oil and sauté the onion and garlic until translucent. Add all the remaining ingredients except the beans and potatoes. Reduce the heat to low, cover, and cook for 5 minutes.

Meanwhile, steam the potatoes and beans over boiling water in a covered pot for 5 to 10 minutes, or until still just a little crisp. Add to the tomato mixture and stir. Cover and simmer over medium heat for 15 to 20 minutes, or until beans are tender. Add some of potato steaming water if necessary to thin the dish. Serve immediately.

Per serving: 193 calories (42 from fat), 5 g total fat, 0 g saturated fat, 0 mg cholesterol, 199 mg sodium, 35.2 g carbohydrate, 5.9 g dietary fiber, 5 g protein

Soupe au Pistou

SERVES 6 TO 8

This recipe has many variations, but the concept is simple. Vegetables are cooked in a liquid long enough to turn them to a thick paste, then some green beans and other fresh vegetables are added for crunch. A dollop of pistou is added just before serving.

- 1 cup white beans
- 2 zucchini, diced
- 2 large carrots, diced
- ¹/₂ pound green beans, trimmed and cut into ¹/₂-inch pieces
- 4 tomatoes, peeled, seeded, and chopped
- 1 large leek, trimmed with the white and half of the soft green top sliced thin
- 2 russet potatoes, peeled and diced
- 10 cups water
- Salt and freshly ground pepper to taste
- 6 ounces ziti or penne pasta

PISTOU
- ¹/₂ bunch fresh basil, coarsely chopped (about 1 cup)
- 6 to 8 cloves garlic, minced
- 1 teaspoon sea salt
- ¹/₄ teaspoon freshly ground black pepper
- 1 cup grated Parmesan cheese
- ¹/₃ cup extra virgin olive oil

Soak the white beans overnight in a large pot. Drain the beans and replace the water with new water to cover. Bring to a boil. Reduce the heat and simmer 30 to 40 minutes, or until beans are tender. (Or use the quick soak method: Put the beans in a large pot and cover by 2 inches with water. Bring to a boil, then turn off the heat and let soak for 1 hour. Drain the beans and replace the water with new water to cover. Cook 30 to 40 minutes, or until beans are tender.) Set the beans aside.

In a large soup pot, combine half the zucchini, half the carrots, and all of the tomatoes, leek, and potatoes. Cover with the 10 cups water and bring to a boil. Reduce heat and simmer 40 to 50 minutes, or until the vegetables are nearly all dissolved into a thick paste. Season with salt and pepper to taste.

Add the remaining carrot, zucchini, and green beans, the cooked white beans, and the pasta, and cook over medium-low heat for 15 minutes, or until the pasta is al dente and the newly added vegetables are cooked but still a little crunchy.

Meanwhile, make the pistou. Combine the basil, garlic, salt, and pepper in a food processor fitted with the metal blade. Process until everything is finely chopped. Add half of the grated cheese and pulse several times. Pour in the olive oil while the machine is still running to make a fine liquid paste.

When the soup is ready to serve, ladle it into soup bowls. Spoon 1 to 2 tablespoons of pistou on top of each serving and swirl around briefly. Sprinkle each plate with a little of the remaining grated cheese.

Per serving: 561 calories (160 from fat), 18.3 g total fat, 5 g saturated fat, 13 mg cholesterol, 719 mg sodium, 79.2 g carbohydrate, 11.6 g dietary fiber, 23.6 g protein

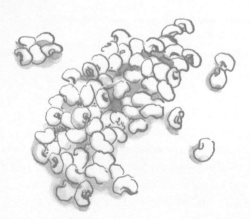

BEETS

To prepare: Scrub the beets and cut off the tops above the stem so they don't bleed while being cooked.

To roast: Preheat the oven to 375°. Rub each beet with a little olive oil and place them in a baking dish. Roast for 40 to 60 minutes, or until tender when pierced with a fork. Let cool before peeling.

To boil or steam: Steam whole beets over boiling water in a covered container until tender, or cook in boiling water until tender. Cooking time varies with the age of the beets. For boiling whole young beets, allow 30 to 40 minutes. For steaming whole young beets, allow 50 to 60 minutes. Cook older whole beets 10 to 15 minutes longer. There should be no resistance when you test them with a knife.

Ginger-Glazed Beets

SERVES 6

Adapted from Cooking at the Natural Cafe in Santa Fe, *by Lynn Walters. A good, simple recipe.*

**1 pound red or golden beets, or 8 ounces of each,
    peeled and cut into chunks**
³/₄ cup water
1 teaspoon minced gingerroot
¹/₄ teaspoon salt
2 tablespoons pure maple syrup

Put the beets, water, and gingerroot in a small saucepan and bring to a boil. Cover and cook over medium heat until the beets are tender. Add the salt and maple syrup and continue to cook, uncovered, until the liquid is almost gone and the beets are shiny with the glaze.

Serve immediately.

Per serving: 39 calories (1 from fat), 0.1 g total fat, 0 g saturated fat, 0 mg cholesterol, 130 mg sodium, 9.3 g carbohydrate, 1.4 g dietary fiber, 0.8 g protein

BASIC BEET RECIPES

Beets with Yogurt Dressing

Cut cooked beets into ¼-inch-thick slices and dress with a mixture of finely chopped red onions, a dash of Dijon-style mustard, a drizzle of white wine vinegar, and enough low-fat yogurt to coat beets. (Horseradish may be used in place of the mustard and vinegar.) Toss in a bowl; add salt and pepper to taste.

Beet Salad

Roast beets, peel, and cut into julienne. Combine the beets in a bowl with equal amounts of watercress and mixed baby greens. Coat with a light vinaigrette dressing made of lemon juice, olive oil, vinegar, and thyme. Sprinkle a little crumbled goat cheese and toasted walnut pieces on top.

Beets with Horseradish-Dill Butter

Make a mixture of butter, minced fresh dill, horseradish, and cider vinegar and simmer together in a small pan. Pour over sliced cooked beets and toss.

Simple Beet Salad

Prepare these elements: diced cooked beets, butter lettuce or mixed baby greens, finely chopped red onion, and Curry-Mustard Vinaigrette (page 92). In a small bowl, dress the beets with a little of the vinaigrette. In a separate bowl, toss the greens with the vinaigrette. Place the greens around the edge of a serving platter, place the beets in the center of the greens, garnish the top of beets with finely chopped onion, and serve.

Beet Borscht

SERVES 6

12 ounces cooked beets (page 394)
1 ½ cups chicken stock
Grated zest and juice of 1 lemon
3 to 4 tablespoons minced fresh dill
¼ teaspoon pepper
6 scallions, chopped
1 cup low-fat sour cream
1 cup low-fat plain yogurt
2 tablespoons minced fresh chives and chive blossoms

In a blender or food processor, combine the beets and stock.

Add the lemon zest and juice, dill, salt, pepper, and scallions. Blend until smooth, pour into a bowl, and blend in the sour cream and yogurt. Cover and refrigerate until very cold. Taste for seasoning; it should be nice and lemony. Garnish each bowl with chopped chives and blossoms.

Per serving: 104 calories (24 from fat), 2.7 g total fat, 1.6 g saturated fat, 10 mg cholesterol, 643 mg sodium, 14.9 g carbohydrate, 1.8 g dietary fiber, 5.6 g protein

Roasted Beets with Braised Kale and Curry Dressing

SERVES 4 TO 6

Serve this warm or as a cold salad. It tastes great the next day because the flavors will meld overnight in the refrigerator.

> 9 small to medium beets
> 3 teaspoons olive oil
> 1 small white or yellow onion, finely chopped
> 1 bunch kale, stemmed and coarsely chopped
> ½ cup vegetable stock or water
> Juice of 1 lemon
> Salt and freshly ground pepper to taste

> DRESSING
> ½ teaspoon kosher salt
> 2 teaspoons Dijon mustard
> 3 tablespoons fresh lemon juice
> 1½ teaspoons curry powder
> 5 tablespoons olive oil

> 1 tablespoon black or yellow mustard seeds for garnish

Preheat the oven to 375°. Rub the beets with 1 teaspoon of the olive oil. Bake for 45 to 50 minutes, or until tender when pierced with a knife. Set aside to cool.

Meanwhile, in a medium skillet over medium heat, heat the remaining 2 teaspoons oil. Add the onion, cover, and cook for 4 to 5 minutes. Add the kale and toss to coat with the oil; add the stock, cover, and braise for 5 to 10 minutes. Uncover and cook until the kale is tender and nearly all the liquid is evaporated, another 15 to 20 minutes. Add water if necessary. Add the lemon juice, salt, and pepper. Set aside and let cool. Squeeze out the excess liquid. Peel the beets and cut them into fine julienne.

To make the dressing, dry the skillet with a paper towel and heat the skillet over medium heat. Dry-roast the mustard seeds for 2 to 3 minutes until aromatic and starting to pop. Set aside to cool.

In a small bowl, mix together the kosher salt, mustard, lemon juice, and curry powder. Gradually whisk in the olive oil.

Place the kale and beets in separate bowls, and dress each with one-third of the dressing. On a serving platter, arrange the kale around the outside and the beets in the center. Drizzle with any remaining dressing and garnish with the toasted mustard seeds.

Serve warm or refrigerate to serve cold.

Per serving: 325 calories (190 from fat), 22.3 g total fat, 3 g saturated fat, 0 mg cholesterol, 625 mg sodium, 29.6 g carbohydrate, 6.8 g dietary fiber, 5.7 g protein

BROCCOLI

To prepare: Break off the florets in big bunches, then break the big florets into smaller ones. Trim the stem ends. The stems can be peeled with a peeler and cut into coins ($1/16$- or $1/8$-inch-thick disks), then sautéed or steamed a little longer than the tops.

To steam: Broccoli is better when steamed rather than cooked in boiling water because it won't get as soggy. Broccoli is better for you when steamed rather than raw because steaming helps release many of broccoli's nutrients. Steam over boiling water in a covered container for 5 to 6 minutes, or until tender.

BASIC BROCCOLI RECIPE

Pasta with Broccoli and Carrots

Peel 3 carrots and 5 broccoli stems. Cut equal amounts into fine julienne. Steam them and set aside. Chop 2 or 3 broccoli florets and grate 1 carrot, then sauté in a little olive oil. Add the steamed vegetables. Season with salt, pepper, herbs, a little garlic, and lemon juice. Serve over 6 ounces hot cooked pasta. Serves 2.

Broccoli with Oil and Lemon

SERVES 4

My mother used to dress steamed broccoli with lemon juice, chopped garlic, olive oil, salt, and pepper. Following her inspiration, I've concocted a special marinade that can be poured over the broccoli the minute it comes out of the steamer. After you've tried the recipe as is a few times, make whatever adjustments to the dressing that may suit your taste.

> 1 large bunch broccoli, separated into florets, stems trimmed, peeled, and cut into $1/8$-inch-thick disks
> 3 cloves garlic, minced
> 1 tablespoon balsamic vinegar
> 2 tablespoons fresh lemon juice
> 2 teaspoons olive oil
> $1/3$ teaspoon kosher salt
> $1/2$ teaspoon pepper

Steam the stem pieces over boiling water in a covered container for 2 to 3 minutes. Add the florets and steam for 9 or 10 minutes, or until the broccoli is tender.

Meanwhile, prepare the dressing by combining all the remaining ingredients in a small dish or cup and whisking with a small whisk or fork.

When the broccoli is cooked, place it in a serving bowl, dress with the dressing, and serve immediately.

Per serving: 33 calories (19 from fat), 2.4 g total fat, 0.3 g saturated fat, 0 mg cholesterol, 163 mg sodium, 3 g carbohydrate, 0.8 g dietary fiber, 0.9 g protein

Broccoli Stems with Cashews

SERVES 3 TO 4 AS A SIDE DISH

This is a good way to use an excess of broccoli stems; we first tasted it at O'mei Restaurant in Santa Cruz, California. The recipe can easily be cut in half if only a few stems are available.

> 5 to 6 large broccoli stems
>
> 1/4 cup unroasted cashews
>
> 2 teaspoons Asian sesame oil
>
> 1 tablespoon grated or minced gingerroot
>
> Freshly ground pepper to taste
>
> 2 tablespoons low-salt soy sauce

Preheat the oven to 350°. Pare each broccoli stem with a potato peeler so that all the tough green outer flesh is removed. With angled cuts, cut stems into 1¹/₂-inch lengths. Then pare each piece of stem into a softly rounded oval nugget.

In a pie pan, toast the cashews in the oven for 5 to 8 minutes, or until just golden brown. Set aside.

Steam the stems over boiling water in a covered pot for 8 to 12 minutes, or until crisp-tender.

In a medium nonstick skillet over medium heat, heat the oil and sauté the gingerroot for a few seconds. Add the broccoli stems and pepper, and sauté for 2 to 3 minutes to coat and reheat the broccoli. Pour in the soy sauce and stir to coat. Transfer to a serving platter, sprinkle with the nuts, and serve immediately.

Per serving: 167 calories (71 from fat), 9.2 g total fat, 1.6 g saturated fat, 0 mg cholesterol, 470 mg sodium, 17.6 g carbohydrate, 0.8 g dietary fiber, 9.9 g protein

Pasta with Broccoli

SERVES 2

Broccoli, garlic, and lemon juice make a simple pasta sauce. For a simpler version, just sauté garlic in olive oil, add broccoli florets and some lemon juice, and pour it over cooked pasta.

> 4 cups small broccoli florets
>
> 4 ounces spaghetti
>
> 3 tablespoons olive oil
>
> 5 cloves garlic, minced
>
> 1 cup raw broccoli stems, peeled and grated
>
> 1/2 cup minced fresh flat-leaf parsley
>
> 1/2 teaspoon salt
>
> Freshly ground pepper to taste
>
> 1/2 teaspoon crushed red pepper flakes (optional)
>
> 1/3 cup fresh lemon juice
>
> Grated Parmesan cheese or toasted bread crumbs for topping

Add 1 inch of water to a skillet or saucepan. Bring to boil, add the broccoli, cover and cook until crisp-tender, 3 to 5 minutes. Set aside.

In a large pot of salted boiling water, cook the pasta and until very al dente, about 8 minutes. Drain, reserving 2 cups of the water.

Meanwhile, in a medium skillet over medium heat, heat the olive oil, add the garlic, and sauté until translucent. Add the grated broccoli stems, parsley, salt, pepper, and pepper flakes and sauté for 2 to 3 minutes. Add the broccoli florets and sauté briefly. Pour in the lemon juice and stir.

Add the pasta to the skillet with the broccoli and add about 1 cup of the pasta water. Turn the heat up to medium-high and stir continuously for 2 to 3 minutes until the water cooks off and the pasta is al dente. Add another cup or so of water and cook off if pasta is not quite done.

Serve sprinkled with Parmesan or toasted bread crumbs.

Per serving: 471 calories (189 from fat), 22 g total fat, 3.0 g saturated fat, 0 mg cholesterol, 584 mg sodium, 59.5 g carbohydrate, 6.4 g dietary fiber, 14.1 g protein

Roasted Broccoli Soup

SERVES 6

Serve with a dollop of red pepper purée (page 85). A sprinkling of paprika or New Mexico chile powder at the table adds a spicy taste and nice color.

- 1 slice white bread or sweet French bread, crust removed
- 2 cups low-fat milk
- 3 cups broccoli florets and coarsely chopped peeled stems
- 2 tablespoons olive oil
- 2 tablespoons fresh lemon juice
- 1/2 teaspoon salt
- 1/2 cup chopped celery
- 1/2 cup chopped onion
- 1 teaspoon minced fresh thyme
- 3 cups low-fat chicken stock

Tear the bread into chunks, place in a bowl, and cover with the milk. Let soak for 20 minutes or so.

Preheat the oven to 375°. Coat the broccoli with 1 tablespoon of the olive oil and the lemon juice; sprinkle with the salt. Put the broccoli on a nonstick baking sheet and bake for 30 minutes, or until slightly brown and tender.

Meanwhile, in a large, heavy saucepan over medium heat, heat the remaining tablespoon of olive oil. Sauté the celery, onion, and thyme until tender, stirring frequently. Squeeze the bread dry and add it to the pot, reserving the milk. Add the broccoli and the stock. Bring to a boil, then reduce heat and simmer for 20 to 25 minutes.

Purée the mixture in a blender or food processor (in batches if necessary). Then strain the mixture and return it to the saucepan. Add the milk and simmer over low heat 10 minutes. Serve piping hot.

Per serving: 114 calories (43 from fat), 5.7 g total fat, 1.2 g saturated fat, 3 mg cholesterol, 521 mg sodium, 11.2 g carbohydrate, 1.8 g dietary fiber, 10.1 g protein

CAULIFLOWER

To prepare: Wash head. Trim the base of the stalk. Break or cut florets into sections.

To cook: Steam 8 to 10 minutes until tender, or steam 2 to 3 minutes and then stir-fry 2 to 3 minutes.

Penne and Cauliflower Casserole

SERVES 6 TO 8

This baked dish is based on a peasant recipe from southern Italy. You can also serve it as a sauced pasta without baking it.

- 1 cauliflower, cut into florets
- 1 pound penne pasta
- 1/4 cup extra virgin olive oil
- 1 large onion, diced
- 6 anchovy fillets, chopped
- 8 tomatoes, peeled, seeded, and coarsely chopped
- 1/2 cup currants or raisins
- 1/2 teaspoon salt
- Freshly ground black pepper to taste
- 1/2 cup fresh bread crumbs
- 1/2 cup pine nuts
- 1/2 cup grated Parmesan, Asiago, or pecorino cheese

In a large pot of salted boiling water, cook the cauliflower florets for 3 to 4 minutes, or until crisp-tender. Remove with a slotted spoon and set aside.

Cook the pasta in the same water until very al dente, about 8 minutes. Drain and let cool, reserving the pasta water.

In a large skillet over medium heat, heat the oil and sauté the onion until translucent. Add the anchovies to the onion and sauté for 1 minute. Add the tomatoes and currants and cook for 5 minutes or so, or until the mixture is blended.

Preheat the oven to 375°. In a large bowl, combine the pasta, 1 cup of the pasta cooking water, cauliflower, and sauce. Toss well. Add the salt and pepper. Pour into a 13 x 9-inch baking dish and sprinkle with the bread crumbs, pine nuts, and cheese.

Bake for 35 to 40 minutes, or until the sauce bubbles and the nuts and crumbs are golden brown.

Per serving: 568 calories (180 from fat), 20.7 g total fat, 4.3 g saturated fat, 10 mg cholesterol, 528 mg sodium, 80.1 g carbohydrate, 6 g dietary fiber, 20.3 g protein

Cauliflower and Green Pea Curry

SERVES 6

1 cauliflower, cut into florets
3 tablespoons butter
1 onion, chopped
2 teaspoons poppy seeds
1¹/₂ tablespoons curry powder
1 tablespoon minced gingerroot
1 teaspoon cumin seed
¹/₄ teaspoon crushed red pepper flakes
1 cup low-fat plain yogurt
1¹/₂ cup cooked peas
Steamed rice or boiled potatoes for serving

Steam the cauliflower over boiling water in a covered container for 8 to 10 minutes, or until crisp-tender. Drain and keep warm.

Meanwhile, in a large skillet, melt the butter over medium-high heat and sauté the onion until brown, about 8 minutes. Add the poppy seeds, curry powder, gingerroot, cumin, and pepper flakes, and stir for 1 minute. Stir in the yogurt, then the peas and cauliflower.

Serve over rice or boiled potatoes.

Per serving: 427 calories (71 from fat), 7.8 g total fat, 4.2 g saturated fat, 18 mg cholesterol, 97 mg sodium, 77.8 g carbohydrate, 2.7 g dietary fiber, 10 g protein

CABBAGE

To prepare: Remove wilted outer leaves and wash head. If you are using the whole head, cut out the core with a peeler (leave core intact if you are using only part of the head). With a large chef's knife, sliver cabbage into ¹/₈-inch slices for raw salads, coleslaw, or vegetable sautés, or chop into 1-inch pieces for stir-fry.

To cook: Steam, sauté, or stir-fry. Steam whole leaves to stuff with cooked rice and vegetables. Then place stuffed leaves in a casserole, cover with red sauce (page 438), and heat through in a 350° oven, 15 to 20 minutes.

Hot Mustard Slaw

SERVES 2

Serve on sandwiches or as a spicy side dish.

2 tablespoons yellow or black mustard seeds
1¹/₂ cups shredded mixed green and red cabbage
¹/₂ cup carrot curls (made with a potato peeler)
1 tablespoon peanut oil
3 tablespoons plain rice wine vinegar
1 teaspoon honey
1 teaspoon mustard
¹/₄ teaspoon salt
¹/₄ teaspoon pepper

In a dry skillet over medium heat, toast the mustard seeds until they are aromatic and begin to pop, 2 to 3 minutes. Set aside to cool.

Put the cabbage and carrot in a medium bowl. Add the oil, vinegar, honey, mustard, salt, and pepper to the skillet with the mustard seeds; heat over medium-low heat until very warm but not boiling. Stir to dissolve the mustard and honey. Pour the hot dressing over the vegetables and toss well. Serve immediately or let cool to room temperature.

Per serving: 359 calories (102 from fat), 11.2 g total fat, 1.5 g saturated fat, 0 mg cholesterol, 486 mg sodium, 54.4 g carbohydrate, 6.8 g dietary fiber, 8.9 g protein

BASIC CABBAGE RECIPE

Red Cabbage Sauté

Sauté 1 cup thinly sliced yellow onion in 2 tablespoons fruity olive oil over medium heat. Add 4 cups shredded red cabbage, 1 teaspoon salt, and 1 teaspoon minced fresh thyme. Cook for 5 to 7 minutes, or until cabbage is tender. Add 2 tablespoons coarsely chopped capers and 1 tablespoon balsamic vinegar. Sauté for 1 minute, or until the vinegar is evaporated.

Remove to a serving bowl and garnish with a little minced fresh parsley. Serves 4.

Chard and Cabbage Kraut

SERVES 4

Serve warm or at room temperature on crostini, as an appetizer, or as a side dish for pork, sausage, or chicken. This may also be used as a sauce for pasta.

- **2 tablespoons olive oil**
- **$^{1}/_{2}$ onion, cut into julienne**
- **1 clove garlic, minced**
- **2 cups shredded Swiss chard**
- **2 cups shredded red cabbage**
- **1 tablespoon tapenade (page 97)**
- **Juice of 1 lemon**
- **1 tablespoon balsamic vinegar**

In a large nonstick skillet over medium heat, heat the olive oil and sauté the onion and garlic until translucent.

Add the Swiss chard and cabbage and sauté for 4 to 5 minutes, or until crisp-tender.

Add the tapenade, lemon juice, and vinegar and sauté for 2 to 3 minutes. Let cool.

Per serving: 84 calories (58 from fat), 6.9 g total fat, 0.9 g saturated fat, 0 mg cholesterol, 46 mg sodium, 6 g carbohydrate, 1.5 g dietary fiber, 1.2 g protein

Vegetable Sauté, Ristorante Avanti

SERVES 2 TO 4

The simplest and best vegetable sauté I've tasted for garden produce is the one at Ristorante Avanti in Santa Cruz, California. The only extra ingredients besides the organic vegetables are kosher salt, fresh black pepper, and olive oil.

- **2 tablespoons olive oil**
- **1 red onion, into 1-inch pieces**
- **1 cup chopped savoy cabbage**
- **1 cup snap peas, cut into bite-sized pieces**
- **$1^{1}/_{2}$ cups chopped red Swiss chard**
- **$1^{1}/_{2}$ cups chopped spinach**
- **$^{1}/_{2}$ teaspoon kosher salt**
- **$^{1}/_{8}$ teaspoon freshly ground black pepper**

In a skillet over medium-high heat, heat the oil and add all the remaining ingredients. Sauté for 3 to 4 minutes, or until the vegetables are crisp-tender. Taste and adjust the seasoning. Serve immediately.

Per serving: 205 calories (120 from fat), 14 g total fat, 1.9 g saturated fat, 0 mg cholesterol, 576 mg sodium, 17.2 g carbohydrate, 6 g dietary fiber, 5.4 g protein

Mimi's Cabbage Borscht

SERVES 10 TO 12

- 8 unpeeled potatoes, halved
- 10 cups water
- 4 tomatoes, peeled, seeded, and chopped
- 1 large carrot, diced
- $1/2$ beet, peeled and chopped
- 1 small whole onion, plus 1 small onion, chopped
- 1 teaspoon salt
- 2 tablespoons olive oil
- 4 cups shredded cabbage
- 2 tablespoons butter
- $1/2$ cup milk
- $1/2$ cup diced green bell pepper
- Freshly ground pepper to taste
- 1 teaspoon minced fresh dill

Cut a few of the potatoes into $1/2$-inch dice so you have $1^1/2$ cups and set aside.

In a large pot, bring the water to a boil. Add the remaining halved potatoes, $1/2$ cup of the tomatoes, the carrot, beet, the whole onion, and salt. Cook until the potatoes are tender, about 5 minutes.

Meanwhile, in a large skillet over medium heat, heat 1 tablespoon of the olive oil and sauté the chopped onion until translucent. Add the remaining tomatoes. Let simmer on the back burner until it becomes a thick sauce, about 30 minutes.

In a medium saucepan over medium heat, heat the remaining 1 tablespoon of olive oil and fry 2 cups of the shredded cabbage until tender but not browned.

With a slotted spoon, transfer the boiled potatoes to a medium bowl. Discard the whole onion to the compost but leave the carrot and beet in the water. Add the butter and the milk to the potatoes and mash with a fork or potato masher.

Add the diced potatoes to the potato water with $1/2$ of the onion-tomato sauce. Cook over medium heat until the potatoes are tender, about 5 minutes. Add the remaining raw cabbage and bring to a boil. Reduce heat and add the mashed potatoes, fried cabbage, the onion-tomato sauce mixture, and the bell pepper. Add the ground pepper and dill. Simmer for 20 to 30 minutes for all the flavors to meld.

Per serving: 315 calories (51 from fat), 5.9 g total fat, 2.1 g saturated fat, 8 mg cholesterol, 283 mg sodium, 60.7 g carbohydrate, 6.7 g dietary fiber, 7.7 g protein

Christie's Coleslaw

SERVES 6

Our good friend and European traveling companion Christie Carlson concocted this recipe. The sugar in the recipe can be replaced with honey. Candied ginger can be purchased in most natural food stores and Asian markets. Combined with the gingerroot in the dressing, it gives this dish a unique flavor.

- 1 small head ($1^1/2$ pounds) red or green cabbage, or a mixture of both, shredded
- 6 carrots, cut into curls with a peeler
- 1 bunch scallions, thinly sliced ($1/2$ cup)
- 1 bunch cilantro, stemmed and coarsely chopped (1cup, loosely packed)

DRESSING
- $1/2$ cup low-fat mayonnaise
- 2 tablespoons grated gingerroot
- 2 tablespoons grated onion
- $1/3$ cup granulated sugar, or 2 tablespoons honey
- $1/2$ cup rice vinegar
- 1 teaspoon salt
- 1 teaspoon pepper

TOPPING
- $1/4$ cup candied ginger, finely chopped
- $1/4$ cup peanuts, chopped

Combine the vegetables and cilantro in a large bowl. Whisk the dressing ingredients together in a medium bowl until well mixed. Dress the slaw with the dressing so that it is well coated. Place the coleslaw in a serving dish and top with the chopped candied ginger and chopped peanuts.

Per serving: 233 calories (76 from fat), 9 g total fat, 1.1 g saturated fat, 13 mg cholesterol, 505 mg sodium, 37.1 g carbohydrate, 6.4 g dietary fiber, 4.8 g protein

Cabbage and Potato Soup

SERVES 6

This is comfort food from the Rosticceria, adapted for home cooking. We've reduced the amount of bacon, butter, and stock, and also eliminated the milk from the recipe.

- 2 slices bacon
- 2 cloves garlic, minced
- 2 onions, diced
- 1 teaspoon minced fresh thyme
- 3 stalks celery, diced
- 2 carrots, thinly sliced
- 4 potatoes, peeled and cubed
- 2 cups low sodium chicken broth or vegetable stock
- 4 cups water
- 1 teaspoon salt
- 1/2 green cabbage, shredded
- Freshly ground pepper to taste

In a skillet over medium heat, sauté the bacon, garlic, onions, and thyme for 5 minutes. Add the celery and carrots and continue to sauté another 10 minutes, or until the vegetables are limp. Add the potatoes, stock, water, and salt. Turn heat to high and bring to a boil; cover and simmer over low heat for 15 minutes. Add half the cabbage and simmer covered until the potatoes and cabbage are tender, about 10 minutes. Let cool.

Purée the soup in a food processor or blender (in batches if necessary). Return to the pot and add the rest of the cabbage and a few grinds of pepper. While stirring frequently, reheat and simmer another 10 minutes or until cabbage is tender. Adjust the seasoning and serve.

Per serving: 264 calories (20 from fat), 2.5 g total fat, 0.5 g saturated fat, 2 mg cholesterol, 462 mg sodium, 55.4 g carbohydrate, 7.5 g dietary fiber, 11.4 g protein

Asian Cabbage

SERVES 3

This is good with bok choy as well.

- 1 1/2 tablespoons peanut oil
- 2 large shallots, minced
- 2 tablespoons chopped gingerroot
- 6 large leaves Lechoy or Mei Ging Choy cabbage, chopped
- 2 tablespoons low-salt soy sauce

In a medium skillet over medium-high heat, heat the oil and sauté the shallots and gingerroot for 2 minutes. Add the cabbage and sauté for 3 or 4 minutes, or until tender. Stir in the soy sauce and stir to coat. Serve immediately.

Per serving: 107 calories (60 from fat), 7.1 g total fat, 1.2 g saturated fat, 0 mg cholesterol, 421 mg sodium, 9.9 g carbohydrate, 2.4 g dietary fiber, 2.6 g protein

CARROTS

To prepare: Wash, trim, and peel or scrape with a sharp knife. Dice, cut into rounds, julienne, or cut diagonally into 1-inch pieces. Grate for salads or cut slivers with a peeler to use in coleslaw or as a garnish.

To cook: Sauté, stir-fry (after steaming slightly), or steam. To roast in the oven (30 to 45 minutes), first drizzle with olive oil and herbs.

BASIC CARROT RECIPES

Moroccan Carrot Salad

Combine julienned or grated carrots with minced shallots, granulated sugar, salt, ground cumin, black pepper, dash of cayenne, lemon juice, and minced fresh parsley. Toss and marinate for 1 hour. Serve at room temperature.

Baby Carrots with Ginger and Sage Butter

Scrub carrots and poach or steam until tender. Melt some butter in a skillet and add a little brown sugar, grated gingerroot, fresh lemon juice, salt, minced garlic, and minced fresh sage. Add the carrots and sauté for a few minutes to blend the flavors.

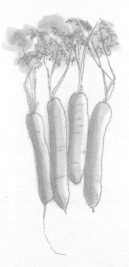

Carrot and Ginger Soup

SERVES 4 TO 6 (AS A FIRST COURSE)

This is a recipe from Gayle's Rosticceria. I've replaced the butter in the original recipe with olive oil and the heavy cream with milk, and added some potatoes as a thickening agent.

- 1¹/₂ tablespoons olive oil
- 1¹/₂ cups chopped onion
- 3 cloves garlic, chopped
- 2 tablespoons chopped gingerroot
- 1 potato, peeled and cubed
- 2 pounds carrots, cut into ¹/₂-inch pieces
- 4 cups low sodium chicken broth or vegetable stock
- ¹/₄ teaspoon salt
- 1 cup milk
- ¹/₈ teaspoon cayenne pepper or New Mexico chile powder
- ¹/₂ cup sour cream or low-fat yogurt mixed with minced scallions or grated gingerroot for garnish
- 2 scallions, chopped

In a large saucepan over medium heat, heat the oil and sauté the onions, garlic, and gingerroot until the onions are translucent. Add the potato, carrots, stock, and salt and bring to a boil. Reduce heat, cover, and simmer until the carrots and potatoes are very tender, 30 to 40 minutes. Remove from heat and let cool.

Purée the soup in a blender or food processor (in batches if necessary). Return to the saucepan and add the milk and cayenne. Simmer uncovered for 10 to 15 minutes. Taste and adjust the seasoning. Serve topped with the sour cream mixture and chopped scallions.

Per serving: 357 calories (126 from fat), 14.6 g total fat, 6.2 g saturated fat, 21 mg cholesterol, 315 mg sodium, 49 g carbohydrate, 8.9 g dietary fiber, 10.7 g protein

Carrot Cake

SERVES 8

1¹/₂ cups vegetable oil

2 cups granulated sugar

4 large eggs, lightly beaten

2 cups all-purpose flour

2 teaspoons baking soda

2 teaspoons baking powder

2 teaspoons ground cinnamon

1 teaspoon salt

3 cups grated carrots (about 4 to 6)

¹/₂ cup raisins

1 cup chopped walnuts (optional)

ICING

8 ounces cream cheese, at room temperature

¹/₂ cup unsalted butter, at room temperature

4 cups sifted confectioners' sugar

1 teaspoon pure vanilla extract

Milk as needed

Preheat the oven to 325°. Grease, flour, and line two 9-inch round cake pans with parchment paper.

In a large bowl, combine the oil and sugar. Beat in the eggs until well blended, about 1 minute.

Combine and sift the dry ingredients together. Add the dry ingredients to the oil mixture and mix until incorporated.

Add the carrots, raisins, and walnuts and mix until just incorporated.

Pour the batter into the prepared pans. Place the pans on a baking sheet and place on the center rack of the oven. Bake for about 30 minutes, or until the cakes are springy to the touch and just start to pull away from the sides of the pans.

Let cool completely in the pans on wire racks, then depan. The cakes may be kept, well wrapped, in the refrigerator for 1 day or frozen for 2 weeks before being iced.

Meanwhile, make the icing. In the bowl of a mixer fitted with the flat beater, cream together the cream cheese and butter, scraping down the bowl and beater twice, until the mixture is fluffy. Add the confectioners' sugar, first mixing on low speed, then increasing the speed to high. Beat until light and fluffy, again scraping down the bowl and beater twice. Blend in the vanilla.

The icing should be a smooth, spreadable consistency, just a little firmer than soft butter. If it is too stiff, add milk, 1 tablespoon at a time, while mixing on medium speed, until the icing is the desired consistency. Use immediately, or refrigerate for up to 2 days, bringing the icing to room temperature before using. (The icing is best when used immediately.)

To assemble: Freeze the layers for about 30 minutes to make them easier to ice. Level the tops of the two cake layers by trimming with a large serrated knife.

Place one cake layer, leveled side up, on a 9-inch cake cardboard. Using a metal icing spatula, spread the top with 1 cup of the icing. Place the other layer, cut-side down, on top of the icing.

Skim coat the entire cake with a very thin layer of the cream cheese icing. Refrigerate for about 30 minutes to let the icing harden.

Remove from the refrigerator and set on a serving platter. Ice the cake by swirling the remaining icing with the rounded end of a metal icing spatula.

The iced cake will keep refrigerated for 3 days. If refrigerated, let it come to room temperature before serving.

Per serving: 1,289 calories (657 from fat), 74.8 g total fat, 19.9 g saturated fat, 172 mg cholesterol, 806 mg sodium, 148.7 g carbohydrate, 3.3 g dietary fiber, 13.2 g protein

CELERY

To prepare: Trim leaves and stem and wash stalks. Peel away strings. Cut into $1/2$-inch half-moon slices, julienne into $1/4$ by 2-inch sticks, or dice.

To cook: Eat raw, cook in soups, or sauté or stir-fry with assorted vegetables.

BASIC CELERY RECIPE

Celery Topping for Soup

Mince some garlic, celery, and celery leaves and sauté in a small amount of fruity olive oil. Use this to garnish your favorite bean soup or minestrone.

Winter Vegetable Salad

SERVES 2

This is refreshing, crunchy, and easy to make.

- 1 stalk celery, sliced thin
- 1 large carrot, shredded
- $1/2$ cucumber, halved lengthwise, seeded, and cut into half-moons
- $1/2$ cup alfalfa sprouts
- Juice of $1/2$ lemon
- 3 tablespoons olive oil
- Salt and freshly ground pepper to taste

Put the vegetables in a medium bowl. Combine the lemon juice and olive oil and pour the dressing over the vegetables. Toss. Add the salt and pepper and toss again.

Per serving: 222 calories (178 from fat), 20.6 g total fat, 2.8 g saturated fat, 0 mg cholesterol, 34 mg sodium, 9.5 g carbohydrate, 2.9 g dietary fiber, 1.9 g protein

SWISS CHARD

To prepare: Discard wilted leaves. Wash remaining leaves. Cut out stems and chop. Chop leaves into 1 or 2 inch pieces or chiffonade (page 48).

To cook: Sauté alone with garlic, olive oil, salt, and pepper, or stir-fry with mixed vegetables like sliced onion and thin coins of carrots. Cook stems a few minutes longer than leaves. Add raw chiffonade to tuna or salmon salad.

Roasted Greens with Bread Crumbs and Pine Nuts

SERVES 4 TO 6

HERB PASTE

- $1/2$ teaspoon salt
- $1/2$ teaspoon pepper
- 1 teaspoon minced garlic
- 1 teaspoon minced fresh sage leaves
- 1 teaspoon minced fresh rosemary
- 1 teaspoon grated lemon zest

GREENS

- $1^1/2$ bunches red or green Swiss chard, spinach, beet greens, or kale (8 cups, roughly chopped)
- $1/4$ cup olive oil
- 2 tablespoons chopped garlic
- $1/4$ cup lemon juice
- 1 tablespoon balsamic vinegar

TOPPING

- 1 cup toasted bread crumbs
- $1/4$ cup pine nuts
- 1 tablespoon grated lemon zest

To make the herb paste, combine all the ingredients in a blender or food processor and pulse several times into a coarse paste. Set aside.

Chop the greens into 2-inch pieces. Reserve the stems.

Preheat the oven to 350°. In a large skillet

over medium heat, heat 2 tablespoons of the oil and sauté the garlic until crisp and golden but not burnt. Remove the garlic with a slotted spoon and reserve. Sauté the chard stems for several minutes, or until just limp.

In a large bowl, place the raw chard leaves with the cooked chard stems and juices on top. Pour on the lemon juice and balsamic vinegar and toss once. Add the herb paste and toss the mixture to coat it well.

Combine the topping ingredients in a small bowl along with the reserved crisp garlic. Add half of the topping mixture to the greens and toss.

Put the greens mixture in individual ramekins on a baking sheet. Top each serving with some of the remaining crumb mixture. Bake for 15 to 20 minutes, or until topping is crisp.

Per serving: 297 calories (176 from fat), 20.5 g total fat, 3 g saturated fat, 0 mg cholesterol, 515 mg sodium, 25.5 g carbohydrate, 2.4 g dietary fiber, 6.2 g protein

BASIC CHARD RECIPE

Chard with Oil and Balsamic Vinegar

Cook 4 to 6 cups chopped wet chard in a sauté pan until wilted. Remove from pan and squeeze out any excess liquid. In the same pan heat a mixture of about 1 tablespoon each olive oil, lemon juice, balsamic vinegar, and minced garlic. Add the chard to the pan and sauté for a few minutes to combine flavors and slightly cook garlic. Add salt and pepper to taste.

Chard and Sun-Dried Tomato Sauté

SERVES 6

$^2/_3$ cup sun-dried tomatoes
2 tablespoons olive oil
3 scallions, minced
6 cloves garlic, minced
4 ounces (6 to 8 slices) prosciutto, coarsely chopped
3 bunches Swiss chard with stems, coarsely chopped
2 tablespoons grated lemon zest
Salt and freshly ground pepper to taste
6 tablespoons toasted bread crumbs, for garnish

If using dry sundried tomatoes, soak them in $^3/_4$ cup hot water for 10 to 15 minutes.

In a large skillet over medium heat, heat the olive oil and sauté the scallions and garlic until translucent. Add the prosciutto and sauté for 1 minute.

Turn the heat to high, add the Swiss chard and the tomatoes with their soaking water. Sauté until most of the liquid has evaporated and the chard is tender, 6 to 8 minutes.

Add the grated lemon zest, salt, and pepper.

Transfer to a serving plate and garnish with the toasted bread crumbs.

Per serving: 151 calories (59 from fat), 6.9 g total fat, 1.3 g saturated fat, 13 mg cholesterol, 726 mg sodium, 15.6 g carbohydrate, 3.5 g dietary fiber, 8.7 g protein

Puttanesca Verde

SERVES 4 TO 6

A traditional puttanesca sauce uses anchovies, capers, black olives, and garlic. This tasty variation does away with the anchovies and substitutes Swiss chard for the tomatoes. The addition of parsley helps give the dish an herbaceous flavor.

- $^1/_4$ cup butter
- 2 tablespoons olive oil
- $^1/_4$ cup minced garlic
- 1 medium bunch Swiss chard, shredded
- 4 tablespoons capers, drained and chopped
- 24 small green olives, pitted and chopped
- $^1/_2$ cup minced fresh flat-leaf parsley
- Juice of 2 lemons
- 12 ounces to 1 pound fresh or dried angel-hair pasta
- $^1/_2$ cup (2 ounces) grated Parmesan cheese

In a large skillet over medium heat, melt 2 tablespoons of the butter with the olive oil. Add the garlic and sauté until translucent. Add the Swiss chard and cook 2 to 3 minutes over medium heat, while stirring. Stir in the capers, olives, parsley, and half the lemon juice.

In a large pot of salted boiling water, cook fresh pasta for 2 to 3 minutes and dried pasta for 4 to 5 minutes, or until al dente. Drain the pasta and place in a serving bowl. Toss with the remaining 2 tablespoons butter and the remaining lemon juice. Add the sauce and toss.

Serve with the Parmesan alongside.

Per serving: 588 calories (234 from fat), 26.2 g total fat, 10.9 g saturated fat, 41 mg cholesterol, 679 mg sodium, 71.8 g carbohydrate, 2.7 g dietary fiber, 17.4 g protein

Purple, Green, and Black Pasta

SERVES 4

- 3 tablespoons olive oil
- 3 skinless, boneless chicken breast halves, cut into $^1/_2$-inch cubes
- 1 cup shredded red cabbage
- 9 leaves spinach or green chard, stemmed and chopped (3 cups)
- $^1/_2$ cup minced fresh flat-leaf parsley
- 12 kalamata olives, pitted and chopped
- $1^1/_2$ tablespoons balsamic vinegar
- 8 ounces angel-hair pasta
- $^3/_4$ cup toasted bread crumbs
- Salt and freshly ground pepper to taste
- $^1/_4$ cup grated Parmesan cheese

In a large skillet over medium heat, heat 2 tablespoons of the olive oil and sauté the chicken until it is golden brown on the outside and opaque throughout. Remove from the skillet with a slotted spoon and keep warm.

Add the remaining 1 tablespoon olive oil to the skillet and sauté the cabbage for 1 minute. Add the spinach, parsley, and olives and sauté for 2 to 3 minutes. Add the balsamic vinegar and stir. Turn off the heat.

Cook the pasta in a large pot of salted boiling water until al dente. Drain, reserving $^3/_4$ cup pasta water.

Return the skillet with the sauce to medium heat and add the chicken and pasta along with the reserved water. Cook for 3 to 4 minutes (stirring to combine), or until the water evaporates. Add salt and pepper to taste.

Place in a serving bowl. Top with the bread crumbs and cheese and toss. Serve immediately.

Per serving: 483 calories (162 from fat), 18.0 g total fat, 3.2 g saturated fat, 18 mg cholesterol, 526 mg sodium, 61.5 g carbohydrate, 4.2 g dietary fiber, 18.7 g protein

CHICORY, ESCAROLE, ENDIVE

To prepare: Wash, remove wilted leaves, cut out core, and remove leaves by hand, breaking up if necessary.

To cook: Serve raw in salads. Chicory can be sautéed and added to soup.

BASIC ESCAROLE AND ENDIVE RECIPES

Escarole Pizza

Sauté 4 cups escarole with a mixture of chopped garlic, olive oil, chopped capers, chopped anchovy fillet, and salt and pepper until wilted. Use along with crumbled feta cheese as a topping for pizza.

Endive Salad

Serve whole endive leaves dressed with a light vinaigrette and garnished with crumbled gorgonzola cheese, raisins, and toasted pinenuts.

Tricolor Salad

SERVES 4 TO 6

> 4 cups shredded Belgian endive
> 4 cups shredded red radicchio
> 4 cups shredded spinach or Swiss chard
> 2 tablespoons minced garlic
> 1 tablespoon Dijon-style mustard
> 1/4 cup fresh lemon juice
> 3 tablespoons light olive oil
> 1 teaspoon salt
> Freshly ground pepper to taste
> 1/2 cup minced fresh flat-leaf parsley

On a large serving platter, place the shredded vegetables in three rows: first the endive, then the raddichio and spinach.

Prepare the dressing by whisking all the remaining ingredients, except the parsley, together in a small bowl. Pour the dressing over the salad. Garnish with the parsley and serve.

Per serving: 135 calories (89 from fat), 10.8 g total fat, 1.4 g saturated fat, 0 mg cholesterol, 649 mg sodium, 8.9 g carbohydrate, 3.1 g dietary fiber, 3.5 g protein

Farfalle Casserole with Escarole and Mushrooms

SERVES 6

Farfalle are bow-tie pasta shapes that really know how to wear a sauce. The recipe was inspired by one by Erica De Mane that appeared in Food & Wine *magazine.*

> 2 heads escarole, coarsely chopped
> 6 tablespoons olive oil
> 6 cloves garlic, thinly sliced
> 1 onion, chopped
> 12 ounces cremini mushrooms, thinly sliced
> 12 ounces farfalle pasta
> Salt and freshly ground black pepper to taste
> 1/4 cup grated Parmesan cheese
> 1/2 cup fresh bread crumbs

In a large saucepan of boiling water, blanch the escarole for 1 minute; drain well and set aside.

In a large skillet over medium heat, heat the olive oil and sauté the garlic until crisp. Using a slotted spoon, transfer the garlic to paper towels to drain. Increase heat to high, add the onion and mushrooms to the pan and cook until brown, 10 to 15 minutes. Add the escarole and sauté briefly to coat with the oil, onion, and mushrooms.

Preheat the oven to 375°. Cook the pasta in a large pot of salted boiling water until very al dente; drain. Place the pasta in a 9 x 13-inch casserole dish and add salt and pepper. Add the escarole and mushroom mixture. Add half of the Parmesan and bread crumbs and toss. Top with the remaining bread crumbs, Parmesan, and garlic. Bake uncovered for 20 minutes, or until the topping is crisp. Bake covered for 10 minutes more, and serve immediately.

Per serving: 390 calories (144 from fat), 16.1 g total fat, 2.9 g saturated fat, 3 mg cholesterol, 109 mg sodium, 50.7 g carbohydrate, 3 g dietary fiber, 11.3 g protein

COLLARDS AND MUSTARD GREENS

To prepare: Wash the greens and spin them dry in a lettuce spinner. When ready to use, trim off any thick stems.

To cook: Leave raw and cut into chiffonade (page 48) for salad toppings. Sauté 2 to 3 minutes in olive oil, until limp. Add $1/8$ to $1/4$ cup water and cover if necessary to cook longer. Dress with champagne or raspberry vinegar.

BASIC MUSTARD GREEN RECIPE

Warm Mustard Green Salad

Bring a large saucepan of water to boil and add salt, pepper, grated onion, and grated gingerroot. Plunge the mustard leaves into the water for 30 seconds to tenderize. Drain, pat dry with paper towels, and chop. Serve warm with your favorite salad dressing. Add chopped onions, almonds, and chopped apple to taste.

Sweet and Bitter Mustard Greens

SERVES 6

2 tablespoons olive oil

1 onion, sliced

$3/4$ cup golden raisins

1 tablespoon minced fresh marjoram or thyme

12 ounces mustard greens, stemmed, rinsed, and coarsely chopped

Salt and freshly ground pepper to taste

In a large skillet over medium-high heat, heat the olive oil and cook the onion, raisins, and herbs for 10 to 15 minutes, or until the onion is tender. Reduce heat to medium.

Add the wet greens and sauté for 2 to 3 minutes, or until tender. Add salt and pepper and serve hot.

Per serving: 127 calories (39 from fat), 4.8 g total fat, 0.7 g saturated fat, 0 mg cholesterol, 18 mg sodium, 21.5 g carbohydrate, 2.4 g dietary fiber, 2.6 g protein

Stir-Fried Collards with Sliced Apple

SERVES 6 AS A SIDE DISH

Adapted from Food & Wine *magazine.*

8 ounces collard greens, stemmed

1¹/₂ tablespoons light olive oil

1 small onion, thinly sliced

1 small tart apple, peeled, cored, halved, and thinly sliced

1 tablespoon balsamic vinegar

Salt and freshly ground pepper to taste

Cook the collards in a little boiling water for 3 to 5 minutes, or until tender. Drain, let cool, and chop coarsely.

In a medium skillet over medium-high heat, heat the oil and sauté the onion until slightly browned, about 4 to 5 minutes. Add the apple and cook a few minutes longer, or until tender.

Stir in the collards and combine. Turn heat to high, stir in the vinegar, and cook until the greens are well coated. Add salt and pepper and serve immediately.

Per serving: 65 calories (30 from fat), 3.6 g total fat, 0.5 g saturated fat, 0 mg cholesterol, 8 mg sodium, 8.5 g carbohydrate, 2.4 g dietary fiber, 0.9 g protein

CORN

To prepare: Remove husks and silk. Leave cobs whole for boiling, or shave kernels with the cob held vertically on a work surface; use a chef's knife to slice downward.

To grill: Remove husks and silk, rewrap with husks, and tie with kitchen twine. Soak in cold water 15 minutes before grilling. Grill over a medium fire for 10 to 15 minutes, until tender.

To boil: Set a large stock pot filled with salted water to boil. Remove husks and silk from corn. Place corn in the boiling water 3 to 6 minutes, or until cooked to desired doneness.

BASIC CORN RECIPE

Corn Cob Stock

After cutting the kernels off the cobs of corn, break the cobs into several pieces and place in a stockpot with 6 cups water. Bring to a boil, reduce heat, and simmer for 20 minutes. Remove the corn cobs and simmer the liquid until reduced to 4 cups. Strain. Makes 4 cups.

Black Bean and Fresh Corn Salad

MAKES 6 SMALL SERVINGS

Delicious. A complete protein with a taste of the Southwest.

- 2 cups black beans
- 3 fresh ears corn, kernels steamed and cut off cob (2 cups)
- 2 tomatoes, peeled, seeded, and diced
- 1/2 red bell pepper, seeded and diced
- 2 jalapeño peppers, seeded and chopped
- 4 scallions, sliced

DRESSING
- 1/2 cup cilantro, minced
- 1/2 cup parsley, minced
- 1/3 cup olive oil
- 1/4 cup lemon juice
- 1 teaspoon ground cumin
- 1 clove garlic, minced
- 1/4 teaspoon crushed red pepper flakes
- 1/4 to 1/2 teaspoon salt

Soak the beans overnight. The next morning, drain the beans, and cover with fresh water. Bring to a boil, then cook on low heat for 1 1/2 to 2 hours or until tender. Meanwhile, combine the dressing ingredients and set aside. Combine the beans, corn kernels, tomatoes, bell pepper, jalapeños, and scallions in a bowl.

Add the dressing to the corn-bean mix and toss to coat evenly. Let sit for 1 hour before serving to blend the flavors.

Per serving: 269 calories (110 from fat), 13 g total fat, 1.8 g saturated fat, 0 mg cholesterol, 112 mg sodium, 33.7 g carbohydrate, 5.7 g dietary fiber, 8.7 g protein

Tomato, Basil, and Corn Soup

SERVES 6

- 1/4 cup olive oil
- 1 onion, chopped
- 1 stalk celery, chopped
- 1 carrot, chopped
- 2 tablespoons minced garlic
- 8 tomatoes, peeled, seeded, and chopped
- 4 cups corn kernels (6 ears)
- 4 cups Corn Cob Stock (page 411)
- 2 cups chopped fresh basil, plus a few leaves for garnish
- 1 jalapeño chile, seeded and chopped
- Salt and freshly ground pepper to taste

In a heavy skillet over medium heat, heat the olive oil and sauté the onion, celery, and carrot for 15 minutes, or until tender. Add the garlic and sauté until the mixture starts to color, another 5 or 10 minutes.

Add the tomatoes and 1 cup of the corn kernels. Sauté briefly till heated through. Add the corn stock, bring to a simmer, reduce heat, and cook for 15 minutes. Add the chopped basil and chile. Let cool slightly and purée in a blender or food processor. Return to the pot, add the remaining corn kernels, and simmer for 10 minutes. Season to taste with salt and pepper. Serve garnished with basil.

Per serving: 245 calories (84 from fat), 10.3 g total fat, 1.4 g saturated fat, 0 mg cholesterol, 30 mg sodium, 38.9 g carbohydrate, 5.6 g dietary fiber, 5.8 g protein

Creamed Corn

SERVES 2 TO 4

- **4 fresh ears corn**
- **5 cups water**
- **$^1/_2$ cup milk**
- **2 teaspoons butter or light oil**
- **$^1/_4$ red bell pepper seeded, deribbed, and finely chopped**
- **$^1/_4$ green bell pepper, deribbed and finely chopped**
- **$^1/_4$ teaspoon cayenne pepper**
- **$^1/_2$ teaspoon salt**

Cut the corn from the cobs with a large knife. Break up the cobs and place them in a pot with the water. Bring to a boil, reduce heat, and simmer for 20 minutes. Remove the cobs from the water and save them for the compost bin. Strain the cooked broth through a sieve lined with cheesecloth. Cook over medium heat to reduce to $^1/_2$ cup.

In a small saucepan, cook the milk over medium heat and add it to the stock. Add the corn kernels and cook for 3 to 4 minutes.

In a small skillet over medium heat, melt the butter or heat the oil and sauté the peppers, cayenne, and salt for 3 or 4 minutes. Add to the corn.

Remove half the corn mixture and purée it in a blender or food processor. Add the purée to the pot and stir to combine.

Per serving: 275 calories (69 from fat), 8.6 g total fat, 4.1 g saturated fat, 19 mg cholesterol, 654 mg sodium, 48.1 g carbohydrate, 6.6 g dietary fiber, 9.7 g protein

Polenta and Corn Pancakes

SERVES 7

Serve these warm, or make ahead and reheat them in the oven or fry them in a little butter until golden brown.

- **2 large fresh ears corn**
- **$5^1/_2$ cups water**
- **$^1/_2$ teaspoon salt**
- **$^1/_2$ cup cornmeal**
- **$^1/_2$ cup polenta**
- **2 tablespoons butter, plus 2 tablespoons (if you're going to fry them later)**
- **1 cup (4 ounces) grated Parmesan cheese**
- **12 to 18 flat-leaf parsley, sage, or tarragon leaves**

Using a large knife, cut the corn kernels from the cobs and set aside.

In a medium saucepan, bring 4 cups of the water to a boil and add the salt. (At this stage, the pot of boiling water can be placed over a double boiler.) Turn down the heat to medium and gradually pour in the cornmeal and polenta in a steady stream, stirring constantly.

Reduce to low and cook the polenta mixture for 30 minutes, stirring frequently. Add up to $1^1/_2$ cups more water if necessary to make the polenta just thin enough so it will pour off the spoon (consistency of thick yogurt).

Add the corn kernels, butter, and cheese. Cook, stirring constantly for 4 minutes.

Spread several pieces of waxed paper or plastic wrap on a large worktable or a few baking trays. Place the assorted herb leaves flat on the waxed paper at 6-inch intervals. Pour $^1/_2$ cup of the polenta mixture on each of the herb clusters, then flatten each mound with a spatula to make pancakes.

Let the pancakes cool for 5 to 10 minutes, or until solidified. Serve them immediately, herbside up. Or reheat later on nonstick cookie sheets in a preheated 425° oven for 15 minutes, or fry them in butter until golden brown.

Per serving: 207 calories (71 from fat), 8 g total fat, 4.8 g saturated fat, 20 mg cholesterol, 468 mg sodium, 25.2 g carbohydrate, 3.3 g dietary fiber, 9.3 g protein

Corn Relish

MAKES 4–5 CUPS (5 SERVINGS)

Serve as a condiment for grilled chicken, fish, or grilled vegetables.

- **2 cups cider vinegar**
- **³/₄ cup granulated sugar**
- **1 teaspoons salt**
- **¹/₂ tablespoon celery seed**
- **1 tablespoon mustard seed**
- **¹/₂ teaspoons ground turmeric**
- **3 cups corn kernels, cut from cobs (3 pounds or 5 ears)**
- **1 onion, chopped**
- **¹/₂ red bell pepper, seeded, deribbed, and finely chopped**
- **¹/₂ green bell pepper, seeded, deribbed**

In a large saucepan, combine the vinegar, sugar, salt, celery, mustard seeds, and turmeric. Bring to a boil and simmer for 2 minutes.

Stir in the corn, onions, and peppers, and cook, stirring constantly until the vegetables are just crisp-tender, about 10 minutes. Turn off heat and let cool. Cover and refrigerate overnight before serving.

Per serving: 200 calories (11 from fat), 1.3 g total fat, 0.2 g saturated fat, 0 mg cholesterol, 433 mg sodium, 50.1 g carbohydrate, 3.2 g dietary fiber, 3.8 g protein

Corn Chowder

SERVES 6

Here is another popular recipe from the Rosticceria. And it's been around a long time. It is rich, but a worthwhile indulgence.

- **¹/₄ cup light olive oil**
- **3 cups chopped onion (2 onions)**
- **¹/₂ teaspoon ground cumin**
- **¹/₂ teaspoon minced fresh sage**
- **1 cup dry white wine**
- **¹/₂ green bell pepper, seeded, deribbed, and chopped**
- **¹/₂ teaspoon ground nutmeg**
- **4 cups corn kernels (5 ears)**
- **2 cups chicken stock or vegetable stock**
- **2 cups milk**
- **Salt and freshly ground pepper to taste**
- **¹/₂ cup shredded Cheddar cheese (optional)**
- **¹/₄ cup minced fresh flat-leaf parsley**
- **Tabasco sauce to taste**

In a large saucepan over medium-high heat, heat the oil and sauté the onion about 5 minutes. Add the cumin and sage and cook over low heat a few minutes more.

Add the wine and cook over medium-high heat until the wine almost evaporates. Add the bell pepper, nutmeg, and 3 cups of the corn. Cook several minutes, until the corn is tender.

Purée the entire mixture in a blender, using some of the stock if necessary to thin. Return the mixture to the saucepan. Add the stock, milk, salt, and pepper, and the remaining 1 cup of corn. Bring to a simmer and cook 5 minutes, until the corn is tender. Serve garnished with cheese, parsley, and Tabasco.

Per serving: 332 calories (148 from fat), 16 g total fat, 5.1 g saturated fat, 21 mg cholesterol, 824 mg sodium, 34.9 g carbohydrate, 4.3 g dietary fiber, 9.8 g protein

CUCUMBERS

To prepare: Scrub. Slice with peel on, peel and slice, or use a peeler to shave off peel vertically at $1/2$-inch intervals, leaving alternating peeled and unpeeled stripes, then slice. To dice, peel, then cut in half lengthwise and remove the seeds with a teaspoon or melon baller; cut into quarters lengthwise, then dice.

To cook: Usually eaten raw, but can be cooked in soups, sautéed, or steamed.

BASIC CUCUMBER RECIPE

Marinated Cucumbers

Dress 8 cups thinly sliced, peeled cucumbers with a mixture of $1/4$ cup each granulated sugar and cider vinegar, 1 tablespoon light olive oil, and $1/8$ teaspoon salt. Toss and refrigerate for several hours.

To make the salad: In a bowl, combine diced cucumbers, diced fresh tomatoes, chopped pitted kalamata olives, and diced feta cheese. Dress with a light vinaigrette (page 90).

Dilled Cucumbers

SERVES 6 TO 8

Serve this dish, from Dr. Kenny Bloom, with gravlax or grilled salmon.

- 3 cucumbers, peeled
- 1 teaspoon salt
- 1 tablespoon granulated sugar
- 2 tablespoons hot water
- $3/4$ cup distilled white vinegar
- 1 teaspoon white pepper
- 2 heaping tablespoons minced fresh dill

Slice the cucumbers very thin with a mandoline. Place the slices in a bowl with $1/2$ teaspoon of the salt and toss. Place them on trays lined with paper towels. Let drain for 2 hours, occasionally pressing them with paper towels. Place the slices in a bowl.

In a small bowl, combine the remaining $1/2$ teaspoon of salt, sugar, and hot water and mix until dissolved. Add the vinegar, pepper, and dill and mix to incorporate.

Pour the dressing over the cucumbers and toss. Refrigerate to chill, about 2 hours, or up to 3 days before serving.

Per serving: 53 calories (3 from fat), 0.4 g total fat, 0.1 g saturated fat, 0 mg cholesterol, 362 mg sodium, 12.4 g carbohydrate, 2.4 g dietary fiber, 2.1 g protein

Cucumber Raita

This dish, adapted from Andrea Chesman's Simply Healthful Skillet Suppers, keeps well in the refrigerator for several days. A refreshing condiment to serve with spicy meals.

- **1 to 2 cups low-fat plain yogurt**
- **2 tablespoons finely chopped onion**
- **1¹/₂ tablespoons minced fresh mint**
- **¹/₈ teaspoon ground cumin**
- **1 teaspoon salt**
- **¹/₂ teaspoon pepper**
- **2 cucumbers, peeled, halved lengthwise, seeded, and thinly sliced**

In a medium bowl, combine the yogurt, onion, mint, cumin, ¹/₂ teaspoon of the salt, and pepper.

Spread the cucumber slices on a tray lined with paper towels, sprinkle with the remaining salt, and let stand for 30 minutes to drain.

Pat the slices dry with paper towels. Dress with the sauce and toss. Cover and refrigerate for at least 30 minutes for the flavors to blend. Serve chilled.

Per serving: 79 calories (11 from fat), 1.3 g total fat, 0.7 g saturated fat, 3 mg cholesterol, 580 mg sodium, 13.1 g carbohydrate, 2.7 g dietary fiber, 5.2 g protein

EGGPLANT

To prepare: Wash and cut off stem. It is not necessary to peel. Slice in ¹/₂- to ¹/₄-inch pieces width- or lengthwise for frying, grilling, or baking. To dice: cut into slices, cut slices into ¹/₂-inch strips, then dice.

To cook: For grilling, frying, or roasting, place slices in one layer on paper towels. Salt first one side, then the other. Leave to drain for 30 minutes. Pat dry before cooking. To roast, place halves, cut side up, on a baking dish. Sprinkle with herbs, salt, and pepper, and drizzle with olive oil. Roast in a 375° oven until a knife slides in easily, about 40 to 50 minutes.

BASIC EGGPLANT RECIPES

Quick-Roasted Ratatouille

Dice equal amounts of eggplant, zucchini, red pepper, tomato, and onion. Place in a baking dish and toss with a little balsamic vinegar, olive oil, minced garlic, herbs (such as parsley, oregano, thyme), salt, and pepper. Roast in a 375° oven, tossing occasionally, for 20 to 30 minutes, until vegetables are tender.

Grilled Eggplant with Pasta

Slice an eggplant lengthwise, ³/₈ inch thick. Use 2 pieces of eggplant per person. Place them on paper towels and salt both sides; let drain for 1 hour. Rinse and pat dry with paper towels. Marinate the slices in olive oil and garlic, then grill over a hot charcoal fire until tender. Keep slices warm. Cook 2 ounces spaghetti per person until al dente and toss with tomato sauce (page 438). Coat each slice of eggplant with sauce, then cover each slice with spaghetti. Roll the eggplant slices up and place, seam side down, on serving plates, 2 rolls per plate.

Aubergines Provençal

SERVES 6

A waiter named Boris from Saint-Rémy de Provence made this simple dish for us when he visited California. It's really eggplant parmigiana without the cheese, so it fits right into our idea of California garden cooking with less saturated fat.

Salt for draining eggplant

3 eggplant, cut into $1/2$-inch-thick crosswise slices

$1/2$ cup extra virgin olive oil

6 to 8 cloves garlic, minced

4 $1/2$ cups tomato sauce (page 000)

$3/4$ cup minced fresh flat-leaf parsley

$1/2$ cup fresh basil leaves, chopped

Lightly salt the eggplant slices on both sides and place them on paper towels. Let drain for 1 hour. Pat the slices dry with paper towels.

In a large nonstick skillet over medium heat, heat $1/4$ cup of the olive oil. Add the garlic and sauté until lightly golden, then remove immediately with a slotted spoon and set aside.

Heat 1 tablespoon of the remaining olive oil in the skillet over medium-high heat and fry 2 or 3 eggplant slices until very tender. (Add 1 tablespoon olive oil just before frying 2 or 3 slices). Transfer to paper towels to drain. Repeat with the remaining eggplant slices and oil.

In a 9 x 9-inch square baking dish, place 3 to 4 tablespoons of the tomato sauce, then a layer of eggplant, then more sauce. Repeat until all the eggplant and sauce is used.

To serve at room temperature, top with the parsley, basil, and crisp garlic. To serve hot, heat in a 375° oven for 30 minutes, then sprinkle with the herbs and garlic.

Per serving: 318 calories (225 from fat), 26.5 g total fat, 3.6 g saturated fat, 0 mg cholesterol, 171 mg sodium, 20.7 g carbohydrate, 7.2 g dietary fiber, 3.8 g protein

Asian Eggplant

SERVES 4 TO 6

$1/4$ cup olive oil

3 tablespoons minced yellow onion

2 tablespoons minced celery

5 Japanese eggplant, cut into diagonal slices, or 1 globe eggplant, cut into 1-inch square strips, then into 3-inch-long diagonal pieces

2 tablespoons low-salt soy sauce

2 tablespoons balsamic vinegar

2 tablespoons Asian sesame oil

2 tablespoons plain rice wine vinegar

1 tablespoon minced fresh oregano

1 tablespoon minced fresh cilantro

3 cloves garlic, minced

3 scallions, chopped fine

In a large skillet over medium heat, heat the olive oil and sauté the onion and celery until translucent.

Add the eggplant and sauté until well browned and tender.

Add the soy sauce, balsamic vinegar, sesame oil, and rice wine vinegar; sauté for a few minutes until the liquid is almost entirely evaporated.

Add the herbs, garlic, and scallions and sauté for 2 minutes. Taste and adjust the seasoning. Serve hot or cold.

Per serving: 228 calories (176 from fat), 20.6 g total fat, 2.8 g saturated fat, 0 mg cholesterol, 310 mg sodium, 11.4 g carbohydrate, 3.7 g dietary fiber, 2.2 g protein

Eggplant Rolls
Maria Grazia

SERVES 6 TO 8 AS A SIDE DISH

Inspired by the restaurant Maria Grazia in Marina del Cantone near Positano, Italy. The recipe was adapted from Nancy Verde Barr's book They Call It Macaroni.

- 3 large eggplant, cut into ¹/₂-inch-thick lengthwise slices
- Salt for draining eggplant
- ¹/₄ cup olive oil
- ¹/₄ cup dried bread crumbs
- 4 cloves garlic, minced
- 1 cup minced fresh flat-leaf parsley
- 2 cups shredded mozzarella cheese
- ³/₄ cup grated Parmesan or Asiago cheese
- 1 egg, beaten
- Salt and freshly ground pepper to taste
- 2 cups tomato sauce (page 438)

Place the eggplant slices on a baking sheet lined with paper towels. Sprinkle on both sides with the salt. Let drain for 1 hour or so.

Preheat the oven to 375°. When the eggplant is ready, pat the slices dry with paper towels. Brush the slices on both sides with the olive oil. Place the slices on nonstick baking sheets and bake for 15 minutes. Turn all the slices over and continue baking another 15 minutes, or until slices are golden and cooked through. Remove with a spatula and drain on paper towels.

In a medium bowl, combine the bread crumbs, garlic, parsley, mozzarella, and all but ¹/₄ cup of the Parmesan. Stir in the egg and season with salt and pepper.

Place half the tomato sauce in two large baking dishes. Spread about 1 tablespoon of the cheese mixture on each slice of eggplant, roll up, and place, seam side down, in the pan. Spoon the remaining sauce over the eggplant rolls and top with any leftover filling. Bake at 375° for 30 minutes, or until sauce is bubbling. Sprinkle with the remaining Parmesan and serve.

Per serving: 395 calories (238 from fat), 27.3 g total fat, 10.4 g saturated fat, 80 mg cholesterol, 524 mg sodium, 22.3 g carbohydrate, 6.9 g dietary fiber, 18.2 g protein

NOTE: To significantly reduce the fat content in this (and other recipes for coating eggplant or zucchini with olive oil), spray a nonstick baking sheet with olive oil spray, then spray the vegetables with a light coating.

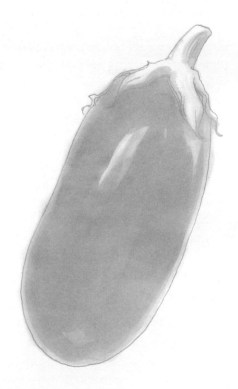

FAVA BEANS

To prepare: Snap the stem end and pull the string down the length of the pod. Open the pod. Remove the pointed stem piece that ties each bean to the pod.

To cook: Young, small favas can be cooked and eaten unpeeled. For larger beans, place them in 1 inch of boiling water in a skillet and cook gently until tender, about 4 or 5 minutes. Snip off the tips and squeeze each bean out of its skin.

Refrigerate whole pods in a brown paper bag up to two weeks.

Fava Bean Purée

SERVES 10 TO 12 AS APPETIZER

- 1 whole bulb garlic
- 4 cups shelled fava beans (3 to 4 pounds before shelling)
- ¼ cup olive oil
- 1 yellow onion, sliced
- 1 teaspoon minced fresh thyme
- 1 teaspoon minced fresh sage
- 1 teaspoon grated lemon zest
- 1 tablespoon fresh lemon juice
- 2 teaspoons sherry wine vinegar
- ½ teaspoon salt
- ½ teaspoon pepper
- Crostini or crackers for serving (optional)

Preheat the oven to 350°. Cut off the top ½ inch of the bulb of garlic and pour in 1 tablespoon of the olive oil. Place in a small baking dish. and bake for 1 hour, or until tender; let cool. Squeeze the insides out of the skins.

Cook the fava beans in a saucepan with boiling water until tender, about 5 to 7 minutes. Drain. If the fava beans are mature, let cool, then peel.

In a medium skillet over medium heat, heat 1 tablespoon of the olive oil and sauté the onion until golden brown.

Purée the favas, garlic, onion mixture, and herbs in a blender or food processor with the remaining 2 tablespoons oil, the lemon zest and juice, and vinegar. If necessary, add a little water or vegetable stock to thin the purée to a creamy paste. Add the salt and pepper. Serve with crostini or crackers.

Per serving: 263 calories (55 from fat), 6.4 g total fat, 0.9 g saturated fat, 0 mg cholesterol, 115 mg sodium, 37.5 g carbohydrate, 15.3 g dietary fiber, 16.1 g protein

Spaghetti with Fava Beans and Chard

SERVES 2

I learned this from Howard Menge, the golf pro at the Par Three Golf Course in Aptos near Cabrillo College, California.

- ¼ cup extra virgin olive oil
- 1 large onion, coarsely chopped
- 4 cups shelled fava beans (3 to 4 pounds before shelling)
- 10 to 12 large leaves Swiss chard, coarsely chopped
- 2 tablespoons minced garlic
- 5 ounces spaghetti, broken into 2-inch pieces
- ¼ cup grated Parmesan cheese

In a large skillet over medium heat, heat the olive oil and sauté the onion until brown but not burnt. Add the fava beans, chard, and garlic and cook, stirring, until the beans are tender.

Meanwhile, cook the broken spaghetti in a large pot of salted boiling water until very al dente; drain, reserving 1 cup of the pasta water. Add the pasta to the fava mixture.

Add the reserved pasta water and stir for several minutes over medium heat, until most of the liquid is evaporated and the pasta is al dente.

Serve with the Parmesan cheese.

Per serving: 1,624 calories (323 from fat), 36.7 g total fat, 7 g saturated fat, 10 mg cholesterol, 301 mg sodium, 237.8 g carbohydrate, 78.3 g dietary fiber, 94.2 g protein

GARLIC

To prepare: Break into cloves and run under cold water. Remove skins. Leave whole or slice into thin slices lengthwise for stir-frying, or cut into thin slices crosswise, flatten with the side of a knife to release the juices, then mince fine.

To dry-sear: Place peeled, whole cloves in a dry skillet and cook over low heat 20 to 30 minutes, turning frequently to caramelize all sides. Use to flavor other dishes.

To roast: Leave the bulb whole, cutting off ½ inch from the top to expose the tops of all the cloves. Rub the entire bulb with a little olive oil and wrap it in aluminum foil, leaving the cut top exposed. Drizzle 1 tablespoon of olive oil inside the bulb and sprinkle with salt. Place the bulb on a baking dish and roast in a 375° oven for 35 to 40 minutes, or until the cloves are soft.

BASIC GARLIC RECIPES

Roasted Artichoke Heart and Garlic Purée

Drain off most of the liquid from a 4- to 6-ounce jar of marinated artichokes. Chop the hearts into ½-inch pieces. Place them in a baking dish along with 8 to 10 whole peeled garlic cloves, mixing the cloves in with the residual marinade. Salt and pepper lightly. Roast in a 375° oven for 25 to 30 minutes, or until the garlic and artichokes are well browned. Purée roughly in a blender and use on pizzas, as a spread for toast, or as a condiment for salads.

Roasted Garlic and Vegetable Sauce

Make a mixture of garlic, onion, potatoes, turnips, mushrooms, and red pepper. Coat with olive oil and a little salt and pepper. Roast until brown. When cool, purée the vegetables; thin with stock, wine, olive oil, or water and use as a sauce for pasta, other vegetables, or meat.

Garlic Roast Chicken

Preheat the oven to 375°. Rinse and dry a roasting chicken. Coat the chicken with oil and sprinkle with salt and pepper inside and out. Put about 8 to 10 unpeeled garlic cloves and 3 or 4 rosemary sprigs in the body cavity of the chicken. Truss the chicken with kitchen twine and stuff a few sprigs of rosemary between the legs and breast. Roast the chicken for 50 to 60 minutes (for a 3- to 4-pound bird), or until the juices run clear when the inner thigh is pierced with a knife.

Garlic Oil

Drop 6 cloves of peeled garlic into a 12- to 16-ounce bottle of extra virgin olive oil. In a few days, the oil will have the flavor of the garlic. It can be used for salad dressings or for dipping raw vegetables.

Whole-Garlic Summer Soup

SERVES 4

Rice and onions can be used instead of cream and flour to thicken soup. Also try using mashed potatoes or puréed steamed vegetables.

- **2 tablespoons olive oil**
- **1 onion, chopped**
- **Peeled cloves from 2 heads garlic**
- **4 cups low sodium chicken broth or vegetable stock**
- **2 tablespoons long-grain rice**
- **4 plum tomatoes, peeled, seeded, and chopped**
- **6 or 8 fresh basil leaves**
- **Salt and freshly ground pepper to taste**
- **Crusty bread or croutons for serving**

In a large saucepan over medium heat, heat the olive oil and sauté the onion until soft. Add the whole garlic cloves, cover the pan, and let the garlic stew for 20 to 25 minutes, stirring occasionally, until browned and tender. Let cool.

Meanwhile, in a large saucepan, combine ¹/₂ cup of the stock and rice. Bring to a boil, reduce heat, and simmer, stirring occasionally, until the rice is tender, about 25 minutes.

Combine the onion, garlic, and stock mixture in a blender or food processor. Purée the mixture (in batches if necessary) and return it to the pan. If it is too thick, add more stock or water.

Pop the garlic from its skins and discard the skins. Add the tomatoes, garlic, basil, and the rest of the stock to the purée. Add salt and pepper. Cook the soup for 2 to 3 minutes. Serve with crusty bread or croutons.

Per serving: 153 calories (66 from fat), 9.8 g total fat, 1 g saturated fat, 0 mg cholesterol, 53 mg sodium, 15.9 g carbohydrate, 2.1 g dietary fiber, 13.1 g protein

KALE

To prepare: Discard wilted leaves and wash remaining leaves. Remove the stems by laying each leaf flat and cutting the stem out with a knife. The stems may be used in vegetable stock in small quantities. Chop leaves coarsely to sauté, or cut into chiffonade by rolling up 2 or 3 leaves at a time and slivering thinly.

To cook: Sauté some minced onion, garlic, or ginger in olive oil. Add some chopped kale and sauté briefly. Stir in a few tablespoons of stock, water, or white wine; cover and cook for 2 or 3 minutes. Uncover and cook until most of the liquid evaporates and the kale is tender; add more liquid if necessary. Splash in some fresh lemon juice and salt and pepper to taste.

Kale and Potato Soup

SERVES 4

- **6 cups water**
- **3 potatoes, peeled and diced**
- **2 tablespoons olive oil**
- **1 onion, chopped**
- **4 cups chopped kale leaves**
- **1 teaspoon Ginger's Gremolata (page 84)**
- **3 cloves garlic, minced**
- **1 beet, peeled and diced**
- **2 cups low sodium chicken broth or vegetable stock**
- **Grated Parmesan cheese for serving (optional)**

In a medium saucepan, bring the water to a boil. Add the potatoes and cook for 10 to 12 minutes, or until tender. Turn off the heat.

Meanwhile, in a medium skillet over medium heat, heat the oil and sauté the onion until translucent. Add the kale and sauté for 5 to 8 minutes, or until tender. Add the gremolata and garlic and sauté for 2 or 3 minutes.

With a slotted spoon, remove half of potatoes from the pan of water and place in the pan with the kale. Turn off the heat.

Add the diced beet and stock to the skillet and cook over medium heat 10 minutes, or until the beets are tender.

Add the kale mixture to the water and remaining potatoes and simmer for 10 minutes. Serve with grated Parmesan cheese.

Per serving: 346 calories (72 from fat), 8.8 g total fat, 1.1 g saturated fat, 0 mg cholesterol, 626 mg sodium, 61.8 g carbohydrate, 5.9 g dietary fiber, 14.2 g protein

LEEKS

To prepare: Thoroughly wash the dirt out of the tops. Trim the stem end and cut off most of the green tops. Slice lengthwise to julienne; slice into disks or 2-inch pieces to steam; or leave whole with green top intact to grill (steam for several minutes first).

To cook: Grill whole, or steam or sauté in pieces.

Leek and Potato Soup

SERVES 8

- 2 tablespoons light olive oil
- 4 leeks, white part and about 1 inch of green tops, cleaned and sliced
- 1 cup chopped onion (1 small onion)
- 6 cups low sodium chicken broth or vegetable stock
- 4 stalks celery, sliced
- 6 potatoes, peeled and diced
- 1 to 2 cups milk
- Salt and freshly ground pepper to taste

In a soup pot over medium-low heat, heat the oil and sauté the leeks and onion until soft but not brown. Add the stock, celery, and diced potatoes. Bring to a boil, cover, and cook until potatoes are tender, about 25 minutes. Purée in a blender or food processor (in batches if necessary). Return to the soup pot and add milk to the desired consistency. Reheat over low heat and add salt and pepper.

Per serving: 322 calories (54 from fat), 6.8 g total fat, 1.2 g saturated fat, 4 mg cholesterol, 91 mg sodium, 62.3 g carbohydrate, 6.1 g dietary fiber, 16.2 g protein

Leeks Vinaigrette

SERVES 4

Jacques Pépin has been a leader in the field of healthy cooking. For years he's been teaching people how to reduce the amount of cream, butter, and cheese in classic French dishes. Here's a recipe inspired by one of his many cooking class demonstrations. We've used his technique with our own ingredient proportions.

- 1/4 cup white wine vinegar
- 6 peppercorns
- 5 large leeks, cleaned and cut into 1-inch pieces
- 1/2 teaspoon kosher salt
- 1 tablespoon minced garlic
- 1 tablespoon Dijon-style mustard
- 1 teaspoon fresh lemon juice
- 2 tablespoons red wine vinegar
- 1/2 cup light olive oil
- 1/4 cup minced fresh flat-leaf parsley, for garnish

Put white wine vinegar, peppercorns, and 1 inch of water in a saucepan. Place a collapsible steamer basket in the pan and add the leeks. Bring to a boil, cover, and steam the leeks for 10 to 20 minutes, or until tender. Let cool.

In a small bowl, mash the salt into the garlic with a fork or the back of a spoon. Add the mustard, lemon juice, and red wine vinegar and mix briefly to incorporate; then whisk in the oil.

Place the leeks on a serving platter, and pour the vinaigrette over. Garnish with the parsley and serve at room temperature, or refrigerate and serve cold.

Per serving: 247 calories (158 from fat), 18.7 g total fat, 2.5 g saturated fat, 0 mg cholesterol, 214 mg sodium, 21 g carbohydrate, 3.9 g dietary fiber, 2.6 g protein

LETTUCE

To prepare: Soak the leaves in a large container of cold water. Remove to a salad spinner, spin several times. Then pat dry with paper towels.

For more notes on salad preparation, see page 280.

BASIC LETTUCE RECIPES

Watercress Salad

Combine the leaves from 1 head butter lettuce and 1 small bunch watercress in a salad bowl. Add 2 finely minced scallions, 1/4 cup currants, and 1/2 cup toasted walnuts. Drizzle with 3 tablespoons walnut oil and toss well. Sprinkle in 1 tablespoon balsamic vinegar, 1/2 teaspoon salt, and freshly ground black pepper to taste. Toss once more and serve. Serves 4.

Low-Fat Salad

Over equal amounts of chopped napa cabbage, radicchio, spinach, and romaine lettuce, sprinkle 1 tablespoon light olive oil and 2 tablespoons champagne or sherry vinegar. Add salt and pepper and toss.

Warm Salad with Prosciutto and Poached Eggs

SERVES 2 AS A MAIN COURSE

- 3 tablespoons sherry vinegar or balsamic vinegar
- 2 eggs
- 1 tablespoon olive oil
- 4 slices prosciutto, chopped (1 ounce)
- 4 tablespoons Dijon-style mustard
- 8 cups chopped mixed romaine lettuce, escarole or frisée, and napa cabbage
- 2 sprigs flat-leaf parsley, minced, for garnish

To poach the eggs, put 6 cups of water and 1 tablespoon of vinegar in a small saucepan over high heat. When the water comes to a boil, turn down the heat and break the eggs gently into the water. Poach for 3 to 4 minutes, until the eggs are just cooked. Remove them with a slotted spoon. Keep warm.

In a small skillet over medium-high heat, heat the olive oil and cook the chopped prosciutto until slightly browned. Add the remaining vinegar and mustard and heat just until warm.

Place the greens in a large bowl. Pour the warm dressing over the greens and toss to coat. Divide between two dinner plates and place a poached egg on top of each serving. Garnish with parsley. Serve immediately.

Per serving: 285 calories (132 from fat), 15.8 g total fat, 3 g saturated fat, 225 mg cholesterol, 935 mg sodium, 22.3 g carbohydrate, 10.7 g dietary fiber, 19.1 g protein

Mock Caesar Salad

SERVES 4

In a true Caesar salad, each ingredient is added individually, and then the salad is tossed after each addition. This is a simple method.

DRESSING

1 egg

2 cloves garlic

2 teaspoons Worcestershire sauce

4 anchovy fillets, minced

2 teaspoons Dijon-style mustard

Juice of 1 lemon

1^1/$_2$ tablespoons balsamic or red wine vinegar

^{3}/$_4$ cup extra virgin olive oil

Salt and freshly ground pepper to taste

CROUTONS

1 tablespoons butter

1 tablespoons olive oil

2 large slices sourdough bread, cut into ^{1}/$_2$-inch cubes

Leaves from 1 head romaine lettuce, torn into bite-sized pieces

^{1}/$_2$ cup grated Parmesan cheese

To make the dressing: Bring a small pot of water to boil. If the egg came straight from the refrigerator, set it in a bowl of warm water for a minute or so first. Place the egg in the boiling water, cover, and turn off the heat. Leave the egg in the water for 4 to 5 minutes. Remove from water and set aside.

Mash the garlic in a mortar and pestle, or squeeze it through a garlic press and place in a small bowl. Add the Worcestershire sauce, anchovies, mustard, lemon juice, egg, and vinegar. Whisk in the olive oil, salt, and pepper.

To make the croutons: In a medium skillet over medium heat, melt the butter with the oil. Sauté in the garlic briefly. Add the bread cubes and sauté for 5 to 8 minutes, or until crisp and golden. Let cool.

Toss the lettuce leaves with the dressing. Sprinkle with the Parmesan cheese. Add the croutons and mix. Serve immediately.

Per serving: 561 calories (461 from fat), 52.2 g total fat, 10.2 g saturated fat, 72 mg cholesterol, 527 mg sodium, 14.9 g carbohydrate, 2.8 g dietary fiber, 10.8 g protein

Salade Frisée au Lardon

SERVES 4

The recipe was inspired by similar salads served at two of my favorite restaurants, Le Vaudeville in Paris and Al Forno in Providence, Rhode Island.

4 tablespoons butter

3 or 4 cloves garlic, crushed

4 slices French bread, cut into 1-inch squares

4 ounces thick-sliced bacon, cut into ^{1}/$_2$-inch squares

Leaves from 3 small heads frisée

1 to 2 tablespoons red wine vinegar

In a skillet over medium-low heat, melt the butter and sauté the garlic until it turns golden. With a slotted spoon, remove the garlic. Sauté the bread cubes in the skillet for 8 to 10 minutes over medium-low heat, or until golden. Remove and let cool.

Cook the bacon squares in a skillet until almost crisp, then remove them with a slotted spoon and drain on paper towels. Reserve the bacon drippings in the skillet.

Place the frisée in a medium bowl and pour 2 to 3 tablespoons of the warm bacon drippings over them, 1 tablespoon at a time, tossing until the leaves are coated. Add the vinegar to taste. Toss well.

Place on serving plates and garnish each with the bacon and croutons.

Per serving: 337 calories (234 from fat), 26.1 g total fat, 12.2 g saturated fat, 55 mg cholesterol, 696 mg sodium, 14.4 g carbohydrate, 1.4 g dietary fiber, 11.4 g protein

Variation: For a main-course salad, place a poached egg on top of each salad.

Gorgonzola and Sun-Dried Tomato Salad

SERVES 4

This is a salad created by Santa Cruz chef Jim Denevan.

- 3 to 4 tablespoons light olive oil
- 1 tablespoon white wine vinegar
- 1 scallion, green and white parts, minced
- Salt and freshly ground pepper to taste
- 3 tablespoons crumbled Gorgonzola cheese
- 1 ounce oil-packed sun-dried tomatoes, halved
- 8 handfuls mixed baby greens

In a medium bowl, whisk together the oil, vinegar, scallion, salt, and pepper. Add the cheese to the mixture and mix gently. Add the tomatoes and let sit for at least 30 minutes.

Put the greens in a salad bowl. Drizzle the dressing over the greens and toss well to coat.

Per serving: 151 calories (109 from fat), 12.8 g total fat, 2.5 g saturated fat, 4 mg cholesterol, 113 mg sodium, 7.5 g carbohydrate, 2.1 g dietary fiber, 3.7 g protein

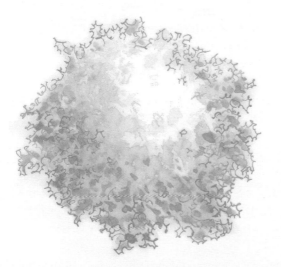

ONIONS

BASIC ONION RECIPE

Pissaladière

Make your favorite French bread or pizza dough. After the first rising, flatten the dough into a sided baking sheet that has been coated with a little olive oil. Spread the top of the dough with caramelized onions (below), a little olive oil, and small pieces of anchovy or minced jalapeño chile. Let the dough rise until doubled in bulk, about 1 hour. Preheat the oven to 375°. Bake for 30 minutes, or until golden brown.

Caramelized Onions

MAKES 2 CUPS (4 SERVINGS)

This preparation can be used to flavor and darken soups, to top pizzas, to garnish hamburgers or tofu burgers, or as an appetizer to serve with French bread.

- $1/4$ cup light olive oil, vegetable oil, or peanut oil
- 2 yellow onions, sliced thin
- 1 tablespoon balsamic vinegar (optional)
- Salt and freshly ground pepper to taste

In a heavy nonreactive skillet over medium-low heat, heat the oil and cook the onions for 25 to 30 minutes, stirring constantly, until golden brown.

Splash with the vinegar and cook for 2 to 3 more minutes. Add salt and pepper. Store in the refrigerator for up to 4 or 5 days.

Per serving: 139 calories (119 from fat), 13.6 g total fat, 1.8 g saturated fat, 0 mg cholesterol, 2 mg sodium, 4.6 g carbohydrate, 0.9 g dietary fiber, 0.6 g protein

PEAS

To prepare: Wash and remove strings from pods.

To cook: Steam 4 to 5 minutes, or boil in water 2 to 3 minutes, unitl tender. Store in a plastic bag in the refrigerator vegetable crisper for up to 4 days. They are best when eaten right away.

Fresh Pea Soup

SERVES 4

Adapted from a recipe from Sibella Kraus.

   3 cups chicken stock or vegetable stock
   2 to 3 pounds green peas, shelled (2 to 3 cups)
   1/4 teaspoon ground turmeric
   1/2 teaspoon ground pasilla chile or New Mexico
      chile powder
   Salt and freshly ground pepper to taste
   1/2 cup low-fat plain yogurt (optional)
   2 tablespoons minced fresh chives or mint

In a medium saucepan, heat the stock. Add the peas and bring to a boil. Reduce heat to low and simmer, covered, for 12 to 15 minutes, or until peas are tender. Purée in a food blender or processor in batches if necessary. Pour back into the saucepan and add the turmeric, chile, salt, and pepper. Heat through. Divide among 4 bowls and top each serving with a dollop of yogurt. Swirl the yogurt through soup with the tip of a small knife. Garnish with chives or mint.

Per serving: 226 calories (25 from fat), 3.3 g total fat, 0.4 g saturated fat, 2 mg cholesterol, 65 mg sodium, 36.6 g carbohydrate, 11.7 g dietary fiber, 22.5 g protein

BASIC PEA RECIPES

Pea Greens

Whole young pea pods, harvested before maturity, can be added to a stir-fry at the last minute.

Snap Peas Dressed with Shallots and Herbs

Blanch snap peas, then sauté in light olive oil seasoned with shallots, raspberry vinegar, and tarragon.

Snap Peas with Green Herb Sauce

Blanch snap peas; let cool. Serve dressed with Green Sauce (page 98).

Snow Pea, Green Pea, and Carrot Salad

SERVES 4

   1 tablespoon red wine vinegar
   1 tablespoon low-salt soy sauce
   1 tablespoon peanut oil
   1/8 teaspoon Asian sesame oil
   12 ounces snow peas, blanched
   8 ounces English peas, shelled and blanched
   1 1/2 carrots, cut into 1-inch-long matchsticks and
      blanched
   Salt and freshly ground pepper to taste
   2 tablespoons minced fresh flat-leaf parsley, for
      garnish

Whisk together the vinegar, soy sauce, peanut oil, and sesame oil. Pour the dressing over the vegetables in a large bowl. Add salt and pepper. Garnish with the chopped parsley and serve.

Per serving: 128 calories (35 from fat), 4.0 g total fat, 0.7 g saturated fat, 0 mg cholesterol, 167 mg sodium, 18.1 g carbohydrate, 5 g dietary fiber, 6 g protein

PEPPERS

To prepare: Cut in half and carve out stem and interior seed pod. Julienne or dice.

To roast: Char whole peppers over a grill or in a broiler, turning frequently to blacken all sides. Place peppers in a plastic or paper bag and close to steam. When cool, peel off the charred skin and discard. Seed peppers and cut into pieces.

BASIC BELL PEPPER RECIPE

Red Pepper Sauce

Sauté ¹/₂ onion and 1 diced red bell pepper in smoking-hot oil until a little burnt. Add a splash of sherry vinegar and a splash of red wine. Cook to reduce by half. Add some chicken stock and cook to reduce some more. Bring to a boil and add a little heavy cream to thicken. Purée in a blender or food processor; then strain the sauce and season with salt and pepper. Use on cooked pasta.

Peperonata

MAKES 4 CUPS, 6 TO 8 SERVINGS

Serve as an appetizer, as an accompaniment for fish or chicken or as a pasta sauce.

- ¹/₃ cup olive oil
- 2 onions, thinly sliced
- 1 tablespoon minced garlic
- 3 tomatoes, peeled, seeded, and diced
- 2 red bell peppers, roasted, seeded, and cut into 1-inch squares
- 2 yellow bell peppers, roasted, seeded, and cut into 1-inch squares
- 2 tablespoons chopped pitted green or black olives
- ¹/₄ cup balsamic vinegar
- 3 tablespoons minced fresh basil, mint, or flat-leaf parsley

In a large skillet over medium heat, heat the oil and sauté the onions and garlic until just browned, stirring frequently; add the tomatoes and cook another few minutes. Add the peppers, olives, vinegar, and herbs and toss just to coat. Serve immediately.

Per serving: 185 calories (108 from fat), 12.8 g total fat, 1.7 g saturated fat, 0 mg cholesterol, 37 mg sodium, 18.1 g carbohydrate, 4 g dietary fiber, 2.6 g protein

Asian-Style Chicken Salad

SERVES 4 TO 6

From the Rosticceria.

- 1 package chow mein noodles (9 ounces)
- 1 red bell pepper, seeded, deribbed, and julienned
- 1 cup snow peas, stemmed and stringed
- ¹/₂ cup Asian-Style Vinaigrette (page 92)
- 1 pound shredded cooked chicken (2 cups)
- 2 scallions, chopped, for garnish
- 3 tablespoons toasted sesame seeds, for garnish

In salted boiling water, cook chow mein noodles until very al dente.

In a large bowl, combine peppers, snow peas, noodles, dressing, and chicken and toss well. Garnish with scallions and sesame seeds and serve.

Per serving: 590 calories (253 from fat), 28.1 g total fat, 4.8 g saturated fat, 96 mg cholesterol, 371 mg sodium, 42 g carbohydrate, 3.8 g dietary fiber, 42.6 g protein

Baked Chiles Rellenos

MAKES 4 SERVINGS

8 tomatoes, peeled, seeded, and coarsely chopped
1 white onion, coarsely chopped
3 cloves garlic, crushed
1 tablespoon minced fresh epazote or fresh oregano
1 cinnamon stick
$1/2$ teaspoon salt
$1/2$ teaspoon pepper
$3/4$ cup (4 ounces) crumbled fresh white goat cheese
1 cup (4 ounces) shredded Monterey jack cheese
8 poblano chiles, roasted and peeled
Flour for dredging, plus $1/4$ cup flour
5 eggs, separated

Purée the tomatoes, onion, and garlic in a blender or food processor. In a large skillet, combine the purée, epazote, cinnamon stick, salt, and pepper. Bring to a boil over medium-high heat, then lower heat and simmer, uncovered, for 5 to 10 minutes, or until slightly thickened. Remove the cinnamon stick.

In a medium bowl, combine the cheeses and mix until well blended. Cut a small slit in the side of each chile and carefully stuff the chiles with the cheese mixture. Dredge the chiles in the flour; set aside. In a medium bowl, beat the egg yolks until pale in color. In a large bowl, beat the egg whites until stiff peaks form. Sprinkle the $1/4$ cup flour into the beaten egg whites. Add the beaten yolks and gently fold together until blended.

Preheat the oven to 350°. Pour the tomato sauce into a 13 x 11–inch baking dish. Gently place one chile at a time into the egg mixture to coat. With a large slotted spoon, carefully place the chile in the sauce. Repeat with the remaining chiles. Bake for 15 minutes, or until golden brown.

Per serving: 495 calories (223 from fat), 25.8 g total fat, 14.4 g saturated fat, 324 mg cholesterol, 629 mg sodium, 41.3 g carbohydrate, 7.3 g dietary fiber, 29.3 g protein

Corn and Chile Pepper Salad

MAKES 6 SERVINGS

DRESSING
$1/3$ cup olive oil
2 tablespoons wine vinegar
1 tablespoon lime or lemon juice
2 teaspoons Dijon-style mustard
1 garlic clove, minced
2 tablespoons snipped cilantro
$1/4$ teaspoon salt

1 Anaheim chile
4 ears fresh corn, (3 cups) steamed and kernels cut off the cob
1 jalapeño chile, seeded and minced
1 Hungarian wax or yellow chile, seeded and minced
1 red bell pepper, seeded and chopped
1 cup chopped red onion (1 medium)
$1/4$ cup minced fresh flat-leaf parsley

Blend together the dressing ingredients. Char the skin of the Anaheim chile by holding it over a flame or by broiling. Place in a bag for 10 to 15 minutes, then peel off the skin, seed, and cut into strips. Combine the corn kernels, chiles, peppers, onion, and parsley in a bowl and toss with the dressing. Serve at room temperature.

Per serving: 206 calories (106 from fat), 12.8 g total fat, 1.7 g saturated fat, 0 mg cholesterol, 117 mg sodium, 23.5 g carbohydrate, 3.5 g dietary fiber, 3.6 g protein

POTATOES

To prepare: Peel to slice, dice, or julienne. Scrub and leave skin on for roasting or grilling.

To cook: Sauté sliced or diced or julienned. Stir-fry (after dicing and steaming) with coarsely chopped mixed vegetables. Roast whole with skin on, or peeled and coarsely chopped, with olive oil, rosemary, salt, and pepper.

Vinaigrette Potato Salad

SERVES 8 TO 10

If you wish, you may cut down on the Parmesan cheese and leave out the hard-boiled eggs for a low-fat version.

- 12 red potatoes (3 pounds), unpeeled, scrubbed, with eyes removed
- 1 cup Basic Vinaigrette (see page 90)
- 1 small red onion, finely chopped
- 1 teaspoon minced garlic
- 1 cup (4 ounces) grated Parmesan cheese
- 1 cup low-fat ricotta cheese
- 3 tablespoons minced fresh flat-leaf parsley
- 2 hard-cooked eggs, chopped
- Salt and freshly ground pepper to taste

Cook the potatoes in salted boiling water until tender. Let cool slightly. Cut the potatoes into 1-inch cubes. Place in a large bowl and dress with the vinaigrette while still warm.

Mix in the remaining ingredients. Season to taste.

Per serving: 358 calories (193 from fat), 21.8 g total fat, 6.4 g saturated fat, 76 mg cholesterol, 403 mg sodium, 27.7 g carbohydrate, 2.5 g dietary fiber, 14.3 g protein

BASIC POTATO RECIPES

Potato-Bean Coulis

Peel and cube 1 Idaho potato. Simmer with 5 peeled garlic cloves in salted water for 15 minutes. Drain.

Place the potatoes and garlic and ¹/₂ cup cooked white beans in a blender or food processor and purée, adding vegetable stock or olive oil to make the mixture the texture of soft mashed potatoes. Stir in 1 tablespoon each fresh minced rosemary and parsley. Serve with grilled chicken or fish.

Potato Focaccia

Make your favorite pizza or French bread dough (or see recipe, page 202), about 1 pound. Take 2 cups cool roasted diced potatoes (page 429) and about 1 cup cool caramelized onions (page 425) and mix half of each into the dough. Coat a baking sheet with a little olive oil and flatten the dough on the sheet into an irregular oval shape. Top with the remaining roasted potatoes and caramelized onions, drizzle some olive oil on top, and let rise for 1 to 1¹/₂ hours, until it doesn't spring back when touched with a finger. Garnish with fresh rosemary leaves. Bake in a preheated 425° oven for 30 minutes, or until golden brown.

Platter-Sized Potato Pancakes

Peel and shred 4 or 5 white potatoes to yield 3 cups. Transfer to a medium bowl (drain excess liquid) and stir in ¹/₄ cup finely chopped onion, 3 lightly beaten eggs, 1 teaspoon salt, and freshly ground pepper. Coat a large, heavy nonstick skillet with vegetable oil and heat over medium heat. Spread ¹/₂ cup batter of the mixture in skillet to form a very thin pancake. Cook 2 to 3 minutes on each side, or until golden brown. Keep warm in a low oven. Repeat to use the remaining batter. Use as an "edible plate" for other vegetable dishes.

Roasted Rosemary Potatoes

SERVES 4

6 unpeeled potatoes, scrubbed and cut into ³/₄-inch cubes

3 tablespoons olive oil

3 tablespoons minced garlic

2 tablespoons minced fresh rosemary leaves

1 teaspoon salt

1 teaspoon black pepper

Preheat the oven to 425°. Put the potatoes in a 13 x 9-inch baking dish. Sprinkle on the remaining ingredients. Toss well. Bake, tossing occasionally, for 30 to 40 minutes, or until golden brown.

Per serving: 526 calories (94 from fat), 10.8 g total fat, 1.5 g saturated fat, 0 mg cholesterol, 567 mg sodium, 99.2 g carbohydrate, 9 g dietary fiber, 11.6 g protein

Roasted Potato and Chicken Salad

SERVES 6 TO 8

4 pounds red potatoes, cut into ³/₄-inch cubes

¹/₄ cup olive oil

2 tablespoons minced garlic

2¹/₂ tablespoons minced fresh oregano

2 teaspoons salt

2 pounds chopped cooked chicken meat

1 red onion, sliced thin

¹/₂ cup minced fresh basil

¹/₂ cup minced fresh flat-leaf parsley

1 cup Basic Vinaigrette (page 000)

Salt and freshly ground pepper to taste

Preheat the oven to 350°. In a large bowl, toss the cubed potatoes with the olive oil, garlic, oregano, and salt. Place on two 13 x 9-inch baking sheets and bake until golden, about 30 minutes. Toss the potatoes with the remaining ingredients.

Per serving: 509 calories (215 from fat), 23.9 g total fat, 4.5 g saturated fat, 96 mg cholesterol, 634 mg sodium, 34.1 g carbohydrate, 3.4 g dietary fiber, 39.2 g protein

Scalloped Potatoes

SERVES 4 TO 6

2 pounds Yukon gold or yellow Finn potatoes, peeled, sliced very thinly

1 teaspoon salt

Freshly ground pepper to taste

5 cloves garlic, minced

2 cups milk

1 cup (4 ounces) shredded Gruyère cheese

Freshly ground nutmeg to taste

Preheat the oven to 425°.

In an ovenproof baking dish about 13 x 9 inches, layer the potatoes in rows so they overlap by about half the diameter of each slice. Season with salt and pepper, then sprinkle on the garlic. Pour on the milk to barely cover. Sprinkle on the cheese and a grating of nutmeg.

Bake for 30 to 40 minutes, or until the milk is almost all evaporated, the potatoes are golden brown and tender, and the cheese is melted.

Per serving: 331 calories (118 from fat), 13.3 g total fat, 7.9 g saturated fat, 47 mg cholesterol, 698 mg sodium, 37.6 g carbohydrate, 2.8 g dietary fiber, 16.1 g protein

Ginger's Sicilian Potatoes

SERVES 4

Christie's sister Ginger is a great cook. Here's a recipe she made up for us to use at the Rosticceria.

- 1¹/₂ cup white wine
- 1 cup low sodium chicken broth, plus extra if needed
- 1¹/₂ pounds yellow Finn, fingerling, or red potatoes, peeled and cut into 1-inch chunks
- 1 tablespoon extra virgin olive oil
- 3 tomatoes, peeled, seeded, and coarsely chopped
- 1 tablespoon plus 1 teaspoon chopped fresh flat-leaf parsley
- 1 teaspoon chopped tarragon
- 1¹/₂ teaspoons salt
- ¹/₈ teaspoon freshly ground black pepper
- ¹/₄ to ¹/₂ cup water or broth (if needed)

Preheat the oven to 425°. In a 12 x 17-inch casserole dish, toss together the wine, 1 cup of the broth, the potatoes, oil, and tomatoes. Sprinkle on the 1 tablespoon parsley and the tarragon, salt, and pepper and toss again.

Bake 1¹/₂ hours, until potatoes start to break down and the liquid is about half evaporated. During baking, toss the potatoes with a large spoon or spatula 3 or 4 times and add a little water or broth if necessary to make sure they don't dry out.

Add salt and pepper to taste, sprinkle with the 1 teaspoon chopped parsley, and serve hot or at room temperature.

Per serving: 214 calories (45 from fat), 4.3 g total fat, 0.5 g saturated fat, 0 mg cholesterol, 830 mg sodium, 30.2 g carbohydrate, 3.1 g dietary fiber, 6.4 g protein

Broccoli Potato Salad

SERVES 6 TO 8

- 10 new potatoes, scrubbed
- 2 heads broccoli, stems trimmed and quartered
- ¹/₃ cup white wine vinegar
- 1 onion, chopped
- 4 hard-boiled eggs, chopped
- 2 to 3 tablespoons chopped dill or dill pickle juice
- 2 stalks celery, thinly sliced
- 3 dill pickles, thinly sliced

DRESSING
- ¹/₂ cup mayonnaise
- ¹/₂ cup nonfat plain yogurt
- 2 teaspoons Dijon-style mustard
- Salt and freshly ground pepper to taste

In a large pot with 2 quarts water, boil the potatoes for 20 minutes, or until tender, over medium-high heat. Add the broccoli to the potatoes. Boil for 5 more minutes, then turn off the heat and drain. Allow potatoes to cool 10 minutes.

When cool, chop the potatoes into large pieces. Put them into a large bowl and drizzle with the vinegar. Coarsely chop the broccoli and add it to the potatoes along with the onion, eggs, dill, celery, and pickle.

Toss in the mayonnaise, yogurt, mustard, and salt and pepper to taste, and serve.

Per serving: 370 calories (167 from fat), 19.5 g total fat, 3.3 g saturated fat, 150 mg cholesterol, 632 mg sodium, 42.4 g carbohydrate, 5.1 g dietary fiber, 11.1 g protein

RADICCHIO

To prepare: Discard wilted outer leaves. Chop for sauté or salads; quarter or halve for grilling.

To cook: Sauté briefly or stir-fry with mixed vegetables.

To store: Store in a brown paper bag in the crisper compartment of the refrigerator for up to a week.

Grilled Radicchio with Pancetta

SERVES 4

Chef Jack Chyle of Chez Renee in Aptos, California, uses radicchio to add color and flavor to his salads. "Some people don't like the bitter taste of radicchio," Chyle says. "But you can grill or roast it with pancetta for a nice appetizer." This is Jack's recipe. You can also make it without the pancetta.

- 2 small heads radicchio
- 8 slices (2 ounces) pancetta (optional)
- 1 tablespoon olive oil
- 1 tablespoon balsamic vinegar
- 1/2 lemon

Quarter each head of radicchio and wrap each piece in a slice of pancetta. Coat with olive oil and grill over hot charcoal or under a broiler for 5 to 8 minutes or until pancetta is crisp. Top with a sprinkle of balsamic vinegar and a squeeze of lemon juice.

Per serving: 62 calories (39 from fat), 4.6 g total fat, 0.9 g saturated fat, 10 mg cholesterol, 383 mg sodium, 1.9 g carbohydrate, 0.1 g dietary fiber, 4.2 g protein

BASIC RADICCHIO RECIPES

Grilled Radicchio with Gorgonzola

Cut radicchio in quarters, leaving the core intact to hold the leaves together. Brush with a little olive oil and sprinkle with salt and pepper. Grill over hot coals or under a broiler until crisp-tender, about 4 to 6 minutes. Serve plain, or sprinkle with a little Gorgonzola cheese, then place under a broiler or in an oven to melt the cheese.

Pasta Sauce of Onion, Lemon Zest, Anchovy, and Radicchio

Sauté a little thinly sliced onion in olive oil, stir in some chopped anchovy, and stir and cook until dissolved. Add a little dry white wine and cook a few minutes more. Stir in some finely slivered radicchio and some grated lemon zest. Cook a few more minutes, stirring. Add a little freshly ground pepper and pour over cooked pasta.

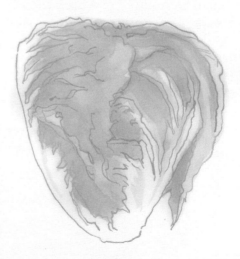

SHALLOTS

To prepare: Cut off stem ends and peel. Chop or mince.

To cook: Sauté in olive oil or butter.

BASIC SHALLOT RECIPES

Shallot Dressing

Blend together ¹/₃ cup thinly sliced shallots, 4 teaspoons Dijon mustard, ¹/₄ cup white wine vinegar, ¹/₂ cup light olive oil, ¹/₄ teaspoon salt, and ¹/₈ teaspoon pepper. Shake or whisk together just before using to dress salad.

Roasted Shallots with Balsamic Vinegar

Coat unpeeled shallots with a little olive oil and place in one layer in a roasting pan. Sprinkle a little balsamic vinegar on top. Bake in a preheated 375° oven until tender. Transfer to a serving platter. Place the pan over medium heat and add a little dry white wine, stirring to scrape up the browned bits from the bottom of the pan. Add a little more balsamic vinegar and 1 teaspoon red currant jelly or apricot jam. Stir to make a sauce. Strain if necessary. Pour the sauce over the shallots.

SPINACH

To clean: Soak in a large sinkful or panful of cold water with a splash of white wine vinegar in it to rid the leaves of dirt. Drain and rinse again.

To prepare: Cut out the large stems on older leaves. Leave them intact on smaller leaves.

To cook: Steam with a little salt about 1 minute until limp but still green. Strain and cool. Gather into a ball and squeeze out moisture. Sauté briefly in garlic and hot olive oil or slice through the ball of greens, making thin shreds.

BASIC SPINACH RECIPES

Joe's Spinach alla Verdura

Wash spinach thoroughly and remove large stems. Place the slightly wet spinach in a large pan and cook over high heat until it withers, tossing frequently with tongs, about 2 to 3 minutes. Cook a few minutes longer, to evaporate moisture. Remove to a dish. When cool, squeeze moisture out of spinach. Sauté a little garlic in a skillet in some olive oil. Add the spinach and toss to coat. Dress with the juice of a 1/2 lemon and a small splash of balsamic vinegar. Add salt and pepper to taste.

Spinach Casserole

Steam or poach stemmed spinach and add salt to taste. Sauté a little garlic in olive oil, toss in the spinach, and stir. Add some raisins, pine nuts, lemon juice, and lemon zest. Remove the mixture to a casserole dish and top with bread crumbs. Bake in a preheated 350° oven for 15 to 20 minutes, or until heated through.

Spinach with Mushrooms in Oyster Sauce

SERVES 4

> 4 tablespoons vegetable oil
> 1 pound spinach, cleaned and stemmed
> Salt to taste
> 1/2 tablespoon grated gingerroot
> 8 ounces mushrooms, cleaned and sliced

> SAUCE
> 1 cup water
> 1 tablespoon oyster sauce
> 1 tablespoon low-salt soy sauce
> 1/2 teaspoon granulated sugar
> 2 teaspoons Asian sesame oil

Heat a wok over high heat, then add 2 table-spoons of the vegetable oil. Stir-fry the spinach until wilted, 2 to 3 minutes. Add salt to taste. Remove and keep warm.

Heat the remaining 2 tablespoons of oil over high heat, add the grated ginger, and sauté the mushrooms for 1 minute. Add all the sauce ingredients. Stir until the sauce is evaporated but not dry.

To serve, place the spinach around the edge of a serving platter, put the mushrooms in the center of the spinach and drizzle the sesame oil over the vegetables.

Per serving: 187 calories (139 from fat), 16.6 g total fat, 2 g saturated fat, 1 mg cholesterol, 400 mg sodium, 8.2 g carbohydrate, 3.8 g dietary fiber, 4.8 g protein

Spinach Sauté

SERVES 4

Here is a variation on San Francisco restaurateur Carlo Middione's simple spinach dish.

> 3 tablespoons raisins or currants
> 4 bunches spinach, washed and stemmed
> 1/3 cup olive oil
> 5 garlic cloves, minced
> 1/4 cup pine nuts
> 1/2 teaspoon salt
> 1/8 teaspoon freshly ground pepper

Soak raisins in hot water to cover for 15 minutes, then drain. Put the wet spinach in a large saucepan and cook over high heat until wilted, stirring constantly. Cook a few minutes longer to evaporate the moisture. Transfer to a dish and let cool. Squeeze as much moisture from the spinach as possible.

In a large skillet over medium heat, heat the olive oil and sauté the garlic until translucent. Add the raisins and pine nuts and cook until the pine nuts are golden brown.

Add the spinach to the skillet and toss until well coated and hot. Season with the salt and pepper and serve at once.

Per serving: 249 calories (195 from fat), 23.3 g total fat, 3.3 g saturated fat, 0 mg cholesterol, 313 mg sodium, 10.1 g carbohydrate, 2.4 g dietary fiber, 4.5 g protein

Spinach-Gorgonzola Pasta

SERVES 6 TO 8

This dish may not be healthy for the body but it does wonders for the spirit. It is a real crowd pleaser at Gayle's Rosticceria. Gayle also teaches this recipe in one of her pasta classes.

GORGONZOLA SAUCE

4 cups milk

3 tablespoons all-purpose flour

3 tablespoons butter

10 ounces Gorgonzola cheese

4 pinches nutmeg

¹/₂ teaspoon pepper

1 pound large pasta shells

2 bunches fresh spinach, cleaned and dried, or
 1 package frozen

³/₄ cup ricotta

3 cloves garlic, minced

Salt and freshly ground pepper to taste

1 cup grated Parmesan cheese

Preheat the oven to 375°. In a heavy saucepan over medium heat, heat the milk until hot but not boiling.

At the same time, combine flour and butter in another heavy saucepan. Stir over medium heat with a wooden spoon or whisk until the mixture has gently bubbled for 2 minutes. Be careful not to brown the flour.

Begin to add the hot milk to the flour mixture a little at a time while whisking vigorously. Continue to add the milk until it is fully incorporated. Bring the mixture to a boil, reduce the heat to low, and simmer, stirring constantly, until the mixture thickens, about 6 to 8 minutes. It will look like heavy cream. Crumble the cheese and add it to the hot béchamel sauce, whisking continuously until smooth. Add the nutmeg and pepper and stir. Remove from heat and let cool.

Cook the pasta in salted boiling water for 8 to 10 minutes, until al dente. Drain and set aside.

If using fresh spinach, blanch it 1 to 2 minutes in a little boiling water. Drain it, let it cool, and squeeze all of the water out several times. If you are using frozen spinach, let it defrost in a sieve over a bowl for at least 3 hours. Squeeze all the water out by hand.

Toss the pasta, Gorgonzola sauce, spinach, ricotta, and garlic in a large bowl until well combined. Taste and correct for salt and pepper.

Place in a 12 x 17-inch casserole dish and top with the Parmesan. Bake for 20 to 30 minutes, until the cheese browns a little. You may make this a day ahead, and before baking, refrigerate well covered.

Per serving: 749 calories (317 from fat), 35.1 g total fat, 21.7 g saturated fat, 102 mg cholesterol, 1,156 mg sodium, 71.1 g carbohydrate, 2.5 g dietary fiber, 36.7 g protein

SQUASH

To prepare winter squash: Slice off the top and bottom (about $1/2$ to $3/4$ inch). Starting from the top, cut off the skin with a paring knife. Cut in half and remove the seeds, then cut into chunks or slices and steam, boil, sauté, or bake.

To bake winter squash: Cut unpeeled winter squash in half and remove the seeds. Brush cut side lightly with a little oil, salt, and pepper. Place, skin side up, on an oiled baking sheet. Bake in a preheated 350° oven for about 40 minutes to 1 hour, or until tender.

To prepare summer squash: Scrub skin with water; dice or cut into coins, or julienne into 2 by $1/4$-inch pieces.

To cook summer squash: Steam, sauté, or roast in chunks. Grill in $1/4$-inch slices cut lengthwise.

Roasted-Zucchini Pasta

SERVES 2

This is a lighter version of a pasta Gayle and I tasted in Italy. Roasting the zucchini intensifies the flavor and creates an aromatic sauce.

> 4 zucchini
> Salt for draining zucchini
> 2 tablespoons olive oil
> 3 large unpeeled cloves garlic
> Freshly ground black pepper to taste
> 4 ounces penne pasta
> $1/2$ cup (2 ounces) grated Parmesan or Asiago
>   cheese

Cut the zucchini into $1/8$-inch-thick coins. Place them on paper towels and salt lightly. After 30 minutes, turn over and salt again. After another 30 minutes, wipe the excess moisture off the zucchini. In a bowl, drizzle 1 tablespoon of olive oil over the zucchini and toss.

Preheat the oven to 375°. Place the zucchini slices on a non-stick baking sheet. Bake for 30 minutes, or until brown. At the same time, roast the garlic cloves for 30 minutes, or until very soft. Let cool.

Squeeze the garlic from its skin into a medium bowl. Finely chop half of the zucchini and add it to the bowl. Mash the garlic and zucchini with a wooden spoon, adding the remaining 1 tablespoon of olive oil and several grinds of pepper.

Preheat the oven to 450°. Cook the penne in a large pot of salted boiling water until very al dente, about 7 to 8 minutes. Drain.

Add the pasta to the zucchini mixture and mix to coat. Add half of the cheese and mix. Pour the zucchini-coated pasta into a small baking dish. Cover with the remaining cheese and zucchini coins and bake, uncovered, for 15 to 20 minutes, or until cheese is crispy.

Let cool for 5 minutes before serving.

Per serving: 488 calories (199 from fat), 22.3 g total fat, 6.8 g saturated fat, 20 mg cholesterol, 482 mg sodium, 52.3 g carbohydrate, 4.6 g dietary fiber, 21 g protein

Stuffed Zucchini Blossoms

SERVES 4

By picking zucchini blossoms just before they start to fruit, you can control the size of your crop. The blossoms, stuffed and sautéed, make a tasty appetizer or side dish.

> 12 to 16 zucchini blossoms
> 1 tablespoon minced garlic
> 1 tablespoon minced onion
> 1 $1/2$ cups (12 ounces) ricotta cheese
> $1/2$ cup (2 ounces) grated Asiago cheese
> 1 beaten egg
> 2 tablespoons minced fresh basil
> Salt and freshly ground pepper to taste
> 4 cups tomato sauce (page 438)

Remove the pistil from each flower, and if necessary, dip the flowers in cold water to clean. Pat them dry on paper towels.

In a medium bowl, combine all the remaining ingredients except the tomato sauce. Stuff the blossoms with the mixture.

In a medium saucepan over low heat, heat the sauce. Set aside and keep warm. Add 1 cup of the sauce to a large skillet and place over medium heat. Place half of the blossoms in the skillet and cook them for 10 to 15 minutes, turning with tongs once. Transfer to a large casserole dish in a warm oven. Repeat with remaining blossoms.

Top the blossoms with the remaining sauce and serve warm or at room temperature.

Per serving: 362 calories (244 from fat), 27.6 g total fat, 11.8 g saturated fat, 110 mg cholesterol, 541 mg sodium, 11.3 g carbohydrate, 1.7 g dietary fiber, 18.7 g protein

Winter Squash with Lemon and Garlic

SERVES 4 TO 6

- **2 winter squash (about 2 pounds)**
- **2 tablespoons olive oil**
- **2 tablespoons minced garlic**
- **$1/2$ teaspoon nutmeg**
- **Juice of $1/2$ lemon**
- **Salt and freshly ground pepper to taste**
- **2 tablespoons minced fresh flat-leaf parsley, for garnish**

Peel and seed the squash and cut them into 2-inch chunks. In a large skillet over medium heat, heat the oil and sauté the garlic until translucent. Add the squash, cover, and cook until tender, about 20 to 30 minutes. Add the nutmeg, lemon juice, salt, and pepper to taste. Remove to a platter and garnish with the parsley.

Per serving: 153 calories (60 from fat), 7.4 g total fat, 1.1 g saturated fat, 0 mg cholesterol, 11 mg sodium, 22 g carbohydrate, 3.6 g dietary fiber, 3.6 g protein

Roasted Winter Squash Soup

SERVES 8

- **2 pounds winter squash, halved and seeded**
- **$1/4$ cup chopped walnuts**
- **2 tablespoons olive oil**
- **1 onion, chopped**
- **1 tablespoon minced fresh thyme**
- **Pinch of ground allspice**
- **1 small apple, peeled, cored, and diced**
- **4 cups low sodium chicken broth or vegetable stock**
- **1 red pepper, roasted, peeled, and chopped**
- **$1/2$ tablespoon fresh lemon juice**
- **Salt to taste**
- **$1/4$ teaspoon pepper**

Preheat the oven to 375°. Place the squash on an oiled baking sheet, cut side down. Bake until tender, about 1 hour. Let cool. Meanwhile, put the walnuts on a baking sheet and toast 10 to 12 minutes, or until slightly brown.

In a sauce pan over medium heat, heat the olive oil. Add onion, thyme, and allspice. Reduce heat to low, cover, and cook until the onion is tender, about 10 minutes. Uncover and stir in the apple and stock. Bring to a simmer and cook until the apple is tender, about 15 minutes.

Scoop out the squash pulp and add it to the pan. Simmer for 5 minutes. Let cool slightly, and add the red pepper. Purée in a blender or food processor (in batches if necessary). Strain. Heat over medium heat and season with lemon, salt, and pepper. Serve in soup bowls and garnish with toasted walnuts.

Per serving: 130 calories (52 from fat), 7.2 g total fat, 0.7 g saturated fat, 0 mg cholesterol, 25 mg sodium, 16.2 g carbohydrate, 2.8 g dietary fiber, 8.5 g protein

TOMATOES

To peel: Drop 1 or 2 tomatoes at a time into a large pot of boiling water. Parboil for 10 to 15 seconds. Retrieve each tomato using a slotted spoon. Set aside and let cool. Cut each tomato in half, squeeze out the seeds, pull off the skin, and cut out the stem-core on top. Tomatoes can also be charred by holding them individually over an open flame with tongs. When cool, peel and seed.

To roast: Cut tomatoes in half horizontally. Place them on a rimmed baking sheet or in a deep baking dish. Dress them lightly with olive oil, chopped garlic, chopped herbs like oregano, sage (not too much), rosemary (minced very fine and not too much), basil, and thyme. Add salt and freshly ground black pepper to taste. Bake in a 350° oven for 1 to 1½ hours until dark and aromatic.

To grill: Place tomatoes on a grill with long tongs. Turn often and very gently to avoid breaking the skin. When slightly charred all around, they're done.

Tomato Sauce

MAKES 4 CUPS (5 SERVINGS)

This simple tomato sauce can be used for everything from eggplant Parmesan to pizza.

- ⅓ cup extra virgin olive oil
- 4 cloves garlic, minced
- 12 to 14 plum tomatoes, peeled, seeded, and coarsely chopped (5 cups prepared)
- ½ teaspoon salt
- ¼ teaspoon black pepper
- 2 tablespoons minced fresh basil, flat-leaf parsley, or 1 teaspoon minced fresh oregano (optional)

In a large saucepan over medium heat, heat the oil and sauté the garlic until translucent. Add the chopped tomatoes, salt, and pepper. Lower heat and simmer uncovered for 30 minutes to 1 hour. Add the herbs 10 minutes before the end of cooking. The sauce will keep for 1 week in refrigerator.

Note: This recipe is designed to be doubled or halved for whatever size batch desired.

Per ¾-cup serving: 120 calories (90 from fat), 10.6 g total fat, 1.4 g saturated fat, 0 mg cholesterol, 213 mg sodium, 6.9 g carbohydrate, 1.6 g dietary fiber, 1.3 g protein

Tomato Soup

SERVES 6 TO 8

This healthful, but flavorful tomato soup uses light olive oil, milk, and the soft crumbs of any white bread to replace the heavy cream and butter in the traditional recipe.

- ¼ cup light olive oil
- 3 yellow onions, chopped
- 12 to 15 plum tomatoes, peeled and seeded
- 2 cups low sodium chicken broth or vegetable stock
- 2 teaspoons gremolata (page 84)
- 1 cup milk
- 2 tablespoons extra virgin olive oil
- 1 cup tightly packed crustless white bread
- Salt and freshly ground pepper to taste
- Chopped chives, for garnish

In a nonstick skillet over medium-low heat, heat the oil and sauté the onions for 20 minutes, stirring occasionally. Add the tomatoes, stock, and gremolata. Simmer for 20 minutes.

Meanwhile, whisk the milk and olive oil together in a small bowl. Add the bread and soak for 15 minutes.

Purée the bread mixture in a blender or food processor until smooth. Purée the tomato mixture separately. Combine the two mixtures in a pot and simmer for 10 minutes to meld the flavors.

Season with salt and pepper and serve immediately, sprinkled with chives.

Per serving: 328 calories (152 from fat), 17.4 g total fat, 3.3 g saturated fat, 6 mg cholesterol, 630 mg sodium, 37.6 g carbohydrate, 4.5 g dietary fiber, 8.2 g protein

Tortilla Soup

SERVES 6

1 onion, peeled and halved

8 whole tomatoes

Corn oil for coating, plus 2 tablespoons

4 cloves garlic, chopped

2 ancho or pasilla chiles (dried), seeded, stemmed, and finely chopped

1 bay leaf

1 sprig epazote or oregano

2 teaspoons ground cumin (optional if using epazote)

8 cups low sodium chicken broth or vegetable stock

Salt to taste

Cayenne or black pepper to taste

GARNISH

1 corn tortilla, cut into thin strips

1 tablespoon vegetable oil for frying

Diced avocado

6 tablespoons crème fraîche or sour cream

Grated Monterey jack or white Mexican cheese

Coat the onion and tomatoes lightly with oil and grill over a medium–hot charcoal fire, turning several times, until charred evenly. Let cool, remove most of the blackened skin and seeds from the tomatoes and break them into chunks with your hands, trying to reserve as much juice as possible. Chop the onion.

In a large stockpot over medium heat, heat the 2 tablespoons oil and fry the garlic and chiles for 5 minutes, stirring frequently. Add the bay leaf, herb sprig, cumin, and stock.

Add the tomatoes with their juice and the onions. Simmer for 30 minutes. Add salt and cayenne. Remove the bay leaf and herb sprig.

To make the garnish: Fry the tortilla strips in hot oil until crisp, or bake in a preheated 350° oven until crisp. Set aside and let cool.

Garnish each bowl of soup with crisp tortilla chips, diced avocado, a tablespoon of crème fraîche, and a little grated cheese.

Per serving: 173 calories (70 from fat), 10.9 g total fat, 0.9 g saturated fat, 0 mg cholesterol, 78 mg sodium, 19.1 g carbohydrate, 2.9 g dietary fiber, 17.1 g protein

Tomato-Basil Pasta Crudo

SERVES 2

This dish uses what is called a crudo *sauce in Italian. Totally uncooked, the sauce relies on the aromatic flavors of the garlic, olive oil, and basil. We learned it from a waiter named Boris at Bistro des Alpilles in Saint-Rémy de Provence.*

2 tomatoes

$1/3$ cup extra virgin olive oil

2 tablespoons chopped garlic

$1/2$ cup finely chopped fresh basil

$1/2$ teaspoon salt

$1/4$ teaspoon freshly ground pepper

6 ounces spaghetti or angel-hair pasta

$1/4$ cup grated Parmesan cheese

Without scalding the tomatoes, carefully peel off the skins, starting from the top with a sharp knife. Cut each tomato in half and squeeze out the seeds. Chop the remaining tomato flesh into $1/4$-inch cubes and place them in a small bowl.

Add the olive oil, garlic, basil, salt, and pepper to the chopped tomatoes. Mix and allow to macerate for at least 30 minutes.

Cook the pasta in rapidly boiling salted water until it is cooked al dente. Drain and place the cooked pasta in bowls. Top with the sauce and serve immediately with the grated Parmesan.

Per serving: 731 calories (370 from fat), 41.4 g total fat, 7.5 g saturated fat, 10 mg cholesterol, 784 mg sodium, 73.2 g carbohydrate, 3.3 g dietary fiber, 17.7 g protein

Mimi's Salsa

SERVES 4 (4 CUPS)

This is an easy food processor salsa that's as good as any you've ever tasted. Thick for dipping with chips. Keeps 5 days refrigerated.

- 3 pickled or 2 fresh jalapeño chiles, stemmed and quartered
- 4 medium tomatoes, stem ends cut off and quartered
- 1 small to medium onion, cut in eighths
- 1 bunch cilantro (1 loosely packed cup), stemmed
- 1 (15-ounce) can tomato sauce
- 1 bell or Anaheim pepper, seeded and cut into eighths (optional)
- Juice of 1/2 lemon
- 1 tablespoon juice from pickled jalapeños
- 1/2 teaspoon salt
- Pinch of cayenne (optional)

If using fresh jalapeños, seed. Place all ingredients in bowl of food processor. Pulse 15 to 20 times until finely chopped.

Per serving: 76 calories (5 from fat), 0.7 g total fat, 0.1 g saturated fat, 0 mg cholesterol, 653 mg sodium, 17.6 g carbohydrate, 3.9 g dietary fiber, 3.1 g protein

Basil, Cherry Tomato, and Mozzarella Salad

MAKES 6 SMALL SERVINGS

Easy to make; great flavors of summer.

- 1 pound (1 basket) cherry tomatoes, halved
- 1/2 cup basil, coarsely chopped
- 1/2 pound mozzarella cheese, cut in 1/2-inch cubes

DRESSING

- 2 teaspoons lemon juice
- 4 tablespoons red wine vinegar
- 6 tablespoons olive oil
- 2 cloves garlic
- 1/2 loosely packed cup basil
- 1/4 loosely packed cup parsley
- 1/4 teaspoon salt or to taste
- Few grinds black pepper

Combine tomatoes, basil and mozzarella in a bowl. Place all dressing ingredients in food processor. Process until basil and parsley are finely chopped.

Add the dressing to the tomato mixture and toss.

Per serving: 261 calories (203 from fat), 23.1 g total fat, 7.7 g saturated fat, 34 mg cholesterol, 254 mg sodium, 5.8 g carbohydrate, 1.1 g dietary fiber, 9.1 g protein

Gazpacho

SERVES 4

2 red onions, coarsely chopped

5 jalapeño chiles, seeded and coarsely chopped

1 tablespoon chopped garlic

12 tomatillos, husked and chopped

4 plum tomatoes, peeled, seeded, and chopped

2 red bell peppers, seeded, deveined, and chopped

2 tablespoons minced fresh cilantro

1/4 cup olive oil

6 tablespoons red wine vinegar

1 teaspoon salt or to taste

2 tablespoons granulated sugar

1 teaspoon minced fresh oregano

Tabasco sauce to taste

Pulse all of the ingredients in a blender or food processor (in batches if necessary) until chunky. Refrigerate for several hours. Ladle into individual bowls or cups.

Per serving: 271 calories (127 from fat), 15.3 g total fat, 1.9 g saturated fat, 0 mg cholesterol, 553 mg sodium, 34.6 g carbohydrate, 7 g dietary fiber, 4.6 g protein

TURNIPS

To prepare: Peel and cut into pieces, or leave whole or in large chunks for roasting.

To cook: Steam, braise, or blanch. Steam lightly before stir frying.

Mashed Turnips and Potatoes

SERVES 6

2 tablespoons olive oil

1 large onion, chopped

3 large heads garlic

1 1/4 pounds turnips, peeled and quartered

1 1/2 pounds russet potatoes, peeled and quartered

1 1/2 cups chicken or vegetable stock

1/4 cup low-fat milk

Salt and freshly ground pepper to taste

Minced fresh flat-leaf parsley for garnish

Preheat the oven to 375°. Pour the oil into a 15 x 10-inch baking pan. Add the onion and mix until coated. Cut the garlic heads in half crosswise. Place the garlic, cut side down, in the pan. Bake until the garlic is very tender and the onions are browned, about 45 minutes. Let cool.

Meanwhile, put the turnips and potatoes in a medium saucepan with the stock. Bring to a boil, then reduce heat, cover, and simmer until the vegetables are tender, 35 minutes or so. Remove the lid and boil if necessary to reduce the liquid to a glaze.

Squeeze the garlic out of the husks and place in a small bowl. With a fork, mash the garlic; mix in the onions and set aside.

Transfer the turnips and potatoes to a large bowl, and with an electric mixer or a potato masher, beat until almost smooth. Add the milk and garlic-onion mixture; beat until smooth and creamy. Add the salt and pepper. Garnish with parsley and serve.

Per serving: 155 calories (44 from fat), 5 g total fat, 0.8 g saturated fat, 1 mg cholesterol, 611 mg sodium, 24.5 g carbohydrate, 3.5 g dietary fiber, 3.6 g protein

Appendices

Bibliography

CHAPTER 1: PLANNING THE COOK'S GARDEN AND SETTING UP THE GARDENER'S KITCHEN

Ausubel, K. *Seeds of Change.* San Francisco: Harper, 1994.

Bartholomew, M. *Square Foot Gardening.* Emmaus, PA: Rodale Press, 1981.

Bubel, N. *The Seed Starters Handbook.* Emmaus, PA: Rodale Press, 1988.

Coleman, E. *The New Organic Grower.* Chelsea, VT: Chelsea Green, 1989.

Creasy, R. *Cooking from the Garden.* San Francisco: Sierra Club Books, 1988.

Hunt, M.B. & B. Bortz. *High-Yield Gardening.* Emmaus, PA: Rodale Press, 1986.

Kimball, C. *The Cook's Bible.* Boston: Little-Brown, 1996.

Kitto, D. *Planning the Organic Vegetable Garden.* Golden, CO: Fulcrum Press, 1993.

Kourik, R. *Drip Irrigation for Every Landscape and All Climates.* Santa Rosa, CA: Metamorphic Press, 1992.

Kourik, R. *Designing and Maintaining Your Edible Landscape Naturally.* Santa Rosa, CA: Metamorphic Press, 1986.

Lyte, C. *The Kitchen Garden.* Somerset, England: Oxford Illustrated Press, 1984.

Miller, M. and M. Kiffen. *Coyote's Pantry.* Berkeley, CA: Ten Speed Press, 1989.

Ogden, S. *Step by Step Organic Vegetable Gardening.* New York: Harper Collins, 1992.

Poisson, L. and G. Poisson. *Solar Gardening: Growing Vegetables Year-Round the American Intensive Way.* White River Junction, VT: Chelsea Green, 1994.

Southern Living staff. *Southern Living Garden Book.* Birmingham, AL: Oxmoor House, 1998.

Sunset staff. *National Garden Book.* Menlo Park: Sunset, 1997.

Sunset staff. *Western Garden Book.* Menlo Park: Sunset, 1995.

Tucker, D.M. *Kitchen Gardening in America.* Ames, Iowa: Iowa State University Press, 1993.

Climate Resources: There are several publications that provide current weather information based on a national network of weather stations. These are available for most states from the National Climatic Center, Federal Building, Asheville, NC 28801.

CHAPTER 2:
UNDERSTANDING SOILS AND FERTILIZERS AND MAKING FLAVORINGS FROM THE GARDEN

Braasch, B. *Improving Your Garden Soil*. San Ramon, CA: Ortho Books, 1992.

Ferrary, J. and L. Fiszer. *Season to Taste: Herbs and Spices in American Cooking*. New York: Simon & Schuster.

Fine Gardening. *Healthy Soil*. Newtown, CT: Taunton Press, 1995.

Gershuny, G. *Start with the Soil*. Emmaus, PA: Rodale Press, 1993.

Hynes, E. *Improving the Soil*. Emmaus, PA: Rodale Press, 1994.

Kohnke, H. & D. P. Franzmeier. *Soil Science Simplified*. Prospect Heights, IL: Waveland Press, 1995.

Ortiz, E. L. *Encyclopedia of Flavorings and Seasonings*. New York: Dorking-Kingersley, 1990.

Parnes, R. *Fertile Soils: A Grower's Guide To Organic and Inorganic Fertilizers*. Davis, CA: agAccess, 1990.

CHAPTER 3:
NOURISHING SOIL AND BODY

Applehof, M. *Worms Eat My Garbage*. City TK: Flower Press, 1982.

Azevedo, J. *Farm Animal Manures*. Berkeley, CA: Calif. Agric. Exper. Sta., Manual 44, Agric. Publ., Univ. Calif., 1974.

Bugg, R. L. and R. Zomer. *Cover Crops Manual*. Davis, CA: Sustainable Agriculture Research and Education Program, UC Davis, 1989.

Campbell, S. *Let it Rot: The Gardener's Guide to Composting*. Charlotte, VT: Garden Way Publ., 1990.

Cheney, D., et al. *Organic Soil Amendments and Fertilizers*. Oakland, CA: UC Sustainable Agriculture Research and Education Program, Publ. 21505. Div. Agric. Nat. Res., Univ. Calif., 1992.

Collen, M. and L. Johnson. *The Urban/Suburban Composter*. New York: St. Martin's Press, 1992.

Hupping, C. *Stocking Up: The Third Edition of the Classic Preserving Guide*. New York: Fireside, 1990.

La Place, V. Verdura: *Vegetables Italian Style*. New York: William Morrow & Co., 1991.

Martin, D. & G. Gershuny (eds.) *The Rodale Book of Composting*. Emmaus, PA: Rodale Press, 1992.

CHAPTER 4:
CONTROLLING GARDEN PESTS AND FEEDING KITCHEN GUESTS

Bumstead, C., A. Knaus, and A. Jones. *Pesticides: A Community Action Guide*. Washington, DC: Concern, Inc., 1986.

Cranshaw, W. *Pests of the West: Prevention and Control for Today's Garden and Small Farm*. Golden, CO: Fulcrum Press, 1992.

Druse, K. *The Natural Habitat Garden*. New York: Clarkson Potter Publ., 1994.

Ferrary, J. and L. Fiszer. *Sweet Onions and Sour Cherries*. New York: Simon & Schuster, 1992.

Gilkeson, L., P. Pierce, and M. Smith. *Rodale's Pest and Disease Problem Solver*. Emmaus, PA: Rodale Press, 1996.

Harper, P. *The Natural Garden Book: A Holistic Approach to Gardening*. New York: Simon & Schuster, 1994.

MacNab, A. *Identifying Diseases of Vegetables*. University Park, PA: Penn. State Univ., College of Agriculture, 1983.

Mott, L. & K. Snyder. *Pesticide Alert: A Guide to Pesticides in Fruits and Vegetables.* San Francisco: Sierra Club Books, 1987.

Olkowski, W., S. Daar, and H. Olkowski. *The Gardener's Guide to Common-Sense Pest Control.* Newtown, CT: The Taunton Press, 1995.

Pleasant, B. *Plant Diseases: Earth Safe Remedies.* Pownal, VT: Storey Communications, Inc., 1995.

Putnam, C. (ed.). *Controlling Vegetable Pests.* San Francisco: Ortho Books, 1991.

Smith, C. (ed.). *The Ortho Home Gardener's Problem Solver.* San Francisco: Ortho Books, 1995.

Smith, M. and A. Carr. *Rodale's Garden Insect, Disease & Weed Identification Guide.* Emmaus, PA: Rodale Press, 1988.

Stein, S. *Noah's Garden: Restoring the Ecology of Our Backyards.* New York: Houghton Mifflin, 1993.

Stokes, D. A *Guide to Observing Insect Lives.* Boston: Little Brown & Co., 1983.

Whitson, T. (ed.), et al. *Weeds of the West.* Newark, CA: Western Society of Weed Science, 1992.

VEGETABLE COMPENDIUM

Aaron, C. *The Great Garlic Book: A Guide With Recipes.* Berkeley, CA: Ten Speed Press, 1997.

Adams, C. *Nutritive Value of American Foods in Common Units.* U.S.D.A. Handbook #456, Agric. Research Service, U.S.D.A., Washington D.C. U.S. Gov. Print. Office, 1975.

Andrews, J. *Peppers: The Domesticated Capsicums.* Austin, TX: Univ. Texas Press, 1984.

Bear, F. et al (eds.). *Hunger Signs in Crops.* Washington D.C.: Amer. Soc. Agron. & Nat. Fert. Assoc., 1949.

Brennan, G., I. Crownin, and S. Glenn. *The New American Vegetable Cookbook.* Berkeley, CA: Aris Books, 1985.

Brennan, G. *Potager: Fresh Garden Cooking in the French Style.* San Francisco: Chronicle Books, 1992.

Burr, F. *Field and Garden Vegetables of America.* Reprint: Boston: J.E. Tilton & Co., 1863.

Coonse, M. *Onions, Leeks, and Garlic: A Handbook for Gardeners.* College Station, TX: Texas A&M University Press, 1995.

Creasy, R. *Cooking From the Garden: Creative Gardening and Contemporary Cuisine.* San Francisco: Sierra Club Books, 1988.

Dahlen, M. and K. Phillips. *A Popular Guide to Chinese Vegetables.* New York: Crown Publishers, 1983.

Dreppe, C. *Breed Your Own Vegetable Varieties.* New York: Little, Brown & Co., 1993.

Engeland, R. *Growing Great Garlic.* Okanogan, WA: Filaree Productions, 1991.

Flint, M. *Integrated Pest Management of Cole Crops and Lettuce.* Oakland, CA: Div. of Agric. & Nat. Res., Univ. Calif., 1985.

Flint, M. *Pests of the Garden and Small Farm: A Growers Guide to Using Less Pesticides.* Oakland, CA: Publ. 3322, Div. Agric. Nat. Res., Univ. Calif., 1990.

Forsyth T. and M. Mohr. *The Harrowsmith Salad Garden.* Ontario, Canada: Cambden House, 1992.

Greene, B. *Greene on Greens.* New York: Workman Press, 1984.

Harrington, G. *Grow Your Own Chinese Vegetables.* Pownal, VT: Storey Communications, Inc., 1978.

Hendrickson, R. *The Great American Tomato Book.* New York: Doubleday & Co., 1977.

Jabs, C. *The Heirloom Gardener.* San Francisco: Sierra Club Books, 1984.

Jeavons, J. *How to Grow More Vegetables.* Berkeley, CA: Ten Speed Press, 1982.

Johnson, R. *Growing Garden Seeds.* Albion, ME: Johnny's Selected Seeds, 1983.

Jones, J., et al. (eds.). *Compendium of Tomato Diseases.* St. Paul, MN: American Phytopathological Society, 1991.

Katzen, M. *Moosewood Cookbook.* Berkeley, CA: Ten Speed Press, 1977.

Kays, S. and J. Silva Dias. *Common Names of Commercially Cultivated Vegetables of the World in 15 Languages.* Economic Botany, 49(2): 115–152.

Kirchner, B. *The Bold Vegetarian.* New York: Haper Collins, 1995.

Larcom, Joy. *Oriental Vegetables: The Complete Guide for Garden and Kitchen.* New York: Kodansha International, 1991.

Maynard, D. and G. Hochmuth. *Knott's Handbook for Vegetable Growers (4th ed.).* New York: John Wiley & Sons, 1997.

Michalak, P. *Rodale's Successful Organic Gardening: Vegetables.* Emmaus, PA: Rodale Press, 1993.

Morash, M. *The Victory Garden Cookbook.* New York: Alfred A. Knopf, 1982.

National Gardening Association. *Gardening: The Complete Guide to Growing America's Favorite Fruits and Vegetables.* Menlo Park, CA: Addison Wesley Publ. Co., Inc., 1985.

National Research Council. *Lost Crops of the Incas.* Washington D.C.: National Academy Press, 1989.

Ogden, S. and E. Ogden. 1989. *The Cook's Garden: Growing and Using the Best-Tasting Vegetable Varieties.* Emmaus, PA: Rodale Press 1989.

Peirce, P. *Golden Gate Gardening.* Davis, CA: agAccess, 1993.

Pennington, J. *Bowe's & Church's Food Values of Portions Commonly Used (16th ed.).* Philadelphia: J. B. Lippincott Co., 1993.

Robertson, L., C. Flinders, and B. Ruppenthal. *Laurel's Kitchen Recipes.* Berkeley, CA: Ten Speed Press, 1993.

Robinson, J. (general ed). *Diagnosis of Mineral Disorders in Plants, Vol. 2: Vegetables.* London: Her Majesty's Stationery Office, 1983.

Schwartz, H. and S. Mohan (eds.). *Compendium of Onion and Garlic Diseases.* St. Paul, MN: American Phytopathological Society, 1994.

Shepherd, R. *Recipes from a Kitchen Garden.* Berkeley, CA: Ten Speed Press, 1987.

Shewell-Cooper. *The Basic Book of Vegetable Growing.* New York: Drake Publishers, Inc., 1973.

Simmonds, N. (ed.). *The Evolution of Crop Plants.* New York: Longman, 1976.

Stone, S. and M. Stone. *The Essential Root Vegetable Cookbook.* New York: Clarkson, Potter, Publ., 1991.

Sunset staff. *Western Garden Book.* Menlo Park, CA: Sunset, 1995.

Tucker, D. M. *Kitchen Gardening in America.* Ames, IA: Iowa State Univ. Press, 1993.

Vilmorin-Andrieus, M. M. *The Vegetable Garden.* Reprint: Berkeley, CA: Ten Speed Press, 1885.

Watson, B. *Heirloom Vegetables.* New York: Houghton Mifflin Co., 1996.

Whealy, K. *Garden Seed Inventory.* Decorah, IA: Seed Savers Publication, 1995.

Zomlefer, W. *Guide To the Flowering Plant Families.* Chapel Hill, NC: Univ. No. Carolina Press, 1994.

Seed Companies

VEGETABLE SEED COMPANIES

Abundant Life Seed Foundation
abundant@olypen.com. Box 772, Port Townsend, WA 98368. This non-profit group is dedicated to the preservation of heirloom and open-pollinated seeds. It specializes in open-pollinated vegetables and herbs grown by a network of regional gardeners.

Bountiful Gardens
18001 Shafer Ranch Rd., Willits, CA 95490. This non-profit project offers untreated open-pollinated vegetables, herbs, flowers, and European heirlooms, many of which are organically grown.

Burpee, W. Atlee Co.
300 Park Ave., Warminster, PA 18991. A seed supplier for American gardens since 1876. Introduced Iceberg lettuce and hybrid tomatoes. They have a large selection of flowers, vegetables, nursery stock, and gardening supplies.

DV Burrell Seed Growers
Box 150, Rocky Ford, CO 81067. They maintain scores of varieties of vegetables, flowers, and herb seeds, in addition to supplies. They specialize in melons.

The Cook's Garden
PO Box 5010, Hodges, SC. Choice kitchen garden list of standard and gourmet vegetables and flowers. Great selection of lettuce, European greens mesclun mixes, and shallots.

Delegeane Garlic Farms
Box 2561, Yountsville, CA 94599. Elephant, red, and white garlic.

Deep Diversity Catalog
Box 15700, Santa Fe, NM 87506. Carries food/fiber plants, herbs, heirlooms, and medicinals.

DiGiorgi Seed Co.
6011 N. St., Omaha, NE 68117. International mix of heirlooms, vegetables, herbs, wildflowers, perennials. hybrids, and open-pollinated.

Evergreen Y.H. Enterprises
Box 17538, Anaheim, CA. Over 200 varieties of Asian vegetables, including Japanese bunching onions.

Fedco Seeds
Box 520, Waterville, ME 04903. Cooperative offering vegetables and herb and flower seeds for northeast climates at low prices.

Filaree Farms
182 Conconully, Okanagan, WA 98840. More than 100 strains of certified, organic garlic.

Fox Hollow Seed Co.
Box 148, McGrann. PA 16236. Heirloom vegetables, herbs, and flowers, plus garlic and herbs.

Garden City Seeds
778 Hwy. 93 N. #3, Hamilton, MT. Untreated heirloom, hybrid, and open-pollinated vegetables, plus garlic, potatoes, and asparagus.

Gurney's Seeds and Nursery
110 Capital St., Yankton, SD 57079. Large selection of traditional and unusual vegetables.

Harris Seeds
60 Saginaw Dr., P.O. Box 22960, Rochester, NY 14623. Very large selection of choice vegetables. They have an informative catalog

Heirloom Seed Project
2451 Kissel Hill Rd., Lancaster, PA 17601. Many traditional heirloom vegetables, herbs, and flower seeds.

Horticultural Enterprises
Box 810082, Dallas, TX 75381. Hot and sweet peppers from around the world. They also grow herbs for Mexican cooking.

Jersey Asparagus Farms
105 Porchtown Rd., Pittsgrove, NJ. Fine selection of asparagus, old and new.

J. L. Hudson, Seedsman
Star Route 2, Box 337, La Honda, CA 94020. European and Native American heirloom vegetables and uncommon alliums.

Irish Eyes Potatoes and Garlic
Box 307, Ellensburg, WA 98920. Over 150 varietes of potatoes, plus garlic, shallots, and other alliums.

Johnny's Selected Seeds
310 Foss Hill Rd., Albion, ME 04910. Fine choice of American, European, and Asian hybrid and open-pollinated vegetables. They have garden and market varieties, and supplies. Mostly for cool, short seasons. A favorite supplier of kitchen gardeners everywhere.

Kalmia Farms
Box 3881, Charlottesville, VA 22903. Specializes in alliums, like garlic, multiplier onions, and shallots.

Kitazawa Seed Co.
111 Chapman St., San Jose, CA 95126. Asian vegetables since 1917.

Landreth Seed Company
Box 6426, Baltimore, MD 21230. Since 1784; a wide variety of new and old vegetables.

Le Jardin du Gourmet
Box 7H, St. Johnsbury Center, VT 05863. French vegetable seeds plus shallots, garlic, bunching onions, and herbs. Known for 25¢ seed packs.

Liberty Seed Company
128 1st Dr. SE, New Philadelphia, OH 44663. Vegetables, flowers, and herbs, plus supplies for the serious gardener.

Lockhart Seeds, Inc.
P.O. Box 1361, Stockton, CA 95205. Packets to pounds of market variety vegetables adapted to West Coast conditions; features onions, broccoli, Asian vegetables, and peppers.

The Montana Garlic Farm
355 Sunny Dene Lane, Kalispell, MT 59901. Maintains world's largest collection of garlic-over 400 varieties.

Monticello Center for Historic Plants
Box 316, Charlottesville, VA 22902. Heirloom seeds and plants, many from the years of Thomas Jefferson.

Native Seeds Search
2509 North Campbell, Tucson, AZ 85710. Collects and preserves Native American crops; corn, beans, tomatillos, etc. Membership.

Nichols Garden Nursery
1190 North Pacific Highway, Albany OR 97321. Traditional, unusual, gourmet and Asian vegetables, plus garlic, shallots, herbs, flowers, and supplies.

Old Sturbridge Village Seeds
1 Old Sturbridge Village Rd., Sturbridge, MA 01566. Heirloom vegetables and flowers

from 19th century kitchen gardens. Non-profit.

P & P Seed Co.
14050 Rt. 2, Collins, NY 14034. Features giant vegetable seeds.

Park Seed Co
1 Parkton Ave., Greenwood, SC 29647. Since 1868. Hundreds of varieties of top-rated vegetables, flowers, and herbs, plus garden supplies.

Pinetree Garden Seeds
Box 300, Route 100, New Gloucester, ME 04260. Specializes in small packets of small packets of vegetable, flower, and herb seeds at reduced prices. They also have tubers, shallots, plants, and supplies.

Plants of the Southwest
Agua Fria, Route 6, Box 11A, Santa Fe, NM 87501. Heirloom Native American varieties of vegetables.

Redwood City Seed Co.
Box 361, Redwood City, CA 94064. RCSC specializes in endangered cultivated plants. Old-fashioned, open-pollinated vegetable and herb seeds. Good selection of Asian vegetables and chiles.

Renee's Garden Seeds
7389 W. Zayante, Felton, CA 95018. Distributes quality European and U.S. kitchen garden seed varieties to independent garden centers and nurseries. Call 888-880-7228 for the nearest supplier.

Seed Savers International
3076 North Winn Rd. Decorah, IA 52101. Non-profit group offering a large selection of regional and old-time vegetables, most are heirloom or open-pollinated. Rare heirloom vegetable and flower seeds from Seed Savers Exchange.

Seeds Blüm
HC33 Idaho City Stage, Boise, ID 83706.

Large selection of heirloom and open-pollinated vegetables and uncommon alliums; delightful, original catalog.

Seeds for the World
Garden Lane, Fair Haven, VT 05743. Snap, shelling, dry beans, traditional and Euro-Asian vegetables.

Seeds of Change
P.O. Box 15700, Santa Fe, NM 87506. Organically grown traditional and heirloom vegetables, herbs, and flowers.

Seed Savers Exchange
Rt. 3, Box 239, Cedorah, IA 52101. members can access hundreds of heirloom, regional, and old-time favorites.

Seeds West Garden Seeds
317 14th St. NW, Albuquerque, NM 87104. Native, rare, heirloom and hybrid vegetable seeds for dry areas and poor soils.

Shepherd's Garden Seeds
30 Irene St., Torrington CT 06790. Vegetable, flower, and herb seeds for today's kitchen garden.

R H Shumway Seedsman
Box 1, Graniteville, SC 29829. Since 1870; specializes in old-fashioned and open-pollinated varieties of vegetables, flowers, and field crops..

Southern Exposure Seed Exchange
Box 170, Earlysville, VA 22936. Untreated open-pollinated and heirloom vegetable seeds, many organically grown. Also, many unusual alliums. A must for kitchen gardeners interested in nonhybrid varieties.

Stokes Seeds
Box 548, Buffalo, NY 14240. Since 1881. Huge selection of over 2500 varieties of vegetable and flower seeds at great prices; includes hybrid and open-pollinated, as well as corn, peppers, cabbage, and Asian varieties. They also have gardening supplies.

Sunrise Oriental Seed Company
Box 330058, West Hartford, CT 06133. Over 100 varieties of Asian vegetables.

Sweetwater Farms Garlic Division
57707 Highway 204, Weston, OR 97886. (503) 566-2756. Lots of garlic, elephant garlic, shallots and other alliums.

Territorial Seed Co.
P.O. Box 157, Cottage Grove, OR 97424. Hybrid, heirloom, and open-pollinated vegetables. Over 300 varieties of vegetables, flowers, and herbs selected for cool, short season gardening. Also carries garden supplies.

Thomas Jefferson Center for Historic Plants
Box 316, Charlottesville, VA 22902. Over 50 varieties of authentic early American vegetables and flowers.

Tomato Growers Supply
Box 2237, Fort Myers, FL 33902. Over 300 tomatoes and 100 peppers in all shapes, sizes, and colors.

Tomato Seed Company.
Over 300 varieties of hybrid, heirloom, and open-pollinated tomatoes.

Totally Tomatoes
Box 1626, Augusta, GA 30902. More than 300 varieties of tomato and pepper seeds. Some supplies.

Twilley Seed Co.
Box 65, Trevose, PA 19053. Large selection of vegetables, nicely described for various regions of the United States.

Willhite Seed, Inc.
Box 23, Poolville, TX 76487. Vegetable seeds, specializing in melons.

Wood Prairie Farms
R.R. 4, Box 164C, Bridgewater, MN 04735. Certified organic seed potatoes. Other vegetables too.

Supply Companies

GENERAL GARDEN SUPPLIES

Charley's Greenhouse Supplies
17979 State Route 536, Mount Vernon, WA 98273. Wide variety of hobby to small commercial greenhouses with the suppliers and equipment necessary.

Denman & Co.
401 W. Chapman Ave., Orange, CA 92866. Manufactures and sells professional grade garden tools.

Design Toscano
1645 Greenleaf, Elk Grove Village, IL 60007. Historical European reproductions of gargoyles, statuary, wall reliefs, etc.

D.I.G. Corp.
130 Bostick Blvd., San Marcos, CA 92082. Drip and mist irrigation supplies.

Gardener's Eden
Box 379907, Las Vegas, NV 89137. Large selection of garden gifts, tools, containers, etc.

Garden Way
1 Garden Way, Troy, NY 12180. (800) 833-6990. Makes and sells mowers and rototillers.

Gardener's Supply Co.
128 Intervale Rd., Burlington, VT 15401. Fine selection of germination systems, irrigation supplies, tools, greenhouses, natural pest controls, etc.

Gardens for Growing People
Box 630, Point Reyes, CA 94956. Children's gardening supplies, books, games.

Hydro-Gardens
Box 25845, Colorado Springs, CO80936. Greenhouse and hydroponic supplies, beneficial insects, fertilizers.

Kinsman Co., Inc.
Box 357, River Rd., Point Pleasant, PA 18950. Importers of English gardening tools, arbors, cold frames.

Langenbach
644 Enterprise Ave., Galesburg, IL 61401. Tools, barrows, Gardena watering products.

Lee Valley Tools, Ltd.
Box 1780, Ogdenburg, NY 13369. Propagation systems, quality tools, season extenders, and more.

A.M. Leonard, Inc.
241 Fox Dr., Box 816, Piqua, OH 45356. Quality hand tools, safety equipment and supplies for gardeners and arborists.

Mellingers, Inc.
2310 W South Range Rd., North Lima, OH 44452. Extensive garden and nursery supplies.

Raindrip, Inc.
Box 1500, 2250 Agate Court, Simi Valley, CA 93065. Drip irrigation systems and supplies

Smith & Hawken
2 Arbor Lane, Box 6900, Lawrence, KY 41022. High quality tools, gifts, clothes, books, bulbs.

Solar Survival
Box 250, Harrisville, NH 03450. Kits for season extenders (solar cones, cloches, etc.)

Urban Farmer Store
2833 Vicente Ave., San Francisco, CA 94116. Drip irrigation, outdoor lighting, pond equipment, tools, clothing.

Winged Weeder
c/o Creative Enterprises, Box 3452, Idaho Falls, ID 83403. Best manual shallow-root weeder.

NATURAL AND ORGANIC SUPPLIES

Arbico
Box 4247, Tucson, AZ 85738. Beneficial insects, rumatodes, and microbes; traps, organic fertilizers, state-of-the-arts.

Gardens Alive
5100 Schenley Pl., Lawrenceburg, IN 47025. Great up-to-date source for natural pest controls on the scale of the home garden.

Harmony Farm Supply and Nursery
Box 460, Graton, CA 95444. Extensive organic gardening supplies.

Integrated Fertility Management
333 Ohme Gardens Rd., Wenatchee, WA 98801. Organic supplies, specializing in organic fruit production.

The Natural Gardener, Inc.
8648 Old Bee Caves Rd., Austin, TX 78735. Complete selection of organic gardening supplies.

Natural Gardening Co.
217 San Anselmo Ave., San Anselmo, CA 94960. Organic seedlings, compost equipment.

Nitron Industries
Box 1447, Fayetteville, AR 72702. Organic soil amendments, conditioners, humates.

Peaceful Valley Farm Supply
Box 2209, Grass Valley, CA 95945. Extensive organic gardening and farming supplies. One of the best in the country. Their catalog is a gardening book.

San Jacinto Environmental Supplies
2221-A West 34th St., Houston, TX 77018. Organic gardening supplies.

Trece, Inc.
Box 6278, Salinas, CA 93912. Makes and sells the Pherocon line of pheromone traps. Large selection from great catalog.

Verdant Brands/Ringer
9555 James Ave. South, Suite 200, Bloomington, MN 55341. Natural lawn and garden care products, fertilizers, tools.

NATURAL PEST CONTROLS

A-1 Insect Control
5504 Sperry Dr., Citrus Heights, CA 95621. Lacewings, praying mantids, Trichogramma, etc.

Beneficial Insectary
14751 Oak Run Rd., Oak Run, CA 96069. Lacewings, praying mantids, Trichogramma, etc.

Buena Biosystems
Box 4008, Ventura, CA 93007. Lacewings, praying mantids, Trichogramma, etc.

Central Coast Insectary
291 Ames Rd., Watsonville, CA 95076. Raises and sells predatory mites.

Digger's Product Development Co.
Box 1551, Soquel, CA 95073. Underground, wire-mesh gopher baskets.

Foothill Agricultural Research, Inc.
510 Foothill Pkwy., Corona, CA 91720. Biocontrols and pheromone traps.

The Ladybug Co.
12857 Oro-Quincy Hwy., Berry Creek, CA 95916. Lacewings, parasitioids, ladybeetles.

Natural Pest Control
8864 Little Creek Dr., Orangevale, CA 95662. Wide variety of beneficial insects.

Mycotech
529 E. Front St., Butte, MT 59702. The insect-eating fungus Beauveria formulated for controlling soft-bodied insects.

Nature's Control
Box 35, Medford, OR 97501. Beneficial insects for indoor and greenhouse pests.

Planet Natural
Box 3416, 1612 Gold Ave., Bozeman, MT 59772. Beneficial insects, pheromone traps, botanical pesticides,etc.

Plant Sciences, Inc.
342 Green Valley Rd., Watsonville, CA 95076. Wide selection of beneficial insects.

Rincon-Vitova Insectaries, Inc.
Box 1554, Ventura, CA 93002. Oldest and largest commercial insectary in the world. Great informational brochures and catalog.

MEASURING DEVICES

Davis Instruments
3465 Diablo Ave., Hayward, CA 94545. Wide variety of weather-monitering devices and systems.

Environmental Concepts
710 Northwest 57th St., Ft, Lauderdale, FL 33309. Meters to measure pH, soil salts, temp., moisture, soil fertility, light intensity.

Pike Lab Supplies
R. R. #2, Box 710, Strong, ME 04983. pH, salinity, soil testing, and sampling instruments for the home gardener.

Reotemp Instrument Corp.
11568 Sorrento Valley Rd., San Diego, CA 92121. Bi-metal thermometersfor soil and compost temperature measurement.

Wind & Weather
1200 N. Main St., Fort Bragg, CA 95437. Everything for the home gardener-weather enthusiast. Books and sundials.

EARLIEST DATES, AND RANGE OF DATES, FOR SAFE SPRING PLANTING OF VEGETABLES IN THE OPEN

(Adapted from U.S. Department of Agriculture Information)

CROP	PLANTING DATES FOR LOCALITIES IN WHICH AVERAGE DATE OF LAST FROST IS...					
	Feb 8	Feb 18	Feb 28	Mar 10	Mar 20	Mar 30
Asparagus[1]				Jan 1-Mar 1	Feb 1-Mar 10	Feb 15-Mar 20
Beans, snap	Feb 1-May 1	Mar 1-May 1	Mar 10-May 15	Mar 15-May 15	Mar 15-May 25	Apr 1-June 1
Beet	Jan 10-Mar 15	Jan 20-Apr 1	Feb 1-Apr 15	Feb 15-June 1	Feb 15-May 15	Mar 1-June 1
Broccoli, sprouting[1]	Jan 1-30	Jan 15-Feb 15	Feb 1-Mar 1	Feb 15-Mar 15	Feb 15-Mar 15	Mar 1-20
Cabbage[1]	Jan 1-Feb 10	Jan 1-Feb 25	Jan 15-Feb 25	Jan 25-Mar 1	Feb 1-Mar 1	Feb 15-Mar 10
Cabbage, Chinese	[2]	[2]	[2]	[2]	[2]	[2]
Carrot	Jan 1-Mar 1	Jan 15-Mar 1	Feb 1-Mar 1	Feb 10-Mar 15	Feb 15-Mar 20	Mar 1-Apr 10
Cauliflower[1]	Jan 1-Feb 1	Jan 10-Feb 10	Jan 20-Feb 20	Feb 1-Mar 1	Feb 10-Mar 10	Feb 20-Mar 20
Chard	Jan 10-Apr 1	Jan 20-Apr 15	Feb 1-May 1	Feb 15-May 15	Feb 20-May 15	Mar 1-May 25
Chervil and chives	Jan 1-Feb 1	Jan 1-Feb 1	Jan 15-Feb 15	Feb 1-Mar 1	Feb 10-Mar 10	Feb 15-Mar 15
Chicory, witloof				June 1-July 1	June 1-July 1	June 1-July 1
Collards[1]	Jan 1-Feb 15	Jan 1-Mar 15	Jan 15-Mar 15	Feb 1-Apr 1	Feb 15-May 1	Mar 1-June 1
Corn, sweet	Feb 10-Apr 1	Feb 20-Apr 15	Mar 1-Apr 15	Mar 10-Apr 15	Mar 15-May 1	Mar 25-May 15
Cucumber	Feb 15-Apr 1	Feb 15-Apr 15	Mar 1-Apr 15	Mar 15-Apr 15	Apr 1-May 1	Apr 10-May 15
Eggplant[1]	Feb 10-Mar 15	Feb 20-Apr 1	Mar 10-Apr 15	Mar 15-Apr 15	Apr 1-May 1	Apr 15-May 15
Endive	Jan 1-Mar 1	Jan 15-Mar 1	Feb 1-Mar 1	Feb 15-Mar 15	Mar 1-Apr 1	Mar 10-Apr 10
Garlic	[2]	[2]	[2]	[2]	Feb 1-Mar 1	Feb 10-Mar 10
Kale	Jan 10-Feb 1	Jan 20-Feb 10	Feb 1-20	Feb 10-Mar 1	Feb 20-Mar 10	Mar 1-20
Leek	Jan 1-Feb 1	Jan 1-Feb 15	Jan 15-Feb 15	Jan 25-Mar 1	Feb 1-Mar 1	Feb 15-Mar 15
Lettuce, head[1]	Jan 1-Feb 1	Jan 1-Feb 1	Jan 15-Feb 15	Feb 1-20	Feb 15-Mar 10	Mar 1-20
Lettuce, leaf	Jan 1-Feb 1	Jan 1-Mar 15	Jan 1-Mar 15	Jan 15-Apr 1	Feb 1-Apr 1	Feb 15-Apr 15
Mustard	Jan 1-Mar 1	Feb 15-Apr 15	Feb 1-Mar 1	Feb 10-Mar 15	Feb 20-Apr 1	Mar 1-Apr 15
Onion[1]	Jan 1-15	Jan 1-15	Jan 1-Feb 1	Jan 15-Feb 15	Feb 10-Mar 10	Feb 15-Mar 15
Onion, seed	Jan 1-15	Jan 1-15	Jan 1-Feb 15	Feb 1-Mar 1	Feb 10-Mar 10	Feb 20-Mar 15
Onion, sets	Jan 1-15	Jan 1-15	Jan 1-Mar 1	Jan 15-Mar 10	Feb 1-Mar 20	Feb 15-Mar 20
Peas, garden	Jan 1-Feb 15	Jan 1-Mar 1	Jan 15-Mar 1	Jan 15-Mar 15	Feb 1-Mar 15	Feb 10-Mar 20
Pepper[1]	Feb 15-Apr 15	Mar 1-May 1	Mar 15-May 1	Apr 1-June 1	Apr 10-June 1	Apr 15-June 1
Potato	Jan 1-Feb 15	Jan 15-Mar 1	Jan 15-Mar 1	Feb 1-Mar 1	Feb 10-Mar 15	Feb 20-Mar 20
Shallot	Jan 1-Feb 10	Jan 1-Feb 20	Jan 1-Mar 1	Jan 15-Mar 1	Feb 1-Mar 10	Feb 15-Mar 15
Sorrel	Jan 1-Mar 1	Jan 15-Mar 1	Feb 1-Mar 10	Feb 10-Mar 15	Feb 10-Mar 20	Feb 20-Apr 1
Spinach	Jan 1-Feb 15	Jan 1-Mar 1	Jan 1-Mar 1	Jan 15-Mar 10	Jan 15-Mar 15	Feb 1-Mar 20
Squash, summer	Feb 15-Apr 15	Mar 1-Apr 15	Mar 15-Apr 15	Mar 15-May 1	Apr 1-May 15	Apr 10-June 1
Tomato	Feb 20-Apr 10	Mar 1-Apr 20	Mar 10-May 1	Mar 20-May 10	Apr 1-May 20	Apr 10-June 1
Turnip	Jan 1-Mar 1	Jan 10-Mar 1	Jan 20-Mar 1	Feb 1-Mar 1	Feb 10-Mar 10	Feb 20-Mar 20

[1] Plants
[2] Generally fall-planted

EARLIEST DATES, AND RANGE OF DATES, FOR SAFE SPRING PLANTING OF VEGETABLES IN THE OPEN—*Continued*

(Adapted from U.S. Department of Agriculture Information)

CROP	PLANTING DATES FOR LOCALITIES IN WHICH AVERAGE DATE OF LAST FROST IS...					
	Apr 10	Apr 20	Apr 30	May 10	May 20	May 30
Asparagus[1]	Mar 10-Apr 10	Mar 15-Apr 15	Mar 20-Apr 15	Mar 10-Apr 30	Apr 20-May 15	May 1-June 1
Beans, snap	Apr 10-June 30	Apr 25-June 30	May 10-June 30	May 10-June 30	May 15-June 30	May 25-June 15
Beet	Mar 10-June 1	Mar 20-June 1	Apr 1-June 15	Apr 15-June 15	Apr 25-June 15	May 1-June 15
Broccoli, sprouting[1]	Mar 15-Apr 15	Mar 25-Apr 20	Apr 1-May 1	Apr 15-June 1	May 1-June 15	May 10-June 10
Cabbage[1]	Mar 1-Apr 1	Mar 10-Apr 1	Mar 15-Apr 10	Apr 1-May 15	May 1-June 15	May 10-June 15
Cabbage, Chinese	[2]	[2]	[2]	Apr 1-May 15	May 1-June 15	May 10-June 15
Carrot	Mar 10-Apr 20	Apr 1-May 15	Apr 10-June 1	Apr 20-June 15	May 1-June 1	May 10-June 1
Cauliflower[1]	Mar 1-20	Mar 15-Apr 20	Apr 10-May 10	Apr 15-May 15	May 10-June 15	May 20-June 1
Chard	Mar 15-June 15	Apr 1-June 15	Apr 15-June 15	Apr 20-June 15	May 10-June 15	May 20-June 1
Chervil and chives	Mar 1-Apr 1	Mar 10-Apr 10	Mar 20-Apr 20	Apr 1-May 1	Apr 15-May 15	May 1-June 1
Chicory, witloof	June 10-July 1	June 15-July 1	June 15-July 1	June 1-20	June 1-15	June 1-15
Collards[1]	Mar 1-June 1	Mar 10-June 1	Apr 1-June 1	Apr 15-June 1	May 1-June 1	May 10-June 1
Corn, sweet	Apr 10-June 1	Apr 25-June 15	May 10-June 15	May 10-June 1	May 15-June 1	May 20-June 1
Cucumber	Apr 20-June 1	May 1-June 15	May 15-June 15	May 20-June 15	June 1-15	
Eggplant[1]	May 1-June 1	May 10-June 1	May 15-June 10	May 20-June 15	June 1-15	
Endive	Mar 15-Apr 15	Mar 25-Apr 15	Apr 1-May 1	Apr 15-May 15	May 1-30	May 1-30
Garlic	Feb 20-Mar 20	Mar 10-Apr 1	Mar 15-Apr 15	Apr 1-May 1	Apr 15-May 15	May 1-30
Kale	Mar 10-Apr 1	Mar 20-Apr 10	Apr 1-20	Apr 10-May 1	Apr 20-May 10	May 1-30
Leek	Mar 1-Apr 1	Mar 15-Apr 15	Apr 1-May 1	Apr 15-May 15	May 1-20	May 1-15
Lettuce, head[1]	Mar 10-Apr 1	Mar 20-Apr 15	Apr 1-May 1	Apr 15-May 15	May 1-June 30	May 10-June 30
Lettuce, leaf	Mar 15-May 15	Mar 20-May 15	Apr 1-June 1	Apr 15-June 15	May 1-June 30	May 10-June 30
Mustard	Mar 10-Apr 20	Mar 20-May 1	Apr 1-May 10	Apr 15-June 1	May 1-June 30	May 10-June 30
Onion1	Mar 1-Apr 1	Mar 15-Apr 10	Apr 1-May 1	Apr 10-May 1	Apr 20-May 15	May 1-30
Onion, seed	Mar 1-Apr 1	Mar 15-Apr 1	Mar 15-Apr 15	Apr 1-May 1	Apr 20-May 15	May 1-30
Onion, sets	Mar 1-Apr 1	Mar 10-Apr 1	Mar 10-Apr 10	Apr 10-May 1	Apr 20-May 15	May 1-30
Parsley	Mar 10-Apr 10	Mar 20-Apr 20	Apr 1-May 1	Apr 15-May 15	May 1-20	May 10-June 1
Peas, garden	Feb 20-Mar 20	Mar 10-Apr 10	Mar 20-May 1	Apr 1-May 15	Apr 15-June 1	May 1-June 15
Pepper[1]	May 1-June 1	May 10-June 1	May 15-June 10	May 20-June 10	May 25-June 15	June 1-15
Potato	Mar 10-Apr 1	Mar 15-Apr 10	Mar 20-May 10	Apr 1-June 1	Apr 15-June 15	May 1-June 15
Shallot	Mar 1-Apr 1	Mar 15-Apr 15	Apr 1-May 1	Apr 10-May 1	Apr 20-May 10	May 1-June 1
Sorrel	Mar 1-Apr 15	Mar 15-May 1	Apr 1-May 15	Apr 15-June 1	May 1-June 1	May 10-June 10
Spinach	Feb 15-Apr 1	Mar 1-Apr 15	Mar 20-Apr 20	Apr 1-June 15	Apr 10-June 15	Apr 20-June 15
Squash, summer	Apr 20-June 1	May 1-June 15	May 1-30	May 10-June 10	May 20-June 15	June 1-20
Tomato	Apr 20-June 1	May 5-June 10	May 10-June 15	May 15-June 10	May 25-June 15	June 5-20
Turnip	Mar 1-Apr 1	Mar 10-Apr 1	Mar 20-May 1	Apr 1-June 1	Apr 15-June 1	May 1-June 15

[1] Plants

[2] Generally fall-planted

LATEST DATES, AND RANGE OF DATES, FOR SAFE FALL PLANTING OF VEGETABLES IN THE OPEN

(Adapted from U.S. Department of Agriculture Information)

CROP	PLANTING DATES FOR LOCALITIES IN WHICH AVERAGE DATE OF FIRST FROST IS...				
	Sept 10	Sept 20	Sept 30	Oct 10	Oct 20
Asparagus[1]			Oct 20-Nov 15	Nov 1-Dec 15	
Beans, snap	May 15-June 15	June 1-July 10	June15-July20	July 1-Aug 1	
Beet	June 1-July 1	June 1-July 10	June 15-July 25	July 1-Aug 5	
Broccoli, sprouting	May 1-June 1	May 1-June 15	June 1-30	June 15-July 15	July 1-Aug 1
Cabbage[1]	May 1-June 1	May 1-June 15	June 1-July 10	June 1-July 15	July 1-20
Cabbage, Chinese	May 15-June 15	June 1-July 1	June 1-July 15	June 15-Aug 1	July 15-Aug 15
Carrot	May 15-June 15	June 1-July 1	June 1-July 10	June 1-July 20	June 15-Aug 1
Cauliflower[1]	May 1-June 1	May 1-July 1	May 10-July 15	June 1-July 25	July 1-Aug 5
Chard	May 15-July 1	June 1-July 1	June 1-July 5	June 1-July 20	June 1-Aug 1
Chervil and chives	May 1-June15	May 15-June 15	[2]	[2]	[2]
Chicory, witloof	May 15-June 15	May 15-June 15	June 1-July 1	June 1-July 1	June 15-July 15
Collards[1]	May 15-June 15	May 15-June 15	June 15-July 15	July 1-Aug 1	July 15-Aug 15
Corn, sweet		June 1-July 1	June 1-July 1	June 1-July 10	June 1-July 20
Cucumber		June 1-15	June 1-July 1	June 1-July 1	June 1-July 15
Eggplant[1]			May 20-June 10	May 15-June 15	June 1-July 1
Endive	June 1-July 1	June 15-July 15	June 15-Aug 1	July 1-Aug 15	July 15-Sept 1
Garlic	[2]	[2]	[2]	[2]	[2]
Kale	May 15-June 15	June 1-July 1	June 15-July 15	July 1-Aug 1	July 15-Aug 15
Leek	May 1-June 1	[2]	[2]	[2]	[2]
Lettuce, head[1]	May 15-July 1	June 1-July 15	June 15-Aug 1	July 15-Aug 15	Aug 1-30
Lettuce, leaf	May 15-July 15	June 1-Aug 1	June 1-Aug 1	July 15-Sept 1	July 15-Sept 1
Mustard	May 15-July 15	June 1-Aug 1	June 15-Aug 1	July 15-Aug 15	Aug 1-Sept 1
Onion	May 1-June 10	[2]	[2]	[2]	[2]
Onion, seed	May 1-June 10	[2]	[2]	[2]	[2]
Onion, sets	May 1-June 10	[2]	[2]	[2]	[2]
Parsley	May 1-June 15	June 1-July 1	June 1-July 15	June 15-Aug 1	July 15-Aug 15
Peas, garden	May 1-July 1	June 1-July 15	June 1-Aug 1	[2]	[2]
Pepper[1]		June 1-20	June 1-July 1	June 1-July 1	June 1-July 10
Potato	May 1-June 15	May 1-June 15	May 1-June 15	May 15-June 15	June 15-July 15
Shallot	[2]	[2]	[2]	[2]	[2]
Sorrel	May 1-June 15	June 1-July 1	June 1-July 15	July 1-Aug 1	July 15-Aug 15
Spinach	June 1-July 15	June 1-Aug 1	July 1-Aug 15	Aug 1-Sept 1	Aug 20-Sept 10
Squash, summer	June 1-20	May 15-July 1	June 1-July 1	June 1-July 15	June 1-July 20
Squash, winter		May 20-June 10	June 1-15	June 1-July 1	June 1-July 1
Tomato	June 10-20	June 1-20	June 1-20	June 1-20	June 1-July 1
Turnip	June 1-July 1	June 1-July 15	June 1-Aug 1	July 1-Aug 1	July 15-Aug 15

[1] Plants
[2] Generally spring-planted

LATEST DATES, AND RANGES OF DATES, FOR SAFE FALL PLANTING OF VEGETABLES IN THE OPEN-*Continued*

(Adapted from U.S. Department of Agriculture Information)

CROP	PLANTING DATES FOR LOCALITIES IN WHICH AVERAGE DATE OF FIRST FROST IS...				
	Oct 30	Nov 10	Nov 20	Nov 30	Dec 10
Asparagus[1]	Nov 15-Jan 1	Dec 1-Jan 1			
Beans, snap	July 1-Aug 15	July 1-Sept 1	July 1-Sept 10	Aug 15-Sept 20	Sept 1-30
Beet	Aug 1-Sept 1	Aug 1-Oct 1	Sept 1-Dec 1	Sept 1-Dec 15	Sept 1-Dec 31
Broccoli, sprouting	July 1-Aug 15	Aug 1-Spet 1	Aug 1-Sept 15	Aug 1-Oct 1	Aug 1-Nov 1
Cabbage[1]	Aug 1-Sept 1	Sept 1-15	Sept 1-Dec 1	Sept 1-Dec 31	Sept 1-Dec 31
Cabbage, Chinese	Aug 1-Sept 15	Aug 15-Oct 1	Sept 1-Oct 15	Sept 1-Nov 1	Sept 1-Nov 15
Carrot	July 1-Aug 15	Aug 1-Sept 1	Sept 1-Nov 1	Sept 15-Dec 1	Sept 15-Dec 1
Cauliflower[1]	July 15-Aug 15	Aug 1-Sept 1	Aug 1-Sept 15	Aug 15-Oct 10	Sept 1-Oct 20
Chard	June 1-Sept 10	June 1-Sept 15	June 1-Oct 1	June 1-Nov 1	June 1-Dec 1
Chervil and chives	[2]	[2]	Nov 1-Dec 31	Nov 1-Dec 31	Nov 1-Dec 31
Chicory, witloof	July 1-Aug 10	July 10-Aug 20	July 20-Sept 1	Aug 15-Sept 30	Aug 15-Oct 15
Collards[1]	Aug 1-Sept 15	Aug 15-Oct 1	Aug 25-Nov 1	Sept 1-Dec 1	Sept 1-Dec 31
Corn, sweet	June 1-Aug 1	June 1-Aug 15	June 1-Sept 1		
Cucumber	June 1-Aug 1	June 1-Aug 15	June 1-Aug 15	July 15-Sept 15	Aug 15-Oct 1
Eggplant[1]	June 1-July 1	June 1-July 15	June 1-Aug 1	July 1-Sept 1	Aug 1-Sept 30
Enidve	July 15-Aug 15	Aug 1-Sept 1	Sept 1-Oct 1	Sept 1-Nov 15	Sept 1-Dec 31
Garlic	[2]	Aug 1-Oct 1	Aug 15-Oct 1	Sept 1-Nov 15	Sept 15-Nov 15
Kale	July 15-Sept 1	Aug 1-Sept 15	Aug 15-Oct 15	Sept 1-Dec 1	Sept 1-Dec 31
Leek	[2]	[2]	Sept 1-Nov 1	Sept 1-Nov 1	Sept 1-Nov 1
Lettuce, head[1]	Aug 1-Sept 15	Aug 15-Oct 15	Sept 1-Nov 1	Sept 1-Dec 1	Sept 15-Dec 31
Lettuce, leaf	Aug 16-Oct 1	Aug 25-Oct 1	Sept 1-Nov 1	Sept 1-Dec 1	Sept 15-Dec 31
Mustard	Aug 15-Oct 15	Aug 15-Nov 1	Sept 1-Dec 1	Sept 1-Dec 1	Sept 1-Dec 1
Onion[1]		Sept 1-Oct 15	Oct 1-Dec 31	Oct 1-Dec 31	Oct 1-Dec 31
Onion, seed			Sept 1-Nov 1	Sept 1-Nov 1	Sept 1-Nov 1
Onion, sets		Oct 1-Dec 1	Nov 1-Dec 31	Nov 1-Dec 31	Nov 1-Dec 31
Parsley	Aug 1-Sept 15	Sept 1-Nov 15	Sept 1-Dec 31	Sept 1-Dec 31	Sept 1-Dec 31
Peas, garden	Aug 1-Sept 15	Sept 1-Nov 1	Oct 1-Dec 1	Oct 1-Dec 31	Oct 1-Dec 31
Pepper[1]	June 1-July 20	June 1-Aug 1	June 1-Aug 15	June 15-Sept 1	Aug 15-Oct 1
Potato	July 20-Aug 10	July 25-Aug 20	Aug 10-Sept 15	Aug 1-Sept 15	Aug 1-Sept 15
Shallot	[2]	Aug 1-Oct 1	Aug 15-Oct 1	Aug 15-Oct 15	Sept 15-Nov 1
Sorrel	Aug 1-Sept 15	Aug 15-Oct 1	Aug 15-Oct 15	Sept 1-Nov 15	Sept 1-Dec 15
Spinach	Sept 1-Oct 1	Sept 15-Nov 1	Oct 1-Dec 1	Oct 1-Dec 31	Oct 1-Dec 31
Squash, summer	June 1-Aug 1	June 1-Aug 10	June 1-Aug 20	June 1-Sept 1	June 1-Sept 15
Squash, winter	June 10-July 10	June 20-July 20	July 1-Aug 1	July 15-Aug 15	Aug 1-Sept 1
Tomato	June 1-July 1	June 1-July 15	June 1-Aug 1	Aug 1-Sept 1	Aug 15-Oct 1
Turnip	Aug 1-Sept 15	Sept 1-Oct 15	Sept 1-Nov 15	Sept 1-Nov 15	Oct 1-Dec 1

[1] Plants

[2] Generally spring-planted

Index